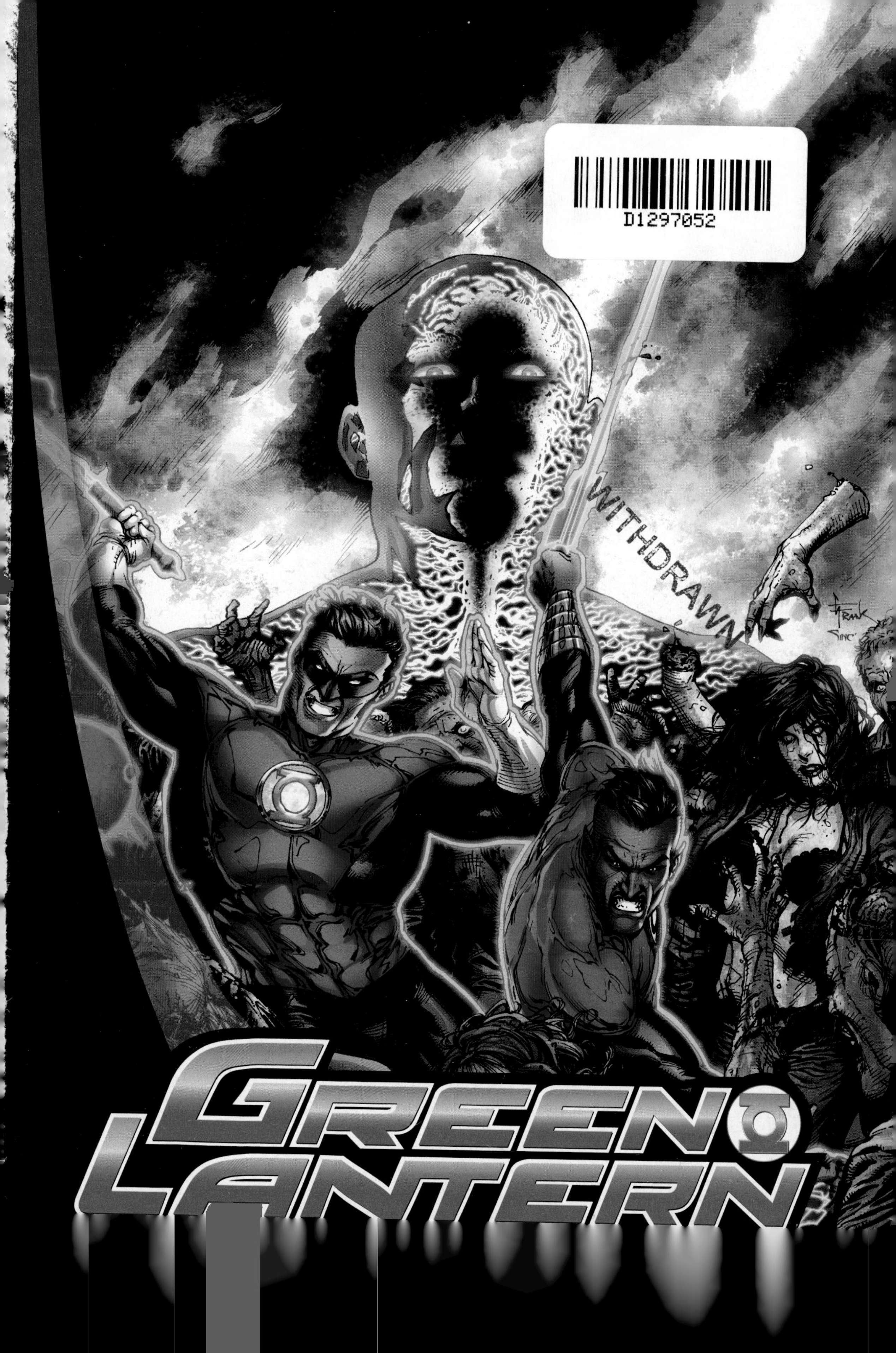
GREEN
LANTERN

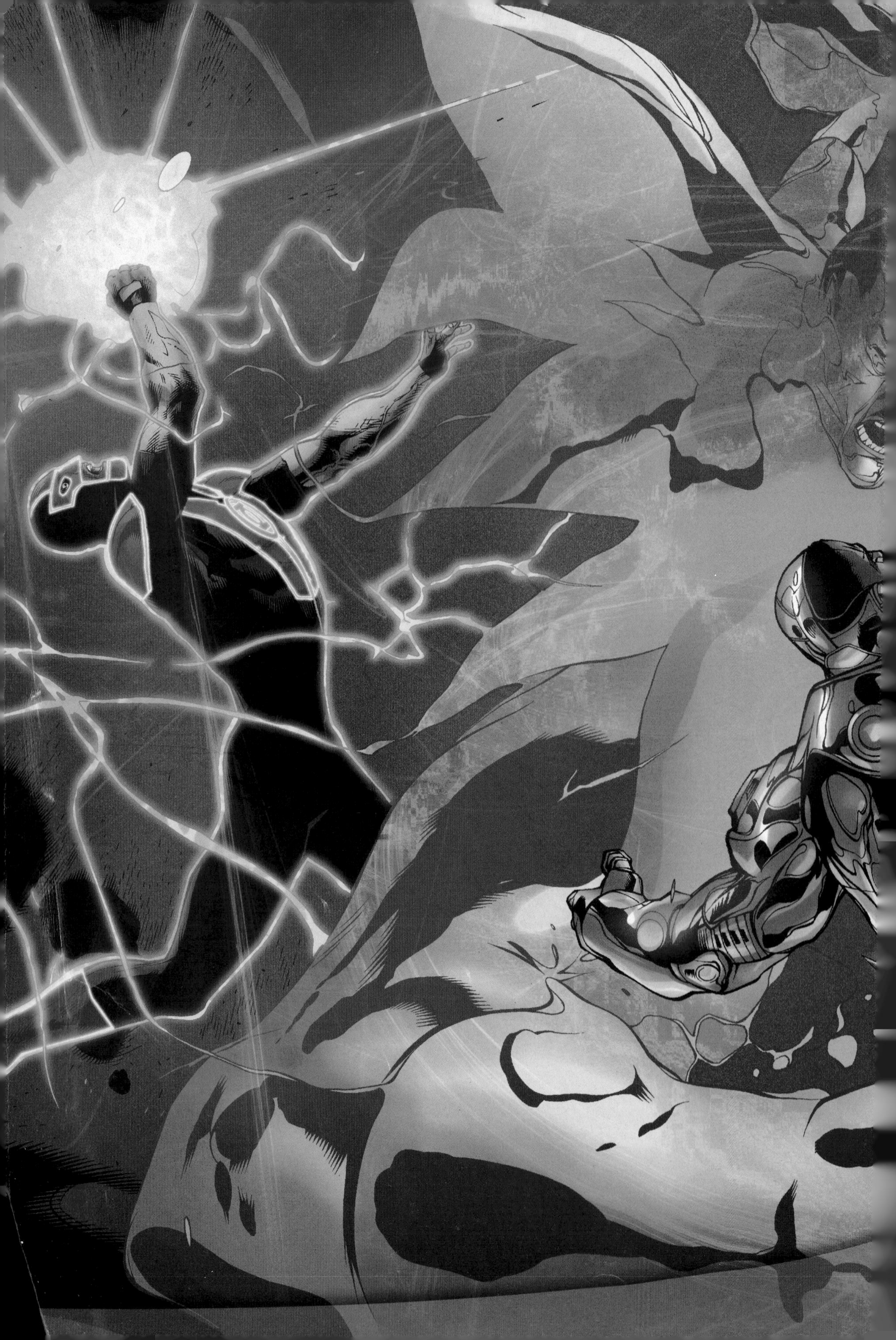

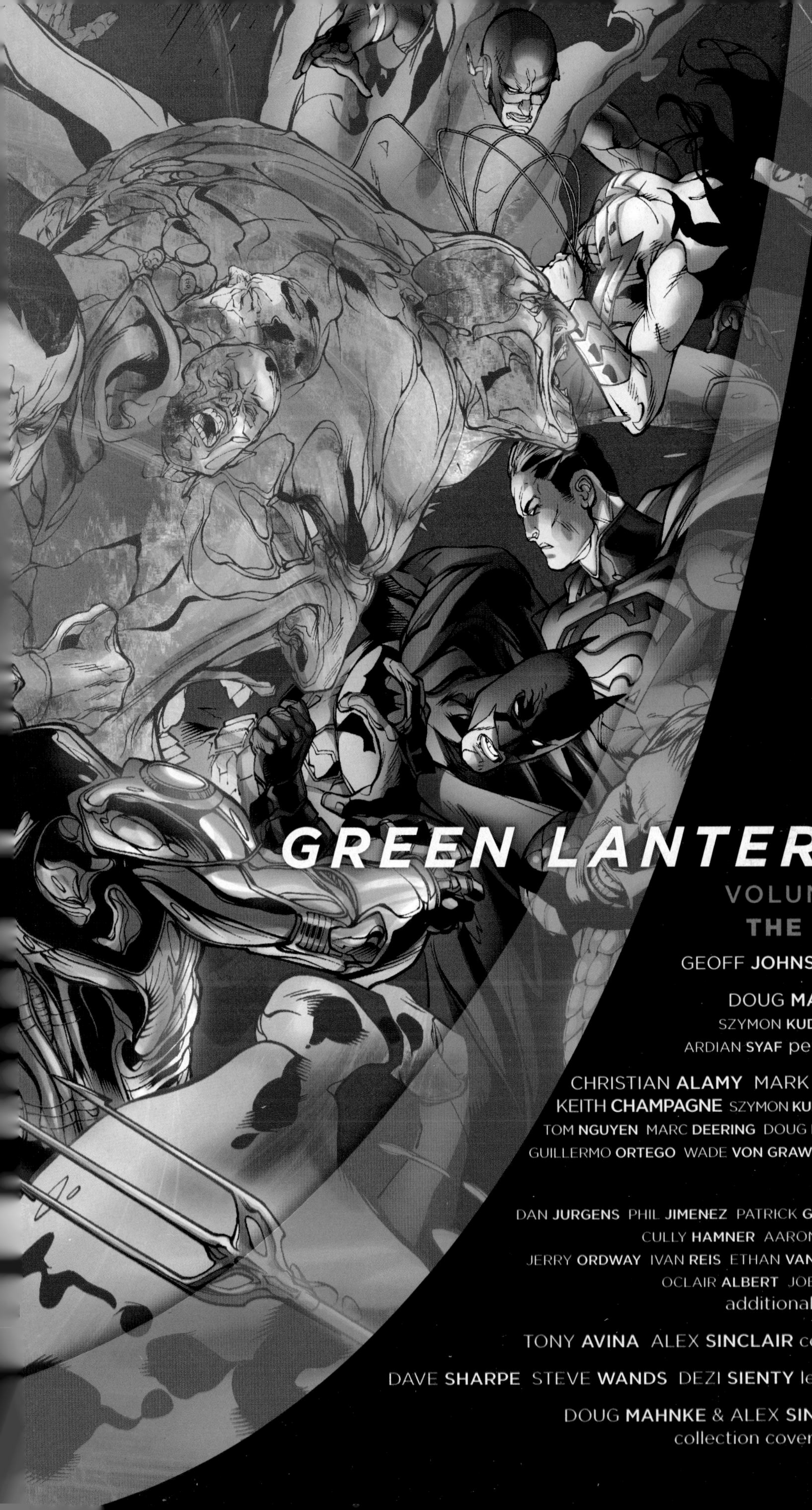

GREEN LANTERN

VOLUME 3
THE END

GEOFF **JOHNS** writer

DOUG **MAHNKE**
SZYMON **KUDRANSKI**
ARDIAN **SYAF** pencillers

CHRISTIAN **ALAMY** MARK **IRWIN**
KEITH **CHAMPAGNE** SZYMON **KUDRANSKI**
TOM **NGUYEN** MARC **DEERING** DOUG **MAHNKE**
GUILLERMO **ORTEGO** WADE **VON GRAWBADGER**
inkers

DAN **JURGENS** PHIL **JIMENEZ** PATRICK **GLEASON**
CULLY **HAMNER** AARON **KUDER**
JERRY **ORDWAY** IVAN **REIS** ETHAN **VAN SCIVER**
OCLAIR **ALBERT** JOE **PRADO**
additional artists

TONY **AVIÑA** ALEX **SINCLAIR** colorists

DAVE **SHARPE** STEVE **WANDS** DEZI **SIENTY** letterers

DOUG **MAHNKE** & ALEX **SINCLAIR**
collection cover artists

MATT IDELSON Editor – Original Series   WIL MOSS   CHRIS CONROY Associate Editors – Original Series
KYLE ANDRUKIEWICZ Assistant Editor – Original Series   PETER HAMBOUSSI Editor
ROBBIN BROSTERMAN Design Director – Books   ROBBIE BIEDERMAN Publication Design

BOB HARRAS Senior VP – Editor-in-Chief, DC Comics

DIANE NELSON President   DAN DIDIO and JIM LEE Co-Publishers
GEOFF JOHNS Chief Creative Officer
JOHN ROOD Executive VP – Sales, Marketing and Business Development
AMY GENKINS Senior VP – Business and Legal Affairs   NAIRI GARDINER Senior VP – Finance
JEFF BOISON VP – Publishing Planning   MARK CHIARELLO VP – Art Direction and Design
JOHN CUNNINGHAM VP – Marketing   TERRI CUNNINGHAM VP – Editorial Administration
ALISON GILL Senior VP – Manufacturing and Operations
HANK KANALZ Senior VP – Vertigo and Integrated Publishing   JAY KOGAN VP – Business and Legal Affairs, Publishing
JACK MAHAN VP – Business Affairs, Talent   NICK NAPOLITANO VP – Manufacturing Administration
SUE POHJA VP – Book Sales   COURTNEY SIMMONS Senior VP – Publicity
BOB WAYNE Senior VP – Sales

GREEN LANTERN VOLUME 3: THE END

DC Comics, 1700 Broadway, New York, NY 10019
A Warner Bros. Entertainment Company.
Printed by RR Donnelley, Salem, VA, USA. 3/21/14. First Printing.

ISBN: 978-1-4012-4684-6

SUSTAINABLE   Certified Chain of Custody
FORESTRY   At Least 20% Certified Forest Content
INITIATIVE   www.sfiprogram.org
             SFI-01042
             APPLIES TO TEXT STOCK ONLY

Library of Congress Cataloging-in-Publication Data

Johns, Geoff, 1973-
Green Lantern. Volume 3, The end / Geoff Johns, Doug Mahnke.
pages cm
"Originally published in single magazine form as Green Lantern, 13-20."
ISBN 978-1-4012-4408-8
1. Graphic novels. I. Mahnke, Doug. II. Title. III. Title: End.
PN6728.G74J6588 2013

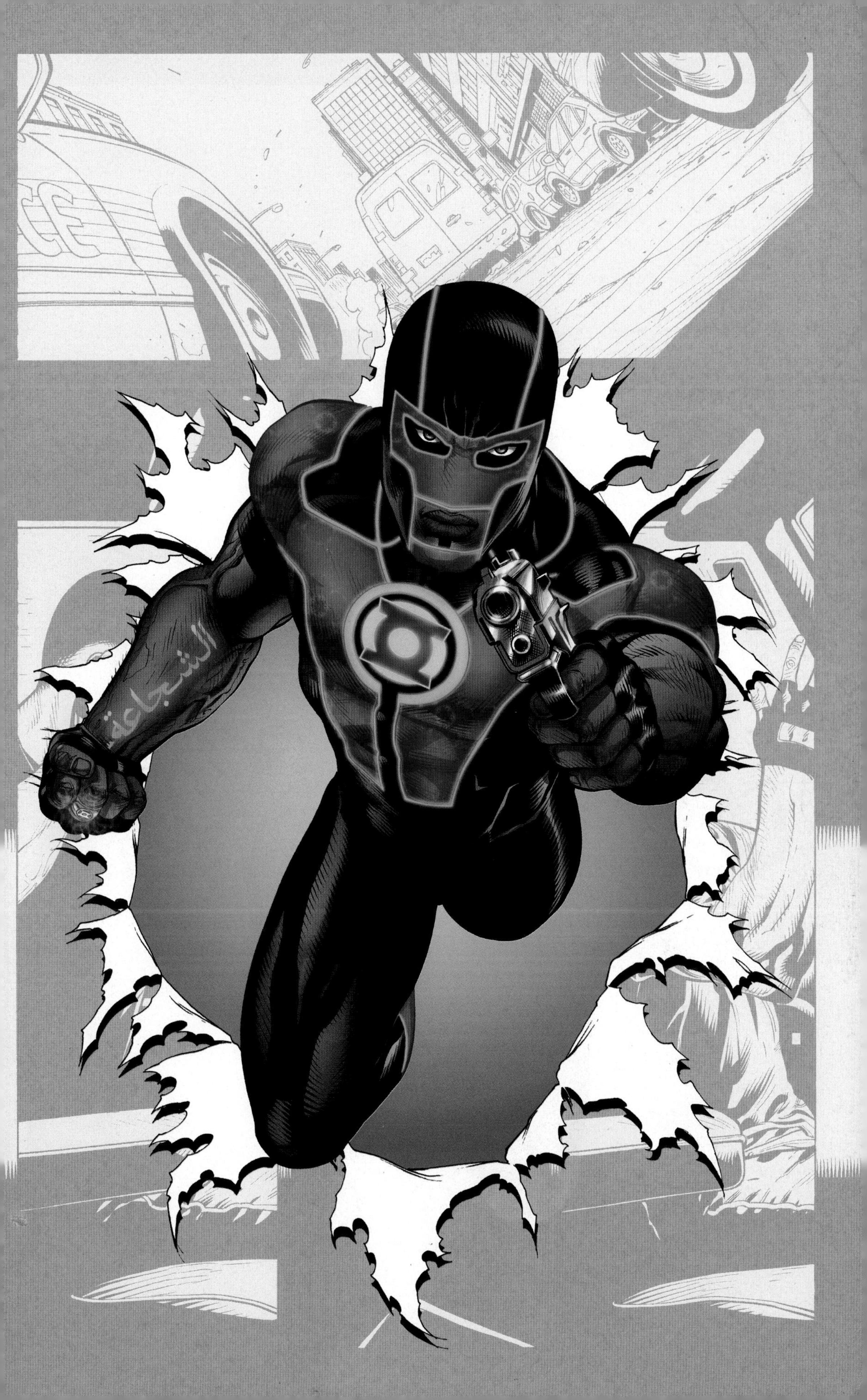
الشجاعة

GEOFF JOHNS writer **DOUG MAHNKE** penciller **CHRISTIAN ALAMY, KEITH CHAMPAGNE & MARK IRWIN** inkers
DOUG MAHNKE, CHRISTIAN ALAMY & ALEX SINCLAIR cover

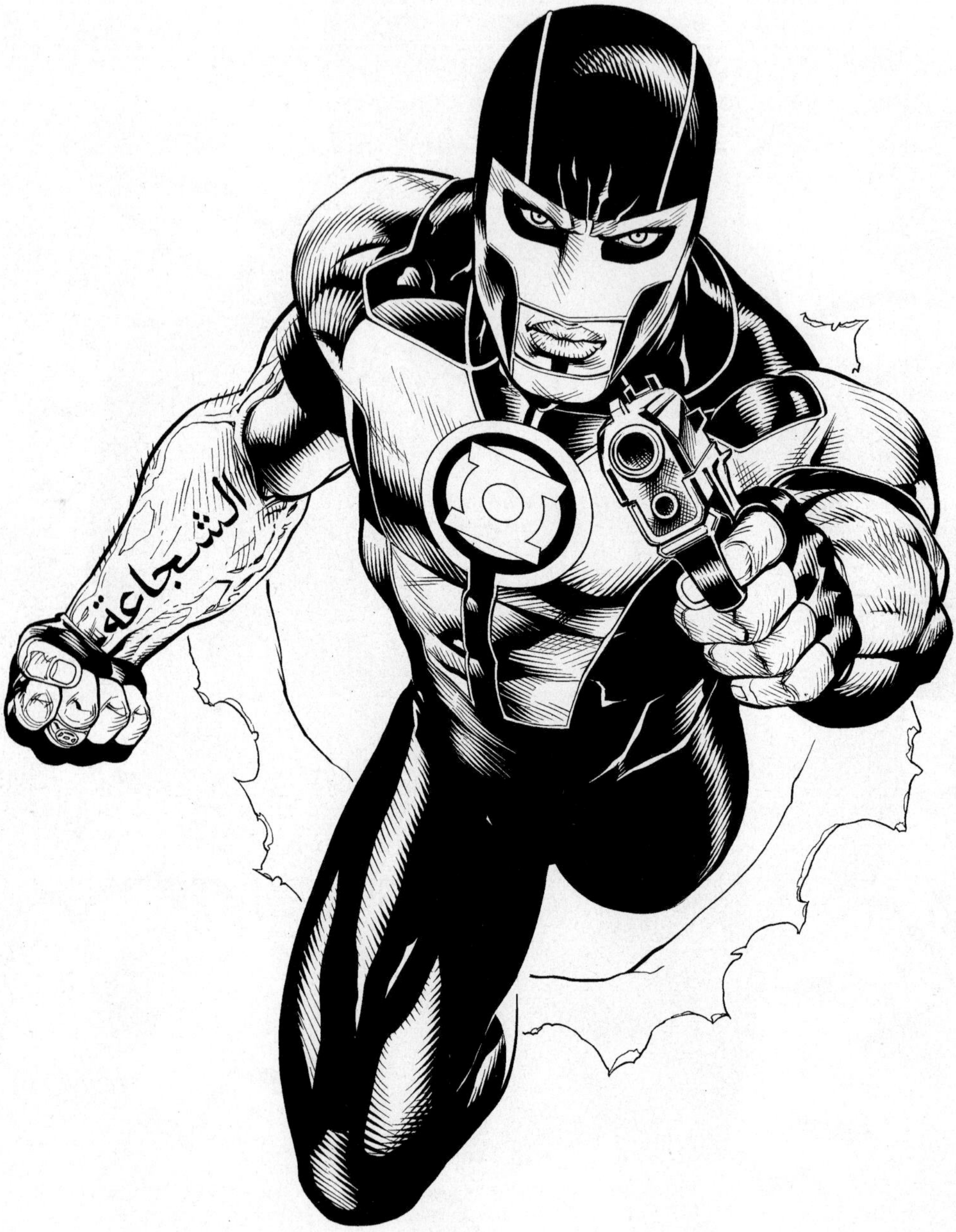
الشجاعة

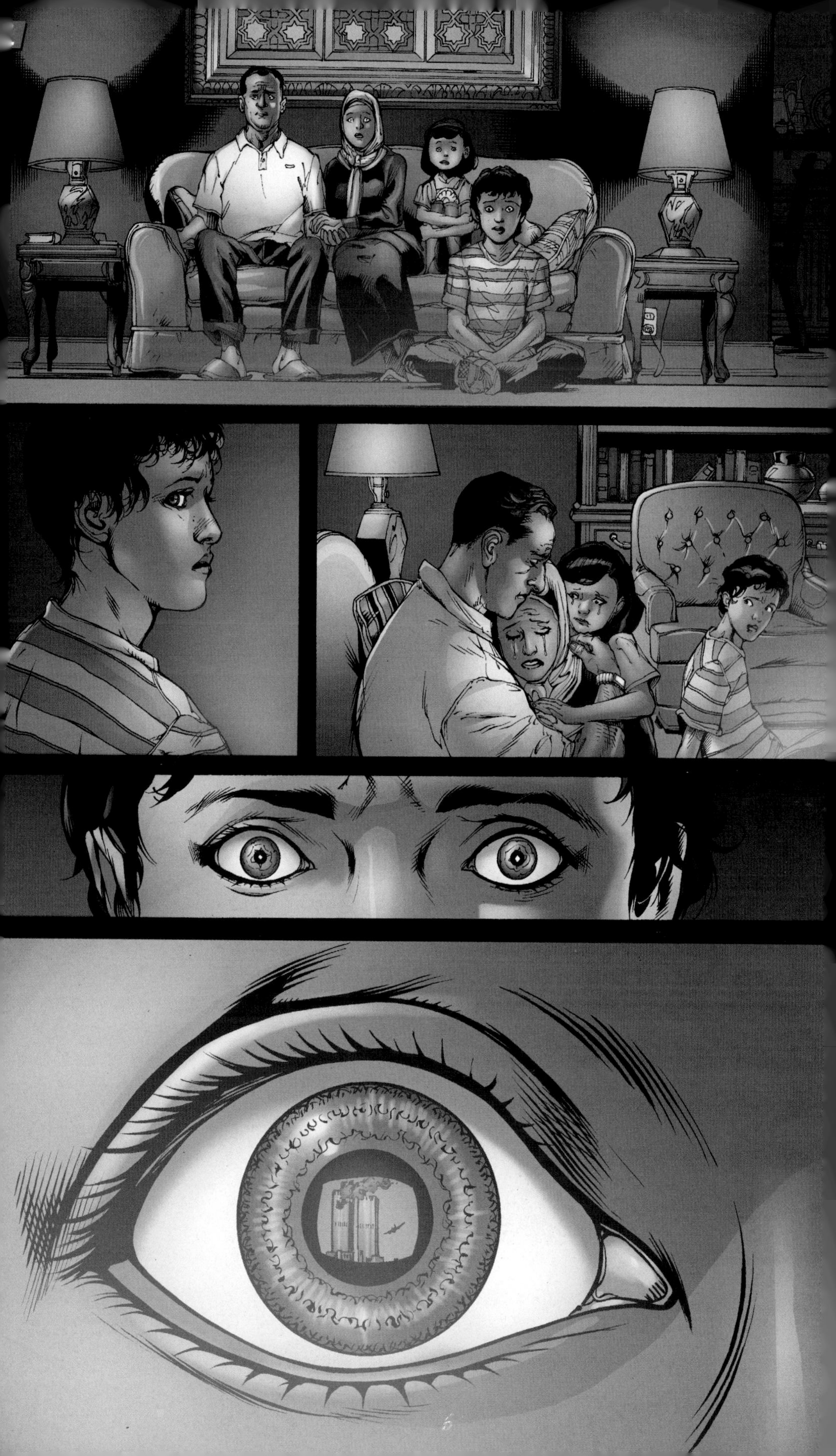

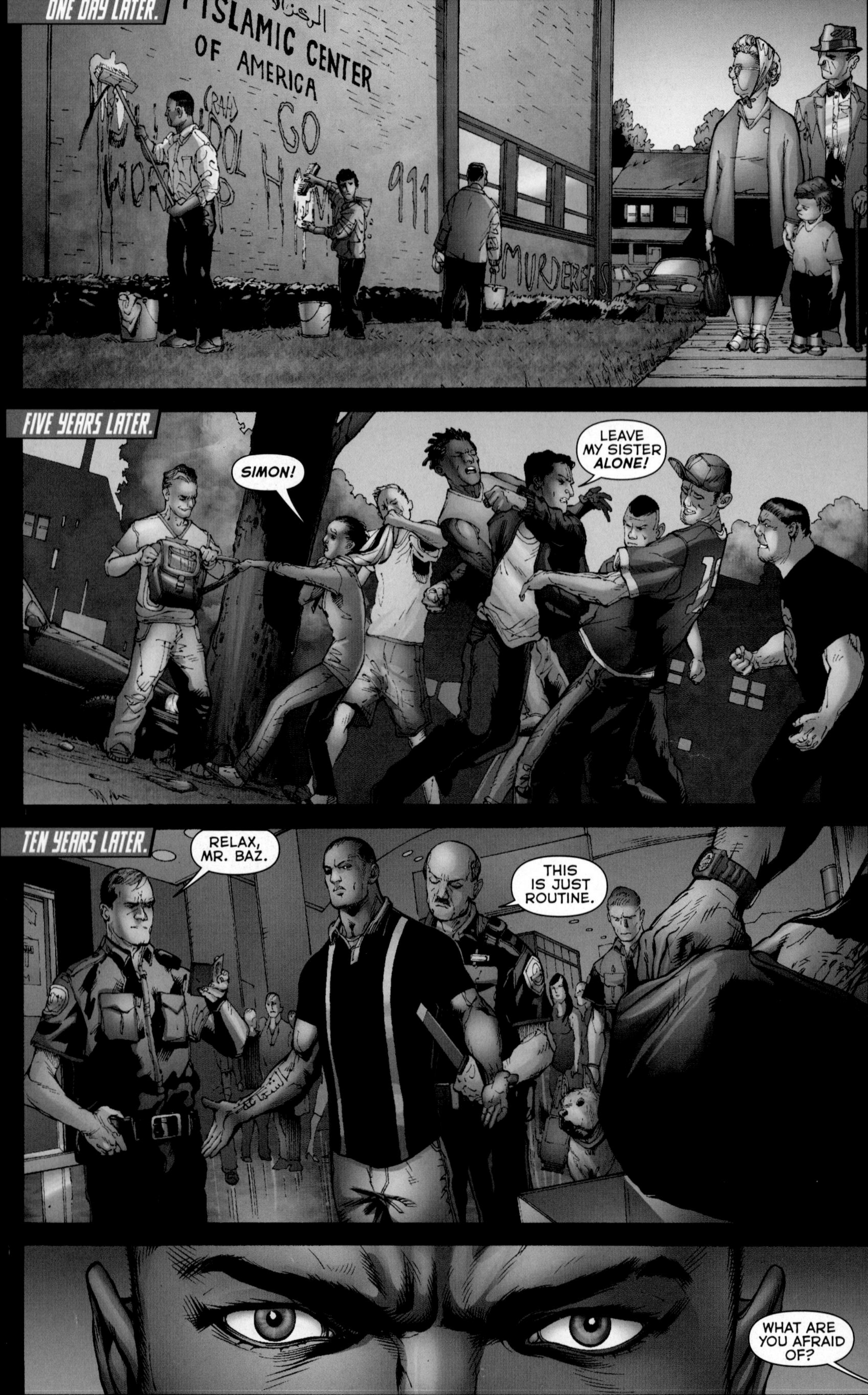
ONE DAY LATER.
ISLAMIC CENTER OF AMERICA
GO
911
MURDERERS
FIVE YEARS LATER.
SIMON!
LEAVE MY SISTER ALONE!
TEN YEARS LATER.
RELAX, MR. BAZ.
THIS IS JUST ROUTINE.
WHAT ARE YOU AFRAID OF?

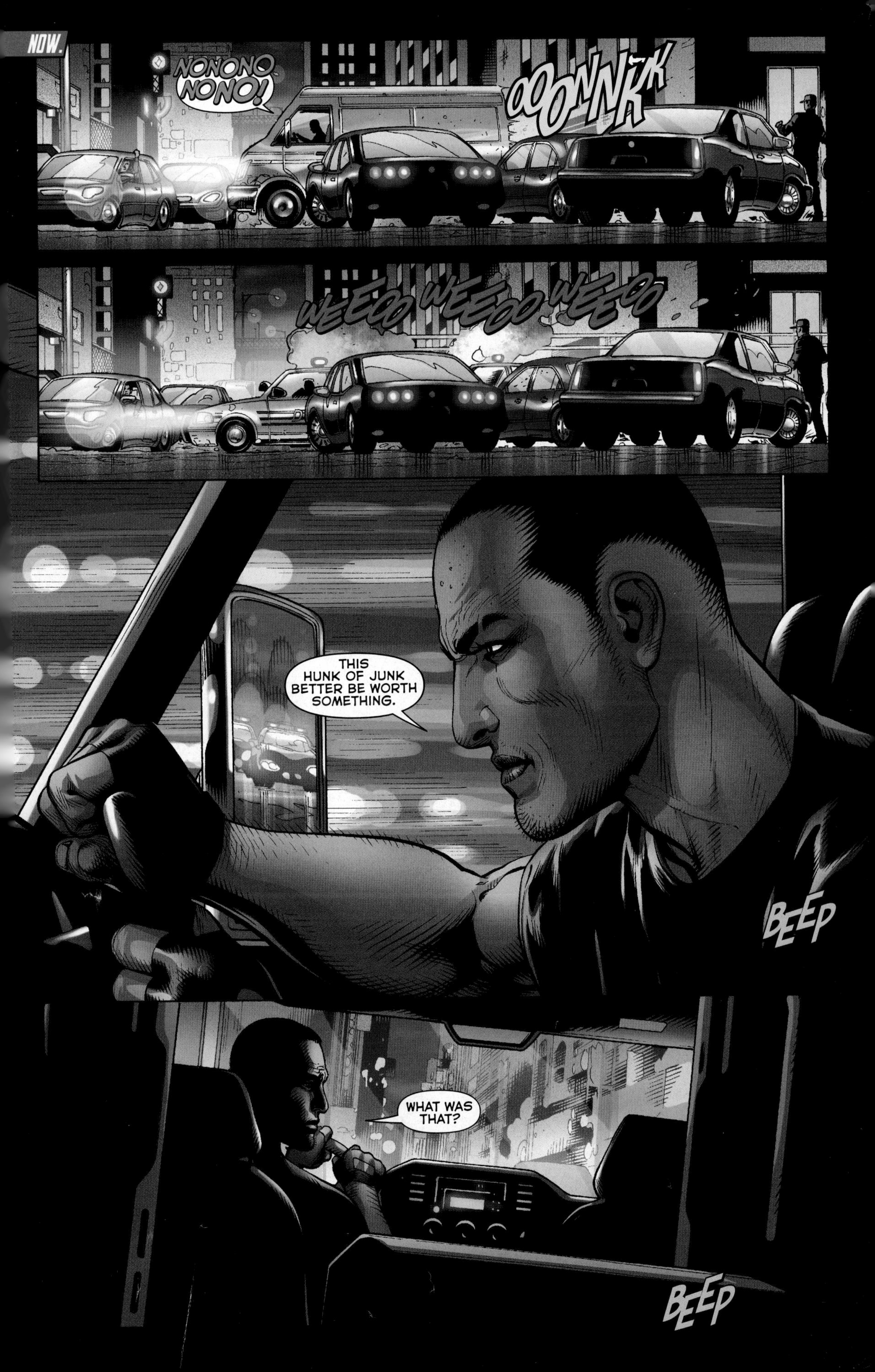
NOW.
NONONO NONO!
OOONNK
WEEOO WEEOO WEEOO
THIS HUNK OF JUNK BETTER BE WORTH SOMETHING.
BEEP
WHAT WAS THAT?
BEEP

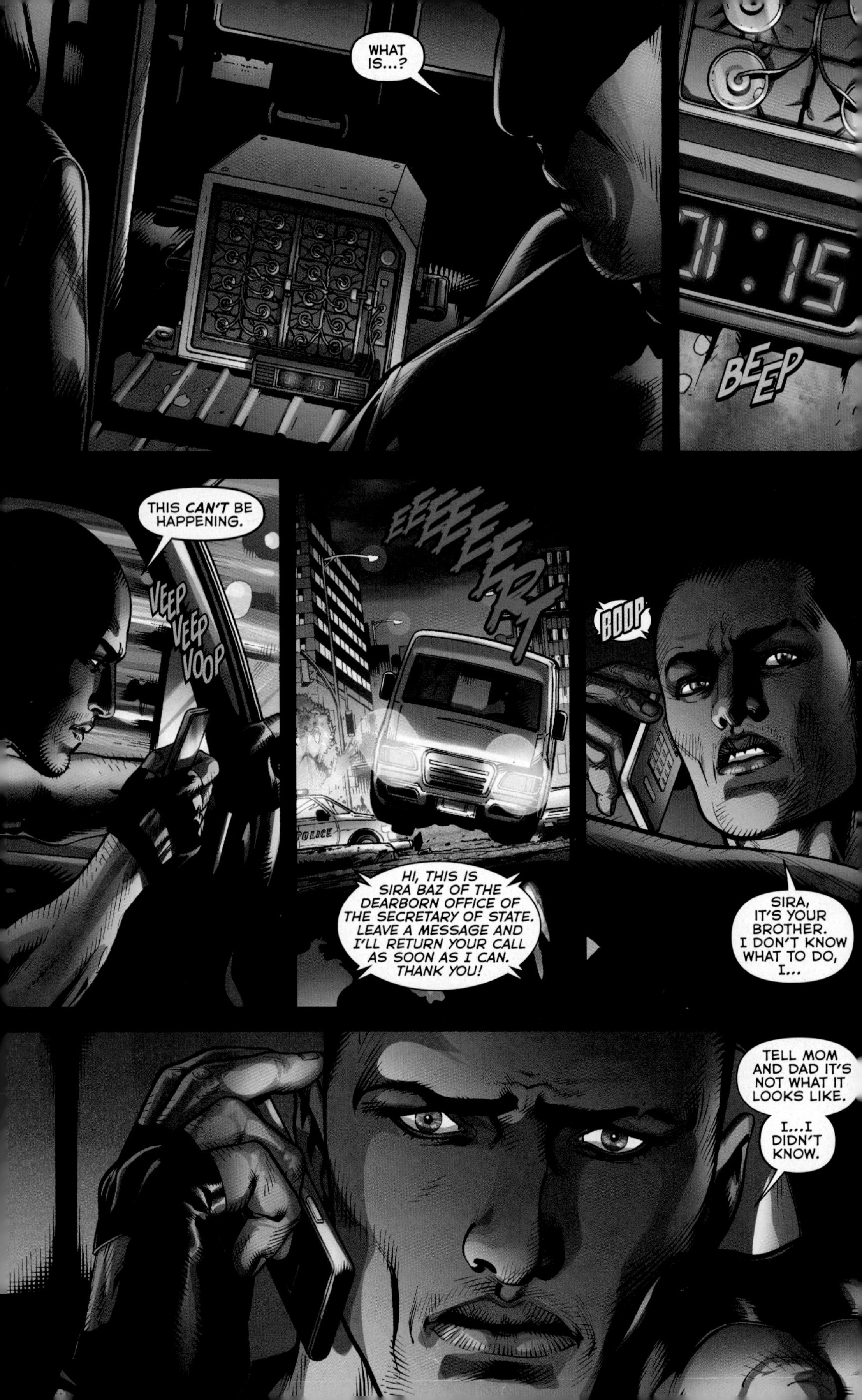
WHAT IS...?
01:16
01:15
BEEP
THIS CAN'T BE HAPPENING.
VEEP VEEP VOOP
EEEEEERR
POLICE
BOOP
HI, THIS IS SIRA BAZ OF THE DEARBORN OFFICE OF THE SECRETARY OF STATE. LEAVE A MESSAGE AND I'LL RETURN YOUR CALL AS SOON AS I CAN. THANK YOU!
SIRA, IT'S YOUR BROTHER. I DON'T KNOW WHAT TO DO, I...
TELL MOM AND DAD IT'S NOT WHAT IT LOOKS LIKE.
I...I DIDN'T KNOW.

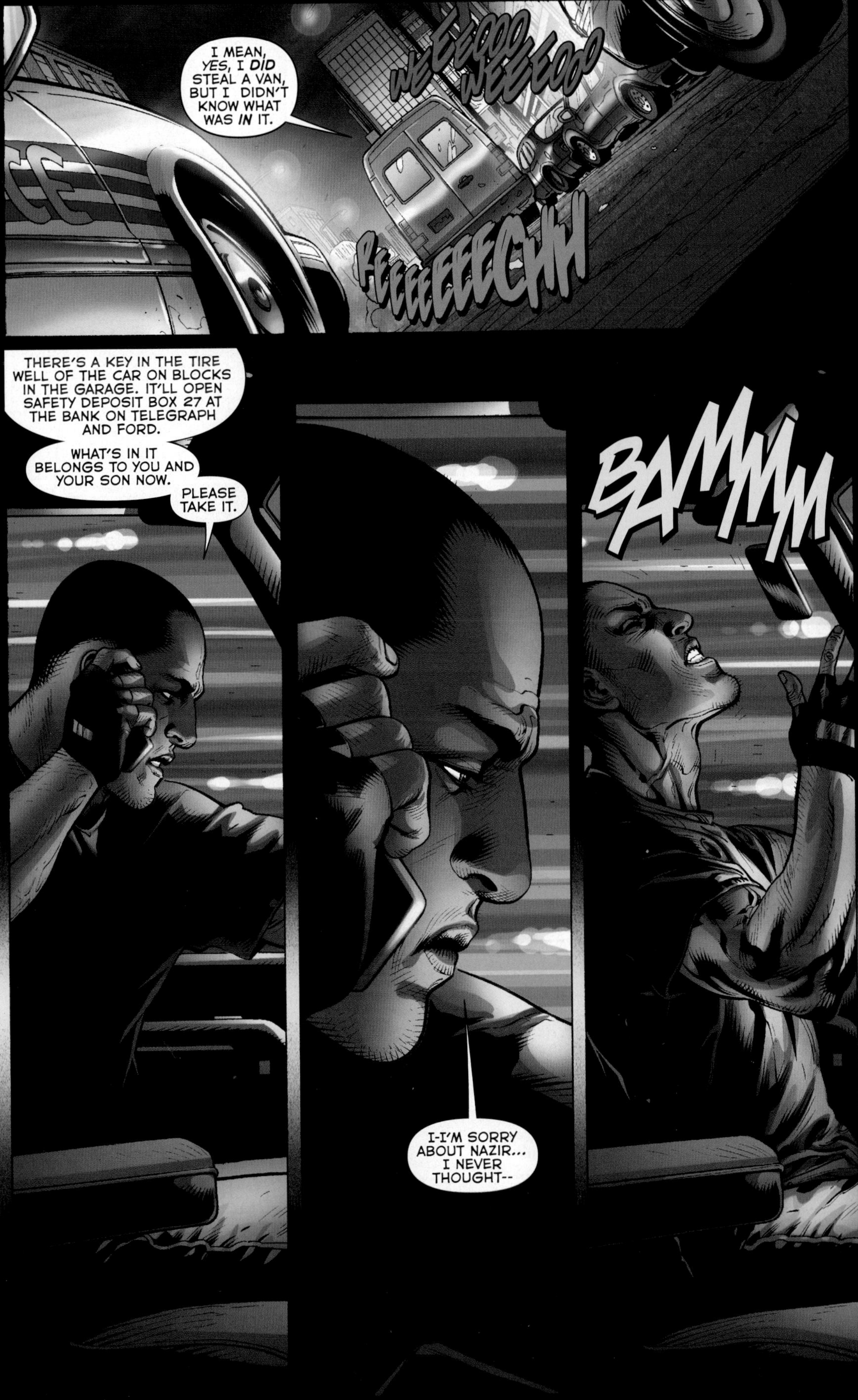

I MEAN, YES, I DID STEAL A VAN, BUT I DIDN'T KNOW WHAT WAS IN IT.
WEEEOOO WEEEOOO
REEEEEEECHH
THERE'S A KEY IN THE TIRE WELL OF THE CAR ON BLOCKS IN THE GARAGE. IT'LL OPEN SAFETY DEPOSIT BOX 27 AT THE BANK ON TELEGRAPH AND FORD.
WHAT'S IN IT BELONGS TO YOU AND YOUR SON NOW.
PLEASE TAKE IT.
I-I'M SORRY ABOUT NAZIR... I NEVER THOUGHT--
BAMMM

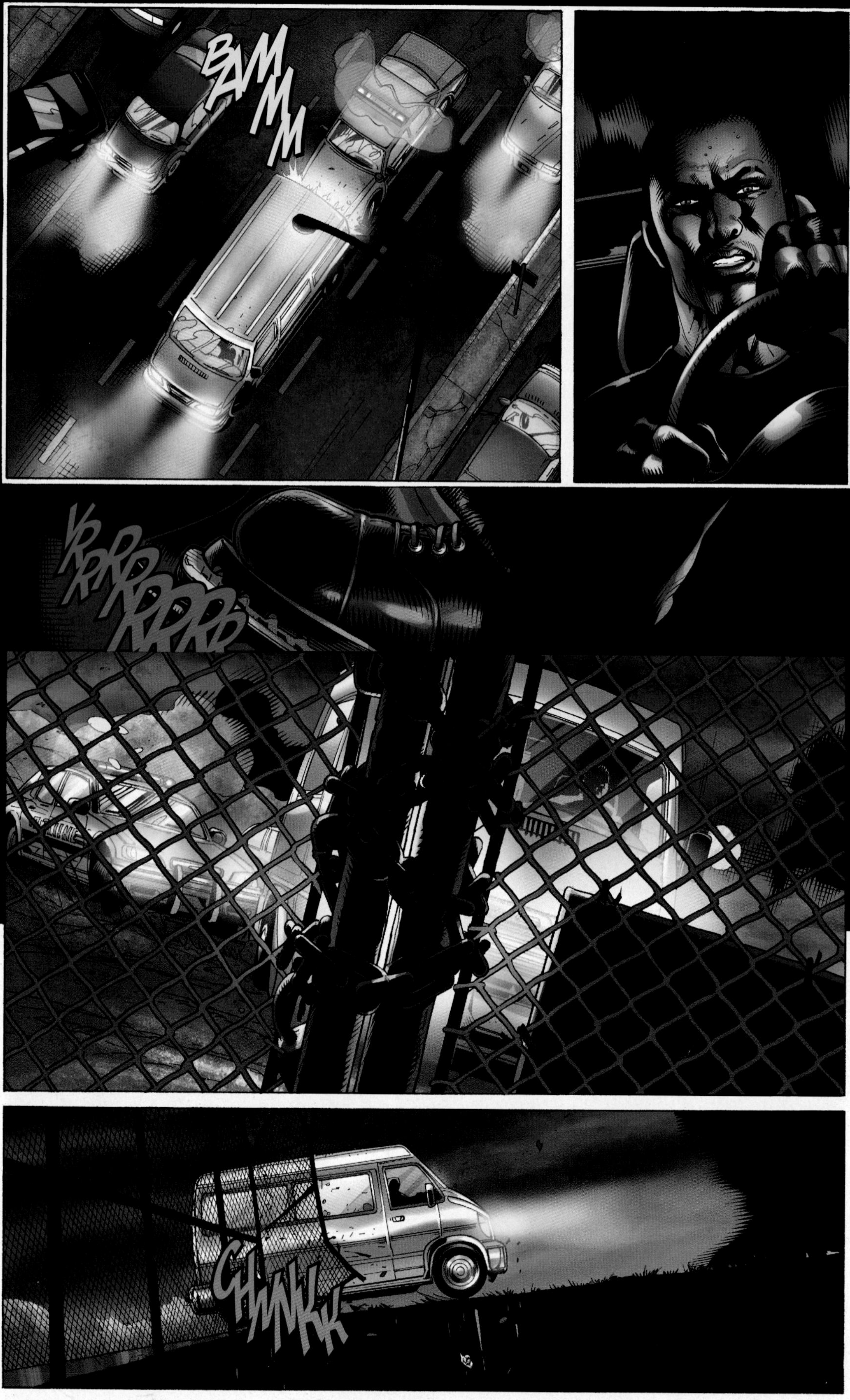
BAMMMM
VRRRRRRRRR
CHNNKK

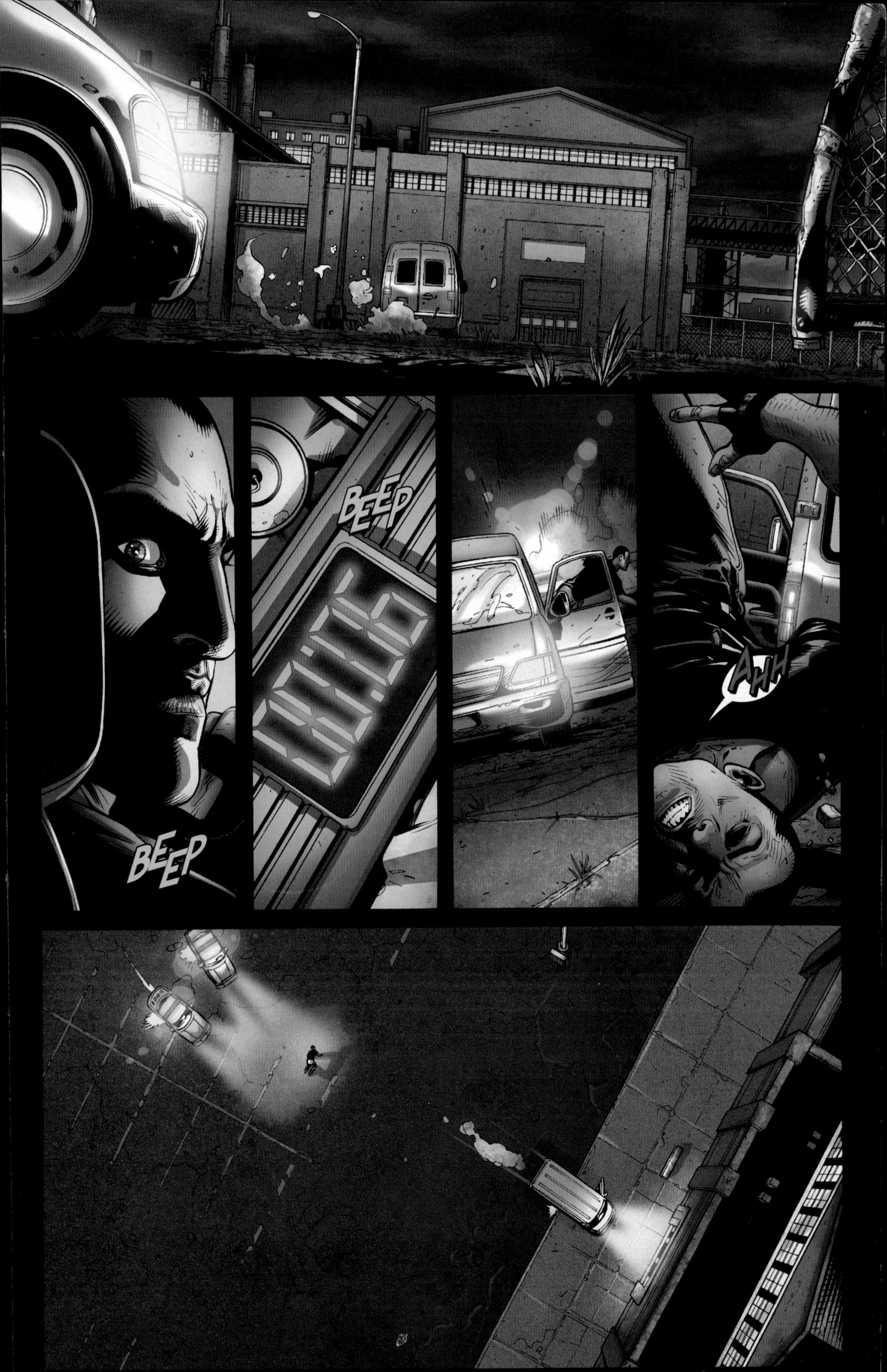
BEEP
BEEP
AHH

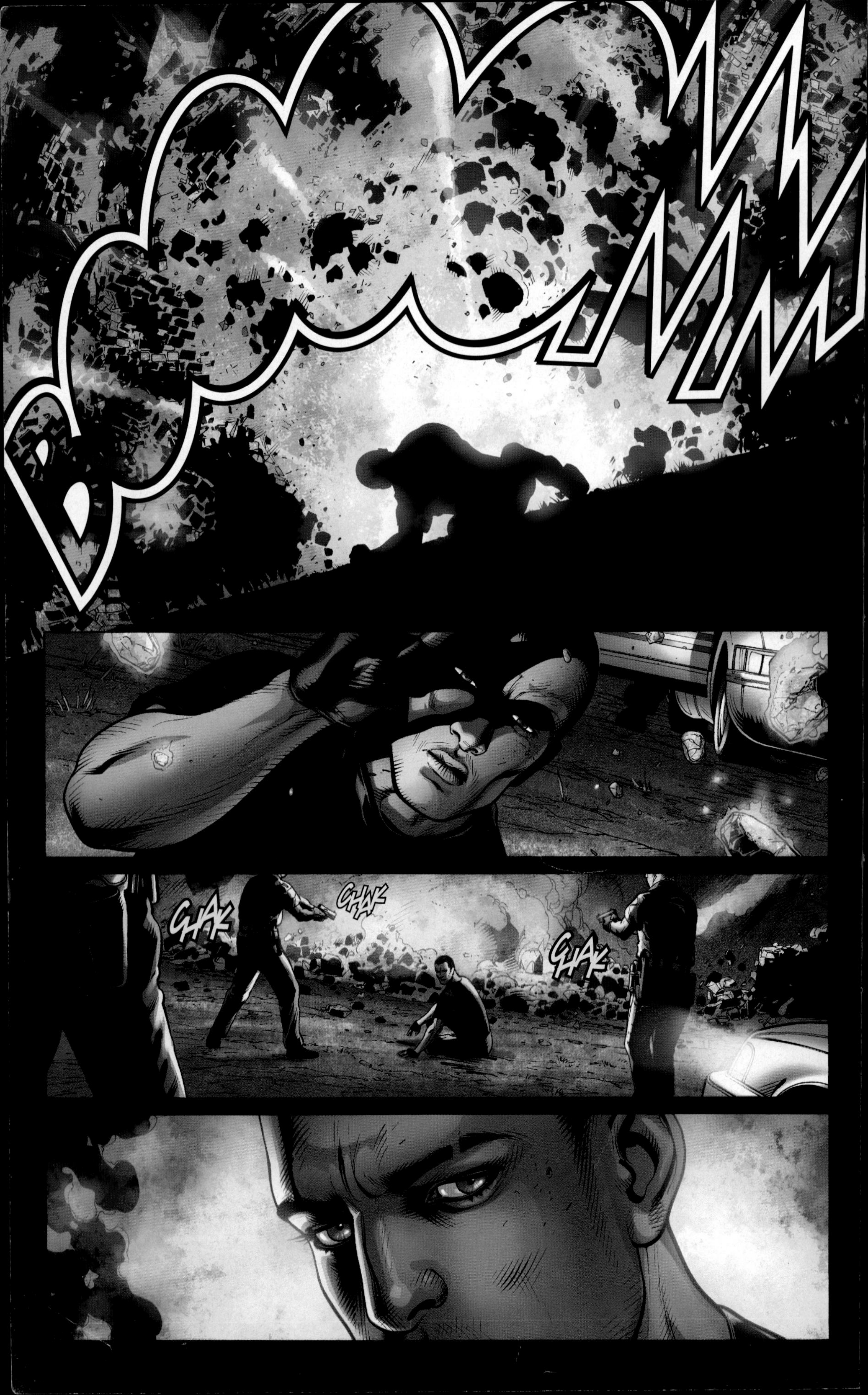

BOOMM
CHAK
CHAK
CHAK

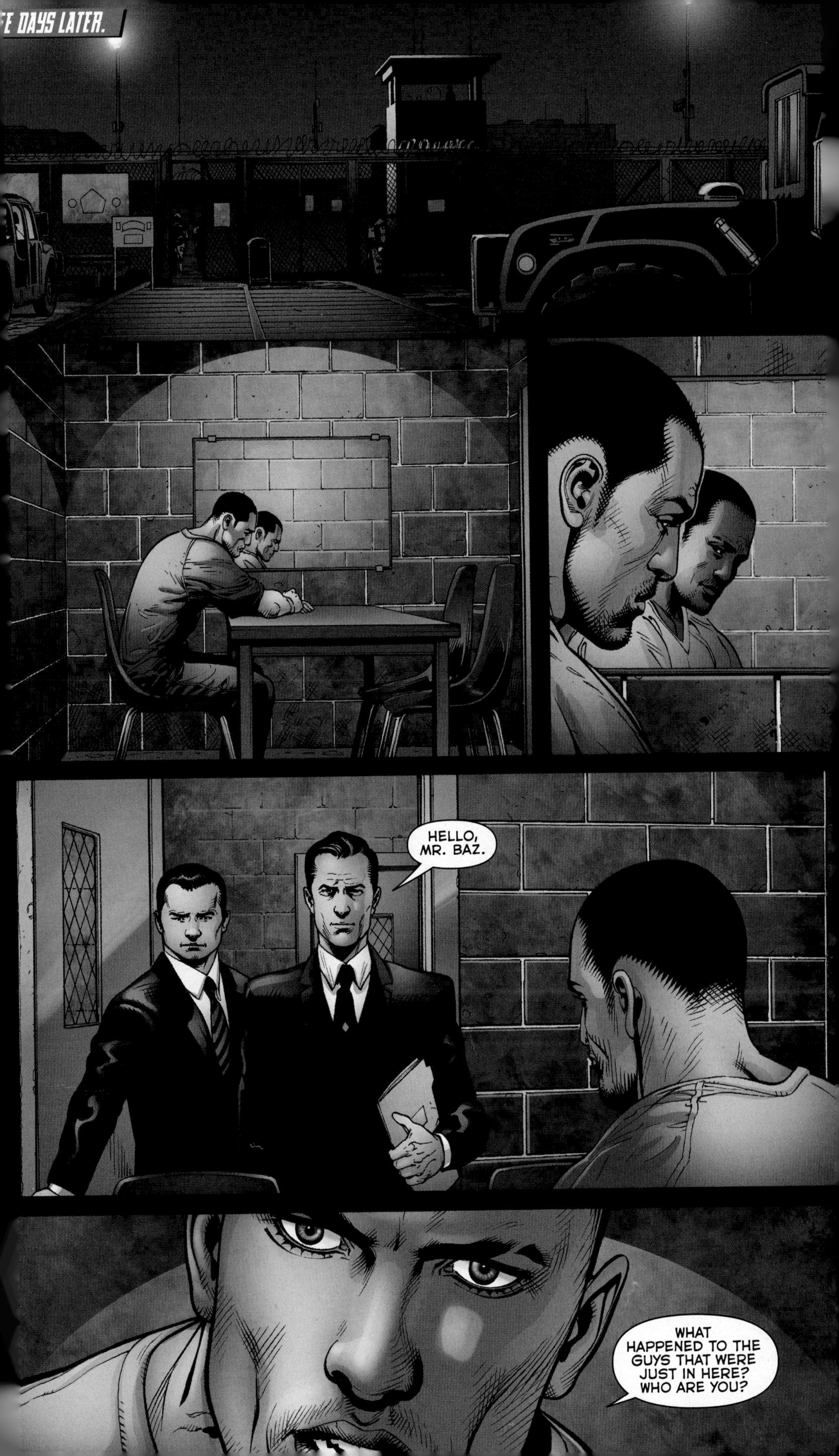
E DAYS LATER.
HELLO, MR. BAZ.
WHAT HAPPENED TO THE GUYS THAT WERE JUST IN HERE? WHO ARE YOU?

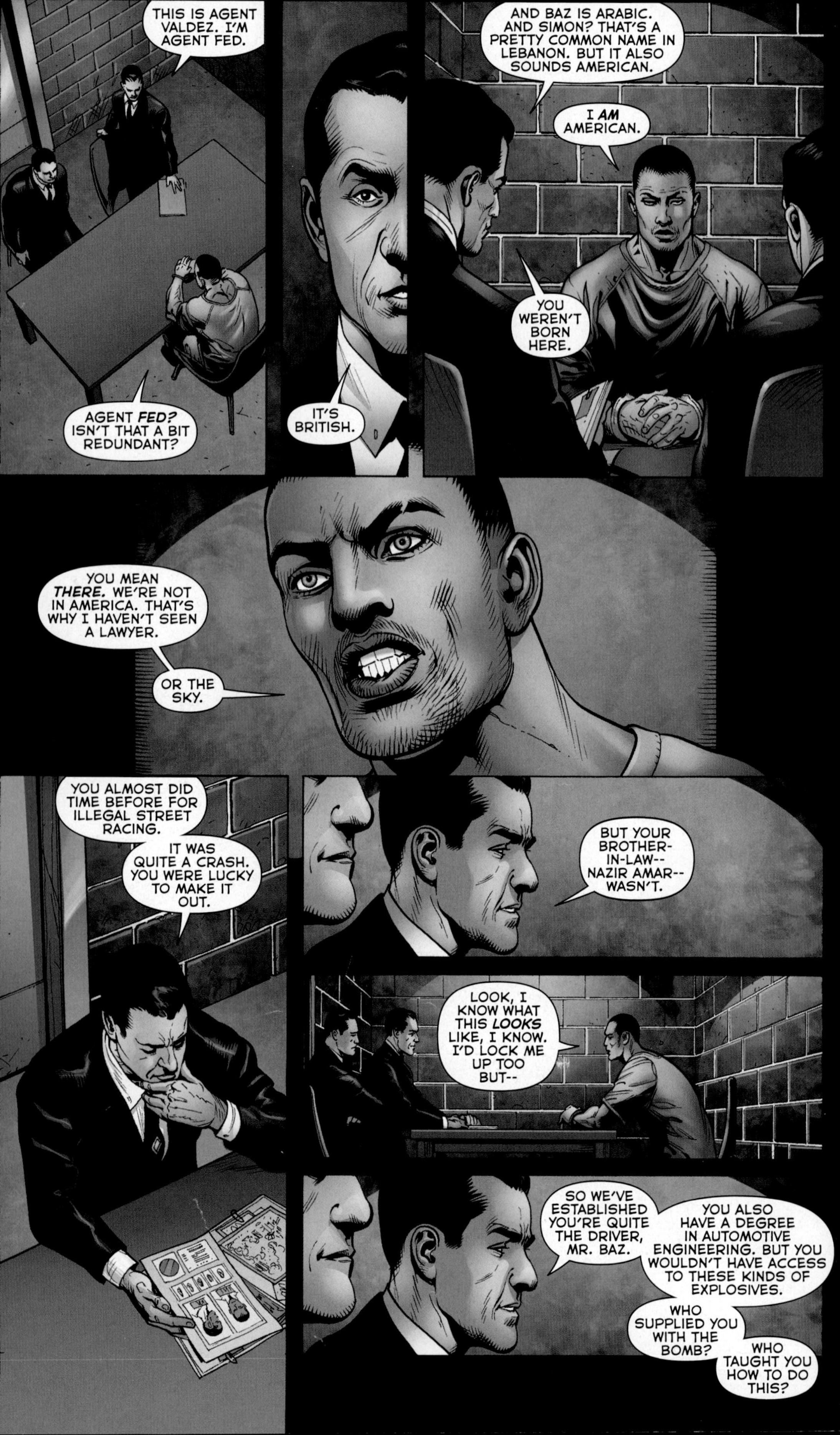
THIS IS AGENT VALDEZ. I'M AGENT FED.
AGENT *FED?* ISN'T THAT A BIT REDUNDANT?
IT'S BRITISH.
AND BAZ IS ARABIC. AND SIMON? THAT'S A PRETTY COMMON NAME IN LEBANON. BUT IT ALSO SOUNDS AMERICAN.
I *AM* AMERICAN.
YOU WEREN'T BORN HERE.
YOU MEAN *THERE.* WE'RE NOT IN AMERICA. THAT'S WHY I HAVEN'T SEEN A LAWYER.
OR THE SKY.
YOU ALMOST DID TIME BEFORE FOR ILLEGAL STREET RACING.
IT WAS QUITE A CRASH. YOU WERE LUCKY TO MAKE IT OUT.
BUT YOUR BROTHER-IN-LAW-- NAZIR AMAR-- WASN'T.
LOOK, I KNOW WHAT THIS *LOOKS* LIKE, I KNOW. I'D LOCK ME UP TOO BUT--
SO WE'VE ESTABLISHED YOU'RE QUITE THE DRIVER, MR. BAZ.
YOU ALSO HAVE A DEGREE IN AUTOMOTIVE ENGINEERING. BUT YOU WOULDN'T HAVE ACCESS TO THESE KINDS OF EXPLOSIVES.
WHO SUPPLIED YOU WITH THE BOMB?
WHO TAUGHT YOU HOW TO DO THIS?

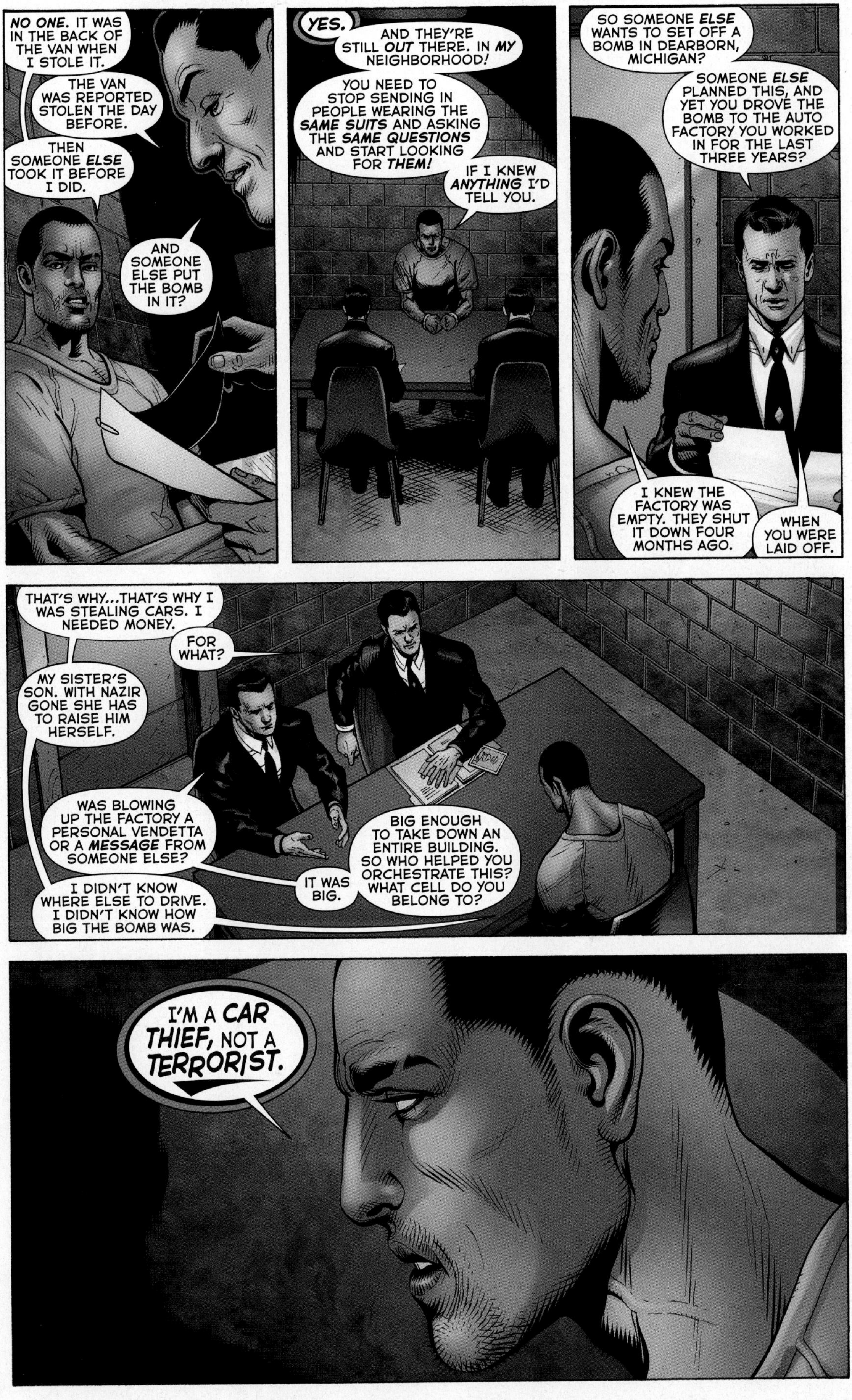
NO ONE. IT WAS IN THE BACK OF THE VAN WHEN I STOLE IT.
THE VAN WAS REPORTED STOLEN THE DAY BEFORE.
THEN SOMEONE ELSE TOOK IT BEFORE I DID.
AND SOMEONE ELSE PUT THE BOMB IN IT?
YES.
AND THEY'RE STILL OUT THERE. IN MY NEIGHBORHOOD!
YOU NEED TO STOP SENDING IN PEOPLE WEARING THE SAME SUITS AND ASKING THE SAME QUESTIONS AND START LOOKING FOR THEM!
IF I KNEW ANYTHING I'D TELL YOU.
SO SOMEONE ELSE WANTS TO SET OFF A BOMB IN DEARBORN, MICHIGAN?
SOMEONE ELSE PLANNED THIS, AND YET YOU DROVE THE BOMB TO THE AUTO FACTORY YOU WORKED IN FOR THE LAST THREE YEARS?
I KNEW THE FACTORY WAS EMPTY. THEY SHUT IT DOWN FOUR MONTHS AGO.
WHEN YOU WERE LAID OFF.
THAT'S WHY...THAT'S WHY I WAS STEALING CARS. I NEEDED MONEY.
FOR WHAT?
MY SISTER'S SON. WITH NAZIR GONE SHE HAS TO RAISE HIM HERSELF.
WAS BLOWING UP THE FACTORY A PERSONAL VENDETTA OR A MESSAGE FROM SOMEONE ELSE?
I DIDN'T KNOW WHERE ELSE TO DRIVE. I DIDN'T KNOW HOW BIG THE BOMB WAS.
IT WAS BIG.
BIG ENOUGH TO TAKE DOWN AN ENTIRE BUILDING. SO WHO HELPED YOU ORCHESTRATE THIS? WHAT CELL DO YOU BELONG TO?
I'M A CAR THIEF, NOT A TERRORIST.

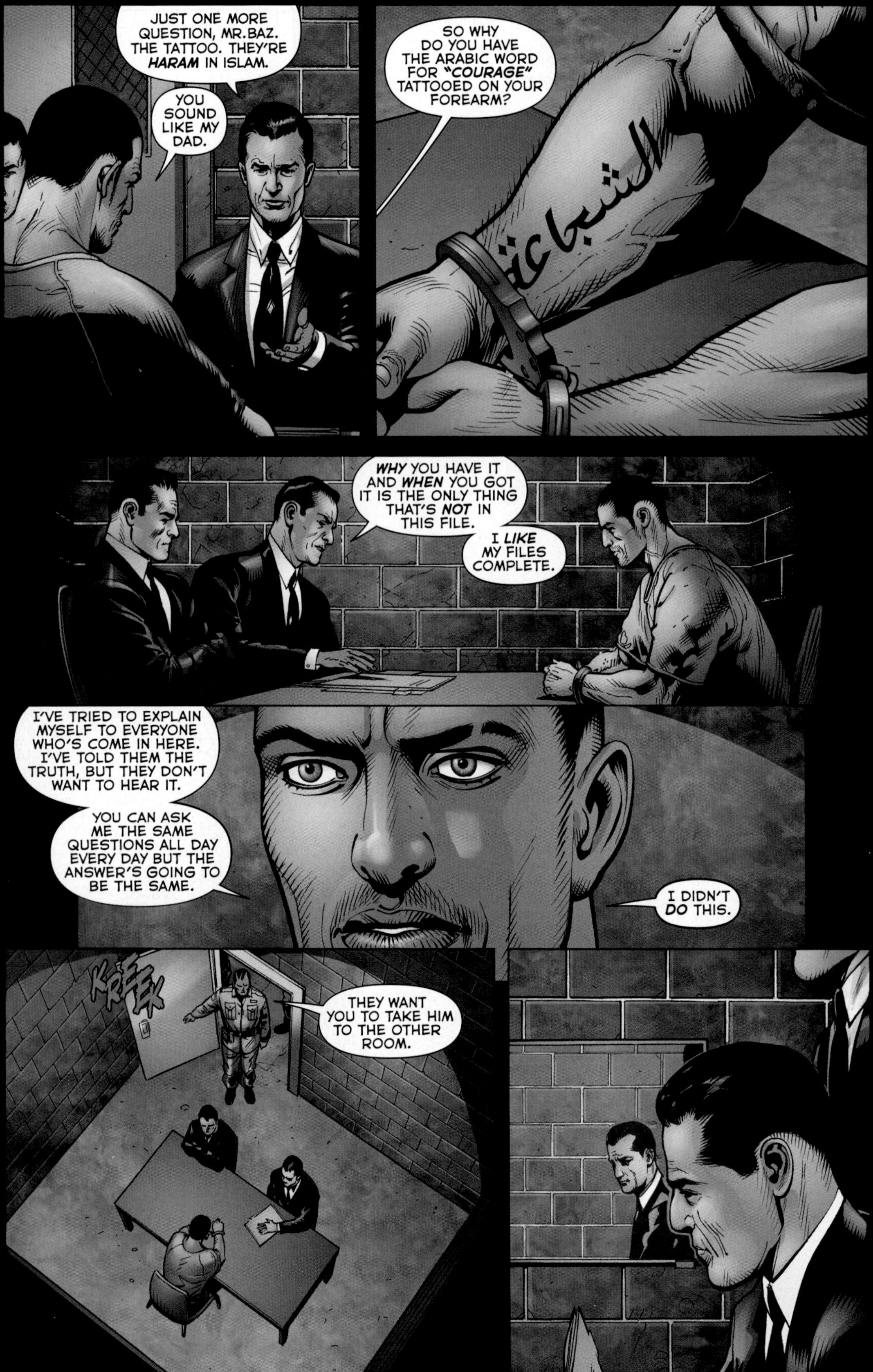

JUST ONE MORE QUESTION, MR.BAZ. THE TATTOO. THEY'RE HARAM IN ISLAM.
YOU SOUND LIKE MY DAD.
SO WHY DO YOU HAVE THE ARABIC WORD FOR "COURAGE" TATTOOED ON YOUR FOREARM?
الشجاعة
WHY YOU HAVE IT AND WHEN YOU GOT IT IS THE ONLY THING THAT'S NOT IN THIS FILE.
I LIKE MY FILES COMPLETE.
I'VE TRIED TO EXPLAIN MYSELF TO EVERYONE WHO'S COME IN HERE. I'VE TOLD THEM THE TRUTH, BUT THEY DON'T WANT TO HEAR IT.
YOU CAN ASK ME THE SAME QUESTIONS ALL DAY EVERY DAY BUT THE ANSWER'S GOING TO BE THE SAME.
I DIDN'T DO THIS.
KREEK
THEY WANT YOU TO TAKE HIM TO THE OTHER ROOM.

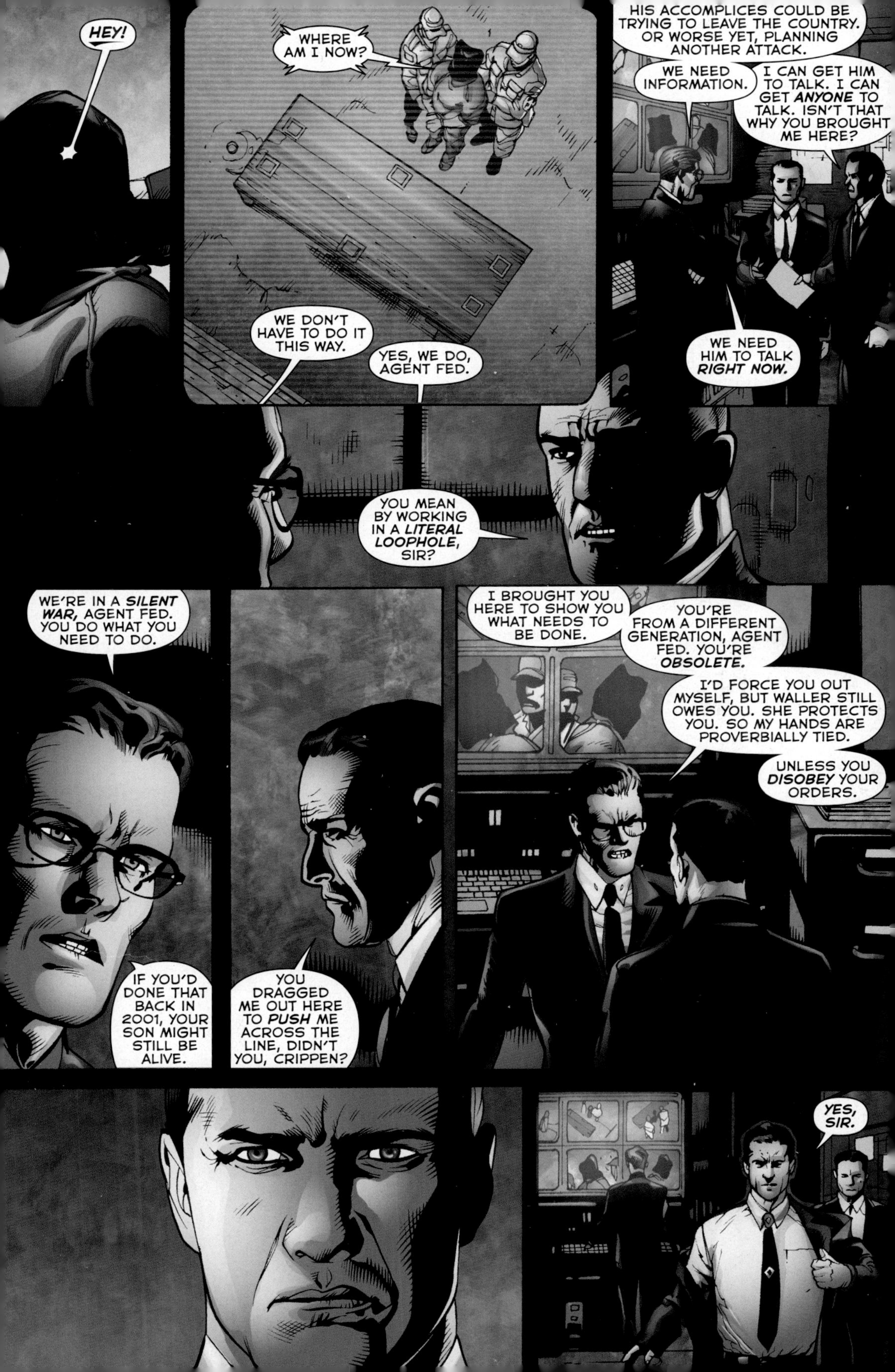

HEY!
WHERE AM I NOW?
WE DON'T HAVE TO DO IT THIS WAY.
YES, WE DO, AGENT FED.
HIS ACCOMPLICES COULD BE TRYING TO LEAVE THE COUNTRY. OR WORSE YET, PLANNING ANOTHER ATTACK.
WE NEED INFORMATION.
I CAN GET HIM TO TALK. I CAN GET ANYONE TO TALK. ISN'T THAT WHY YOU BROUGHT ME HERE?
WE NEED HIM TO TALK RIGHT NOW.
YOU MEAN BY WORKING IN A LITERAL LOOPHOLE, SIR?
WE'RE IN A SILENT WAR, AGENT FED. YOU DO WHAT YOU NEED TO DO.
IF YOU'D DONE THAT BACK IN 2001, YOUR SON MIGHT STILL BE ALIVE.
YOU DRAGGED ME OUT HERE TO PUSH ME ACROSS THE LINE, DIDN'T YOU, CRIPPEN?
I BROUGHT YOU HERE TO SHOW YOU WHAT NEEDS TO BE DONE.
YOU'RE FROM A DIFFERENT GENERATION, AGENT FED. YOU'RE OBSOLETE.
I'D FORCE YOU OUT MYSELF, BUT WALLER STILL OWES YOU. SHE PROTECTS YOU. SO MY HANDS ARE PROVERBIALLY TIED.
UNLESS YOU DISOBEY YOUR ORDERS.
YES, SIR.

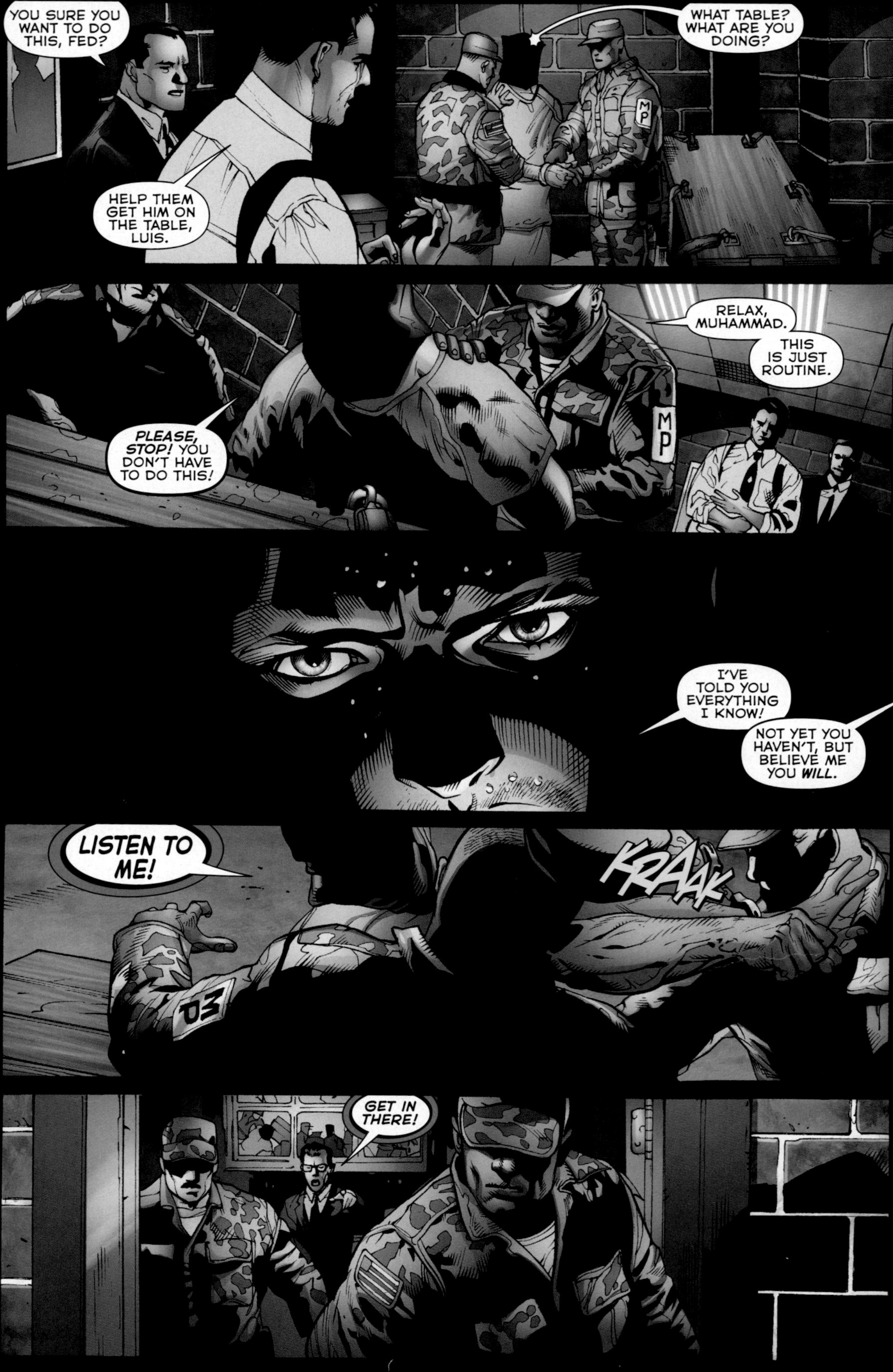
YOU SURE YOU WANT TO DO THIS, FED?
HELP THEM GET HIM ON THE TABLE, LUIS.
WHAT TABLE? WHAT ARE YOU DOING?
MP
PLEASE, STOP! YOU DON'T HAVE TO DO THIS!
RELAX, MUHAMMAD.
THIS IS JUST ROUTINE.
MP
I'VE TOLD YOU EVERYTHING I KNOW!
NOT YET YOU HAVEN'T, BUT BELIEVE ME YOU WILL.
LISTEN TO ME!
KRAAAK
GET IN THERE!

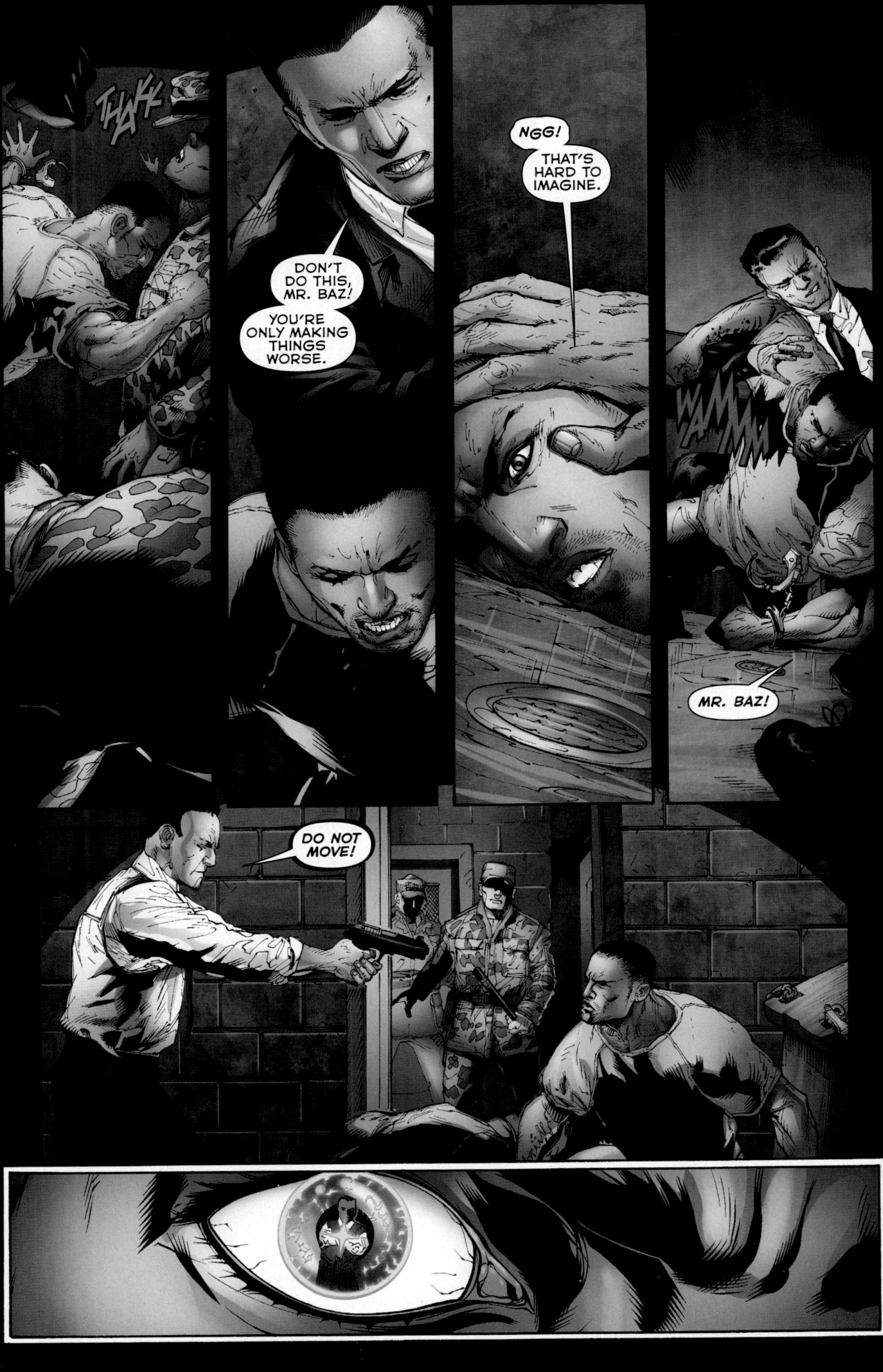
THAKK
DON'T DO THIS, MR. BAZ!
YOU'RE ONLY MAKING THINGS WORSE.
NGG!
THAT'S HARD TO IMAGINE.
WAMM
MR. BAZ!
DO NOT MOVE!

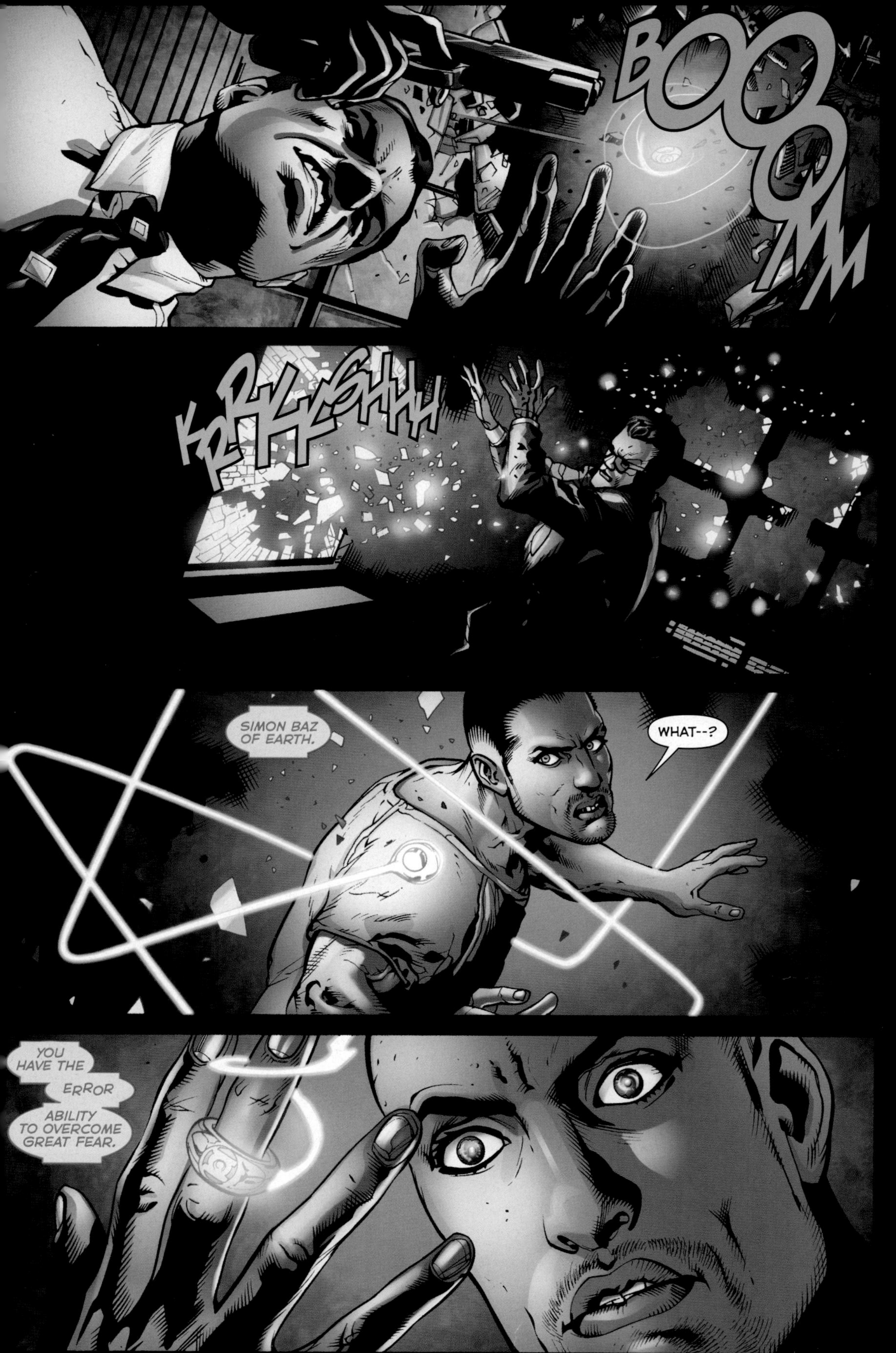
BOOOOM
KRRKKSHHH
SIMON BAZ OF EARTH.
WHAT--?
YOU HAVE THE
ERROR
ABILITY TO OVERCOME GREAT FEAR.

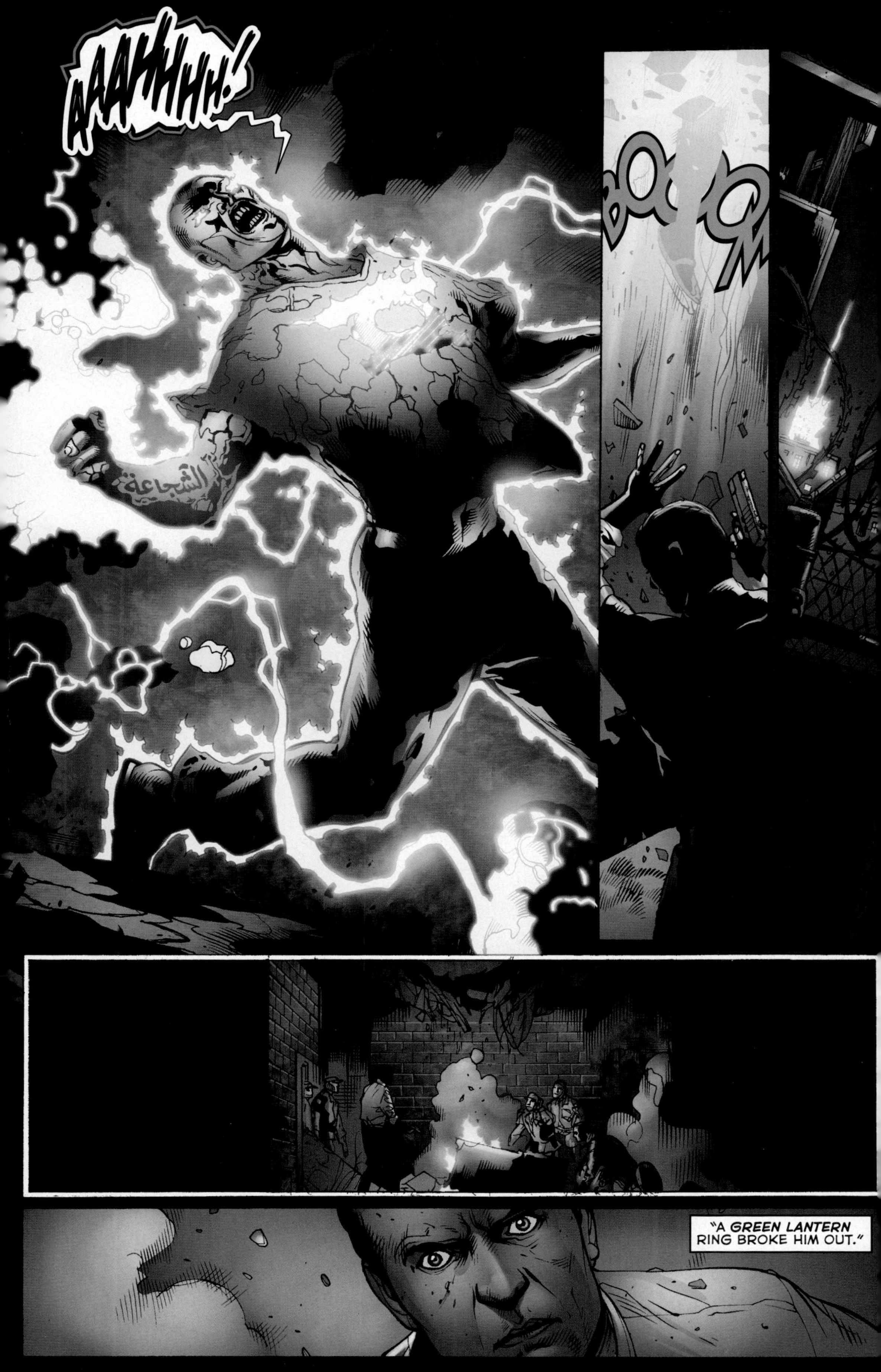
AAAHHHH!
BOOOM
الشجاعة
"A GREEN LANTERN RING BROKE HIM OUT."

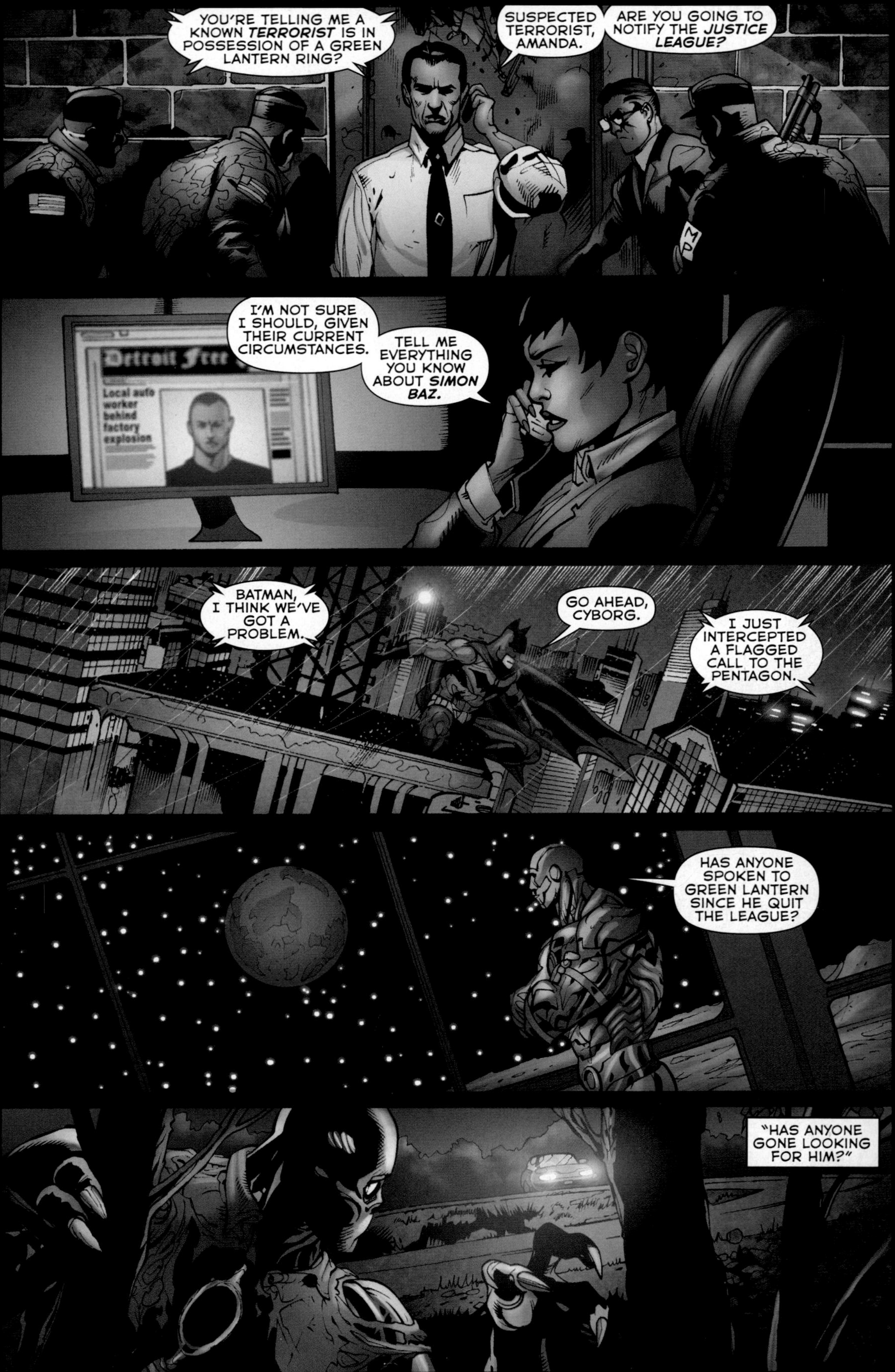

YOU'RE TELLING ME A KNOWN TERRORIST IS IN POSSESSION OF A GREEN LANTERN RING?
SUSPECTED TERRORIST, AMANDA.
ARE YOU GOING TO NOTIFY THE JUSTICE LEAGUE?
MP
Detroit Free
Local auto worker behind factory explosion
I'M NOT SURE I SHOULD, GIVEN THEIR CURRENT CIRCUMSTANCES.
TELL ME EVERYTHING YOU KNOW ABOUT SIMON BAZ.
BATMAN, I THINK WE'VE GOT A PROBLEM.
GO AHEAD, CYBORG.
I JUST INTERCEPTED A FLAGGED CALL TO THE PENTAGON.
HAS ANYONE SPOKEN TO GREEN LANTERN SINCE HE QUIT THE LEAGUE?
"HAS ANYONE GONE LOOKING FOR HIM?"

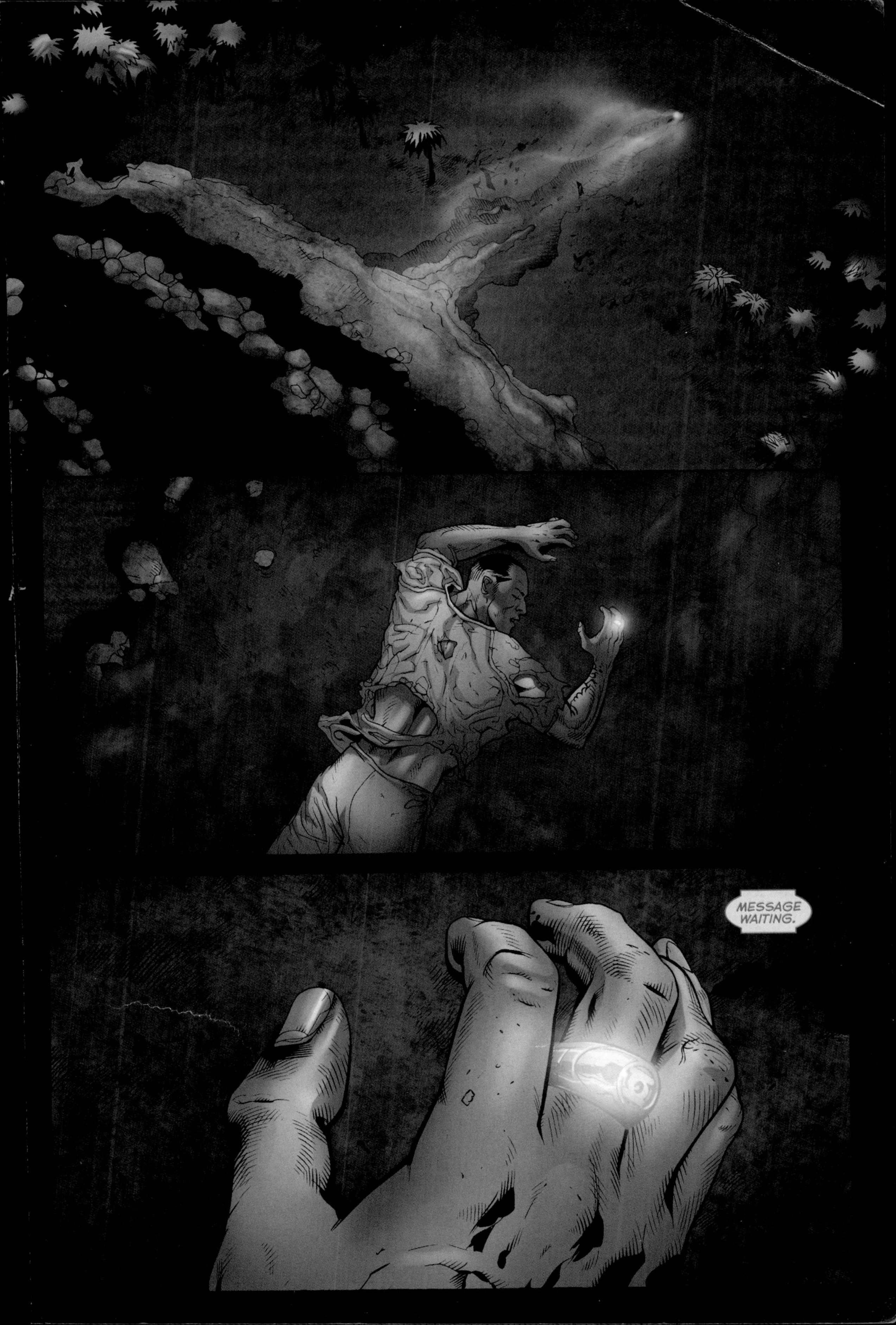
MESSAGE WAITING.

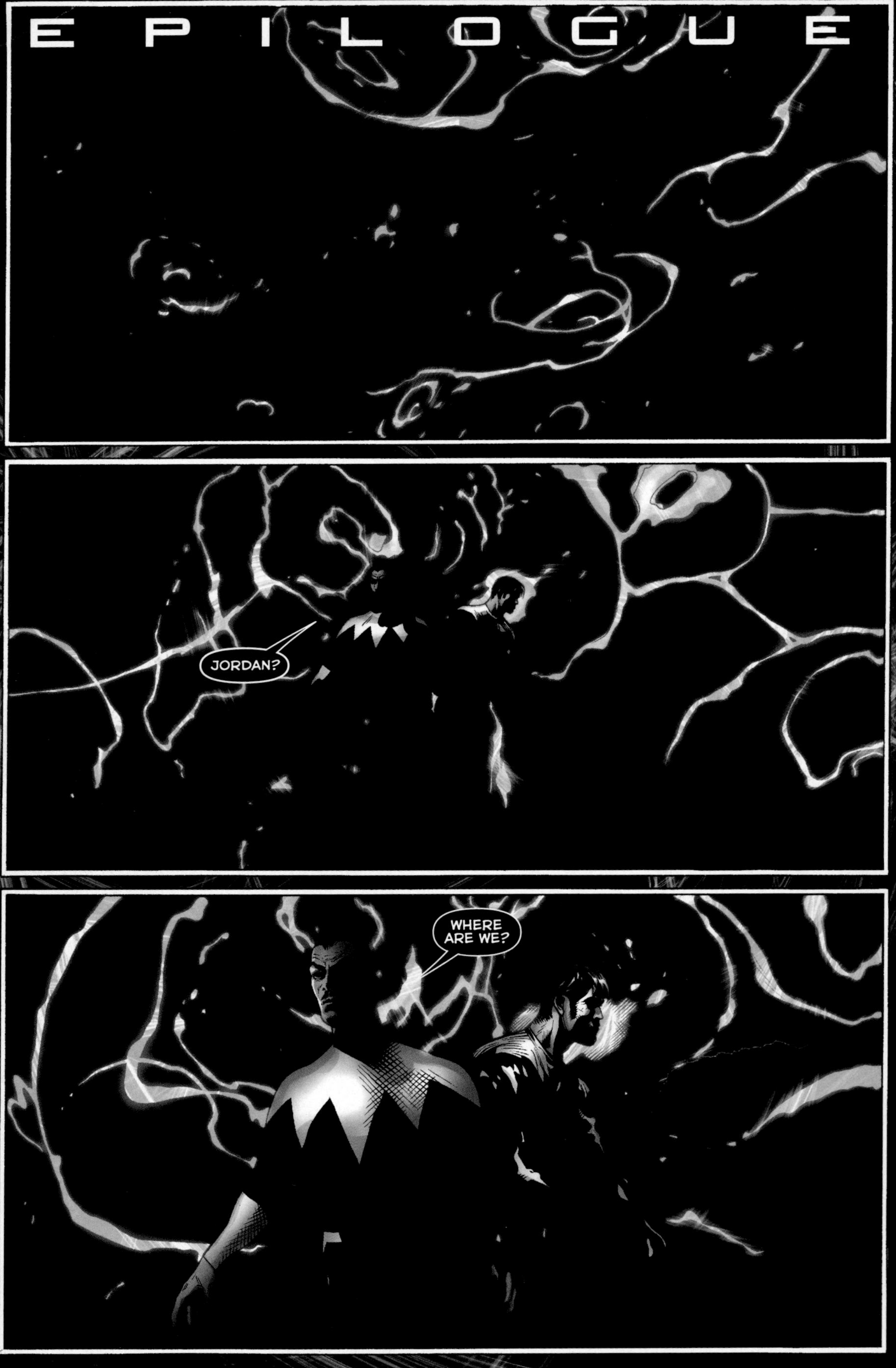
EPILOGUE
JORDAN?
WHERE ARE WE?

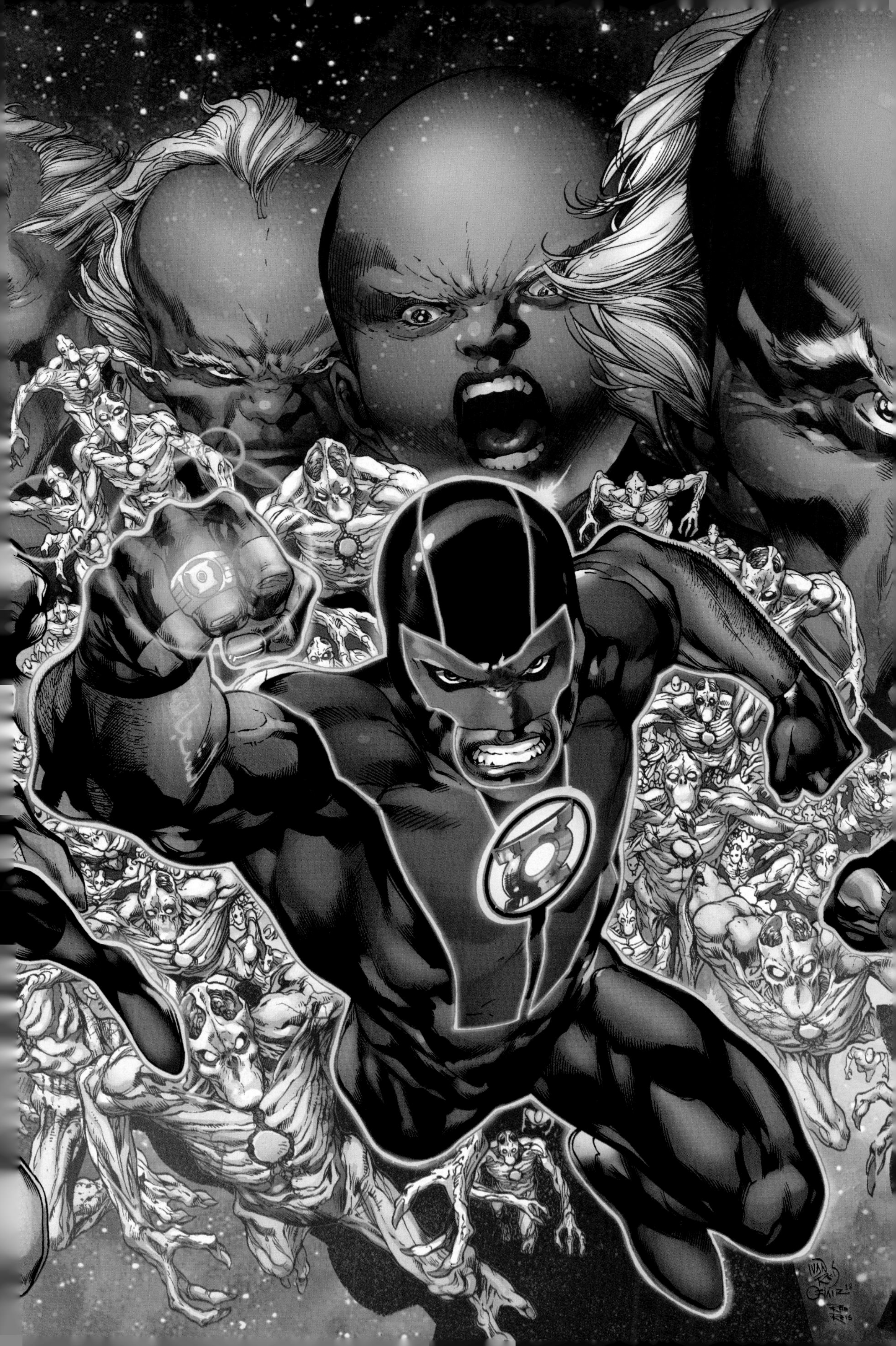

GEOFF JOHNS writer **DOUG MAHNKE** penciller **CHRISTIAN ALAMY, MARK IRWIN, TOM NGUYEN, KEITH CHAMPAGNE & MARC DEERING** inkers
IVAN REIS, OCLAIR ALBERT & ROD REIS cover

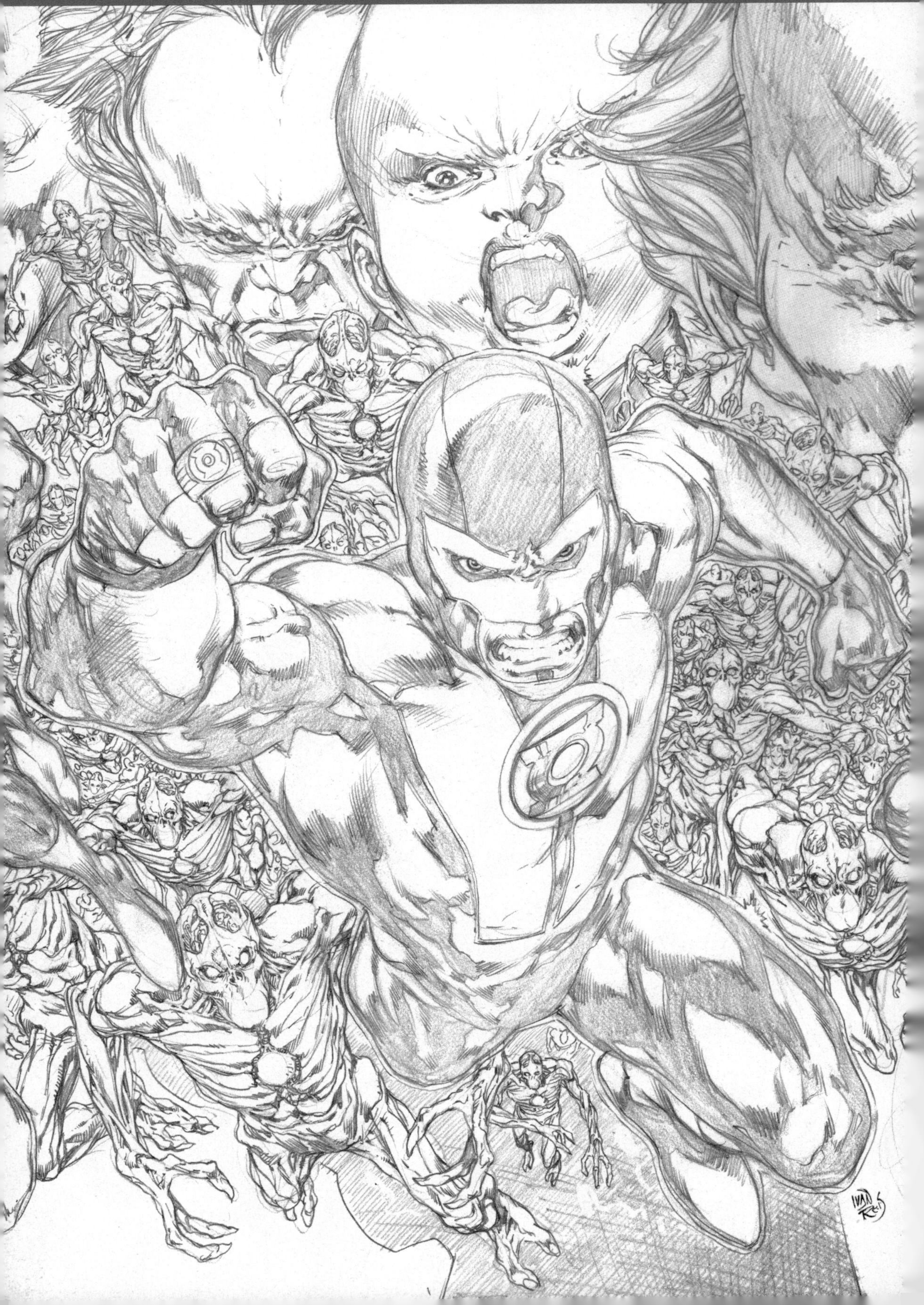

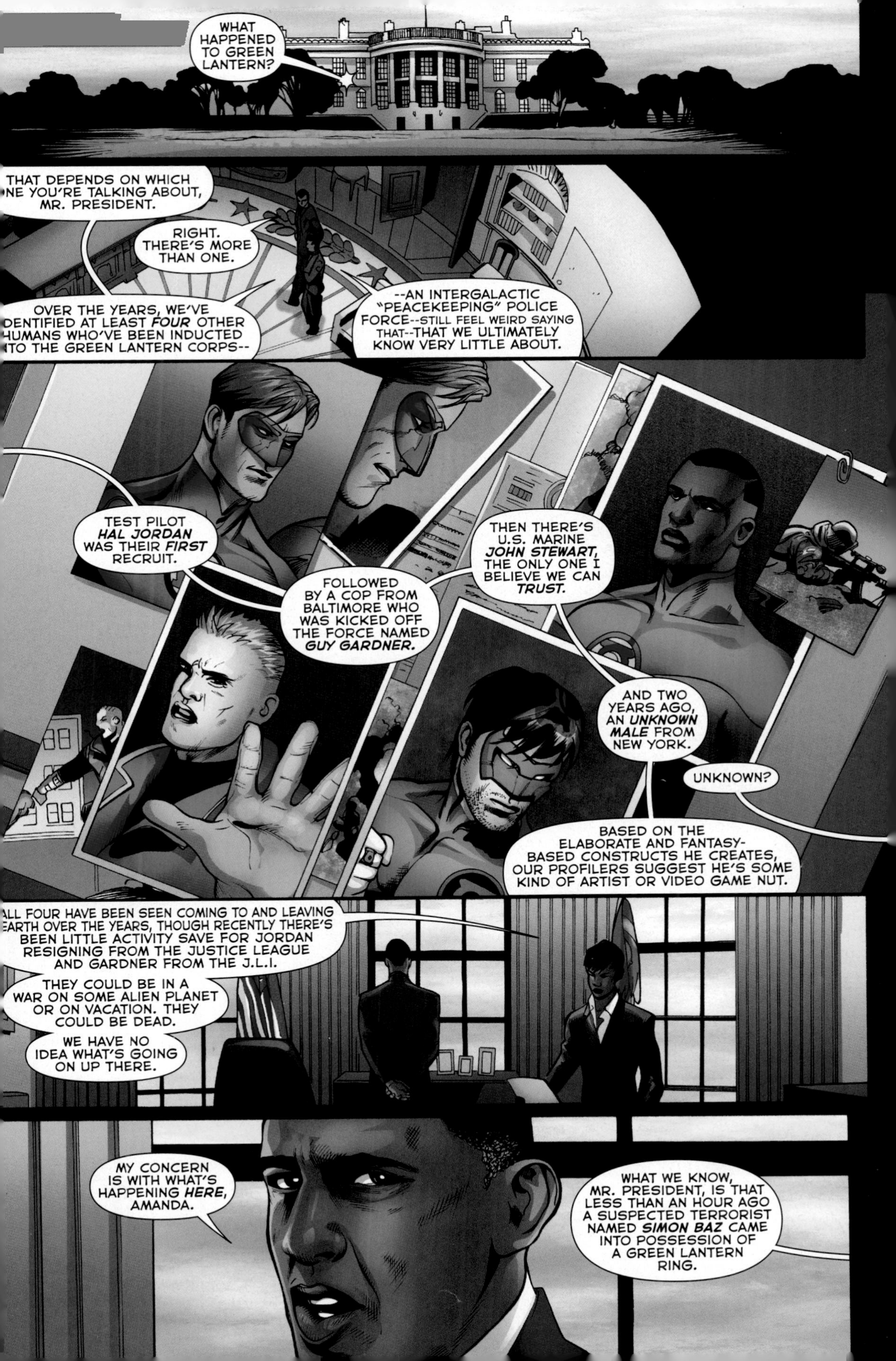
WHAT HAPPENED TO GREEN LANTERN?
THAT DEPENDS ON WHICH NE YOU'RE TALKING ABOUT, MR. PRESIDENT.
RIGHT. THERE'S MORE THAN ONE.
OVER THE YEARS, WE'VE DENTIFIED AT LEAST FOUR OTHER HUMANS WHO'VE BEEN INDUCTED NTO THE GREEN LANTERN CORPS--
--AN INTERGALACTIC "PEACEKEEPING" POLICE FORCE--STILL FEEL WEIRD SAYING THAT--THAT WE ULTIMATELY KNOW VERY LITTLE ABOUT.
TEST PILOT HAL JORDAN WAS THEIR FIRST RECRUIT.
FOLLOWED BY A COP FROM BALTIMORE WHO WAS KICKED OFF THE FORCE NAMED GUY GARDNER.
THEN THERE'S U.S. MARINE JOHN STEWART, THE ONLY ONE I BELIEVE WE CAN TRUST.
AND TWO YEARS AGO, AN UNKNOWN MALE FROM NEW YORK.
UNKNOWN?
BASED ON THE ELABORATE AND FANTASY-BASED CONSTRUCTS HE CREATES, OUR PROFILERS SUGGEST HE'S SOME KIND OF ARTIST OR VIDEO GAME NUT.
ALL FOUR HAVE BEEN SEEN COMING TO AND LEAVING EARTH OVER THE YEARS, THOUGH RECENTLY THERE'S BEEN LITTLE ACTIVITY SAVE FOR JORDAN RESIGNING FROM THE JUSTICE LEAGUE AND GARDNER FROM THE J.L.I.
THEY COULD BE IN A WAR ON SOME ALIEN PLANET OR ON VACATION. THEY COULD BE DEAD.
WE HAVE NO IDEA WHAT'S GOING ON UP THERE.
MY CONCERN IS WITH WHAT'S HAPPENING HERE, AMANDA.
WHAT WE KNOW, MR. PRESIDENT, IS THAT LESS THAN AN HOUR AGO A SUSPECTED TERRORIST NAMED SIMON BAZ CAME INTO POSSESSION OF A GREEN LANTERN RING.

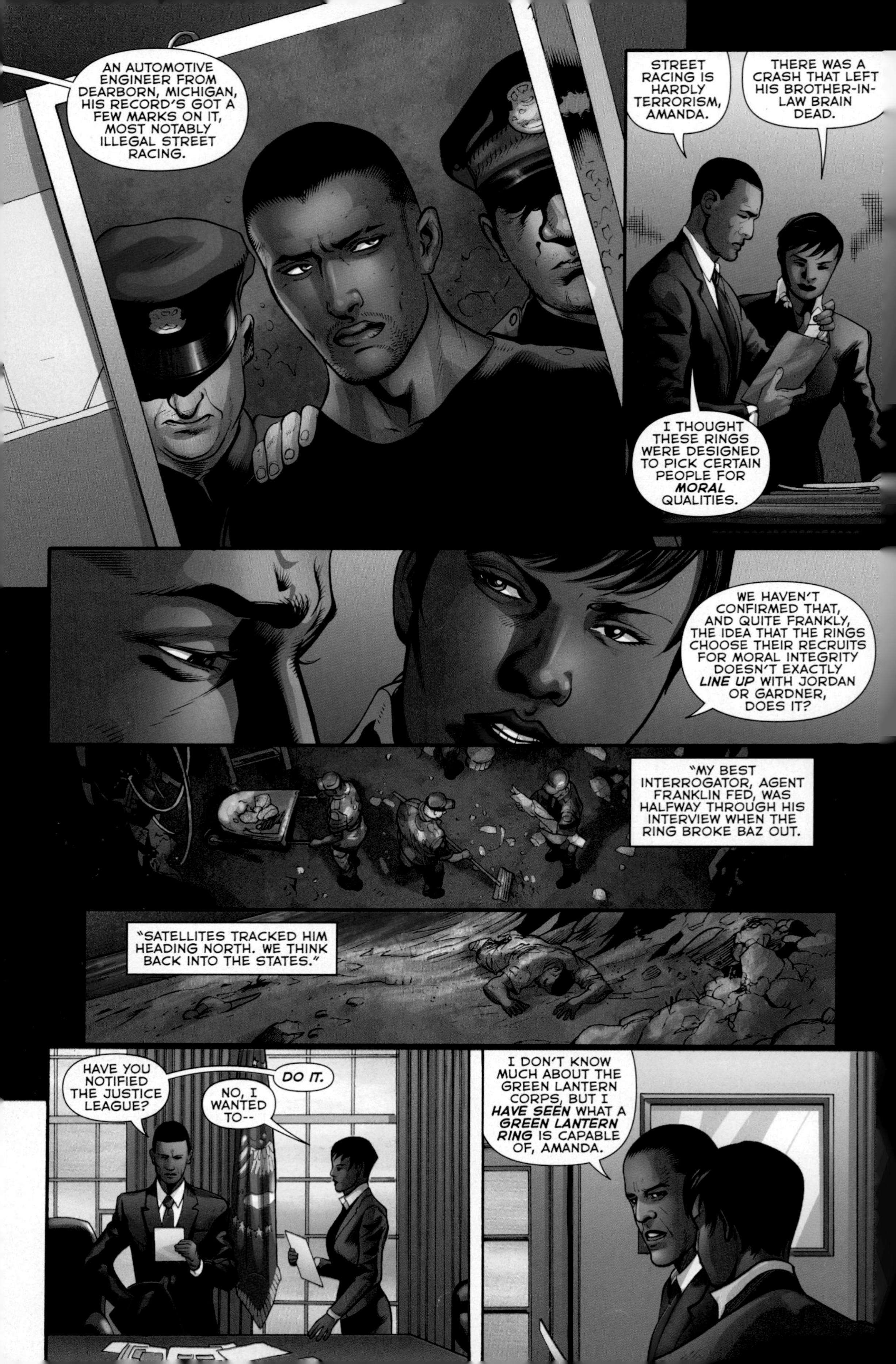
AN AUTOMOTIVE ENGINEER FROM DEARBORN, MICHIGAN, HIS RECORD'S GOT A FEW MARKS ON IT, MOST NOTABLY ILLEGAL STREET RACING.
STREET RACING IS HARDLY TERRORISM, AMANDA.
THERE WAS A CRASH THAT LEFT HIS BROTHER-IN-LAW BRAIN DEAD.
I THOUGHT THESE RINGS WERE DESIGNED TO PICK CERTAIN PEOPLE FOR MORAL QUALITIES.
WE HAVEN'T CONFIRMED THAT, AND QUITE FRANKLY, THE IDEA THAT THE RINGS CHOOSE THEIR RECRUITS FOR MORAL INTEGRITY DOESN'T EXACTLY LINE UP WITH JORDAN OR GARDNER, DOES IT?
"MY BEST INTERROGATOR, AGENT FRANKLIN FED, WAS HALFWAY THROUGH HIS INTERVIEW WHEN THE RING BROKE BAZ OUT.
"SATELLITES TRACKED HIM HEADING NORTH. WE THINK BACK INTO THE STATES."
HAVE YOU NOTIFIED THE JUSTICE LEAGUE?
NO, I WANTED TO--
DO IT.
I DON'T KNOW MUCH ABOUT THE GREEN LANTERN CORPS, BUT I HAVE SEEN WHAT A GREEN LANTERN RING IS CAPABLE OF, AMANDA.

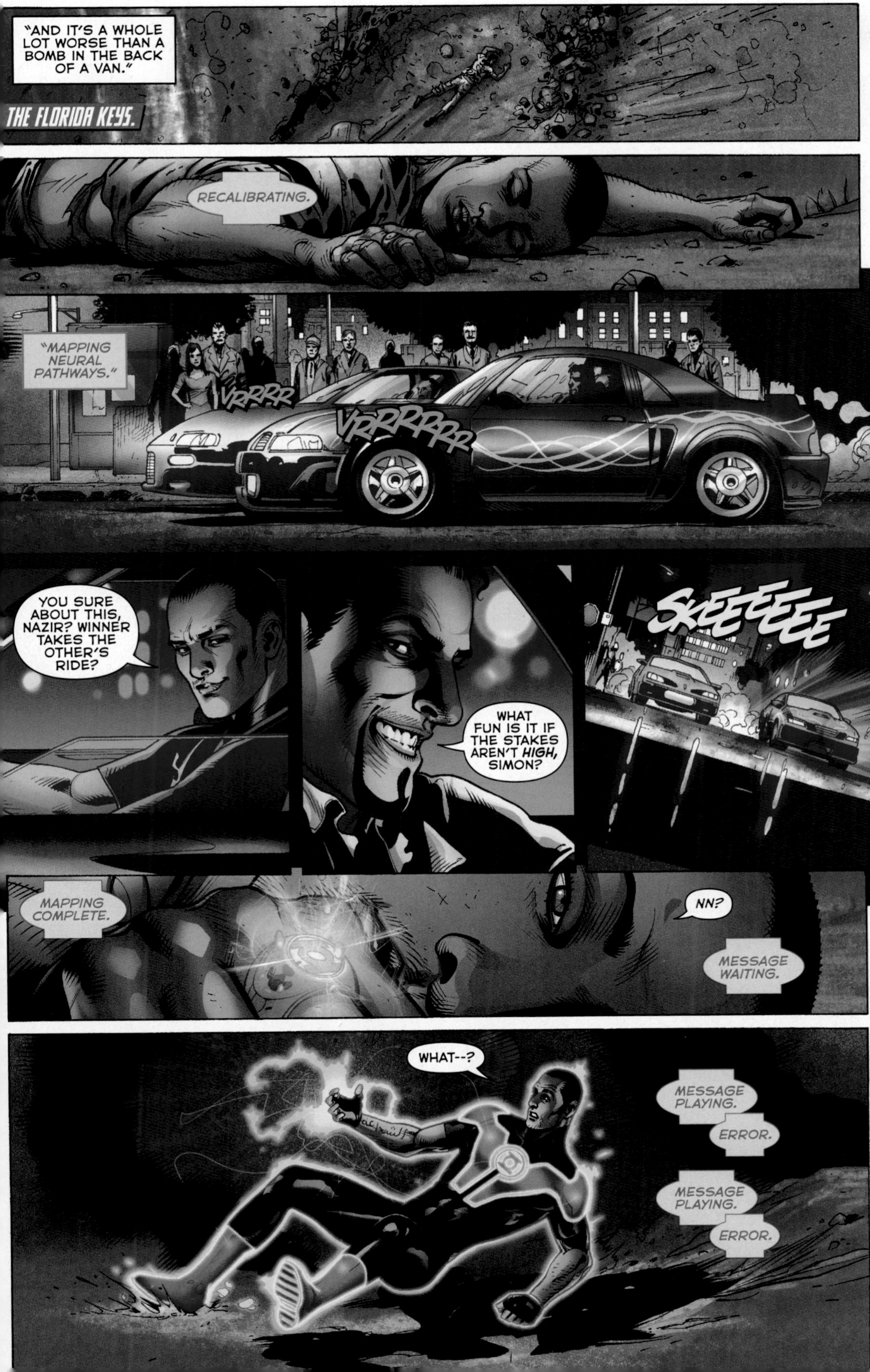
"AND IT'S A WHOLE LOT WORSE THAN A BOMB IN THE BACK OF A VAN."
THE FLORIDA KEYS.
RECALIBRATING.
"MAPPING NEURAL PATHWAYS."
VRRRR
VRRRRRRR
YOU SURE ABOUT THIS, NAZIR? WINNER TAKES THE OTHER'S RIDE?
WHAT FUN IS IT IF THE STAKES AREN'T HIGH, SIMON?
SKEEEEEEE
MAPPING COMPLETE.
NN?
MESSAGE WAITING.
WHAT--?
MESSAGE PLAYING.
ERROR.
MESSAGE PLAYING.
ERROR.

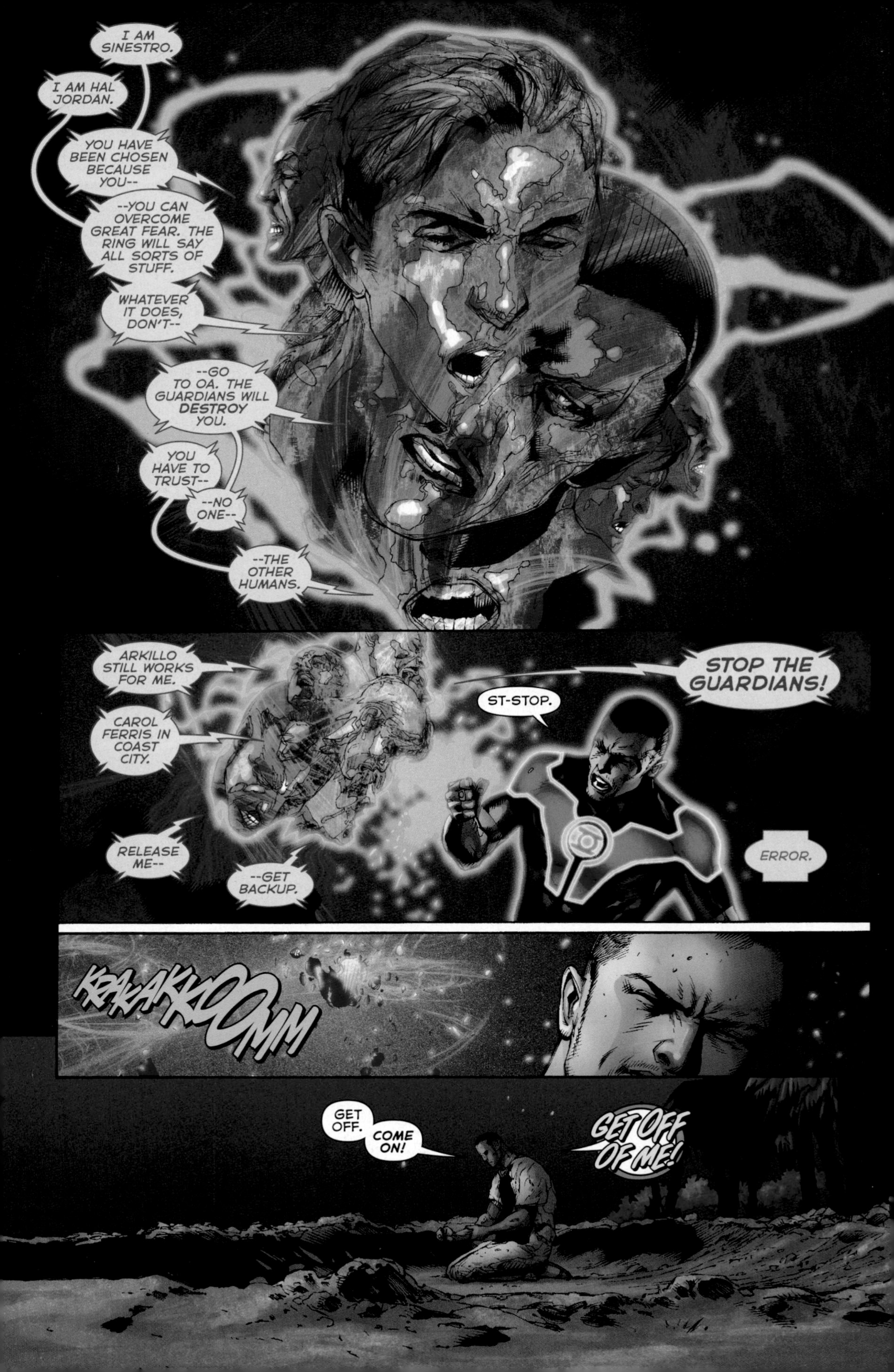
I AM SINESTRO.
I AM HAL JORDAN.
YOU HAVE BEEN CHOSEN BECAUSE YOU--
--YOU CAN OVERCOME GREAT FEAR. THE RING WILL SAY ALL SORTS OF STUFF.
WHATEVER IT DOES, DON'T--
--GO TO OA. THE GUARDIANS WILL DESTROY YOU.
YOU HAVE TO TRUST--
--NO ONE--
--THE OTHER HUMANS.
ARKILLO STILL WORKS FOR ME.
CAROL FERRIS IN COAST CITY.
RELEASE ME--
--GET BACKUP.
STOP THE GUARDIANS!
ST-STOP.
ERROR.
KRAKAKKOOMM
GET OFF.
COME ON!
GET OFF OF ME!

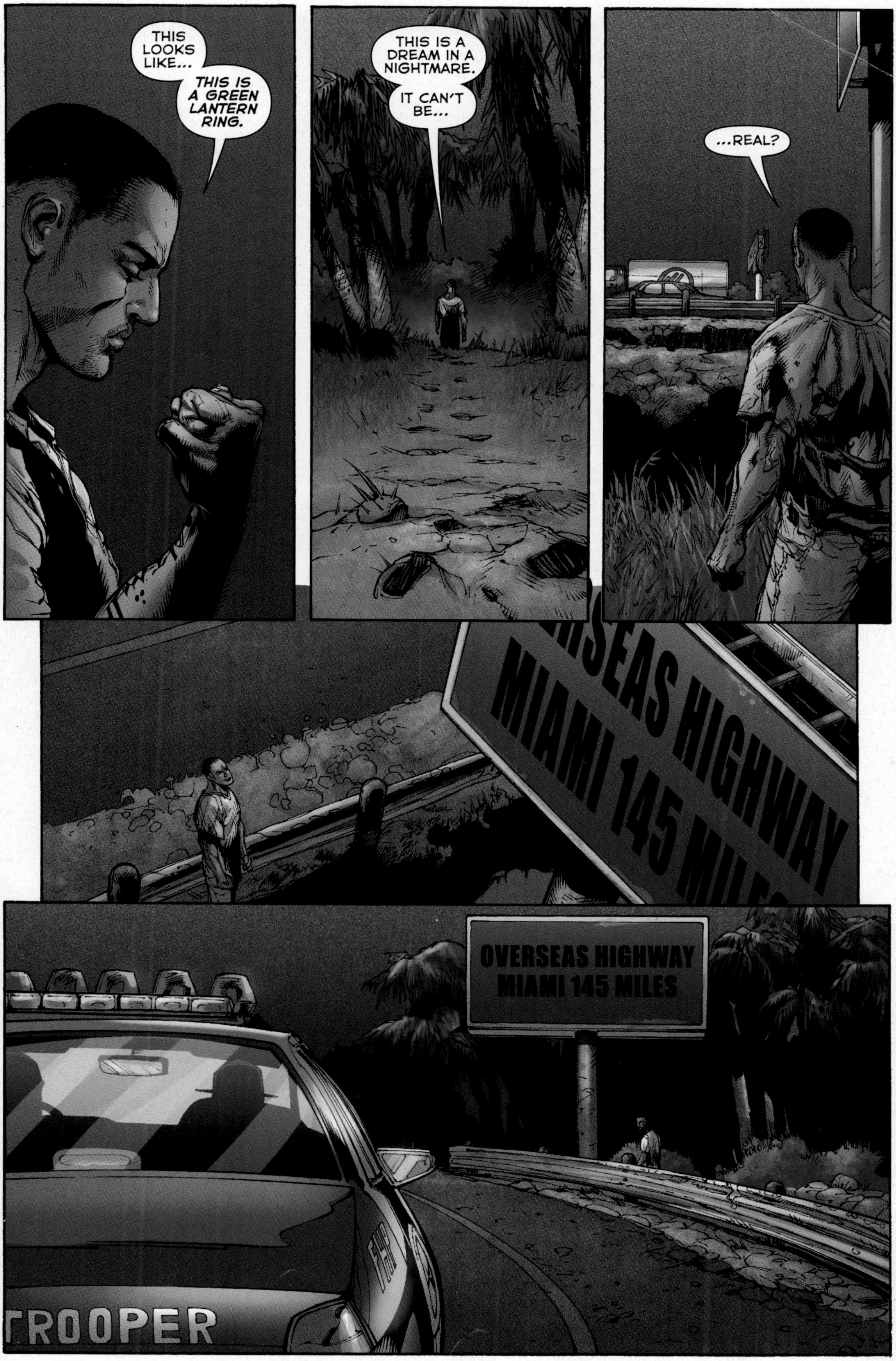
THIS LOOKS LIKE...
THIS IS A GREEN LANTERN RING.
THIS IS A DREAM IN A NIGHTMARE.
IT CAN'T BE...
...REAL?
OVERSEAS HIGHWAY MIAMI 145 MILES
OVERSEAS HIGHWAY
MIAMI 145 MILES
TROOPER

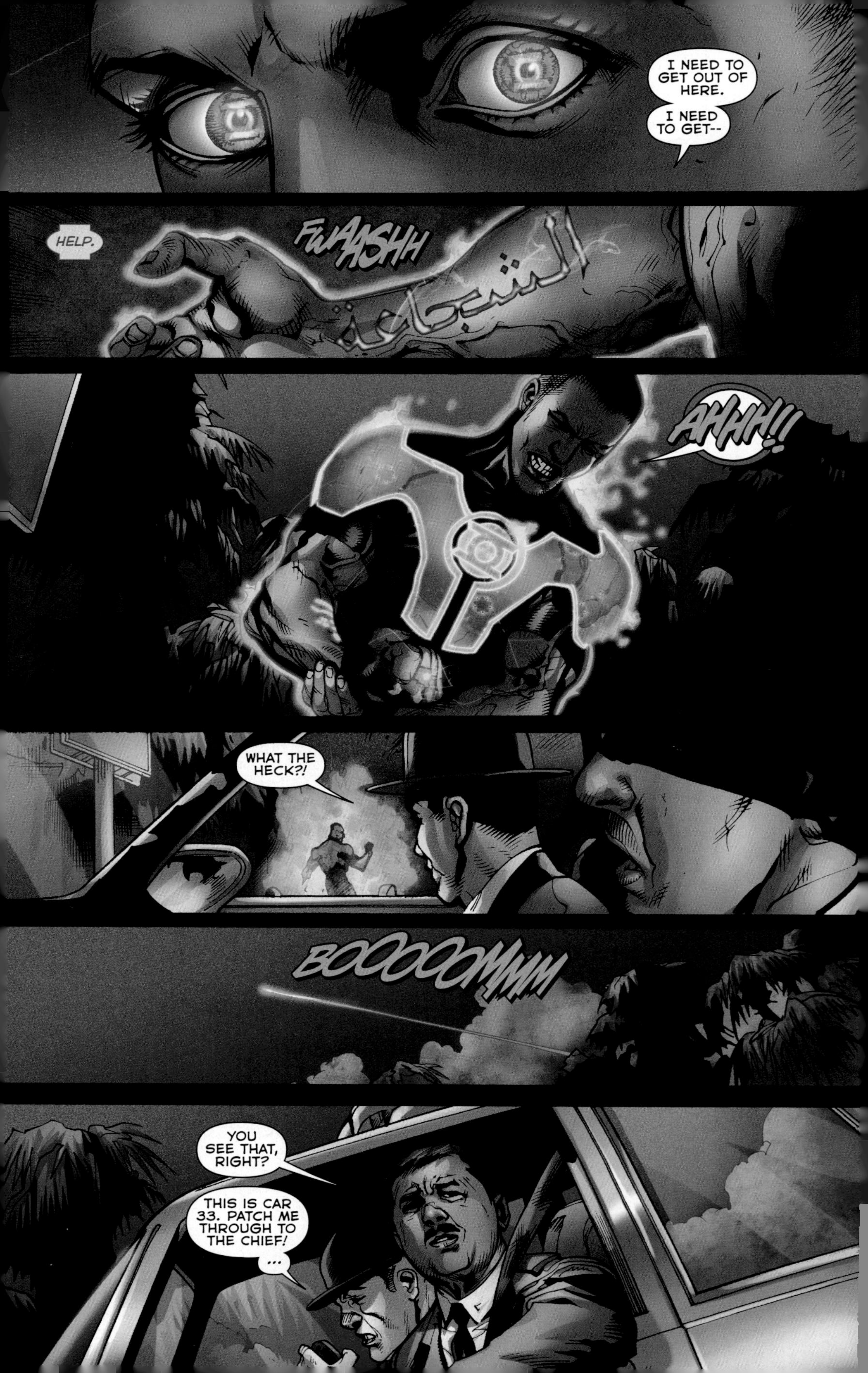
I NEED TO GET OUT OF HERE.
I NEED TO GET--
HELP.
FWAASHH
الشجاعة
AHHH!!
WHAT THE HECK?!
BOOOOOOMMM
YOU SEE THAT, RIGHT?
THIS IS CAR 33. PATCH ME THROUGH TO THE CHIEF!
...

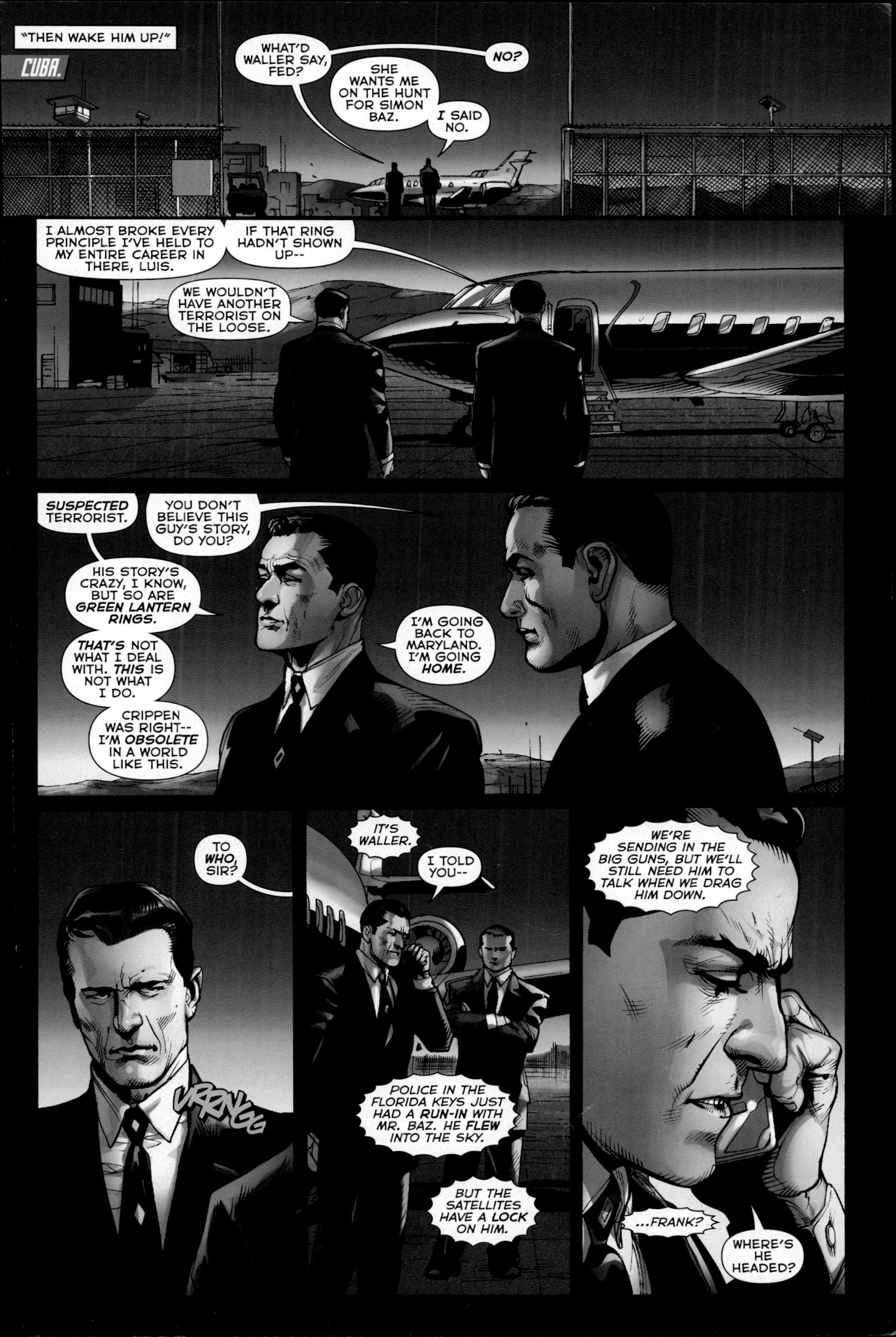
"THEN WAKE HIM UP!"
CUBA.
WHAT'D WALLER SAY, FED?
SHE WANTS ME ON THE HUNT FOR SIMON BAZ.
NO?
I SAID NO.
I ALMOST BROKE EVERY PRINCIPLE I'VE HELD TO MY ENTIRE CAREER IN THERE, LUIS.
IF THAT RING HADN'T SHOWN UP--
WE WOULDN'T HAVE ANOTHER TERRORIST ON THE LOOSE.
SUSPECTED TERRORIST.
YOU DON'T BELIEVE THIS GUY'S STORY, DO YOU?
HIS STORY'S CRAZY, I KNOW, BUT SO ARE GREEN LANTERN RINGS.
THAT'S NOT WHAT I DEAL WITH. THIS IS NOT WHAT I DO.
CRIPPEN WAS RIGHT-- I'M OBSOLETE IN A WORLD LIKE THIS.
I'M GOING BACK TO MARYLAND. I'M GOING HOME.
TO WHO, SIR?
VRRNGG
IT'S WALLER.
I TOLD YOU--
POLICE IN THE FLORIDA KEYS JUST HAD A RUN-IN WITH MR. BAZ. HE FLEW INTO THE SKY.
BUT THE SATELLITES HAVE A LOCK ON HIM.
WE'RE SENDING IN THE BIG GUNS, BUT WE'LL STILL NEED HIM TO TALK WHEN WE DRAG HIM DOWN.
...FRANK?
WHERE'S HE HEADED?

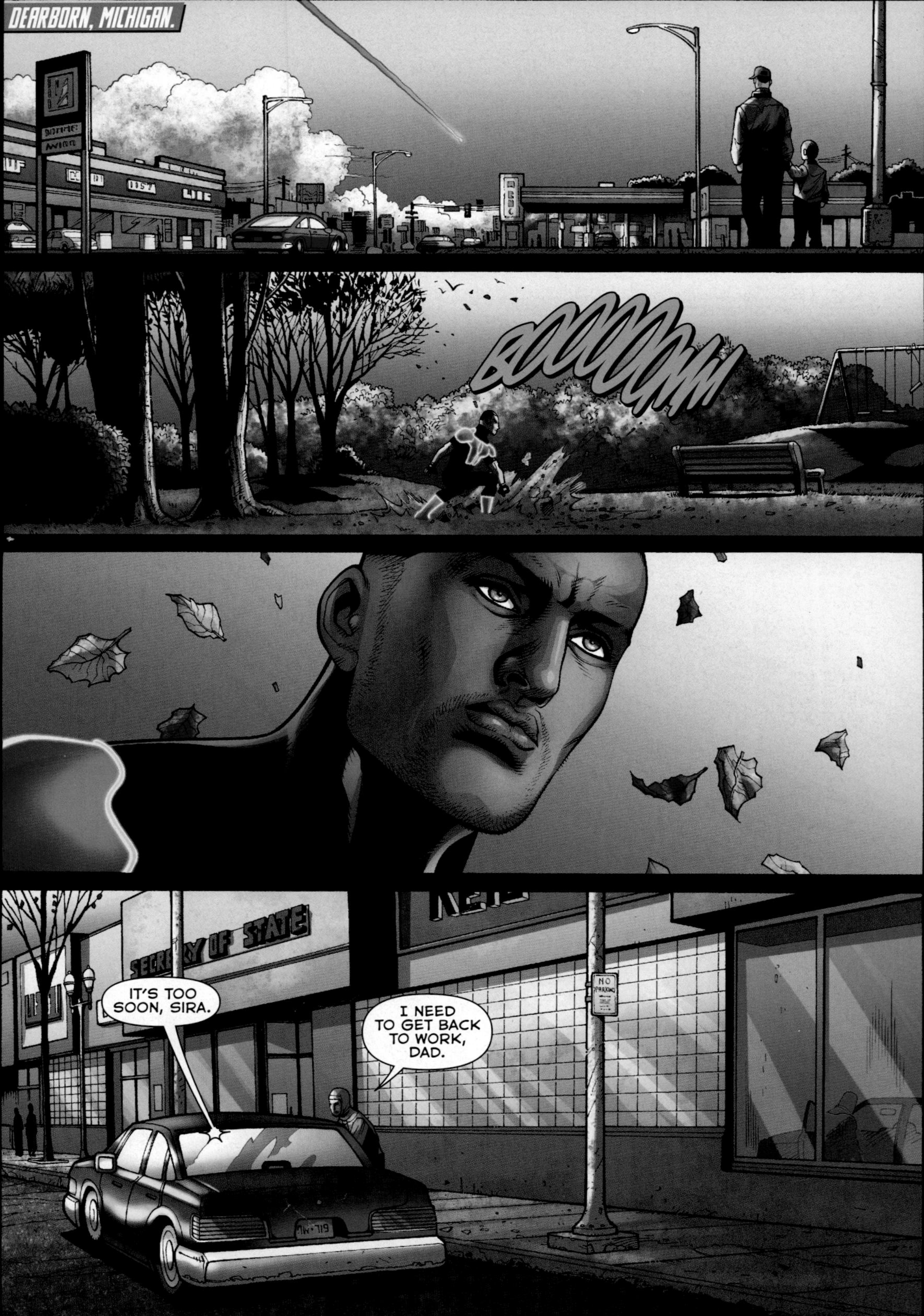
DEARBORN, MICHIGAN.
BOOOOOMM
IT'S TOO SOON, SIRA.
I NEED TO GET BACK TO WORK, DAD.

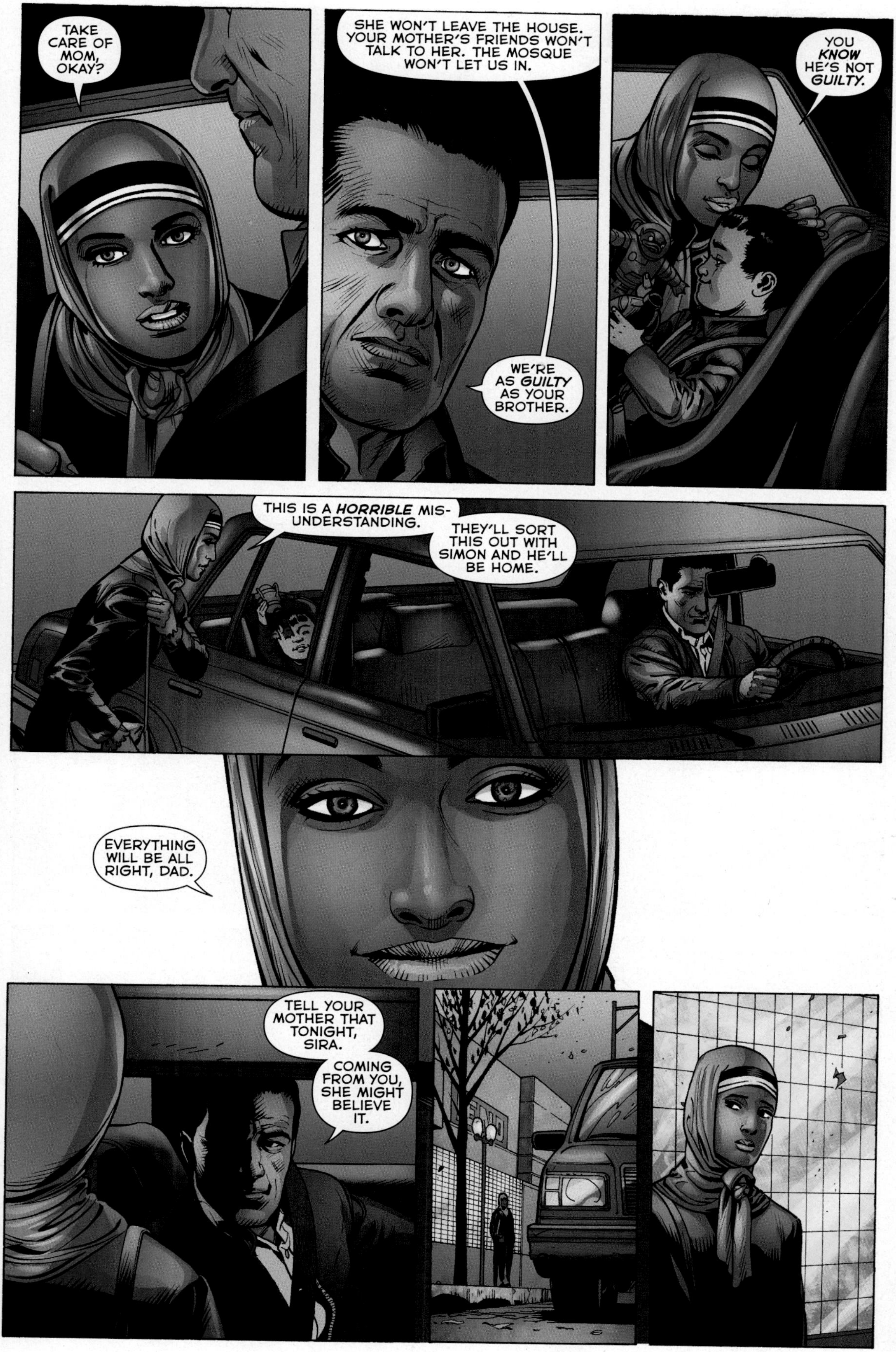
TAKE CARE OF MOM, OKAY?
SHE WON'T LEAVE THE HOUSE. YOUR MOTHER'S FRIENDS WON'T TALK TO HER. THE MOSQUE WON'T LET US IN.
WE'RE AS GUILTY AS YOUR BROTHER.
YOU KNOW HE'S NOT GUILTY.
THIS IS A HORRIBLE MIS-UNDERSTANDING.
THEY'LL SORT THIS OUT WITH SIMON AND HE'LL BE HOME.
EVERYTHING WILL BE ALL RIGHT, DAD.
TELL YOUR MOTHER THAT TONIGHT, SIRA.
COMING FROM YOU, SHE MIGHT BELIEVE IT.

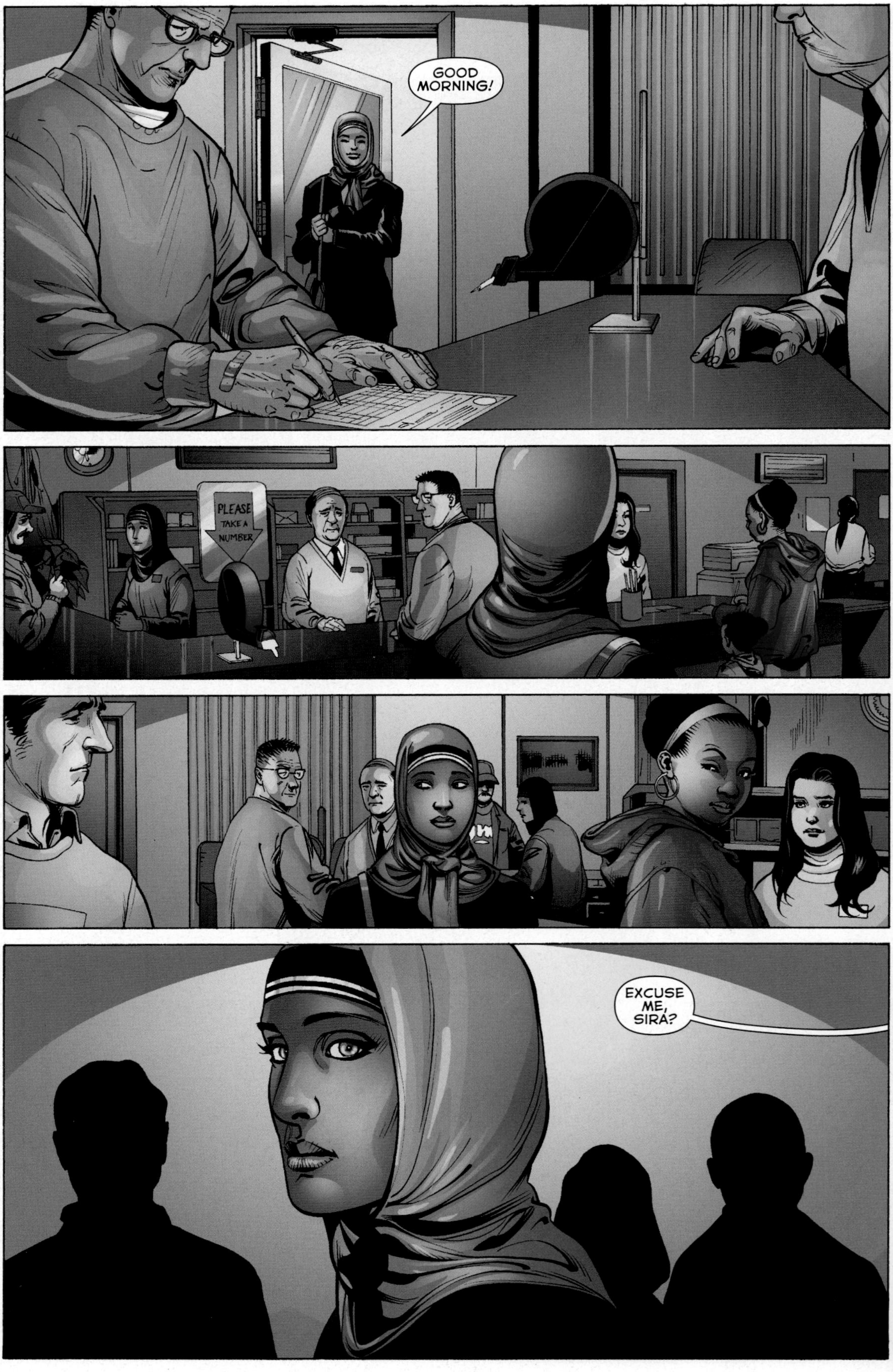
GOOD MORNING!
PLEASE TAKE A NUMBER
EXCUSE ME, SIRA?

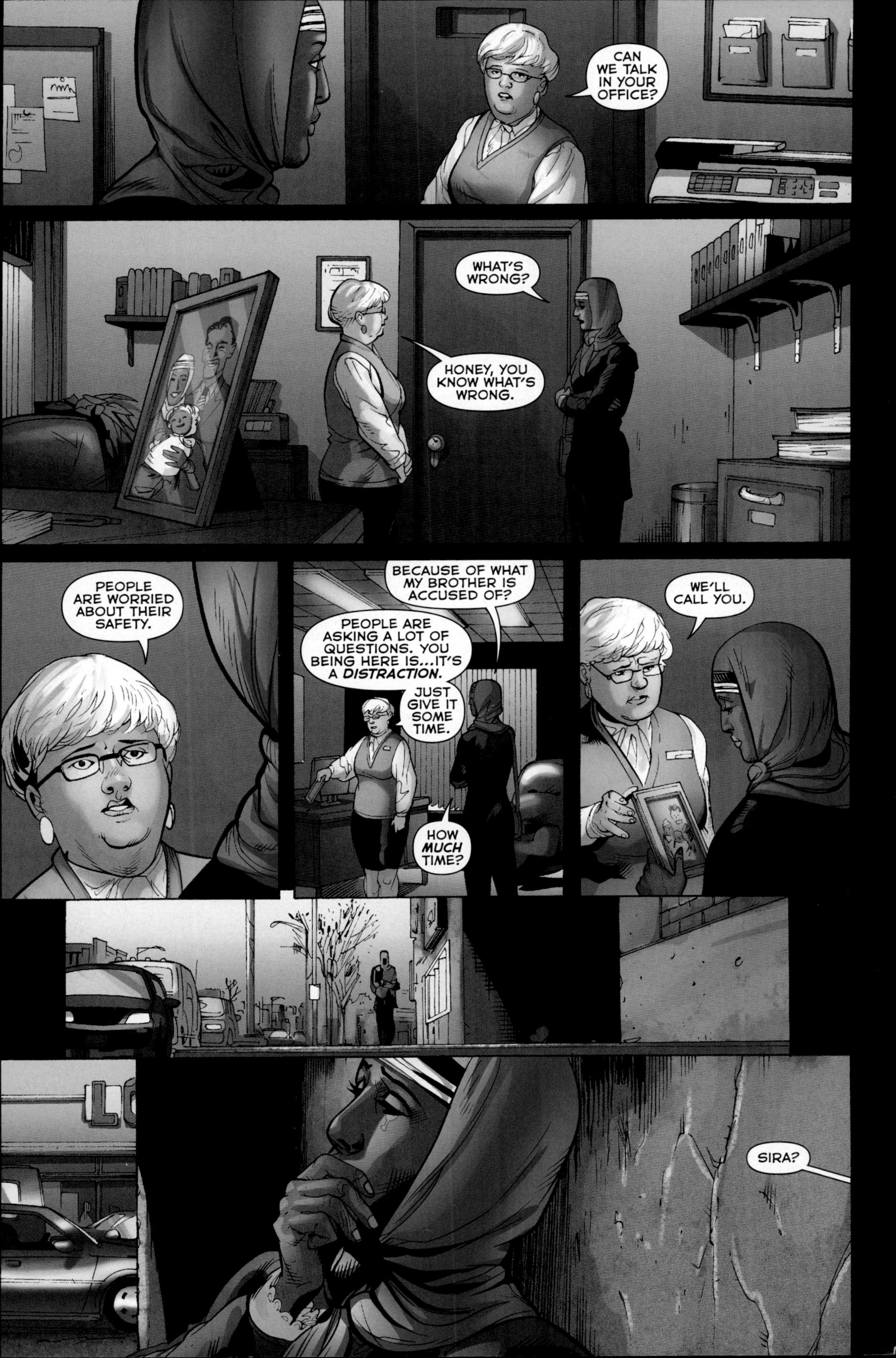
CAN WE TALK IN YOUR OFFICE?
WHAT'S WRONG?
HONEY, YOU KNOW WHAT'S WRONG.
PEOPLE ARE WORRIED ABOUT THEIR SAFETY.
BECAUSE OF WHAT MY BROTHER IS ACCUSED OF?
PEOPLE ARE ASKING A LOT OF QUESTIONS. YOU BEING HERE IS...IT'S A *DISTRACTION*.
JUST GIVE IT SOME TIME.
HOW *MUCH* TIME?
WE'LL CALL YOU.
SIRA?

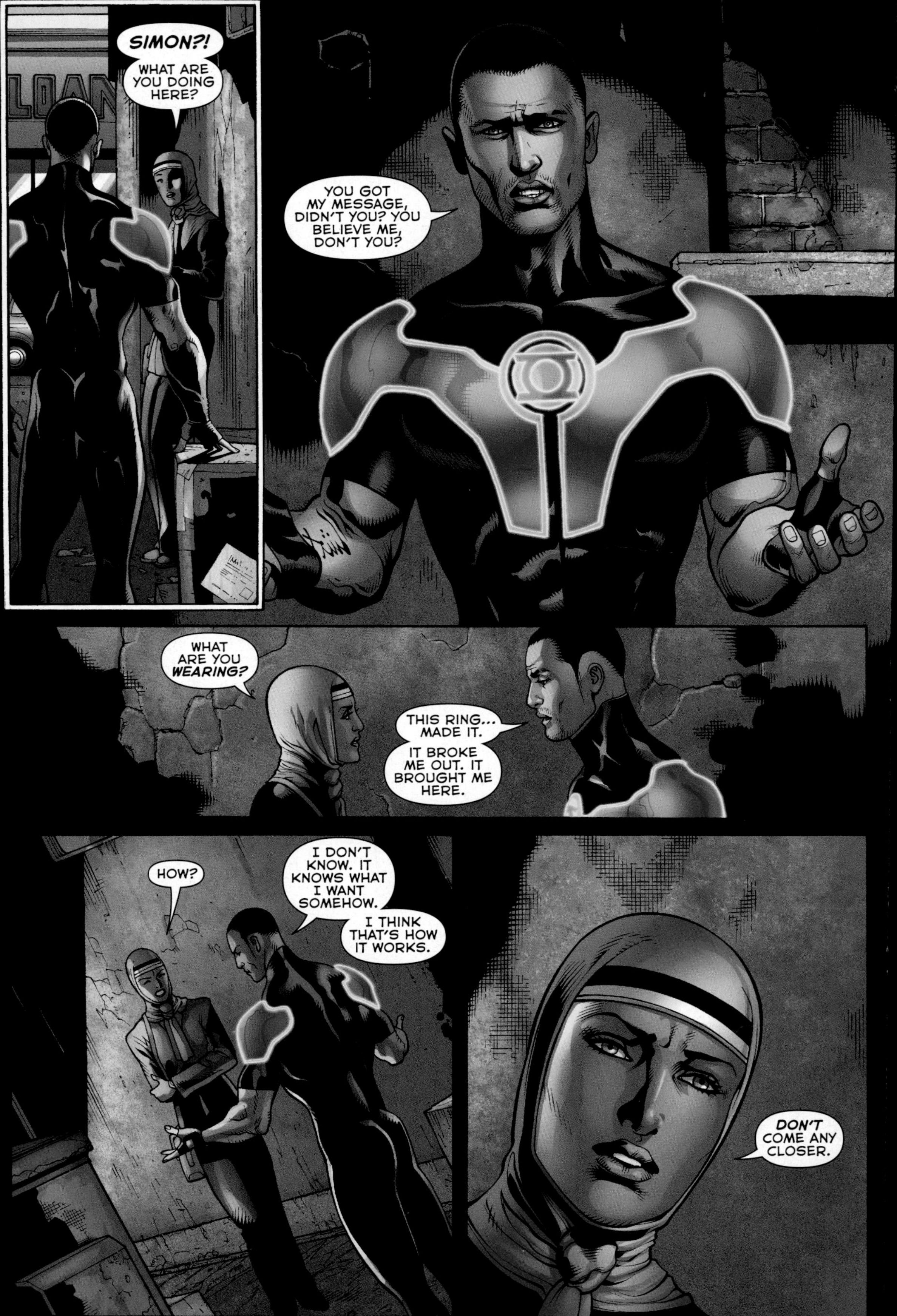
LOAN
SIMON?! WHAT ARE YOU DOING HERE?
YOU GOT MY MESSAGE, DIDN'T YOU? YOU BELIEVE ME, DON'T YOU?
WHAT ARE YOU *WEARING?*
THIS RING... MADE IT.
IT BROKE ME OUT. IT BROUGHT ME HERE.
HOW?
I DON'T KNOW. IT KNOWS WHAT I WANT SOMEHOW.
I THINK THAT'S HOW IT WORKS.
DON'T COME ANY CLOSER.

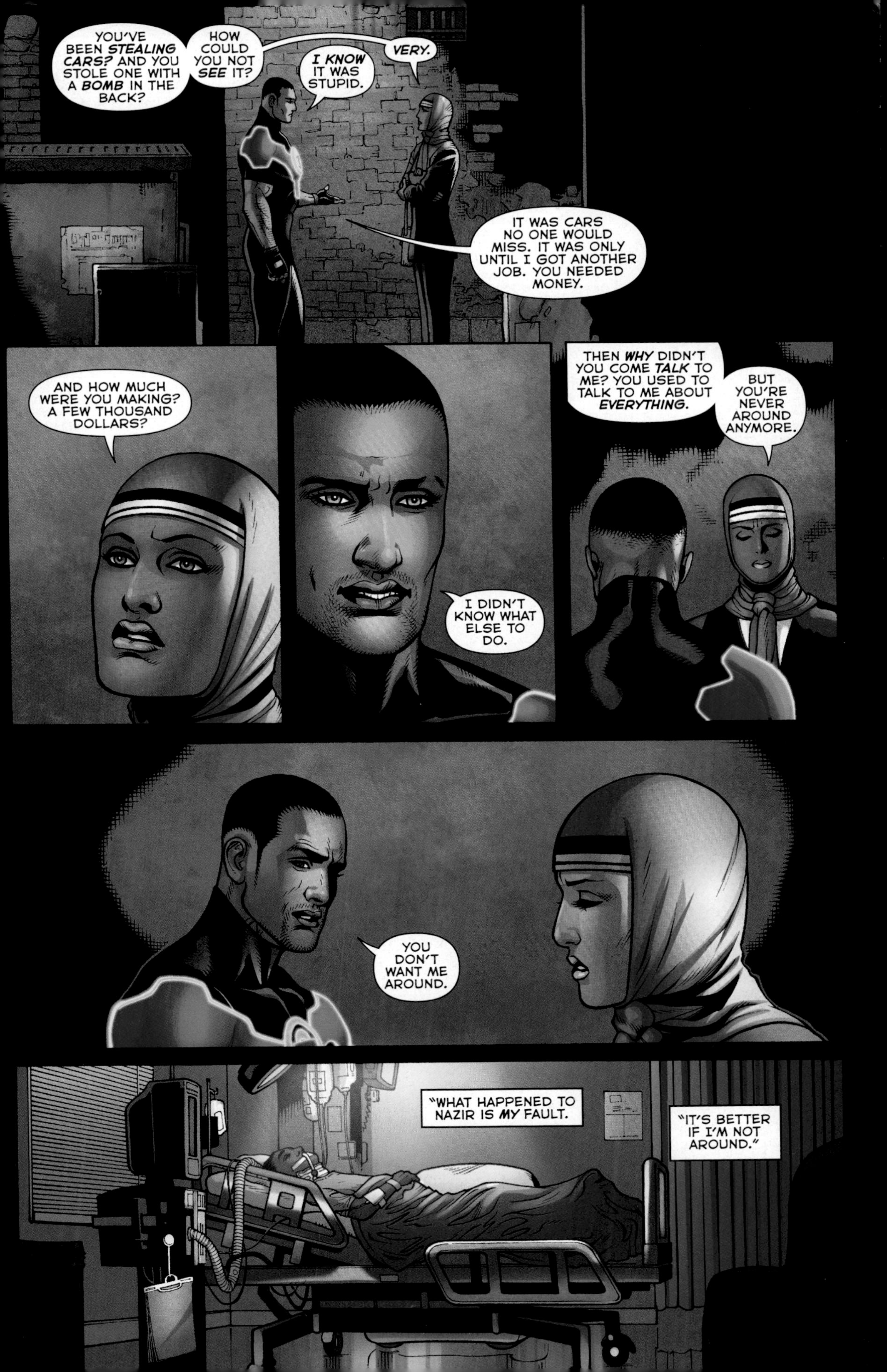
YOU'VE BEEN STEALING CARS? AND YOU STOLE ONE WITH A BOMB IN THE BACK?
HOW COULD YOU NOT SEE IT?
VERY.
I KNOW IT WAS STUPID.
IT WAS CARS NO ONE WOULD MISS. IT WAS ONLY UNTIL I GOT ANOTHER JOB. YOU NEEDED MONEY.
AND HOW MUCH WERE YOU MAKING? A FEW THOUSAND DOLLARS?
I DIDN'T KNOW WHAT ELSE TO DO.
THEN WHY DIDN'T YOU COME TALK TO ME? YOU USED TO TALK TO ME ABOUT EVERYTHING.
BUT YOU'RE NEVER AROUND ANYMORE.
YOU DON'T WANT ME AROUND.
"WHAT HAPPENED TO NAZIR IS MY FAULT.
"IT'S BETTER IF I'M NOT AROUND."

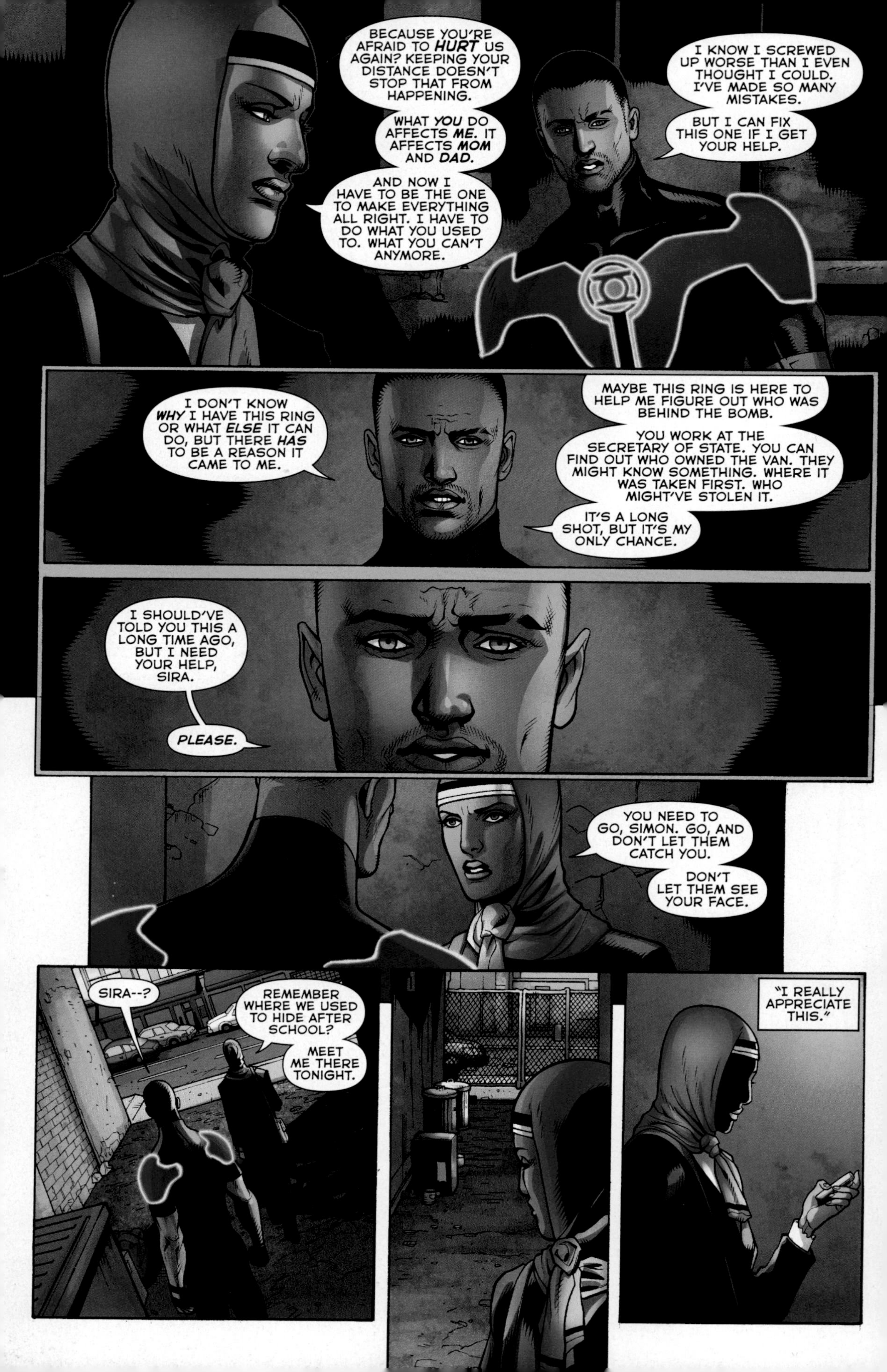
BECAUSE YOU'RE AFRAID TO HURT US AGAIN? KEEPING YOUR DISTANCE DOESN'T STOP THAT FROM HAPPENING.
WHAT YOU DO AFFECTS ME. IT AFFECTS MOM AND DAD.
AND NOW I HAVE TO BE THE ONE TO MAKE EVERYTHING ALL RIGHT. I HAVE TO DO WHAT YOU USED TO. WHAT YOU CAN'T ANYMORE.
I KNOW I SCREWED UP WORSE THAN I EVEN THOUGHT I COULD. I'VE MADE SO MANY MISTAKES.
BUT I CAN FIX THIS ONE IF I GET YOUR HELP.
I DON'T KNOW WHY I HAVE THIS RING OR WHAT ELSE IT CAN DO, BUT THERE HAS TO BE A REASON IT CAME TO ME.
MAYBE THIS RING IS HERE TO HELP ME FIGURE OUT WHO WAS BEHIND THE BOMB.
YOU WORK AT THE SECRETARY OF STATE. YOU CAN FIND OUT WHO OWNED THE VAN. THEY MIGHT KNOW SOMETHING. WHERE IT WAS TAKEN FIRST. WHO MIGHT'VE STOLEN IT.
IT'S A LONG SHOT, BUT IT'S MY ONLY CHANCE.
I SHOULD'VE TOLD YOU THIS A LONG TIME AGO, BUT I NEED YOUR HELP, SIRA.
PLEASE.
YOU NEED TO GO, SIMON. GO, AND DON'T LET THEM CATCH YOU.
DON'T LET THEM SEE YOUR FACE.
SIRA--?
REMEMBER WHERE WE USED TO HIDE AFTER SCHOOL?
MEET ME THERE TONIGHT.
"I REALLY APPRECIATE THIS."

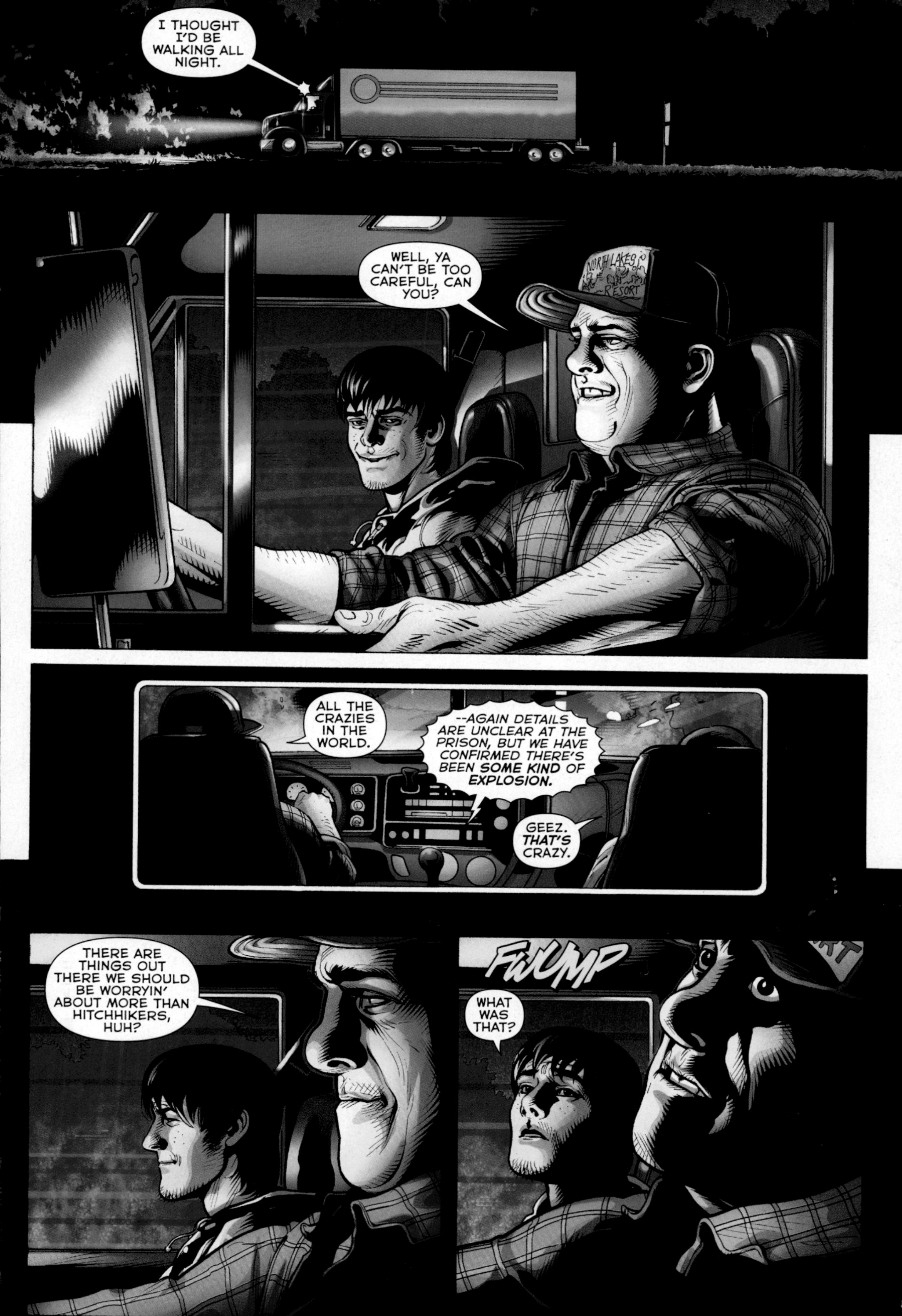

I THOUGHT I'D BE WALKING ALL NIGHT.
WELL, YA CAN'T BE TOO CAREFUL, CAN YOU?
NORTH LAKES RESORT
ALL THE CRAZIES IN THE WORLD.
--AGAIN DETAILS ARE UNCLEAR AT THE PRISON, BUT WE HAVE CONFIRMED THERE'S BEEN **SOME KIND** OF **EXPLOSION.**
GEEZ. **THAT'S** CRAZY.
THERE ARE THINGS OUT THERE WE SHOULD BE WORRYIN' ABOUT MORE THAN HITCHHIKERS, HUH?
FWUMP
WHAT WAS THAT?

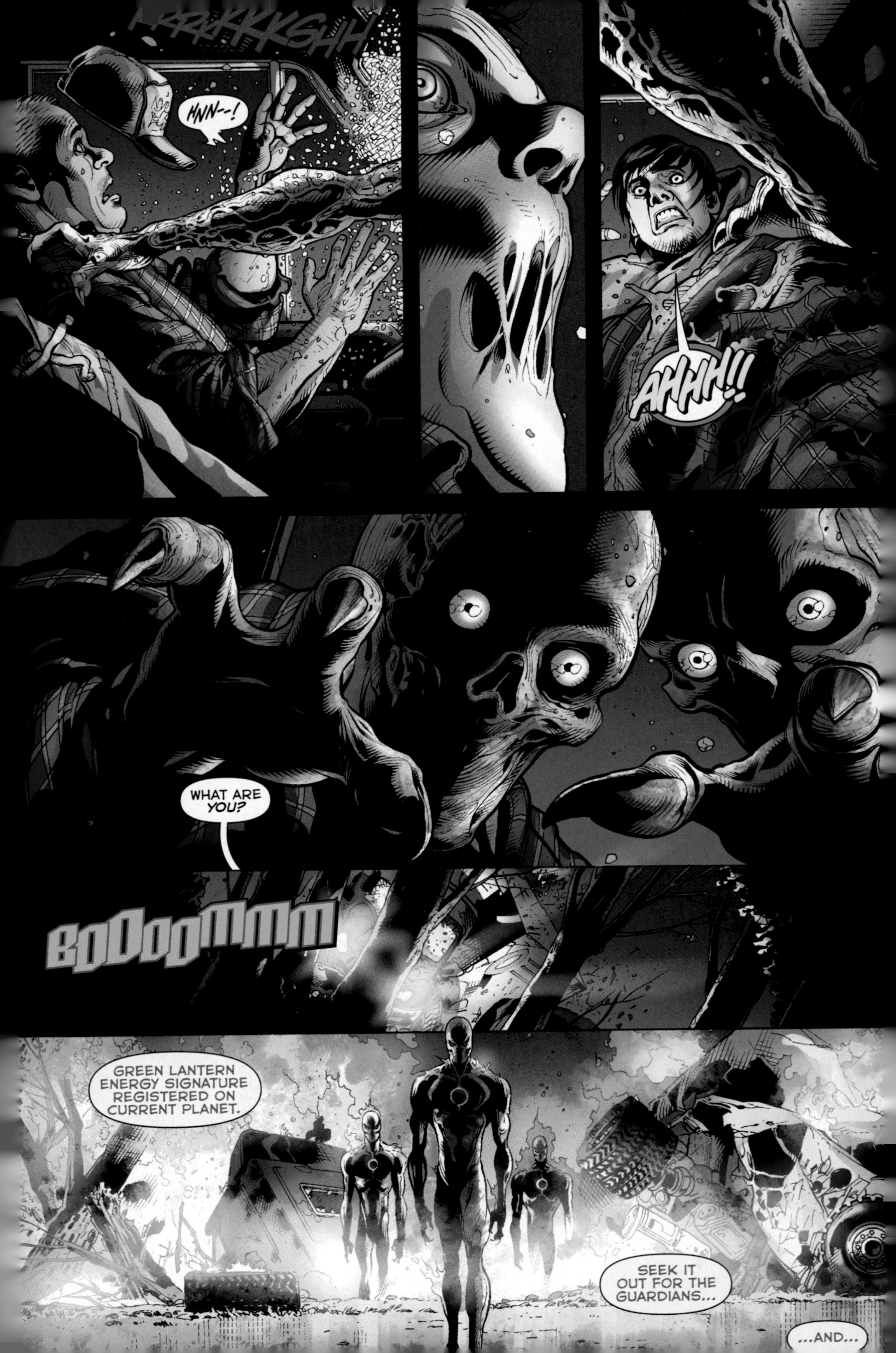
KRRKKKSHH
HNN--!
AHHH!!
WHAT ARE YOU?
BOOOOMMMM
GREEN LANTERN ENERGY SIGNATURE REGISTERED ON CURRENT PLANET.
SEEK IT OUT FOR THE GUARDIANS...
...AND...

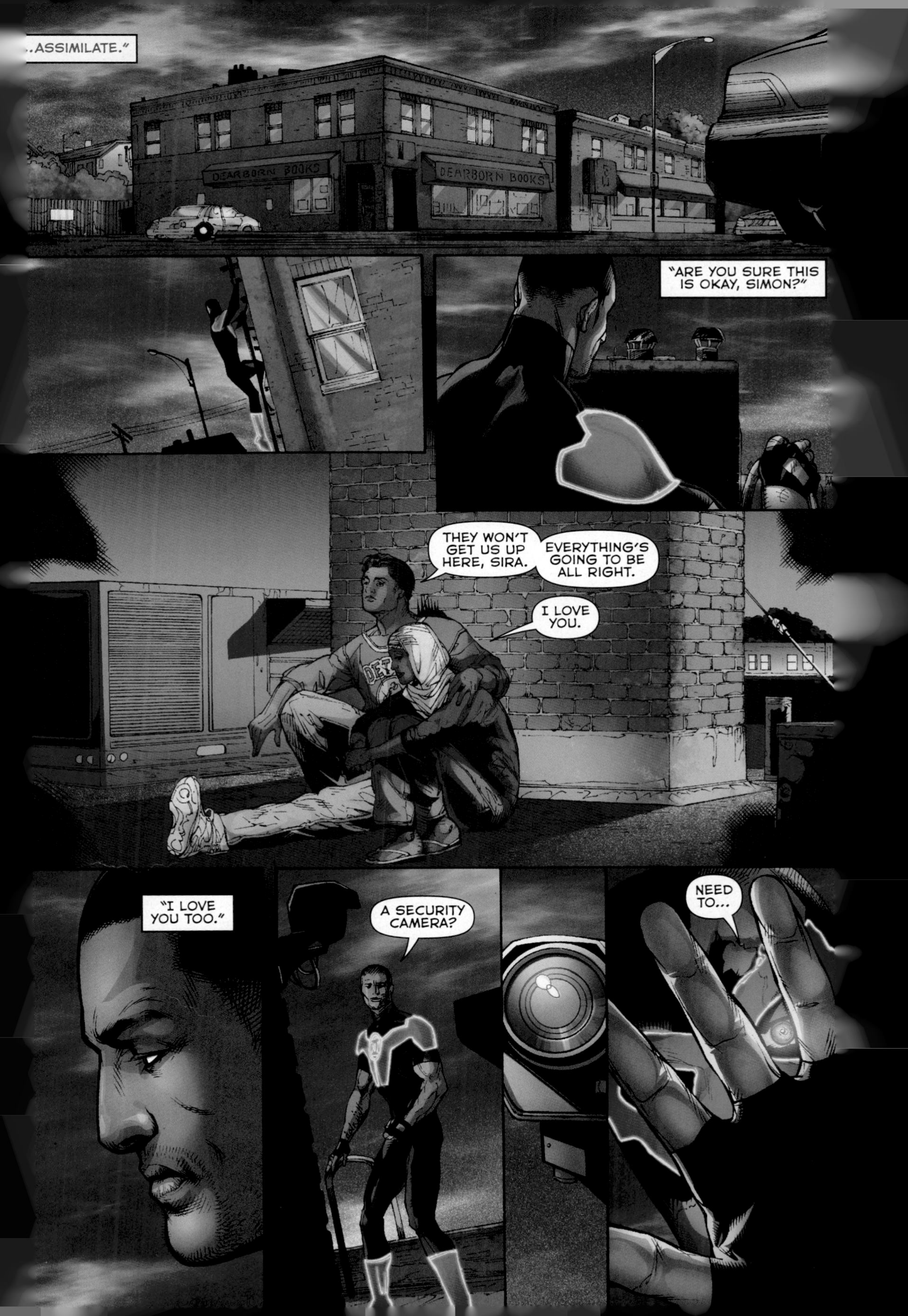

...ASSIMILATE."
DEARBORN BOOKS
DEARBORN BOOKS
"ARE YOU SURE THIS IS OKAY, SIMON?"
THEY WON'T GET US UP HERE, SIRA.
EVERYTHING'S GOING TO BE ALL RIGHT.
I LOVE YOU.
"I LOVE YOU TOO."
A SECURITY CAMERA?
NEED TO...

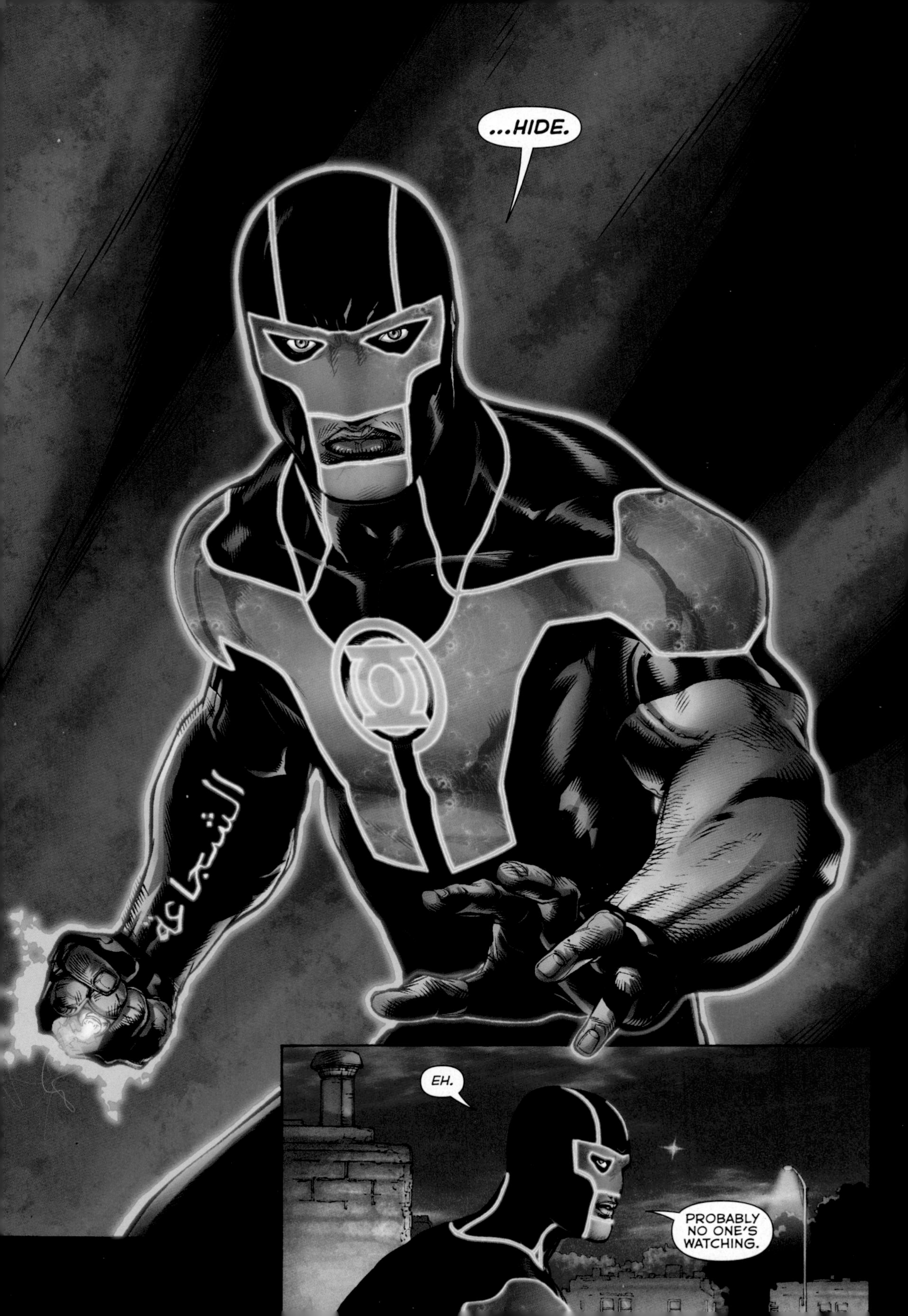
...HIDE.
الشجاعة
EH.
PROBABLY NO ONE'S WATCHING.

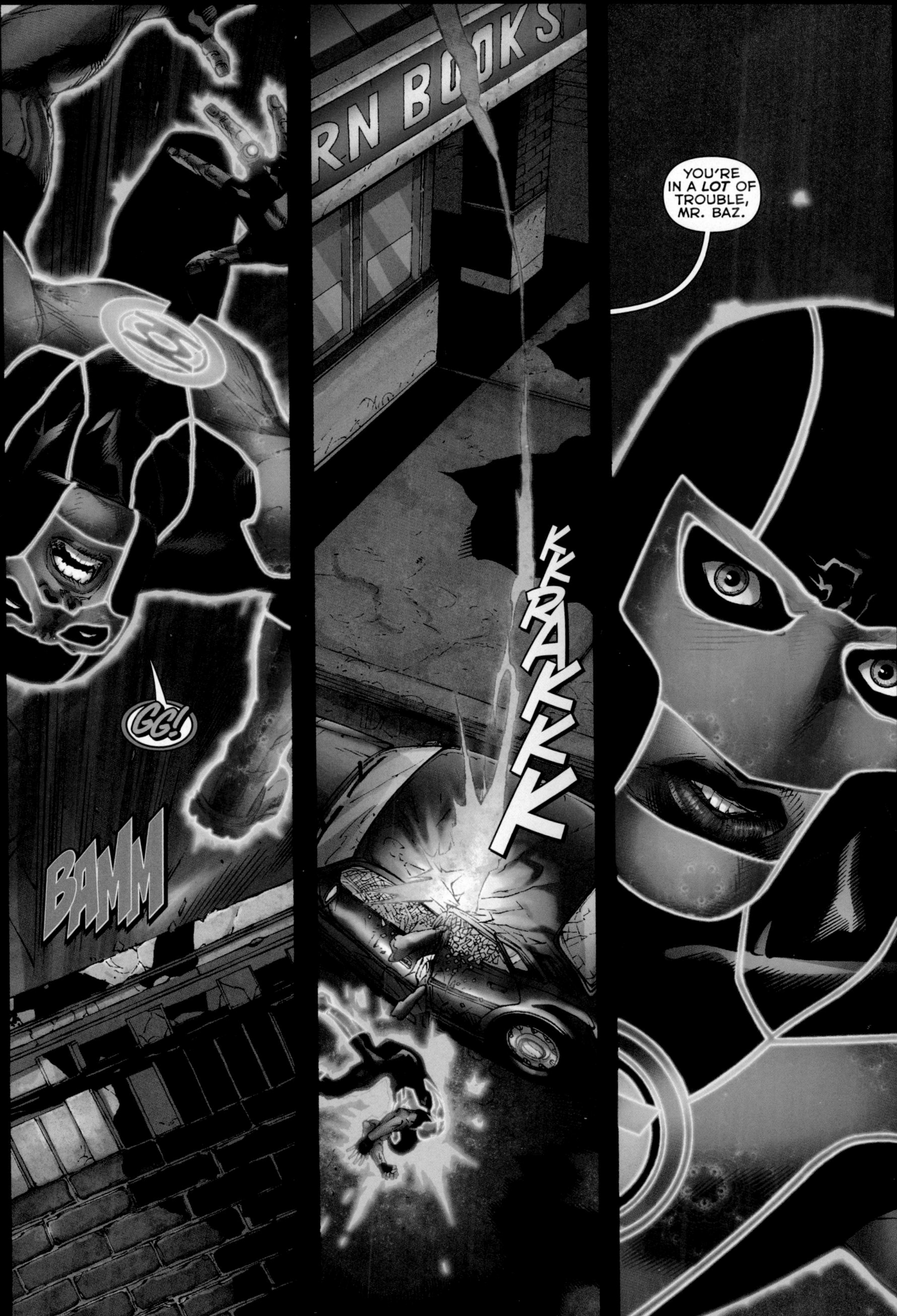
GG!
BAMM
RN BOOKS
KKRAKKK
YOU'RE IN A LOT OF TROUBLE, MR. BAZ.

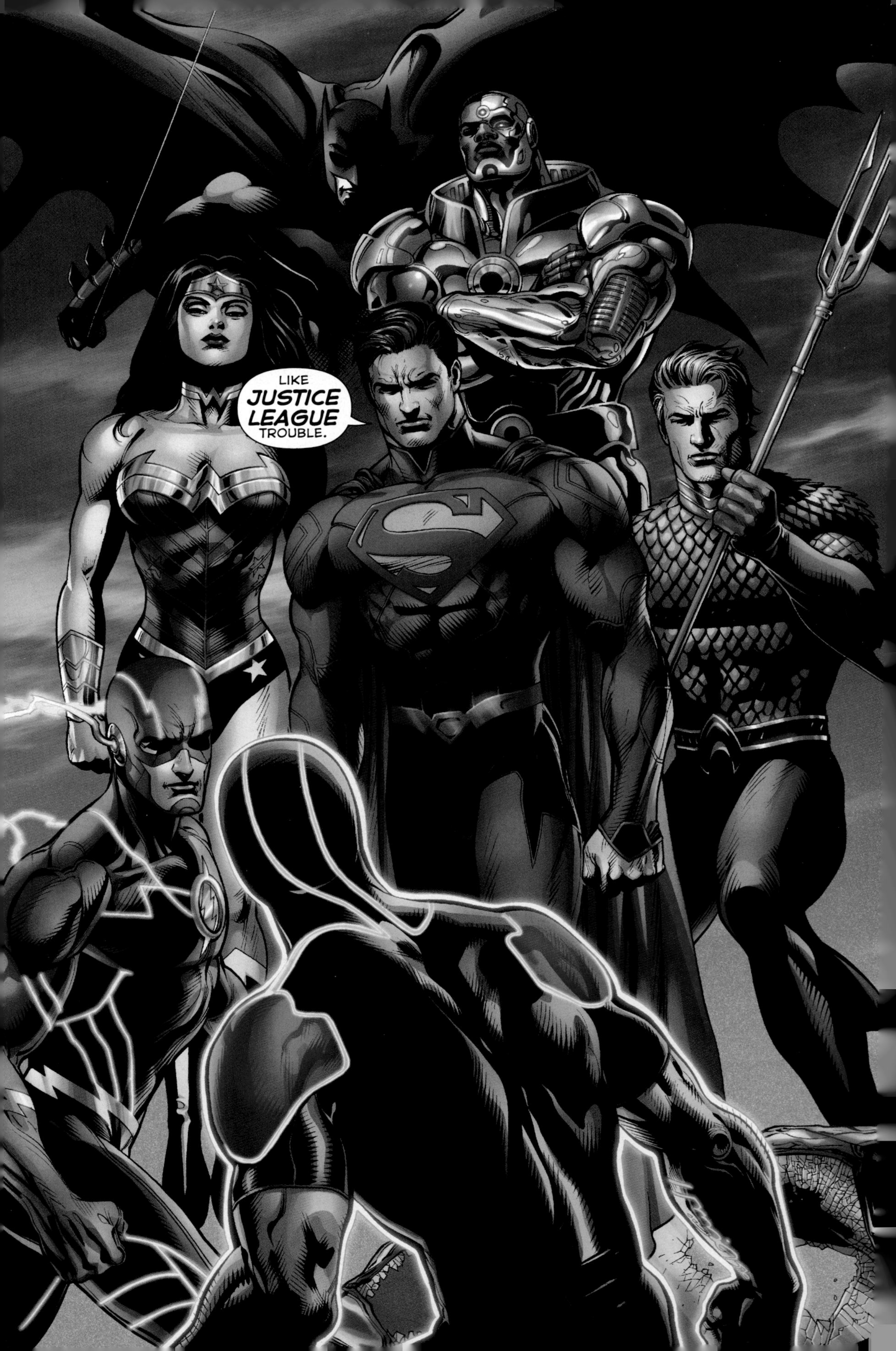
LIKE JUSTICE LEAGUE TROUBLE.

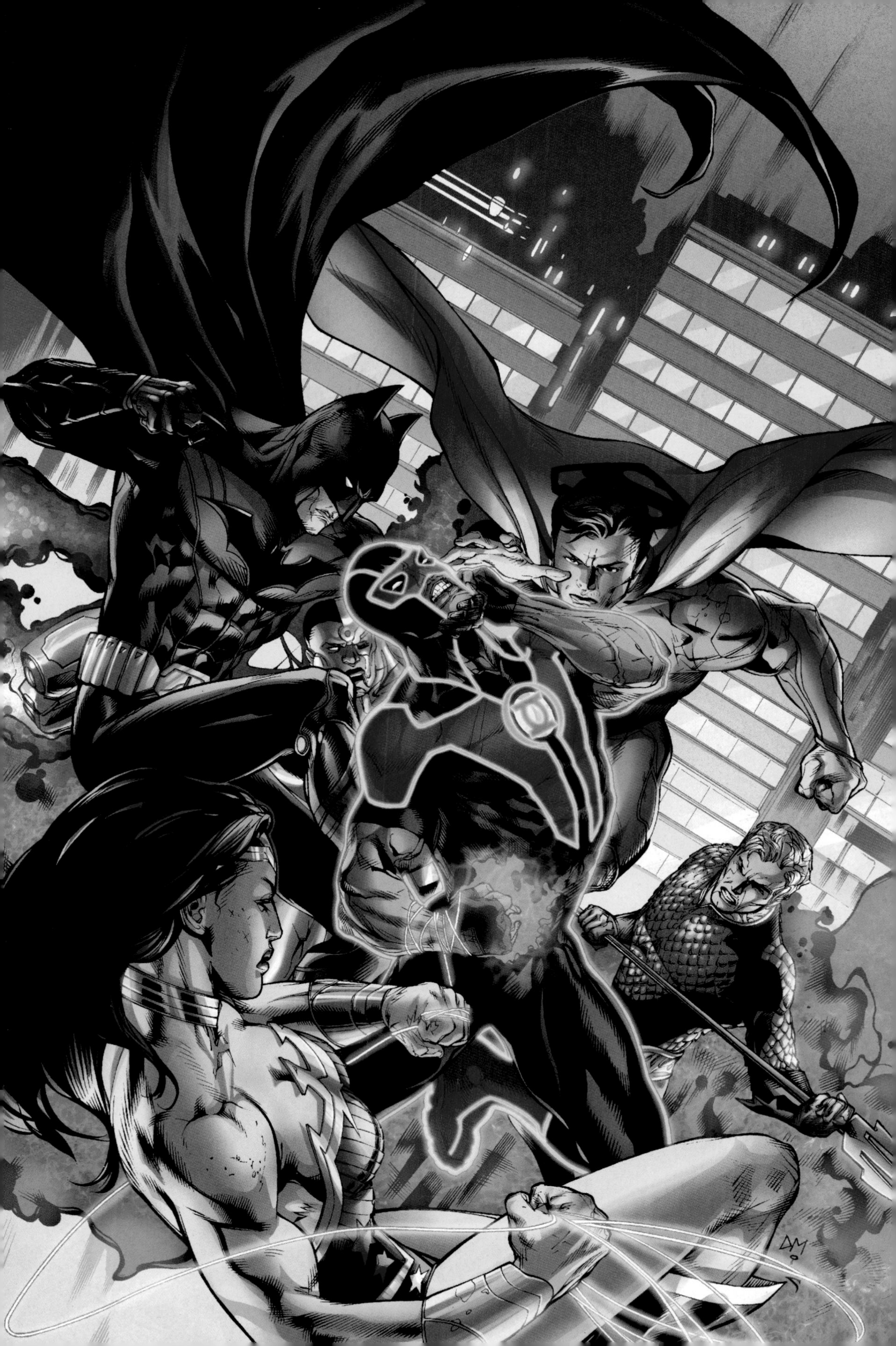

GEOFF JOHNS writer DOUG MAHNKE penciller CHRISTIAN ALAMY, MARK IRWIN, KEITH CHAMPAGNE & TOM NGUYEN inkers
DOUG MAHNKE, MARK IRWIN & ALEX SINCLAIR cover

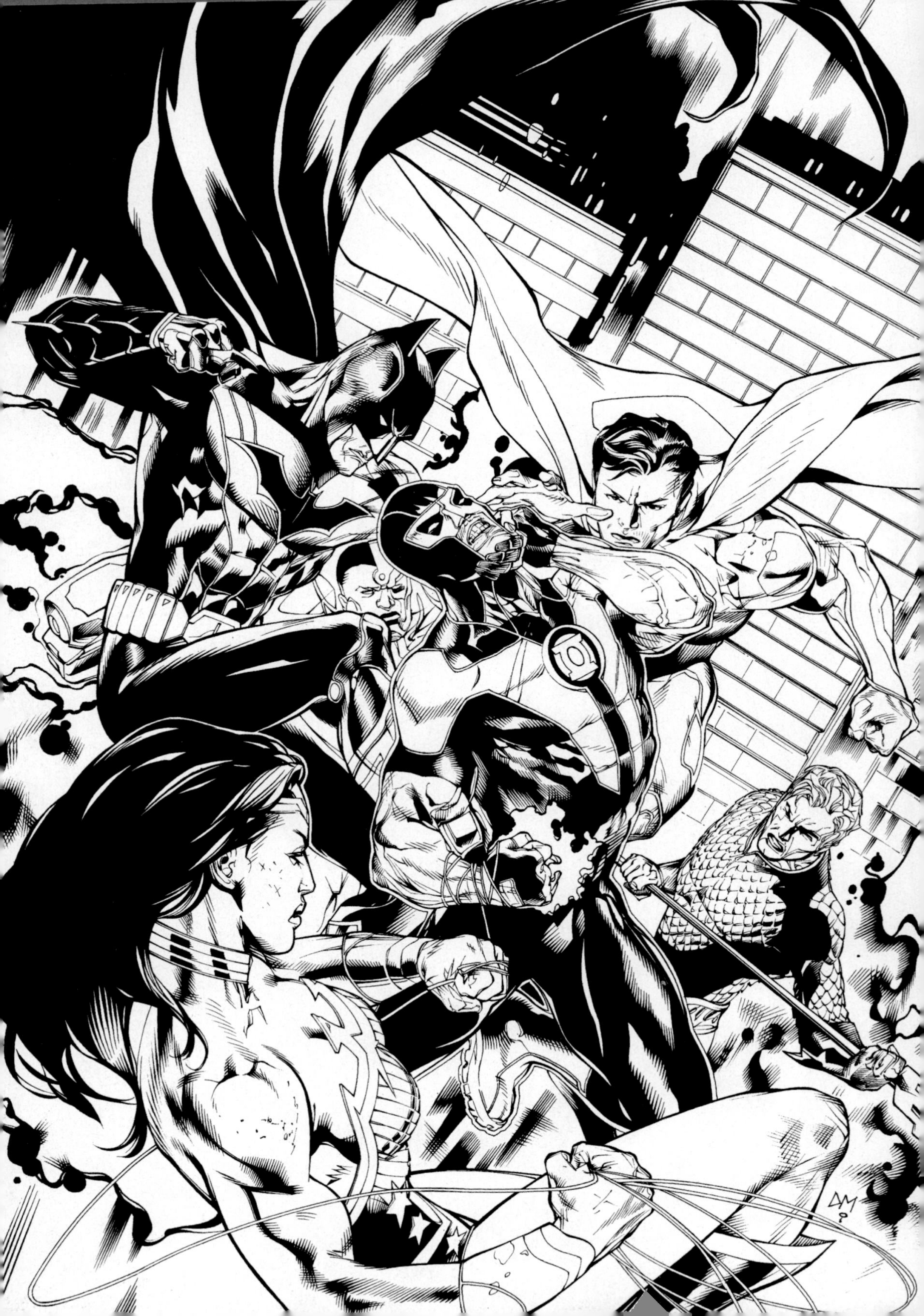

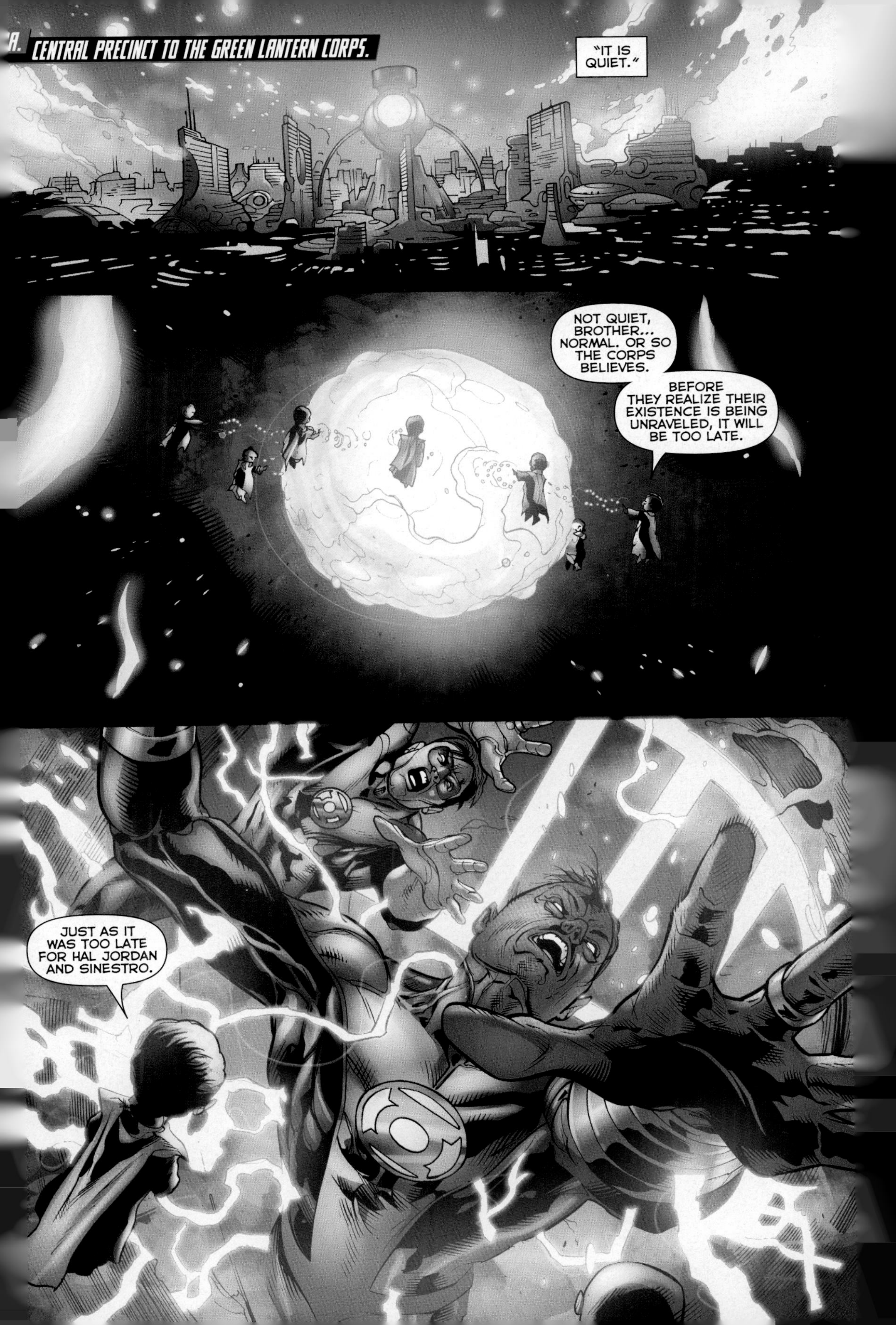
A. CENTRAL PRECINCT TO THE GREEN LANTERN CORPS.
"IT IS QUIET."
NOT QUIET, BROTHER... NORMAL. OR SO THE CORPS BELIEVES.
BEFORE THEY REALIZE THEIR EXISTENCE IS BEING UNRAVELED, IT WILL BE TOO LATE.
JUST AS IT WAS TOO LATE FOR HAL JORDAN AND SINESTRO.

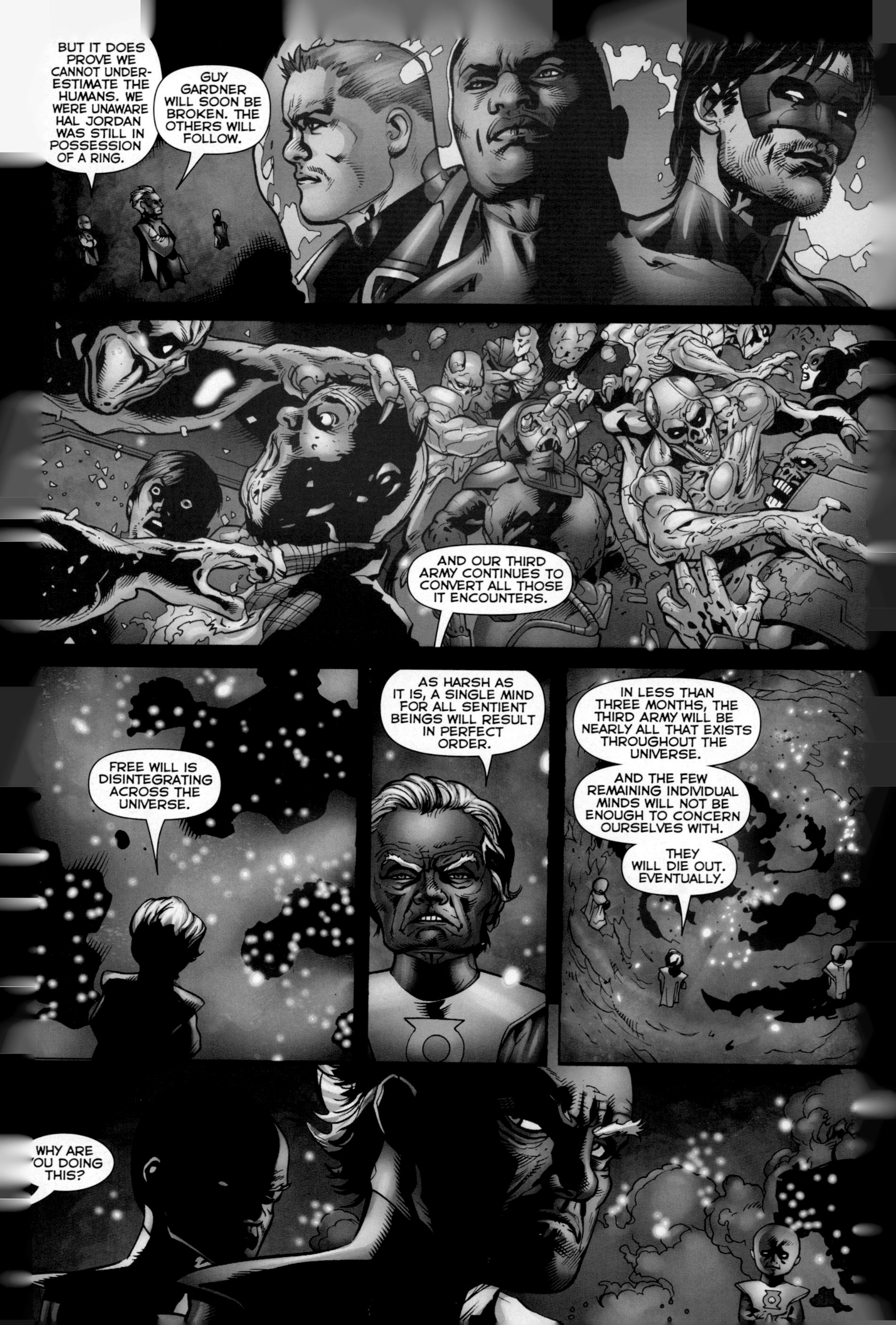
BUT IT DOES PROVE WE CANNOT UNDER-ESTIMATE THE HUMANS. WE WERE UNAWARE HAL JORDAN WAS STILL IN POSSESSION OF A RING.
GUY GARDNER WILL SOON BE BROKEN. THE OTHERS WILL FOLLOW.
AND OUR THIRD ARMY CONTINUES TO CONVERT ALL THOSE IT ENCOUNTERS.
FREE WILL IS DISINTEGRATING ACROSS THE UNIVERSE.
AS HARSH AS IT IS, A SINGLE MIND FOR ALL SENTIENT BEINGS WILL RESULT IN PERFECT ORDER.
IN LESS THAN THREE MONTHS, THE THIRD ARMY WILL BE NEARLY ALL THAT EXISTS THROUGHOUT THE UNIVERSE.
AND THE FEW REMAINING INDIVIDUAL MINDS WILL NOT BE ENOUGH TO CONCERN OURSELVES WITH.
THEY WILL DIE OUT. EVENTUALLY.
WHY ARE YOU DOING THIS?

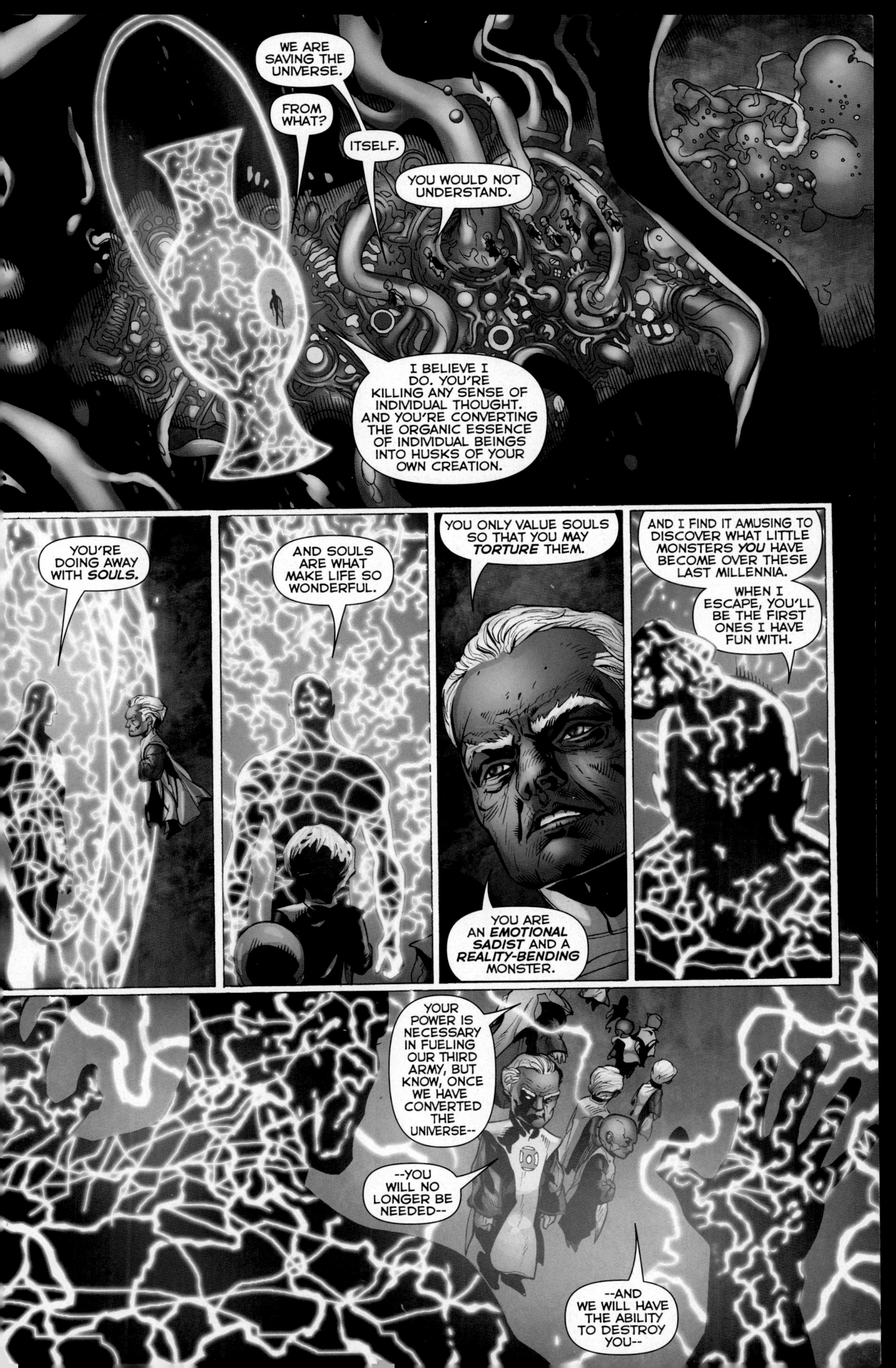
WE ARE SAVING THE UNIVERSE.
FROM WHAT?
ITSELF.
YOU WOULD NOT UNDERSTAND.
I BELIEVE I DO. YOU'RE KILLING ANY SENSE OF INDIVIDUAL THOUGHT. AND YOU'RE CONVERTING THE ORGANIC ESSENCE OF INDIVIDUAL BEINGS INTO HUSKS OF YOUR OWN CREATION.
YOU'RE DOING AWAY WITH SOULS.
AND SOULS ARE WHAT MAKE LIFE SO WONDERFUL.
YOU ONLY VALUE SOULS SO THAT YOU MAY TORTURE THEM.
YOU ARE AN EMOTIONAL SADIST AND A REALITY-BENDING MONSTER.
AND I FIND IT AMUSING TO DISCOVER WHAT LITTLE MONSTERS YOU HAVE BECOME OVER THESE LAST MILLENNIA.
WHEN I ESCAPE, YOU'LL BE THE FIRST ONES I HAVE FUN WITH.
YOUR POWER IS NECESSARY IN FUELING OUR THIRD ARMY, BUT KNOW, ONCE WE HAVE CONVERTED THE UNIVERSE--
--YOU WILL NO LONGER BE NEEDED--
--AND WE WILL HAVE THE ABILITY TO DESTROY YOU--

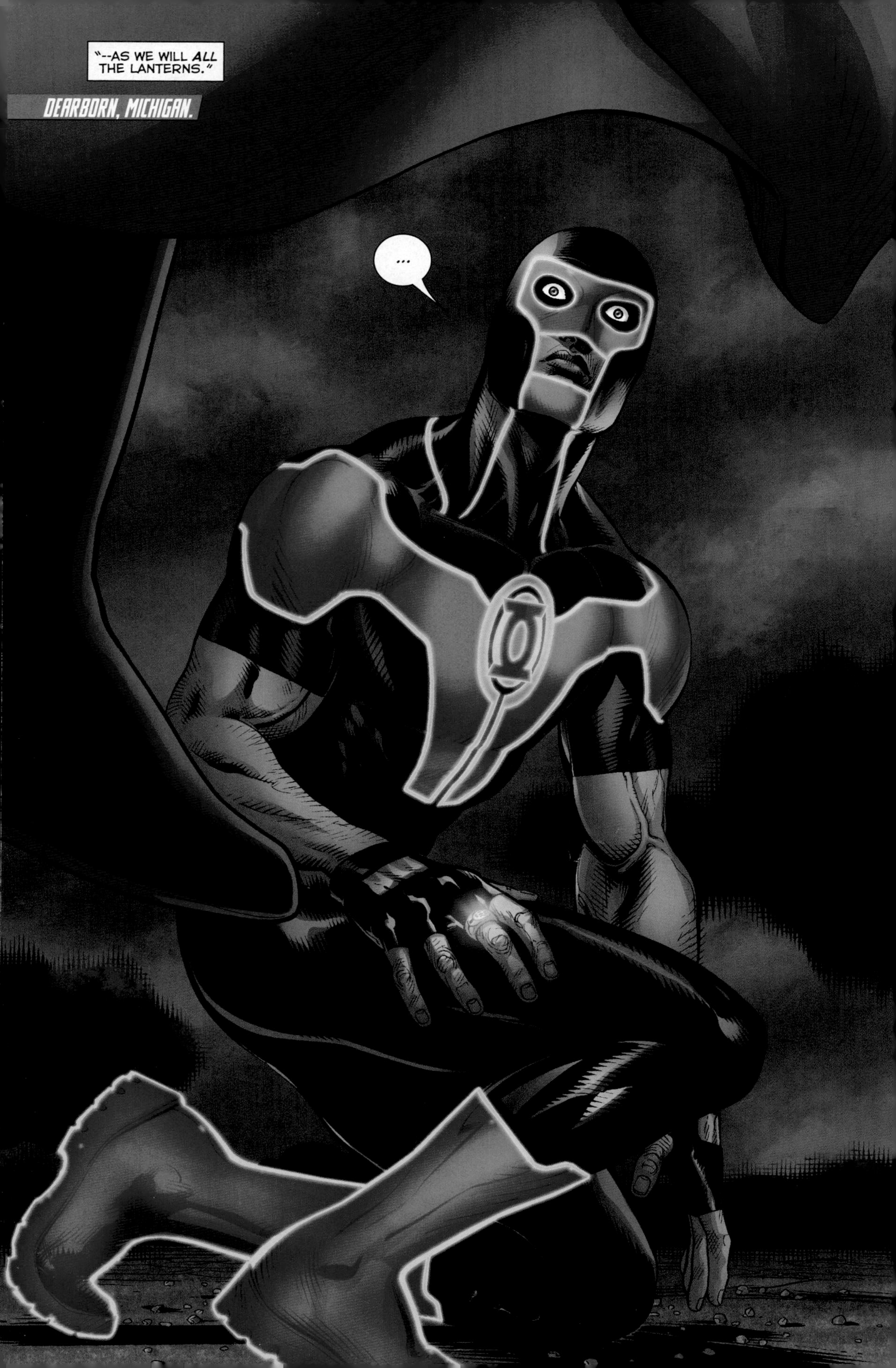
"--AS WE WILL ALL THE LANTERNS."
DEARBORN, MICHIGAN.
...

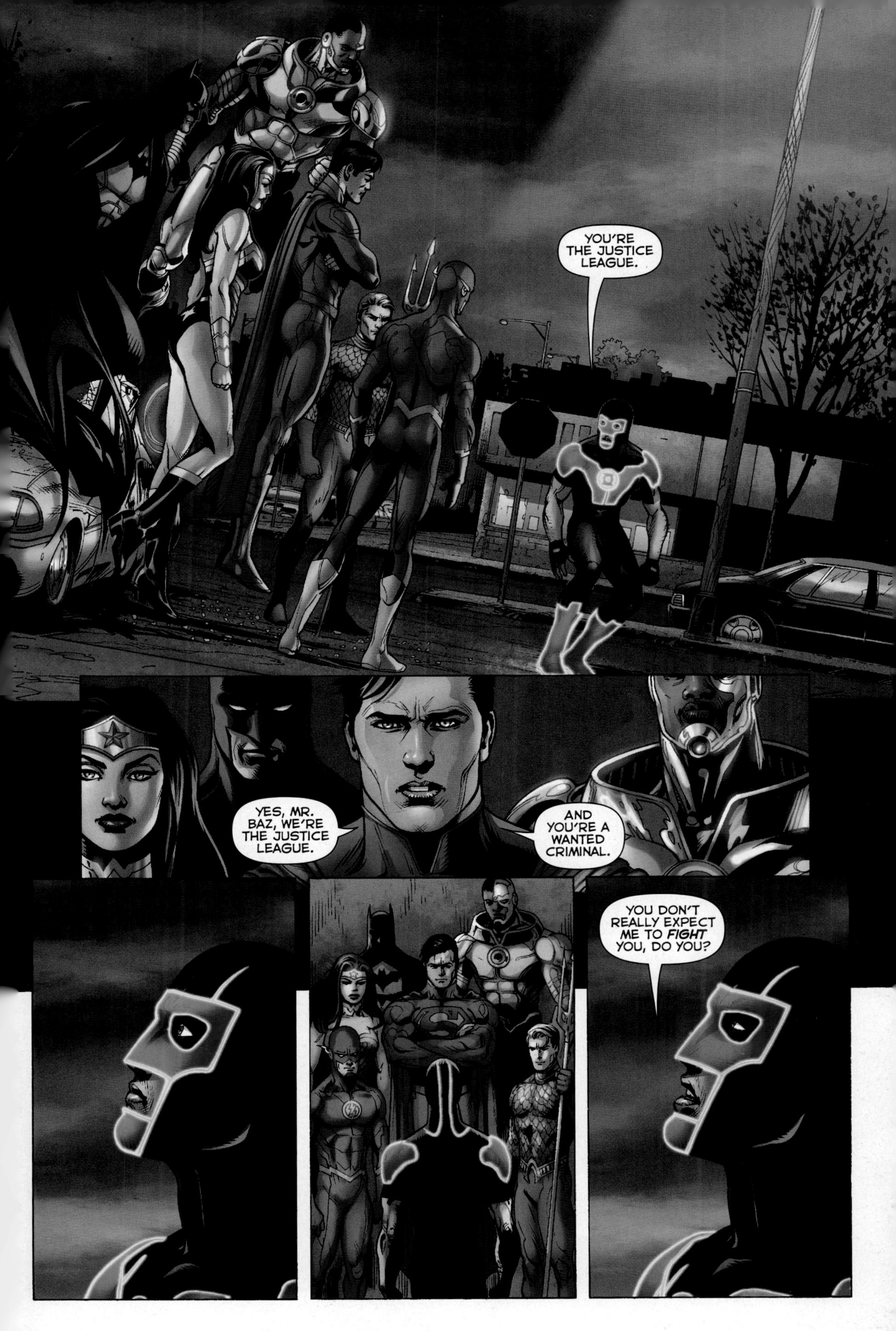
YOU'RE THE JUSTICE LEAGUE.
YES, MR. BAZ, WE'RE THE JUSTICE LEAGUE.
AND YOU'RE A WANTED CRIMINAL.
YOU DON'T REALLY EXPECT ME TO *FIGHT* YOU, DO YOU?

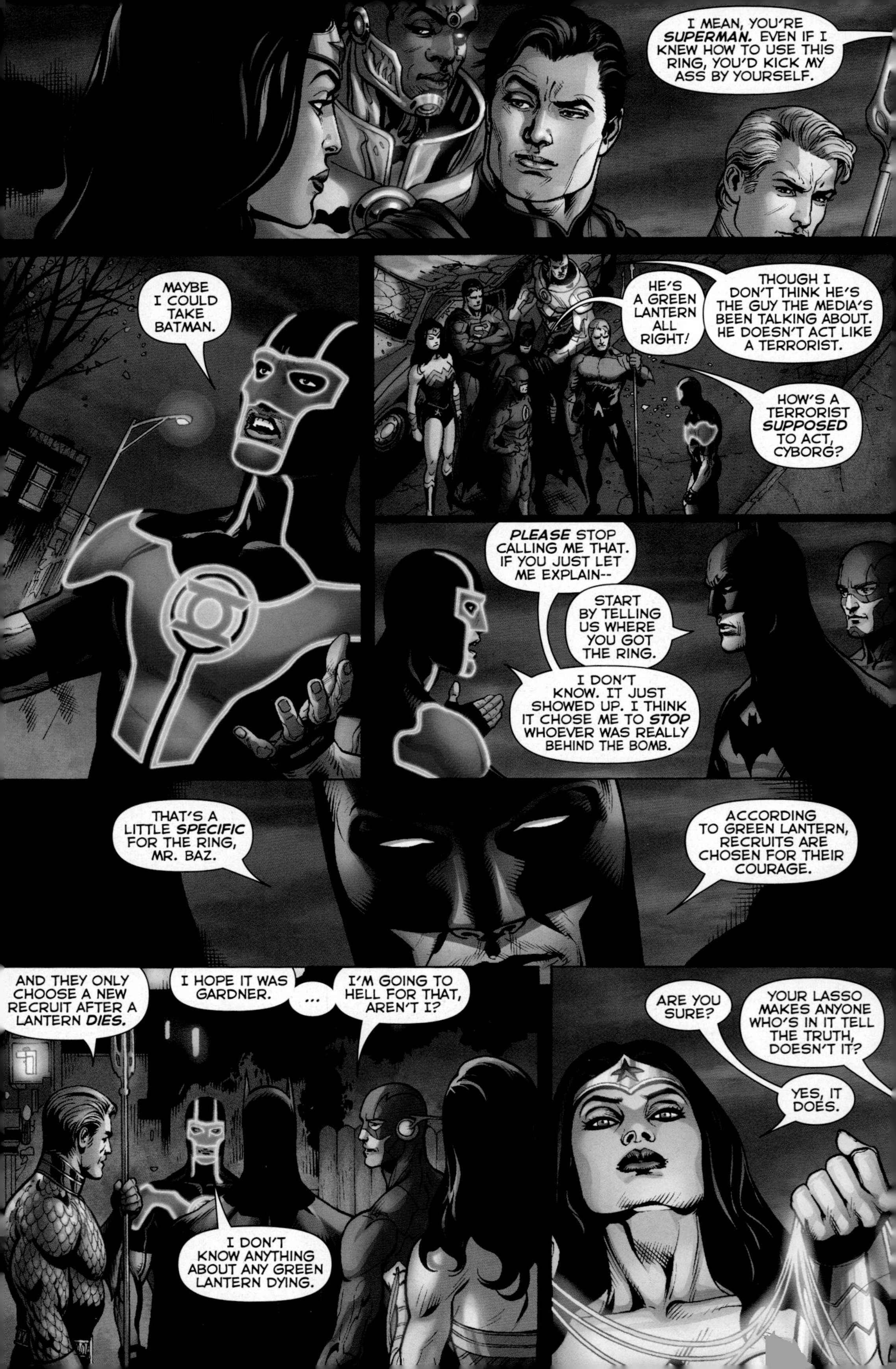

I MEAN, YOU'RE SUPERMAN. EVEN IF I KNEW HOW TO USE THIS RING, YOU'D KICK MY ASS BY YOURSELF.
MAYBE I COULD TAKE BATMAN.
HE'S A GREEN LANTERN ALL RIGHT!
THOUGH I DON'T THINK HE'S THE GUY THE MEDIA'S BEEN TALKING ABOUT. HE DOESN'T ACT LIKE A TERRORIST.
HOW'S A TERRORIST SUPPOSED TO ACT, CYBORG?
PLEASE STOP CALLING ME THAT. IF YOU JUST LET ME EXPLAIN--
START BY TELLING US WHERE YOU GOT THE RING.
I DON'T KNOW. IT JUST SHOWED UP. I THINK IT CHOSE ME TO STOP WHOEVER WAS REALLY BEHIND THE BOMB.
THAT'S A LITTLE SPECIFIC FOR THE RING, MR. BAZ.
ACCORDING TO GREEN LANTERN, RECRUITS ARE CHOSEN FOR THEIR COURAGE.
AND THEY ONLY CHOOSE A NEW RECRUIT AFTER A LANTERN DIES.
I HOPE IT WAS GARDNER.
...
I'M GOING TO HELL FOR THAT, AREN'T I?
I DON'T KNOW ANYTHING ABOUT ANY GREEN LANTERN DYING.
ARE YOU SURE?
YOUR LASSO MAKES ANYONE WHO'S IN IT TELL THE TRUTH, DOESN'T IT?
YES, IT DOES.

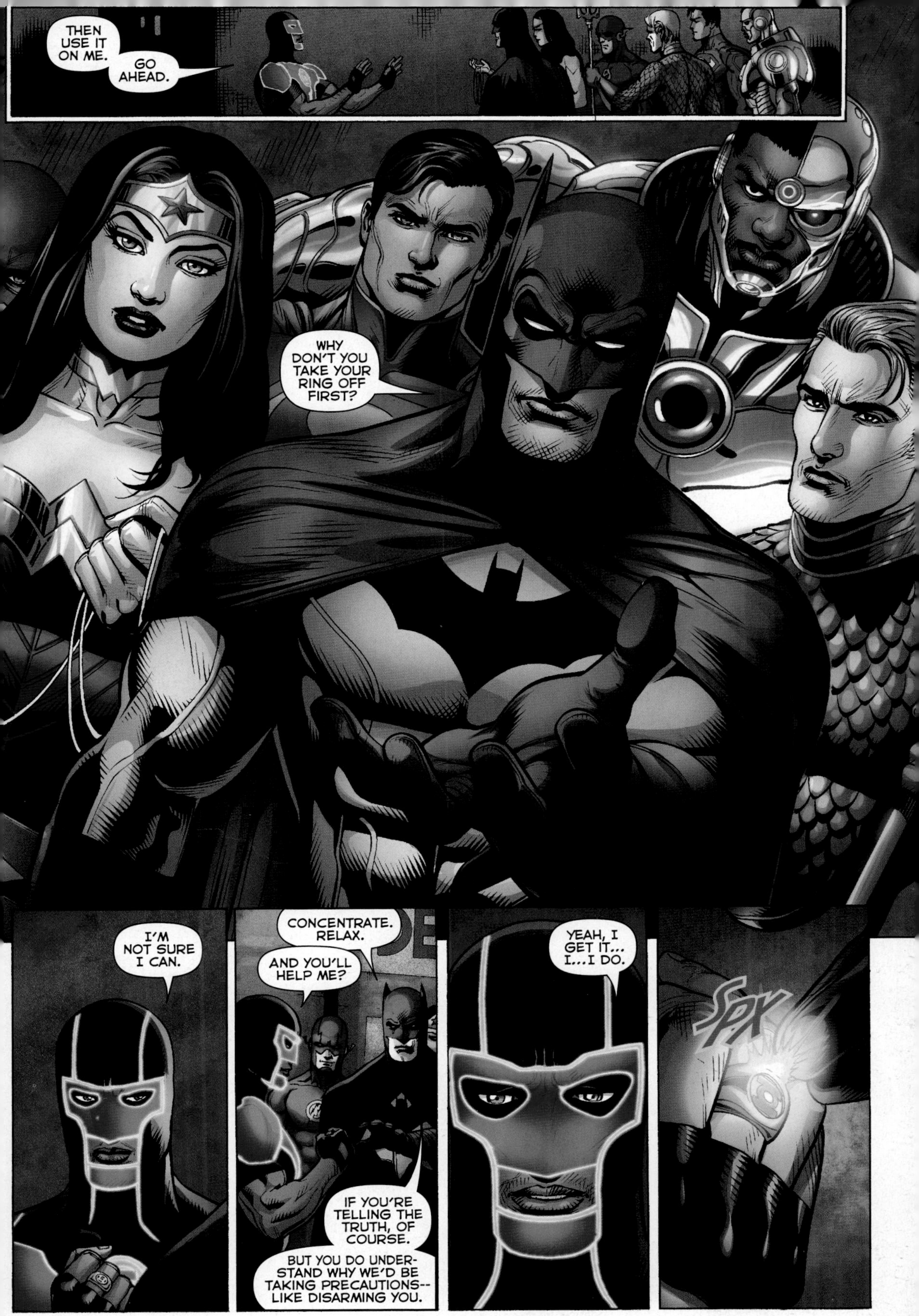
THEN USE IT ON ME.
GO AHEAD.
WHY DON'T YOU TAKE YOUR RING OFF FIRST?
I'M NOT SURE I CAN.
CONCENTRATE. RELAX.
AND YOU'LL HELP ME?
IF YOU'RE TELLING THE TRUTH, OF COURSE.
BUT YOU DO UNDERSTAND WHY WE'D BE TAKING PRECAUTIONS--LIKE DISARMING YOU.
YEAH, I GET IT... I...I DO.
SPX

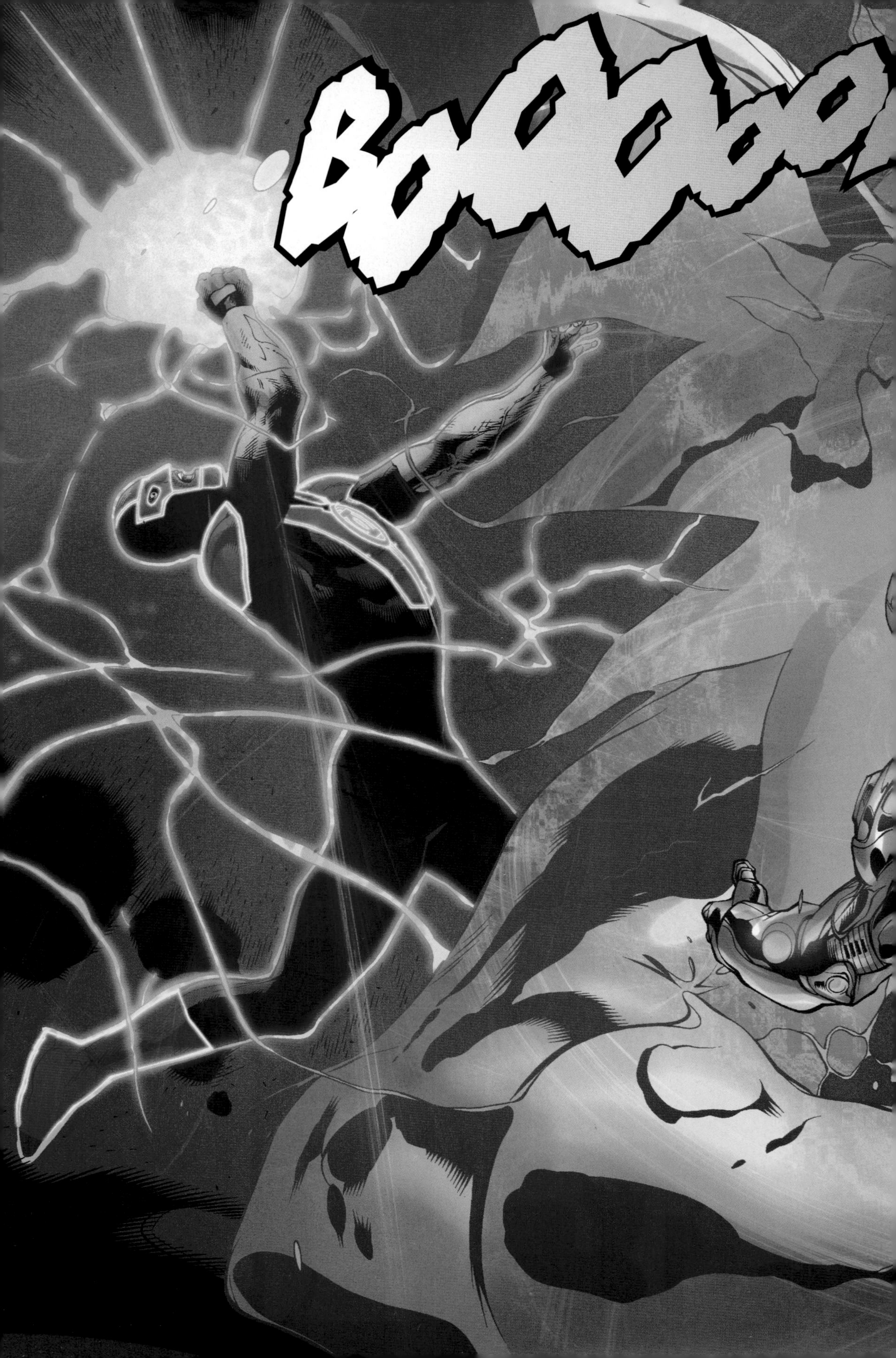
BOOOOO

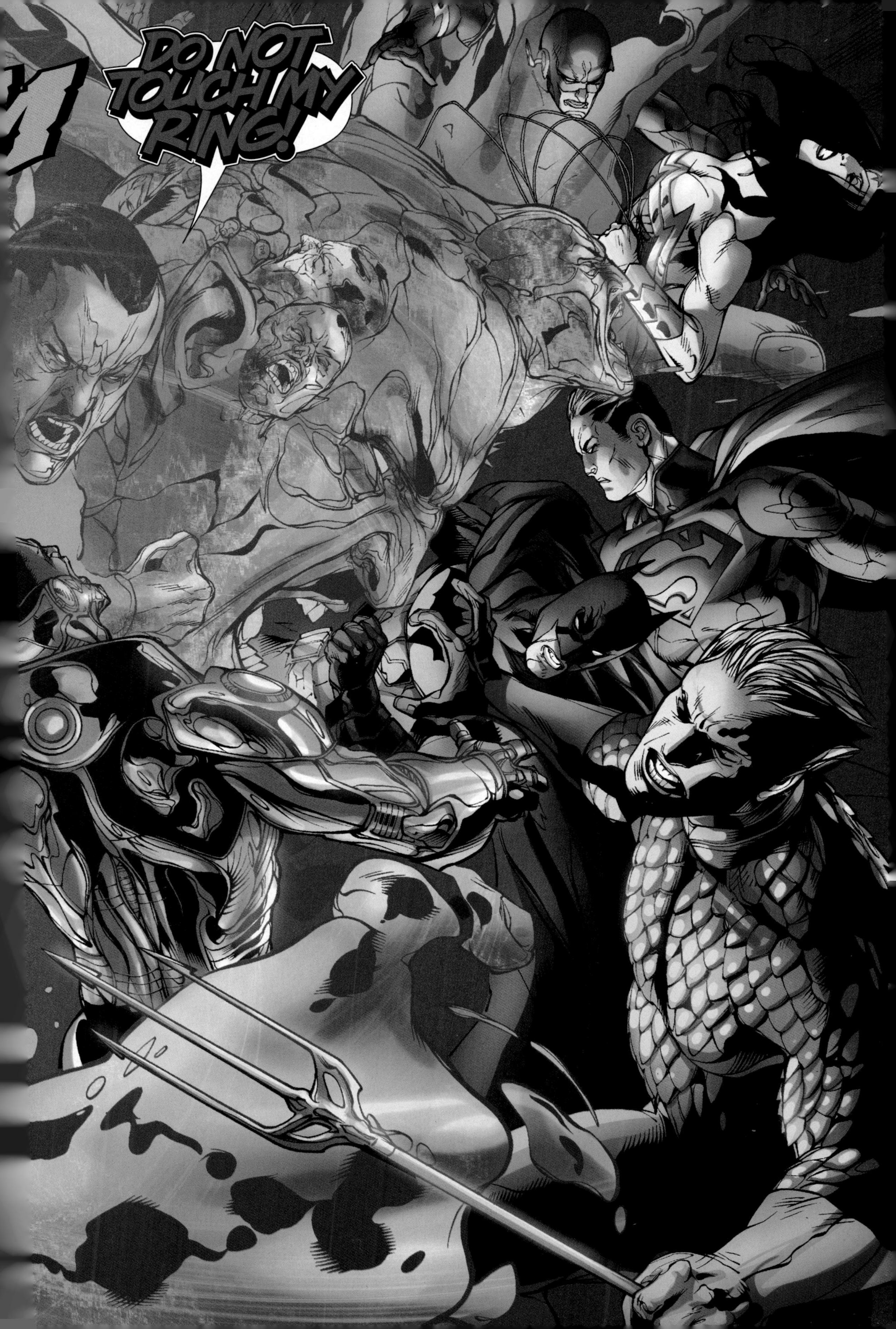
DO NOT TOUCH MY RING!

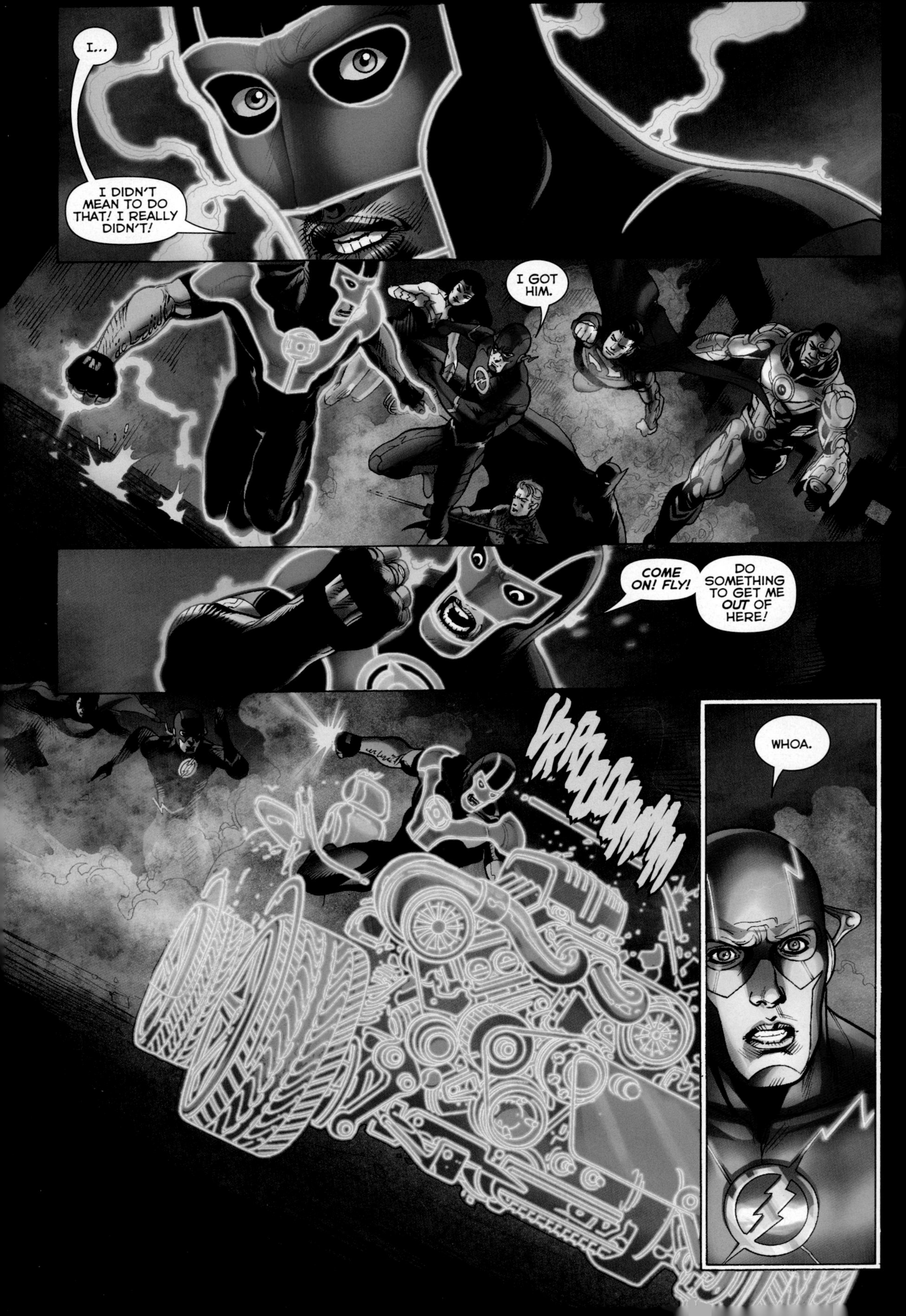
I...
I DIDN'T MEAN TO DO THAT! I REALLY DIDN'T!
I GOT HIM.
COME ON! FLY!
DO SOMETHING TO GET ME OUT OF HERE!
VRROOOMMM
WHOA.

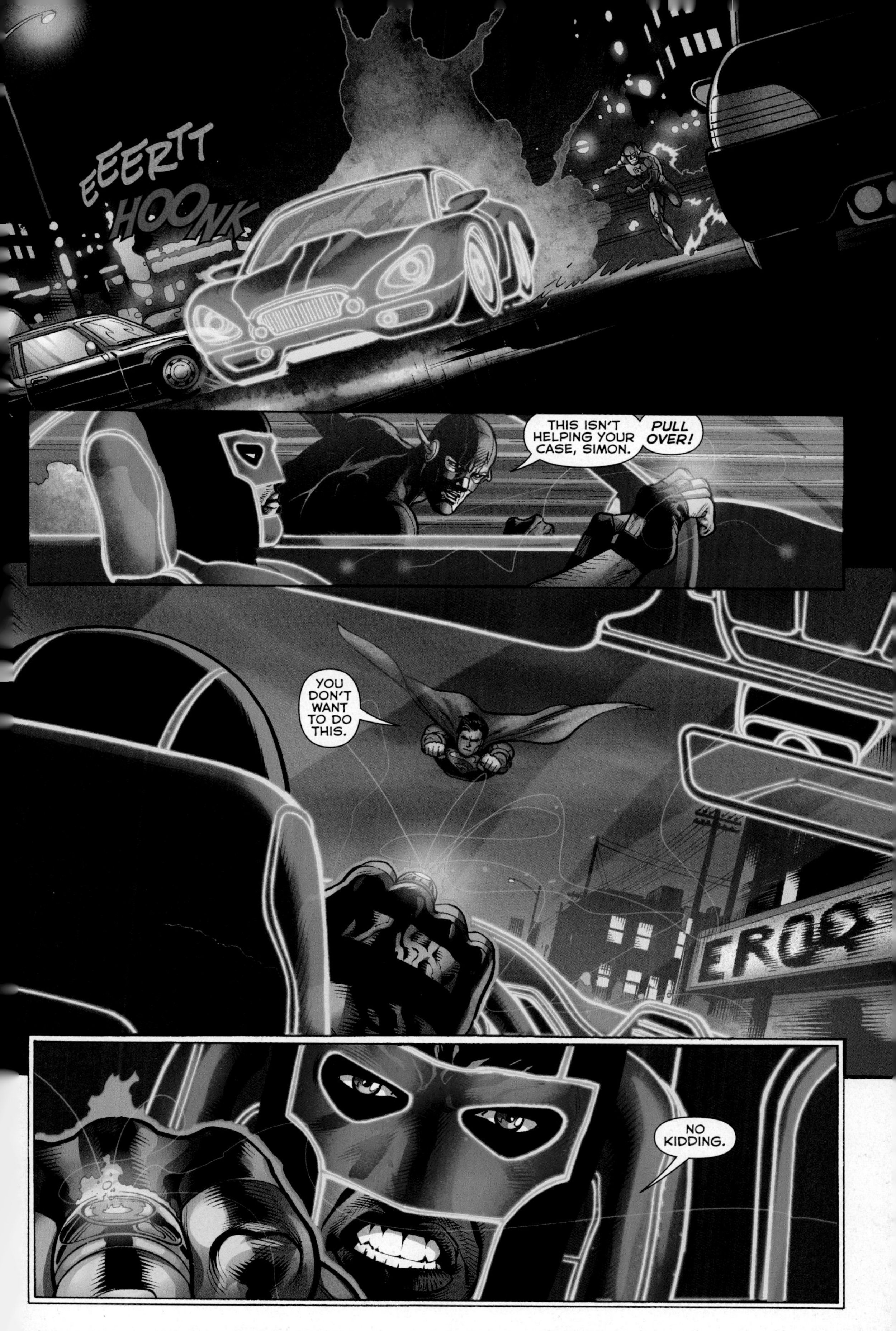
EEERTT
HOONK
THIS ISN'T HELPING YOUR CASE, SIMON.
PULL OVER!
YOU DON'T WANT TO DO THIS.
NO KIDDING.

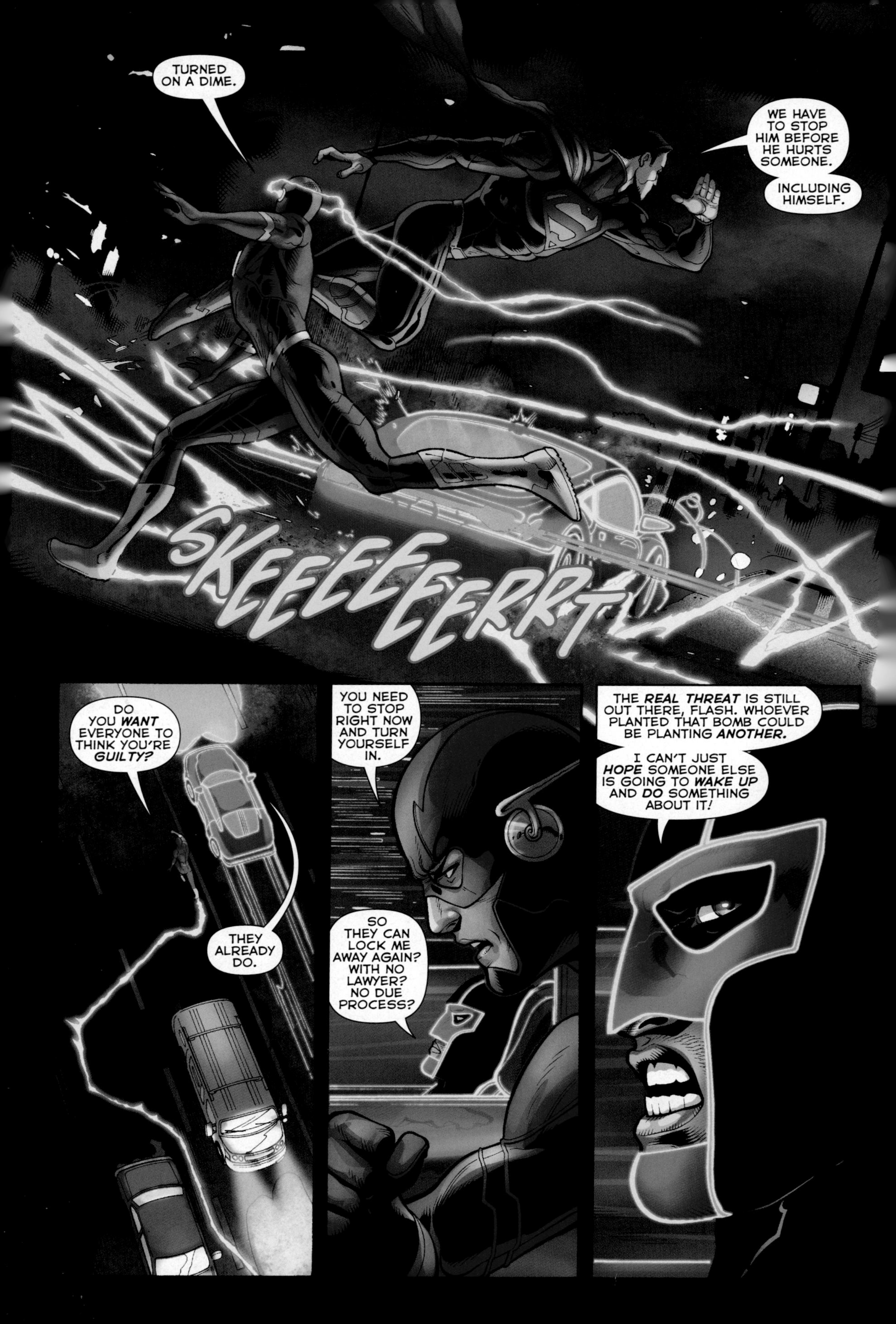
TURNED ON A DIME.
WE HAVE TO STOP HIM BEFORE HE HURTS SOMEONE.
INCLUDING HIMSELF.
SKEEEEEEERRRT
DO YOU WANT EVERYONE TO THINK YOU'RE GUILTY?
THEY ALREADY DO.
YOU NEED TO STOP RIGHT NOW AND TURN YOURSELF IN.
SO THEY CAN LOCK ME AWAY AGAIN? WITH NO LAWYER? NO DUE PROCESS?
THE REAL THREAT IS STILL OUT THERE, FLASH. WHOEVER PLANTED THAT BOMB COULD BE PLANTING ANOTHER.
I CAN'T JUST HOPE SOMEONE ELSE IS GOING TO WAKE UP AND DO SOMETHING ABOUT IT!

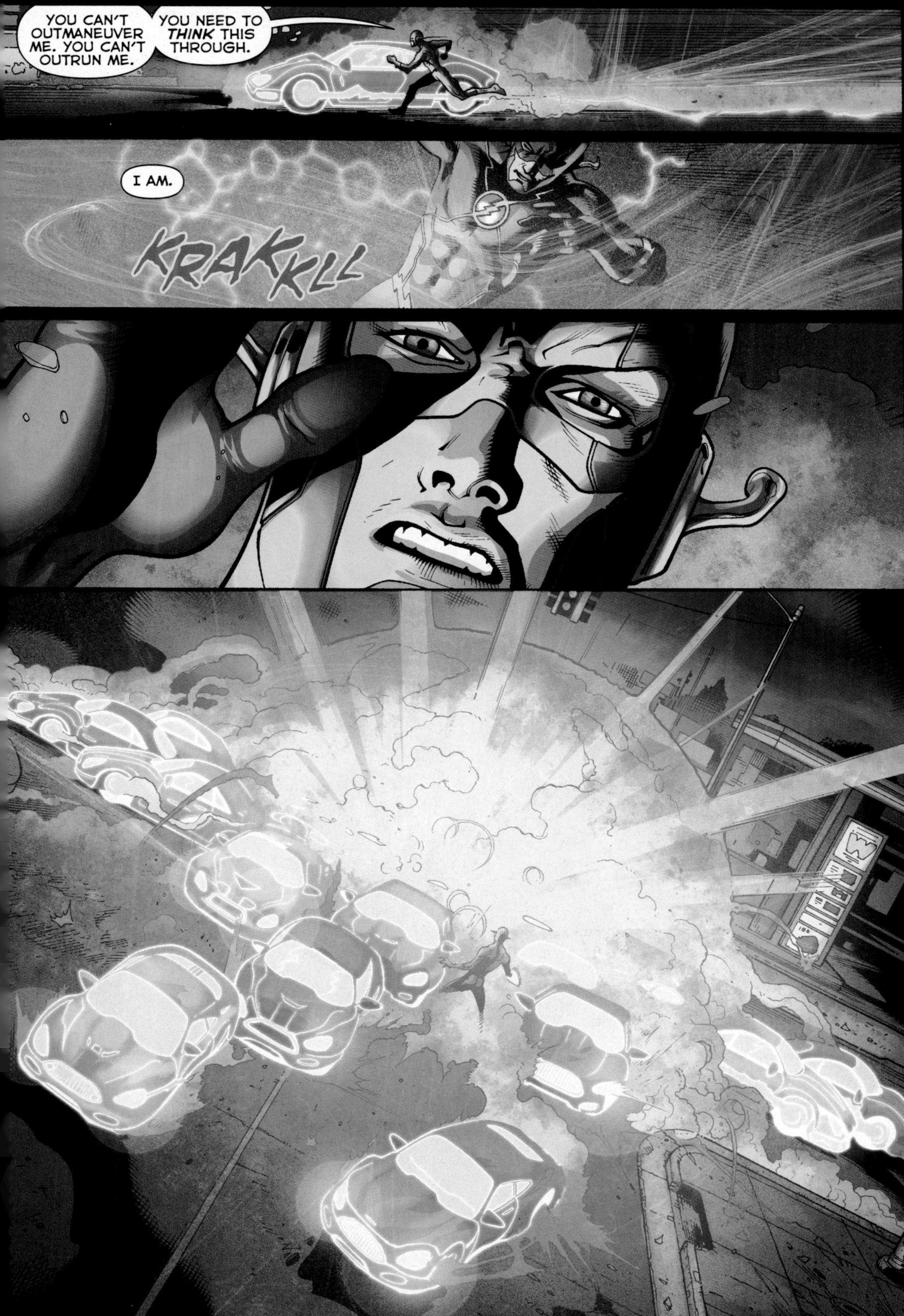
YOU CAN'T OUTMANEUVER ME. YOU CAN'T OUTRUN ME.
YOU NEED TO *THINK* THIS THROUGH.
I AM.
KRAKKLL

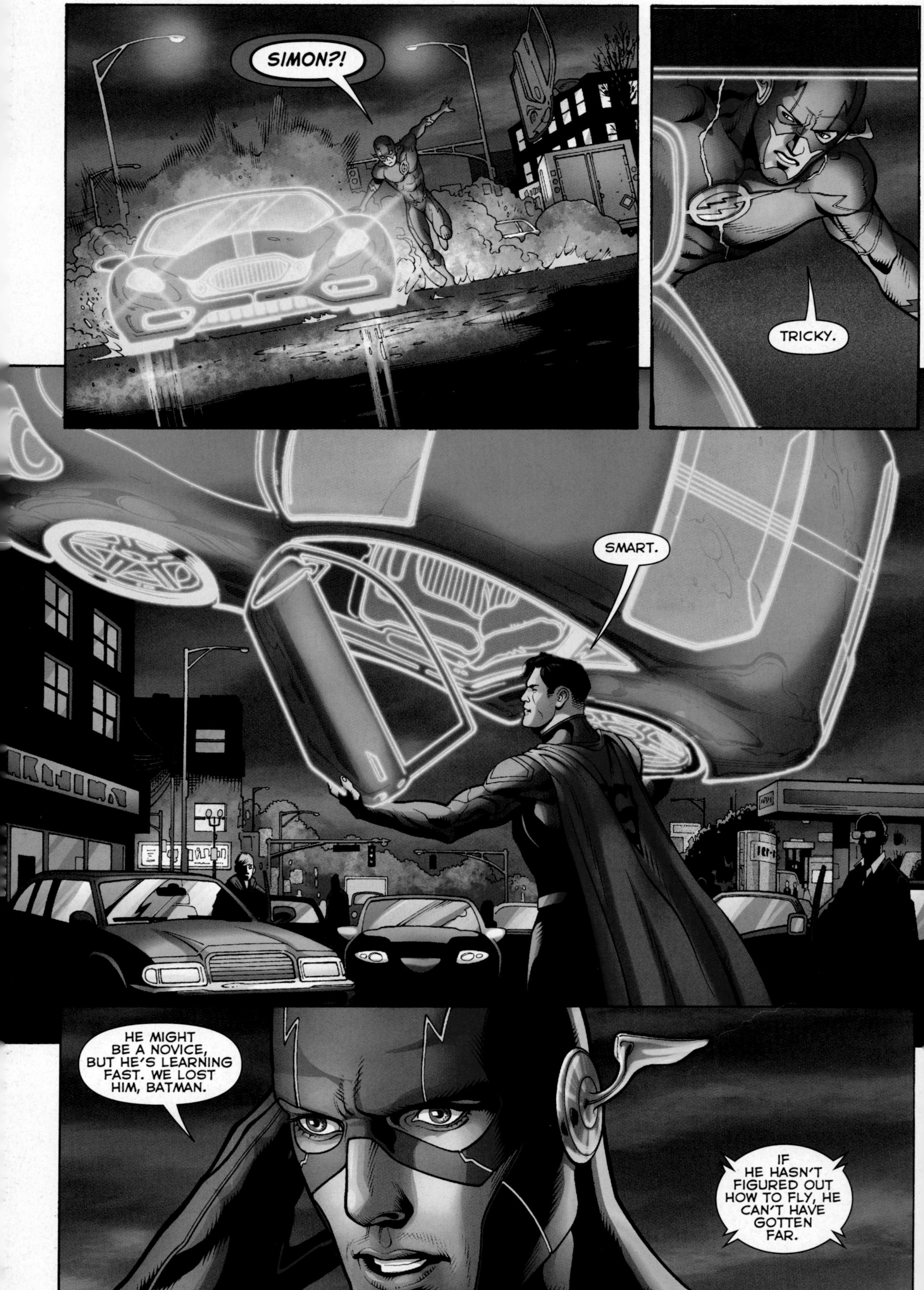
SIMON?!
TRICKY.
SMART.
HE MIGHT BE A NOVICE, BUT HE'S LEARNING FAST. WE LOST HIM, BATMAN.
IF HE HASN'T FIGURED OUT HOW TO FLY, HE CAN'T HAVE GOTTEN FAR.

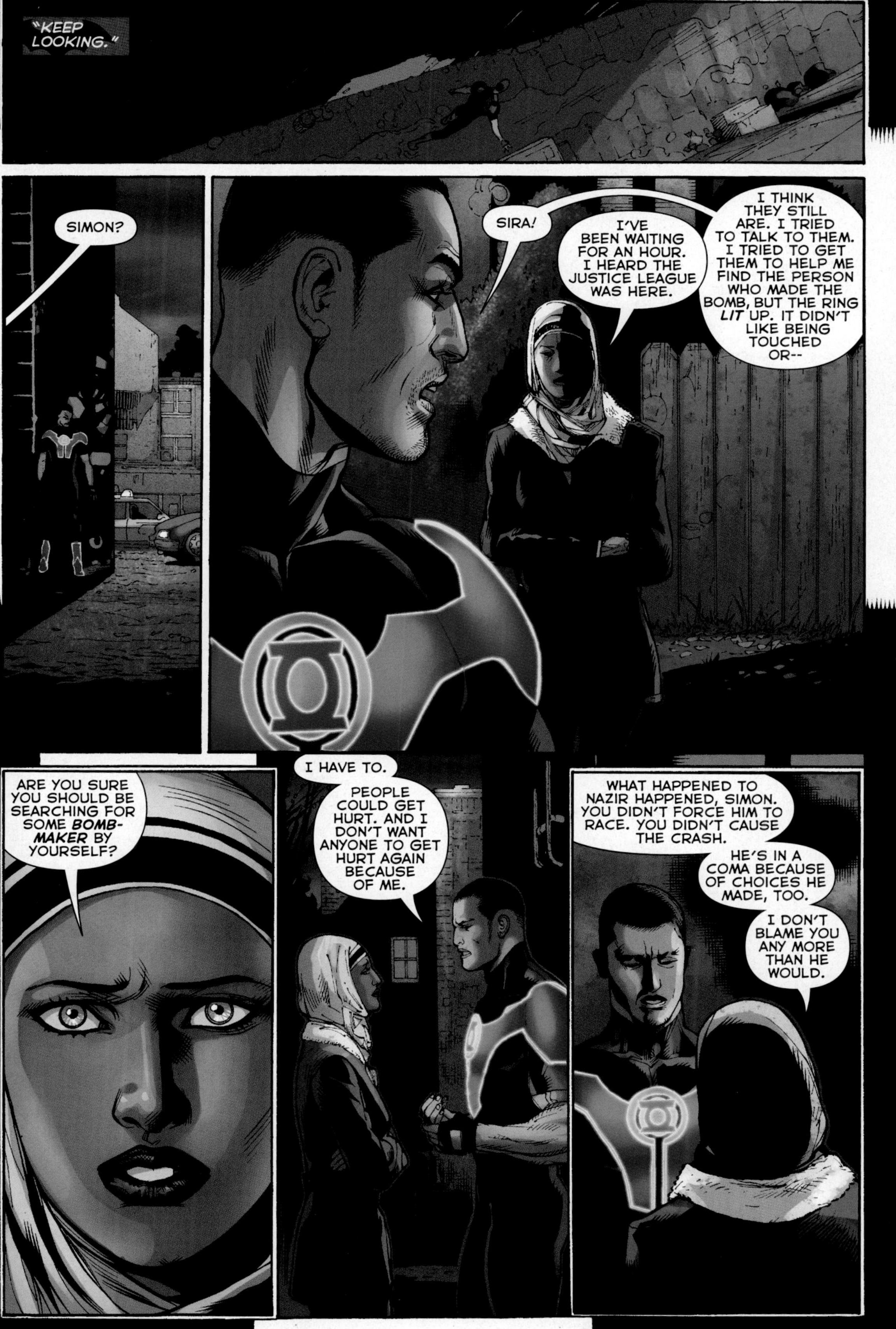
"KEEP LOOKING."
SIMON?
SIRA!
I'VE BEEN WAITING FOR AN HOUR. I HEARD THE JUSTICE LEAGUE WAS HERE.
I THINK THEY STILL ARE. I TRIED TO TALK TO THEM. I TRIED TO GET THEM TO HELP ME FIND THE PERSON WHO MADE THE BOMB, BUT THE RING LIT UP. IT DIDN'T LIKE BEING TOUCHED OR--
ARE YOU SURE YOU SHOULD BE SEARCHING FOR SOME BOMB-MAKER BY YOURSELF?
I HAVE TO.
PEOPLE COULD GET HURT. AND I DON'T WANT ANYONE TO GET HURT AGAIN BECAUSE OF ME.
WHAT HAPPENED TO NAZIR HAPPENED, SIMON. YOU DIDN'T FORCE HIM TO RACE. YOU DIDN'T CAUSE THE CRASH.
HE'S IN A COMA BECAUSE OF CHOICES HE MADE, TOO.
I DON'T BLAME YOU ANY MORE THAN HE WOULD.

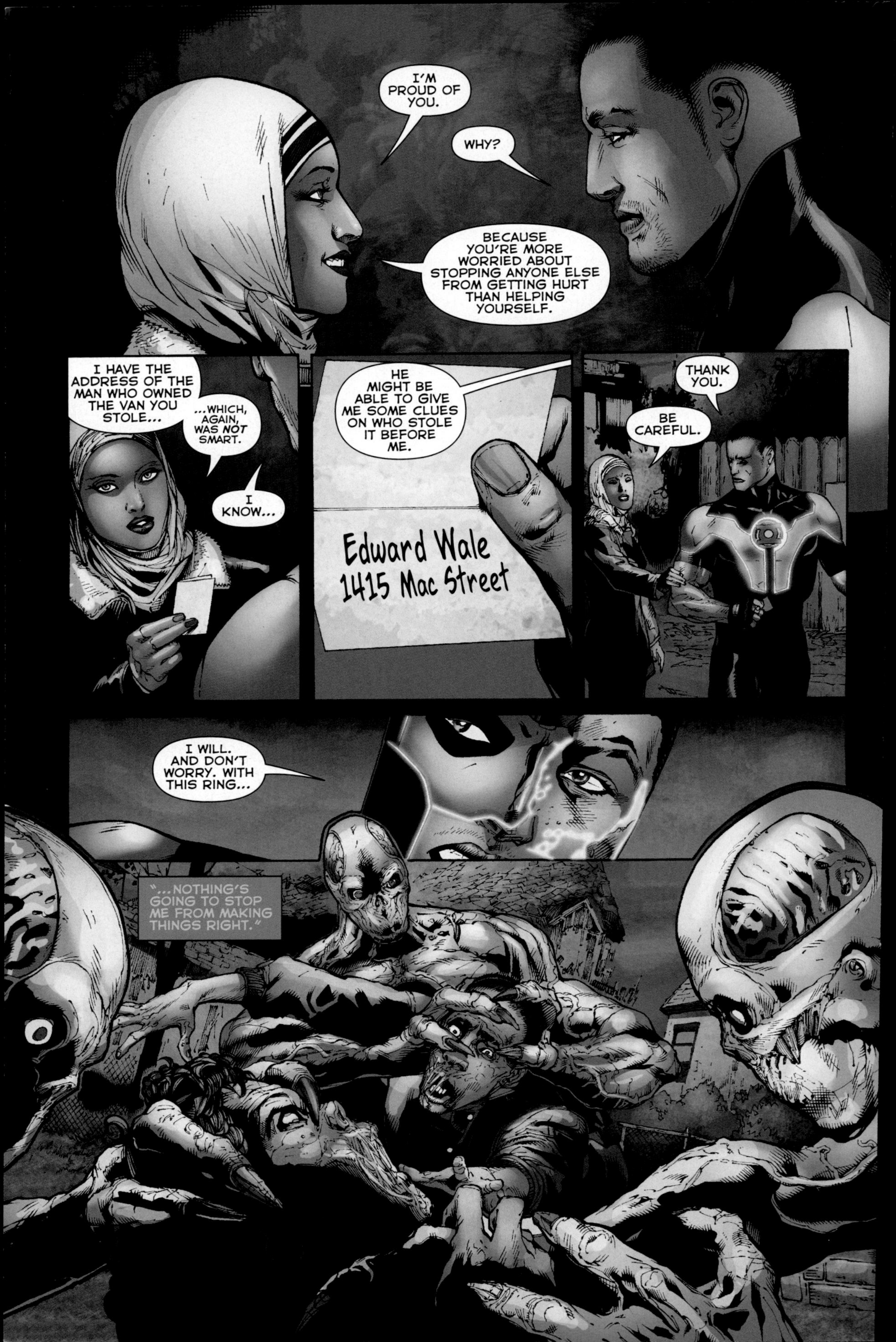
I'M PROUD OF YOU.
WHY?
BECAUSE YOU'RE MORE WORRIED ABOUT STOPPING ANYONE ELSE FROM GETTING HURT THAN HELPING YOURSELF.
I HAVE THE ADDRESS OF THE MAN WHO OWNED THE VAN YOU STOLE...
...WHICH, AGAIN, WAS NOT SMART.
I KNOW...
HE MIGHT BE ABLE TO GIVE ME SOME CLUES ON WHO STOLE IT BEFORE ME.
Edward Wale
1415 Mac Street
THANK YOU.
BE CAREFUL.
I WILL. AND DON'T WORRY. WITH THIS RING...
"...NOTHING'S GOING TO STOP ME FROM MAKING THINGS RIGHT."

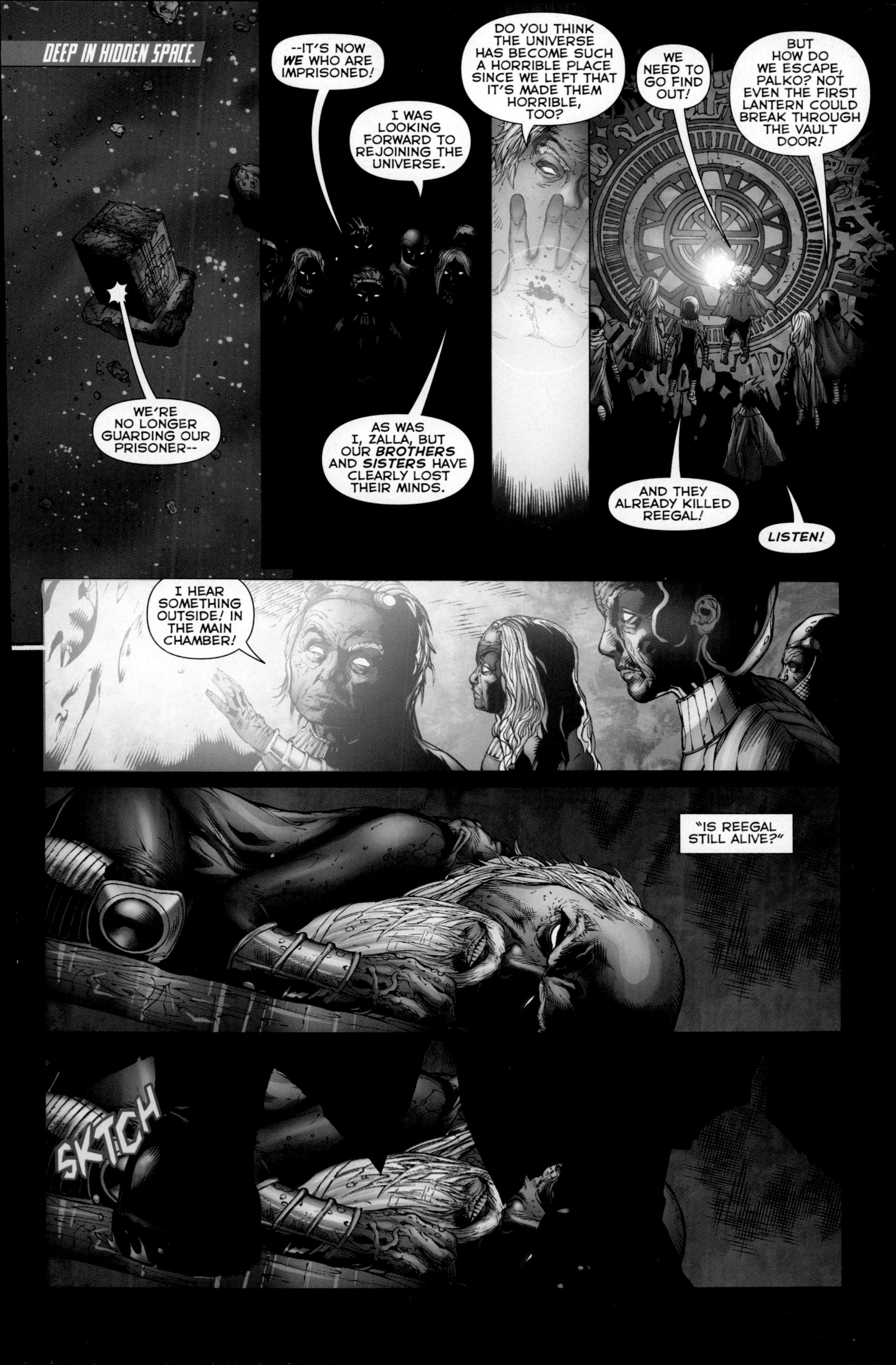
DEEP IN HIDDEN SPACE.
WE'RE NO LONGER GUARDING OUR PRISONER--
--IT'S NOW WE WHO ARE IMPRISONED!
I WAS LOOKING FORWARD TO REJOINING THE UNIVERSE.
AS WAS I, ZALLA, BUT OUR BROTHERS AND SISTERS HAVE CLEARLY LOST THEIR MINDS.
DO YOU THINK THE UNIVERSE HAS BECOME SUCH A HORRIBLE PLACE SINCE WE LEFT THAT IT'S MADE THEM HORRIBLE, TOO?
WE NEED TO GO FIND OUT!
AND THEY ALREADY KILLED REEGAL!
BUT HOW DO WE ESCAPE, PALKO? NOT EVEN THE FIRST LANTERN COULD BREAK THROUGH THE VAULT DOOR!
LISTEN!
I HEAR SOMETHING OUTSIDE! IN THE MAIN CHAMBER!
"IS REEGAL STILL ALIVE?"
SKTCH

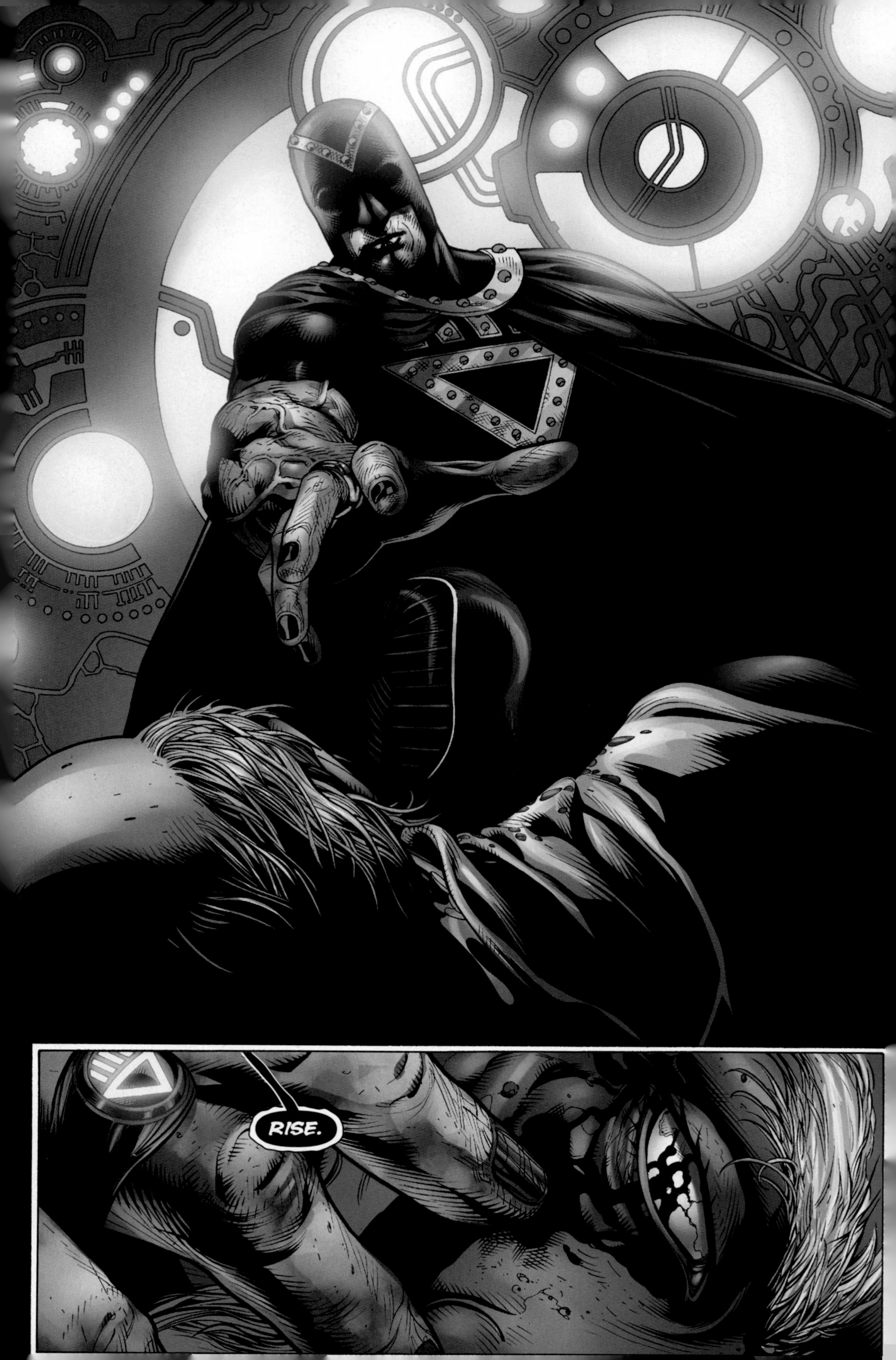
RISE.

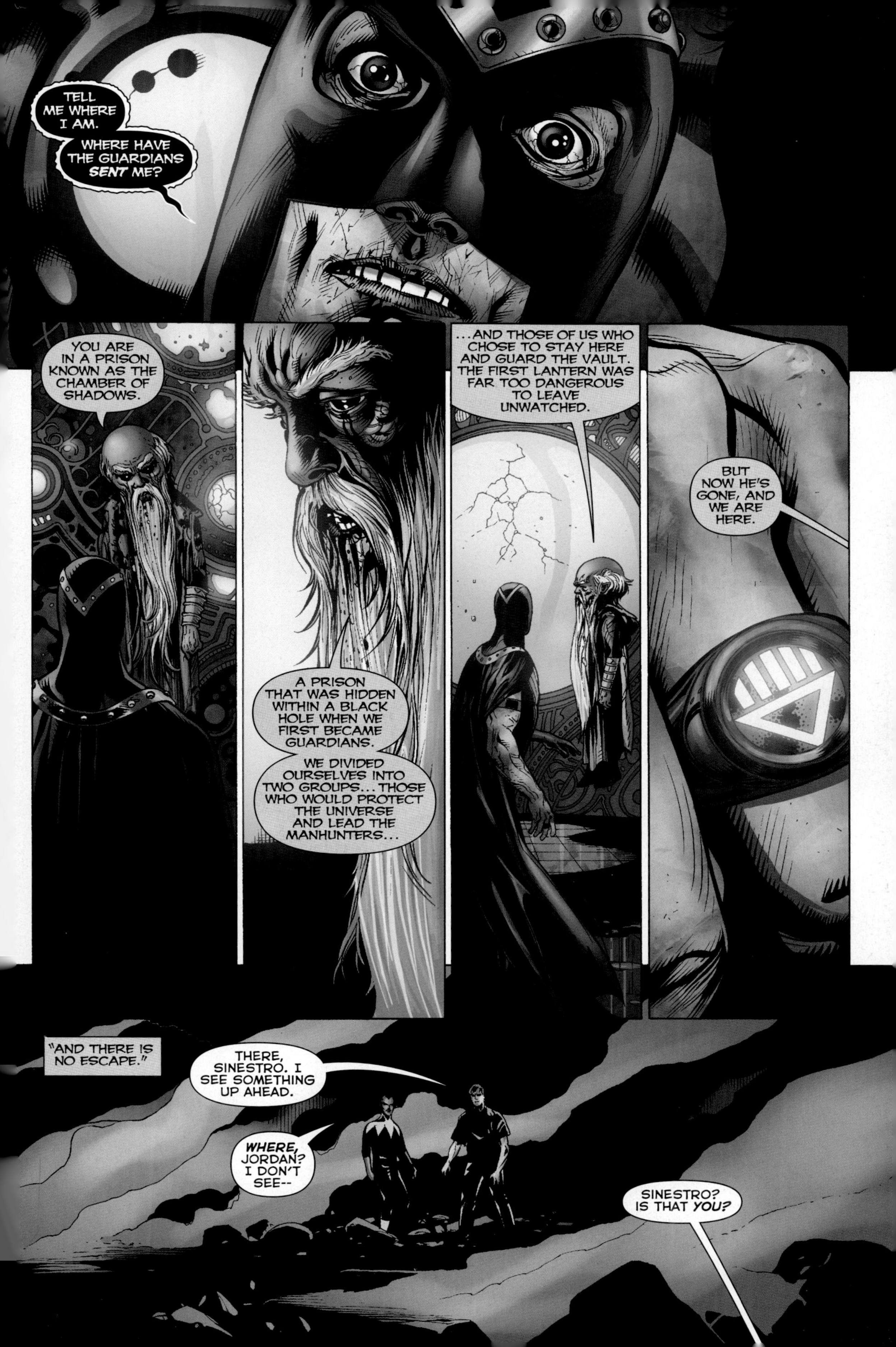

TELL ME WHERE I AM.
WHERE HAVE THE GUARDIANS *SENT* ME?
YOU ARE IN A PRISON KNOWN AS THE CHAMBER OF SHADOWS.
A PRISON THAT WAS HIDDEN WITHIN A BLACK HOLE WHEN WE FIRST BECAME GUARDIANS.
WE DIVIDED OURSELVES INTO TWO GROUPS... THOSE WHO WOULD PROTECT THE UNIVERSE AND LEAD THE MANHUNTERS...
...AND THOSE OF US WHO CHOSE TO STAY HERE AND GUARD THE VAULT. THE FIRST LANTERN WAS FAR TOO DANGEROUS TO LEAVE UNWATCHED.
BUT NOW HE'S GONE, AND WE ARE HERE.
"AND THERE IS NO ESCAPE."
THERE, SINESTRO. I SEE SOMETHING UP AHEAD.
WHERE, JORDAN? I DON'T SEE--
SINESTRO? IS THAT *YOU?*

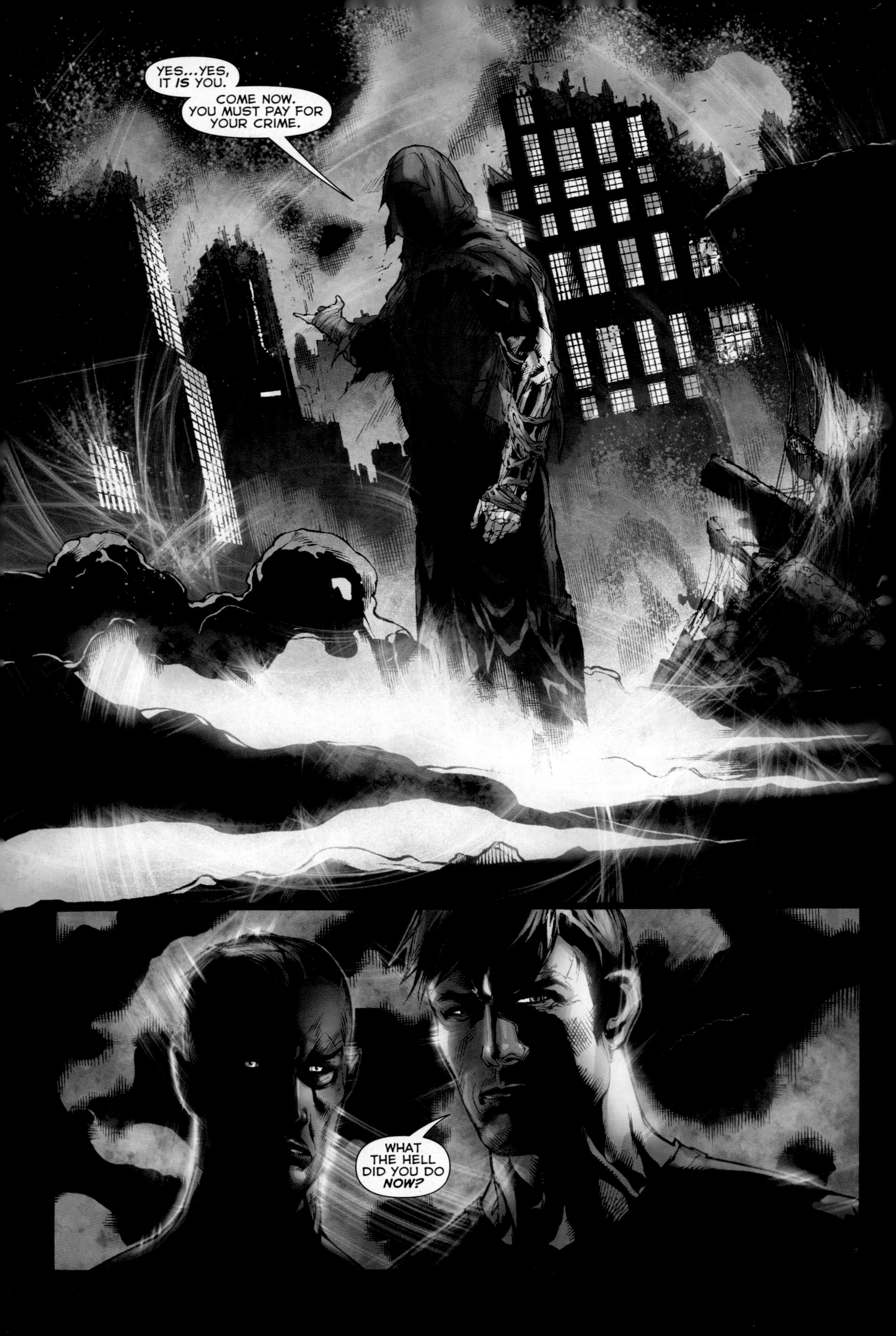
YES...YES, IT IS YOU.
COME NOW. YOU MUST PAY FOR YOUR CRIME.
WHAT THE HELL DID YOU DO NOW?

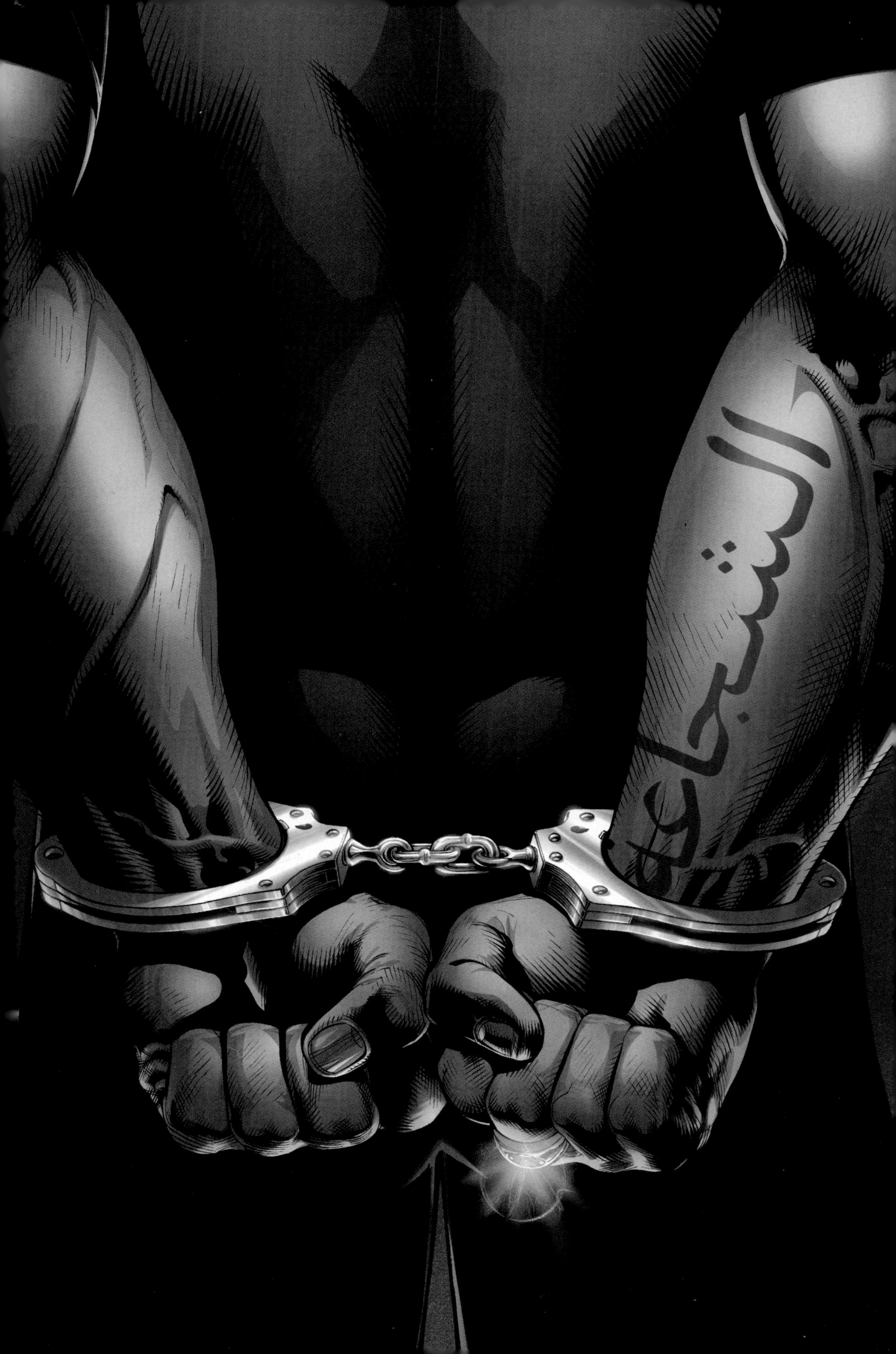
الشجاع

GEOFF JOHNS writer DOUG MAHNKE penciller KEITH CHAMPAGNE, CHRISTIAN ALAMY, MARK IRWIN, TOM NGUYEN & DOUG MAHNKE inkers
DOUG MAHNKE, CHRISTIAN ALAMY & ALEX SINCLAIR cover

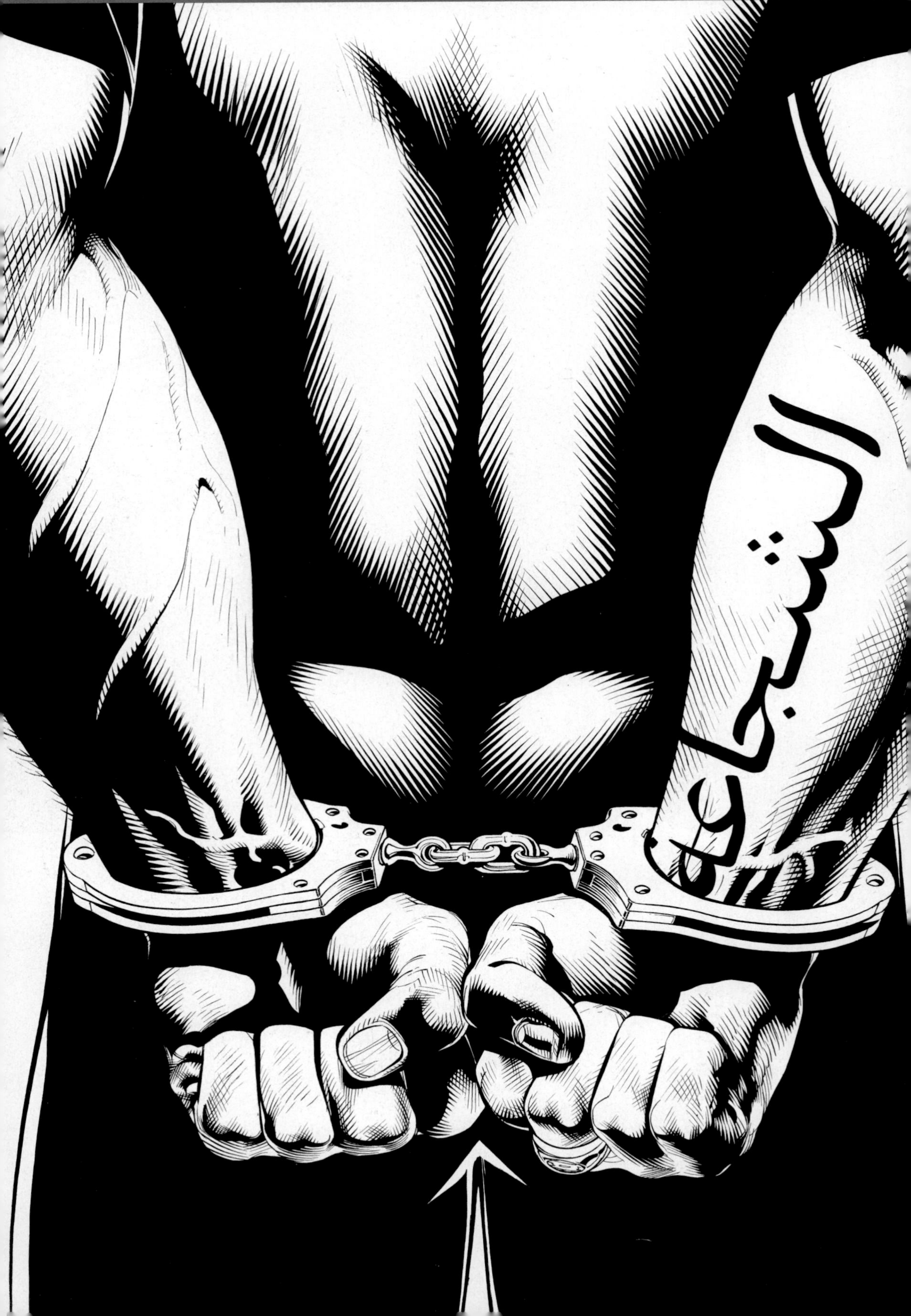

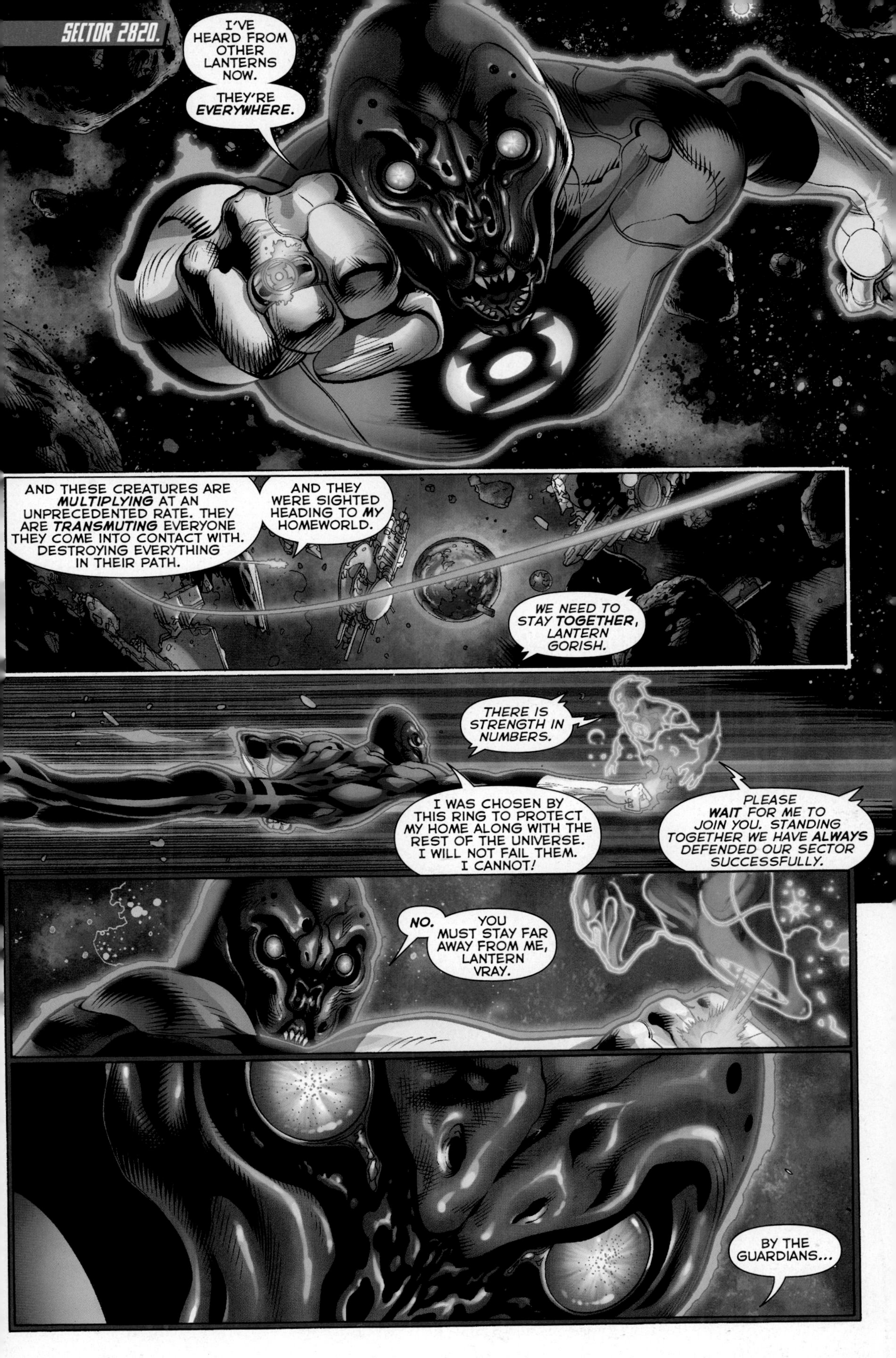
SECTOR 2820.
I'VE HEARD FROM OTHER LANTERNS NOW.
THEY'RE EVERYWHERE.
AND THESE CREATURES ARE MULTIPLYING AT AN UNPRECEDENTED RATE. THEY ARE TRANSMUTING EVERYONE THEY COME INTO CONTACT WITH. DESTROYING EVERYTHING IN THEIR PATH.
AND THEY WERE SIGHTED HEADING TO MY HOMEWORLD.
WE NEED TO STAY TOGETHER, LANTERN GORISH.
THERE IS STRENGTH IN NUMBERS.
I WAS CHOSEN BY THIS RING TO PROTECT MY HOME ALONG WITH THE REST OF THE UNIVERSE. I WILL NOT FAIL THEM. I CANNOT!
PLEASE WAIT FOR ME TO JOIN YOU. STANDING TOGETHER WE HAVE ALWAYS DEFENDED OUR SECTOR SUCCESSFULLY.
NO. YOU MUST STAY FAR AWAY FROM ME, LANTERN VRAY.
BY THE GUARDIANS...

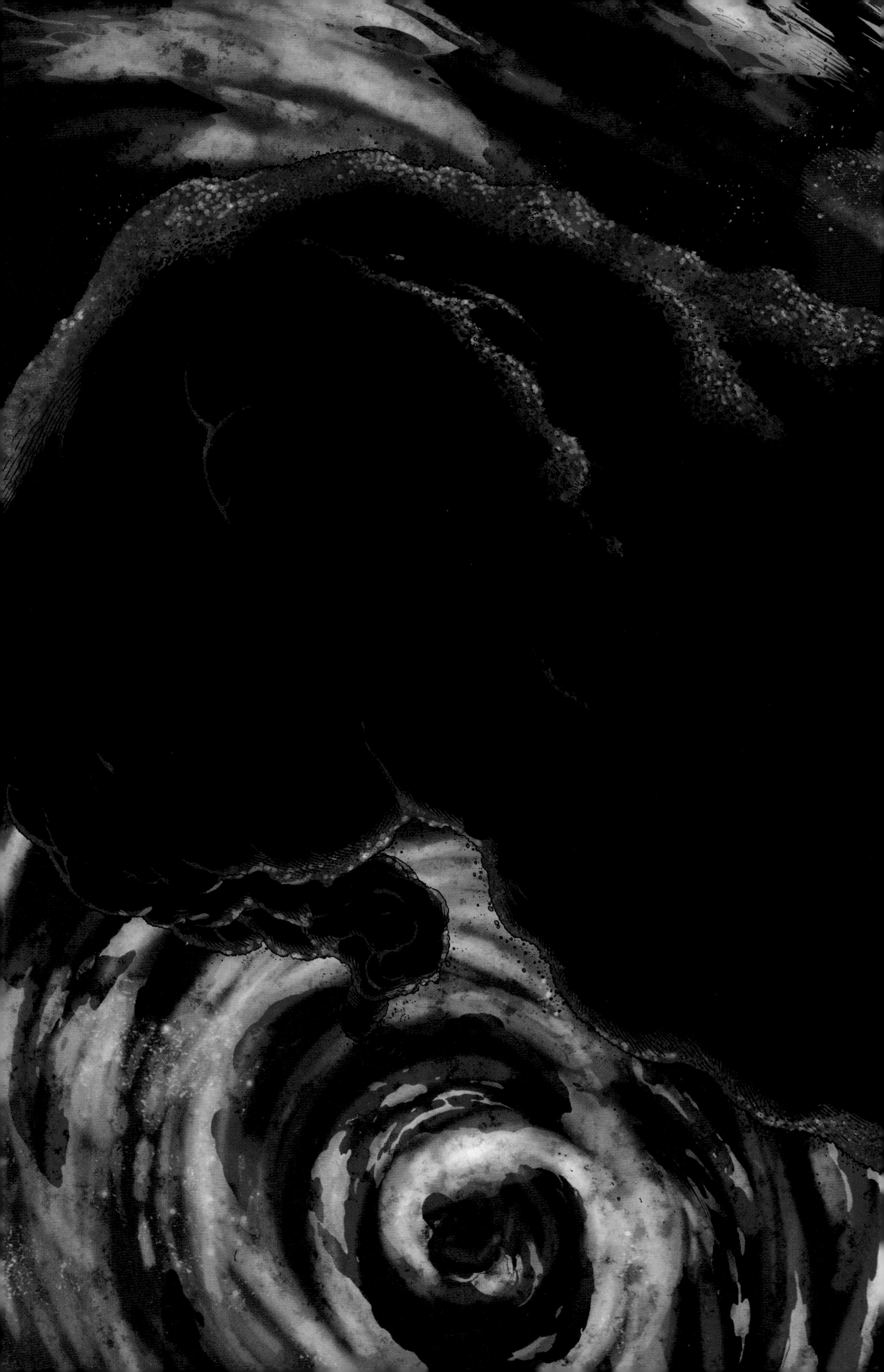

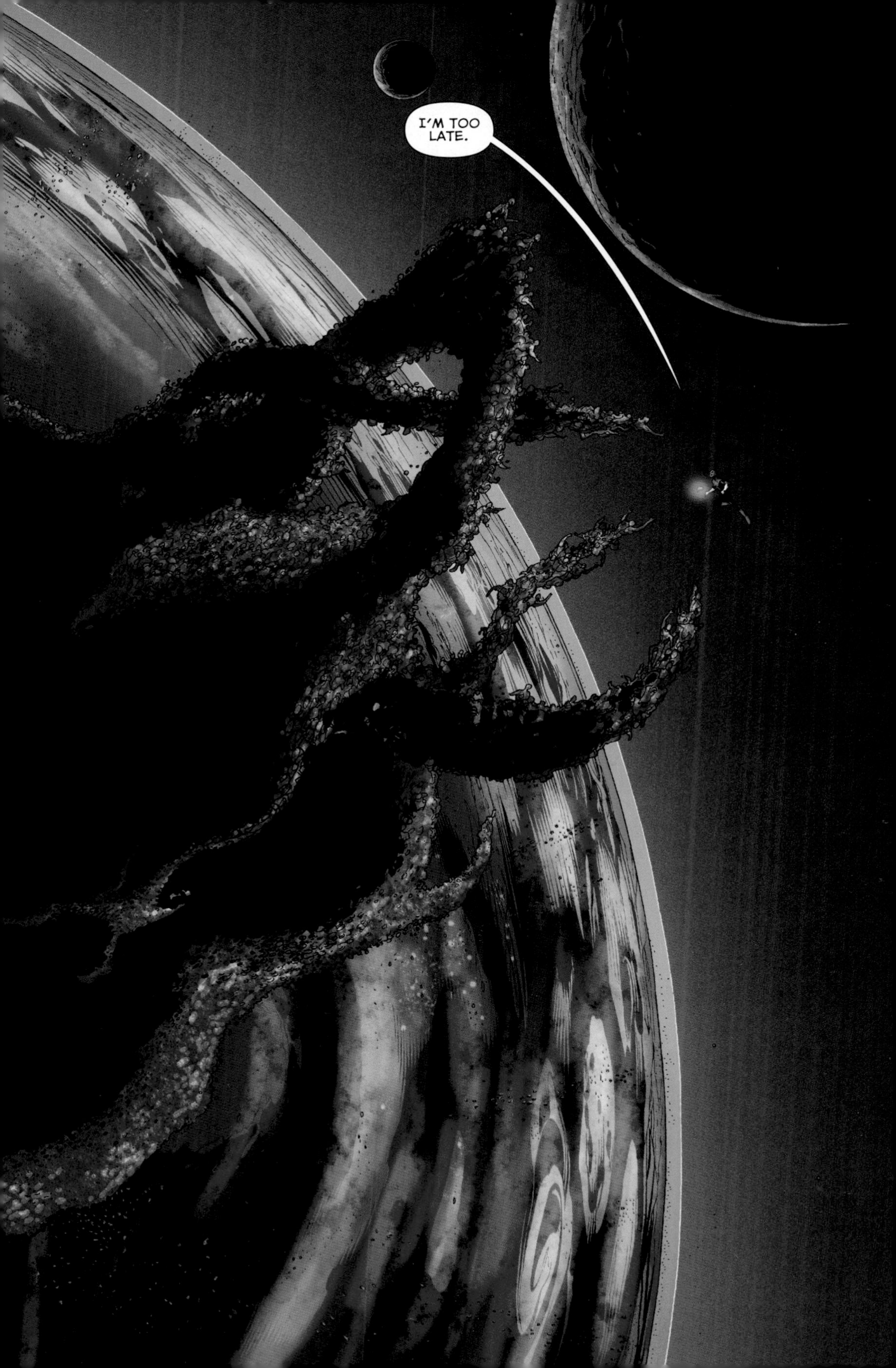
I'M TOO LATE.

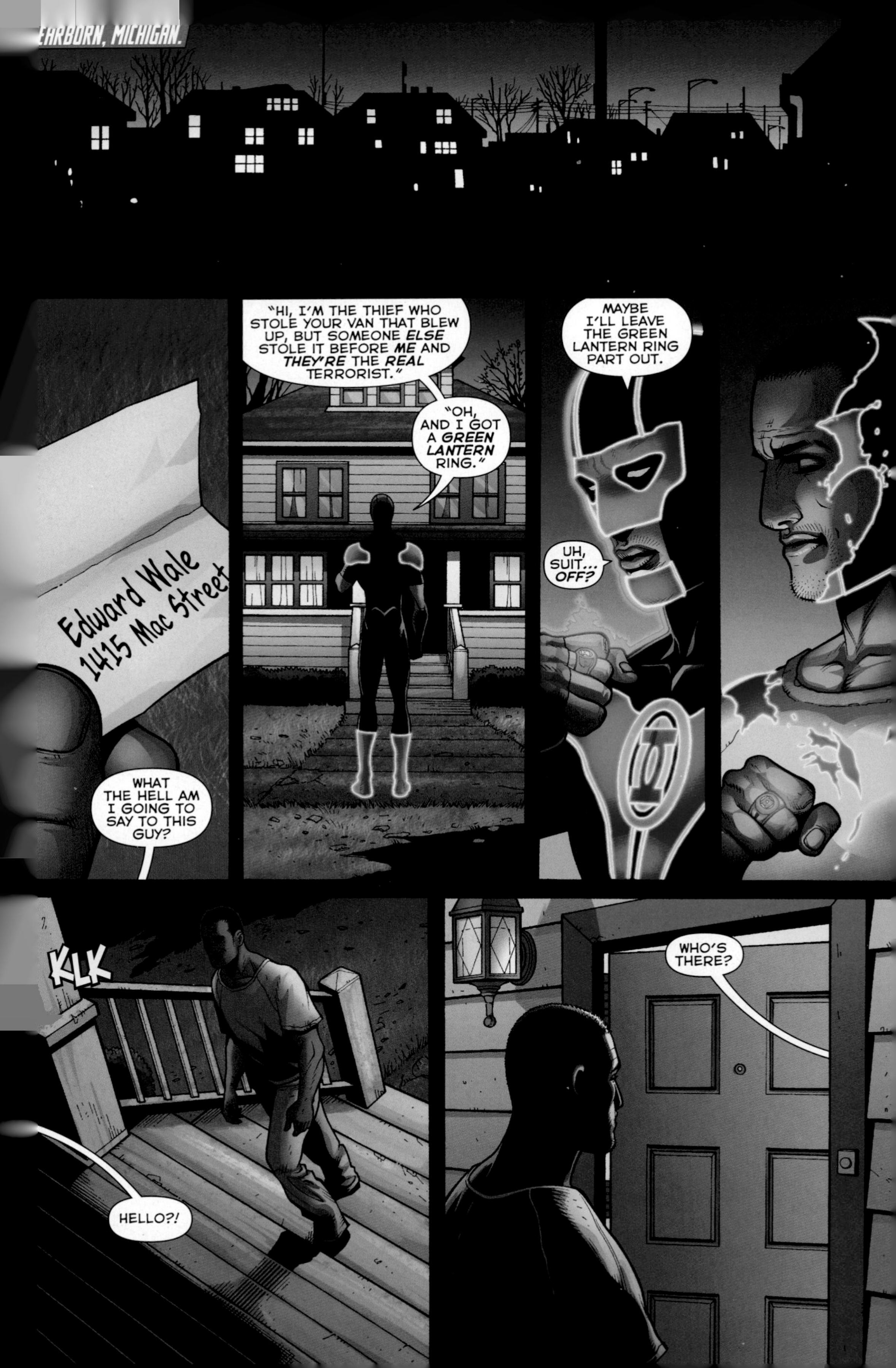

EARBORN, MICHIGAN.
Edward Wale
1415 Mac Street
WHAT THE HELL AM I GOING TO SAY TO THIS GUY?
"HI, I'M THE THIEF WHO STOLE YOUR VAN THAT BLEW UP, BUT SOMEONE ELSE STOLE IT BEFORE ME AND THEY'RE THE REAL TERRORIST."
"OH, AND I GOT A GREEN LANTERN RING."
MAYBE I'LL LEAVE THE GREEN LANTERN RING PART OUT.
UH, SUIT... OFF?
KLK
HELLO?!
WHO'S THERE?

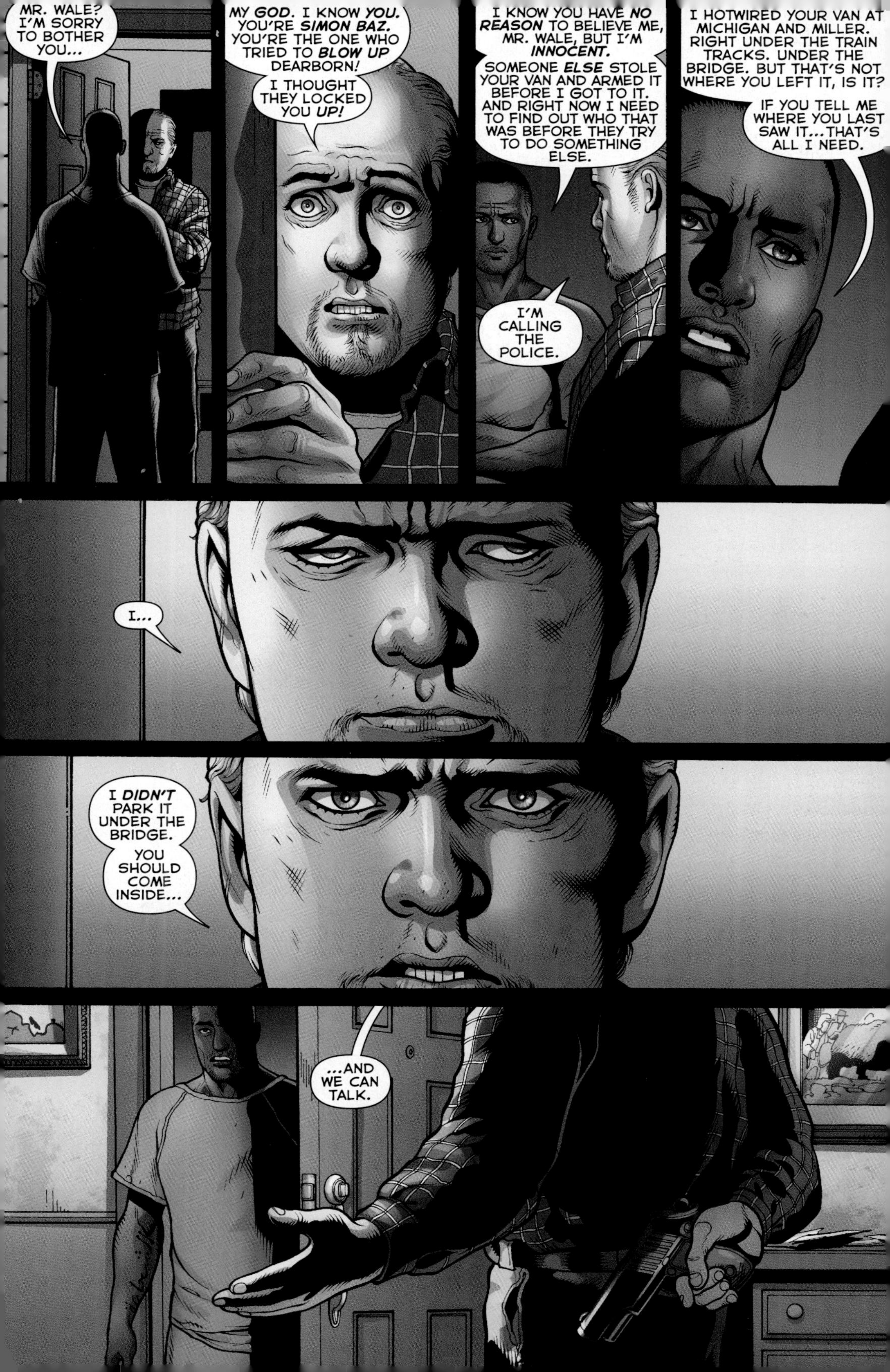
MR. WALE? I'M SORRY TO BOTHER YOU...
MY *GOD*. I KNOW *YOU*. YOU'RE *SIMON BAZ*. YOU'RE THE ONE WHO TRIED TO *BLOW UP* DEARBORN!
I THOUGHT THEY LOCKED YOU *UP!*
I KNOW YOU HAVE *NO REASON* TO BELIEVE ME, MR. WALE, BUT I'M *INNOCENT.*
SOMEONE *ELSE* STOLE YOUR VAN AND ARMED IT BEFORE I GOT TO IT. AND RIGHT NOW I NEED TO FIND OUT WHO THAT WAS BEFORE THEY TRY TO DO SOMETHING ELSE.
I'M CALLING THE POLICE.
I HOTWIRED YOUR VAN AT MICHIGAN AND MILLER. RIGHT UNDER THE TRAIN TRACKS. UNDER THE BRIDGE. BUT THAT'S NOT WHERE YOU LEFT IT, IS IT?
IF YOU TELL ME WHERE YOU LAST SAW IT...THAT'S ALL I NEED.
I...
I *DIDN'T* PARK IT UNDER THE BRIDGE.
YOU SHOULD COME INSIDE...
...AND WE CAN TALK.

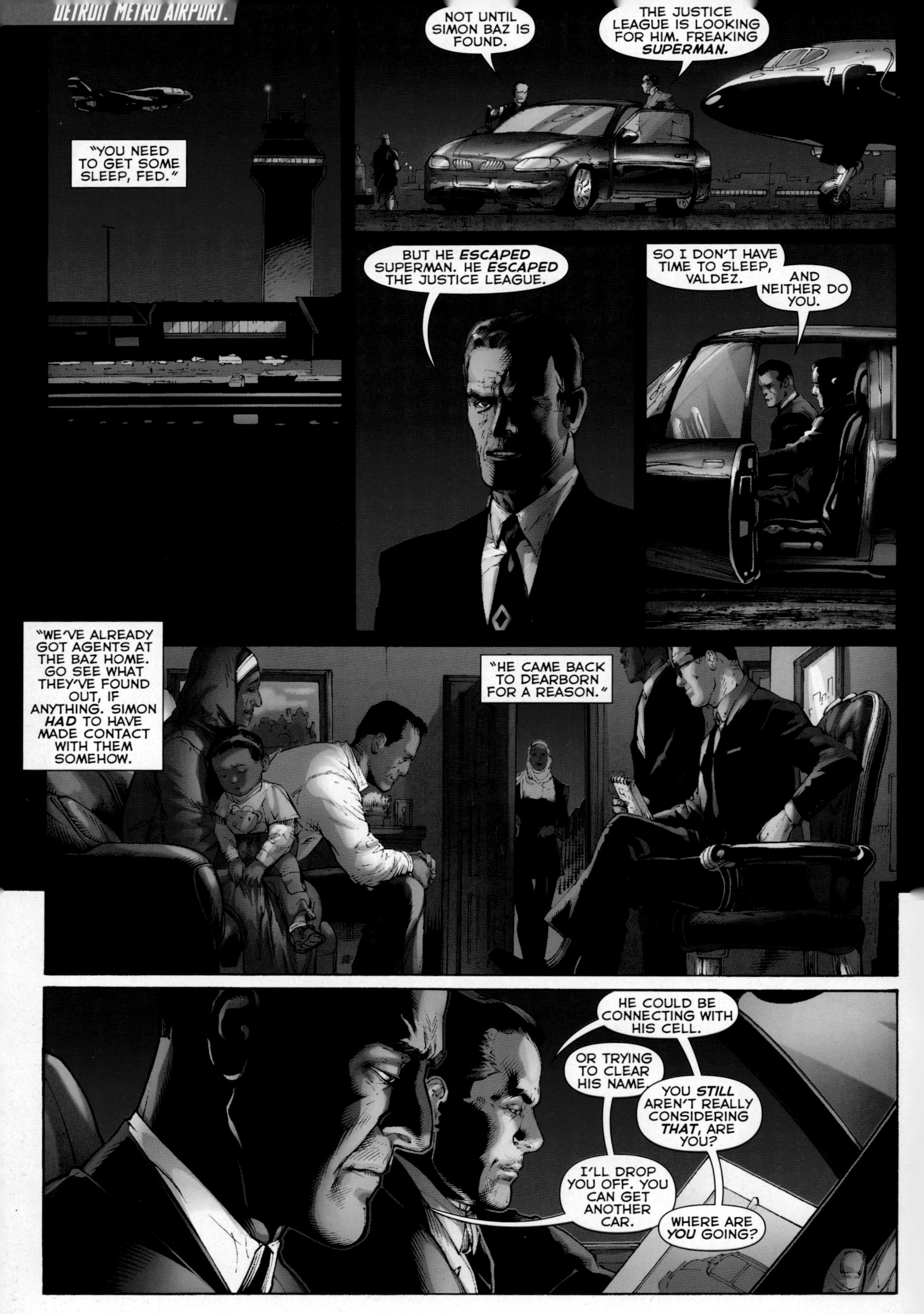
DETROIT METRO AIRPORT.
"YOU NEED TO GET SOME SLEEP, FED."
NOT UNTIL SIMON BAZ IS FOUND.
THE JUSTICE LEAGUE IS LOOKING FOR HIM. FREAKING SUPERMAN.
BUT HE ESCAPED SUPERMAN. HE ESCAPED THE JUSTICE LEAGUE.
SO I DON'T HAVE TIME TO SLEEP, VALDEZ.
AND NEITHER DO YOU.
"WE'VE ALREADY GOT AGENTS AT THE BAZ HOME. GO SEE WHAT THEY'VE FOUND OUT, IF ANYTHING. SIMON HAD TO HAVE MADE CONTACT WITH THEM SOMEHOW.
"HE CAME BACK TO DEARBORN FOR A REASON."
HE COULD BE CONNECTING WITH HIS CELL.
OR TRYING TO CLEAR HIS NAME.
YOU STILL AREN'T REALLY CONSIDERING THAT, ARE YOU?
I'LL DROP YOU OFF. YOU CAN GET ANOTHER CAR.
WHERE ARE YOU GOING?

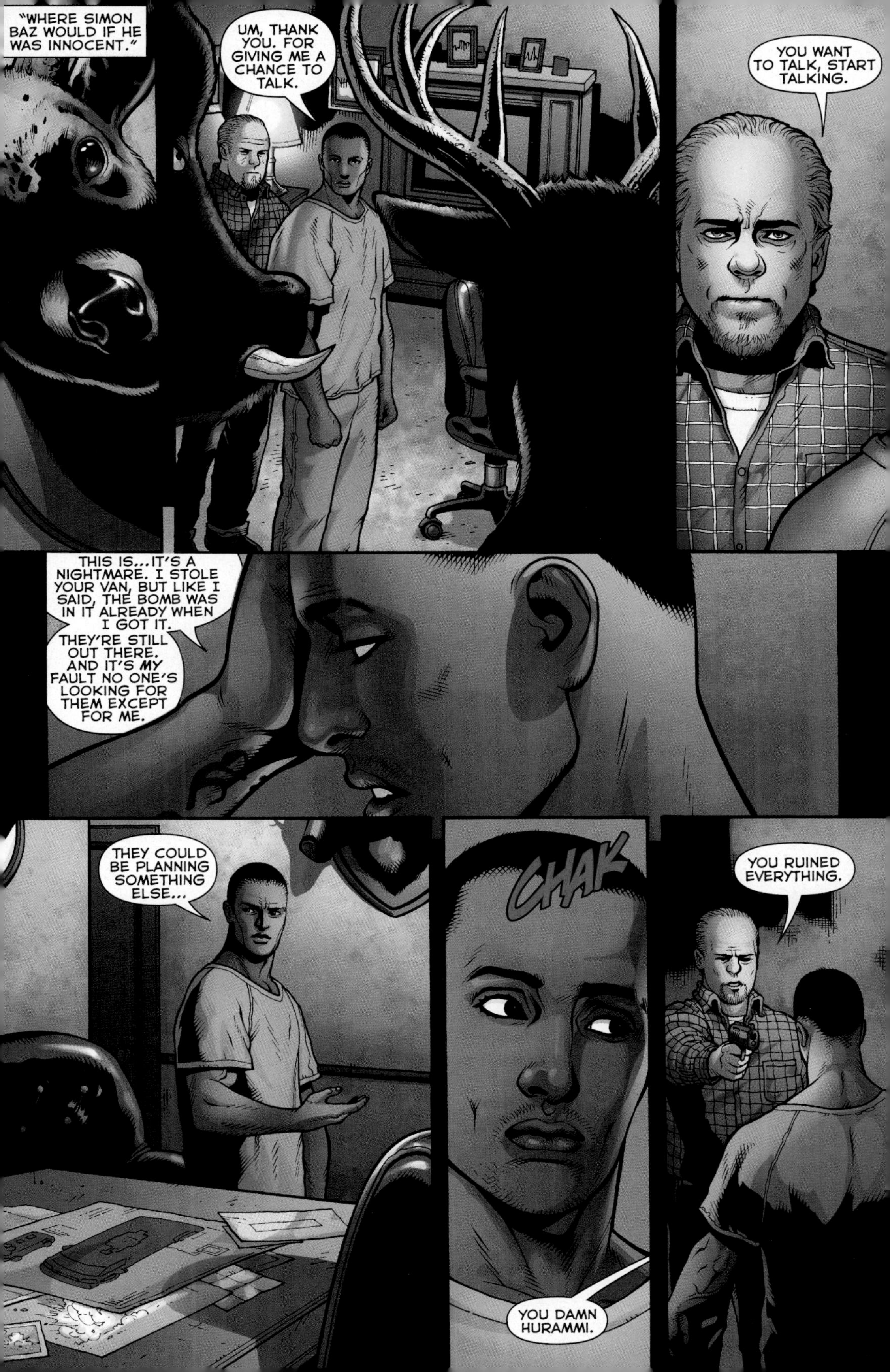
"WHERE SIMON BAZ WOULD IF HE WAS INNOCENT."
UM, THANK YOU. FOR GIVING ME A CHANCE TO TALK.
YOU WANT TO TALK, START TALKING.
THIS IS...IT'S A NIGHTMARE. I STOLE YOUR VAN, BUT LIKE I SAID, THE BOMB WAS IN IT ALREADY WHEN I GOT IT.
THEY'RE STILL OUT THERE. AND IT'S MY FAULT NO ONE'S LOOKING FOR THEM EXCEPT FOR ME.
THEY COULD BE PLANNING SOMETHING ELSE...
CHAK
YOU DAMN HURAMMI.
YOU RUINED EVERYTHING.

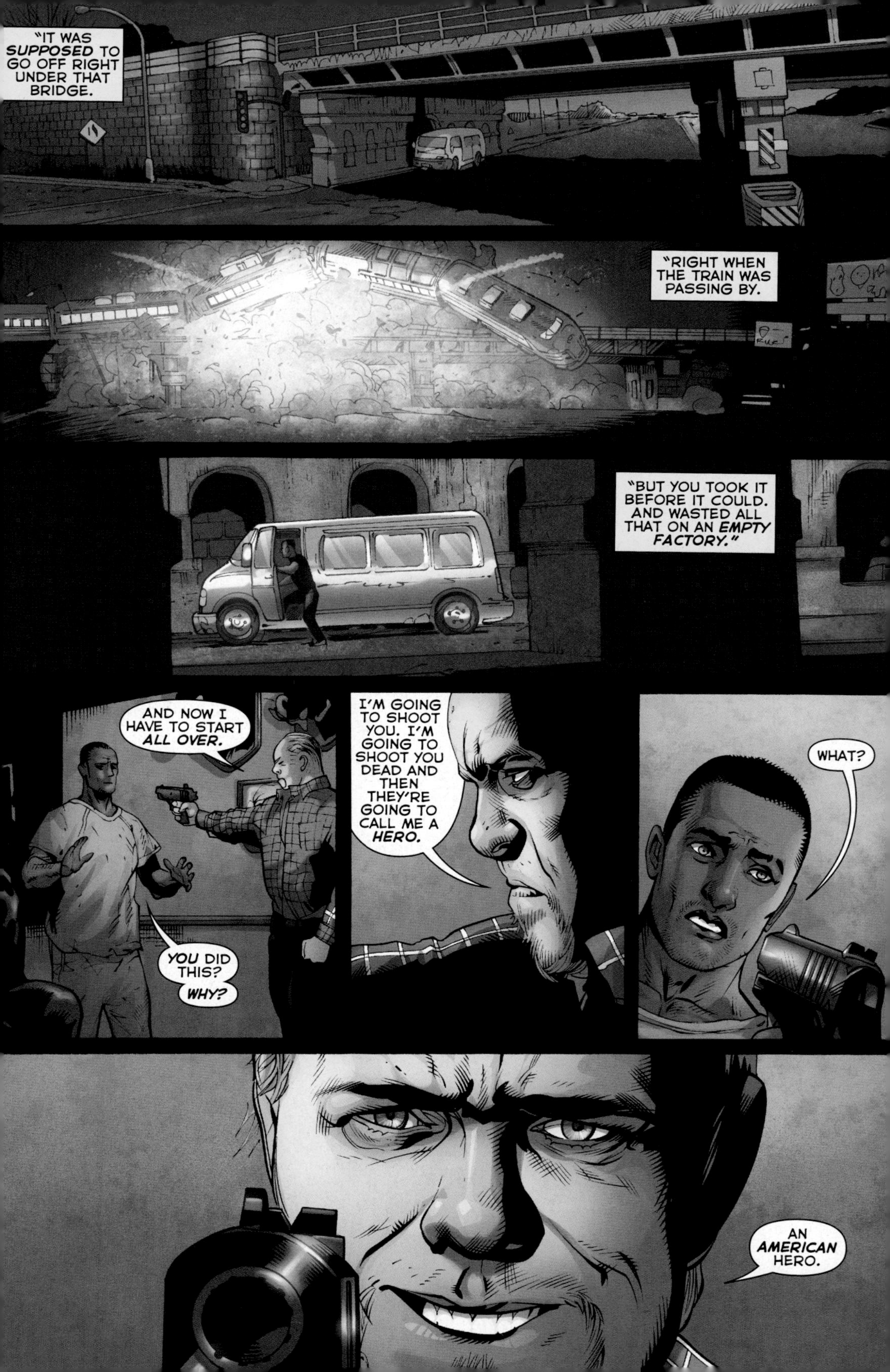
"IT WAS SUPPOSED TO GO OFF RIGHT UNDER THAT BRIDGE.
"RIGHT WHEN THE TRAIN WAS PASSING BY.
"BUT YOU TOOK IT BEFORE IT COULD. AND WASTED ALL THAT ON AN EMPTY FACTORY."
AND NOW I HAVE TO START ALL OVER.
YOU DID THIS? WHY?
I'M GOING TO SHOOT YOU. I'M GOING TO SHOOT YOU DEAD AND THEN THEY'RE GOING TO CALL ME A HERO.
WHAT?
AN AMERICAN HERO.

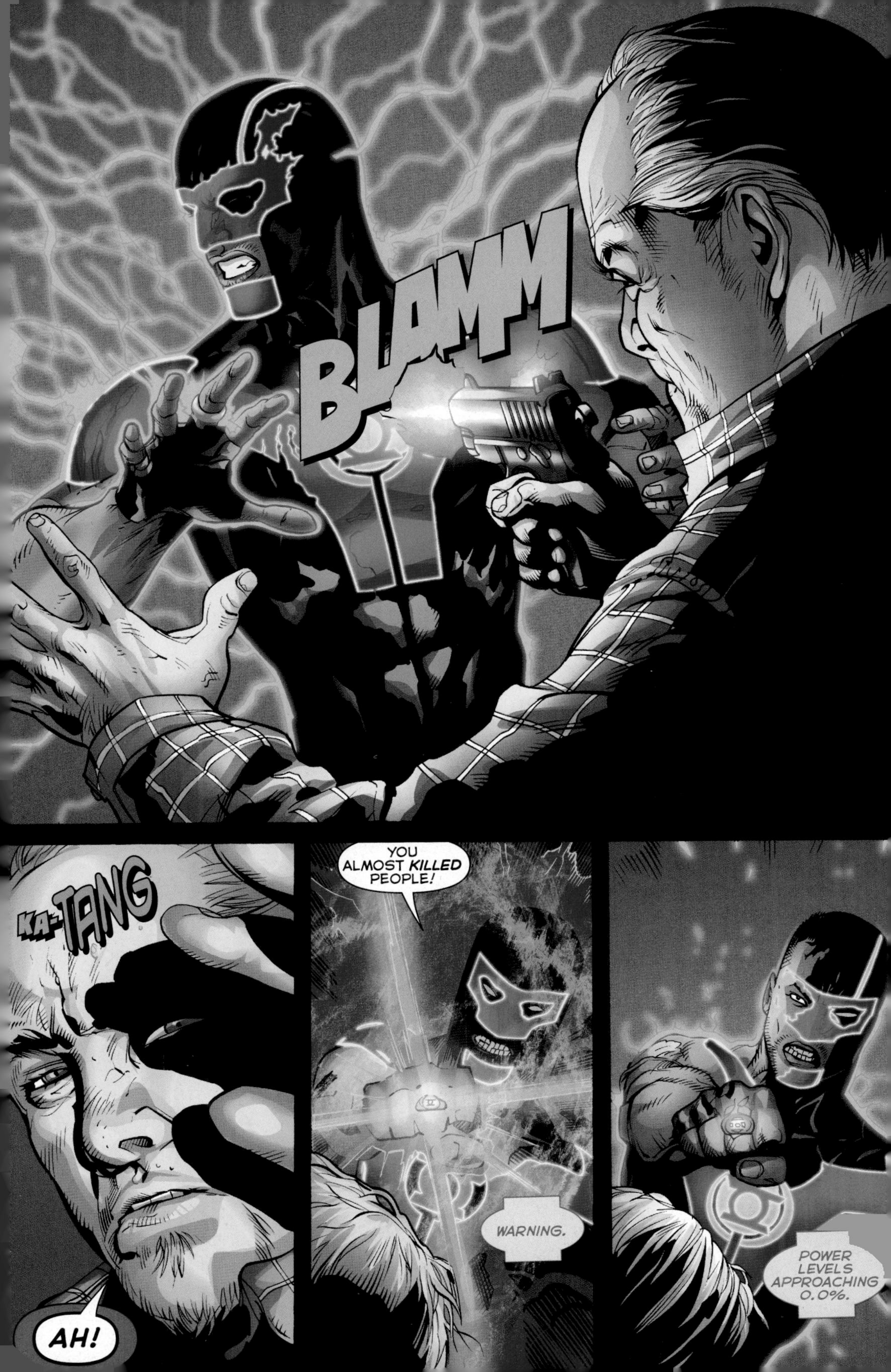
BLAMM
KA-TANG
AH!
YOU ALMOST *KILLED* PEOPLE!
WARNING.
POWER LEVELS APPROACHING 0.0%.

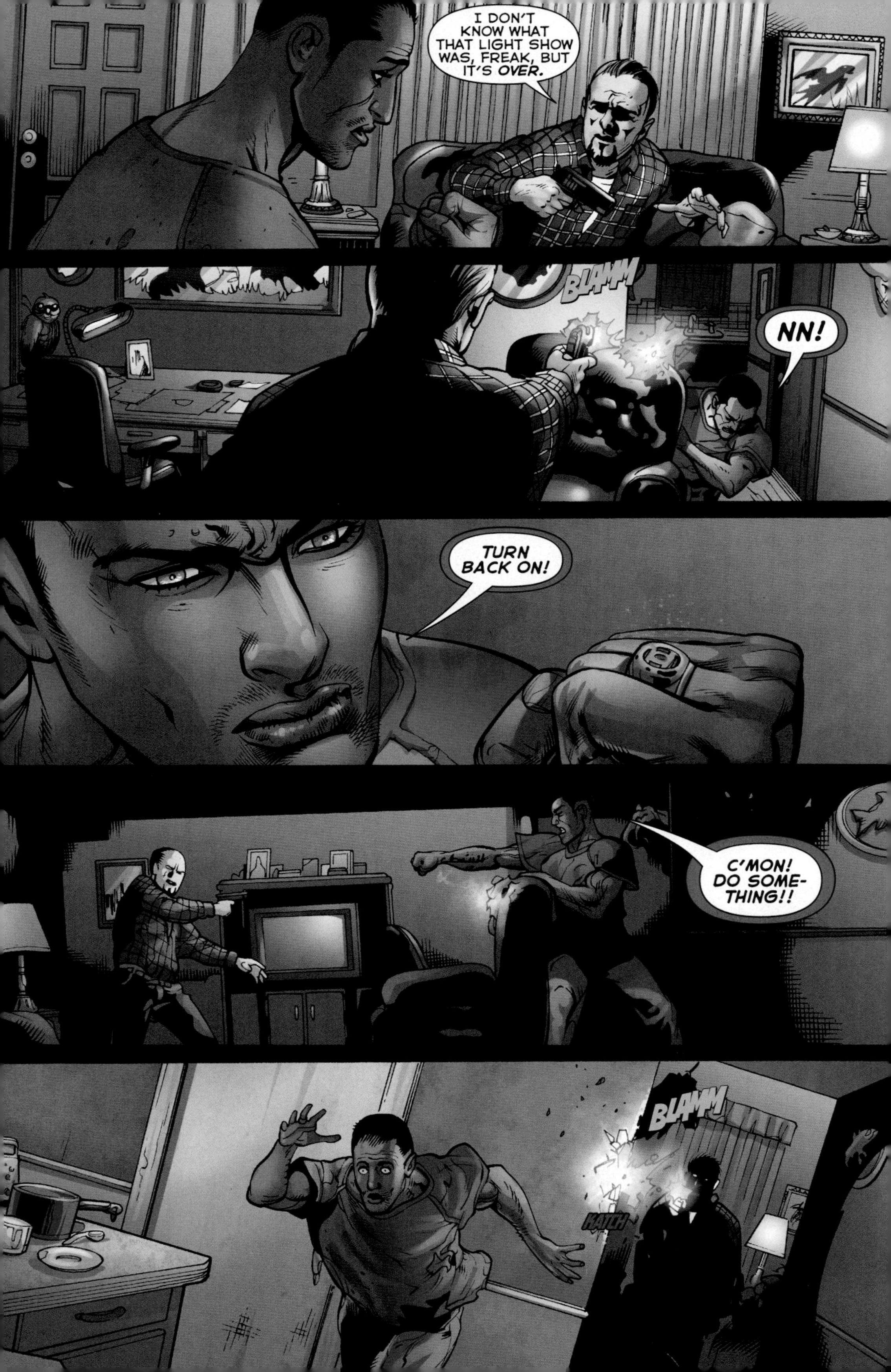

I DON'T KNOW WHAT THAT LIGHT SHOW WAS, FREAK, BUT IT'S *OVER.*
BLAMM
NN!
TURN BACK ON!
C'MON! DO SOME-THING!!
BLAMM
KATCH

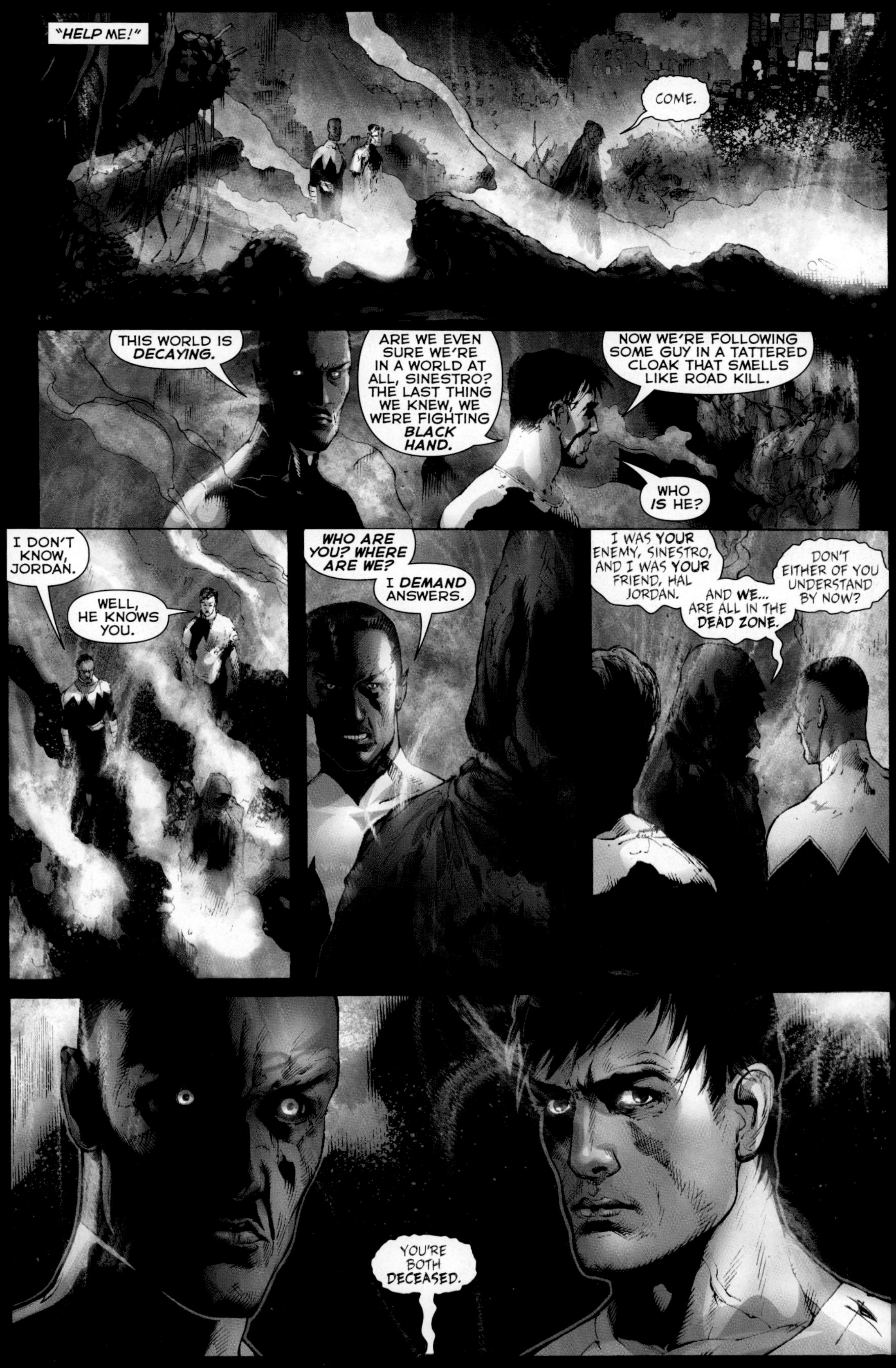
"HELP ME!"
COME.
THIS WORLD IS DECAYING.
ARE WE EVEN SURE WE'RE IN A WORLD AT ALL, SINESTRO? THE LAST THING WE KNEW, WE WERE FIGHTING BLACK HAND.
NOW WE'RE FOLLOWING SOME GUY IN A TATTERED CLOAK THAT SMELLS LIKE ROAD KILL.
WHO IS HE?
I DON'T KNOW, JORDAN.
WELL, HE KNOWS YOU.
WHO ARE YOU? WHERE ARE WE?
I DEMAND ANSWERS.
I WAS YOUR ENEMY, SINESTRO, AND I WAS YOUR FRIEND, HAL JORDAN.
AND WE... ARE ALL IN THE DEAD ZONE.
DON'T EITHER OF YOU UNDERSTAND BY NOW?
YOU'RE BOTH DECEASED.

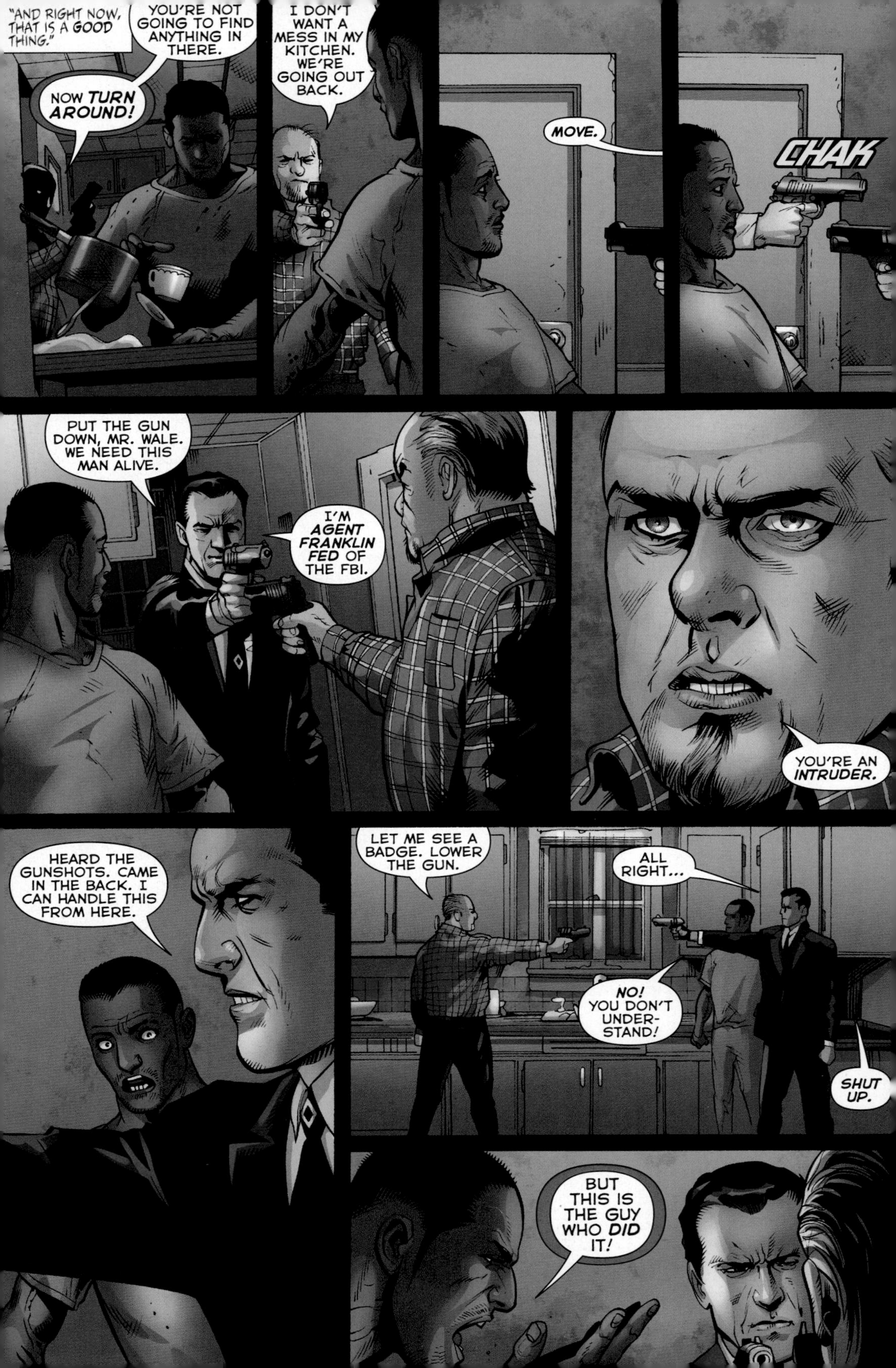
"AND RIGHT NOW, THAT IS A GOOD THING."
YOU'RE NOT GOING TO FIND ANYTHING IN THERE.
NOW TURN AROUND!
I DON'T WANT A MESS IN MY KITCHEN. WE'RE GOING OUT BACK.
MOVE.
CHAK
PUT THE GUN DOWN, MR. WALE. WE NEED THIS MAN ALIVE.
I'M AGENT FRANKLIN FED OF THE FBI.
YOU'RE AN INTRUDER.
HEARD THE GUNSHOTS. CAME IN THE BACK. I CAN HANDLE THIS FROM HERE.
LET ME SEE A BADGE. LOWER THE GUN.
ALL RIGHT...
NO! YOU DON'T UNDER- STAND!
SHUT UP.
BUT THIS IS THE GUY WHO DID IT!

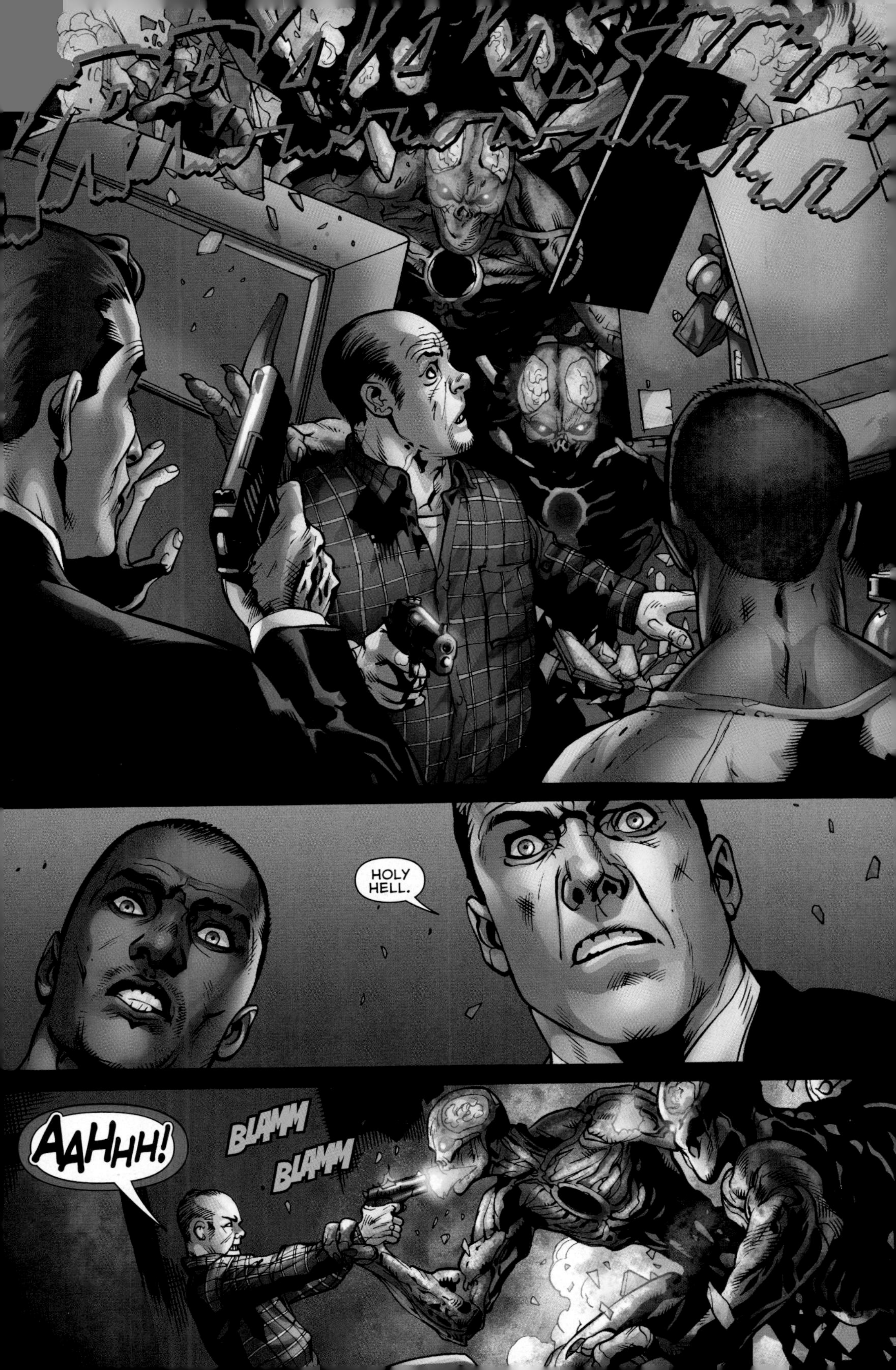
HOLY HELL.
AAHHH!
BLAMM
BLAMM

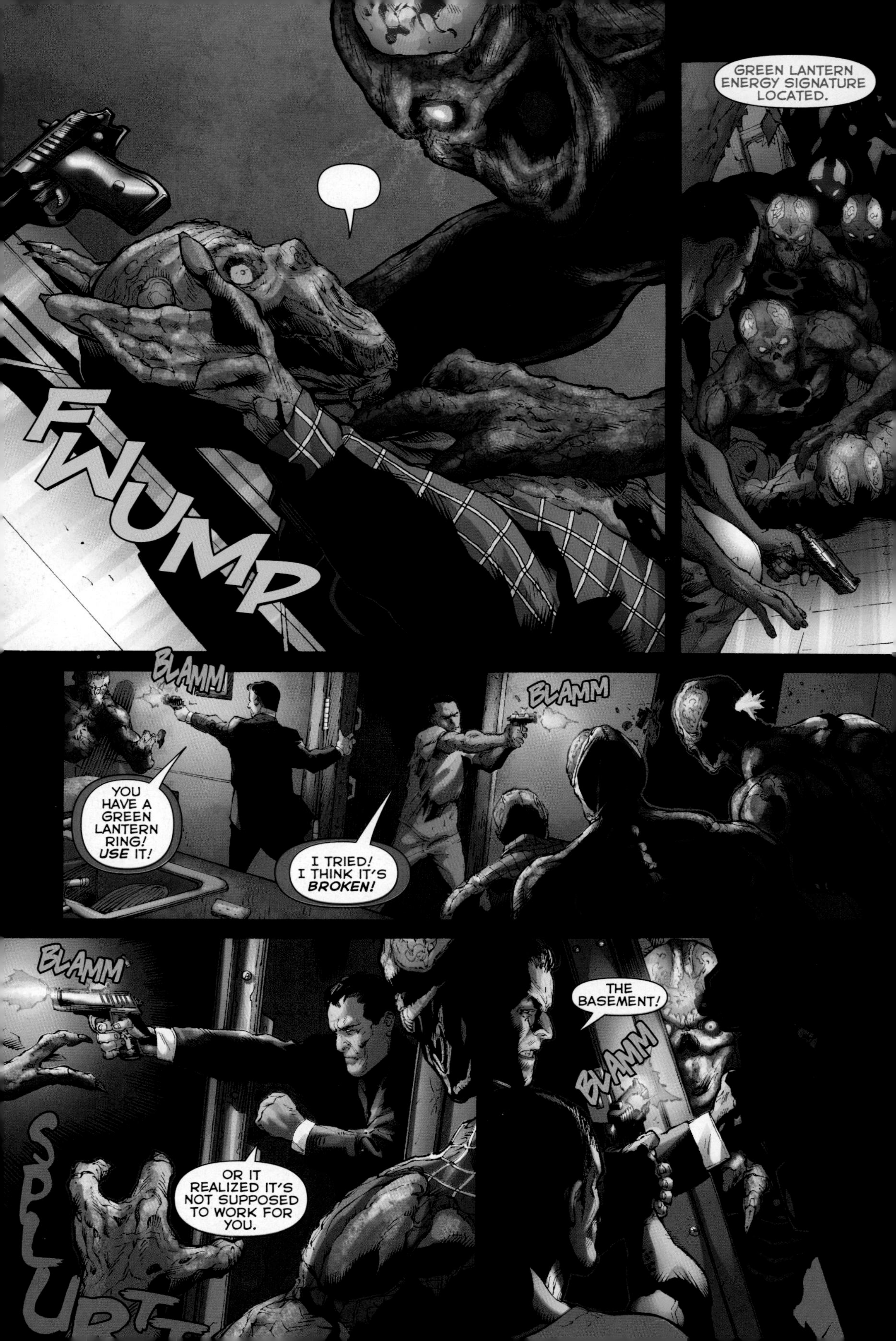

FWUMP
GREEN LANTERN ENERGY SIGNATURE LOCATED.
BLAMM
BLAMM
YOU HAVE A GREEN LANTERN RING! USE IT!
I TRIED! I THINK IT'S BROKEN!
BLAMM
THE BASEMENT!
BLAMM
OR IT REALIZED IT'S NOT SUPPOSED TO WORK FOR YOU.

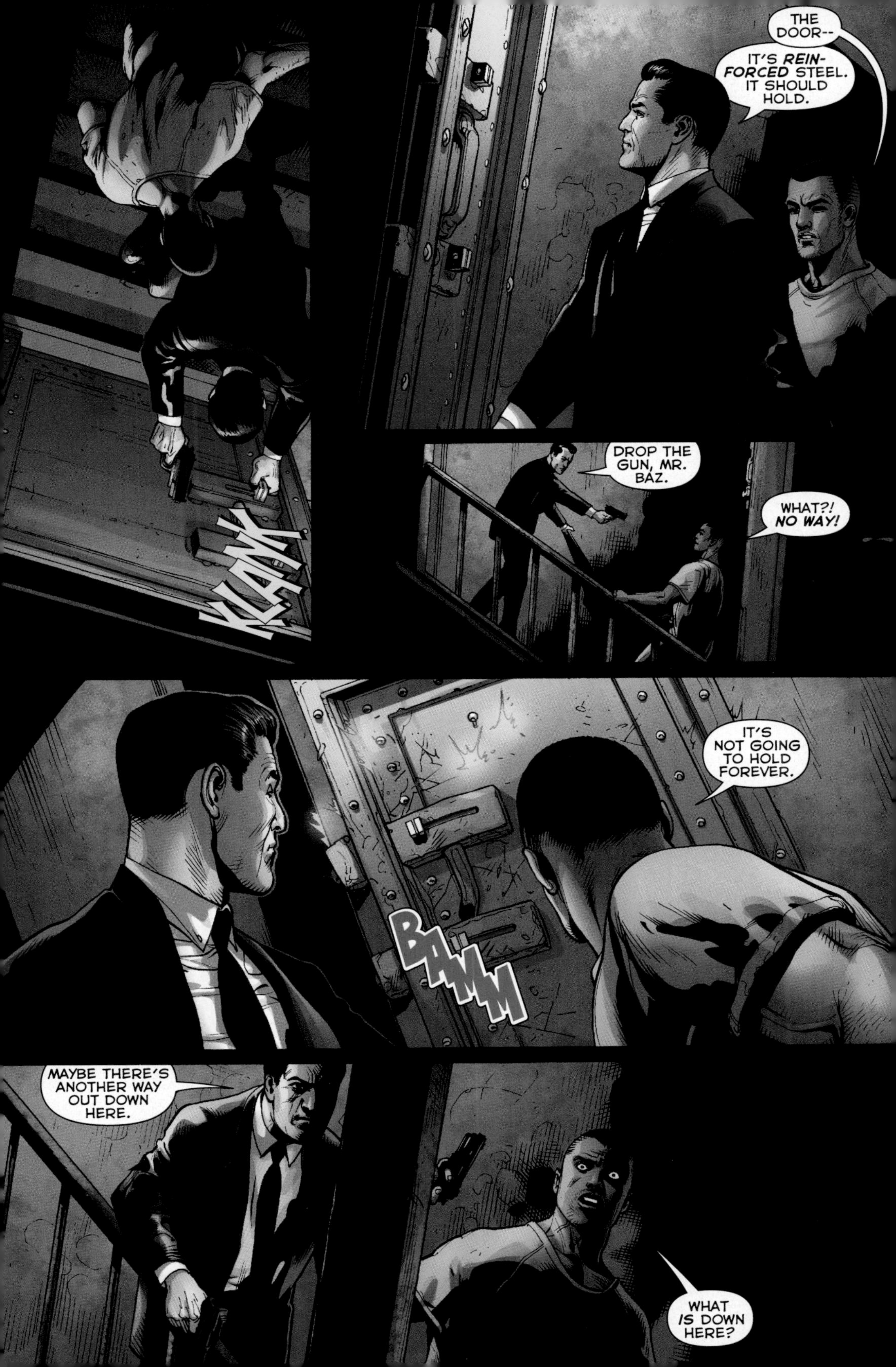
THE DOOR--
IT'S **REIN-FORCED** STEEL. IT SHOULD HOLD.
KLANK
DROP THE GUN, MR. BAZ.
WHAT?! **NO WAY!**
IT'S NOT GOING TO HOLD FOREVER.
BAMM
MAYBE THERE'S ANOTHER WAY OUT DOWN HERE.
WHAT ***IS*** DOWN HERE?

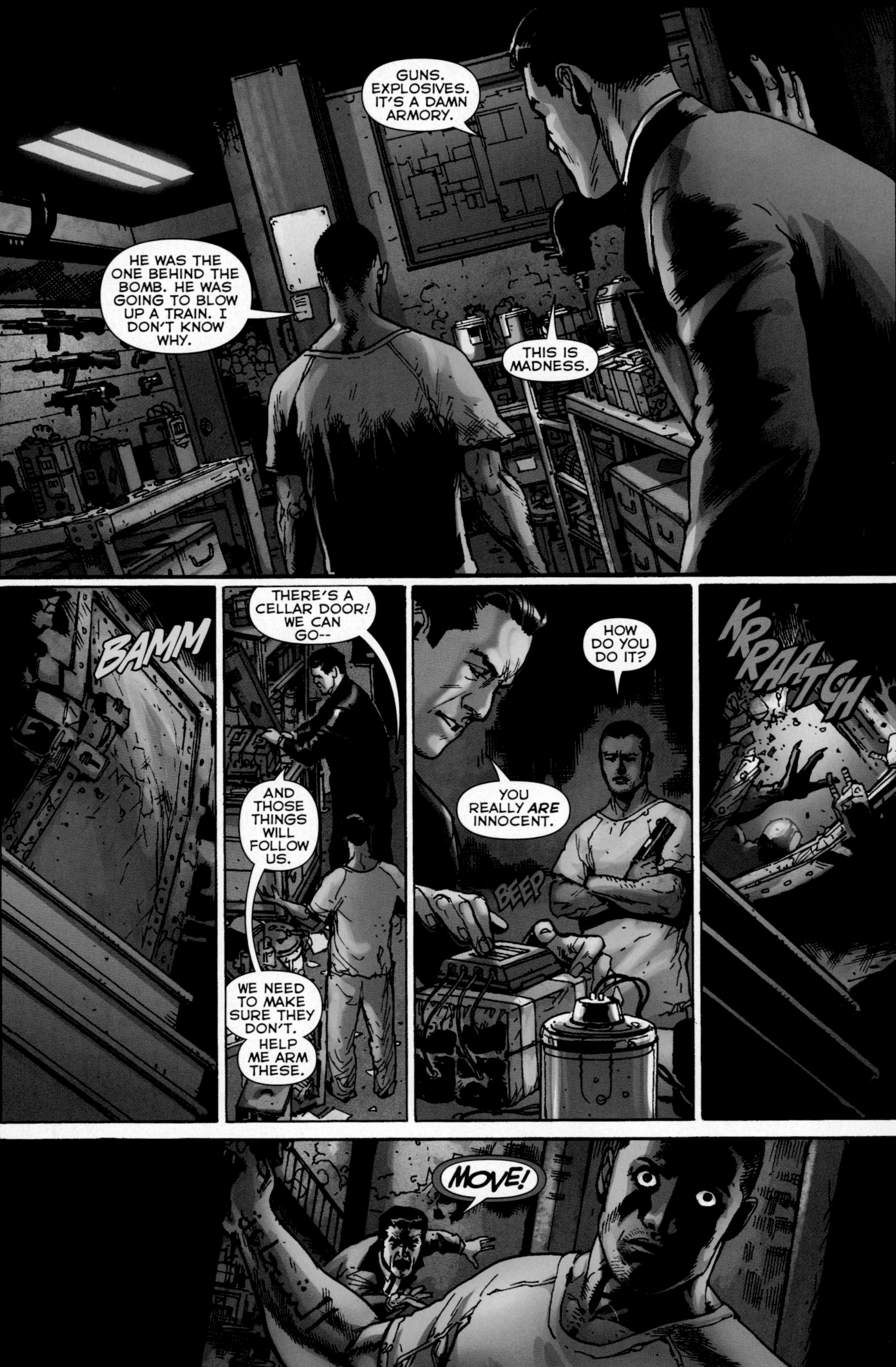
GUNS. EXPLOSIVES. IT'S A DAMN ARMORY.
HE WAS THE ONE BEHIND THE BOMB. HE WAS GOING TO BLOW UP A TRAIN. I DON'T KNOW WHY.
THIS IS MADNESS.
BAMM
THERE'S A CELLAR DOOR! WE CAN GO--
AND THOSE THINGS WILL FOLLOW US.
WE NEED TO MAKE SURE THEY DON'T.
HELP ME ARM THESE.
HOW DO YOU DO IT?
YOU REALLY *ARE* INNOCENT.
BEEP
KRRAATCH
MOVE!

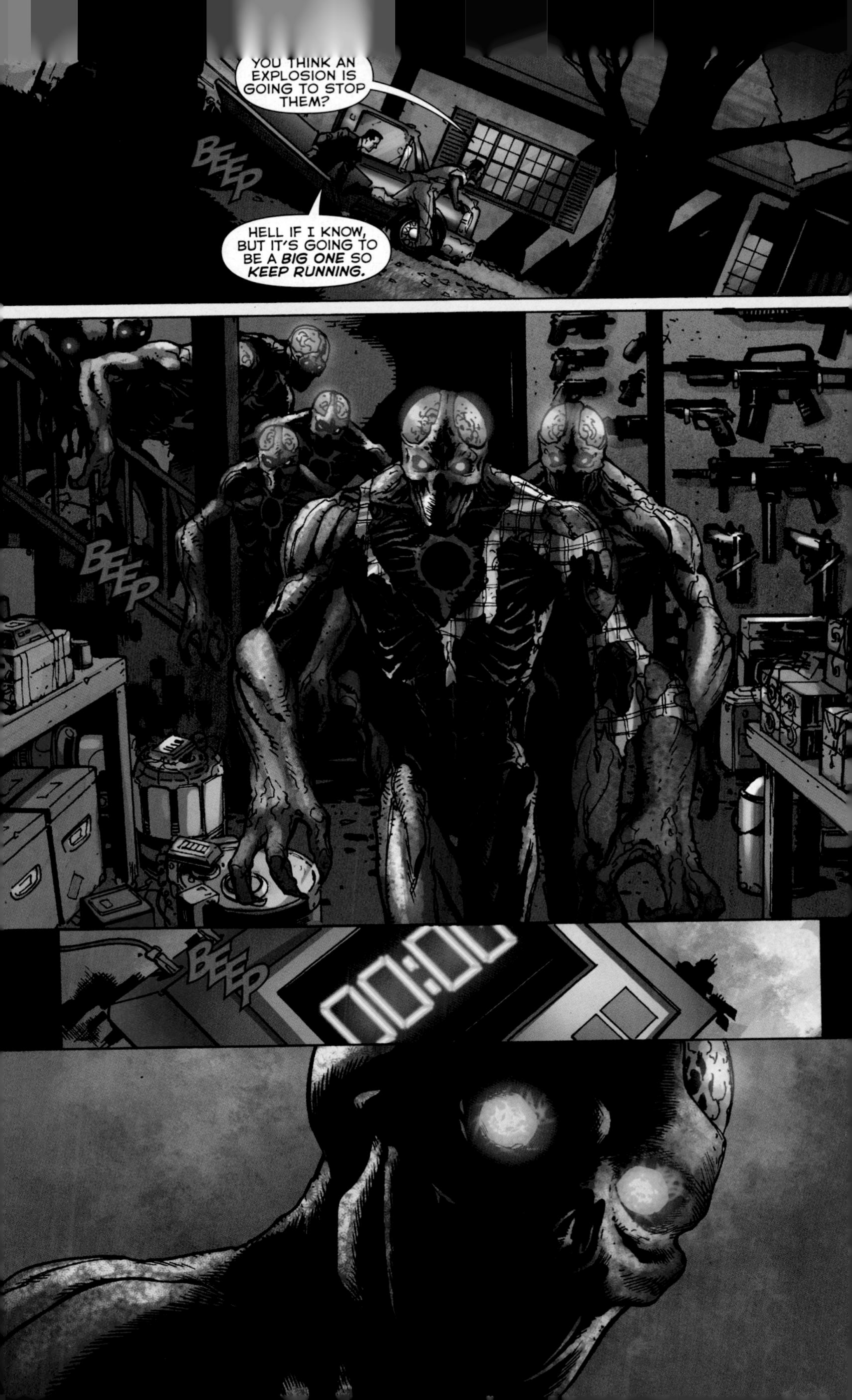
YOU THINK AN EXPLOSION IS GOING TO STOP THEM?
BEEP
HELL IF I KNOW, BUT IT'S GOING TO BE A *BIG ONE* SO *KEEP RUNNING.*
BEEP
BEEP
00:00

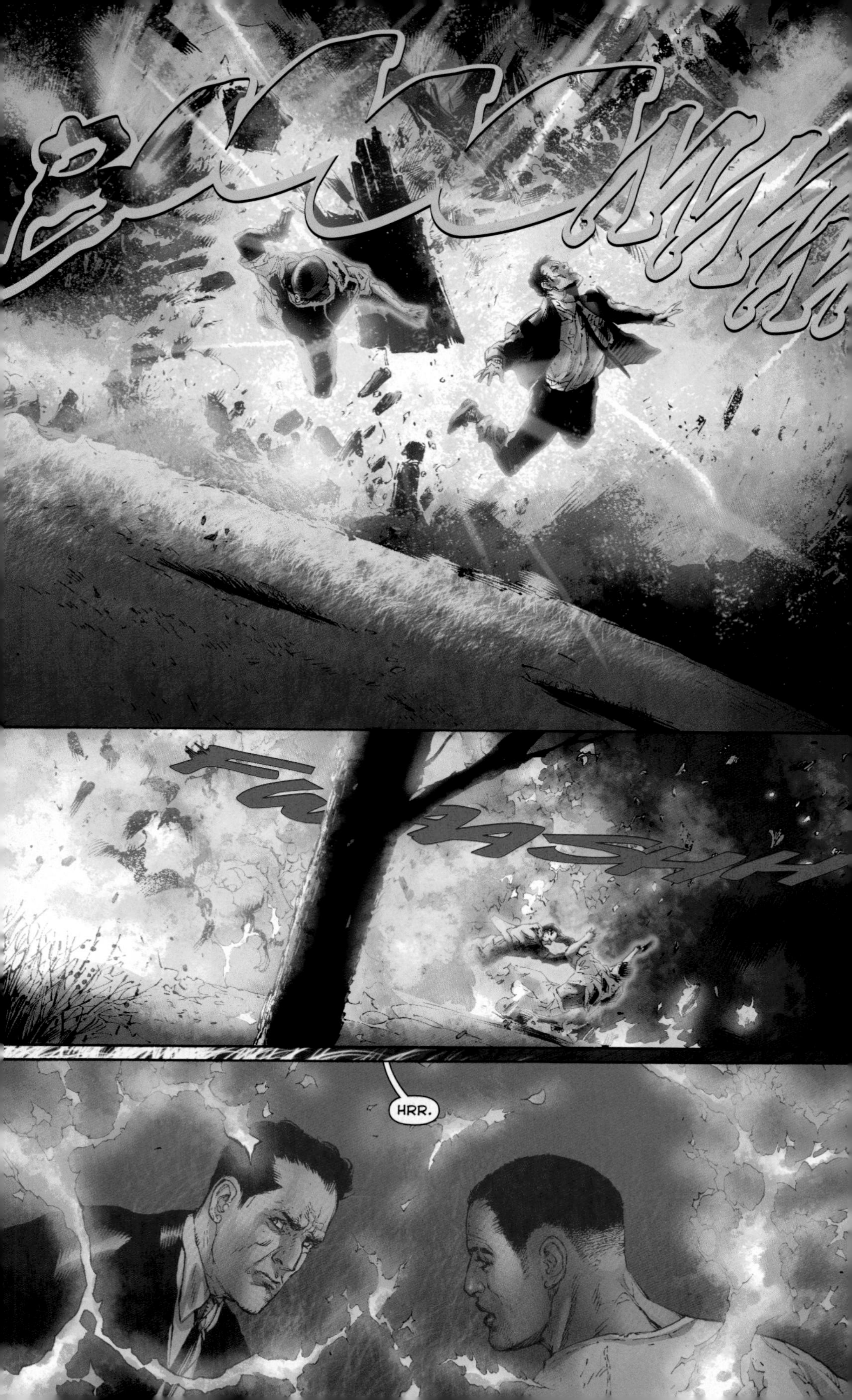
HRR.

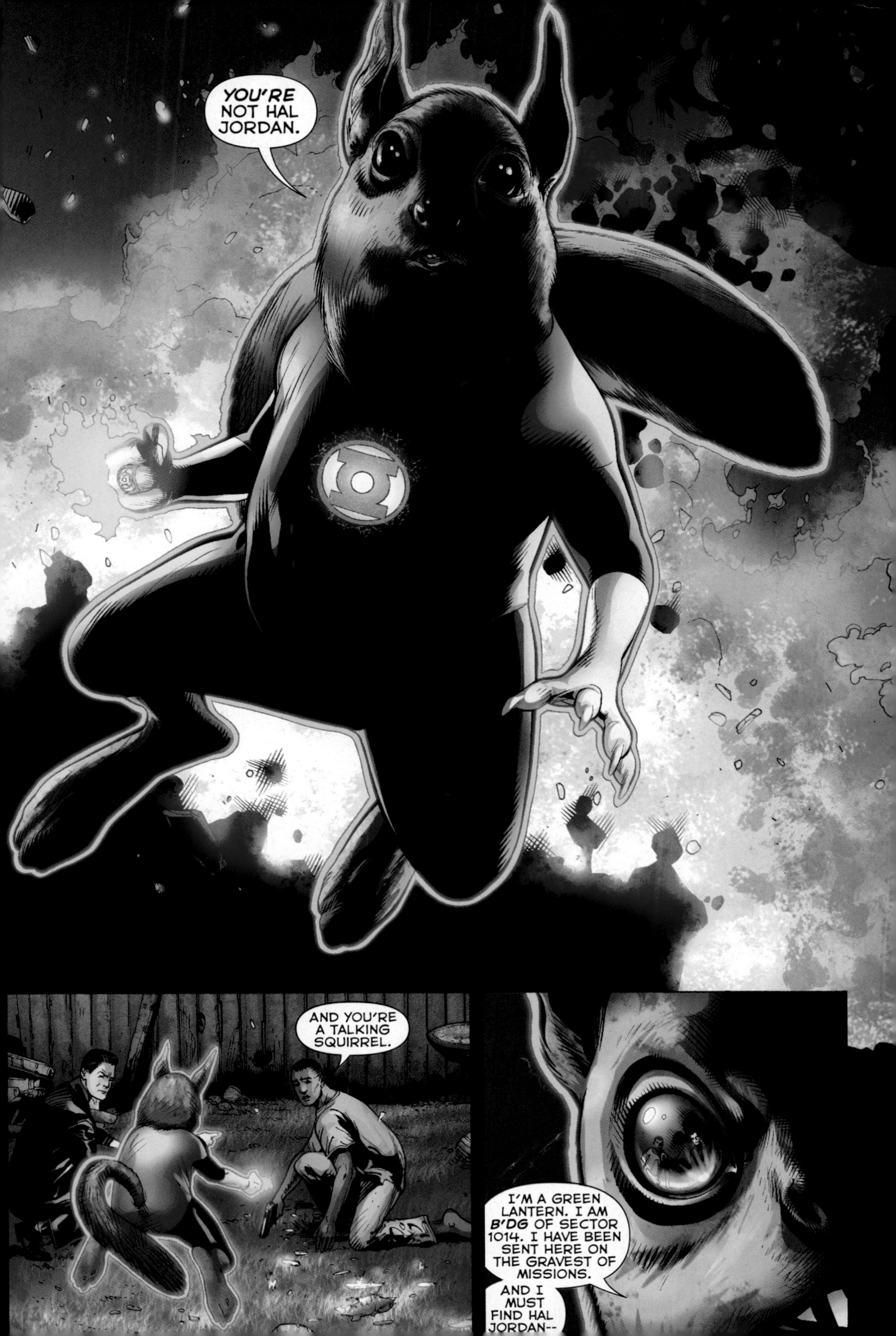
YOU'RE NOT HAL JORDAN.
AND YOU'RE A TALKING SQUIRREL.
I'M A GREEN LANTERN. I AM B'DG OF SECTOR 1014. I HAVE BEEN SENT HERE ON THE GRAVEST OF MISSIONS.
AND I MUST FIND HAL JORDAN--

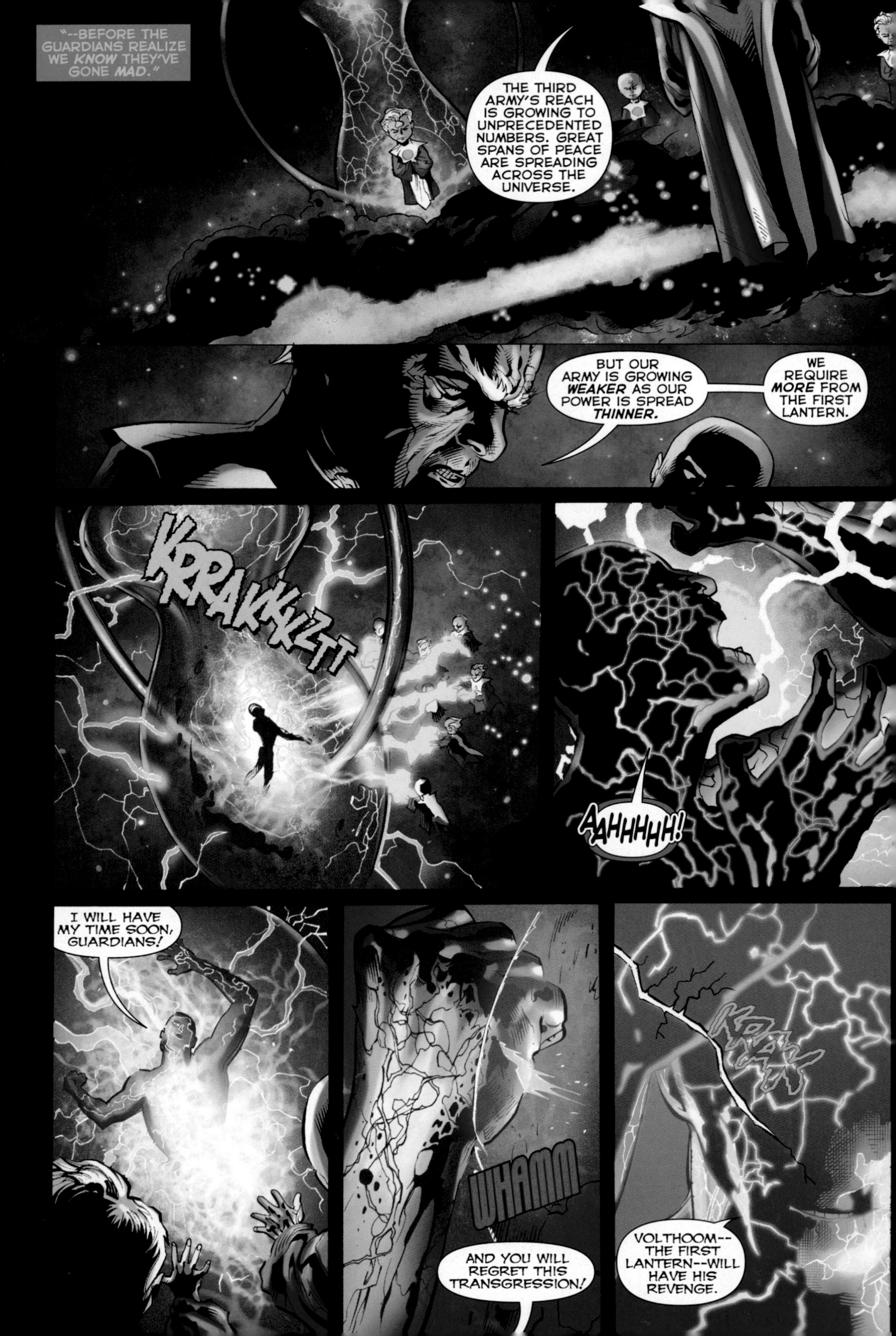
"--BEFORE THE GUARDIANS REALIZE WE KNOW THEY'VE GONE MAD."
THE THIRD ARMY'S REACH IS GROWING TO UNPRECEDENTED NUMBERS. GREAT SPANS OF PEACE ARE SPREADING ACROSS THE UNIVERSE.
BUT OUR ARMY IS GROWING WEAKER AS OUR POWER IS SPREAD THINNER.
WE REQUIRE MORE FROM THE FIRST LANTERN.
KRRAKKKZTT
AAHHHHH!
I WILL HAVE MY TIME SOON, GUARDIANS!
WHAMM
AND YOU WILL REGRET THIS TRANSGRESSION!
VOLTHOOM-- THE FIRST LANTERN--WILL HAVE HIS REVENGE.

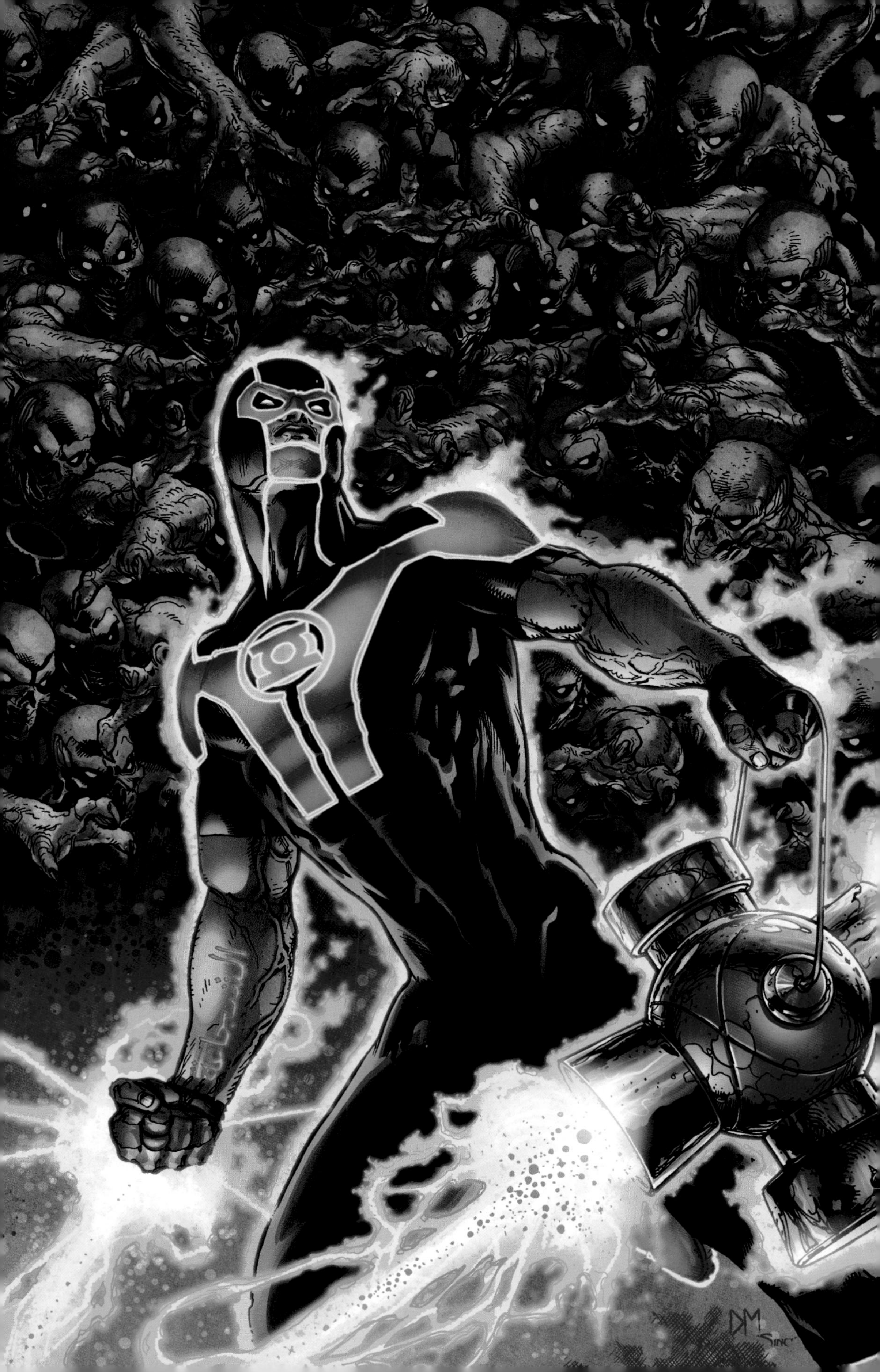

GEOFF JOHNS writer DOUG MAHNKE penciller CHRISTIAN ALAMY, KEITH CHAMPAGNE, TOM NGUYEN, MARK IRWIN & DOUG MAHNKE inkers
DOUG MAHNKE & ALEX SINCLAIR cover

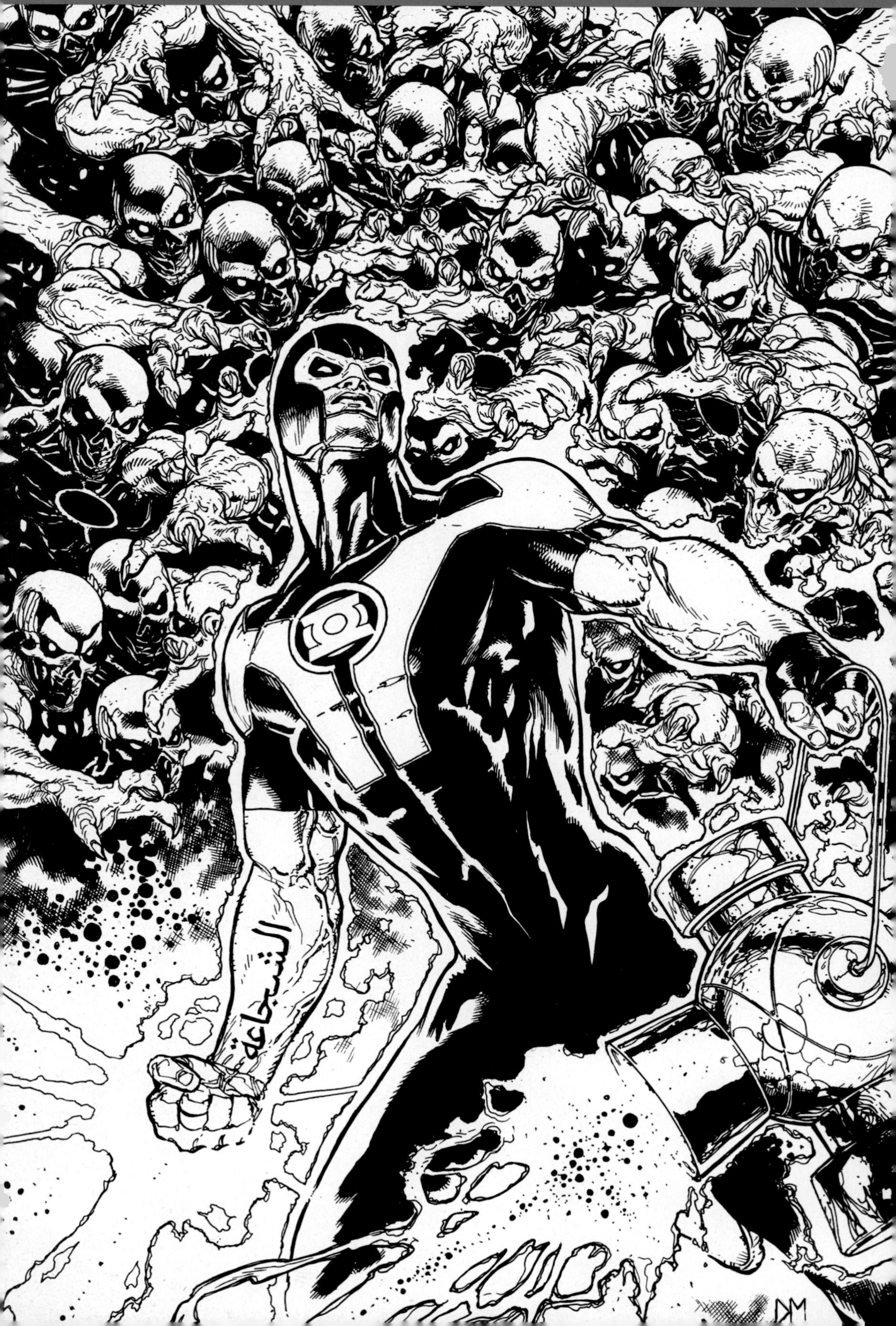

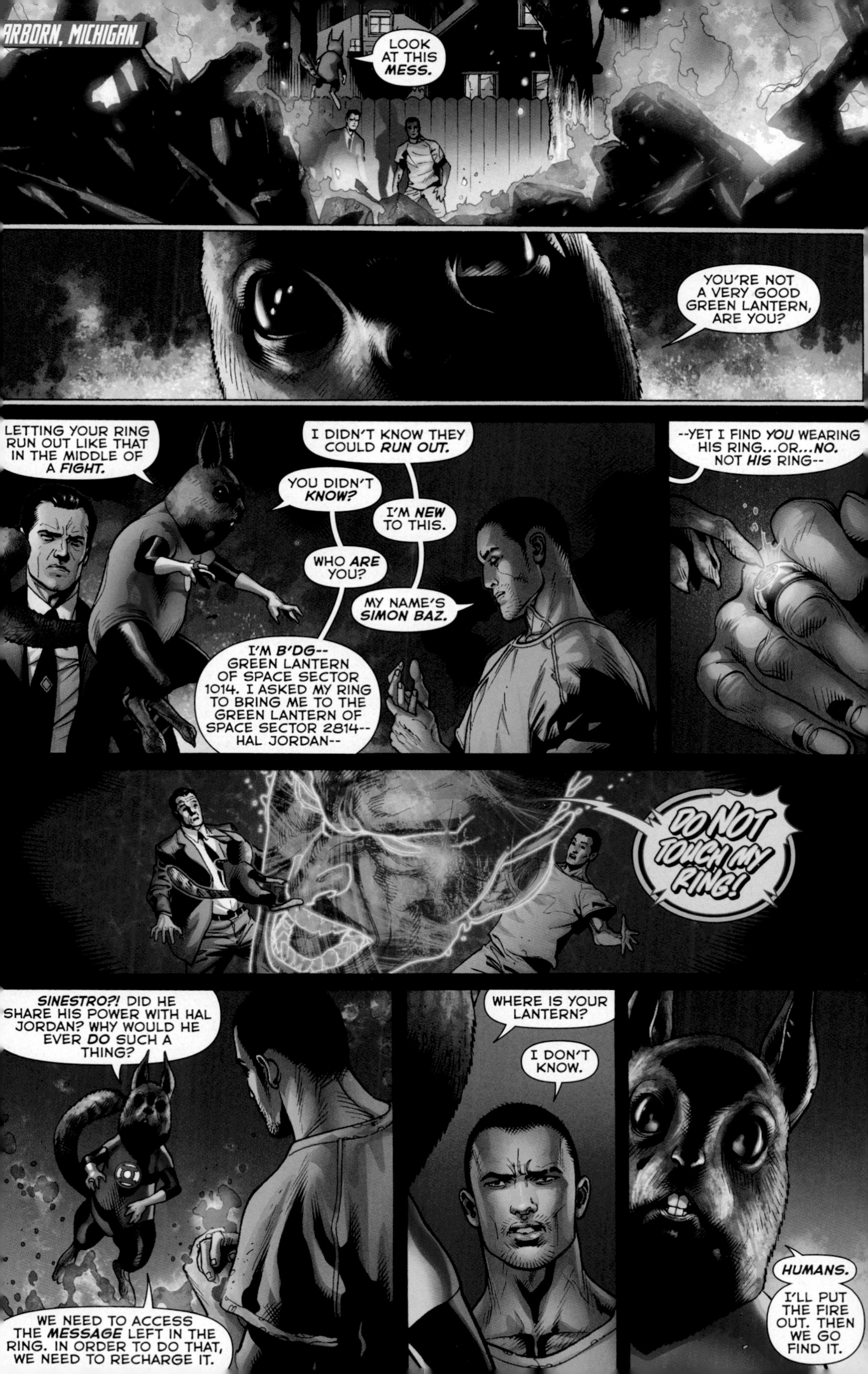
ARBORN, MICHIGAN.
LOOK AT THIS MESS.
YOU'RE NOT A VERY GOOD GREEN LANTERN, ARE YOU?
LETTING YOUR RING RUN OUT LIKE THAT IN THE MIDDLE OF A FIGHT.
I DIDN'T KNOW THEY COULD RUN OUT.
YOU DIDN'T KNOW?
I'M NEW TO THIS.
WHO ARE YOU?
MY NAME'S SIMON BAZ.
I'M B'DG-- GREEN LANTERN OF SPACE SECTOR 1014. I ASKED MY RING TO BRING ME TO THE GREEN LANTERN OF SPACE SECTOR 2814-- HAL JORDAN--
--YET I FIND YOU WEARING HIS RING...OR...NO. NOT HIS RING--
DO NOT TOUCH MY RING!
SINESTRO?! DID HE SHARE HIS POWER WITH HAL JORDAN? WHY WOULD HE EVER DO SUCH A THING?
WE NEED TO ACCESS THE MESSAGE LEFT IN THE RING. IN ORDER TO DO THAT, WE NEED TO RECHARGE IT.
WHERE IS YOUR LANTERN?
I DON'T KNOW.
HUMANS.
I'LL PUT THE FIRE OUT. THEN WE GO FIND IT.

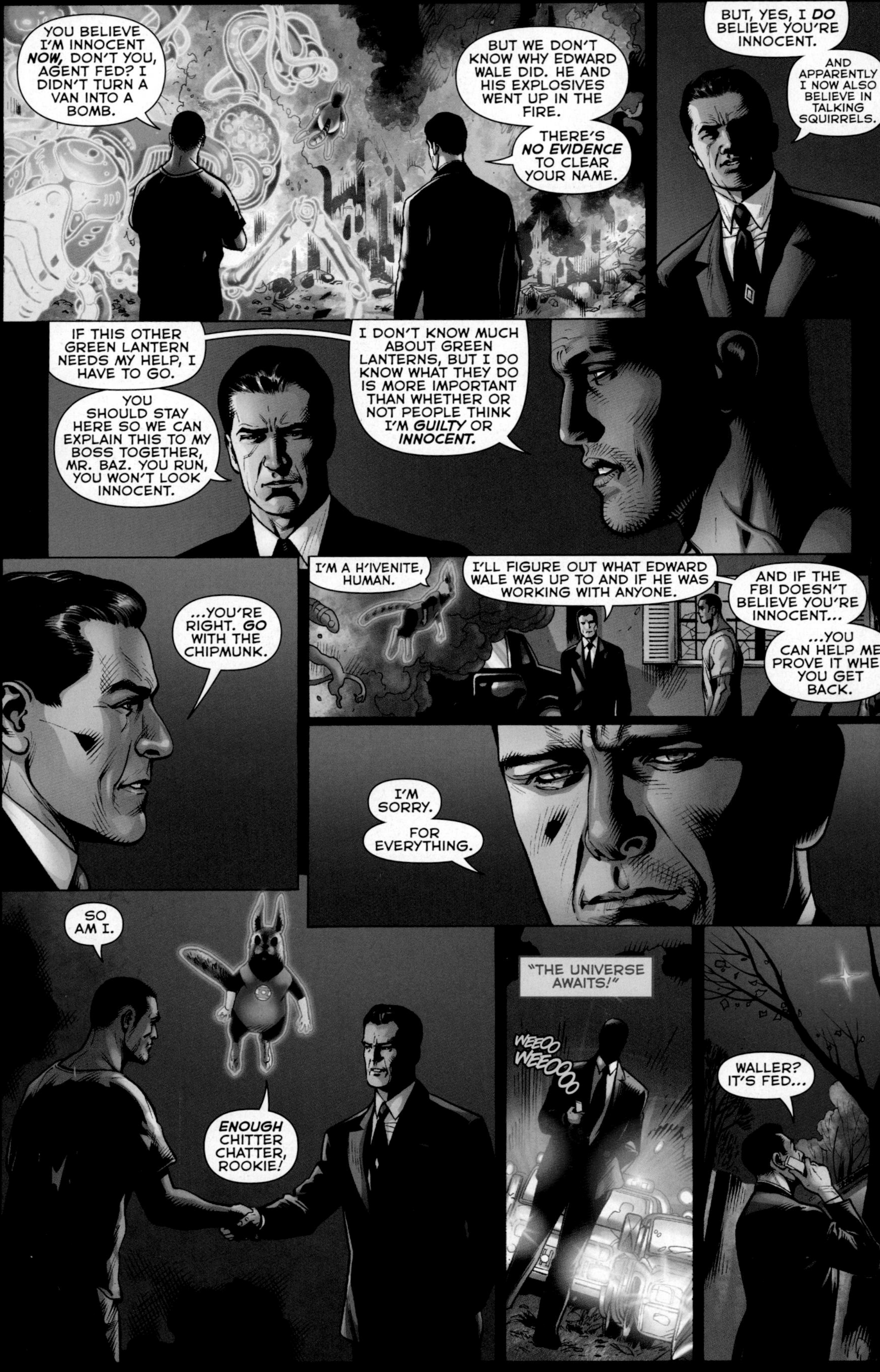
YOU BELIEVE I'M INNOCENT NOW, DON'T YOU, AGENT FED? I DIDN'T TURN A VAN INTO A BOMB.
BUT WE DON'T KNOW WHY EDWARD WALE DID. HE AND HIS EXPLOSIVES WENT UP IN THE FIRE.
THERE'S NO EVIDENCE TO CLEAR YOUR NAME.
BUT, YES, I DO BELIEVE YOU'RE INNOCENT.
AND APPARENTLY I NOW ALSO BELIEVE IN TALKING SQUIRRELS.
IF THIS OTHER GREEN LANTERN NEEDS MY HELP, I HAVE TO GO.
YOU SHOULD STAY HERE SO WE CAN EXPLAIN THIS TO MY BOSS TOGETHER, MR. BAZ. YOU RUN, YOU WON'T LOOK INNOCENT.
I DON'T KNOW MUCH ABOUT GREEN LANTERNS, BUT I DO KNOW WHAT THEY DO IS MORE IMPORTANT THAN WHETHER OR NOT PEOPLE THINK I'M GUILTY OR INNOCENT.
...YOU'RE RIGHT. GO WITH THE CHIPMUNK.
I'M A H'IVENITE, HUMAN.
I'LL FIGURE OUT WHAT EDWARD WALE WAS UP TO AND IF HE WAS WORKING WITH ANYONE.
AND IF THE FBI DOESN'T BELIEVE YOU'RE INNOCENT...
...YOU CAN HELP ME PROVE IT WHEN YOU GET BACK.
I'M SORRY.
FOR EVERYTHING.
SO AM I.
ENOUGH CHITTER CHATTER, ROOKIE!
"THE UNIVERSE AWAITS!"
WEEOO WEEOOOO
WALLER? IT'S FED...

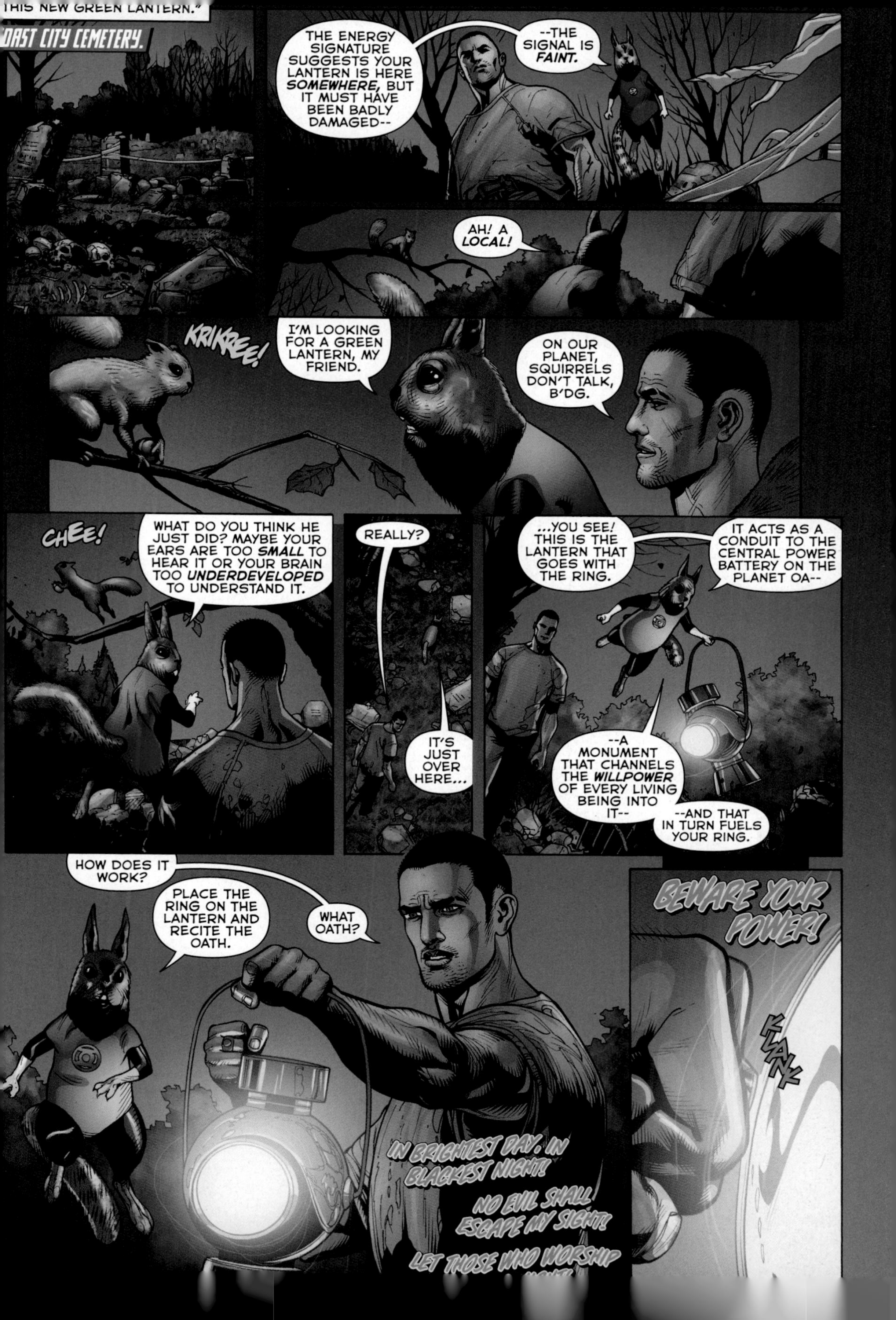
THIS NEW GREEN LANTERN."
COAST CITY CEMETERY.
THE ENERGY SIGNATURE SUGGESTS YOUR LANTERN IS HERE SOMEWHERE, BUT IT MUST HAVE BEEN BADLY DAMAGED--
--THE SIGNAL IS FAINT.
AH! A LOCAL!
KRIKREE!
I'M LOOKING FOR A GREEN LANTERN, MY FRIEND.
ON OUR PLANET, SQUIRRELS DON'T TALK, B'DG.
CHEE!
WHAT DO YOU THINK HE JUST DID? MAYBE YOUR EARS ARE TOO SMALL TO HEAR IT OR YOUR BRAIN TOO UNDERDEVELOPED TO UNDERSTAND IT.
REALLY?
IT'S JUST OVER HERE...
...YOU SEE! THIS IS THE LANTERN THAT GOES WITH THE RING.
IT ACTS AS A CONDUIT TO THE CENTRAL POWER BATTERY ON THE PLANET OA--
--A MONUMENT THAT CHANNELS THE WILLPOWER OF EVERY LIVING BEING INTO IT--
--AND THAT IN TURN FUELS YOUR RING.
HOW DOES IT WORK?
PLACE THE RING ON THE LANTERN AND RECITE THE OATH.
WHAT OATH?
IN BRIGHTEST DAY, IN BLACKEST NIGHT!
NO EVIL SHALL ESCAPE MY SIGHT!
LET THOSE WHO WORSHIP
BEWARE YOUR POWER!
KLANK

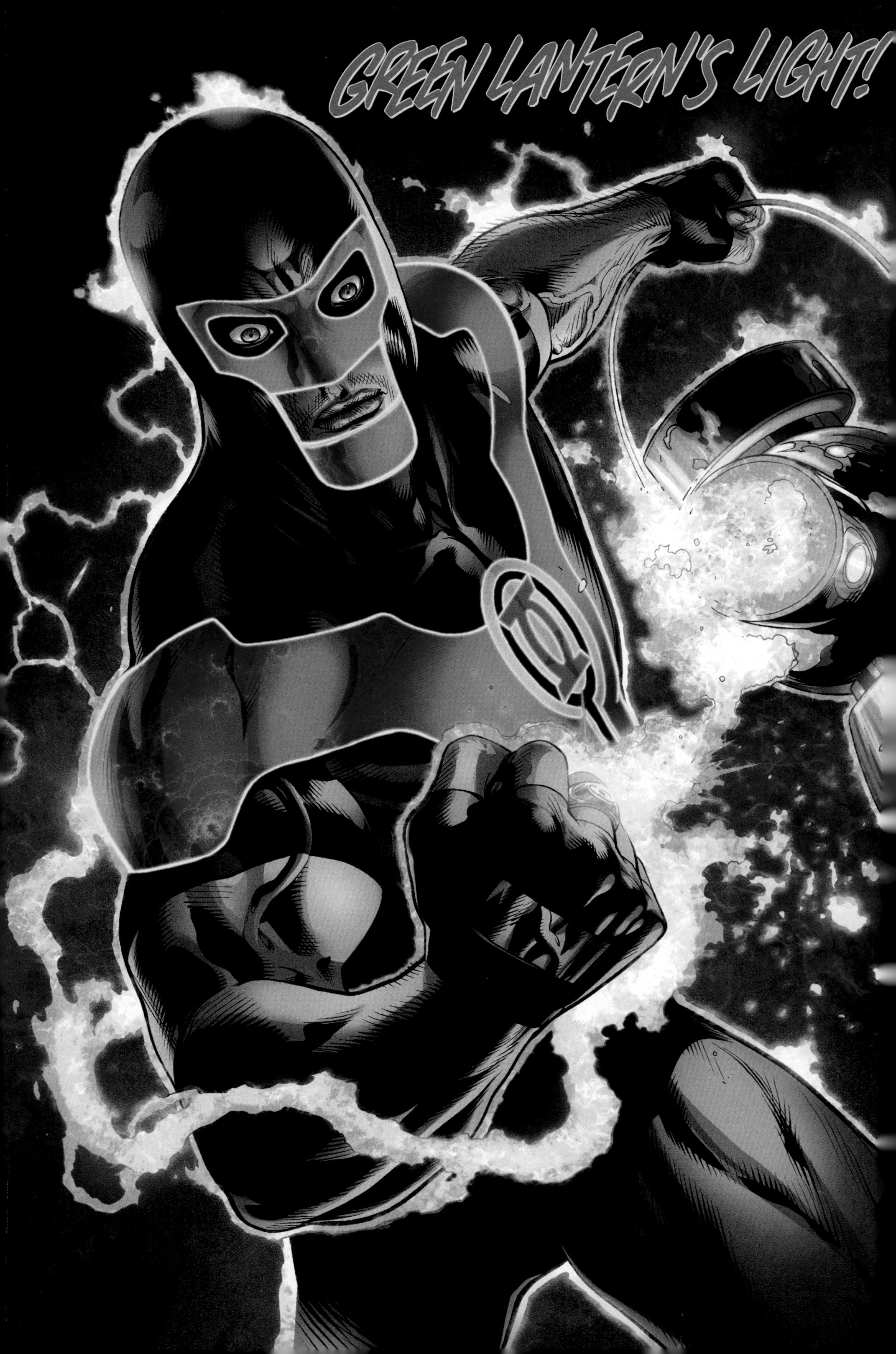
GREEN LANTERN'S LIGHT!

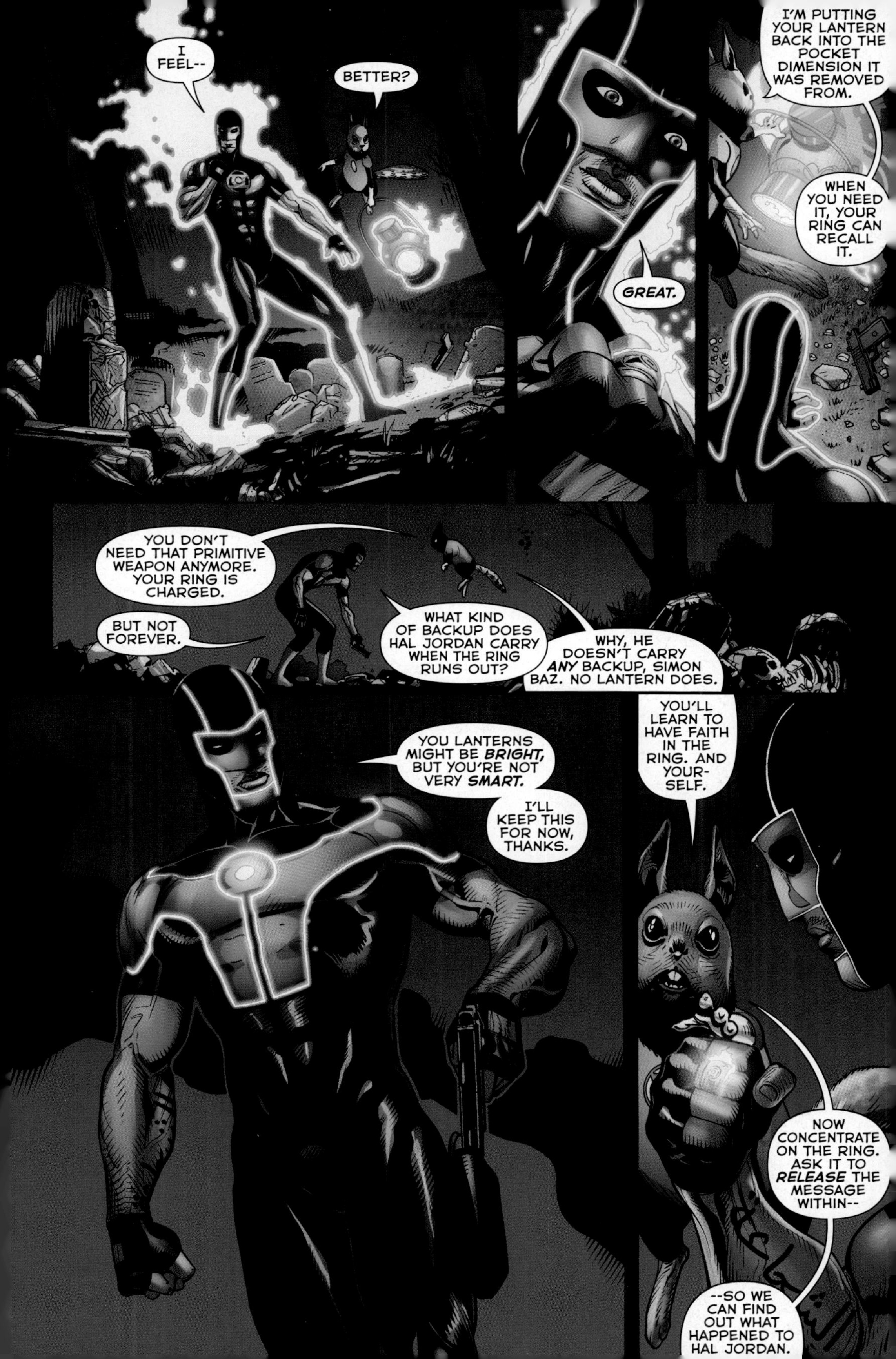
I FEEL--
BETTER?
GREAT.
I'M PUTTING YOUR LANTERN BACK INTO THE POCKET DIMENSION IT WAS REMOVED FROM.
WHEN YOU NEED IT, YOUR RING CAN RECALL IT.
YOU DON'T NEED THAT PRIMITIVE WEAPON ANYMORE. YOUR RING IS CHARGED.
BUT NOT FOREVER.
WHAT KIND OF BACKUP DOES HAL JORDAN CARRY WHEN THE RING RUNS OUT?
WHY, HE DOESN'T CARRY ANY BACKUP, SIMON BAZ. NO LANTERN DOES.
YOU LANTERNS MIGHT BE BRIGHT, BUT YOU'RE NOT VERY SMART.
I'LL KEEP THIS FOR NOW, THANKS.
YOU'LL LEARN TO HAVE FAITH IN THE RING. AND YOURSELF.
NOW CONCENTRATE ON THE RING. ASK IT TO RELEASE THE MESSAGE WITHIN--
--SO WE CAN FIND OUT WHAT HAPPENED TO HAL JORDAN.

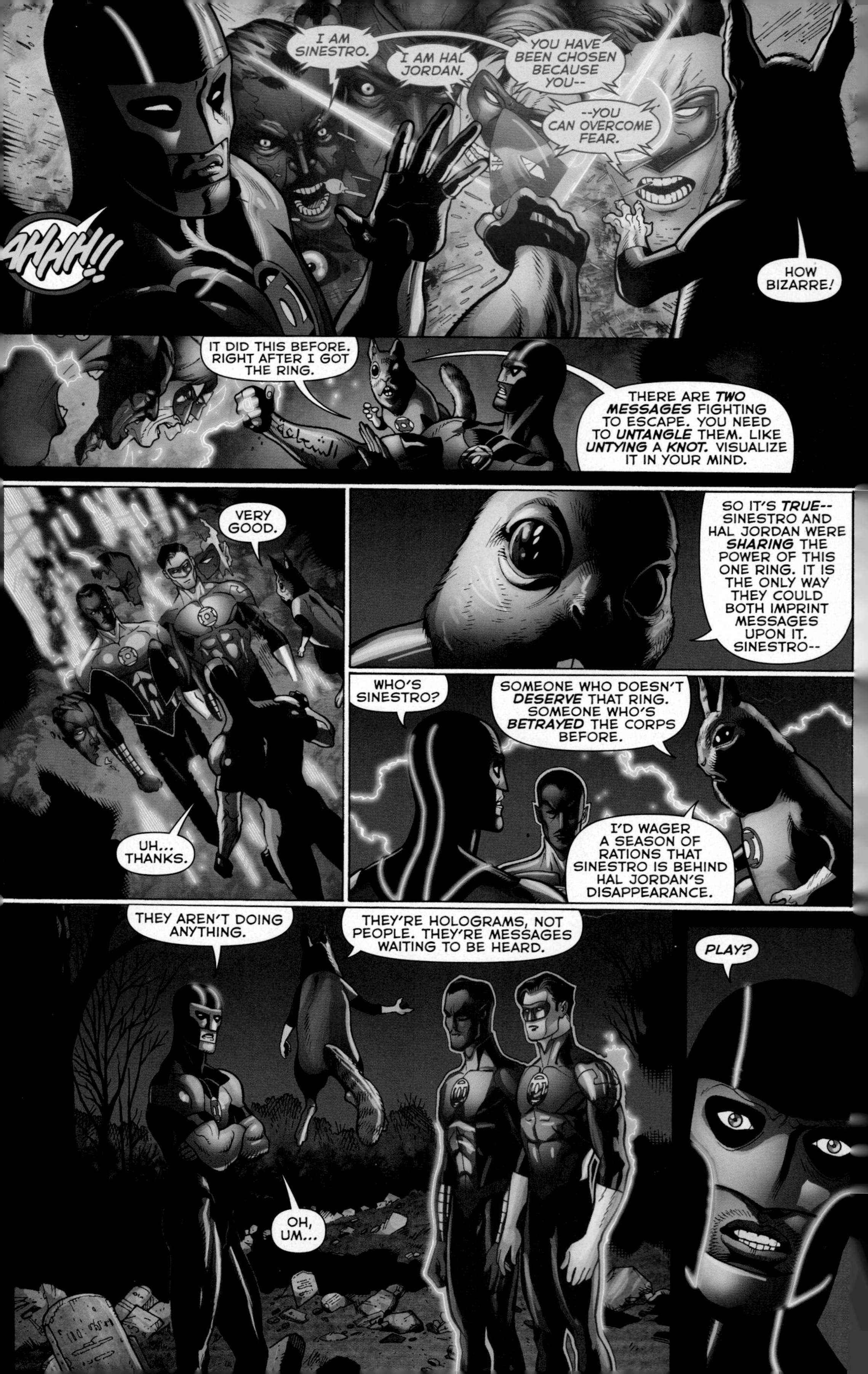
I AM SINESTRO.
I AM HAL JORDAN.
YOU HAVE BEEN CHOSEN BECAUSE YOU--
--YOU CAN OVERCOME FEAR.
AHHH!!
HOW BIZARRE!
IT DID THIS BEFORE. RIGHT AFTER I GOT THE RING.
THERE ARE TWO MESSAGES FIGHTING TO ESCAPE. YOU NEED TO UNTANGLE THEM. LIKE UNTYING A KNOT. VISUALIZE IT IN YOUR MIND.
VERY GOOD.
UH... THANKS.
SO IT'S TRUE-- SINESTRO AND HAL JORDAN WERE SHARING THE POWER OF THIS ONE RING. IT IS THE ONLY WAY THEY COULD BOTH IMPRINT MESSAGES UPON IT. SINESTRO--
WHO'S SINESTRO?
SOMEONE WHO DOESN'T DESERVE THAT RING. SOMEONE WHO'S BETRAYED THE CORPS BEFORE.
I'D WAGER A SEASON OF RATIONS THAT SINESTRO IS BEHIND HAL JORDAN'S DISAPPEARANCE.
THEY AREN'T DOING ANYTHING.
THEY'RE HOLOGRAMS, NOT PEOPLE. THEY'RE MESSAGES WAITING TO BE HEARD.
OH, UM...
PLAY?

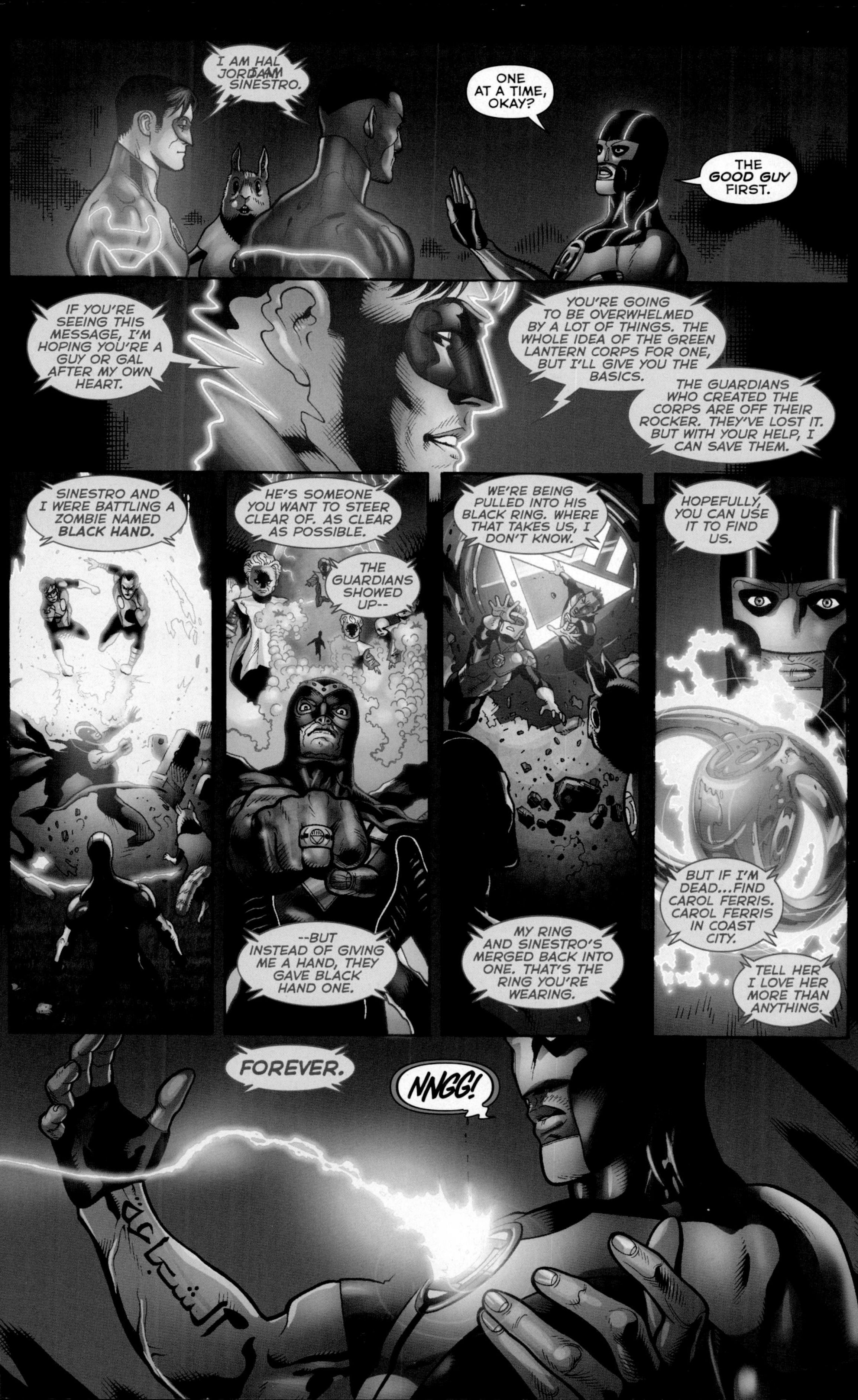
I AM HAL JORDI AM SINESTRO.
ONE AT A TIME, OKAY?
THE GOOD GUY FIRST.
IF YOU'RE SEEING THIS MESSAGE, I'M HOPING YOU'RE A GUY OR GAL AFTER MY OWN HEART.
YOU'RE GOING TO BE OVERWHELMED BY A LOT OF THINGS. THE WHOLE IDEA OF THE GREEN LANTERN CORPS FOR ONE, BUT I'LL GIVE YOU THE BASICS.
THE GUARDIANS WHO CREATED THE CORPS ARE OFF THEIR ROCKER. THEY'VE LOST IT. BUT WITH YOUR HELP, I CAN SAVE THEM.
SINESTRO AND I WERE BATTLING A ZOMBIE NAMED BLACK HAND.
HE'S SOMEONE YOU WANT TO STEER CLEAR OF. AS CLEAR AS POSSIBLE.
THE GUARDIANS SHOWED UP--
--BUT INSTEAD OF GIVING ME A HAND, THEY GAVE BLACK HAND ONE.
WE'RE BEING PULLED INTO HIS BLACK RING. WHERE THAT TAKES US, I DON'T KNOW.
MY RING AND SINESTRO'S MERGED BACK INTO ONE. THAT'S THE RING YOU'RE WEARING.
HOPEFULLY, YOU CAN USE IT TO FIND US.
BUT IF I'M DEAD...FIND CAROL FERRIS. CAROL FERRIS IN COAST CITY.
TELL HER I LOVE HER MORE THAN ANYTHING.
FOREVER.
NNGG!

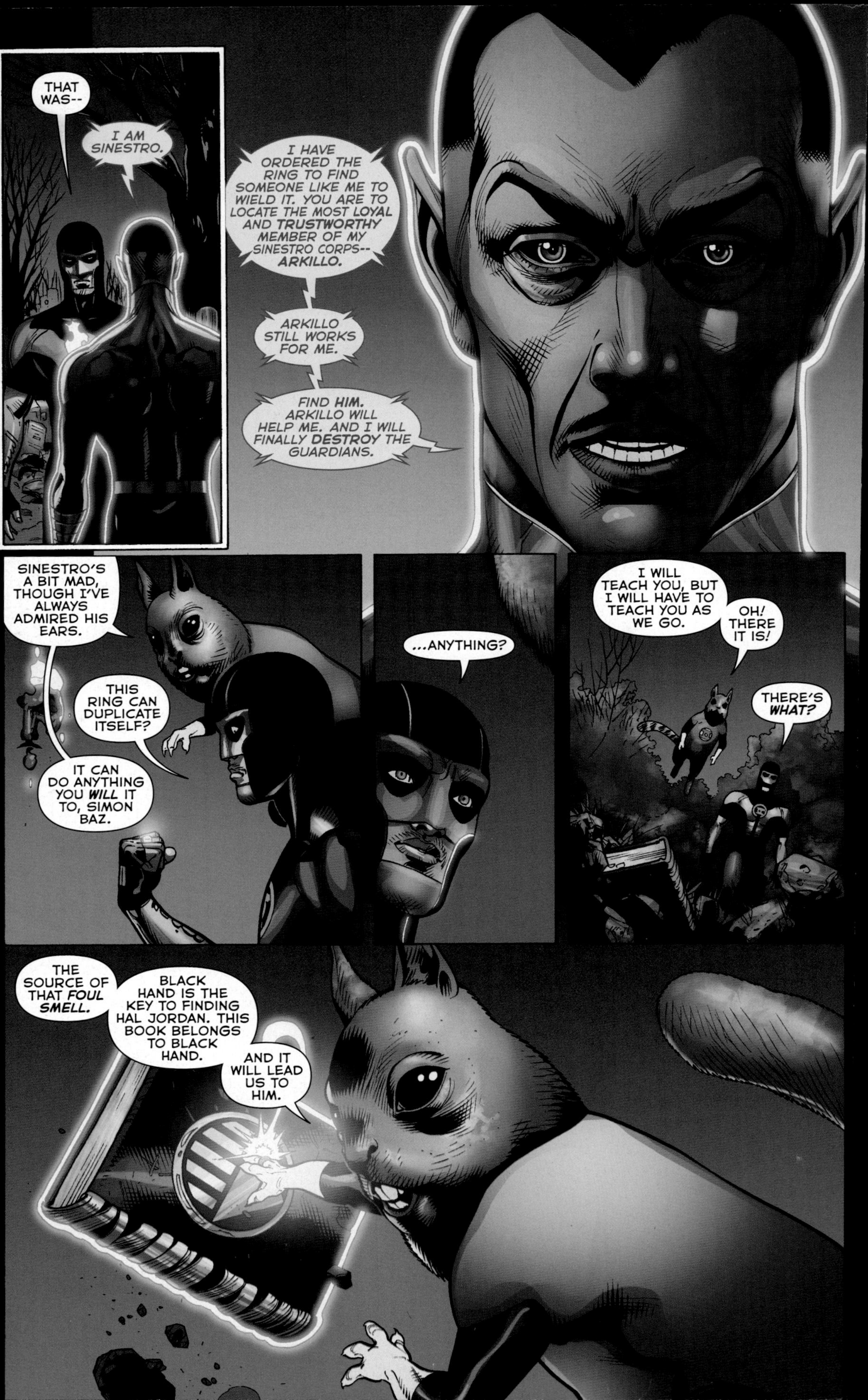
THAT WAS--
I AM SINESTRO.
I HAVE ORDERED THE RING TO FIND SOMEONE LIKE ME TO WIELD IT. YOU ARE TO LOCATE THE MOST LOYAL AND TRUSTWORTHY MEMBER OF MY SINESTRO CORPS-- ARKILLO.
ARKILLO STILL WORKS FOR ME.
FIND HIM. ARKILLO WILL HELP ME. AND I WILL FINALLY DESTROY THE GUARDIANS.
SINESTRO'S A BIT MAD, THOUGH I'VE ALWAYS ADMIRED HIS EARS.
THIS RING CAN DUPLICATE ITSELF?
IT CAN DO ANYTHING YOU WILL IT TO, SIMON BAZ.
...ANYTHING?
I WILL TEACH YOU, BUT I WILL HAVE TO TEACH YOU AS WE GO.
OH! THERE IT IS!
THERE'S WHAT?
THE SOURCE OF THAT FOUL SMELL.
BLACK HAND IS THE KEY TO FINDING HAL JORDAN. THIS BOOK BELONGS TO BLACK HAND.
AND IT WILL LEAD US TO HIM.

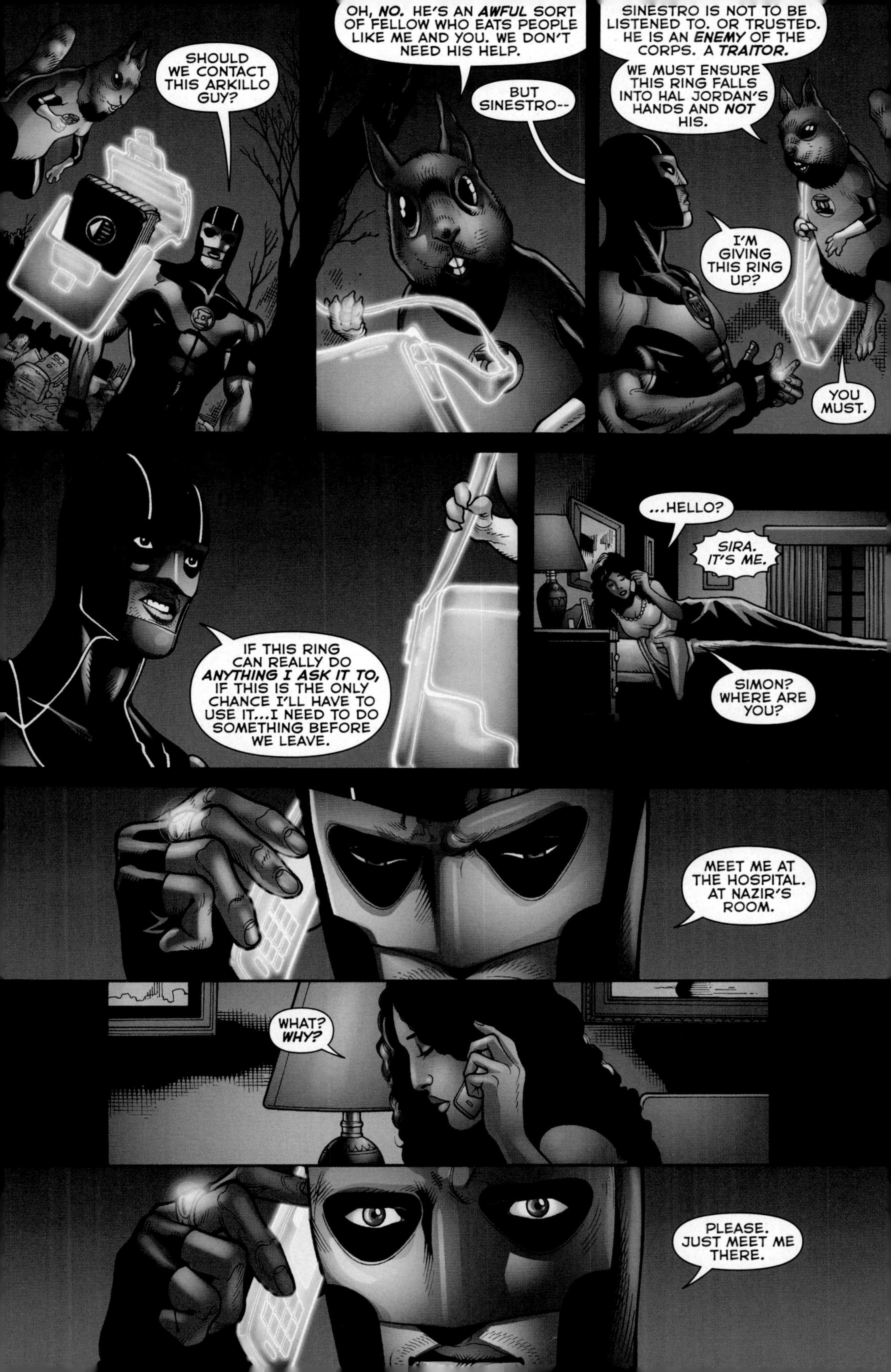
SHOULD WE CONTACT THIS ARKILLO GUY?
OH, NO. HE'S AN AWFUL SORT OF FELLOW WHO EATS PEOPLE LIKE ME AND YOU. WE DON'T NEED HIS HELP.
BUT SINESTRO--
SINESTRO IS NOT TO BE LISTENED TO. OR TRUSTED. HE IS AN ENEMY OF THE CORPS. A TRAITOR.
WE MUST ENSURE THIS RING FALLS INTO HAL JORDAN'S HANDS AND NOT HIS.
I'M GIVING THIS RING UP?
YOU MUST.
IF THIS RING CAN REALLY DO ANYTHING I ASK IT TO, IF THIS IS THE ONLY CHANCE I'LL HAVE TO USE IT...I NEED TO DO SOMETHING BEFORE WE LEAVE.
...HELLO?
SIRA. IT'S ME.
SIMON? WHERE ARE YOU?
MEET ME AT THE HOSPITAL. AT NAZIR'S ROOM.
WHAT? WHY?
PLEASE. JUST MEET ME THERE.

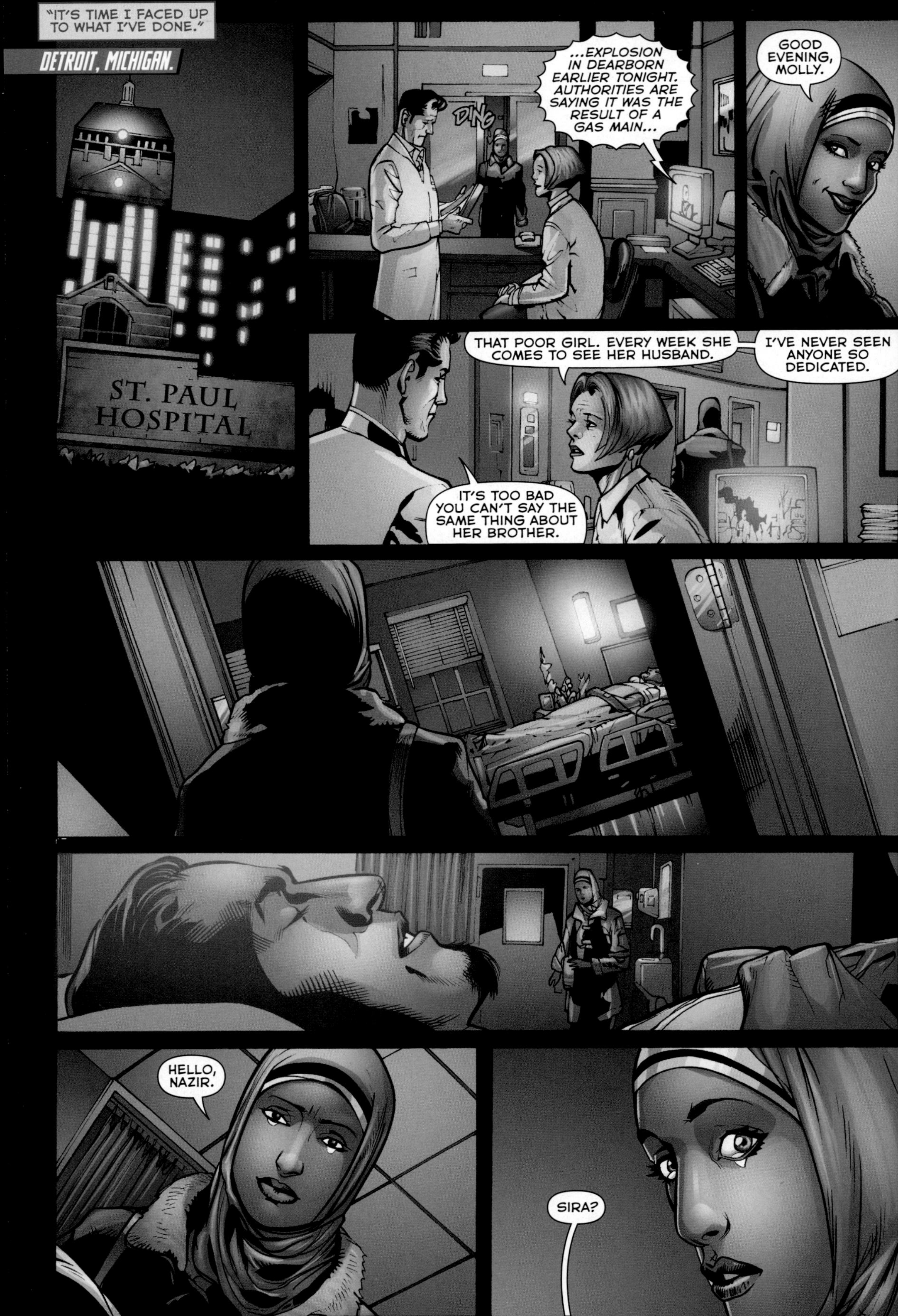
"IT'S TIME I FACED UP TO WHAT I'VE DONE."
DETROIT, MICHIGAN.
ST. PAUL HOSPITAL
...EXPLOSION IN DEARBORN EARLIER TONIGHT. AUTHORITIES ARE SAYING IT WAS THE RESULT OF A GAS MAIN...
DING
GOOD EVENING, MOLLY.
THAT POOR GIRL. EVERY WEEK SHE COMES TO SEE HER HUSBAND.
I'VE NEVER SEEN ANYONE SO DEDICATED.
IT'S TOO BAD YOU CAN'T SAY THE SAME THING ABOUT HER BROTHER.
HELLO, NAZIR.
SIRA?

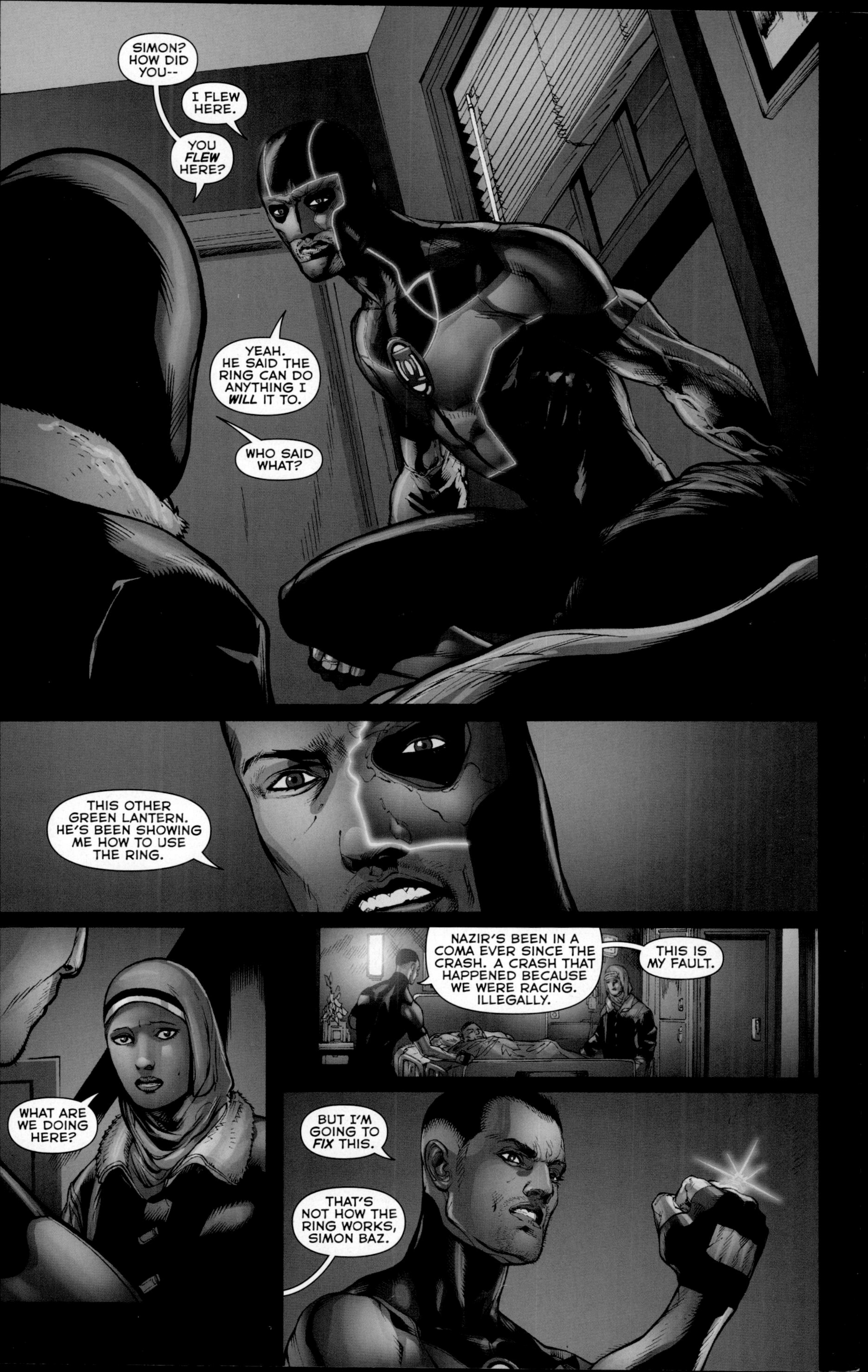
SIMON? HOW DID YOU--
I FLEW HERE.
YOU FLEW HERE?
YEAH. HE SAID THE RING CAN DO ANYTHING I WILL IT TO.
WHO SAID WHAT?
THIS OTHER GREEN LANTERN. HE'S BEEN SHOWING ME HOW TO USE THE RING.
WHAT ARE WE DOING HERE?
NAZIR'S BEEN IN A COMA EVER SINCE THE CRASH. A CRASH THAT HAPPENED BECAUSE WE WERE RACING. ILLEGALLY.
THIS IS MY FAULT.
BUT I'M GOING TO FIX THIS.
THAT'S NOT HOW THE RING WORKS, SIMON BAZ.

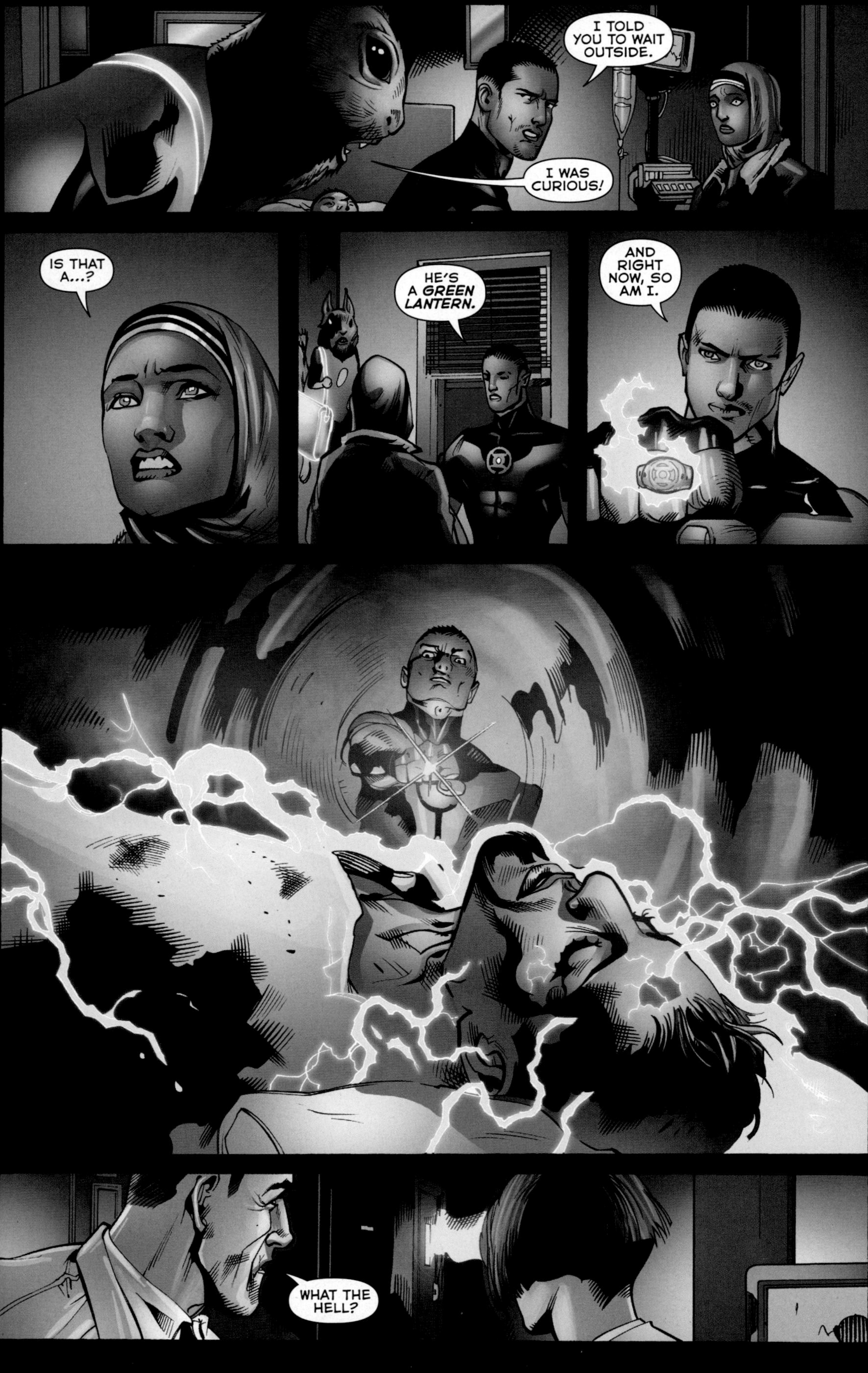
I TOLD YOU TO WAIT OUTSIDE.
I WAS CURIOUS!
IS THAT A...?
HE'S A GREEN LANTERN.
AND RIGHT NOW, SO AM I.
WHAT THE HELL?

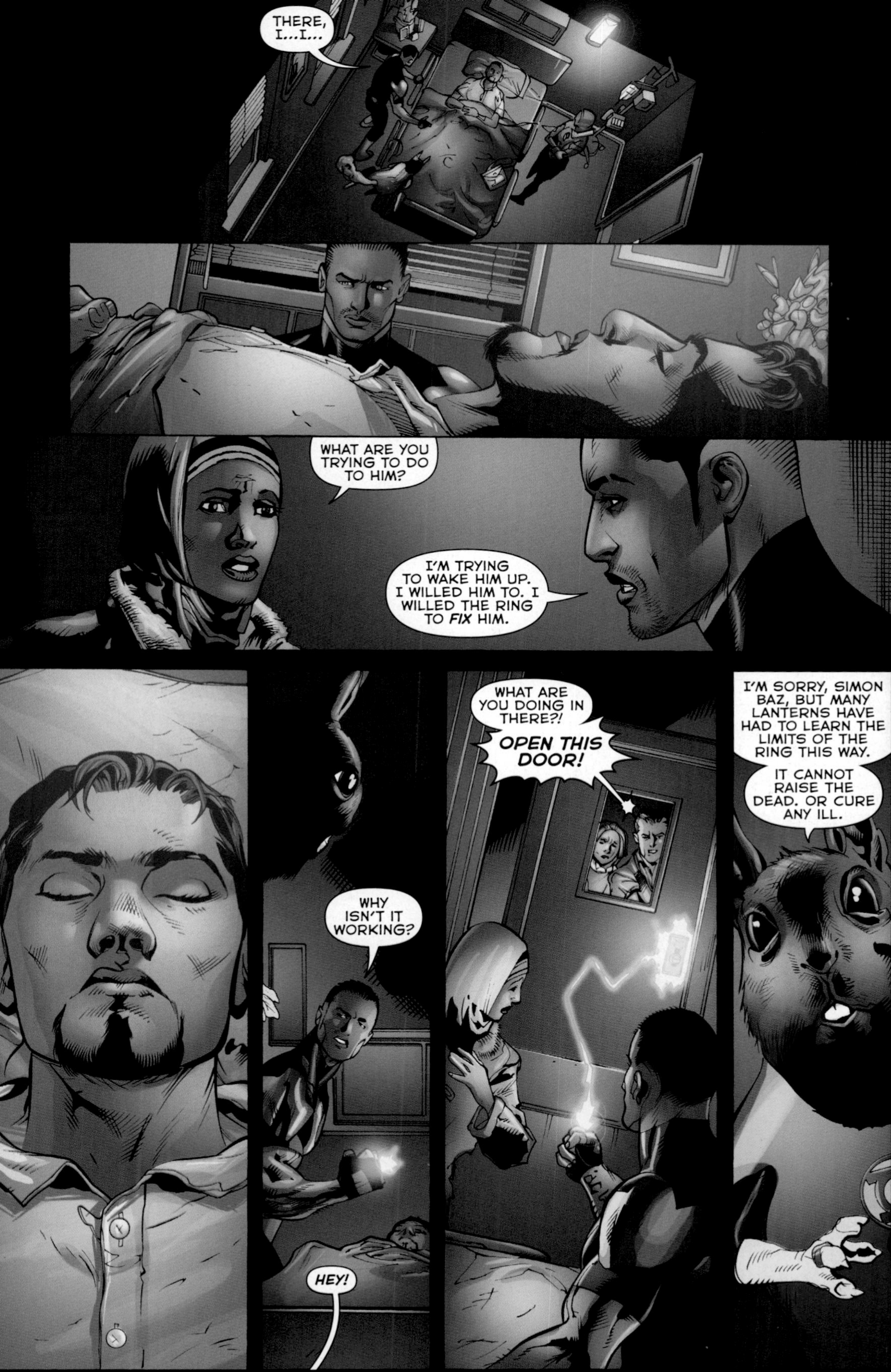

THERE, I...I...
WHAT ARE YOU TRYING TO DO TO HIM?
I'M TRYING TO WAKE HIM UP. I WILLED HIM TO. I WILLED THE RING TO *FIX* HIM.
WHY ISN'T IT WORKING?
HEY!
WHAT ARE YOU DOING IN THERE?!
OPEN THIS DOOR!
I'M SORRY, SIMON BAZ, BUT MANY LANTERNS HAVE HAD TO LEARN THE LIMITS OF THE RING THIS WAY.
IT CANNOT RAISE THE DEAD. OR CURE ANY ILL.

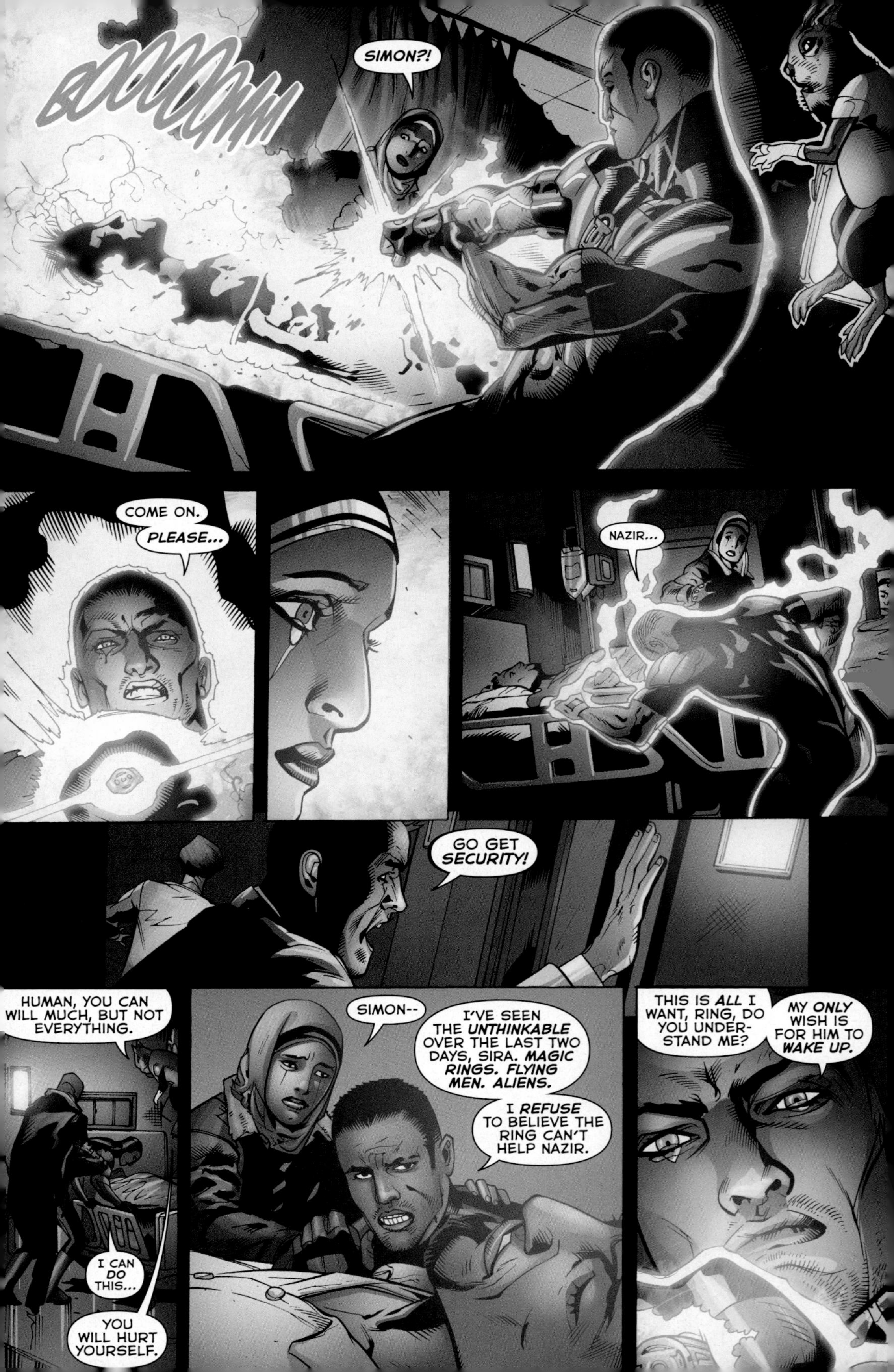
BOOOOOOM
SIMON?!
COME ON.
PLEASE...
NAZIR...
GO GET SECURITY!
HUMAN, YOU CAN WILL MUCH, BUT NOT EVERYTHING.
I CAN DO THIS...
YOU WILL HURT YOURSELF.
SIMON--
I'VE SEEN THE UNTHINKABLE OVER THE LAST TWO DAYS, SIRA. MAGIC RINGS. FLYING MEN. ALIENS.
I REFUSE TO BELIEVE THE RING CAN'T HELP NAZIR.
THIS IS ALL I WANT, RING, DO YOU UNDERSTAND ME?
MY ONLY WISH IS FOR HIM TO WAKE UP.

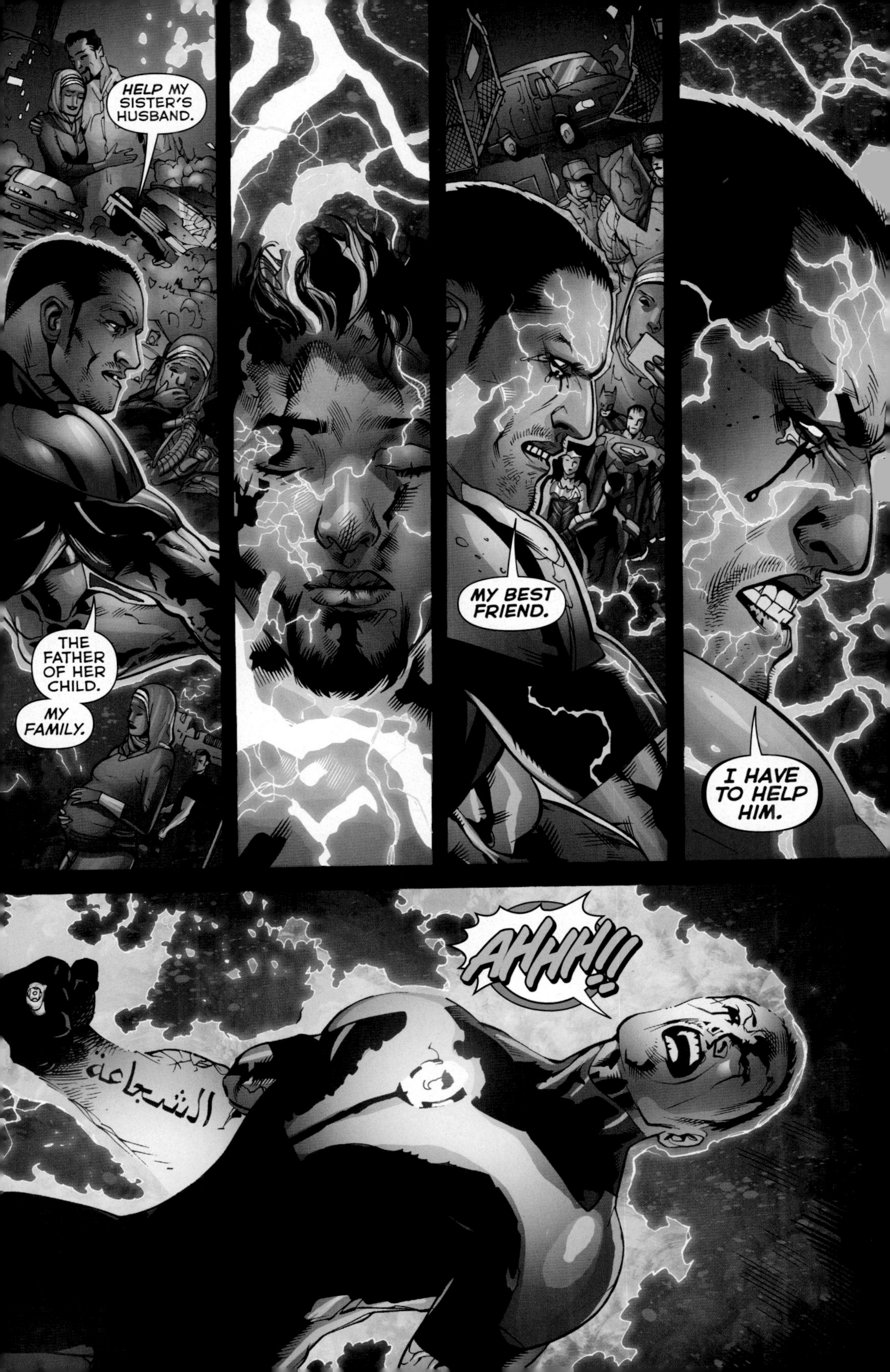

HELP MY SISTER'S HUSBAND.
THE FATHER OF HER CHILD.
MY FAMILY.
MY BEST FRIEND.
I HAVE TO HELP HIM.
AHHH!!
الشجاعة

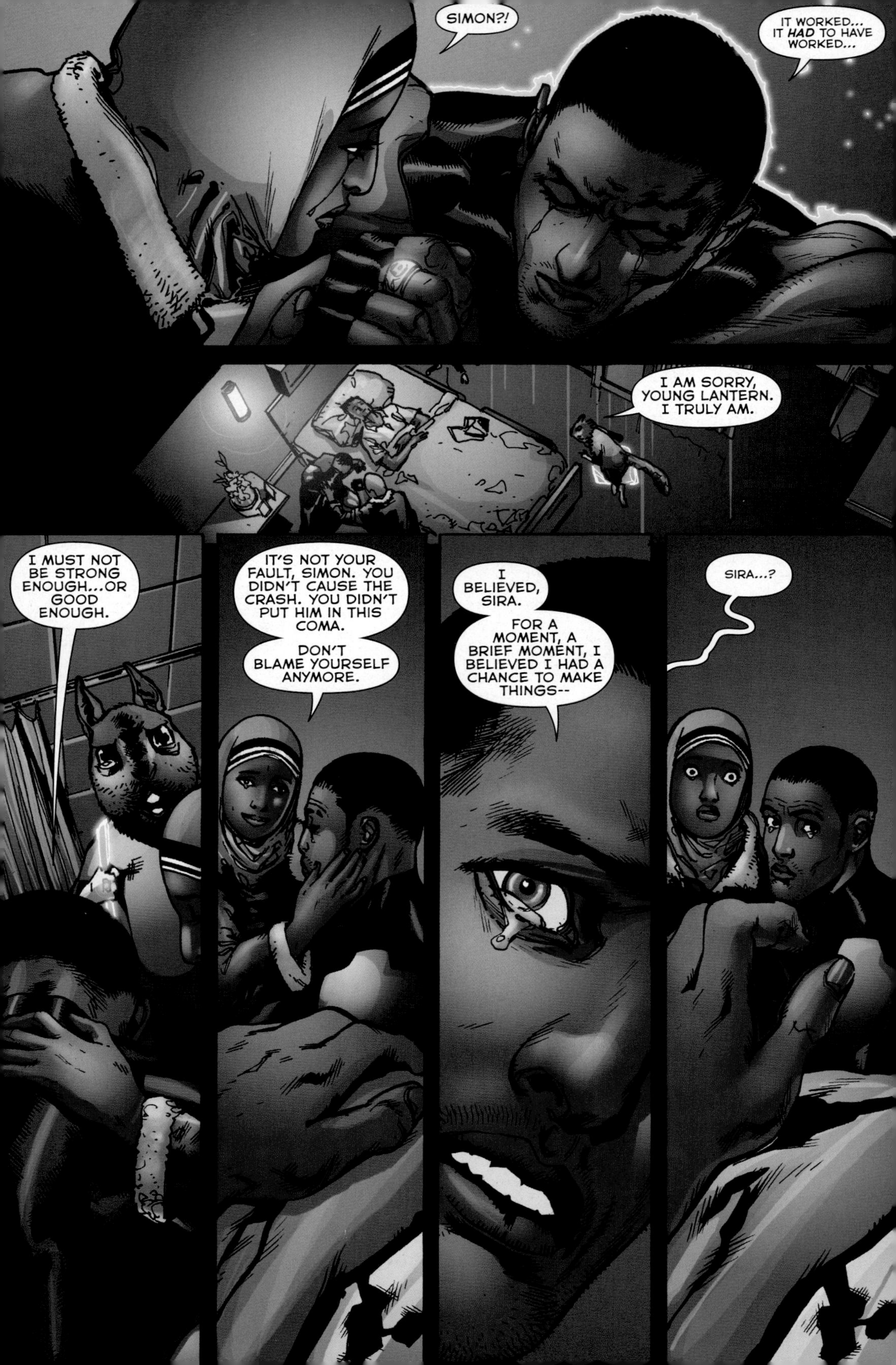
SIMON?!
IT WORKED... IT HAD TO HAVE WORKED...
I AM SORRY, YOUNG LANTERN. I TRULY AM.
I MUST NOT BE STRONG ENOUGH...OR GOOD ENOUGH.
IT'S NOT YOUR FAULT, SIMON. YOU DIDN'T CAUSE THE CRASH. YOU DIDN'T PUT HIM IN THIS COMA.
DON'T BLAME YOURSELF ANYMORE.
I BELIEVED, SIRA.
FOR A MOMENT, A BRIEF MOMENT, I BELIEVED I HAD A CHANCE TO MAKE THINGS--
SIRA...?

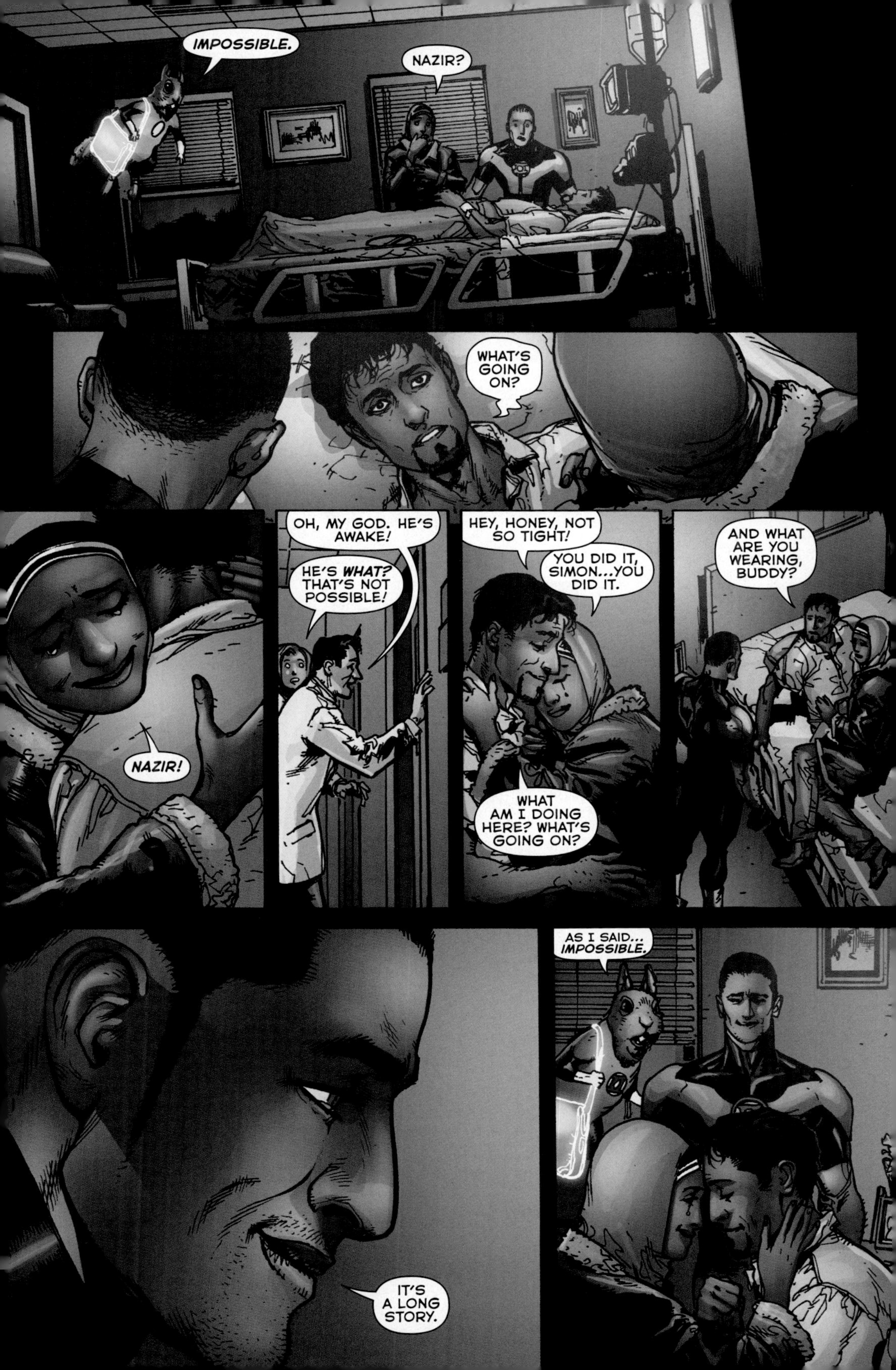
IMPOSSIBLE.
NAZIR?
WHAT'S GOING ON?
NAZIR!
OH, MY GOD. HE'S AWAKE!
HE'S WHAT? THAT'S NOT POSSIBLE!
HEY, HONEY, NOT SO TIGHT!
YOU DID IT, SIMON...YOU DID IT.
WHAT AM I DOING HERE? WHAT'S GOING ON?
AND WHAT ARE YOU WEARING, BUDDY?
IT'S A LONG STORY.
AS I SAID... IMPOSSIBLE.

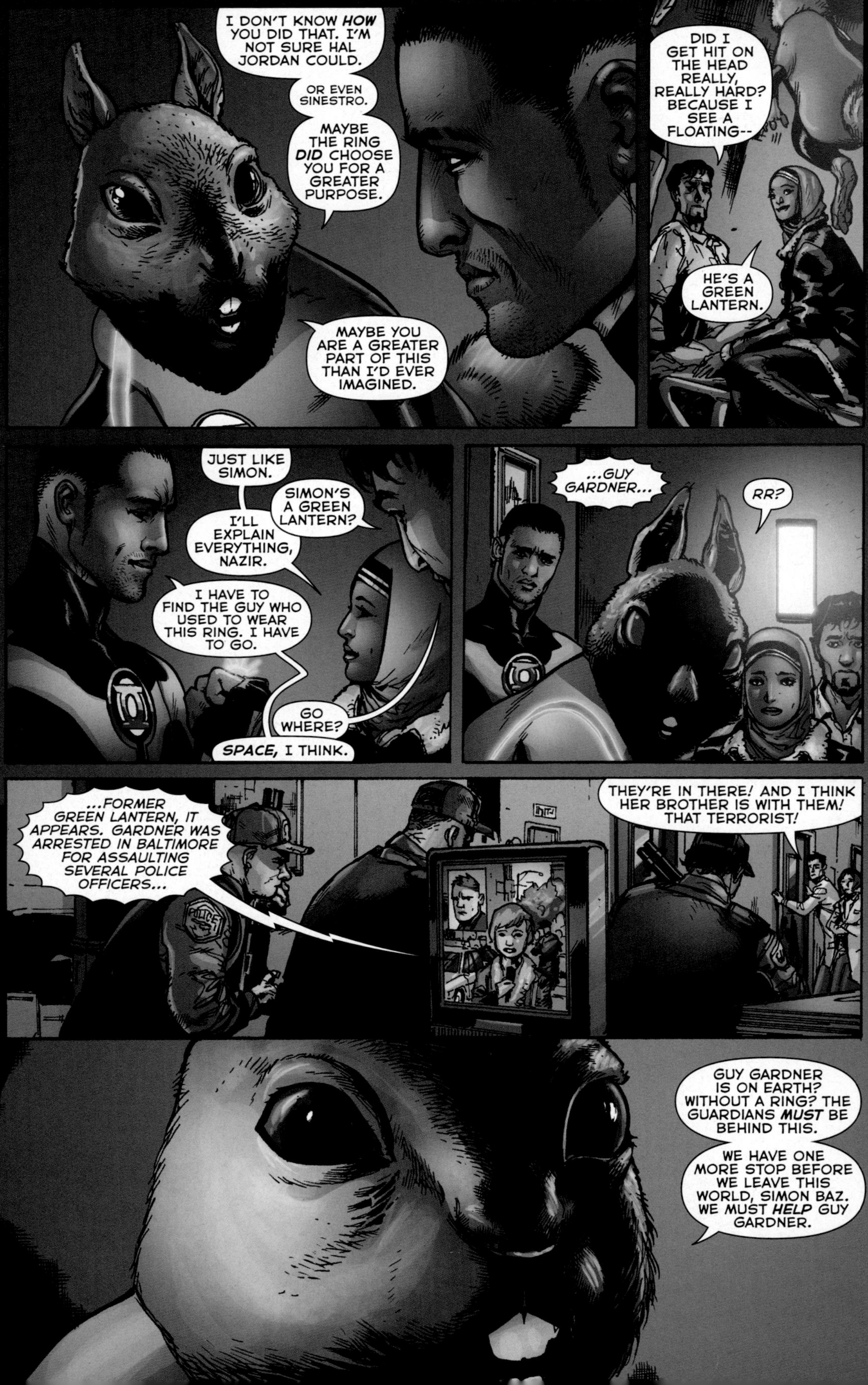
I DON'T KNOW *HOW* YOU DID THAT. I'M NOT SURE HAL JORDAN COULD.
OR EVEN SINESTRO.
MAYBE THE RING *DID* CHOOSE YOU FOR A GREATER PURPOSE.
MAYBE YOU ARE A GREATER PART OF THIS THAN I'D EVER IMAGINED.
DID I GET HIT ON THE HEAD REALLY, REALLY HARD? BECAUSE I SEE A FLOATING--
HE'S A GREEN LANTERN.
JUST LIKE SIMON.
SIMON'S A GREEN LANTERN?
I'LL EXPLAIN EVERYTHING, NAZIR.
I HAVE TO FIND THE GUY WHO USED TO WEAR THIS RING. I HAVE TO GO.
GO WHERE?
SPACE, I THINK.
...GUY GARDNER...
RR?
...FORMER GREEN LANTERN, IT APPEARS. GARDNER WAS ARRESTED IN BALTIMORE FOR ASSAULTING SEVERAL POLICE OFFICERS...
THEY'RE IN THERE! AND I THINK HER BROTHER IS WITH THEM! THAT TERRORIST!
GUY GARDNER IS ON EARTH? WITHOUT A RING? THE GUARDIANS *MUST* BE BEHIND THIS.
WE HAVE ONE MORE STOP BEFORE WE LEAVE THIS WORLD, SIMON BAZ. WE MUST *HELP* GUY GARDNER.

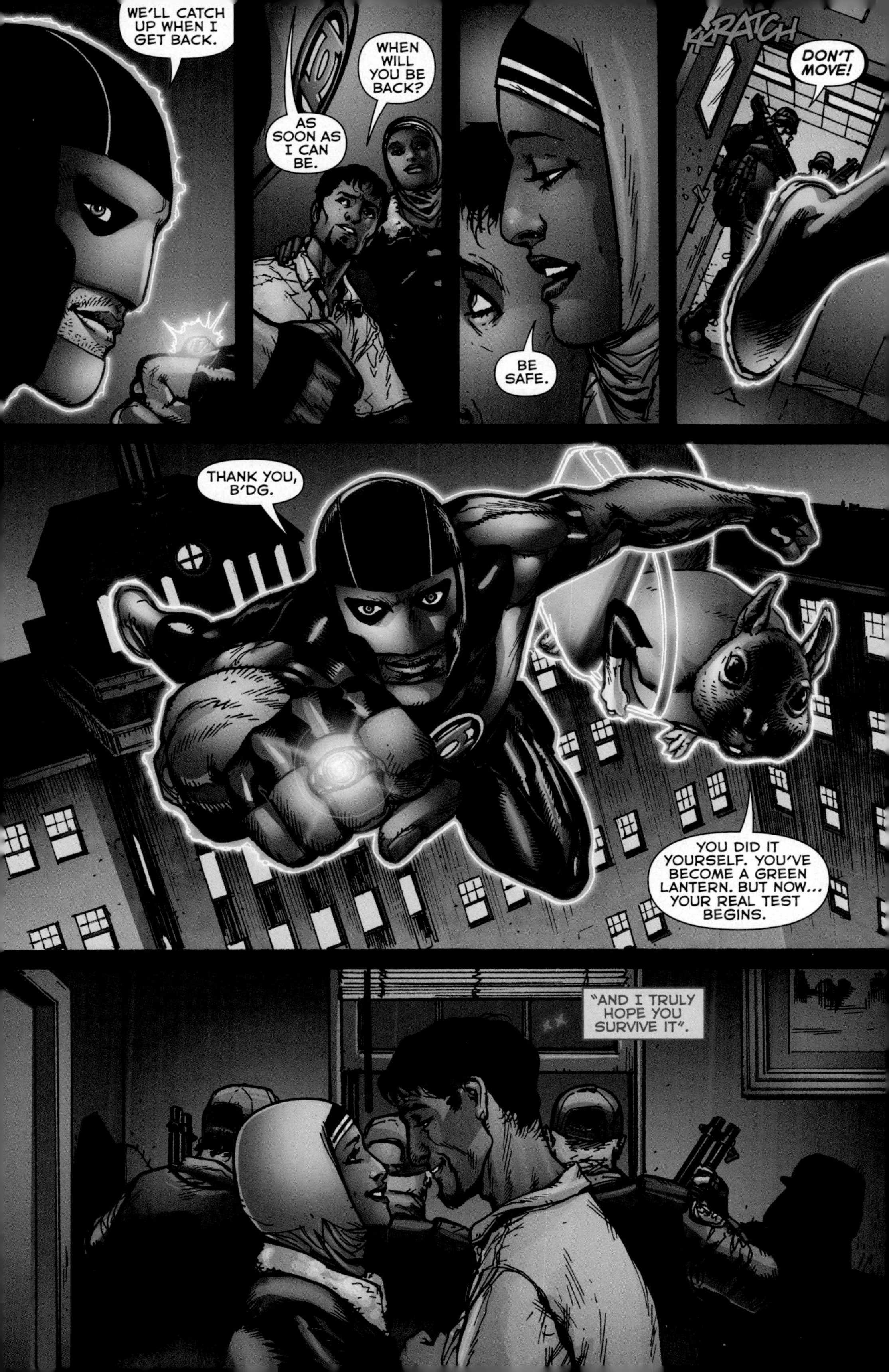
WE'LL CATCH UP WHEN I GET BACK.
WHEN WILL YOU BE BACK?
AS SOON AS I CAN BE.
BE SAFE.
KKRATCH
DON'T MOVE!
THANK YOU, B'DG.
YOU DID IT YOURSELF. YOU'VE BECOME A GREEN LANTERN. BUT NOW... YOUR REAL TEST BEGINS.
"AND I TRULY HOPE YOU SURVIVE IT".

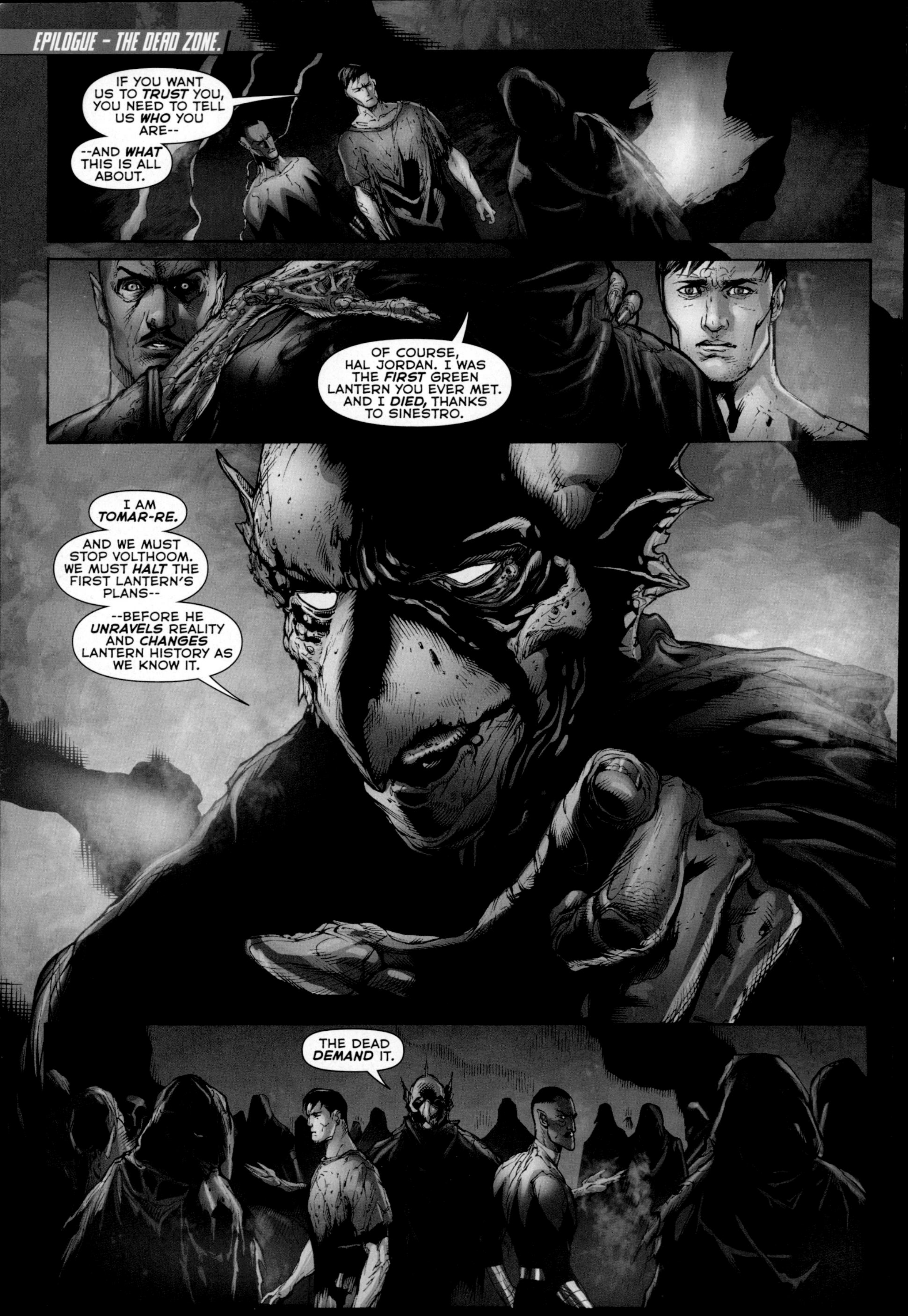
EPILOGUE - THE DEAD ZONE.
IF YOU WANT US TO TRUST YOU, YOU NEED TO TELL US WHO YOU ARE--
--AND WHAT THIS IS ALL ABOUT.
OF COURSE, HAL JORDAN. I WAS THE FIRST GREEN LANTERN YOU EVER MET. AND I DIED, THANKS TO SINESTRO.
I AM TOMAR-RE.
AND WE MUST STOP VOLTHOOM. WE MUST HALT THE FIRST LANTERN'S PLANS--
--BEFORE HE UNRAVELS REALITY AND CHANGES LANTERN HISTORY AS WE KNOW IT.
THE DEAD DEMAND IT.

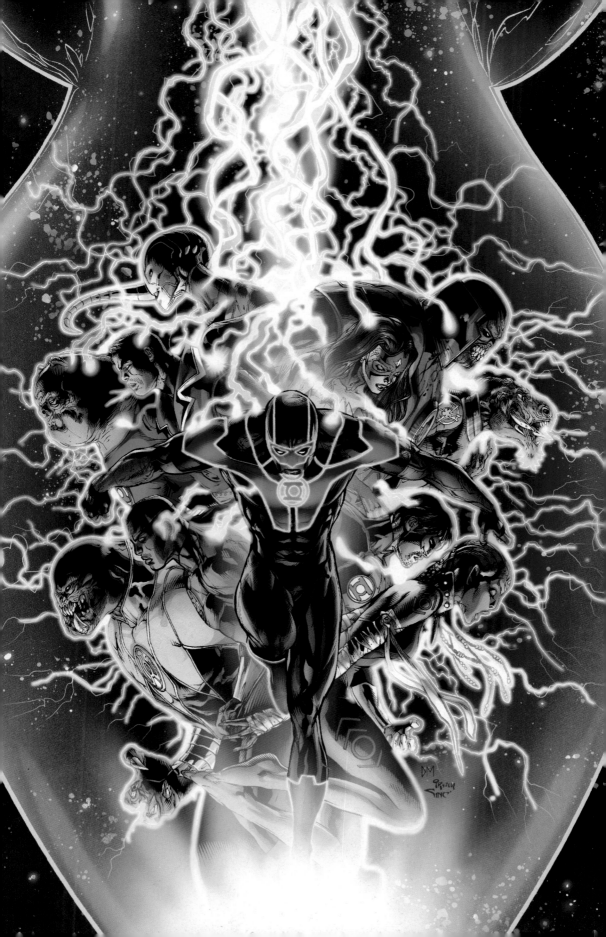

GEOFF JOHNS writer **DOUG MAHNKE** penciller **TOM NGUYEN, KEITH CHAMPAGNE, CHRISTIAN ALAMY, MARK IRWIN & DOUG MAHNKE** inkers
DAN JURGENS prologue layouts **PHIL JIMENEZ** prologue finishes **DOUG MAHNKE, MARK IRWIN & ALEX SINCLAIR** cover

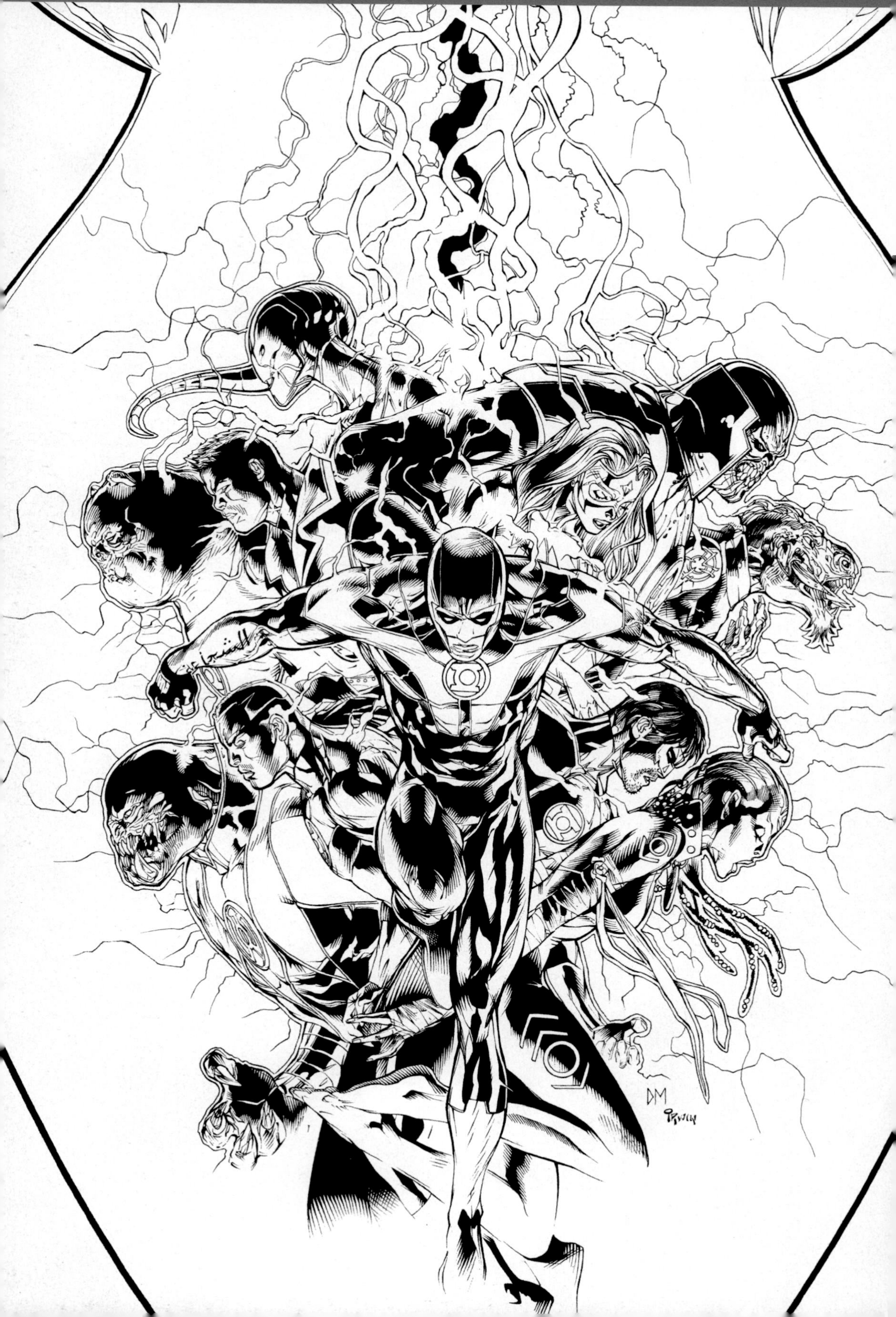

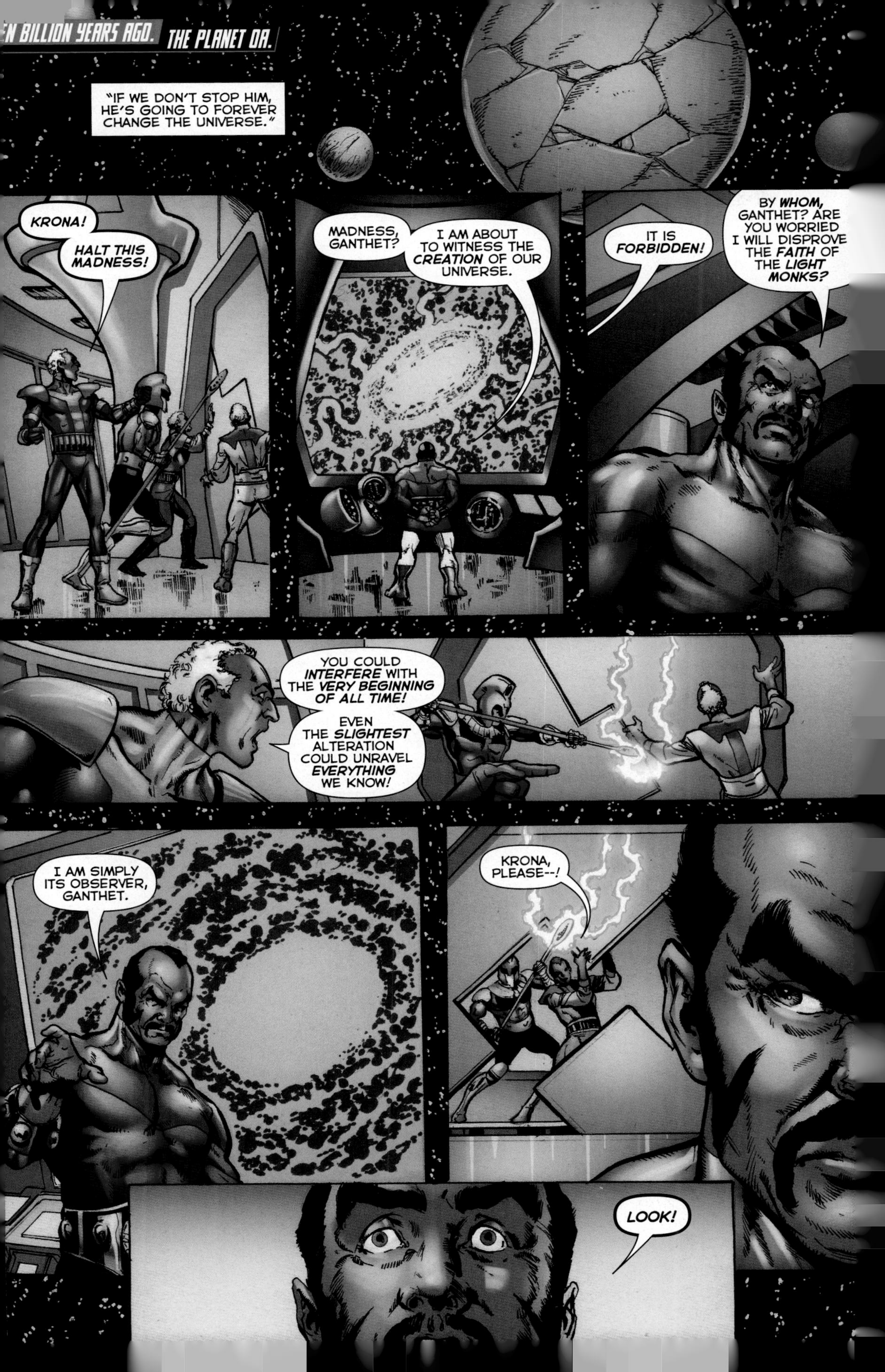
EN BILLION YEARS AGO.
THE PLANET OA.
"IF WE DON'T STOP HIM, HE'S GOING TO FOREVER CHANGE THE UNIVERSE."
KRONA!
HALT THIS MADNESS!
MADNESS, GANTHET?
I AM ABOUT TO WITNESS THE CREATION OF OUR UNIVERSE.
IT IS FORBIDDEN!
BY WHOM, GANTHET? ARE YOU WORRIED I WILL DISPROVE THE FAITH OF THE LIGHT MONKS?
YOU COULD INTERFERE WITH THE VERY BEGINNING OF ALL TIME!
EVEN THE SLIGHTEST ALTERATION COULD UNRAVEL EVERYTHING WE KNOW!
I AM SIMPLY ITS OBSERVER, GANTHET.
KRONA, PLEASE--!
LOOK!

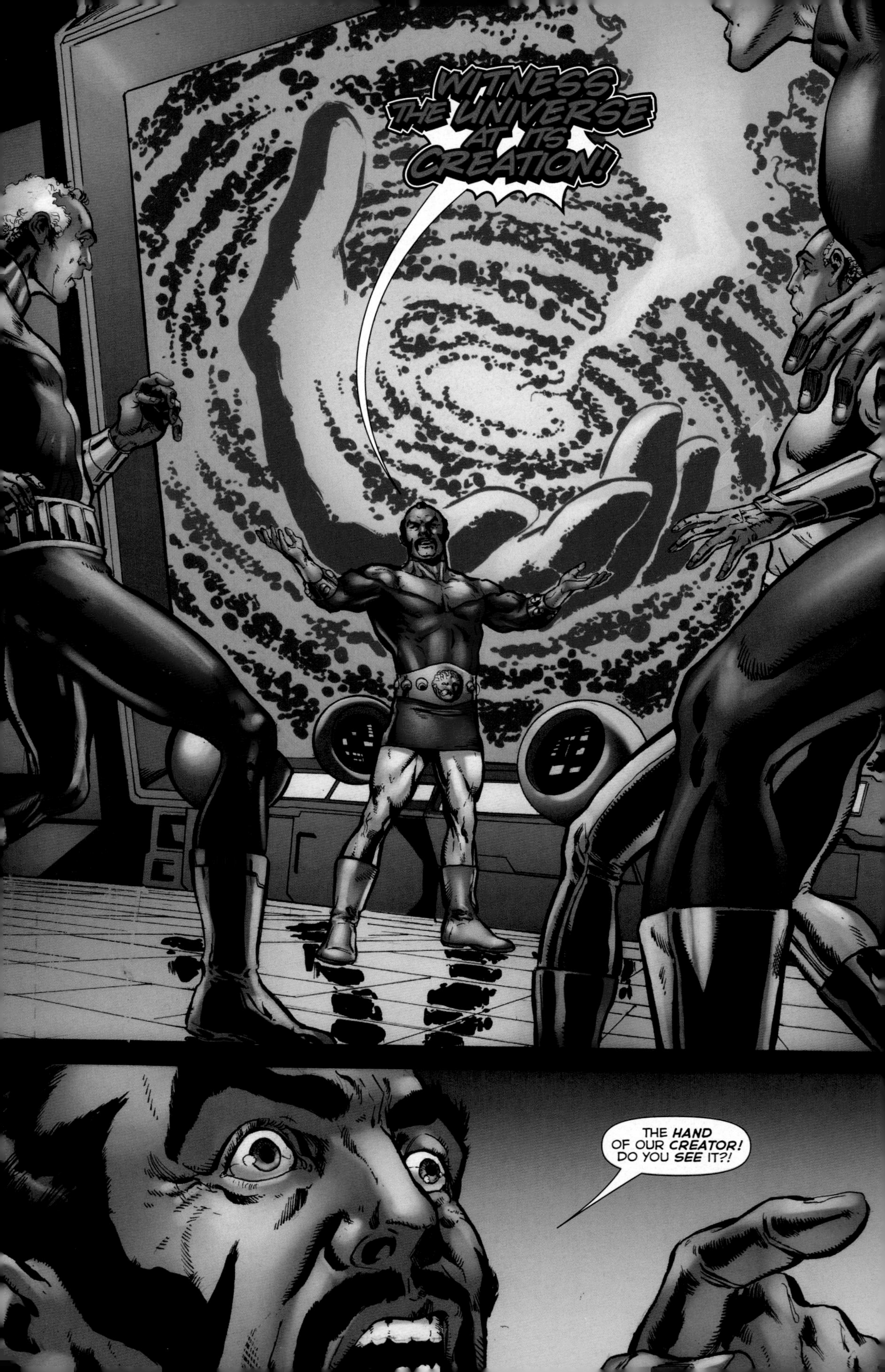
WITNESS THE UNIVERSE AT ITS CREATION!
THE HAND OF OUR CREATOR! DO YOU SEE IT?!

KRONA, YOU *KNOW* THE LEGENDS...

BAH! SUCH STORIES ARE TALES ONLY *FOOLS* WOULD FEAR.

I SEEK TO LEARN THE *ORIGIN OF THE UNIVERSE!*

AND YOU TALK OF LEGENDS OF *DESTRUCTION* SHOULD I LEARN THE TRUTH.

KRONA! THE HAND...

...WHAT IS *ON* IT?

A *RING*--?

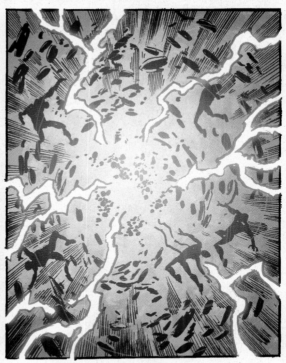

I... I MADE IT. I *SURVIVED!*

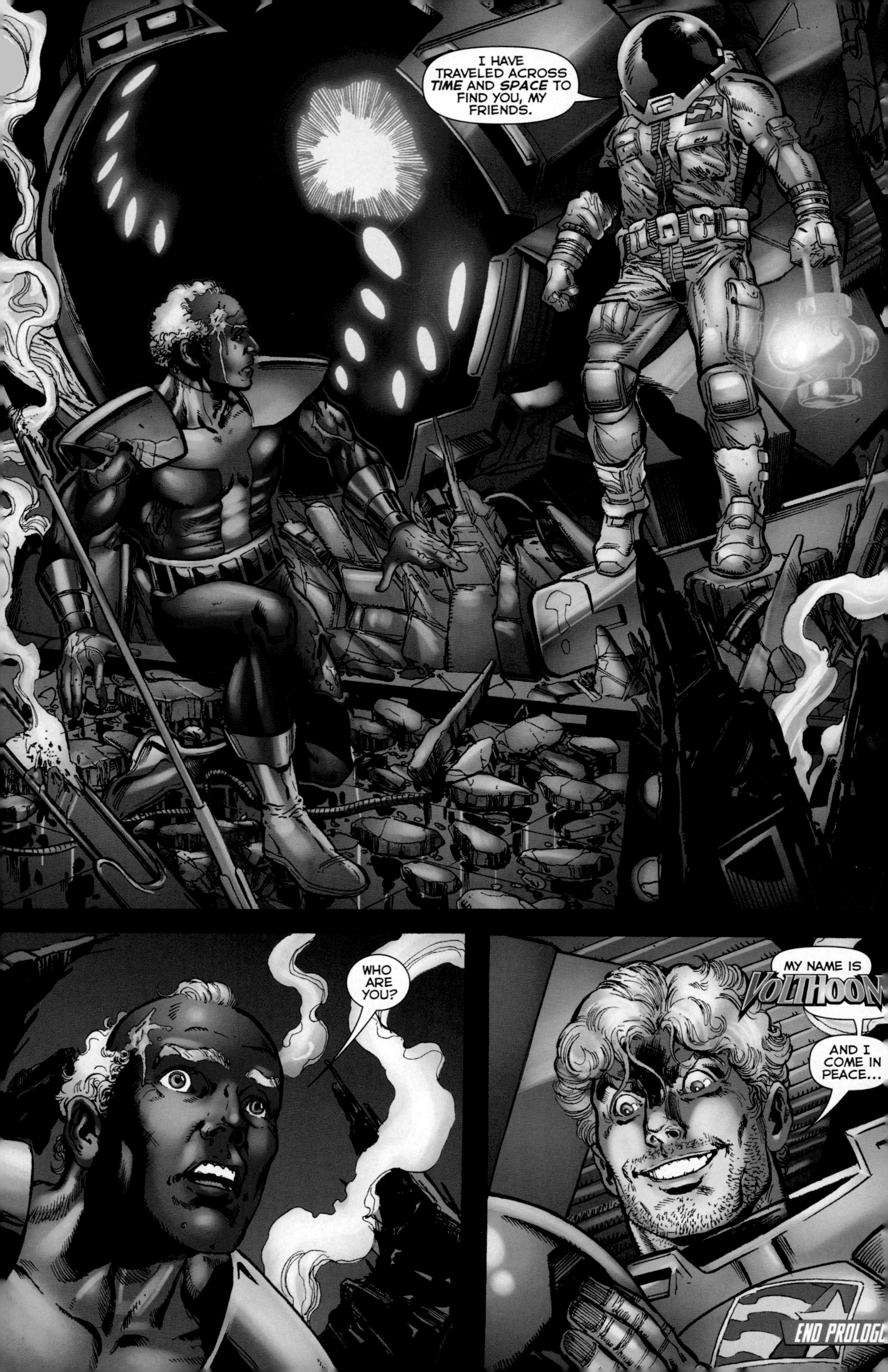
I HAVE TRAVELED ACROSS TIME AND SPACE TO FIND YOU, MY FRIENDS.
WHO ARE YOU?
MY NAME IS VOLTHOON
AND I COME IN PEACE...
END PROLOGU

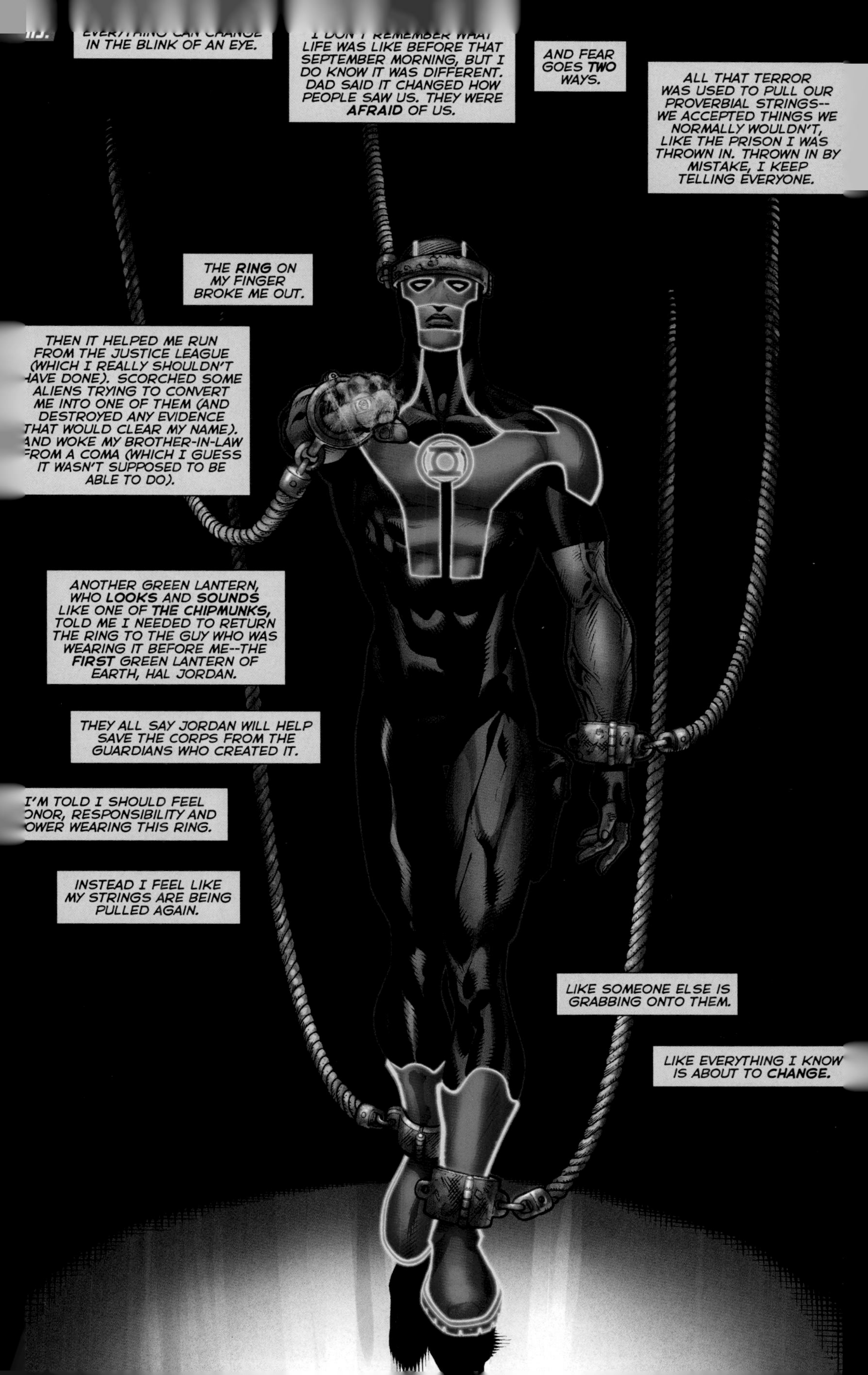

EVERYTHING CAN CHANGE IN THE BLINK OF AN EYE.

I DON'T REMEMBER WHAT LIFE WAS LIKE BEFORE THAT SEPTEMBER MORNING, BUT I DO KNOW IT WAS DIFFERENT. DAD SAID IT CHANGED HOW PEOPLE SAW US. THEY WERE AFRAID OF US.

AND FEAR GOES TWO WAYS.

ALL THAT TERROR WAS USED TO PULL OUR PROVERBIAL STRINGS-- WE ACCEPTED THINGS WE NORMALLY WOULDN'T, LIKE THE PRISON I WAS THROWN IN. THROWN IN BY MISTAKE, I KEEP TELLING EVERYONE.

THE RING ON MY FINGER BROKE ME OUT.

THEN IT HELPED ME RUN FROM THE JUSTICE LEAGUE (WHICH I REALLY SHOULDN'T HAVE DONE). SCORCHED SOME ALIENS TRYING TO CONVERT ME INTO ONE OF THEM (AND DESTROYED ANY EVIDENCE THAT WOULD CLEAR MY NAME). AND WOKE MY BROTHER-IN-LAW FROM A COMA (WHICH I GUESS IT WASN'T SUPPOSED TO BE ABLE TO DO).

ANOTHER GREEN LANTERN, WHO LOOKS AND SOUNDS LIKE ONE OF THE CHIPMUNKS, TOLD ME I NEEDED TO RETURN THE RING TO THE GUY WHO WAS WEARING IT BEFORE ME--THE FIRST GREEN LANTERN OF EARTH, HAL JORDAN.

THEY ALL SAY JORDAN WILL HELP SAVE THE CORPS FROM THE GUARDIANS WHO CREATED IT.

I'M TOLD I SHOULD FEEL HONOR, RESPONSIBILITY AND POWER WEARING THIS RING.

INSTEAD I FEEL LIKE MY STRINGS ARE BEING PULLED AGAIN.

LIKE SOMEONE ELSE IS GRABBING ONTO THEM.

LIKE EVERYTHING I KNOW IS ABOUT TO CHANGE.

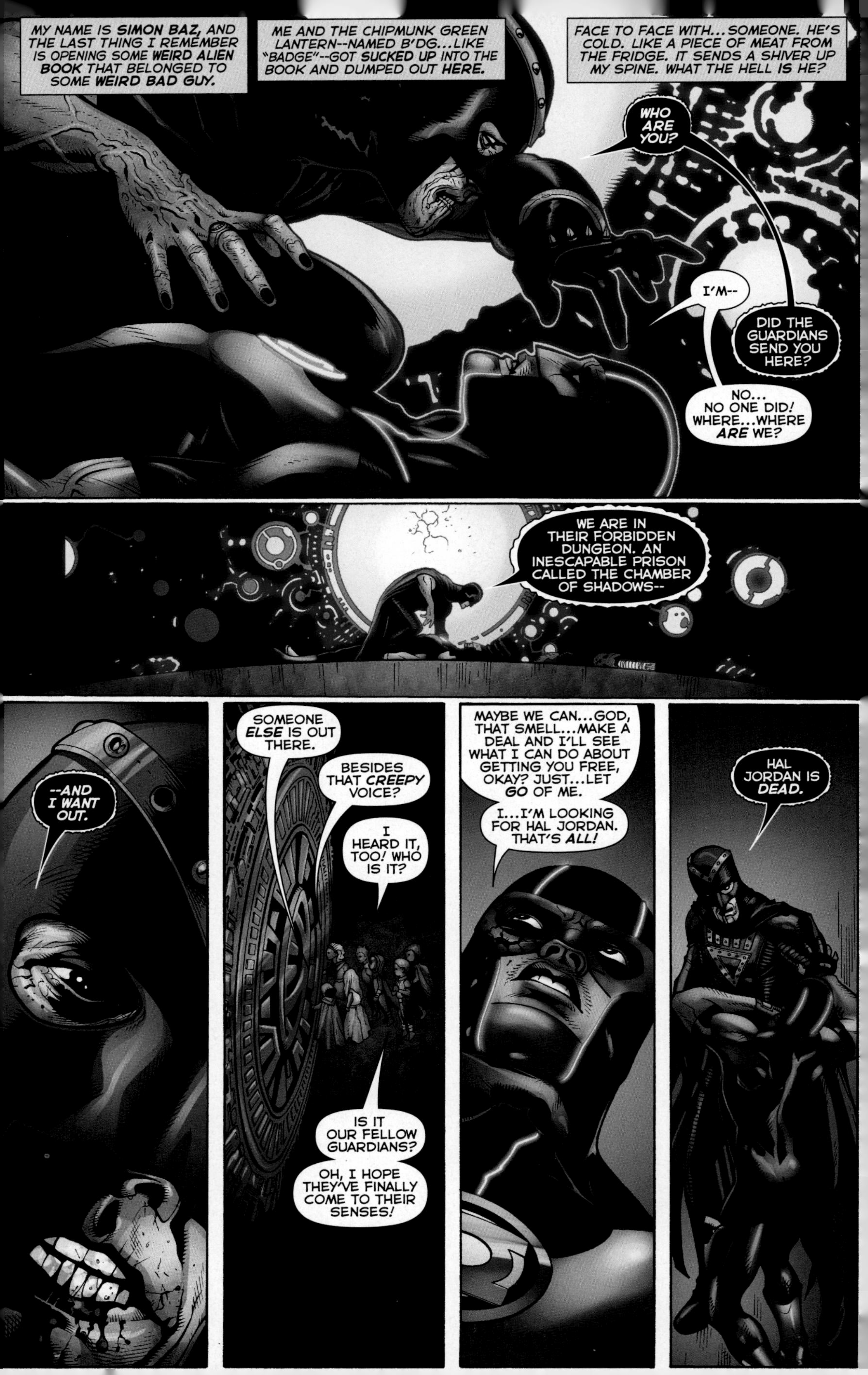
MY NAME IS SIMON BAZ, AND THE LAST THING I REMEMBER IS OPENING SOME WEIRD ALIEN BOOK THAT BELONGED TO SOME WEIRD BAD GUY.
ME AND THE CHIPMUNK GREEN LANTERN--NAMED B'DG...LIKE "BADGE"--GOT SUCKED UP INTO THE BOOK AND DUMPED OUT HERE.
FACE TO FACE WITH...SOMEONE. HE'S COLD. LIKE A PIECE OF MEAT FROM THE FRIDGE. IT SENDS A SHIVER UP MY SPINE. WHAT THE HELL IS HE?
WHO ARE YOU?
I'M--
DID THE GUARDIANS SEND YOU HERE?
NO... NO ONE DID! WHERE...WHERE ARE WE?
WE ARE IN THEIR FORBIDDEN DUNGEON. AN INESCAPABLE PRISON CALLED THE CHAMBER OF SHADOWS--
--AND I WANT OUT.
SOMEONE ELSE IS OUT THERE.
BESIDES THAT CREEPY VOICE?
I HEARD IT, TOO! WHO IS IT?
IS IT OUR FELLOW GUARDIANS?
OH, I HOPE THEY'VE FINALLY COME TO THEIR SENSES!
MAYBE WE CAN...GOD, THAT SMELL...MAKE A DEAL AND I'LL SEE WHAT I CAN DO ABOUT GETTING YOU FREE, OKAY? JUST...LET GO OF ME.
I...I'M LOOKING FOR HAL JORDAN. THAT'S ALL!
HAL JORDAN IS DEAD.

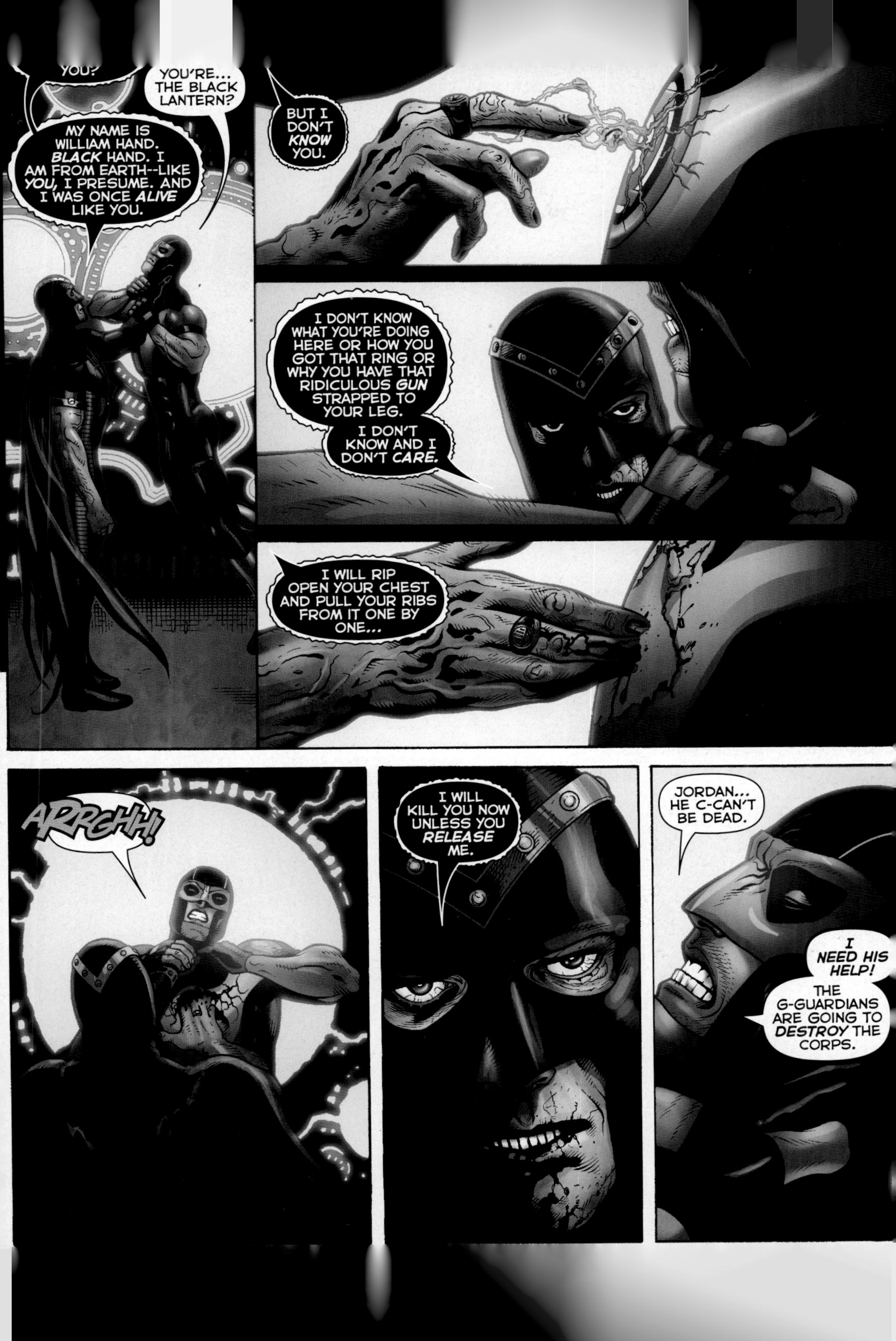

YOU?
YOU'RE... THE BLACK LANTERN?
MY NAME IS WILLIAM HAND. BLACK HAND. I AM FROM EARTH--LIKE YOU, I PRESUME. AND I WAS ONCE ALIVE LIKE YOU.
BUT I DON'T KNOW YOU.
I DON'T KNOW WHAT YOU'RE DOING HERE OR HOW YOU GOT THAT RING OR WHY YOU HAVE THAT RIDICULOUS GUN STRAPPED TO YOUR LEG.
I DON'T KNOW AND I DON'T CARE.
I WILL RIP OPEN YOUR CHEST AND PULL YOUR RIBS FROM IT ONE BY ONE...
ARRGHH!
I WILL KILL YOU NOW UNLESS YOU RELEASE ME.
JORDAN... HE C-CAN'T BE DEAD.
I NEED HIS HELP!
THE G-GUARDIANS ARE GOING TO DESTROY THE CORPS.

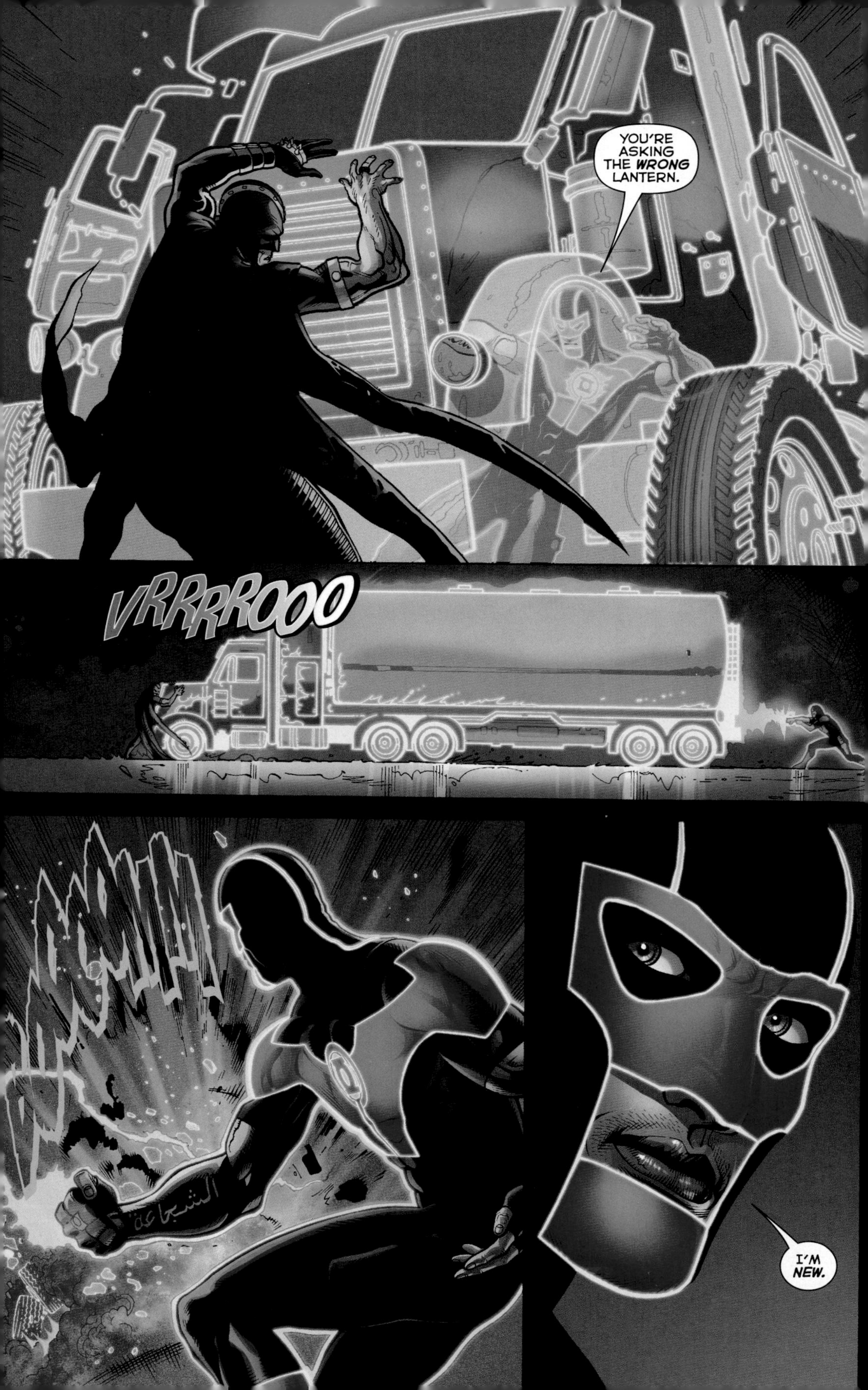
YOU'RE ASKING THE *WRONG* LANTERN.
VRRRROOO
الشجاعة
I'M *NEW.*

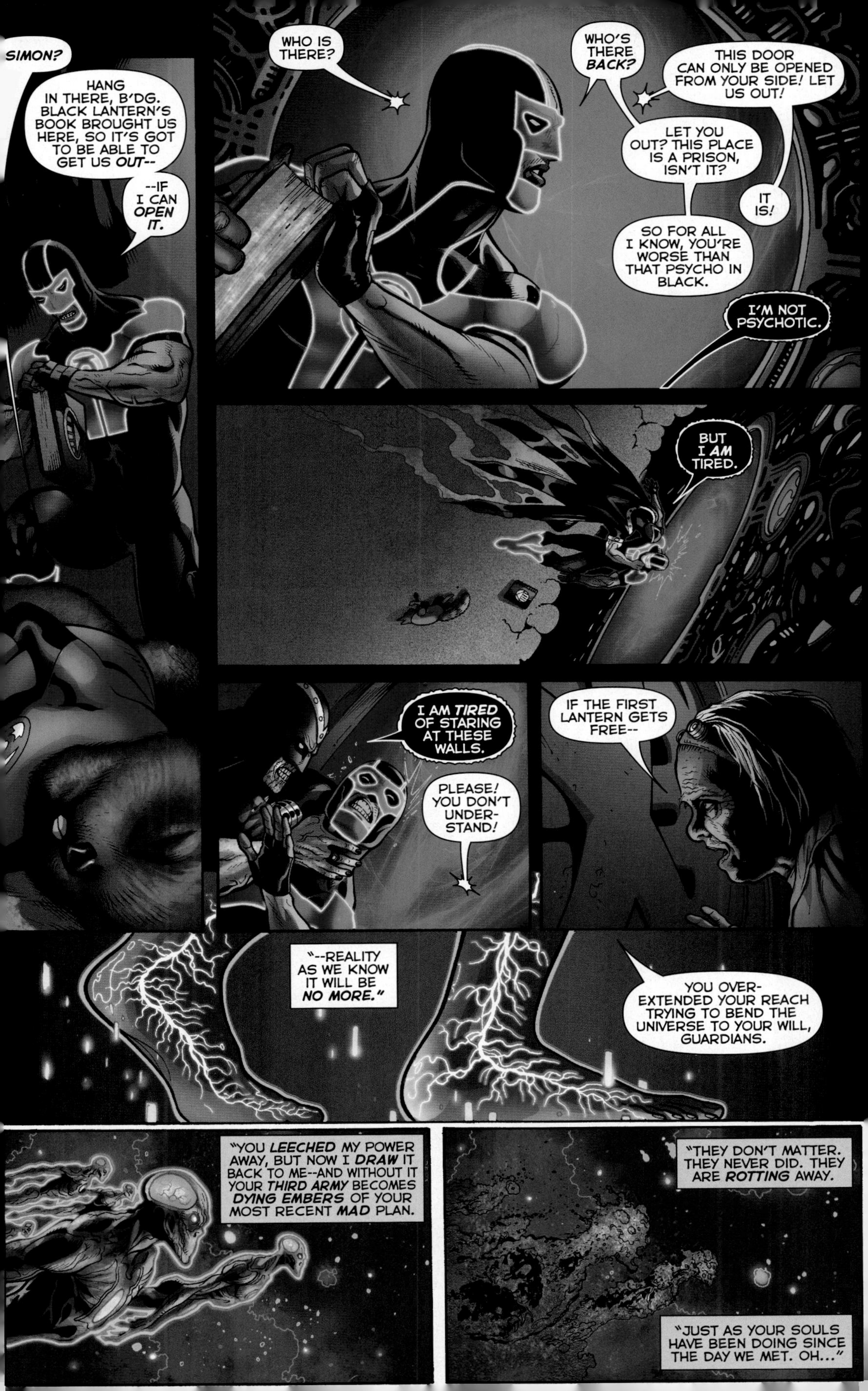

SIMON?
HANG IN THERE, B'DG. BLACK LANTERN'S BOOK BROUGHT US HERE, SO IT'S GOT TO BE ABLE TO GET US OUT--
--IF I CAN OPEN IT.
WHO IS THERE?
WHO'S THERE BACK?
THIS DOOR CAN ONLY BE OPENED FROM YOUR SIDE! LET US OUT!
LET YOU OUT? THIS PLACE IS A PRISON, ISN'T IT?
IT IS!
SO FOR ALL I KNOW, YOU'RE WORSE THAN THAT PSYCHO IN BLACK.
I'M NOT PSYCHOTIC.
BUT I AM TIRED.
I AM TIRED OF STARING AT THESE WALLS.
PLEASE! YOU DON'T UNDER-STAND!
IF THE FIRST LANTERN GETS FREE--
"--REALITY AS WE KNOW IT WILL BE NO MORE."
YOU OVER-EXTENDED YOUR REACH TRYING TO BEND THE UNIVERSE TO YOUR WILL, GUARDIANS.
"YOU LEECHED MY POWER AWAY, BUT NOW I DRAW IT BACK TO ME--AND WITHOUT IT YOUR THIRD ARMY BECOMES DYING EMBERS OF YOUR MOST RECENT MAD PLAN.
"THEY DON'T MATTER. THEY NEVER DID. THEY ARE ROTTING AWAY.
"JUST AS YOUR SOULS HAVE BEEN DOING SINCE THE DAY WE MET. OH..."

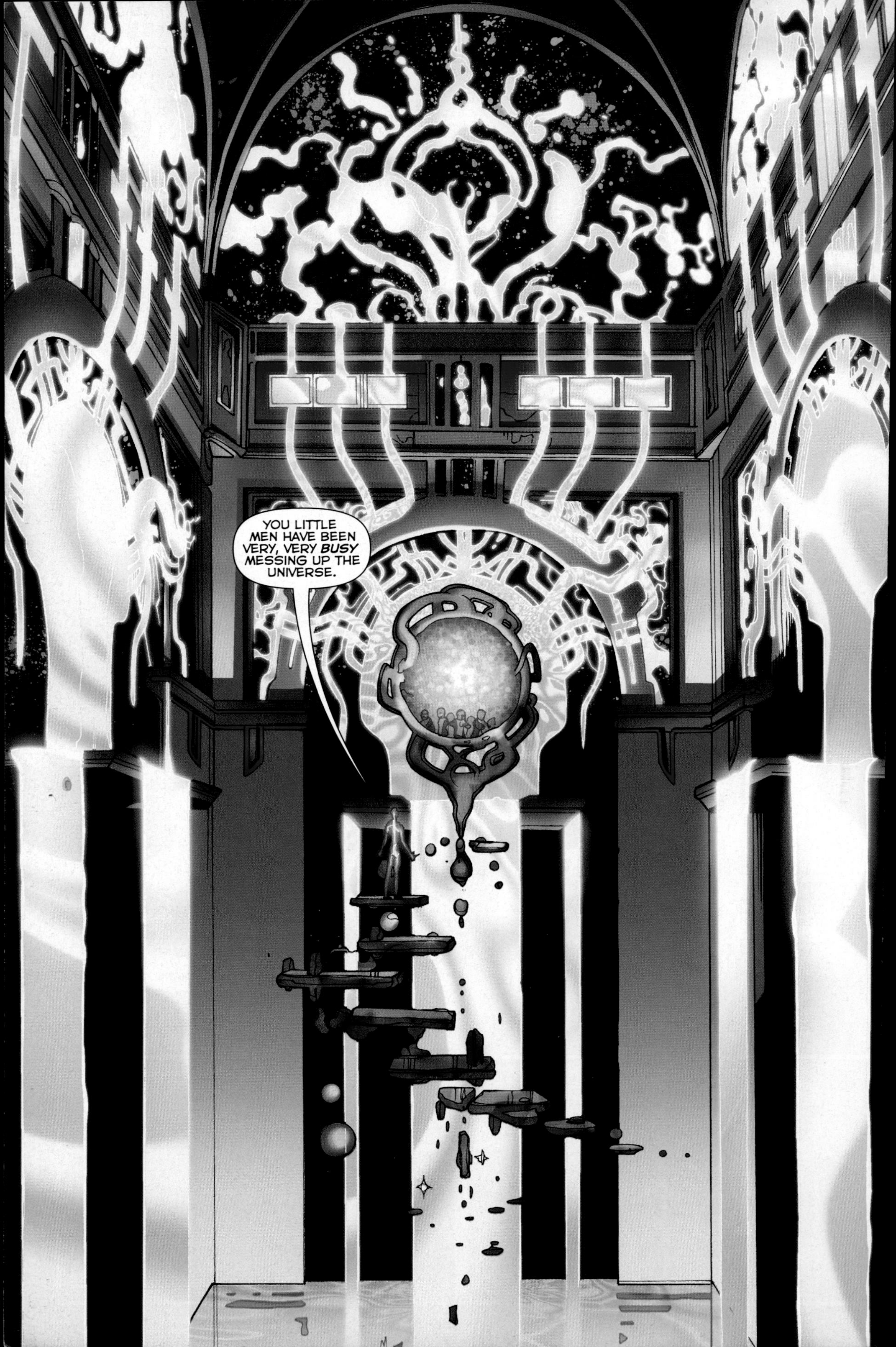
YOU LITTLE MEN HAVE BEEN VERY, VERY BUSY MESSING UP THE UNIVERSE.

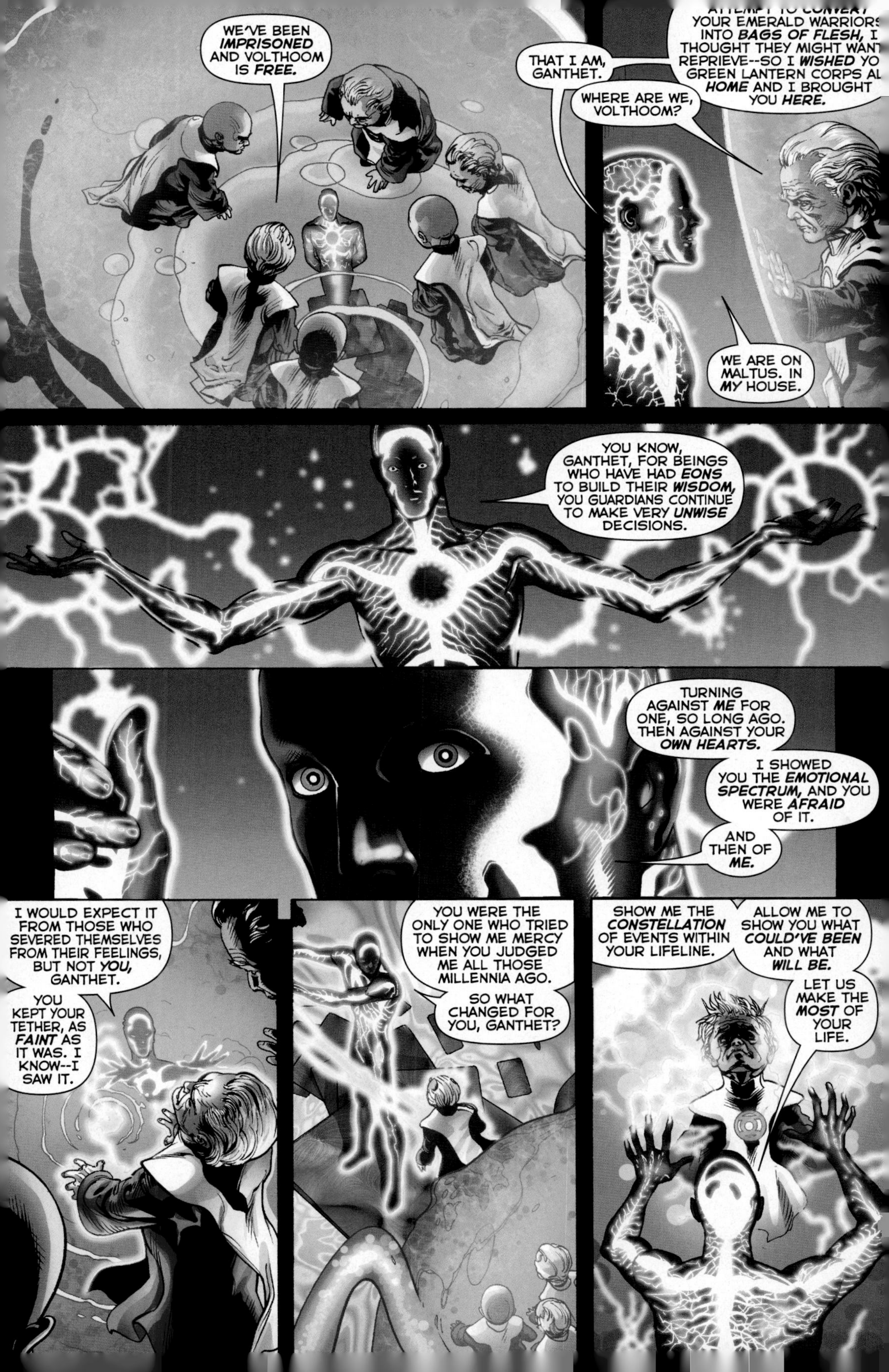

WE'VE BEEN IMPRISONED AND VOLTHOOM IS FREE.
THAT I AM, GANTHET.
YOUR EMERALD WARRIORS INTO BAGS OF FLESH, I THOUGHT THEY MIGHT WANT REPRIEVE--SO I WISHED YO GREEN LANTERN CORPS AL HOME AND I BROUGHT YOU HERE.
WHERE ARE WE, VOLTHOOM?
WE ARE ON MALTUS. IN MY HOUSE.
YOU KNOW, GANTHET, FOR BEINGS WHO HAVE HAD EONS TO BUILD THEIR WISDOM, YOU GUARDIANS CONTINUE TO MAKE VERY UNWISE DECISIONS.
TURNING AGAINST ME FOR ONE, SO LONG AGO. THEN AGAINST YOUR OWN HEARTS.
I SHOWED YOU THE EMOTIONAL SPECTRUM, AND YOU WERE AFRAID OF IT.
AND THEN OF ME.
I WOULD EXPECT IT FROM THOSE WHO SEVERED THEMSELVES FROM THEIR FEELINGS, BUT NOT YOU, GANTHET.
YOU KEPT YOUR TETHER, AS FAINT AS IT WAS. I KNOW--I SAW IT.
YOU WERE THE ONLY ONE WHO TRIED TO SHOW ME MERCY WHEN YOU JUDGED ME ALL THOSE MILLENNIA AGO.
SO WHAT CHANGED FOR YOU, GANTHET?
SHOW ME THE CONSTELLATION OF EVENTS WITHIN YOUR LIFELINE.
ALLOW ME TO SHOW YOU WHAT COULD'VE BEEN AND WHAT WILL BE.
LET US MAKE THE MOST OF YOUR LIFE.

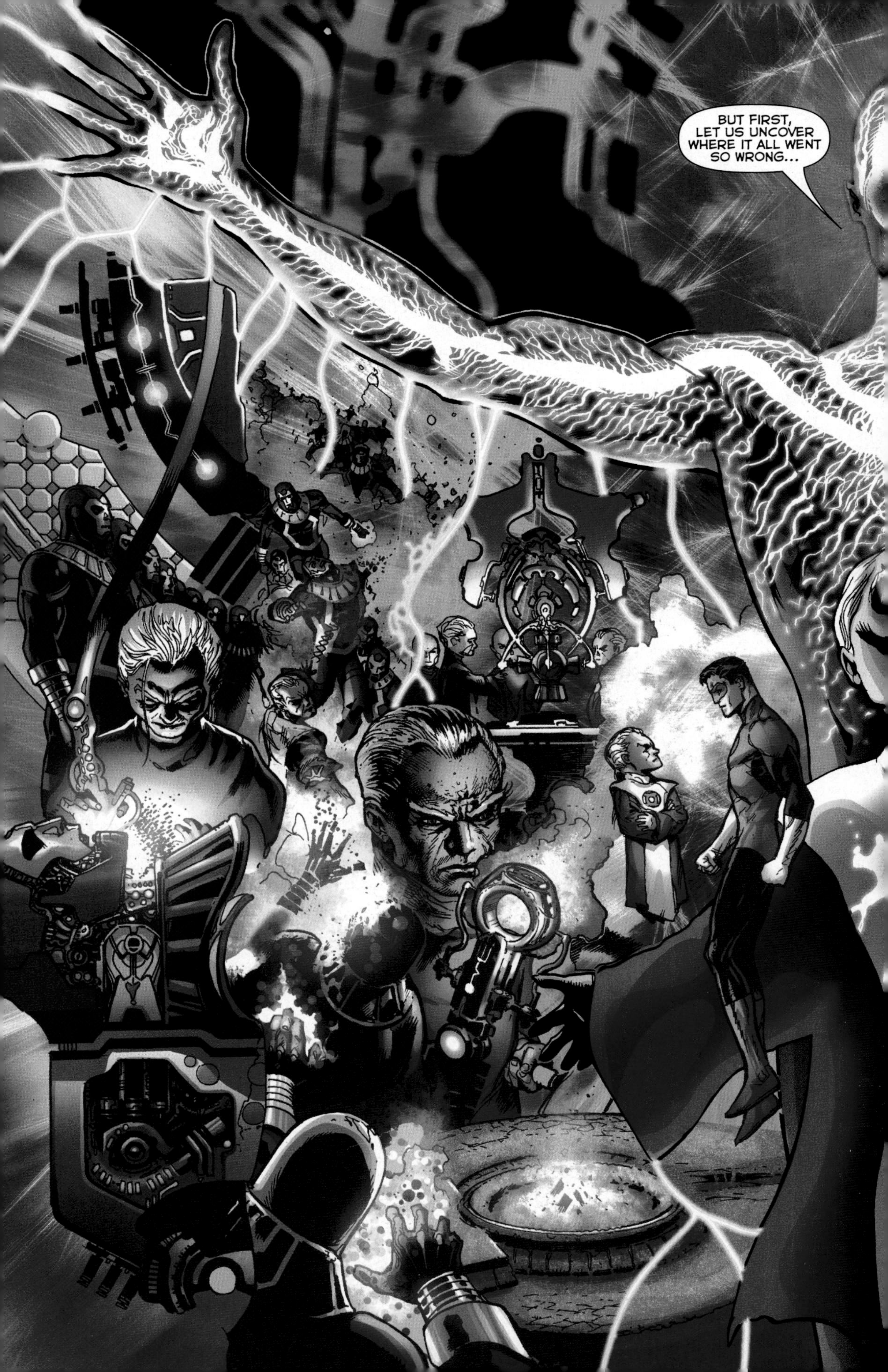
BUT FIRST, LET US UNCOVER WHERE IT ALL WENT SO WRONG...

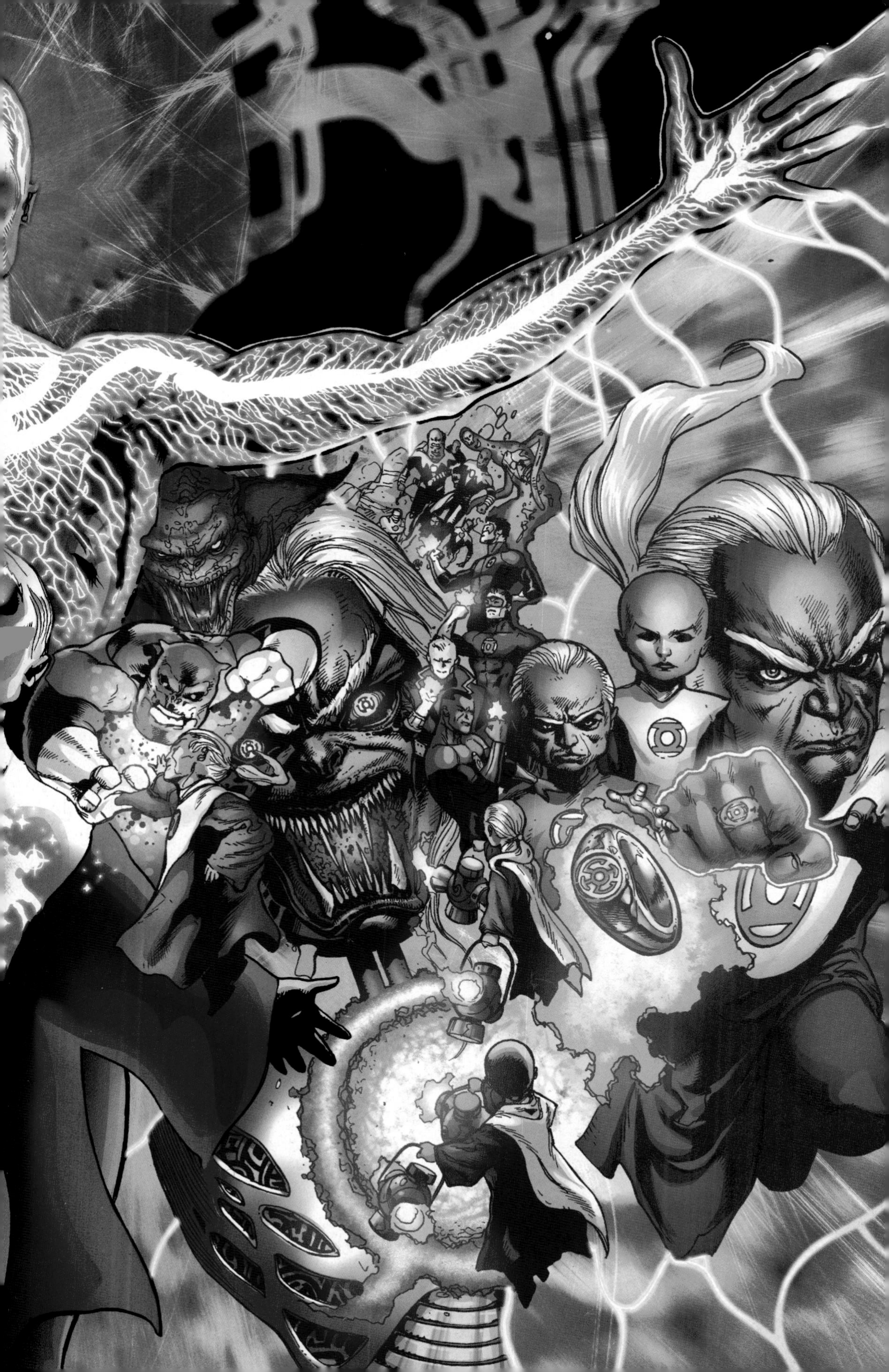

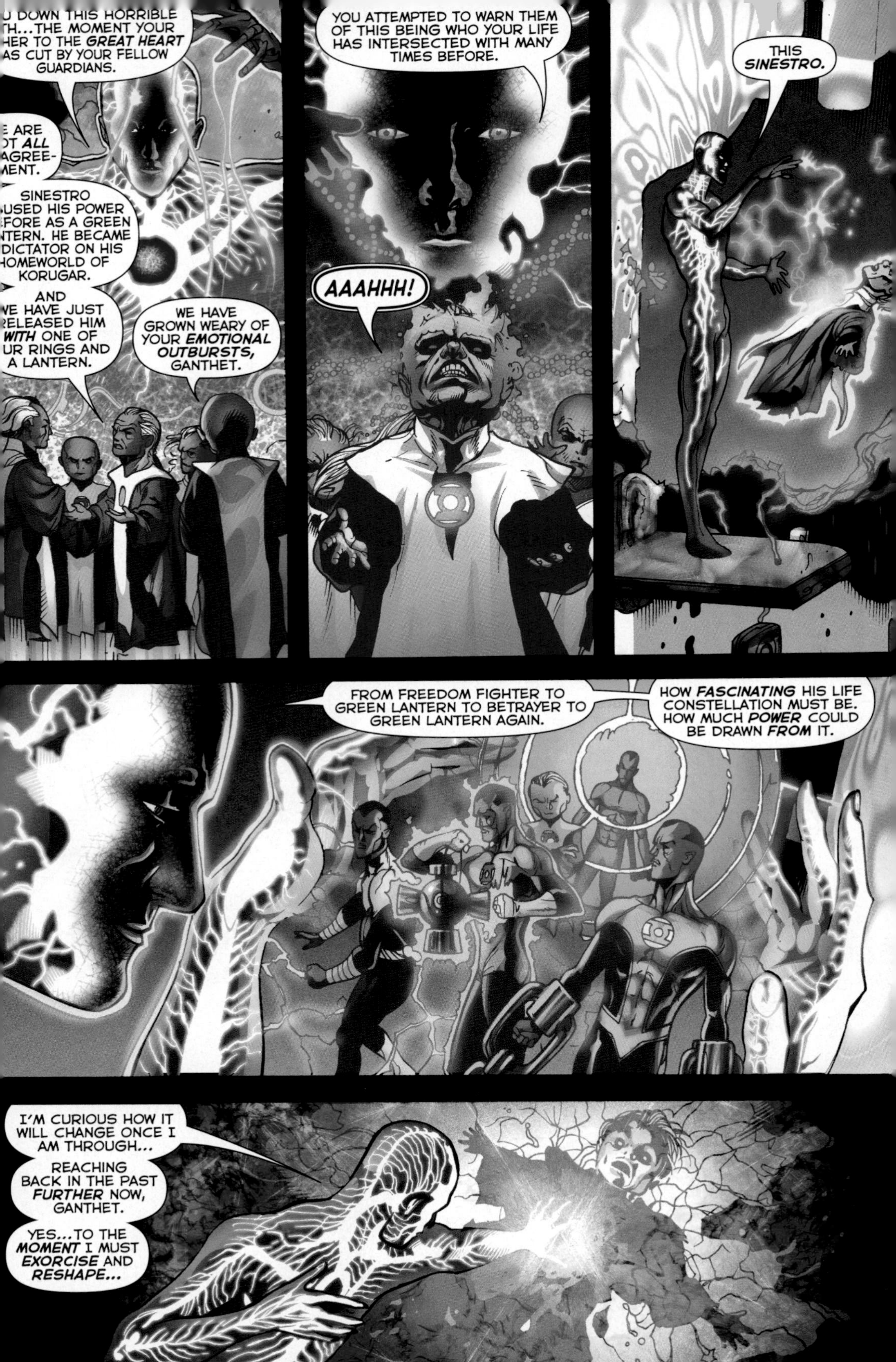

U DOWN THIS HORRIBLE TH...THE MOMENT YOUR HER TO THE GREAT HEART AS CUT BY YOUR FELLOW GUARDIANS.
E ARE OT ALL AGREE-MENT.
SINESTRO USED HIS POWER EFORE AS A GREEN NTERN. HE BECAME DICTATOR ON HIS HOMEWORLD OF KORUGAR.
AND WE HAVE JUST RELEASED HIM WITH ONE OF UR RINGS AND A LANTERN.
WE HAVE GROWN WEARY OF YOUR EMOTIONAL OUTBURSTS, GANTHET.
YOU ATTEMPTED TO WARN THEM OF THIS BEING WHO YOUR LIFE HAS INTERSECTED WITH MANY TIMES BEFORE.
AAAHHH!
THIS SINESTRO.
FROM FREEDOM FIGHTER TO GREEN LANTERN TO BETRAYER TO GREEN LANTERN AGAIN.
HOW FASCINATING HIS LIFE CONSTELLATION MUST BE. HOW MUCH POWER COULD BE DRAWN FROM IT.
I'M CURIOUS HOW IT WILL CHANGE ONCE I AM THROUGH...
REACHING BACK IN THE PAST FURTHER NOW, GANTHET.
YES...TO THE MOMENT I MUST EXORCISE AND RESHAPE...

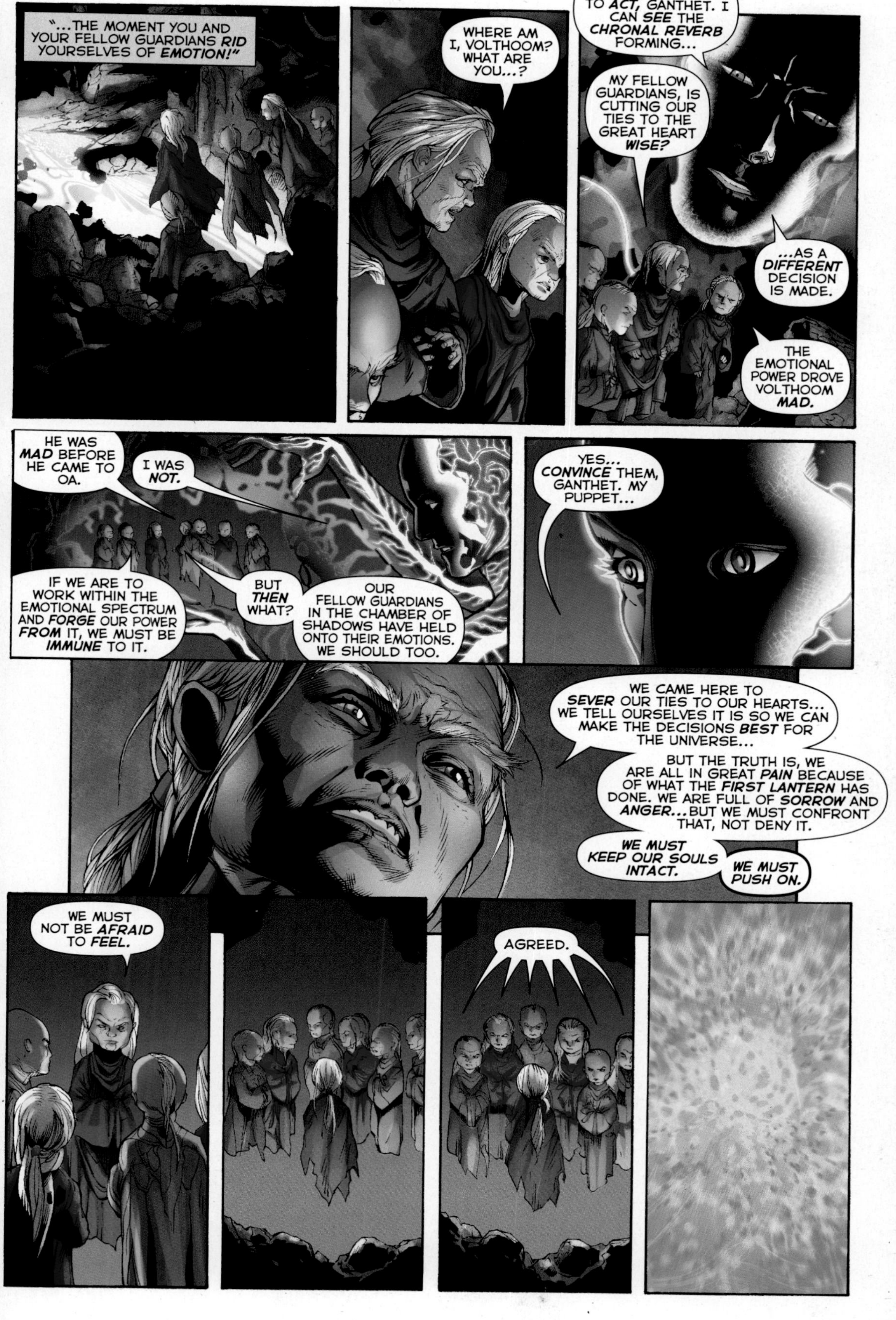
"...THE MOMENT YOU AND YOUR FELLOW GUARDIANS RID YOURSELVES OF EMOTION!"
WHERE AM I, VOLTHOOM? WHAT ARE YOU...?
YOU WILL ACT THE WAY I WILL YOU TO ACT, GANTHET. I CAN SEE THE CHRONAL REVERB FORMING...
MY FELLOW GUARDIANS, IS CUTTING OUR TIES TO THE GREAT HEART WISE?
...AS A DIFFERENT DECISION IS MADE.
THE EMOTIONAL POWER DROVE VOLTHOOM MAD.
HE WAS MAD BEFORE HE CAME TO OA.
I WAS NOT.
IF WE ARE TO WORK WITHIN THE EMOTIONAL SPECTRUM AND FORGE OUR POWER FROM IT, WE MUST BE IMMUNE TO IT.
BUT THEN WHAT?
OUR FELLOW GUARDIANS IN THE CHAMBER OF SHADOWS HAVE HELD ONTO THEIR EMOTIONS. WE SHOULD TOO.
YES... CONVINCE THEM, GANTHET. MY PUPPET...
WE CAME HERE TO SEVER OUR TIES TO OUR HEARTS... WE TELL OURSELVES IT IS SO WE CAN MAKE THE DECISIONS BEST FOR THE UNIVERSE...
BUT THE TRUTH IS, WE ARE ALL IN GREAT PAIN BECAUSE OF WHAT THE FIRST LANTERN HAS DONE. WE ARE FULL OF SORROW AND ANGER...BUT WE MUST CONFRONT THAT, NOT DENY IT.
WE MUST KEEP OUR SOULS INTACT.
WE MUST PUSH ON.
WE MUST NOT BE AFRAID TO FEEL.
AGREED.

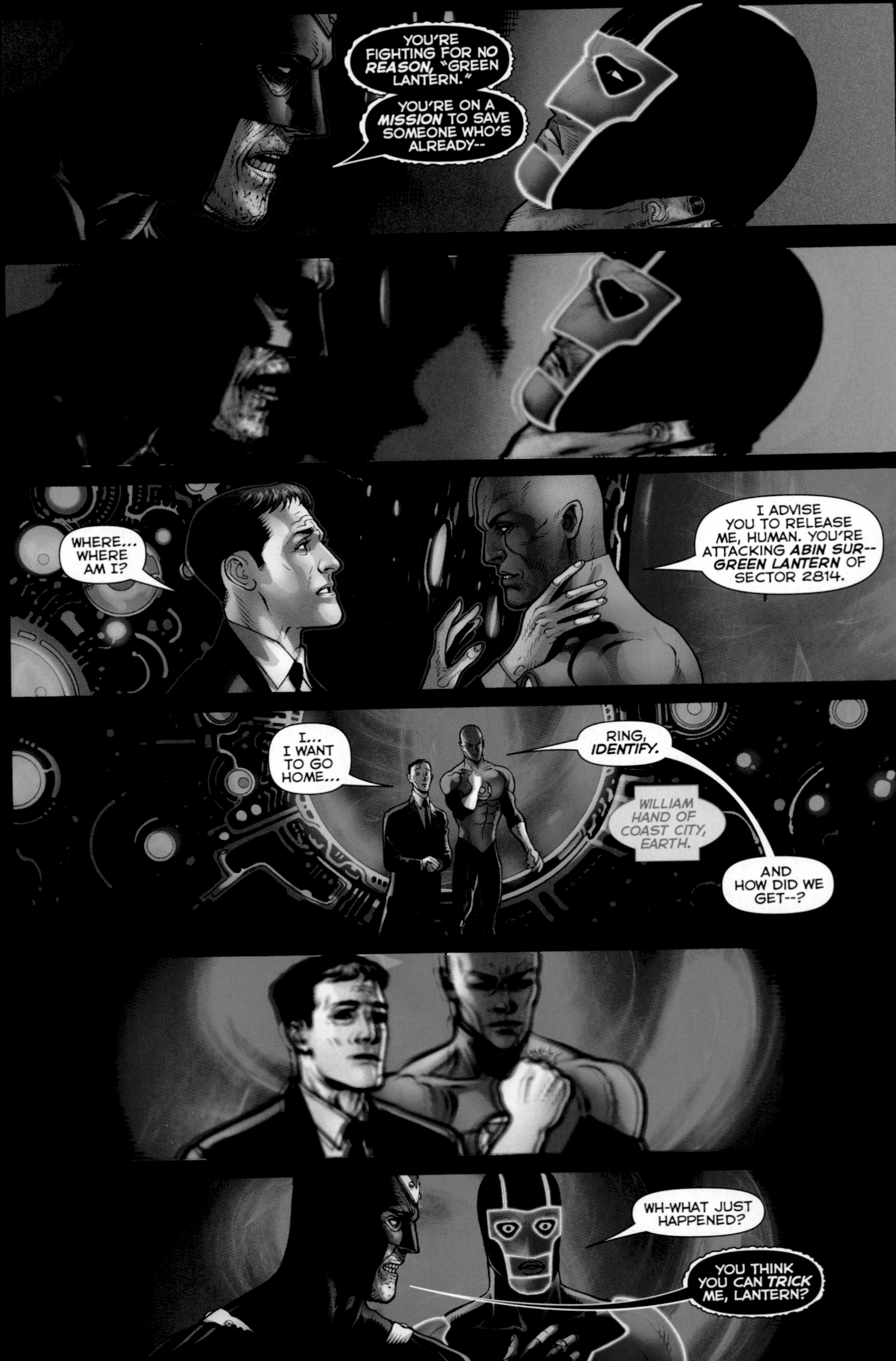
YOU'RE FIGHTING FOR NO REASON, "GREEN LANTERN."
YOU'RE ON A MISSION TO SAVE SOMEONE WHO'S ALREADY--
WHERE... WHERE AM I?
I ADVISE YOU TO RELEASE ME, HUMAN. YOU'RE ATTACKING ABIN SUR--GREEN LANTERN OF SECTOR 2814.
I... I WANT TO GO HOME...
RING, IDENTIFY.
WILLIAM HAND OF COAST CITY, EARTH.
AND HOW DID WE GET--?
WH-WHAT JUST HAPPENED?
YOU THINK YOU CAN TRICK ME, LANTERN?

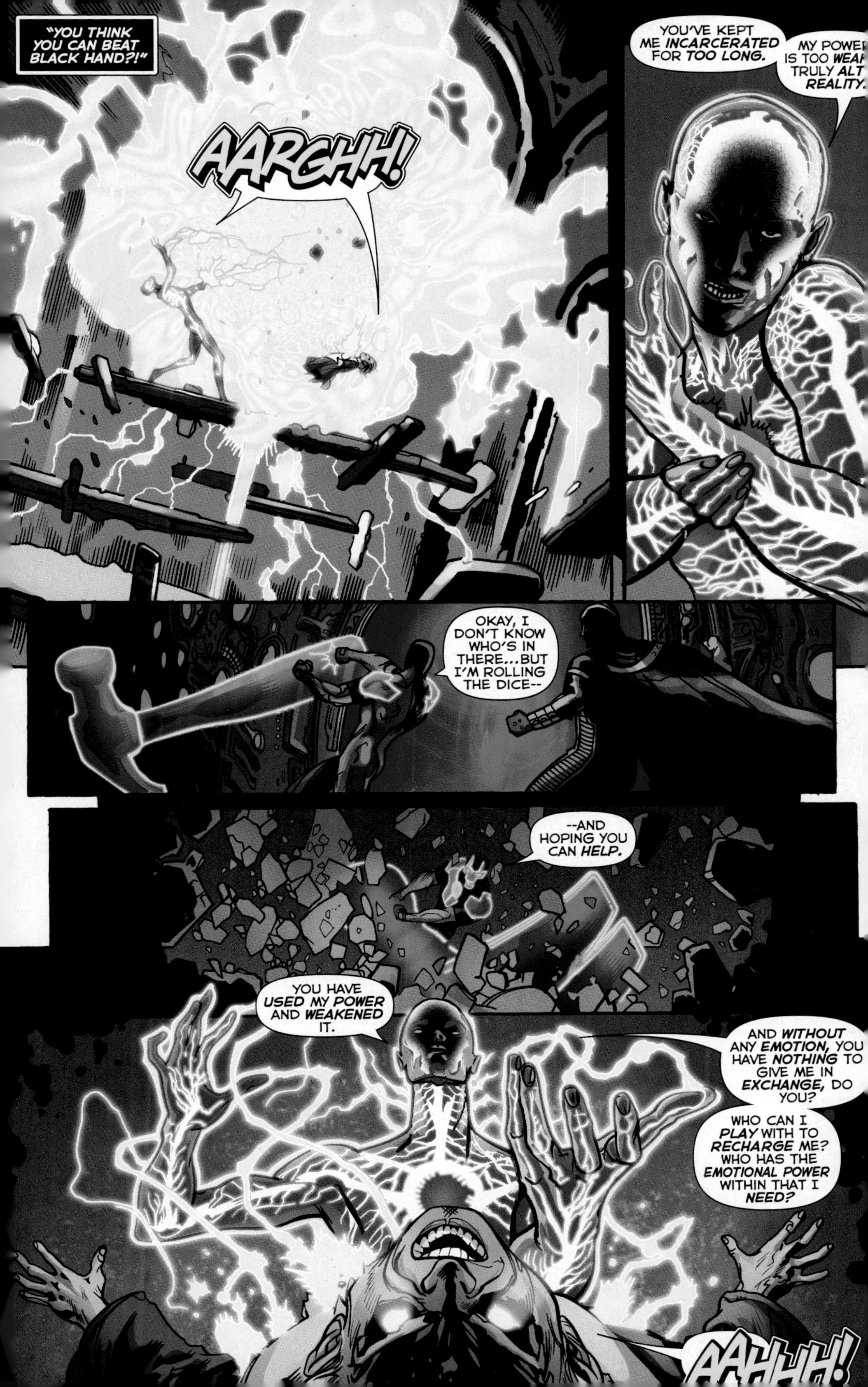
"YOU THINK YOU CAN BEAT BLACK HAND?!"
AARGHH!
YOU'VE KEPT ME INCARCERATED FOR TOO LONG.
MY POWE IS TOO WEA TRULY ALT REALITY.
OKAY, I DON'T KNOW WHO'S IN THERE...BUT I'M ROLLING THE DICE--
--AND HOPING YOU CAN HELP.
YOU HAVE USED MY POWER AND WEAKENED IT.
AND WITHOUT ANY EMOTION, YOU HAVE NOTHING TO GIVE ME IN EXCHANGE, DO YOU?
WHO CAN I PLAY WITH TO RECHARGE ME? WHO HAS THE EMOTIONAL POWER WITHIN THAT I NEED?
AAHHH!

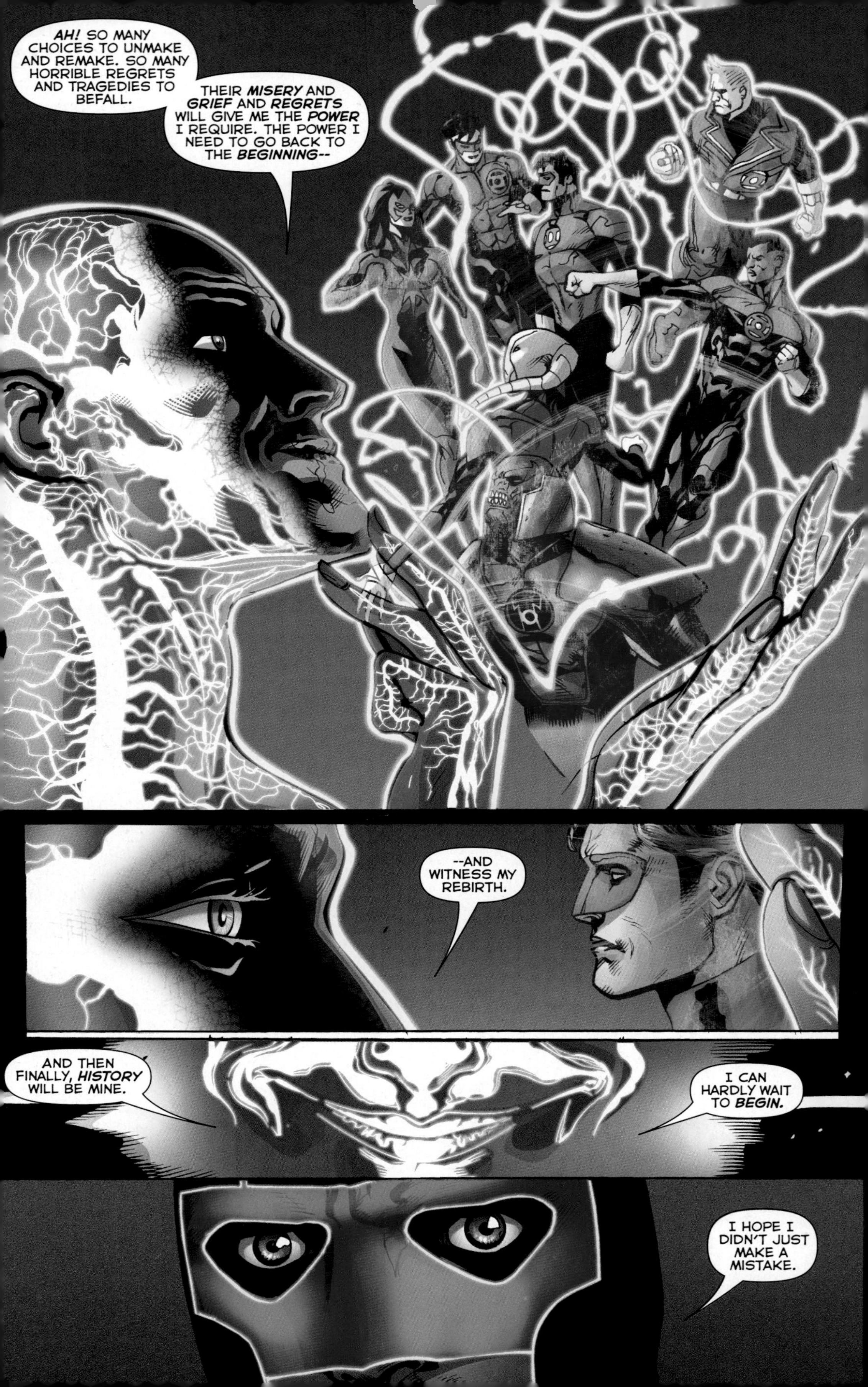
AH! SO MANY CHOICES TO UNMAKE AND REMAKE. SO MANY HORRIBLE REGRETS AND TRAGEDIES TO BEFALL.
THEIR MISERY AND GRIEF AND REGRETS WILL GIVE ME THE POWER I REQUIRE. THE POWER I NEED TO GO BACK TO THE BEGINNING--
--AND WITNESS MY REBIRTH.
AND THEN FINALLY, HISTORY WILL BE MINE.
I CAN HARDLY WAIT TO BEGIN.
I HOPE I DIDN'T JUST MAKE A MISTAKE.

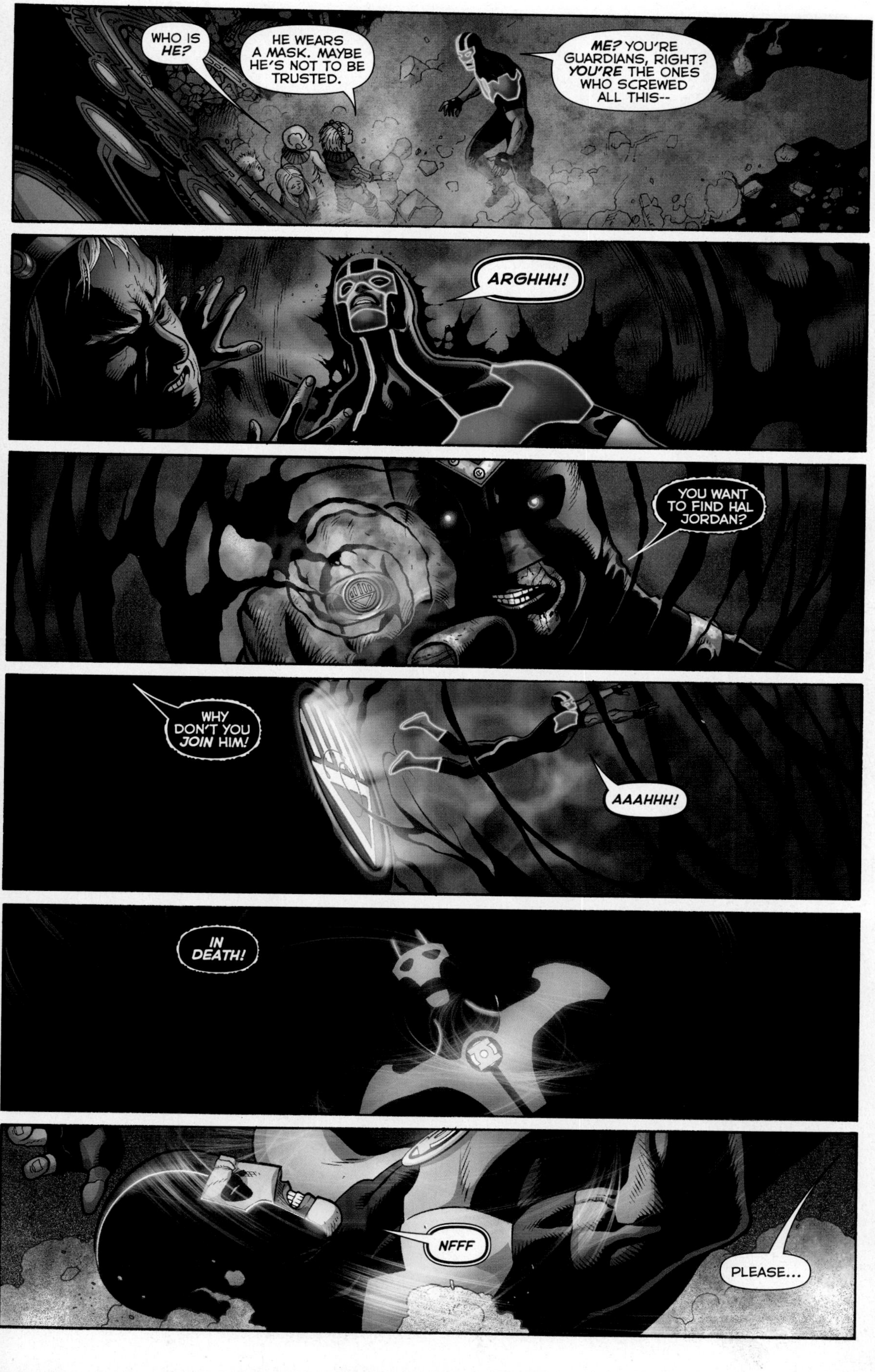
WHO IS HE?
HE WEARS A MASK. MAYBE HE'S NOT TO BE TRUSTED.
ME? YOU'RE GUARDIANS, RIGHT? YOU'RE THE ONES WHO SCREWED ALL THIS--
ARGHHH!
YOU WANT TO FIND HAL JORDAN?
WHY DON'T YOU JOIN HIM!
AAAHHH!
IN DEATH!
NFFF
PLEASE...

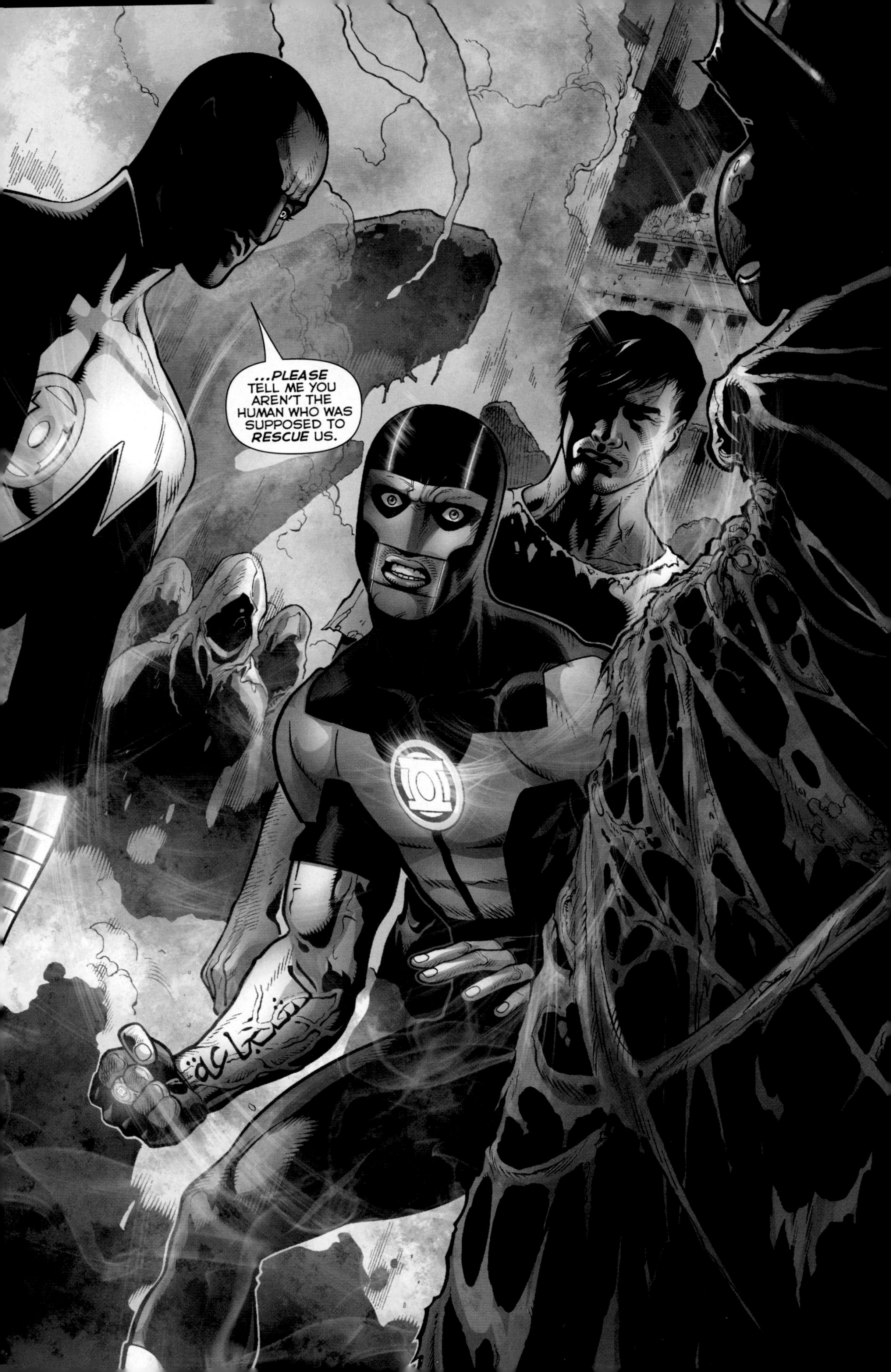
...PLEASE TELL ME YOU AREN'T THE HUMAN WHO WAS SUPPOSED TO RESCUE US.

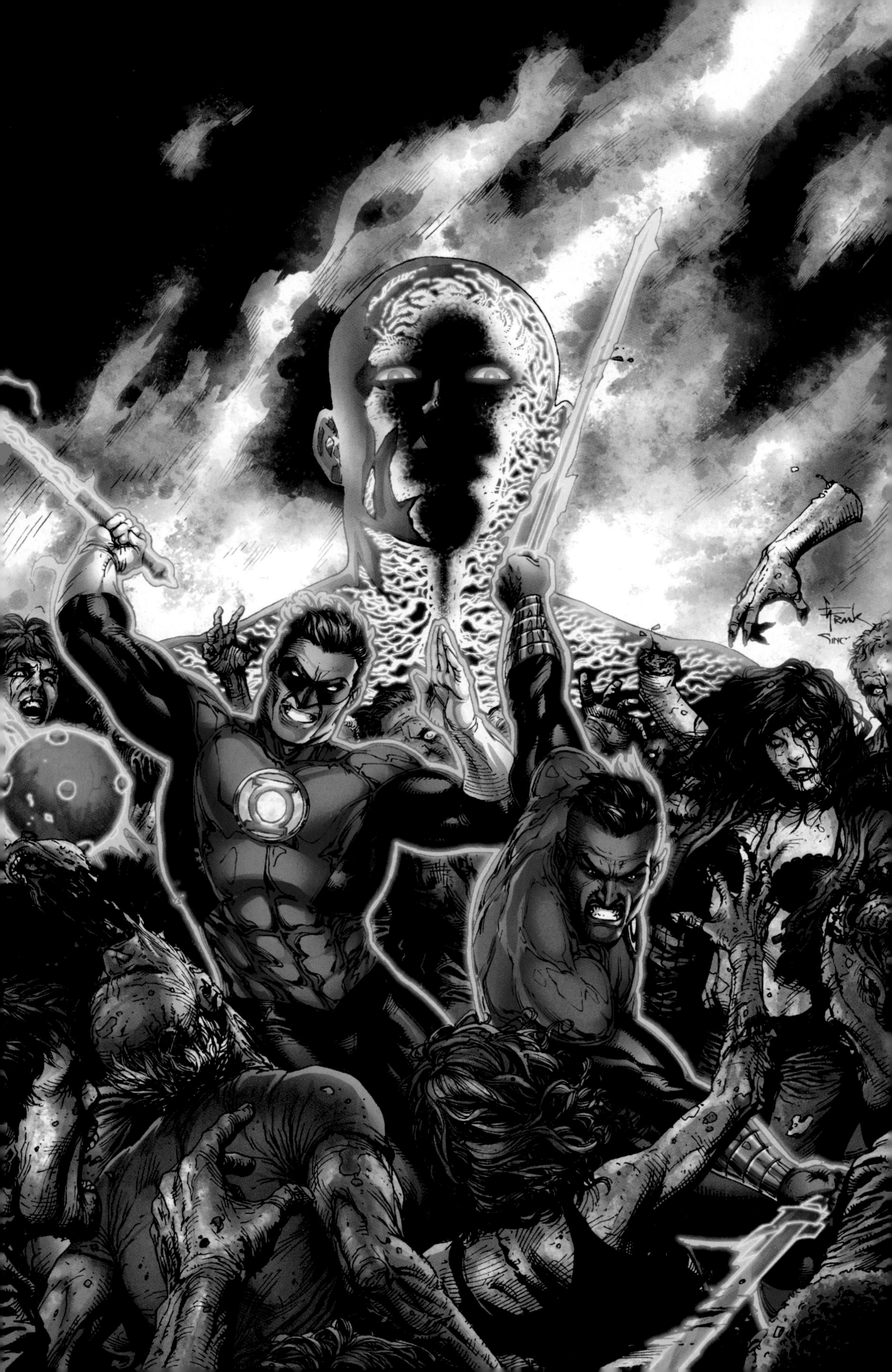

GEOFF JOHNS writer **SZYMON KUDRANSKI** artist – main sequence **ARDIAN SYAF** penciller – Chamber of Shadows sequence
MARK IRWIN inker – Chamber of Shadows sequence **GARY FRANK & ALEX SINCLAIR** cover

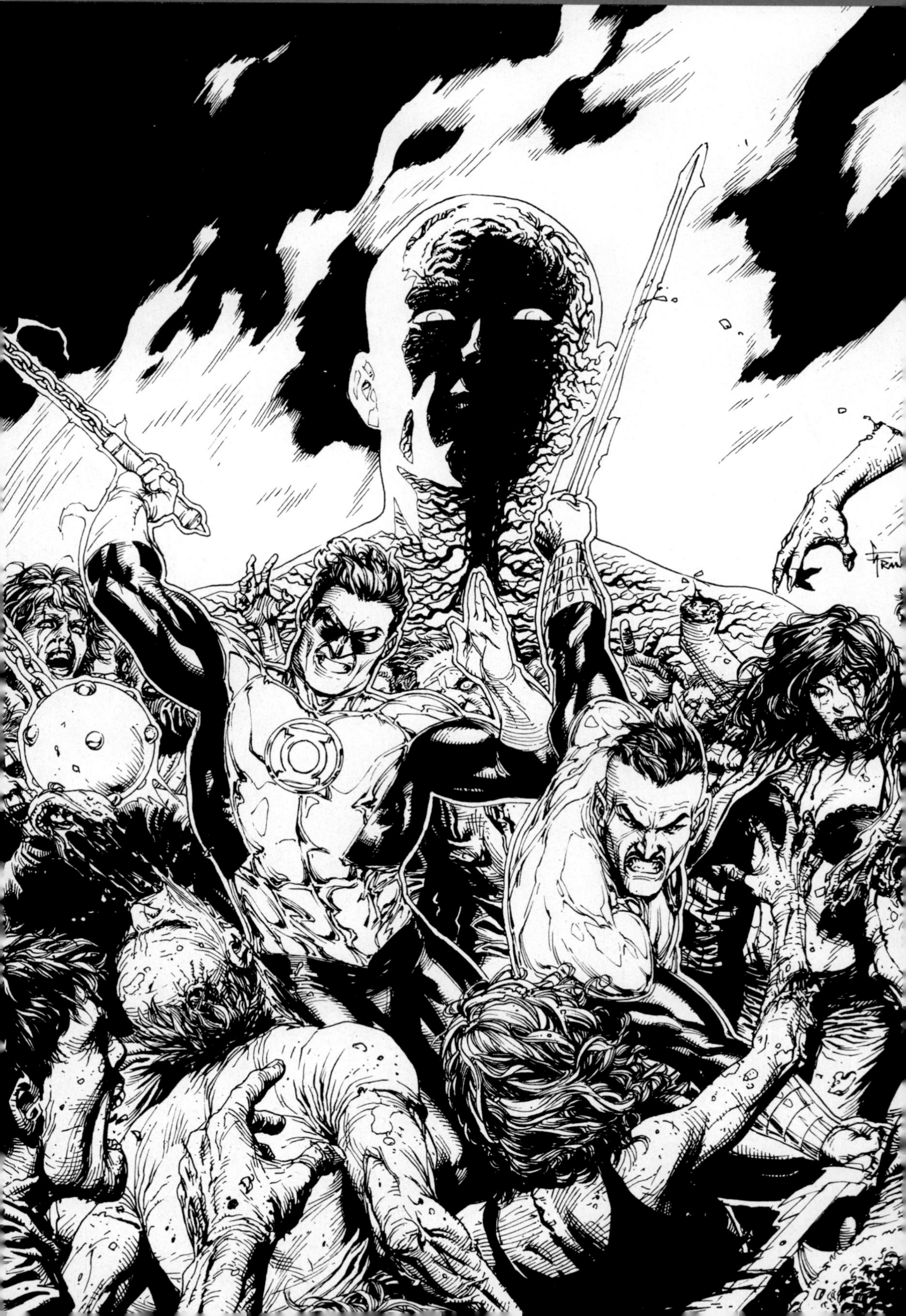

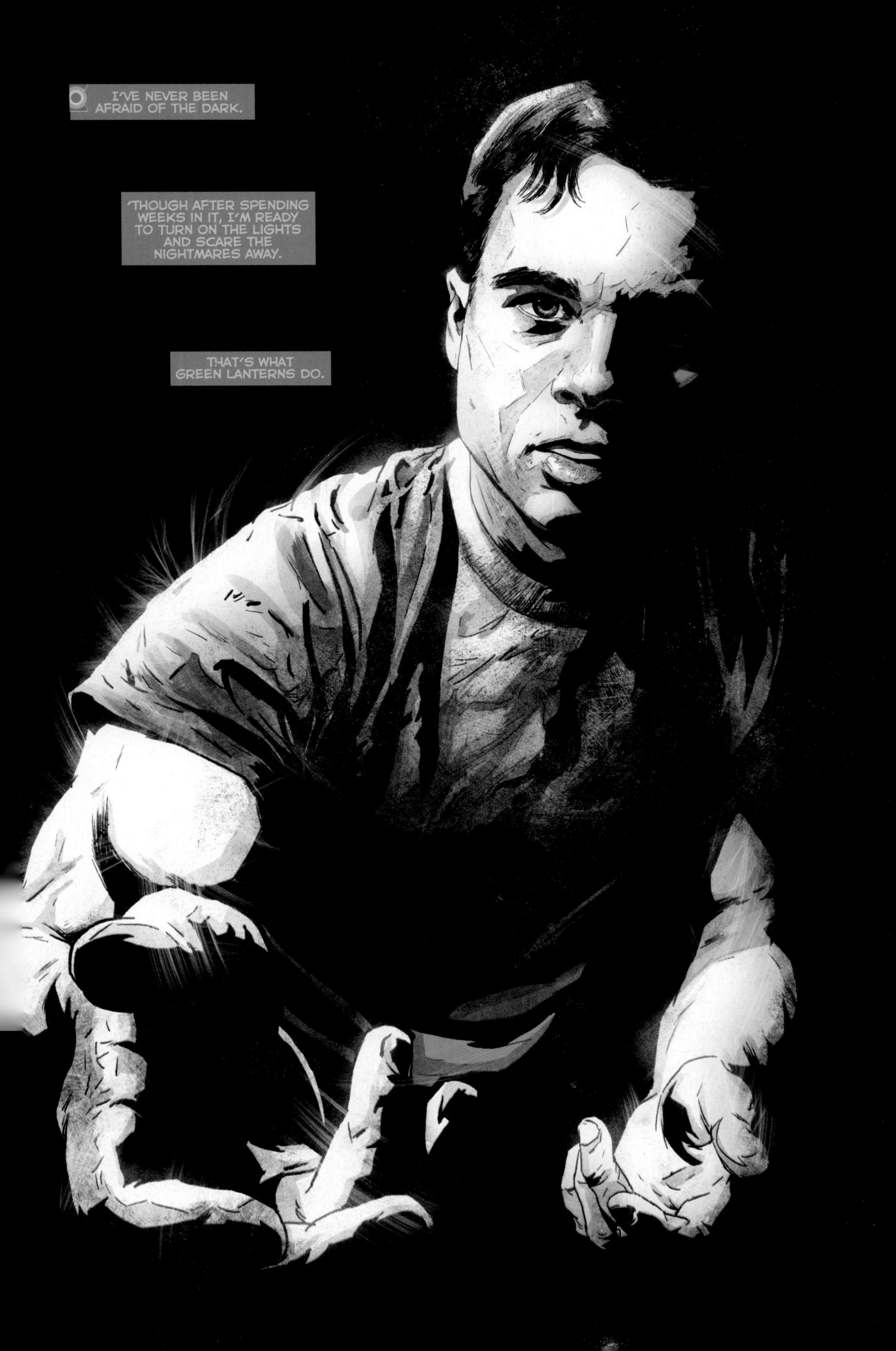
I'VE NEVER BEEN AFRAID OF THE DARK.
'THOUGH AFTER SPENDING WEEKS IN IT, I'M READY TO TURN ON THE LIGHTS AND SCARE THE NIGHTMARES AWAY.
THAT'S WHAT GREEN LANTERNS DO.

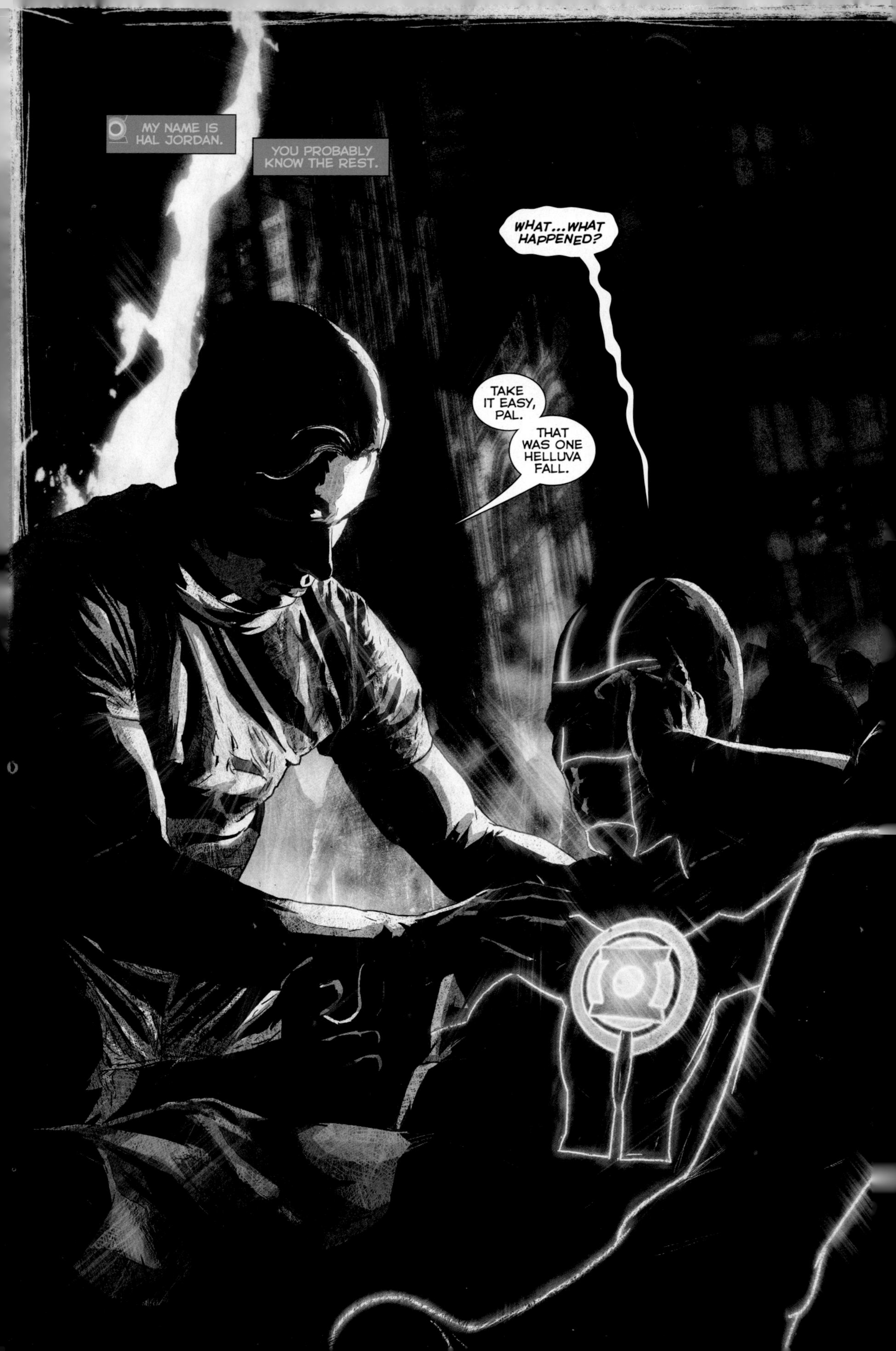
MY NAME IS HAL JORDAN.
YOU PROBABLY KNOW THE REST.
WHAT...WHAT HAPPENED?
TAKE IT EASY, PAL.
THAT WAS ONE HELLUVA FALL.

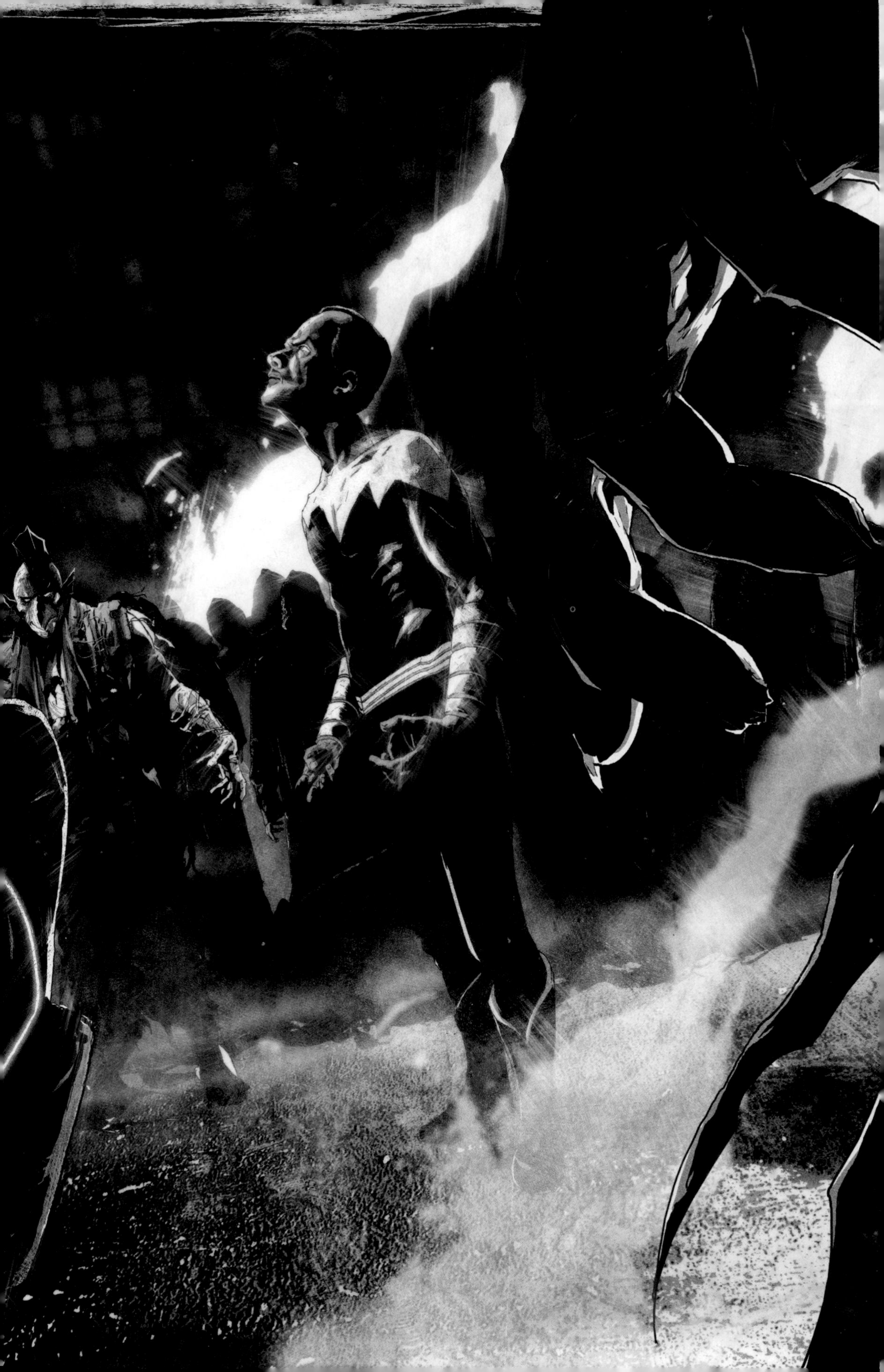

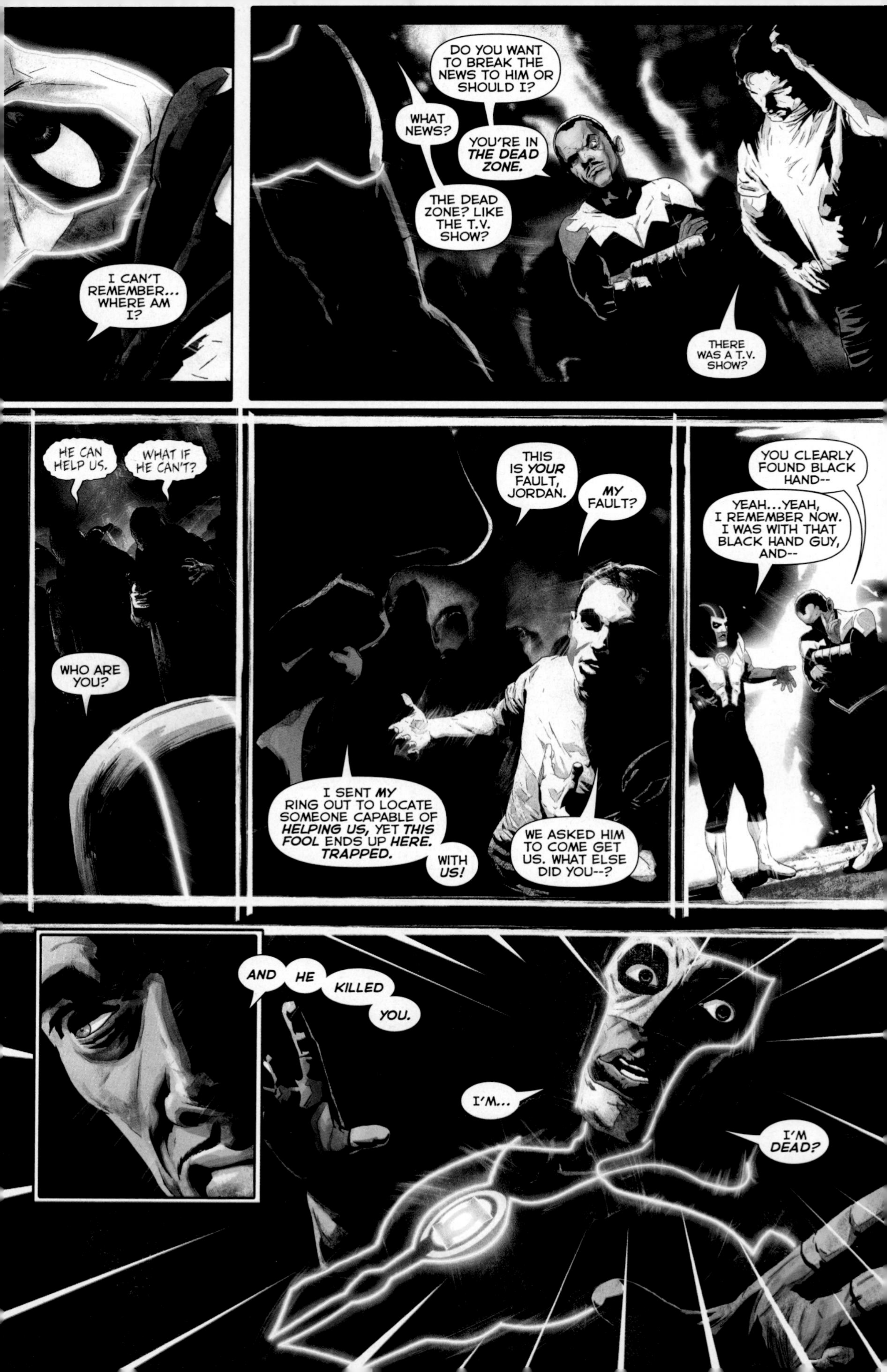
I CAN'T REMEMBER... WHERE AM I?
DO YOU WANT TO BREAK THE NEWS TO HIM OR SHOULD I?
WHAT NEWS?
YOU'RE IN *THE DEAD ZONE.*
THE DEAD ZONE? LIKE THE T.V. SHOW?
THERE WAS A T.V. SHOW?
HE CAN HELP US.
WHAT IF HE CAN'T?
WHO ARE YOU?
THIS IS *YOUR* FAULT, JORDAN.
MY FAULT?
I SENT *MY* RING OUT TO LOCATE SOMEONE CAPABLE OF *HELPING US,* YET *THIS FOOL* ENDS UP *HERE. TRAPPED.*
WITH *US!*
WE ASKED HIM TO COME GET US. WHAT ELSE DID YOU--?
YOU CLEARLY FOUND BLACK HAND--
YEAH...YEAH, I REMEMBER NOW. I WAS WITH THAT BLACK HAND GUY, AND--
AND HE KILLED YOU.
I'M...
I'M *DEAD?*

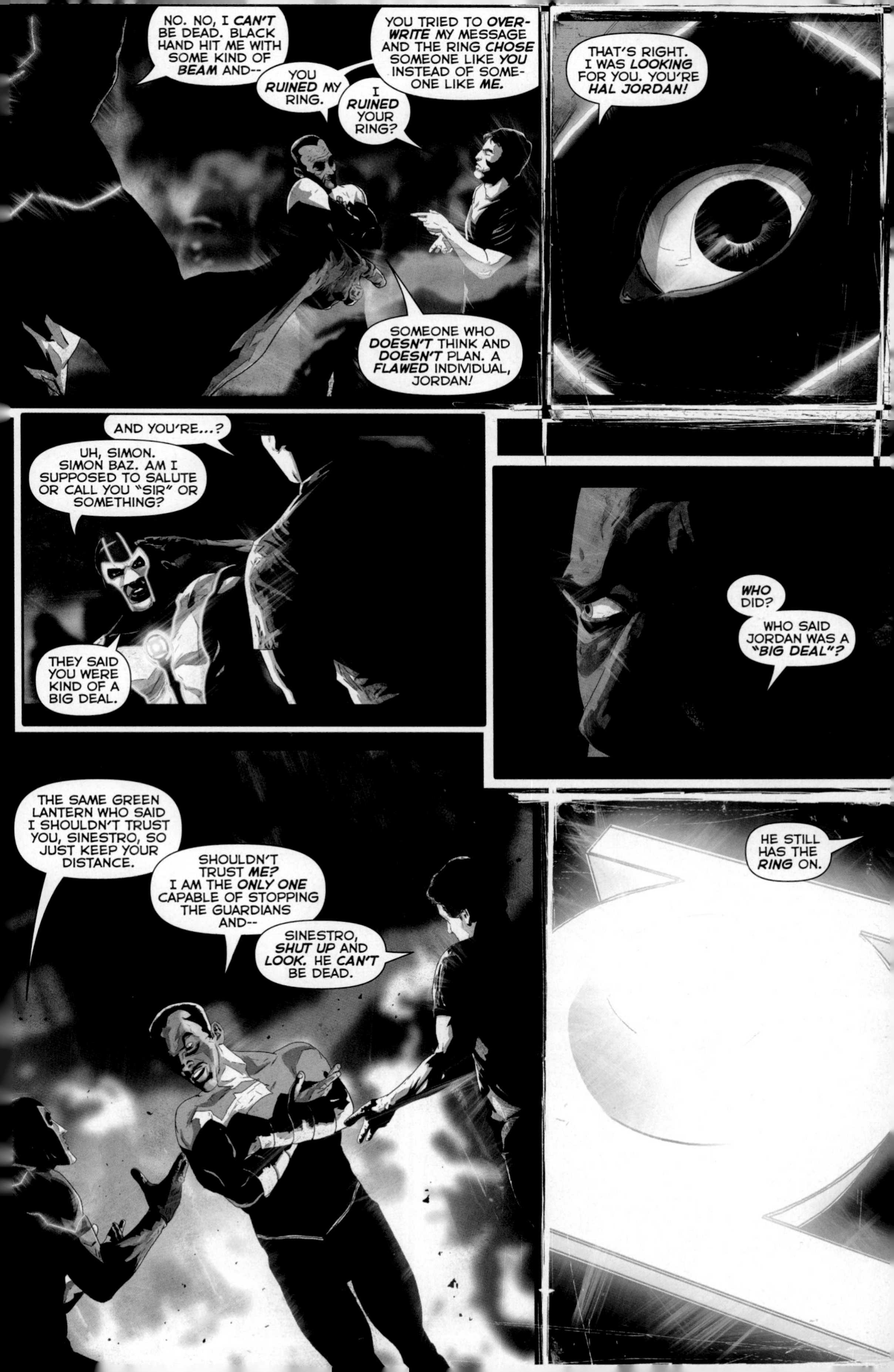
NO. NO, I CAN'T BE DEAD. BLACK HAND HIT ME WITH SOME KIND OF BEAM AND--
YOU RUINED MY RING.
YOU TRIED TO OVER-WRITE MY MESSAGE AND THE RING CHOSE SOMEONE LIKE YOU INSTEAD OF SOME-ONE LIKE ME.
I RUINED YOUR RING?
SOMEONE WHO DOESN'T THINK AND DOESN'T PLAN. A FLAWED INDIVIDUAL, JORDAN!
THAT'S RIGHT. I WAS LOOKING FOR YOU. YOU'RE HAL JORDAN!
AND YOU'RE...?
UH, SIMON. SIMON BAZ. AM I SUPPOSED TO SALUTE OR CALL YOU "SIR" OR SOMETHING?
THEY SAID YOU WERE KIND OF A BIG DEAL.
WHO DID?
WHO SAID JORDAN WAS A "BIG DEAL"?
THE SAME GREEN LANTERN WHO SAID I SHOULDN'T TRUST YOU, SINESTRO, SO JUST KEEP YOUR DISTANCE.
SHOULDN'T TRUST ME? I AM THE ONLY ONE CAPABLE OF STOPPING THE GUARDIANS AND--
SINESTRO, SHUT UP AND LOOK. HE CAN'T BE DEAD.
HE STILL HAS THE RING ON.

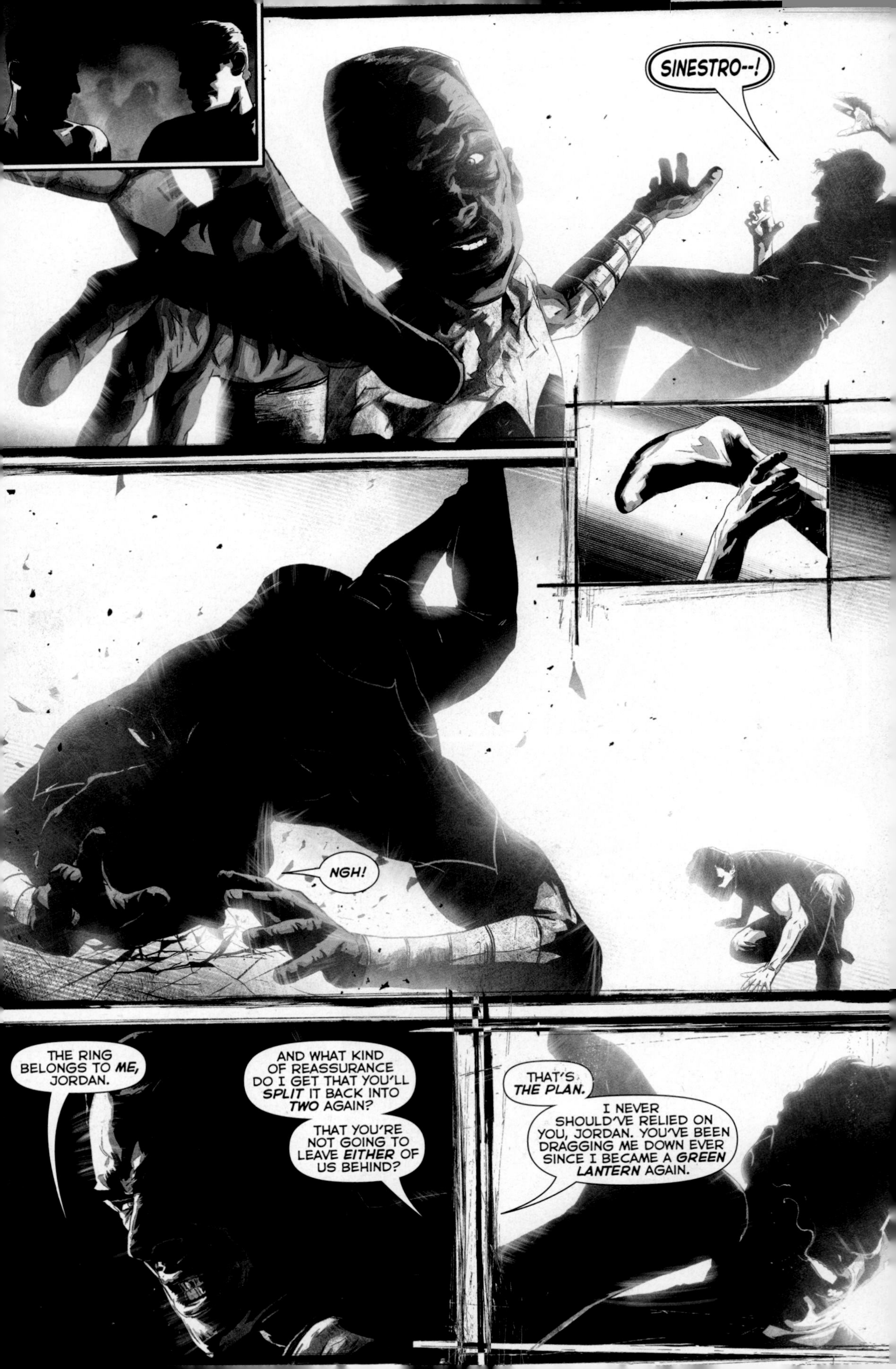
SINESTRO--!
NGH!
THE RING BELONGS TO ME, JORDAN.
AND WHAT KIND OF REASSURANCE DO I GET THAT YOU'LL SPLIT IT BACK INTO TWO AGAIN?
THAT YOU'RE NOT GOING TO LEAVE EITHER OF US BEHIND?
THAT'S THE PLAN.
I NEVER SHOULD'VE RELIED ON YOU, JORDAN. YOU'VE BEEN DRAGGING ME DOWN EVER SINCE I BECAME A GREEN LANTERN AGAIN.

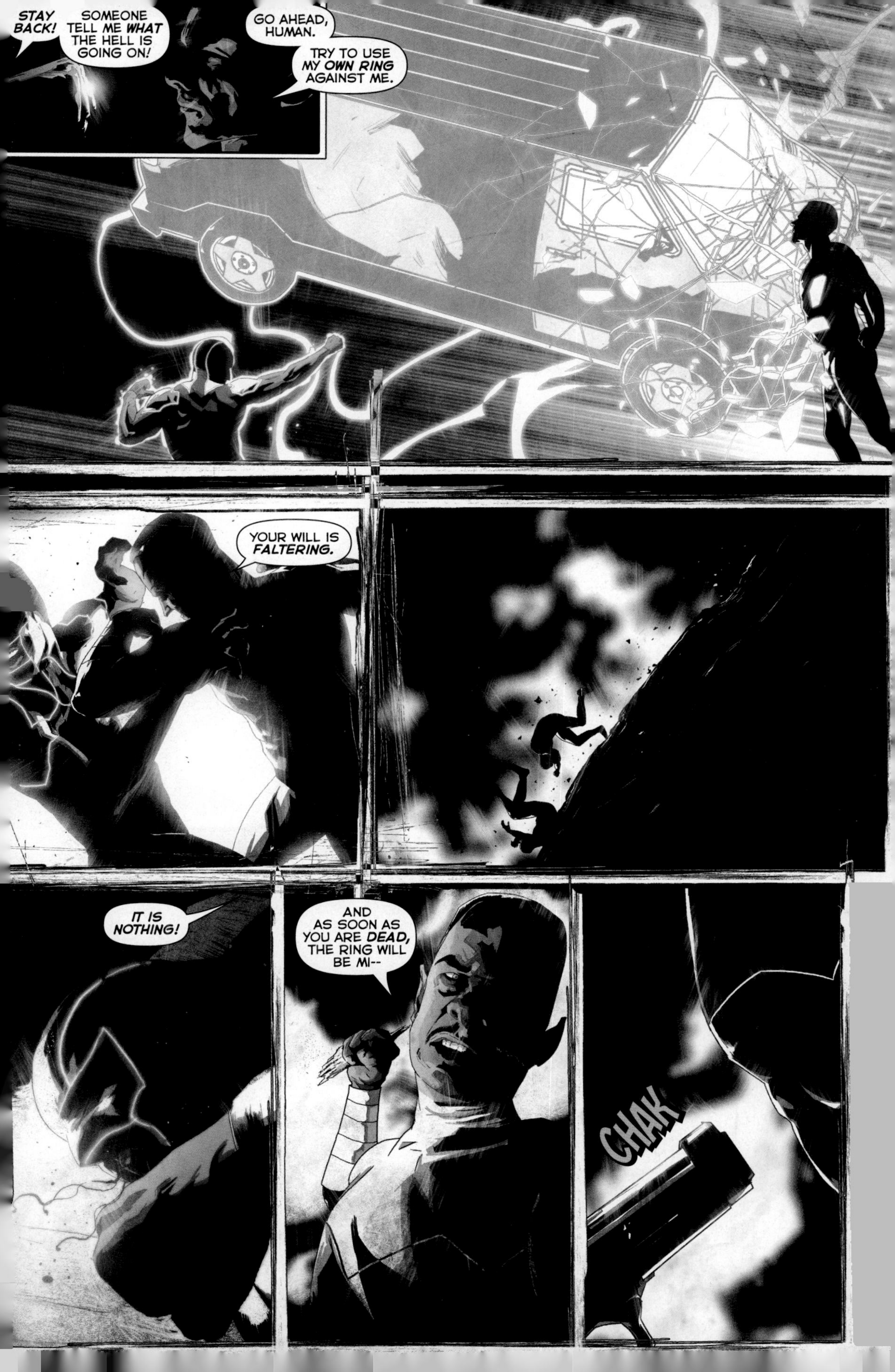
STAY BACK!
SOMEONE TELL ME WHAT THE HELL IS GOING ON!
GO AHEAD, HUMAN.
TRY TO USE MY OWN RING AGAINST ME.
YOUR WILL IS FALTERING.
IT IS NOTHING!
AND AS SOON AS YOU ARE DEAD, THE RING WILL BE MI--
CHAK

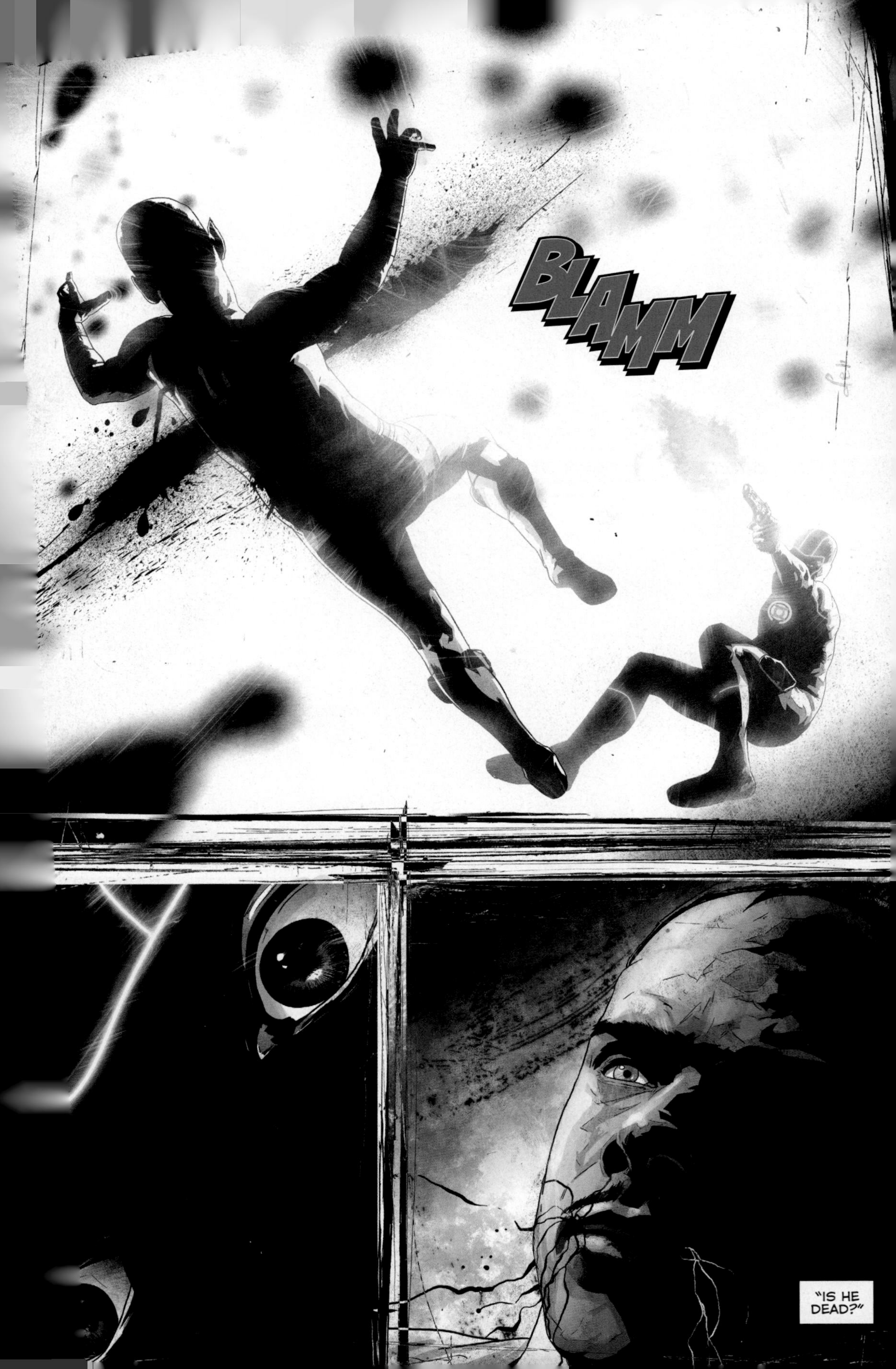
BLAMM
"IS HE DEAD?"

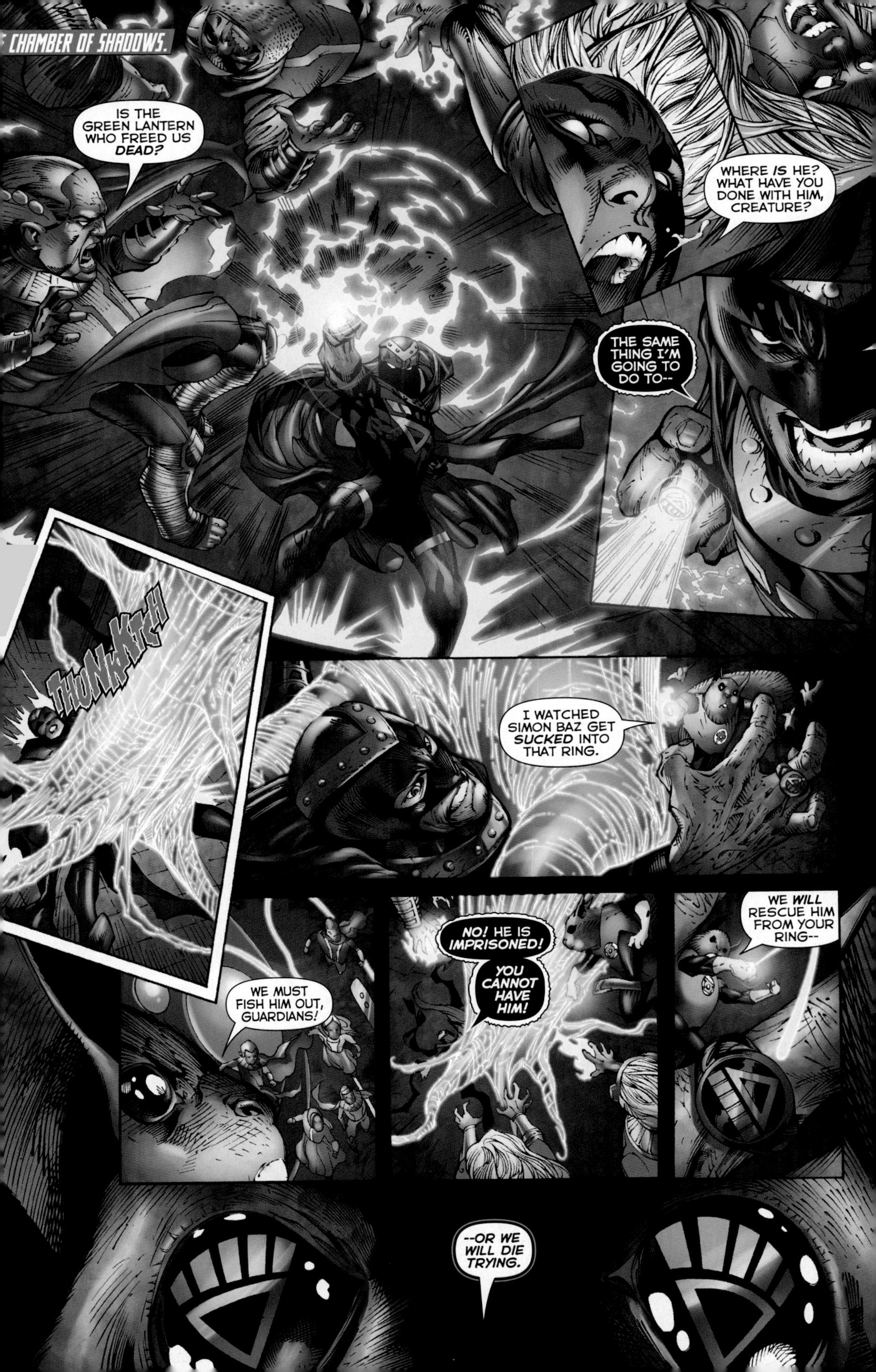
CHAMBER OF SHADOWS.
IS THE GREEN LANTERN WHO FREED US DEAD?
WHERE IS HE? WHAT HAVE YOU DONE WITH HIM, CREATURE?
THE SAME THING I'M GOING TO DO TO--
THUNKKTCH
I WATCHED SIMON BAZ GET SUCKED INTO THAT RING.
WE MUST FISH HIM OUT, GUARDIANS!
NO! HE IS IMPRISONED!
YOU CANNOT HAVE HIM!
WE WILL RESCUE HIM FROM YOUR RING--
--OR WE WILL DIE TRYING.

PERHAPS SINESTRO WAS INCORRECT REGARDING THE RING'S *CHOICE* OF INDIVIDUAL. HE MAY BE MORE LIKE SINESTRO THAN WE THOUGHT.

I... I THOUGHT HE WAS GOING TO *KILL* ME.

IS SINESTRO DEAD, TOMAR?

YES.

BUT AS I SAID BEFORE, HAL, WE'RE *ALL* DEAD IN HERE. UNLIKE ME, HOWEVER, YOU AND SINESTRO AND SIMON BAZ STILL HAVE *ONE FOOT* PLANTED ON THE *OTHER SIDE.*

NNGGK!

YOU *SEE?* YOU CANNOT *DIE* IN HERE AS LONG AS YOU HAVE THE *WILL* TO LIVE.

HEY, MAN, UH, SORRY ABOUT THAT?

JUST YOU WAIT UNTIL THAT RING IS MINE AGAIN, HUMAN.

YOU HAVE MORE TO WORRY ABOUT THAN *PETTY REVENGE,* SINESTRO.

YOUR *EMOTIONAL* VOLATILITY HAS ALWAYS BEEN YOUR WEAKNESS.

AND *TRUSTING* IN OTHERS WAS YOURS, TOMAR-RE. YOU TRUSTED TOO FREELY. YOU PUT YOUR LIFE AND THE LIVES OF OTHERS INTO THE HANDS OF THOSE CLOSE TO YOU.

BUT THEY *FAILED* YOU AND YOU *DIED* AS A RESULT.

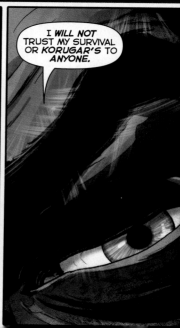

I WILL NOT TRUST MY SURVIVAL OR *KORUGAR'S* TO *ANYONE.*

AS LONG AS THE GUARDIANS BELIEVE I AM DEAD, MY PLANET IS SAFE.

NO PLANET IS SAFE, SINESTRO. NOT KORUGAR. NOT EARTH.

I'M TIRED OF LISTENING TO YOUR NONSENSE. WE KNOW FULL WELL THE GUARDIANS HAVE TURNED AGAINST THE UNIVERSE. EVEN NOW THEY--

THEY ARE AT SOMEONE ELSE'S MERCY, SINESTRO.

HOW DO YOU KNOW THAT?

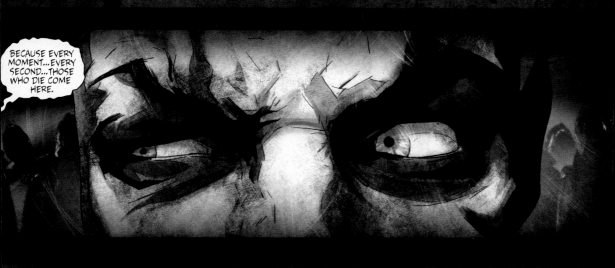

BECAUSE EVERY MOMENT...EVERY SECOND...THOSE WHO DIE COME HERE.

AND WORD SPREADS QUICKLY WHEN IT COMES TO VOLTHOOM.

THAT NAME AGAIN--AS IF IT WERE SUPPOSED TO MEAN SOMETHING TO US.

VOLTHOOM IS RESPONSIBLE FOR THE DEATH OF ALL THOSE YOU SEE HERE.

THOSE THINGS STARING AT US? THERE ARE MAYBE A HUNDRED--

A HUNDRED?

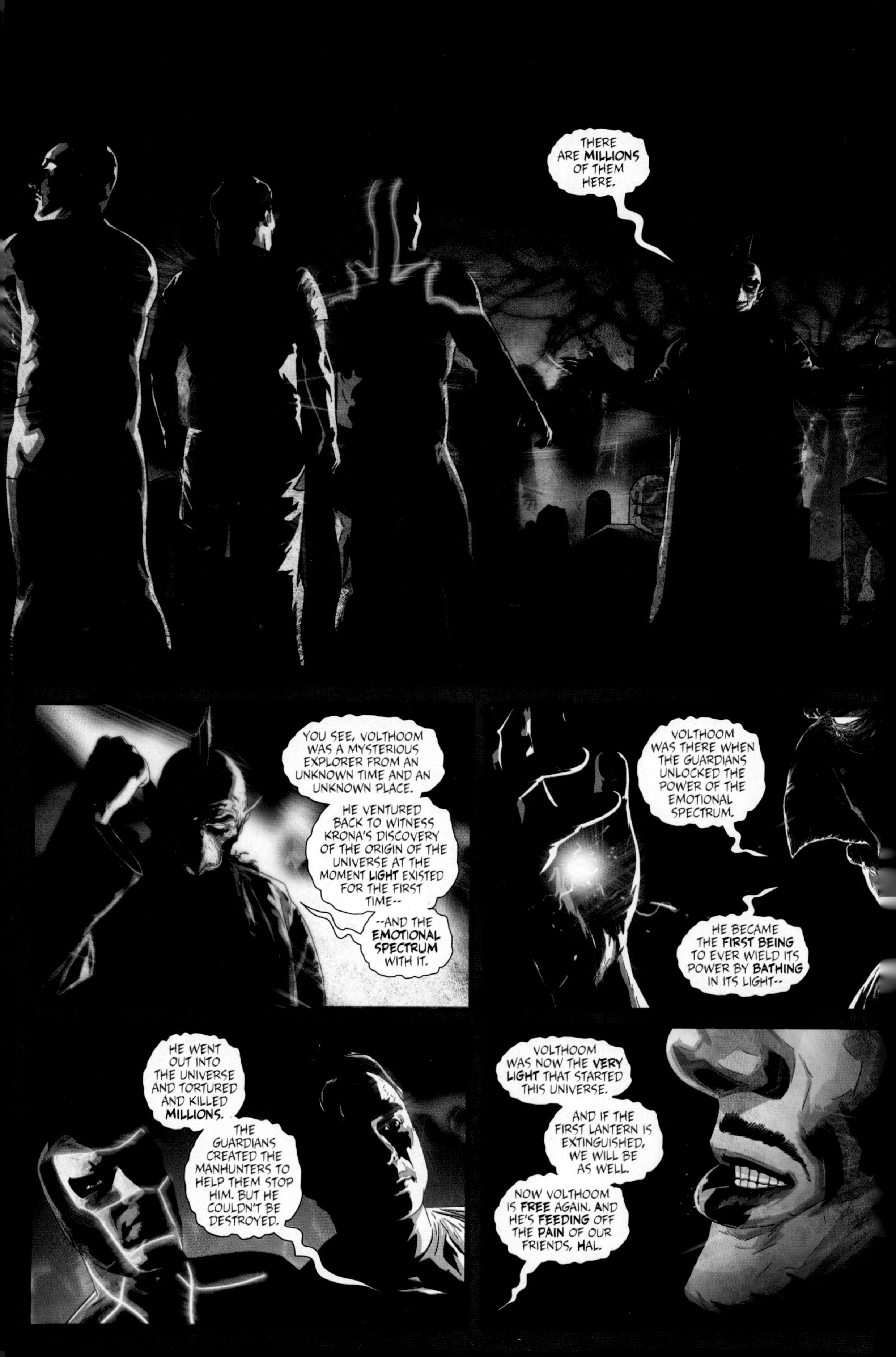
THERE ARE MILLIONS OF THEM HERE.
YOU SEE, VOLTHOOM WAS A MYSTERIOUS EXPLORER FROM AN UNKNOWN TIME AND AN UNKNOWN PLACE.
HE VENTURED BACK TO WITNESS KRONA'S DISCOVERY OF THE ORIGIN OF THE UNIVERSE AT THE MOMENT LIGHT EXISTED FOR THE FIRST TIME--
--AND THE EMOTIONAL SPECTRUM WITH IT.
VOLTHOOM WAS THERE WHEN THE GUARDIANS UNLOCKED THE POWER OF THE EMOTIONAL SPECTRUM.
HE BECAME THE FIRST BEING TO EVER WIELD ITS POWER BY BATHING IN ITS LIGHT--
HE WENT OUT INTO THE UNIVERSE AND TORTURED AND KILLED MILLIONS.
THE GUARDIANS CREATED THE MANHUNTERS TO HELP THEM STOP HIM. BUT HE COULDN'T BE DESTROYED.
VOLTHOOM WAS NOW THE VERY LIGHT THAT STARTED THIS UNIVERSE.
AND IF THE FIRST LANTERN IS EXTINGUISHED, WE WILL BE AS WELL.
NOW VOLTHOOM IS FREE AGAIN. AND HE'S FEEDING OFF THE PAIN OF OUR FRIENDS, HAL.

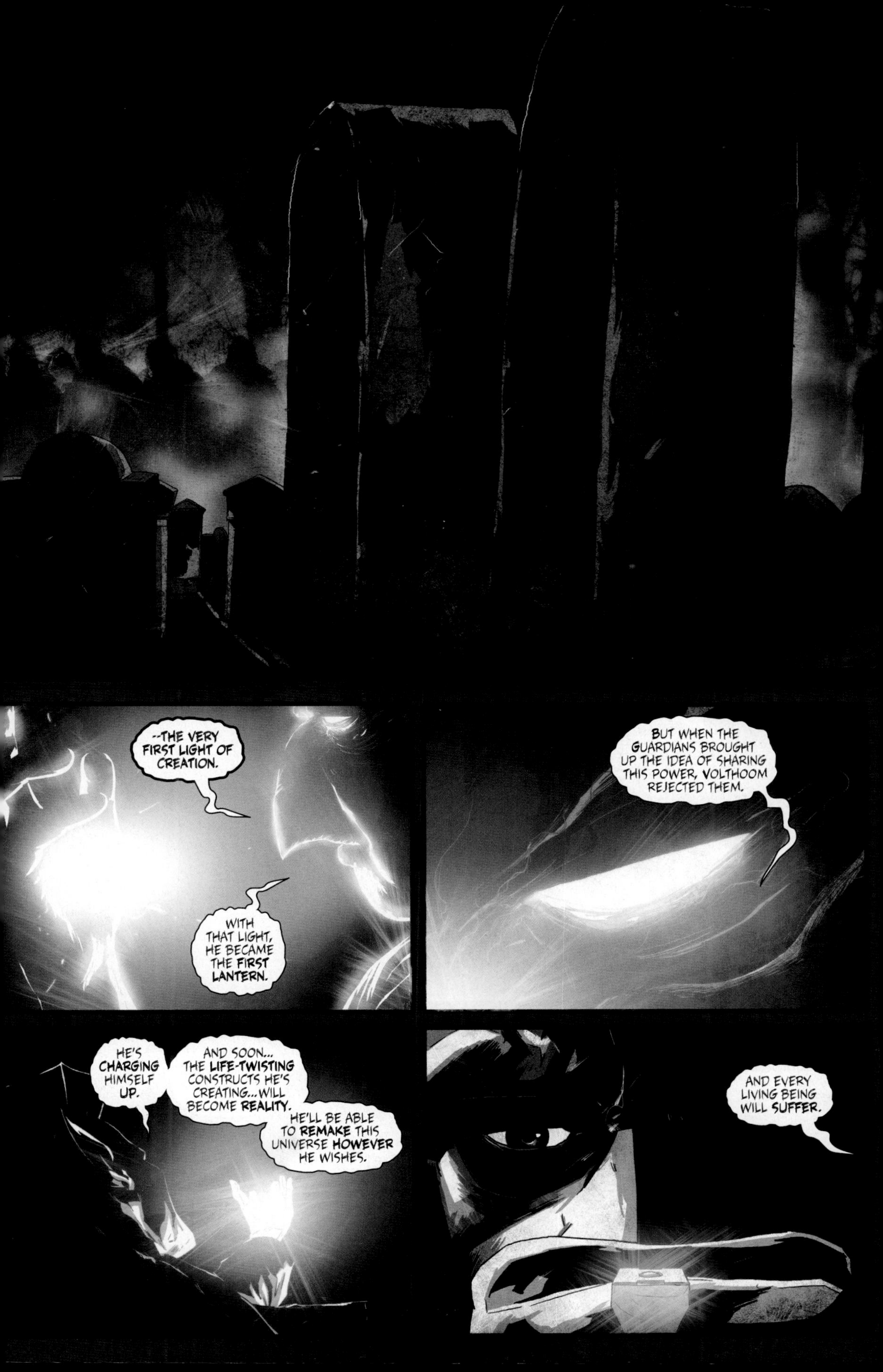
--THE VERY FIRST LIGHT OF CREATION.
WITH THAT LIGHT, HE BECAME THE FIRST LANTERN.
BUT WHEN THE GUARDIANS BROUGHT UP THE IDEA OF SHARING THIS POWER, VOLTHOOM REJECTED THEM.
HE'S CHARGING HIMSELF UP.
AND SOON... THE LIFE-TWISTING CONSTRUCTS HE'S CREATING...WILL BECOME REALITY.
HE'LL BE ABLE TO REMAKE THIS UNIVERSE HOWEVER HE WISHES.
AND EVERY LIVING BEING WILL SUFFER.

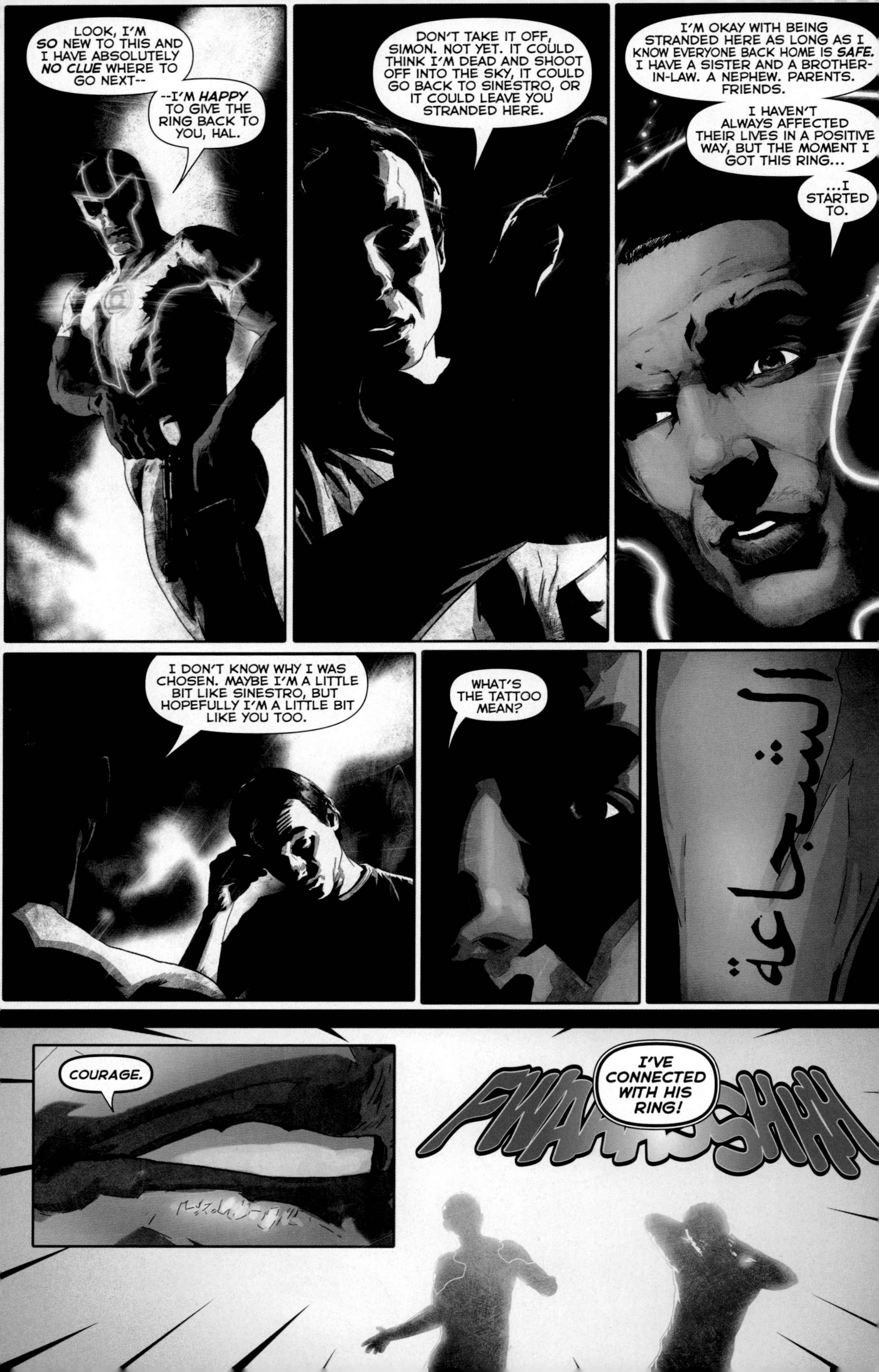
LOOK, I'M SO NEW TO THIS AND I HAVE ABSOLUTELY NO CLUE WHERE TO GO NEXT--
--I'M HAPPY TO GIVE THE RING BACK TO YOU, HAL.
DON'T TAKE IT OFF, SIMON. NOT YET. IT COULD THINK I'M DEAD AND SHOOT OFF INTO THE SKY, IT COULD GO BACK TO SINESTRO, OR IT COULD LEAVE YOU STRANDED HERE.
I'M OKAY WITH BEING STRANDED HERE AS LONG AS I KNOW EVERYONE BACK HOME IS SAFE. I HAVE A SISTER AND A BROTHER-IN-LAW. A NEPHEW. PARENTS. FRIENDS.
I HAVEN'T ALWAYS AFFECTED THEIR LIVES IN A POSITIVE WAY, BUT THE MOMENT I GOT THIS RING...
...I STARTED TO.
I DON'T KNOW WHY I WAS CHOSEN. MAYBE I'M A LITTLE BIT LIKE SINESTRO, BUT HOPEFULLY I'M A LITTLE BIT LIKE YOU TOO.
WHAT'S THE TATTOO MEAN?
الشجاعة
COURAGE.
I'VE CONNECTED WITH HIS RING!

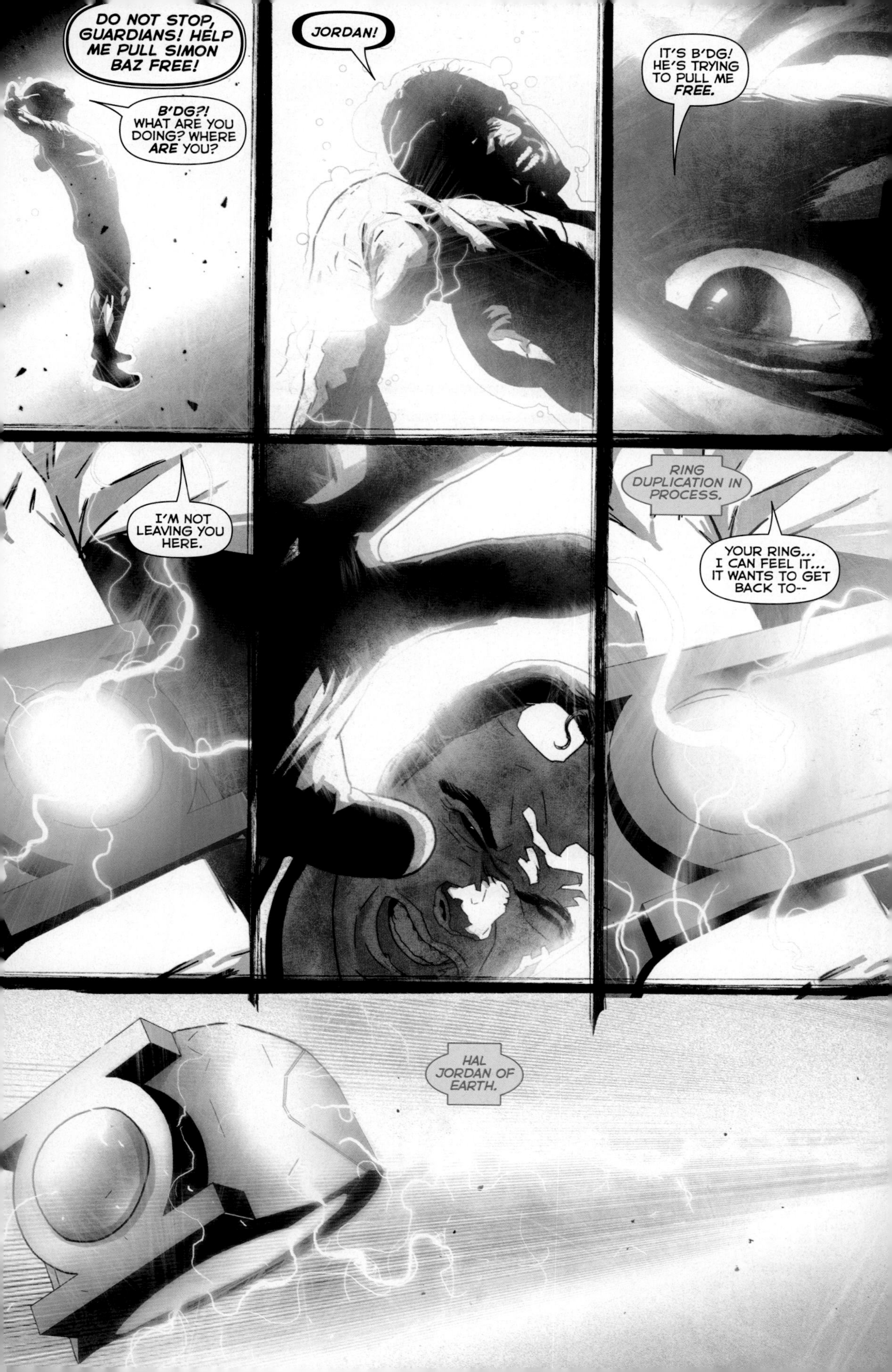
DO NOT STOP, GUARDIANS! HELP ME PULL SIMON BAZ FREE!
B'DG?! WHAT ARE YOU DOING? WHERE ARE YOU?
JORDAN!
IT'S B'DG! HE'S TRYING TO PULL ME FREE.
I'M NOT LEAVING YOU HERE.
RING DUPLICATION IN PROCESS.
YOUR RING... I CAN FEEL IT... IT WANTS TO GET BACK TO--
HAL JORDAN OF EARTH.

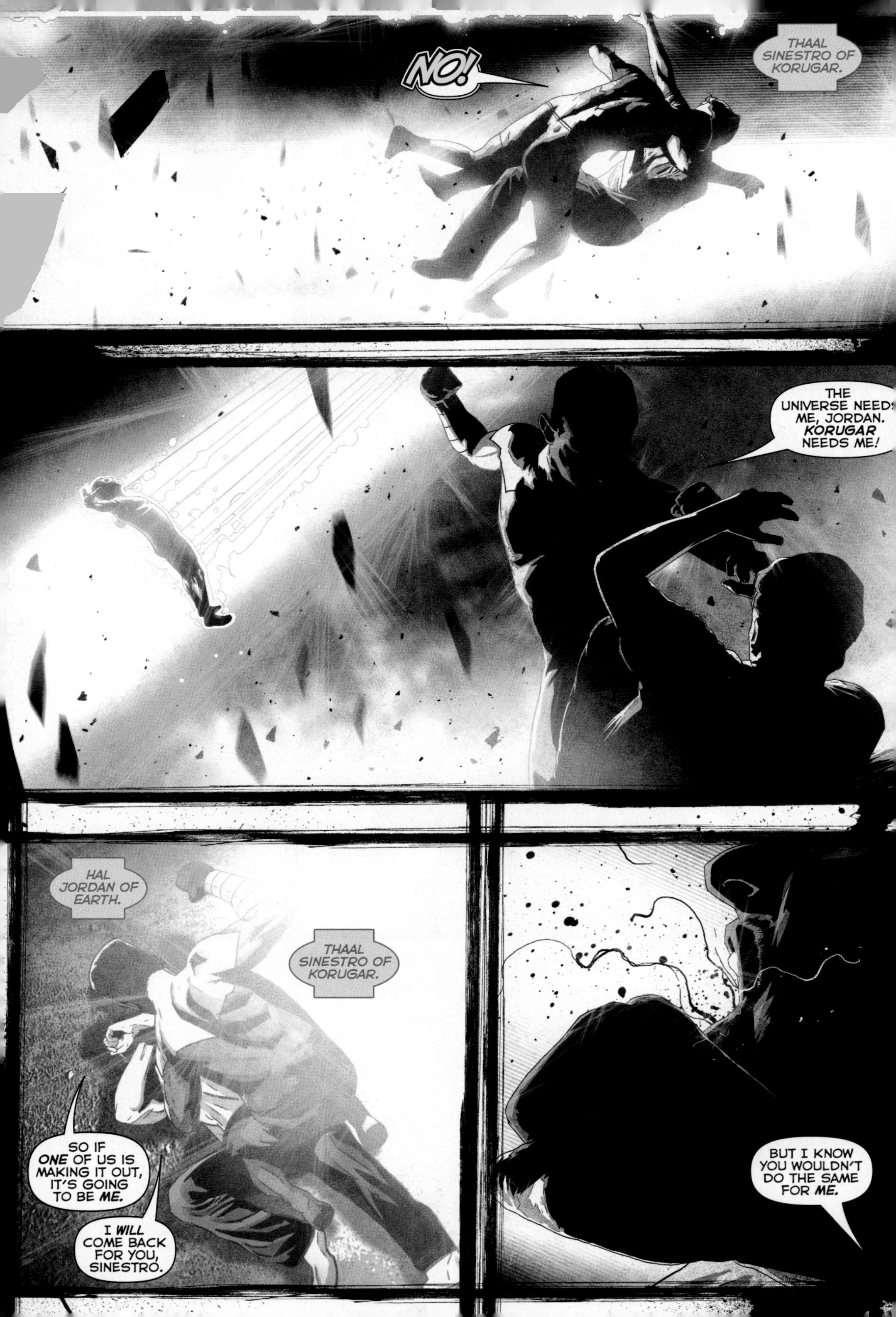
THAAL SINESTRO OF KORUGAR.
NO!
THE UNIVERSE NEEDS ME, JORDAN. KORUGAR NEEDS ME!
HAL JORDAN OF EARTH.
THAAL SINESTRO OF KORUGAR.
SO IF ONE OF US IS MAKING IT OUT, IT'S GOING TO BE ME.
I WILL COME BACK FOR YOU, SINESTRO.
BUT I KNOW YOU WOULDN'T DO THE SAME FOR ME.

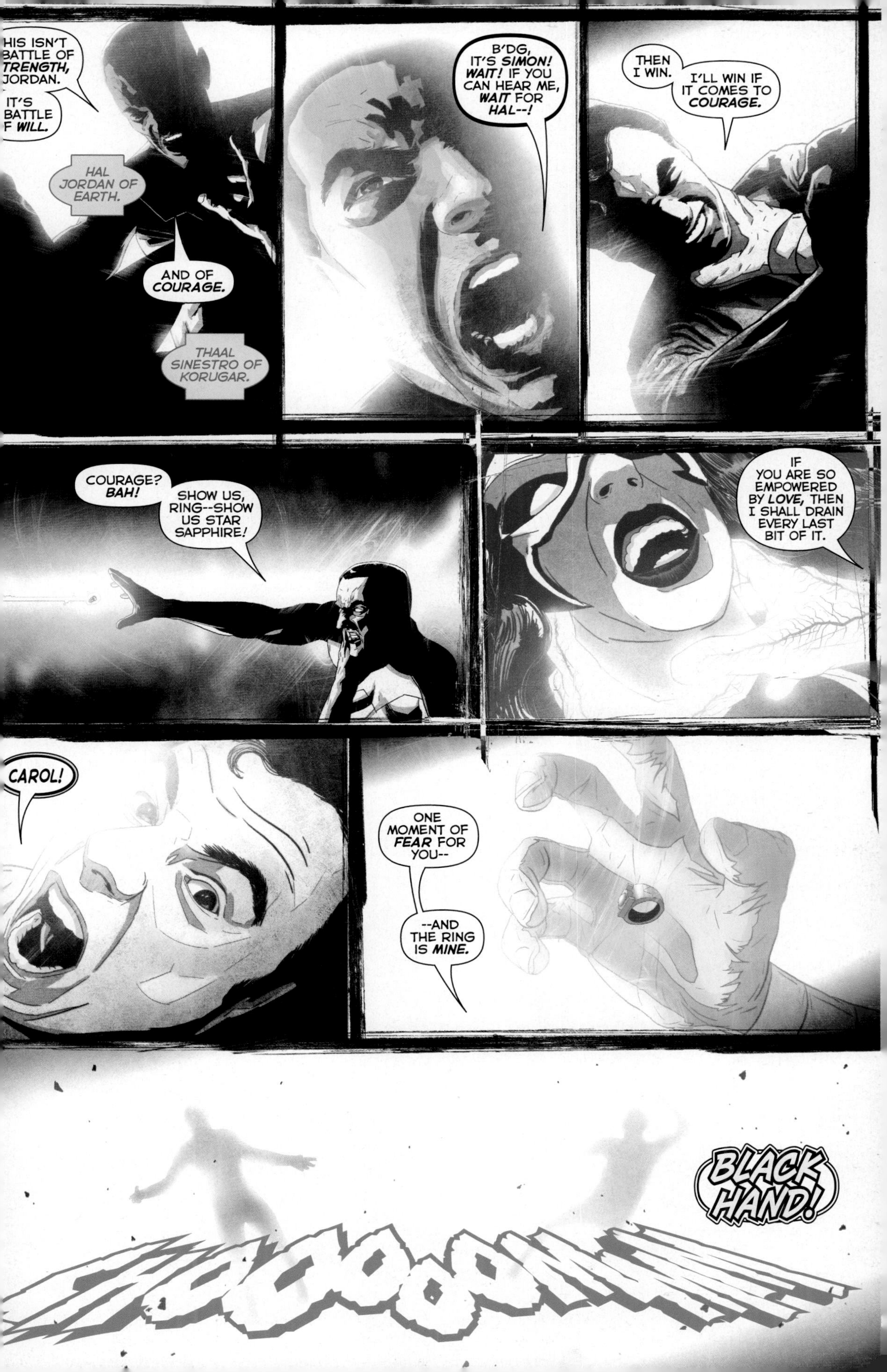

HIS ISN'T BATTLE OF TRENGTH, JORDAN.
IT'S BATTLE F WILL.
HAL JORDAN OF EARTH.
AND OF COURAGE.
THAAL SINESTRO OF KORUGAR.
B'DG, IT'S SIMON! WAIT! IF YOU CAN HEAR ME, WAIT FOR HAL--!
THEN I WIN.
I'LL WIN IF IT COMES TO COURAGE.
COURAGE? BAH!
SHOW US, RING--SHOW US STAR SAPPHIRE!
IF YOU ARE SO EMPOWERED BY LOVE, THEN I SHALL DRAIN EVERY LAST BIT OF IT.
CAROL!
ONE MOMENT OF FEAR FOR YOU--
--AND THE RING IS MINE.
BLACK HAND!

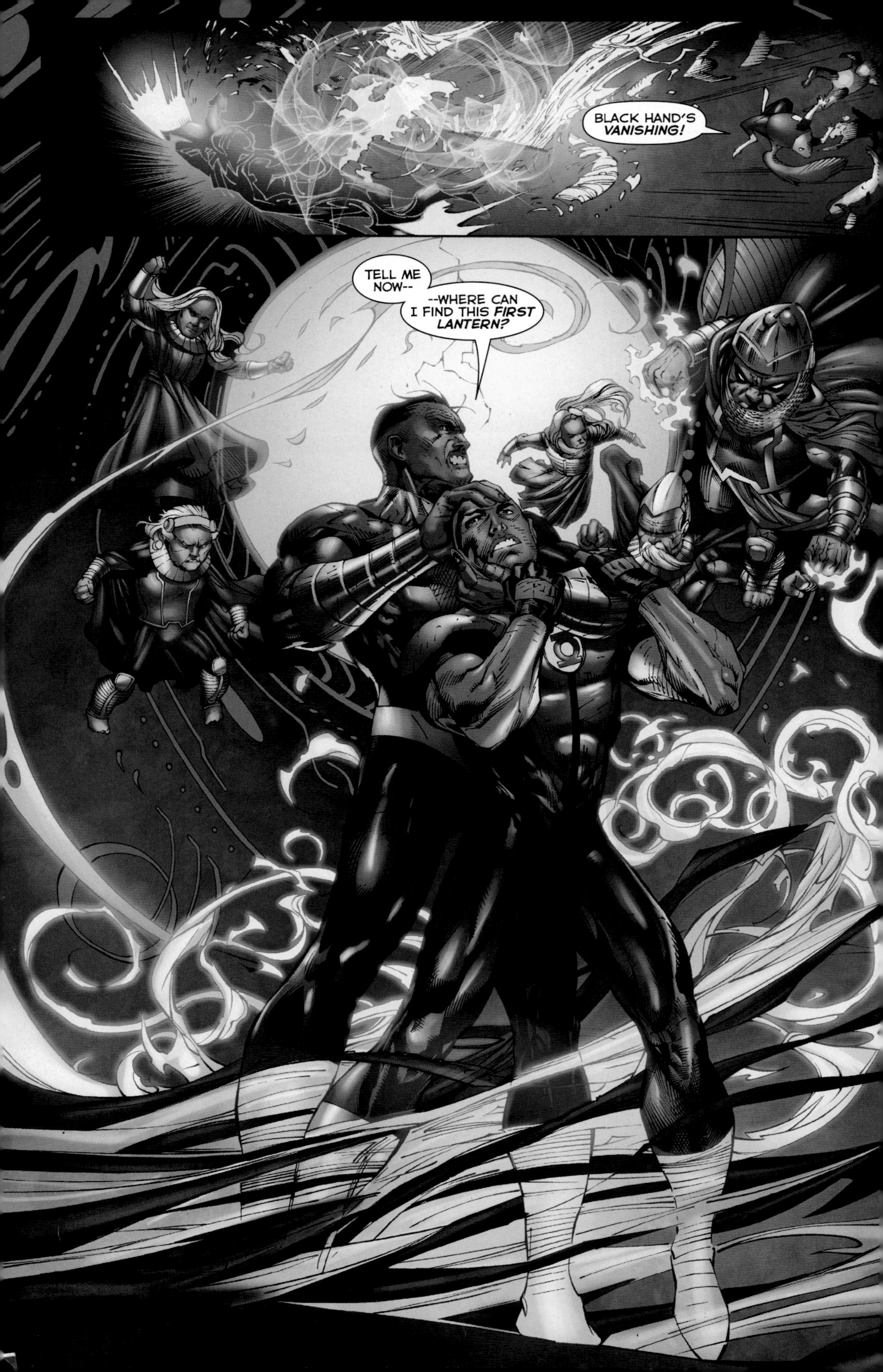
BLACK HAND'S *VANISHING!*
TELL ME NOW--
--WHERE CAN I FIND THIS *FIRST LANTERN?*

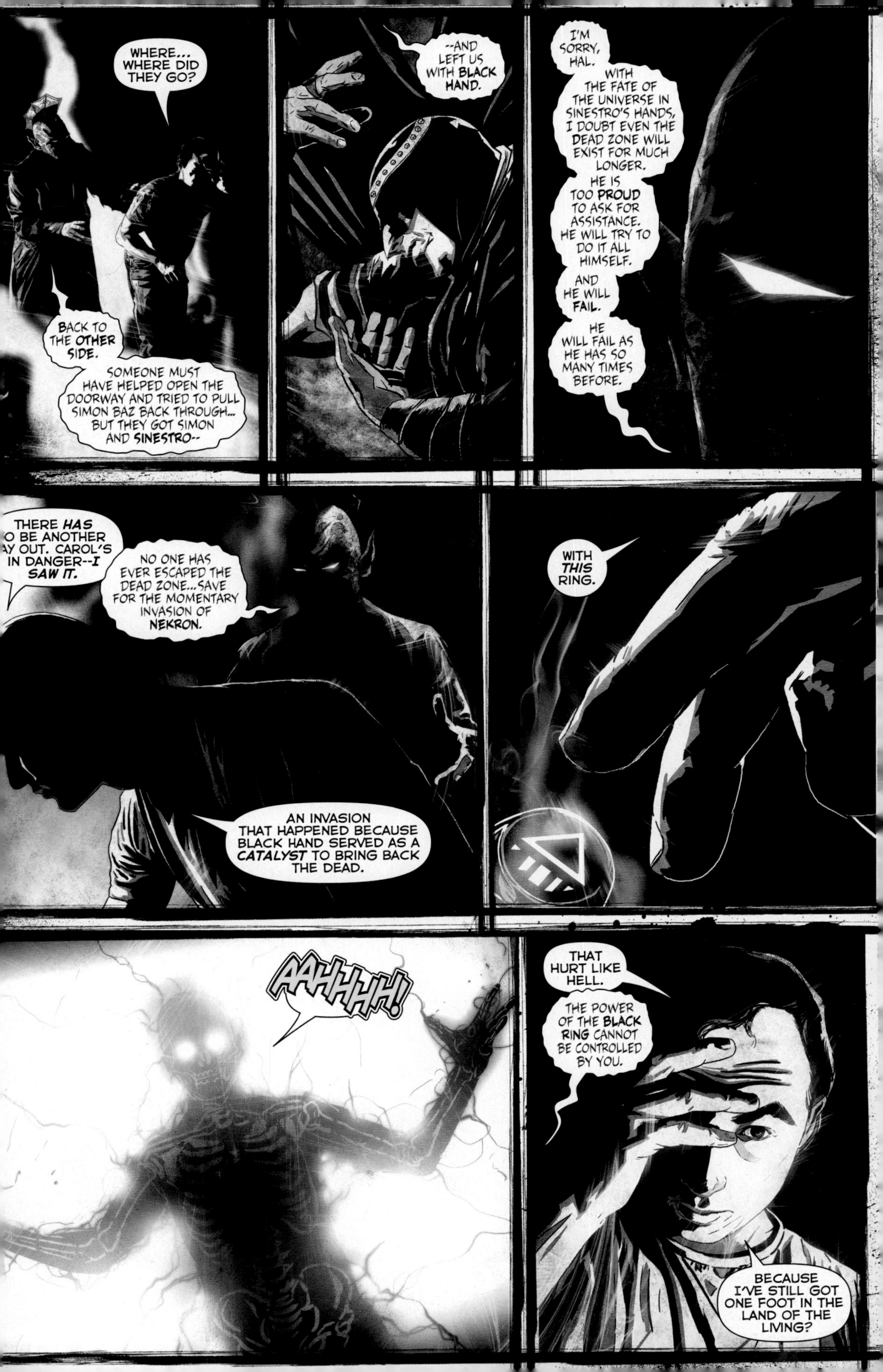
WHERE... WHERE DID THEY GO?
BACK TO THE OTHER SIDE.
SOMEONE MUST HAVE HELPED OPEN THE DOORWAY AND TRIED TO PULL SIMON BAZ BACK THROUGH... BUT THEY GOT SIMON AND SINESTRO--
--AND LEFT US WITH BLACK HAND.
I'M SORRY, HAL.
WITH THE FATE OF THE UNIVERSE IN SINESTRO'S HANDS, I DOUBT EVEN THE DEAD ZONE WILL EXIST FOR MUCH LONGER.
HE IS TOO PROUD TO ASK FOR ASSISTANCE. HE WILL TRY TO DO IT ALL HIMSELF.
AND HE WILL FAIL.
HE WILL FAIL AS HE HAS SO MANY TIMES BEFORE.
THERE HAS O BE ANOTHER AY OUT. CAROL'S IN DANGER--I SAW IT.
NO ONE HAS EVER ESCAPED THE DEAD ZONE...SAVE FOR THE MOMENTARY INVASION OF NEKRON.
AN INVASION THAT HAPPENED BECAUSE BLACK HAND SERVED AS A CATALYST TO BRING BACK THE DEAD.
WITH THIS RING.
AAHHHH!
THAT HURT LIKE HELL.
THE POWER OF THE BLACK RING CANNOT BE CONTROLLED BY YOU.
BECAUSE I'VE STILL GOT ONE FOOT IN THE LAND OF THE LIVING?

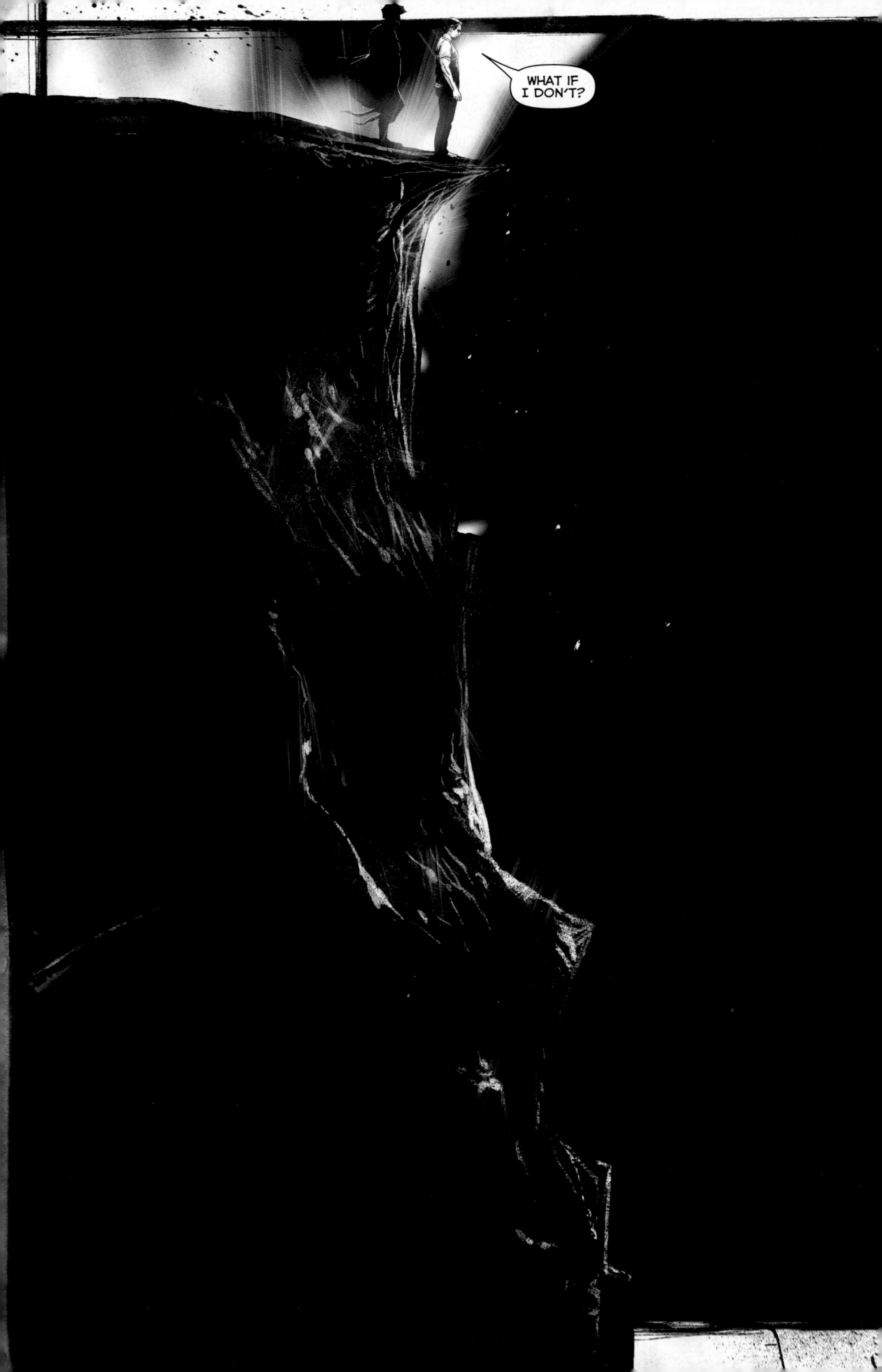
WHAT IF I DON'T?

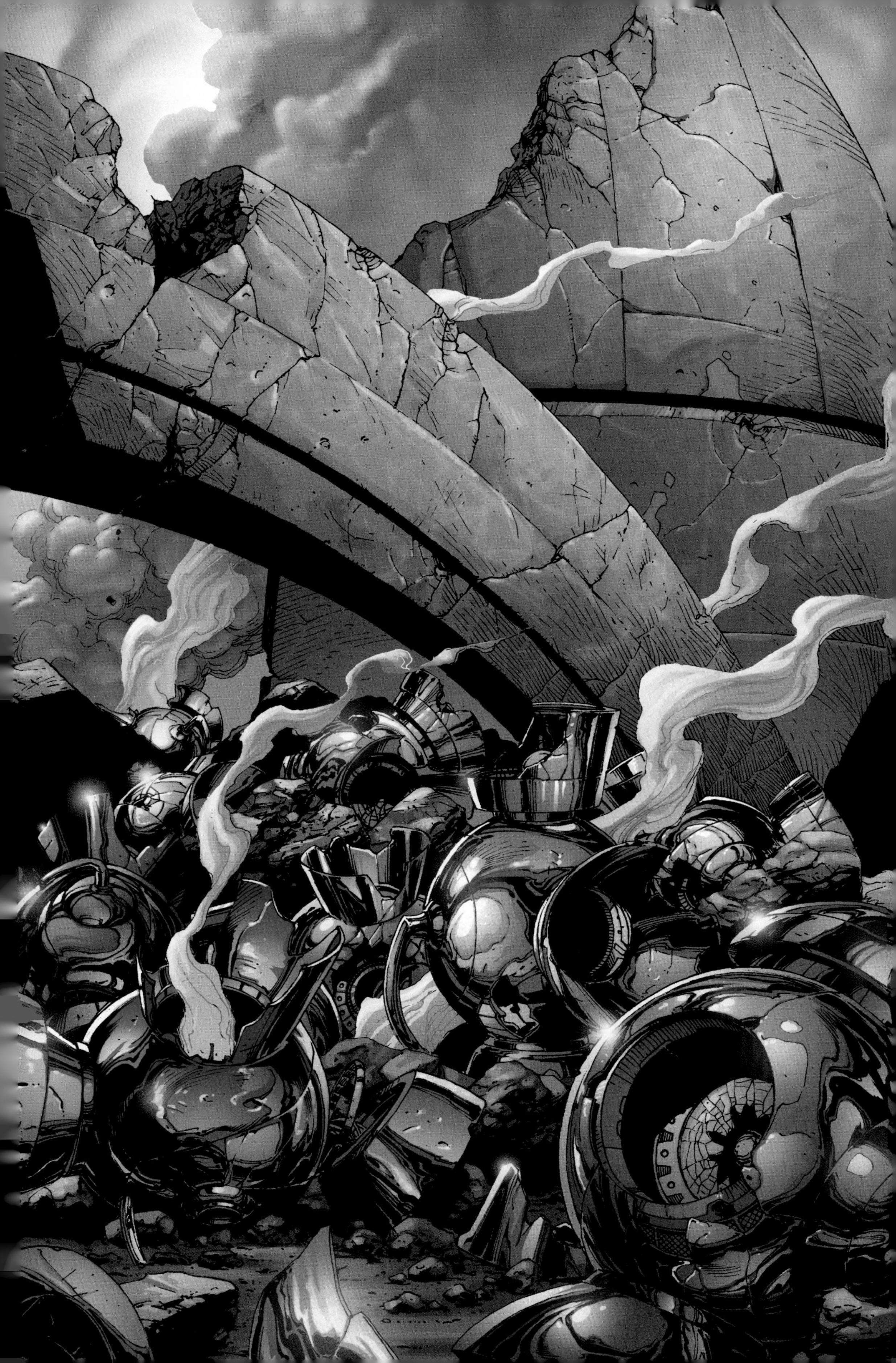

GEOFF JOHNS writer ARDIAN SYAF penciller – main sequence MARK IRWIN & GUILLERMO ORTEGO inkers – main sequence
SZYMON KUDRANSKI artist – Dead Zone sequence GARY FRANK & BRAD ANDERSON cover

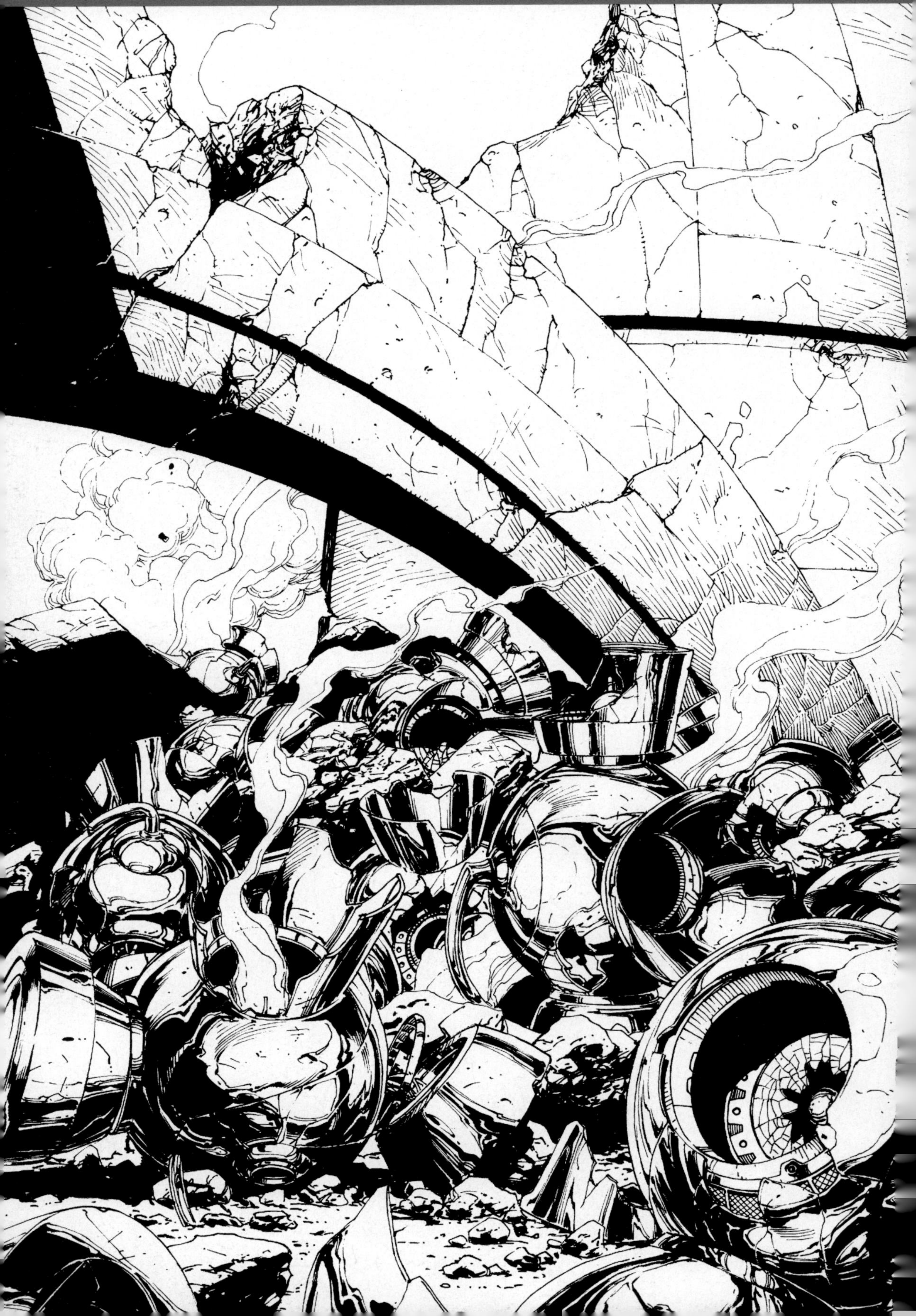

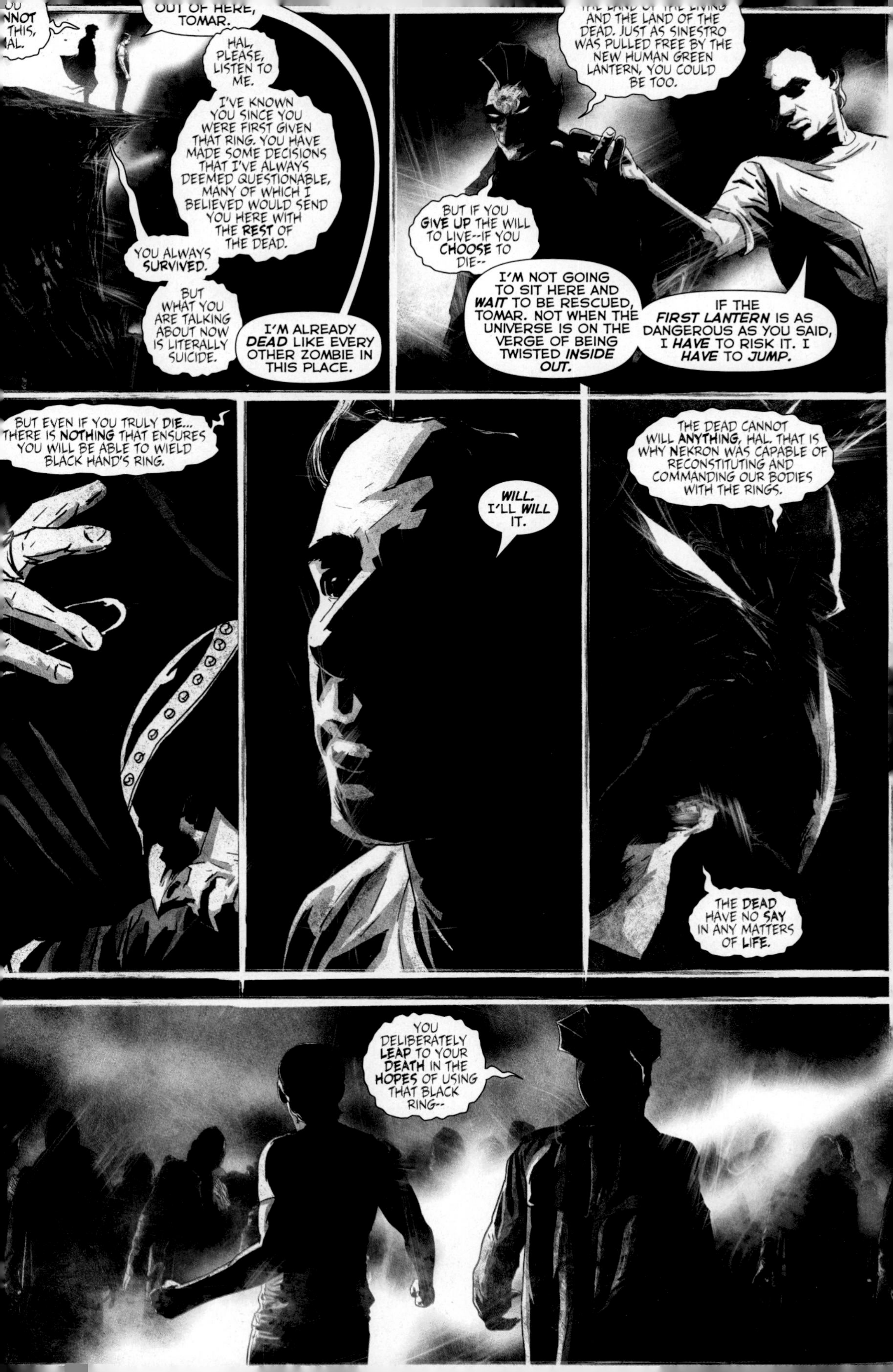

OUT OF HERE, TOMAR.
HAL, PLEASE, LISTEN TO ME.
I'VE KNOWN YOU SINCE YOU WERE FIRST GIVEN THAT RING. YOU HAVE MADE SOME DECISIONS THAT I'VE ALWAYS DEEMED QUESTIONABLE, MANY OF WHICH I BELIEVED WOULD SEND YOU HERE WITH THE REST OF THE DEAD.
YOU ALWAYS SURVIVED.
BUT WHAT YOU ARE TALKING ABOUT NOW IS LITERALLY SUICIDE.
I'M ALREADY DEAD LIKE EVERY OTHER ZOMBIE IN THIS PLACE.
AND THE LAND OF THE DEAD. JUST AS SINESTRO WAS PULLED FREE BY THE NEW HUMAN GREEN LANTERN, YOU COULD BE TOO.
BUT IF YOU GIVE UP THE WILL TO LIVE--IF YOU CHOOSE TO DIE--
I'M NOT GOING TO SIT HERE AND WAIT TO BE RESCUED, TOMAR. NOT WHEN THE UNIVERSE IS ON THE VERGE OF BEING TWISTED INSIDE OUT.
IF THE FIRST LANTERN IS AS DANGEROUS AS YOU SAID, I HAVE TO RISK IT. I HAVE TO JUMP.
BUT EVEN IF YOU TRULY DIE... THERE IS NOTHING THAT ENSURES YOU WILL BE ABLE TO WIELD BLACK HAND'S RING.
WILL. I'LL WILL IT.
THE DEAD CANNOT WILL ANYTHING, HAL. THAT IS WHY NEKRON WAS CAPABLE OF RECONSTITUTING AND COMMANDING OUR BODIES WITH THE RINGS.
THE DEAD HAVE NO SAY IN ANY MATTERS OF LIFE.
YOU DELIBERATELY LEAP TO YOUR DEATH IN THE HOPES OF USING THAT BLACK RING--

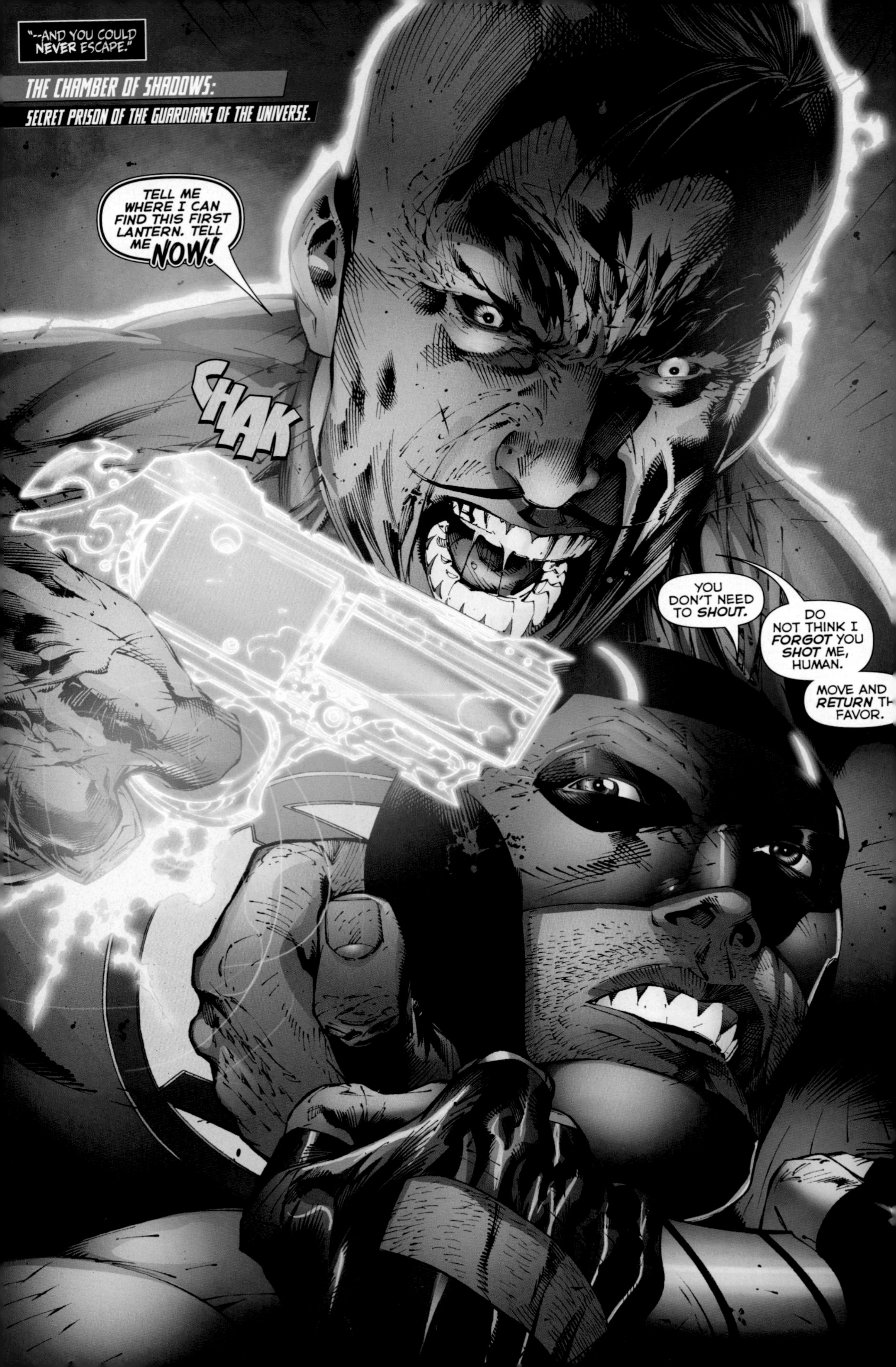
"--AND YOU COULD NEVER ESCAPE."
THE CHAMBER OF SHADOWS:
SECRET PRISON OF THE GUARDIANS OF THE UNIVERSE.
TELL ME WHERE I CAN FIND THIS FIRST LANTERN. TELL ME NOW!
CHAK
YOU DON'T NEED TO SHOUT.
DO NOT THINK I FORGOT YOU SHOT ME, HUMAN.
MOVE AND RETURN TH FAVOR.

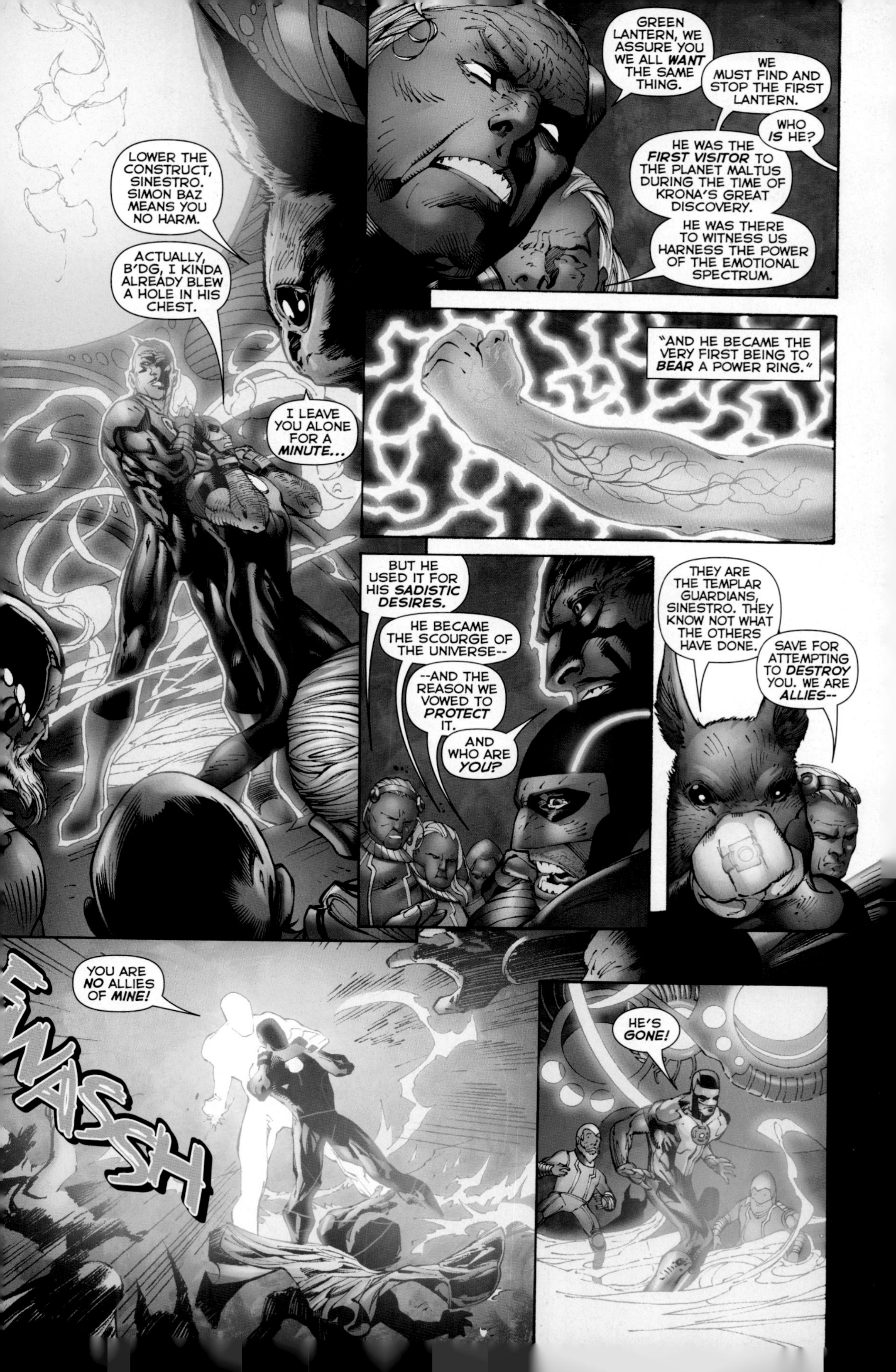
LOWER THE CONSTRUCT, SINESTRO. SIMON BAZ MEANS YOU NO HARM.
ACTUALLY, B'DG, I KINDA ALREADY BLEW A HOLE IN HIS CHEST.
I LEAVE YOU ALONE FOR A MINUTE...
GREEN LANTERN, WE ASSURE YOU WE ALL WANT THE SAME THING.
WE MUST FIND AND STOP THE FIRST LANTERN.
WHO IS HE?
HE WAS THE FIRST VISITOR TO THE PLANET MALTUS DURING THE TIME OF KRONA'S GREAT DISCOVERY.
HE WAS THERE TO WITNESS US HARNESS THE POWER OF THE EMOTIONAL SPECTRUM.
"AND HE BECAME THE VERY FIRST BEING TO BEAR A POWER RING."
BUT HE USED IT FOR HIS SADISTIC DESIRES.
HE BECAME THE SCOURGE OF THE UNIVERSE--
--AND THE REASON WE VOWED TO PROTECT IT.
AND WHO ARE YOU?
THEY ARE THE TEMPLAR GUARDIANS, SINESTRO. THEY KNOW NOT WHAT THE OTHERS HAVE DONE.
SAVE FOR ATTEMPTING TO DESTROY YOU. WE ARE ALLIES--
YOU ARE NO ALLIES OF MINE!
FWASSH
HE'S GONE!

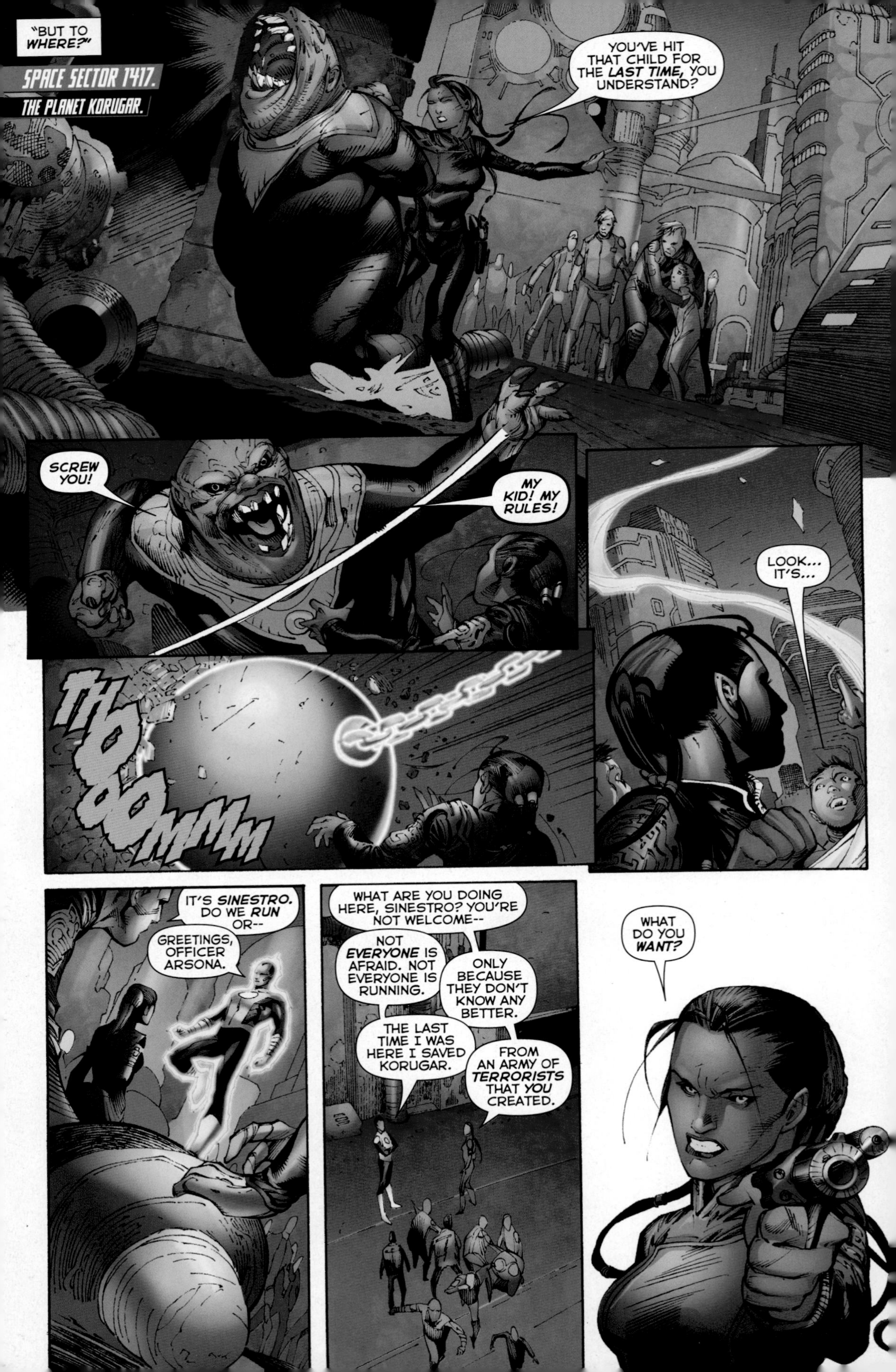
"BUT TO WHERE?"
SPACE SECTOR 1417.
THE PLANET KORUGAR.
YOU'VE HIT THAT CHILD FOR THE LAST TIME, YOU UNDERSTAND?
SCREW YOU!
MY KID! MY RULES!
THOOOMMMM
LOOK... IT'S...
IT'S SINESTRO. DO WE RUN OR--
GREETINGS, OFFICER ARSONA.
WHAT ARE YOU DOING HERE, SINESTRO? YOU'RE NOT WELCOME--
NOT EVERYONE IS AFRAID. NOT EVERYONE IS RUNNING.
ONLY BECAUSE THEY DON'T KNOW ANY BETTER.
THE LAST TIME I WAS HERE I SAVED KORUGAR.
FROM AN ARMY OF TERRORISTS THAT YOU CREATED.
WHAT DO YOU WANT?

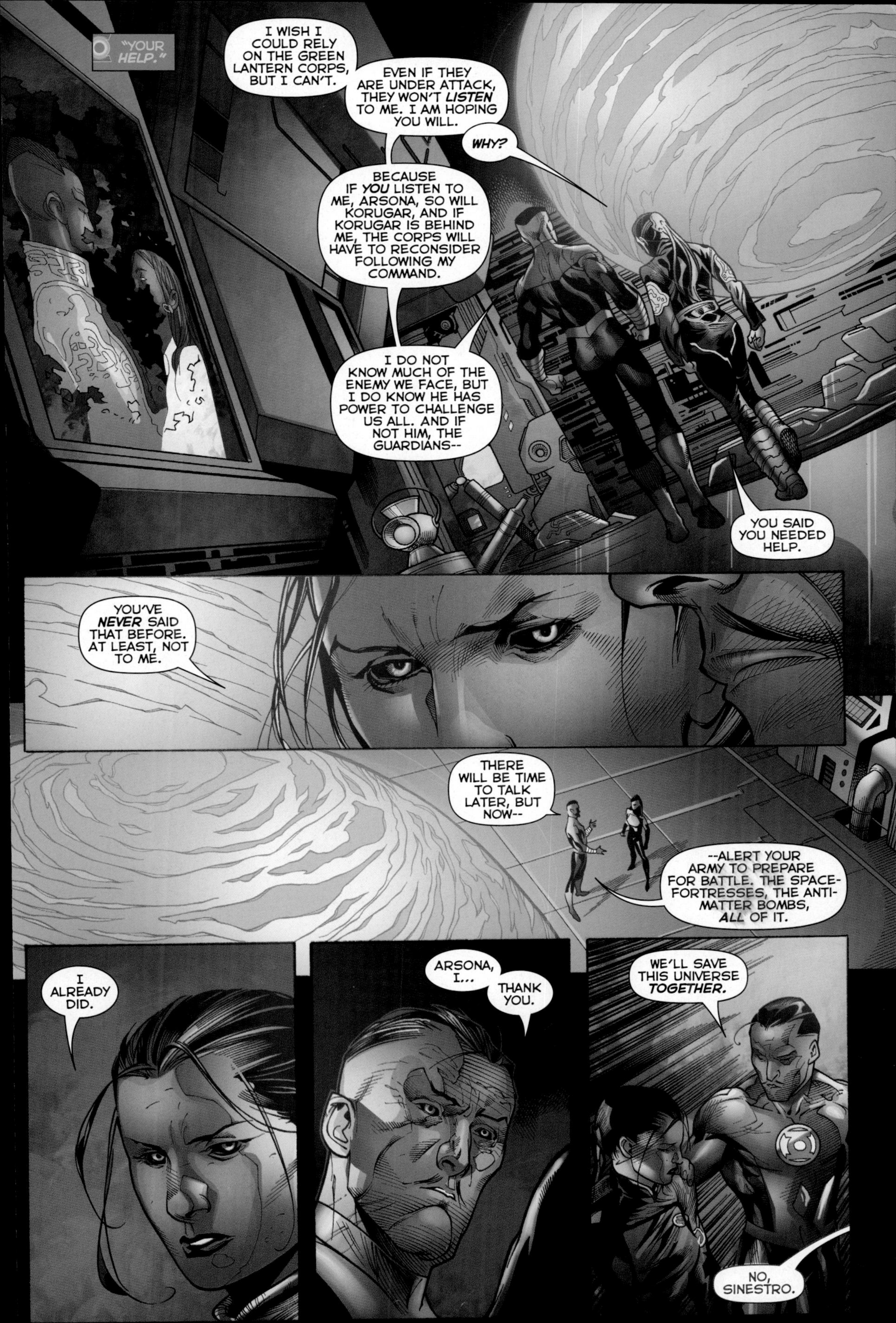
"YOUR HELP."
I WISH I COULD RELY ON THE GREEN LANTERN CORPS, BUT I CAN'T.
EVEN IF THEY ARE UNDER ATTACK, THEY WON'T LISTEN TO ME. I AM HOPING YOU WILL.
WHY?
BECAUSE IF YOU LISTEN TO ME, ARSONA, SO WILL KORUGAR, AND IF KORUGAR IS BEHIND ME, THE CORPS WILL HAVE TO RECONSIDER FOLLOWING MY COMMAND.
I DO NOT KNOW MUCH OF THE ENEMY WE FACE, BUT I DO KNOW HE HAS POWER TO CHALLENGE US ALL. AND IF NOT HIM, THE GUARDIANS--
YOU SAID YOU NEEDED HELP.
YOU'VE NEVER SAID THAT BEFORE. AT LEAST, NOT TO ME.
THERE WILL BE TIME TO TALK LATER, BUT NOW--
--ALERT YOUR ARMY TO PREPARE FOR BATTLE. THE SPACE-FORTRESSES, THE ANTI-MATTER BOMBS, ALL OF IT.
I ALREADY DID.
ARSONA, I...
THANK YOU.
WE'LL SAVE THIS UNIVERSE TOGETHER.
NO, SINESTRO.

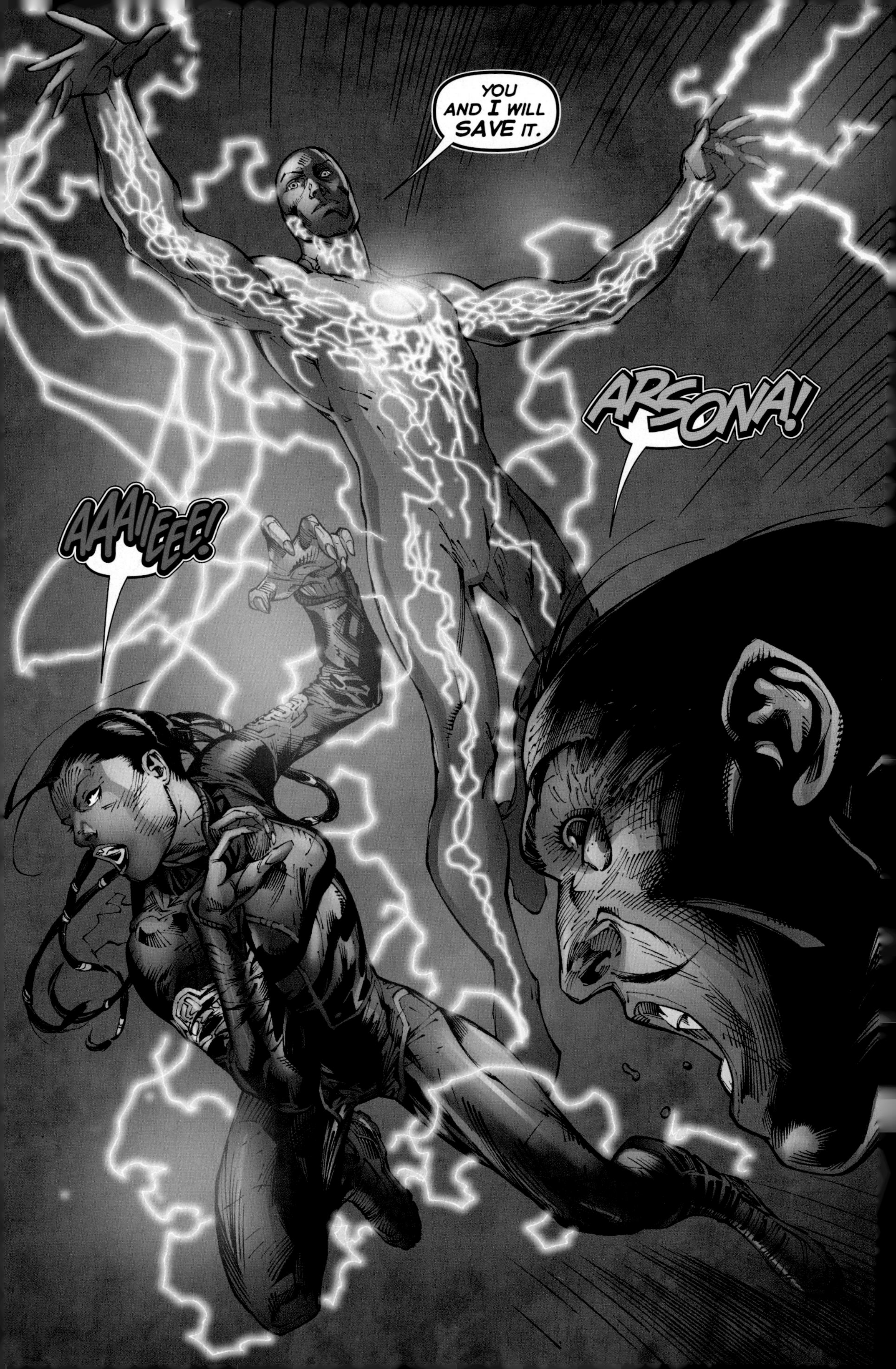
YOU AND I WILL SAVE IT.
ARSONA!
AAAIIEEEE!

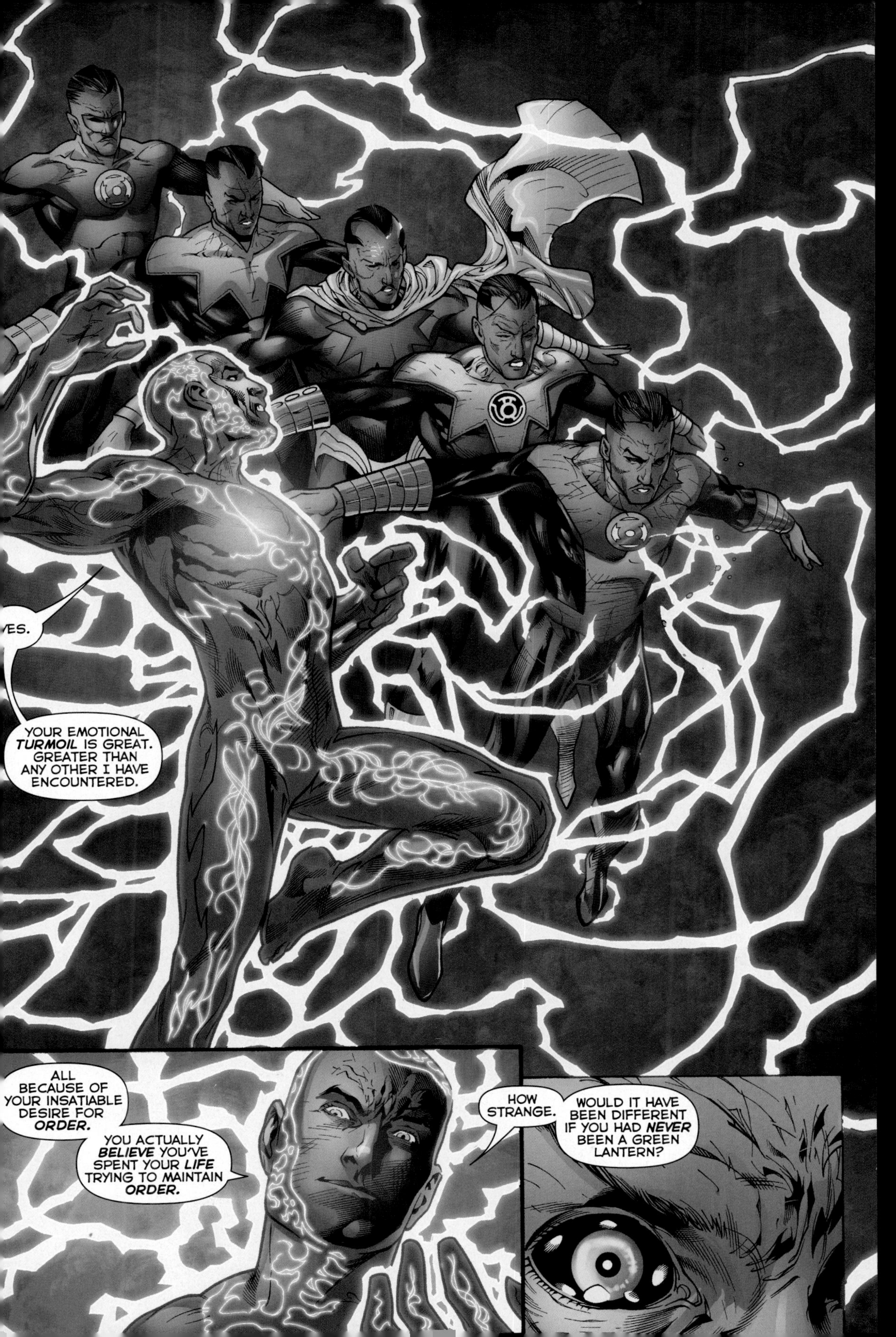

YES.
YOUR EMOTIONAL TURMOIL IS GREAT. GREATER THAN ANY OTHER I HAVE ENCOUNTERED.
ALL BECAUSE OF YOUR INSATIABLE DESIRE FOR ORDER.
YOU ACTUALLY BELIEVE YOU'VE SPENT YOUR LIFE TRYING TO MAINTAIN ORDER.
HOW STRANGE.
WOULD IT HAVE BEEN DIFFERENT IF YOU HAD NEVER BEEN A GREEN LANTERN?

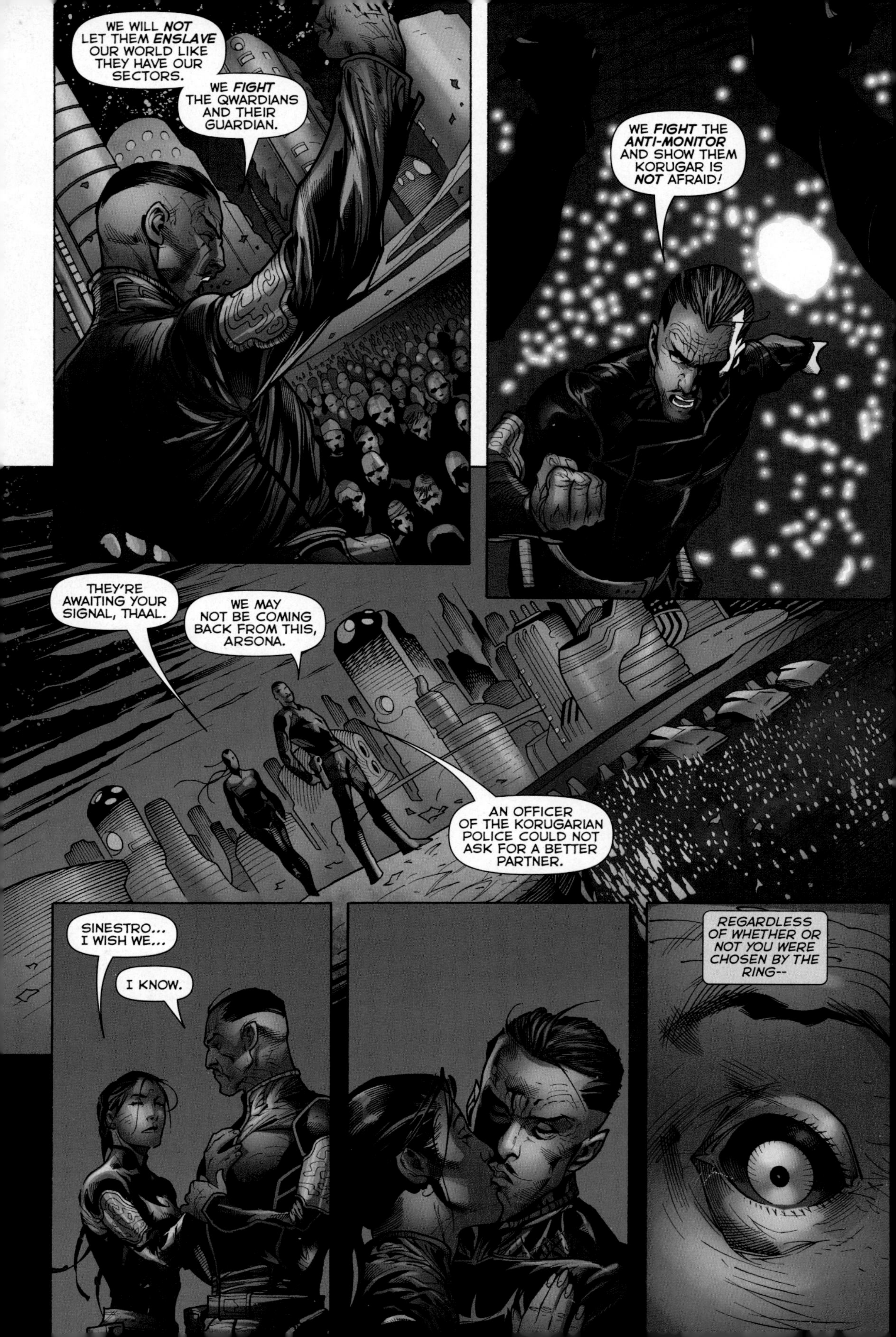
WE WILL *NOT* LET THEM *ENSLAVE* OUR WORLD LIKE THEY HAVE OUR SECTORS.
WE *FIGHT* THE QWARDIANS AND THEIR GUARDIAN.
WE *FIGHT* THE *ANTI-MONITOR* AND SHOW THEM KORUGAR IS *NOT* AFRAID!
THEY'RE AWAITING YOUR SIGNAL, THAAL.
WE MAY NOT BE COMING BACK FROM THIS, ARSONA.
AN OFFICER OF THE KORUGARIAN POLICE COULD NOT ASK FOR A BETTER PARTNER.
SINESTRO... I WISH WE...
I KNOW.
REGARDLESS OF WHETHER OR NOT YOU WERE CHOSEN BY THE RING--

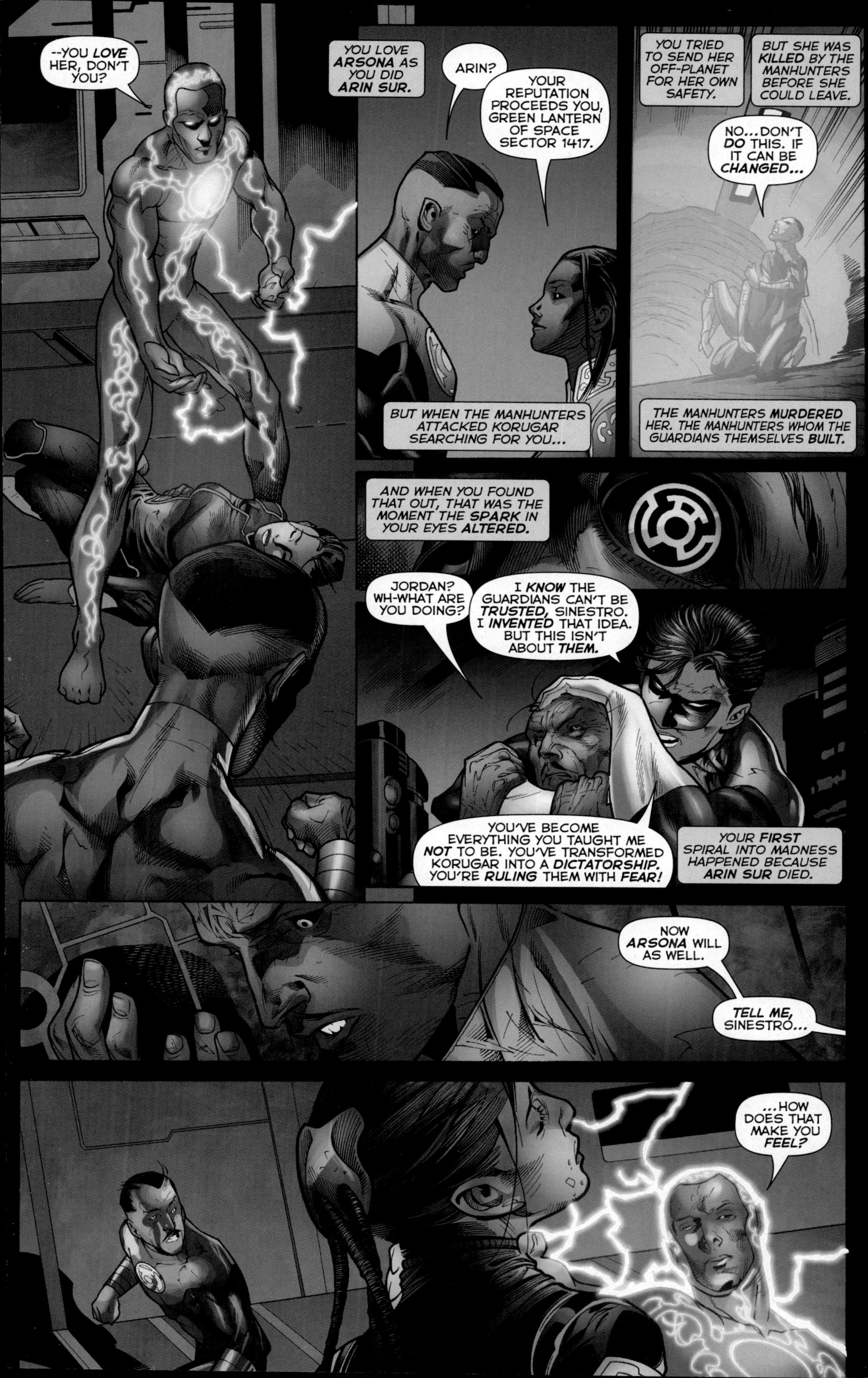
--YOU LOVE HER, DON'T YOU?
YOU LOVE ARSONA AS YOU DID ARIN SUR.
ARIN?
YOUR REPUTATION PROCEEDS YOU, GREEN LANTERN OF SPACE SECTOR 1417.
BUT WHEN THE MANHUNTERS ATTACKED KORUGAR SEARCHING FOR YOU...
YOU TRIED TO SEND HER OFF-PLANET FOR HER OWN SAFETY.
BUT SHE WAS KILLED BY THE MANHUNTERS BEFORE SHE COULD LEAVE.
NO...DON'T DO THIS. IF IT CAN BE CHANGED...
THE MANHUNTERS MURDERED HER. THE MANHUNTERS WHOM THE GUARDIANS THEMSELVES BUILT.
AND WHEN YOU FOUND THAT OUT, THAT WAS THE MOMENT THE SPARK IN YOUR EYES ALTERED.
JORDAN? WH-WHAT ARE YOU DOING?
I KNOW THE GUARDIANS CAN'T BE TRUSTED, SINESTRO. I INVENTED THAT IDEA. BUT THIS ISN'T ABOUT THEM.
YOU'VE BECOME EVERYTHING YOU TAUGHT ME NOT TO BE. YOU'VE TRANSFORMED KORUGAR INTO A DICTATORSHIP. YOU'RE RULING THEM WITH FEAR!
YOUR FIRST SPIRAL INTO MADNESS HAPPENED BECAUSE ARIN SUR DIED.
NOW ARSONA WILL AS WELL.
TELL ME, SINESTRO...
...HOW DOES THAT MAKE YOU FEEL?

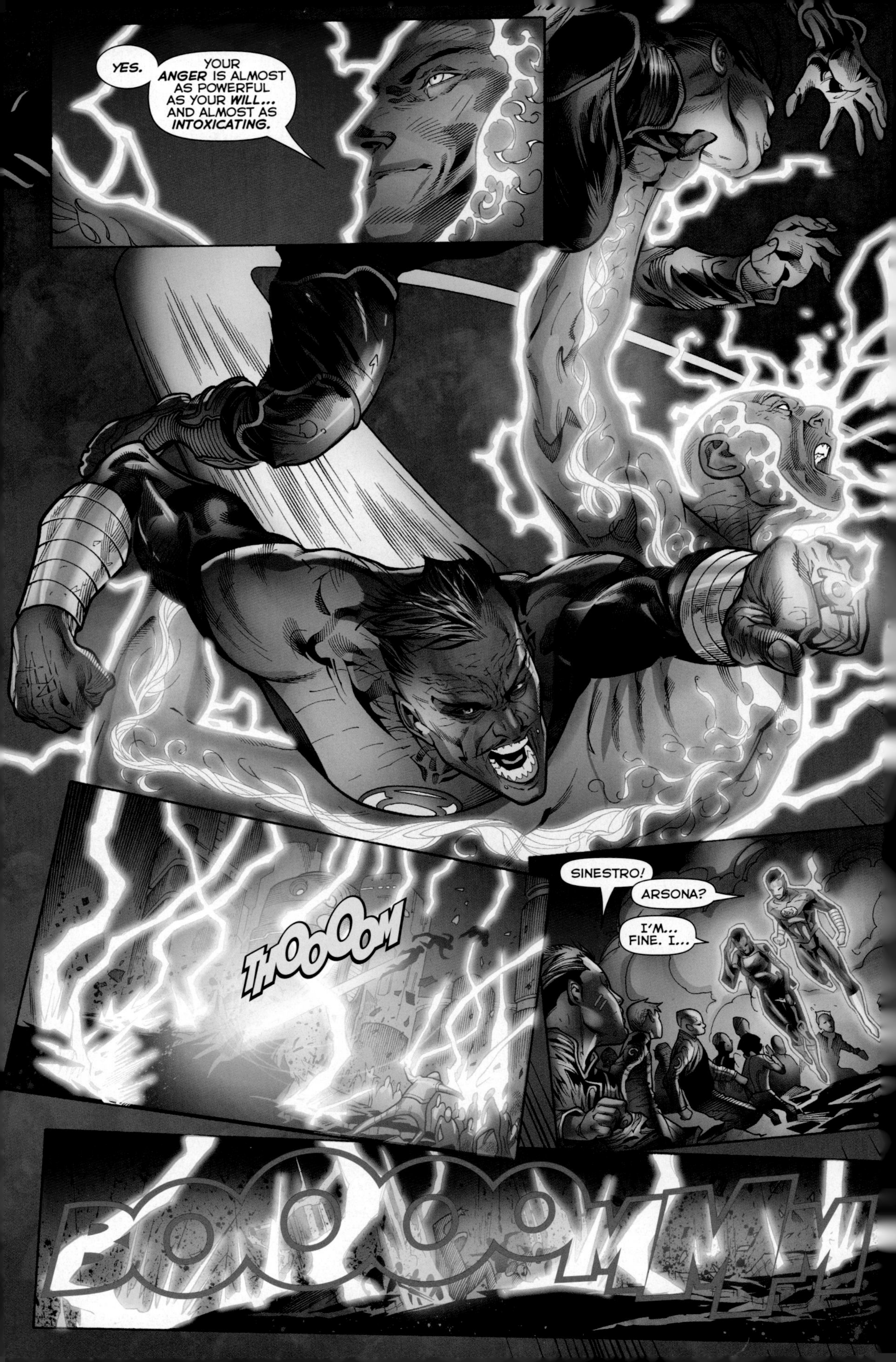
YES.
YOUR ANGER IS ALMOST AS POWERFUL AS YOUR WILL... AND ALMOST AS INTOXICATING.
THOOOOM
SINESTRO!
ARSONA?
I'M... FINE. I...
BOOOOMMM

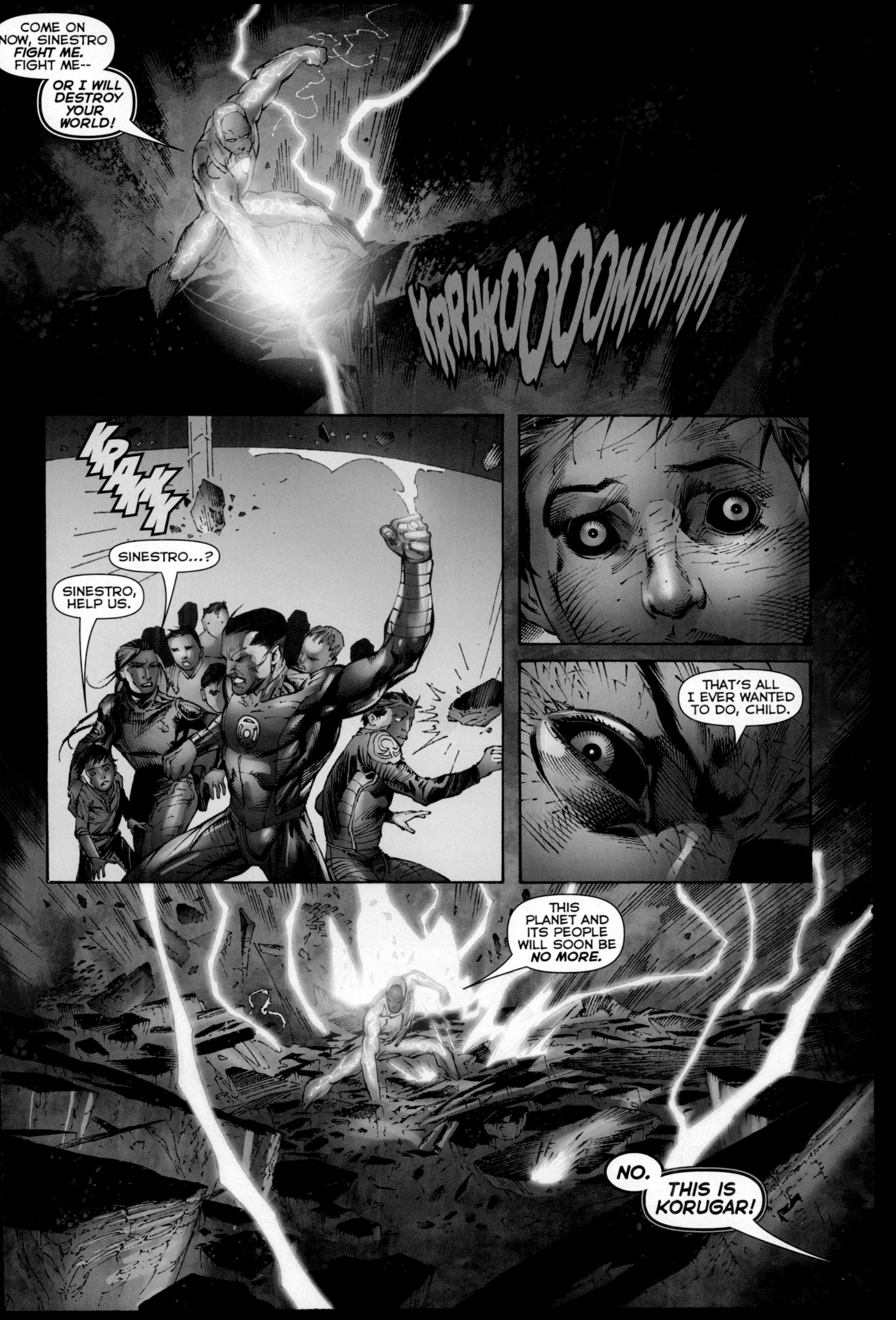

COME ON NOW, SINESTRO FIGHT ME. FIGHT ME--
OR I WILL DESTROY YOUR WORLD!
KRRAKOOOOMMMM
KRAKKK
SINESTRO...?
SINESTRO, HELP US.
THAT'S ALL I EVER WANTED TO DO, CHILD.
THIS PLANET AND ITS PEOPLE WILL SOON BE NO MORE.
NO.
THIS IS KORUGAR!

AND MY OATH ABOVE ALL OTHERS IS TO PROTECT IT!

VZZZZZZZ

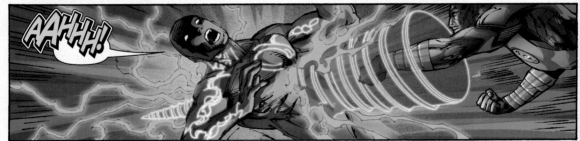

AAHHH!

YOU ACTUALLY... HURT ME...

BUT YOU'VE ALSO DONE *EXACTLY* WHAT I WISHED. YOU'VE CREATED *SUCH* EMOTION HERE ON KORUGAR OVER THE YEARS.

YOU SEE, I'M NOT REALLY HERE FOR *YOU*, SINESTRO.

I'M HERE FOR *YOUR* WORLD.

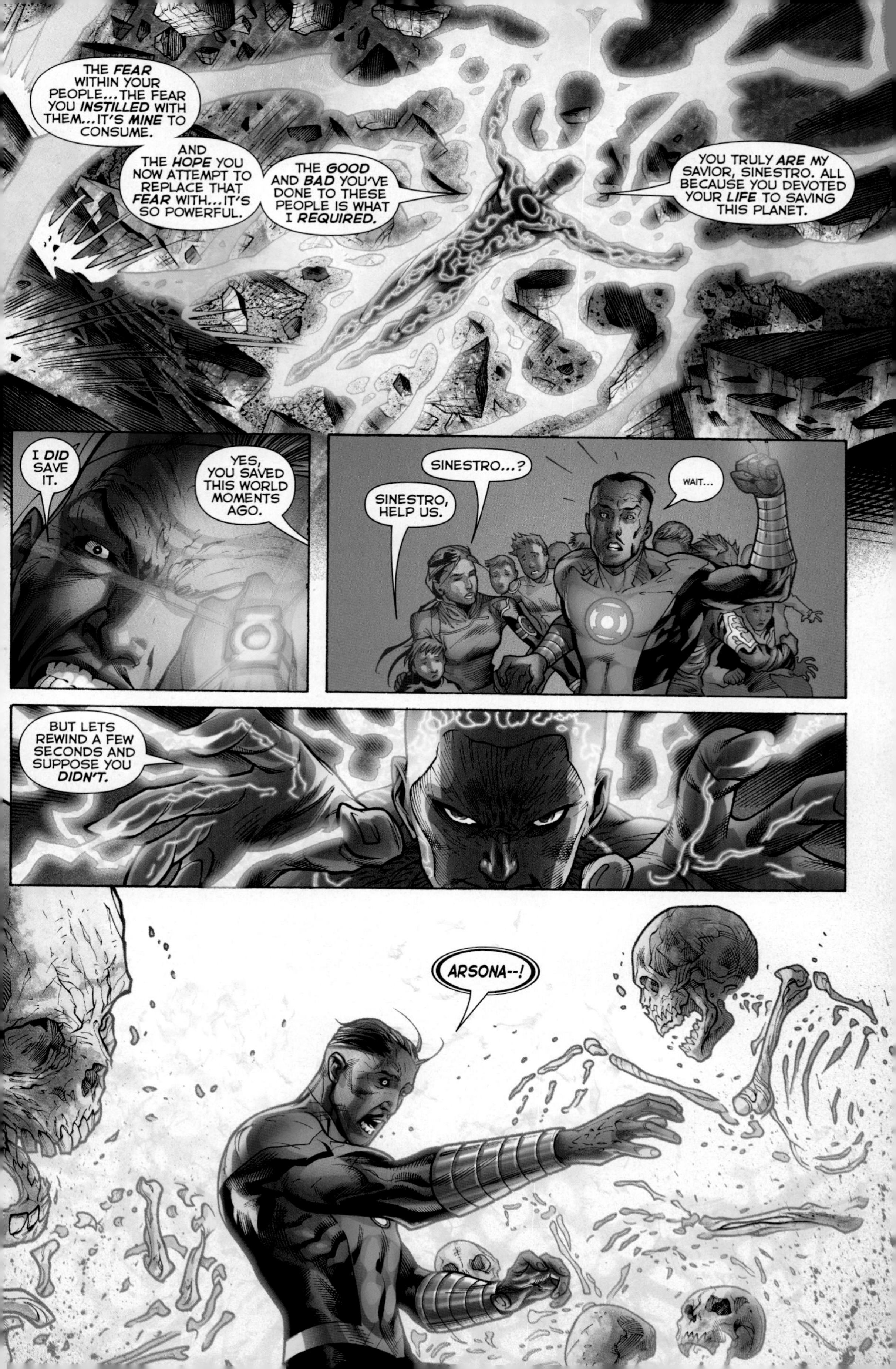
THE FEAR WITHIN YOUR PEOPLE...THE FEAR YOU INSTILLED WITH THEM...IT'S MINE TO CONSUME.
AND THE HOPE YOU NOW ATTEMPT TO REPLACE THAT FEAR WITH...IT'S SO POWERFUL.
THE GOOD AND BAD YOU'VE DONE TO THESE PEOPLE IS WHAT I REQUIRED.
YOU TRULY ARE MY SAVIOR, SINESTRO. ALL BECAUSE YOU DEVOTED YOUR LIFE TO SAVING THIS PLANET.
I DID SAVE IT.
YES, YOU SAVED THIS WORLD MOMENTS AGO.
SINESTRO, HELP US.
SINESTRO...?
WAIT...
BUT LETS REWIND A FEW SECONDS AND SUPPOSE YOU DIDN'T.
ARSONA--!

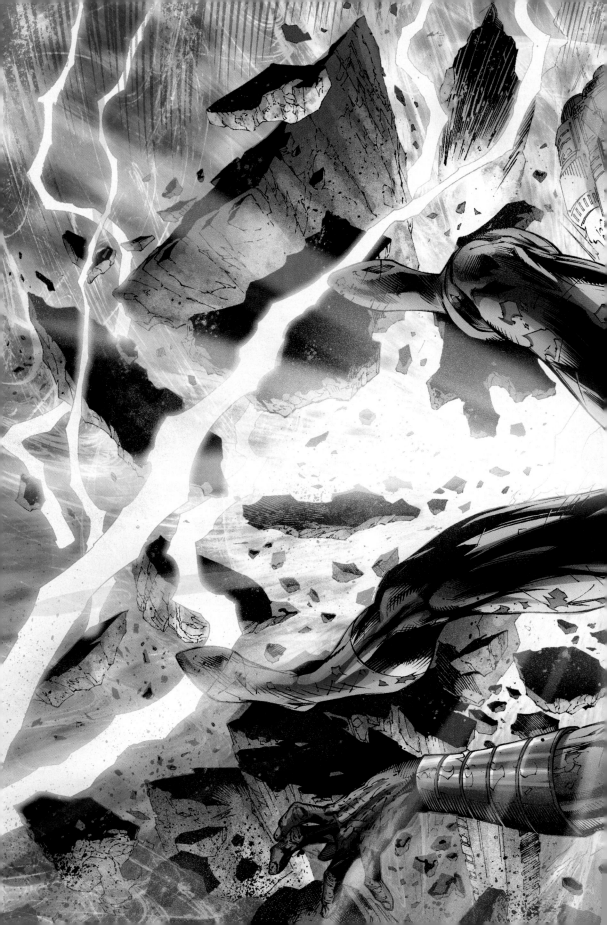

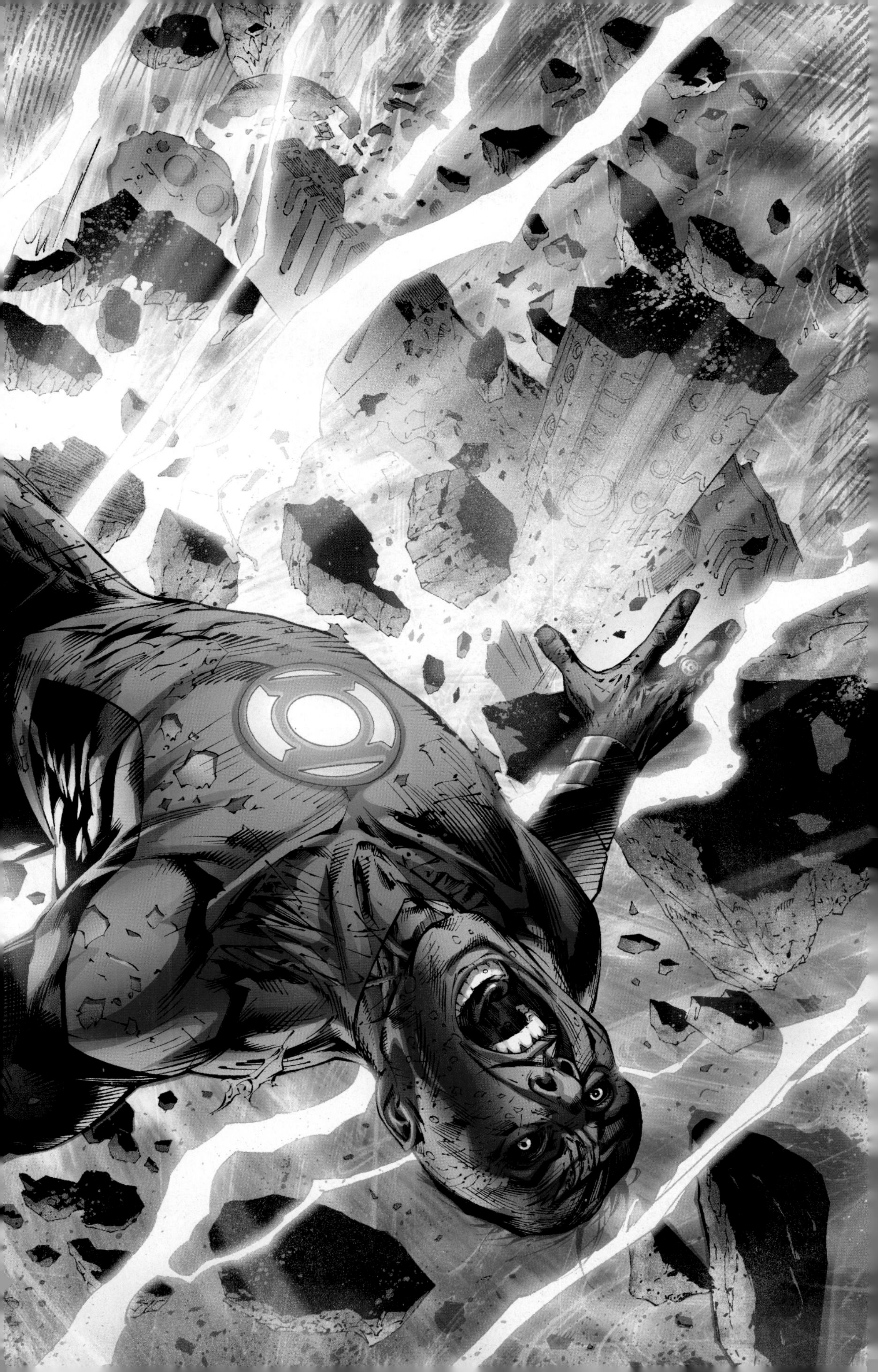

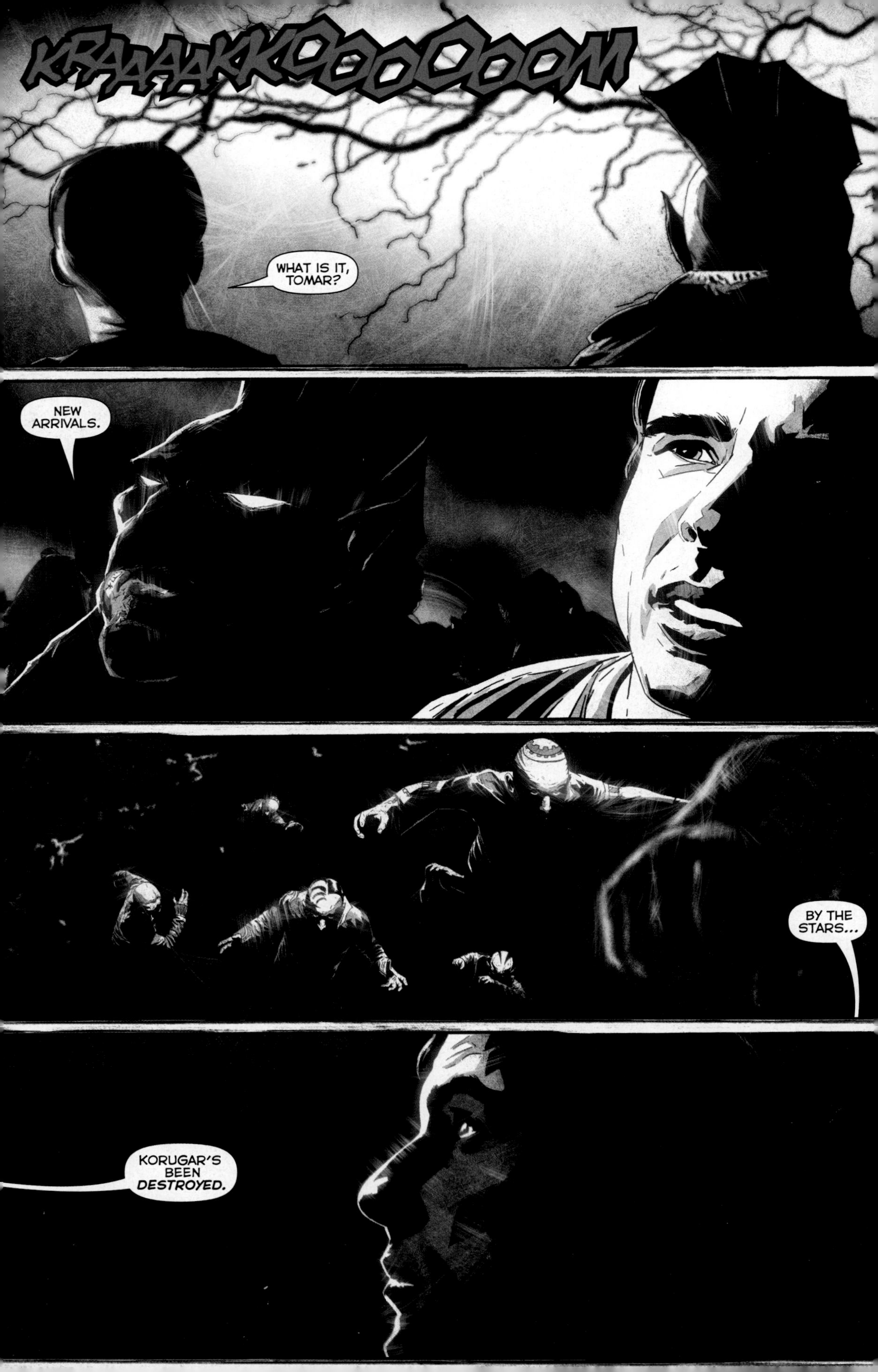
KRAAAAKKOOOOOOOM
WHAT IS IT, TOMAR?
NEW ARRIVALS.
BY THE STARS...
KORUGAR'S BEEN DESTROYED.

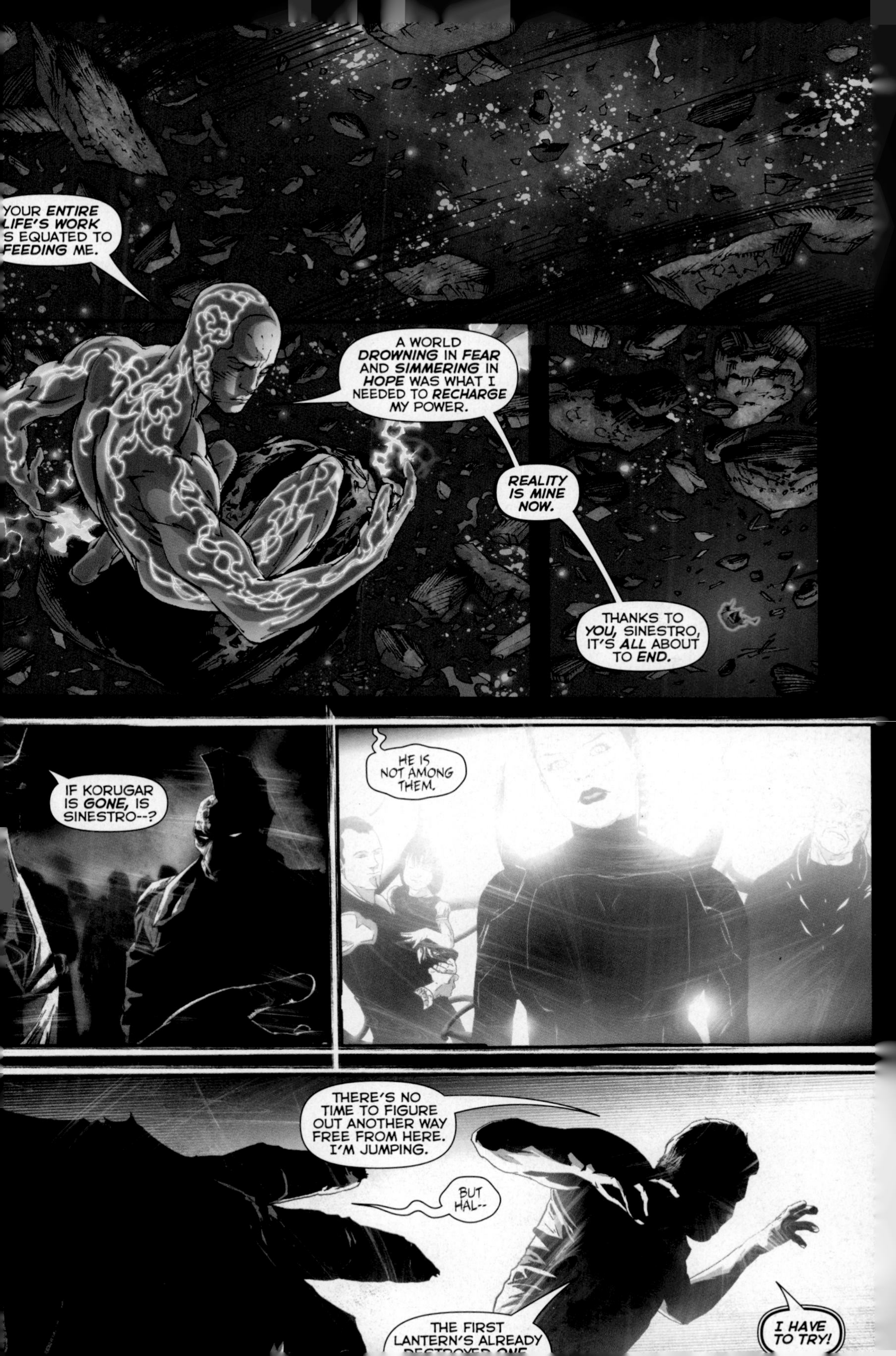
YOUR ENTIRE LIFE'S WORK S EQUATED TO FEEDING ME.
A WORLD DROWNING IN FEAR AND SIMMERING IN HOPE WAS WHAT I NEEDED TO RECHARGE MY POWER.
REALITY IS MINE NOW.
THANKS TO YOU, SINESTRO, IT'S ALL ABOUT TO END.
IF KORUGAR IS GONE, IS SINESTRO--?
HE IS NOT AMONG THEM.
THERE'S NO TIME TO FIGURE OUT ANOTHER WAY FREE FROM HERE. I'M JUMPING.
BUT HAL--
THE FIRST LANTERN'S ALREADY
I HAVE TO TRY!

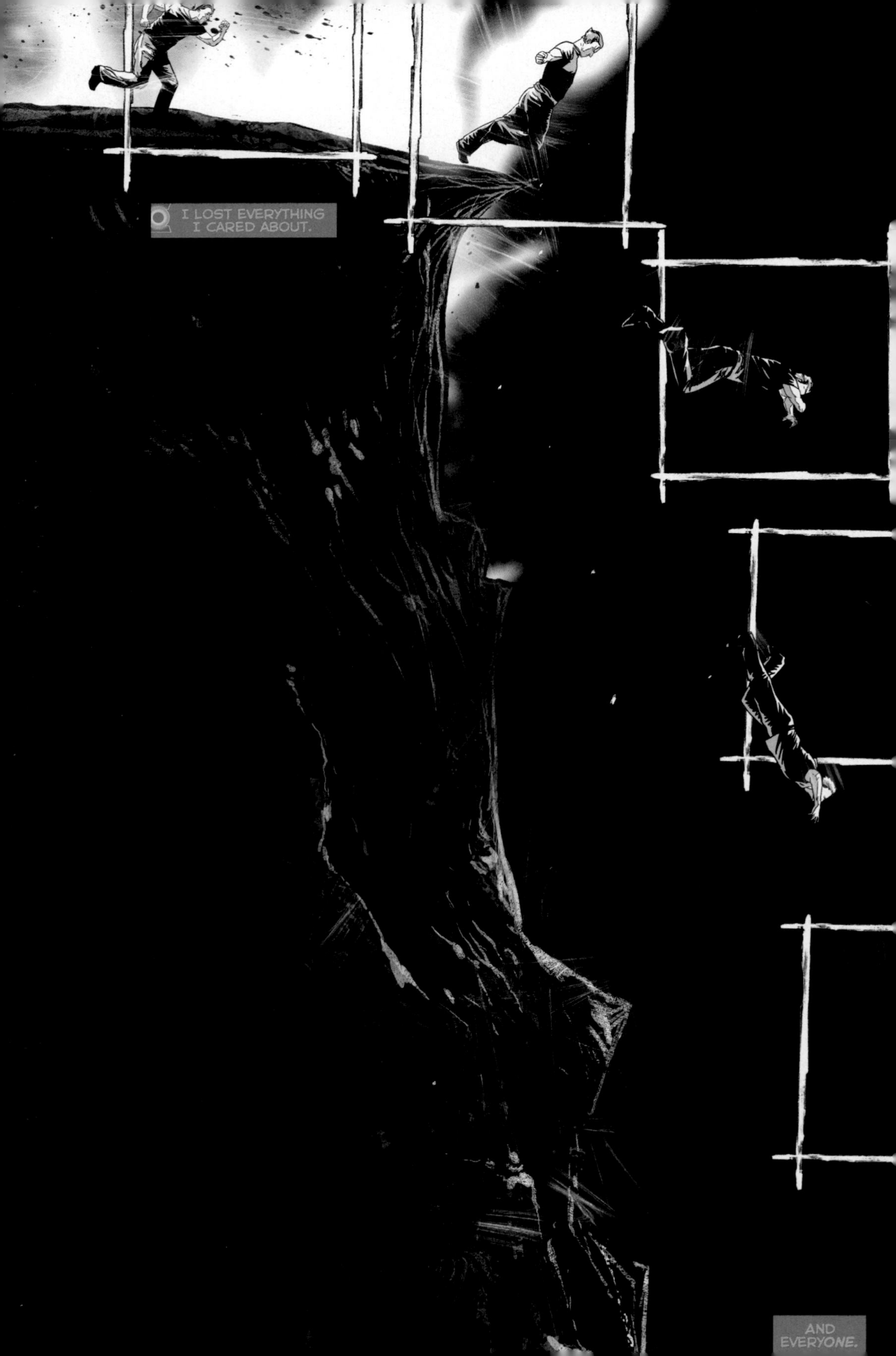

I LOST EVERYTHING I CARED ABOUT.
AND EVERYONE.

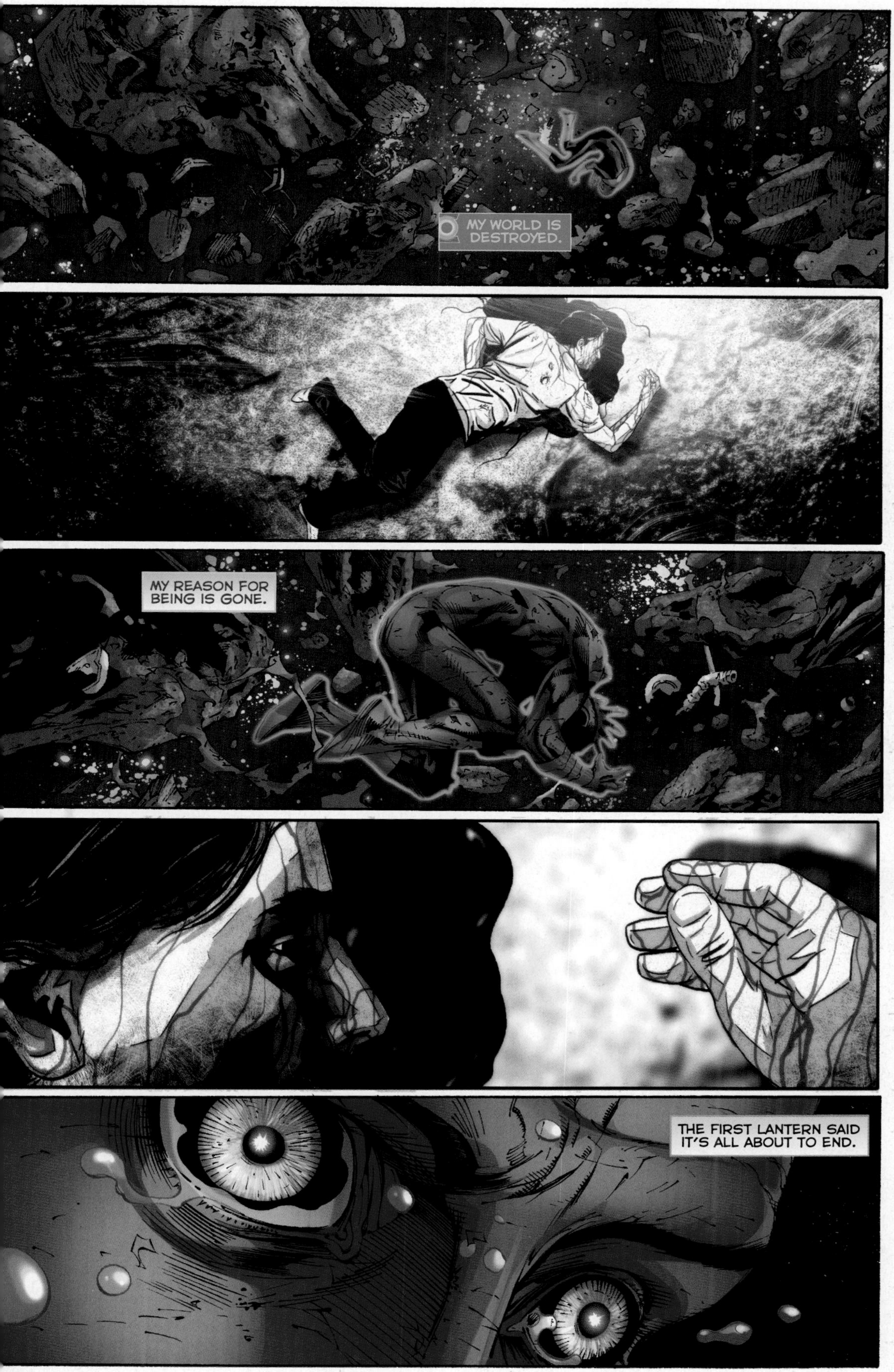
MY WORLD IS DESTROYED.
MY REASON FOR BEING IS GONE.
THE FIRST LANTERN SAID IT'S ALL ABOUT TO END.

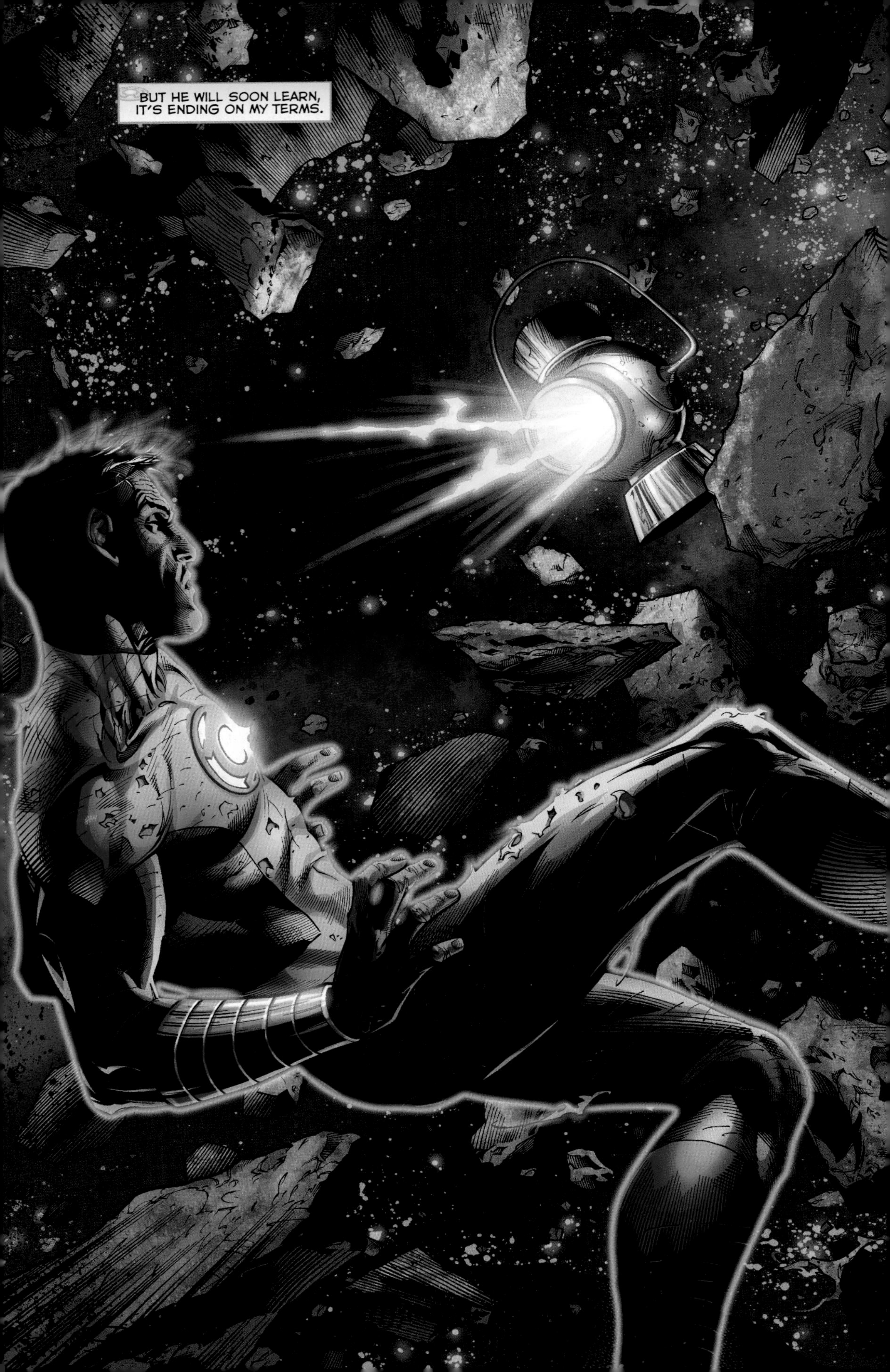
BUT HE WILL SOON LEARN, IT'S ENDING ON MY TERMS.

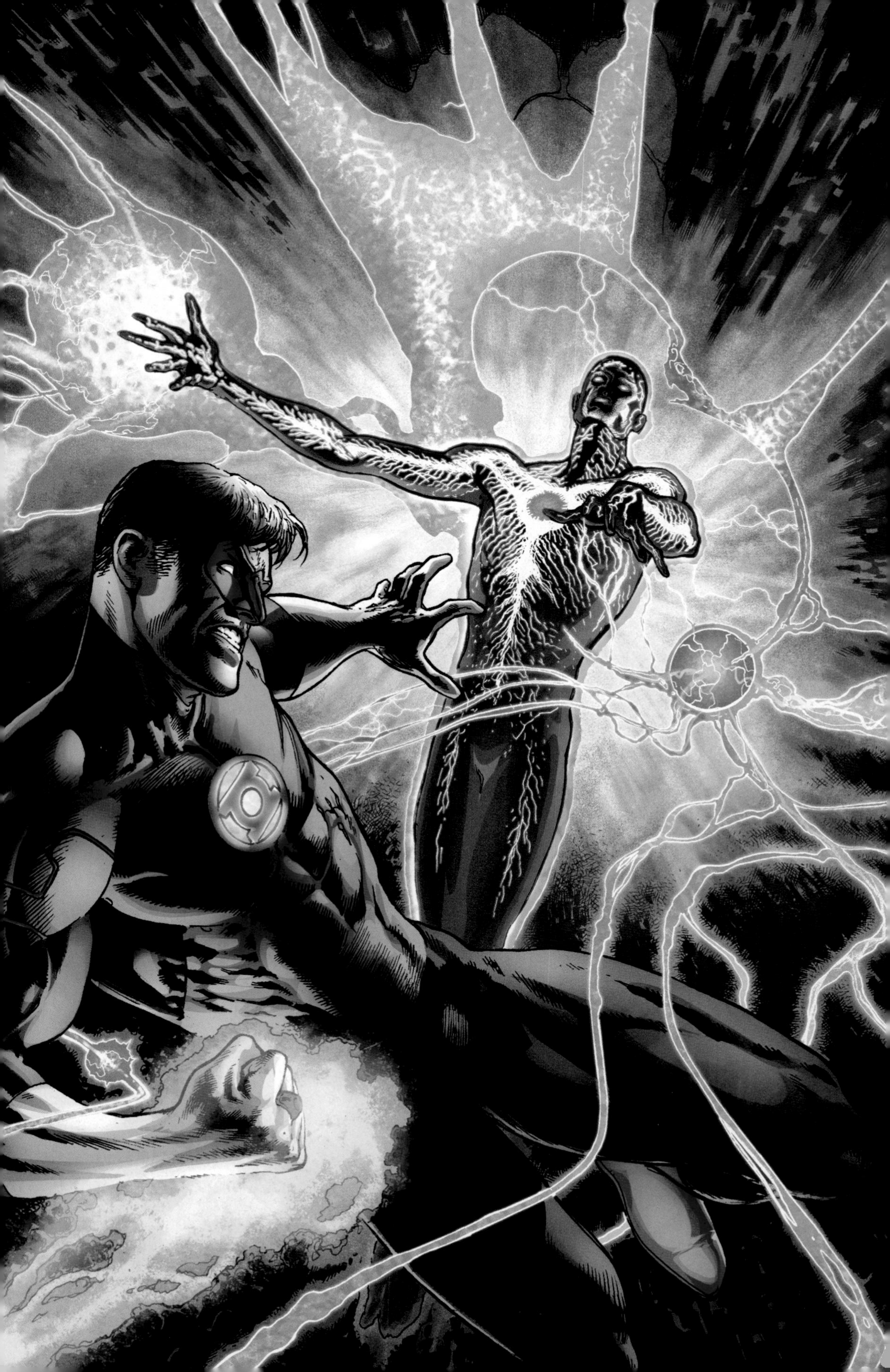

GEOFF JOHNS writer **DOUG MAHNKE** penciller
CHRISTIAN ALAMY, KEITH CHAMPAGNE, MARC DEERING, MARK IRWIN, WADE VON GRAWBADGER, TOM NGUYEN & DOUG MAHNKE inkers
PATRICK GLEASON, CULLY HAMNER, AARON KUDER, JERRY ORDWAY, IVAN REIS, ETHAN VAN SCIVER, OCLAIR ALBERT & JOE PRADO guest art
DOUG MAHNKE & ALEX SINCLAIR cover

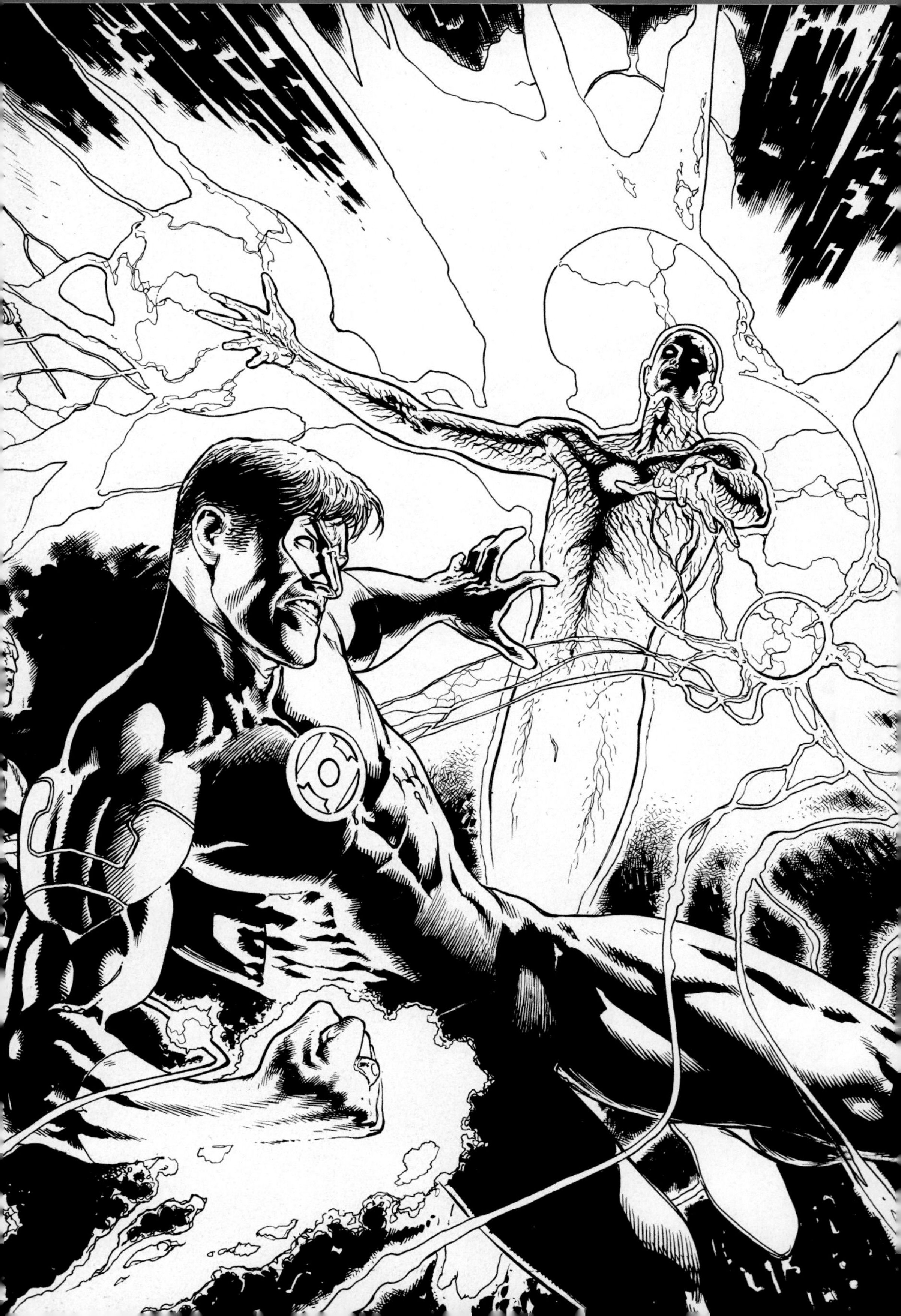

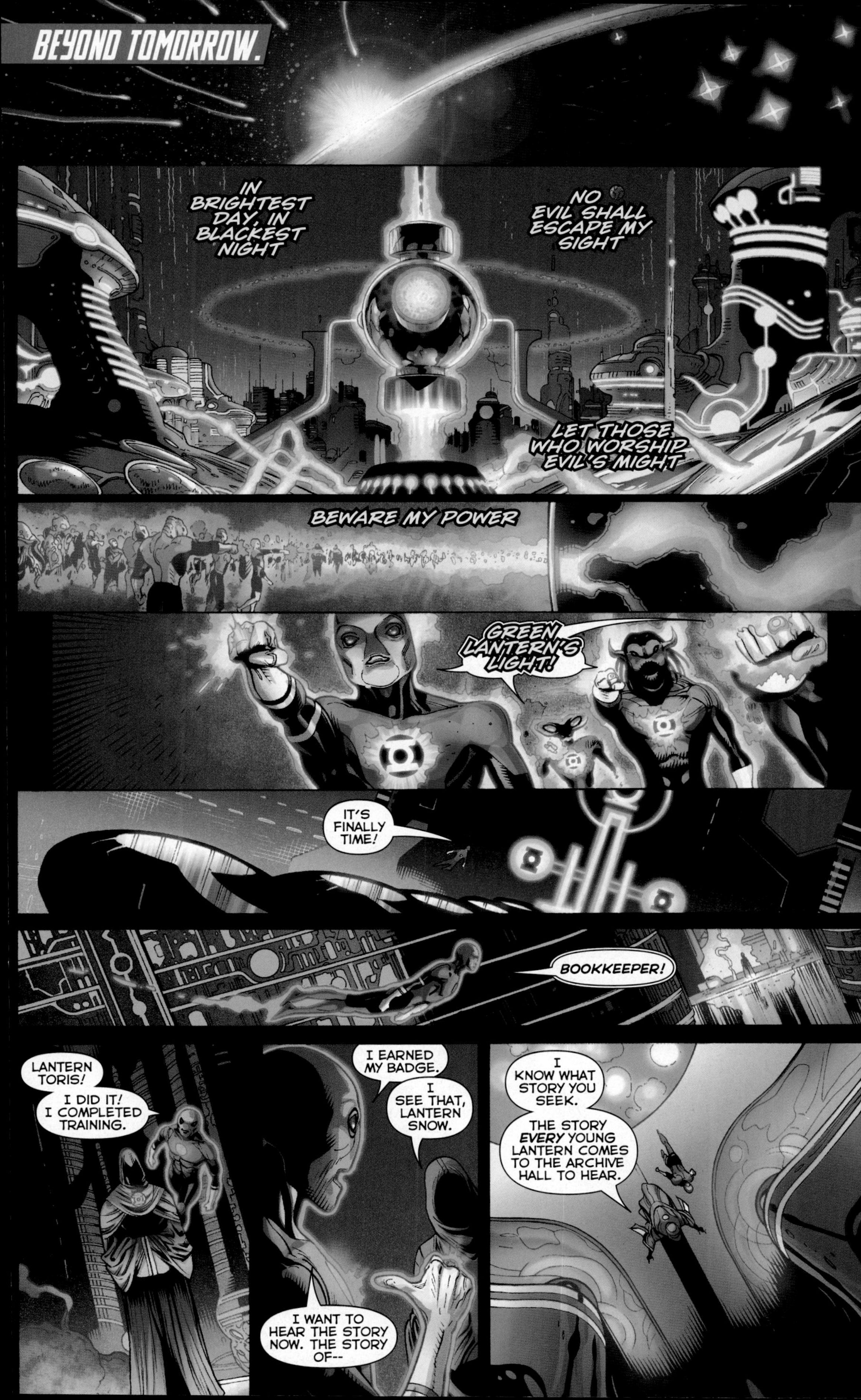
BEYOND TOMORROW.
IN BRIGHTEST DAY, IN BLACKEST NIGHT
NO EVIL SHALL ESCAPE MY SIGHT
LET THOSE WHO WORSHIP EVIL'S MIGHT
BEWARE MY POWER
GREEN LANTERN'S LIGHT!
IT'S FINALLY TIME!
BOOKKEEPER!
LANTERN TORIS!
I DID IT! I COMPLETED TRAINING.
I EARNED MY BADGE.
I SEE THAT, LANTERN SNOW.
I WANT TO HEAR THE STORY NOW. THE STORY OF--
I KNOW WHAT STORY YOU SEEK.
THE STORY EVERY YOUNG LANTERN COMES TO THE ARCHIVE HALL TO HEAR.

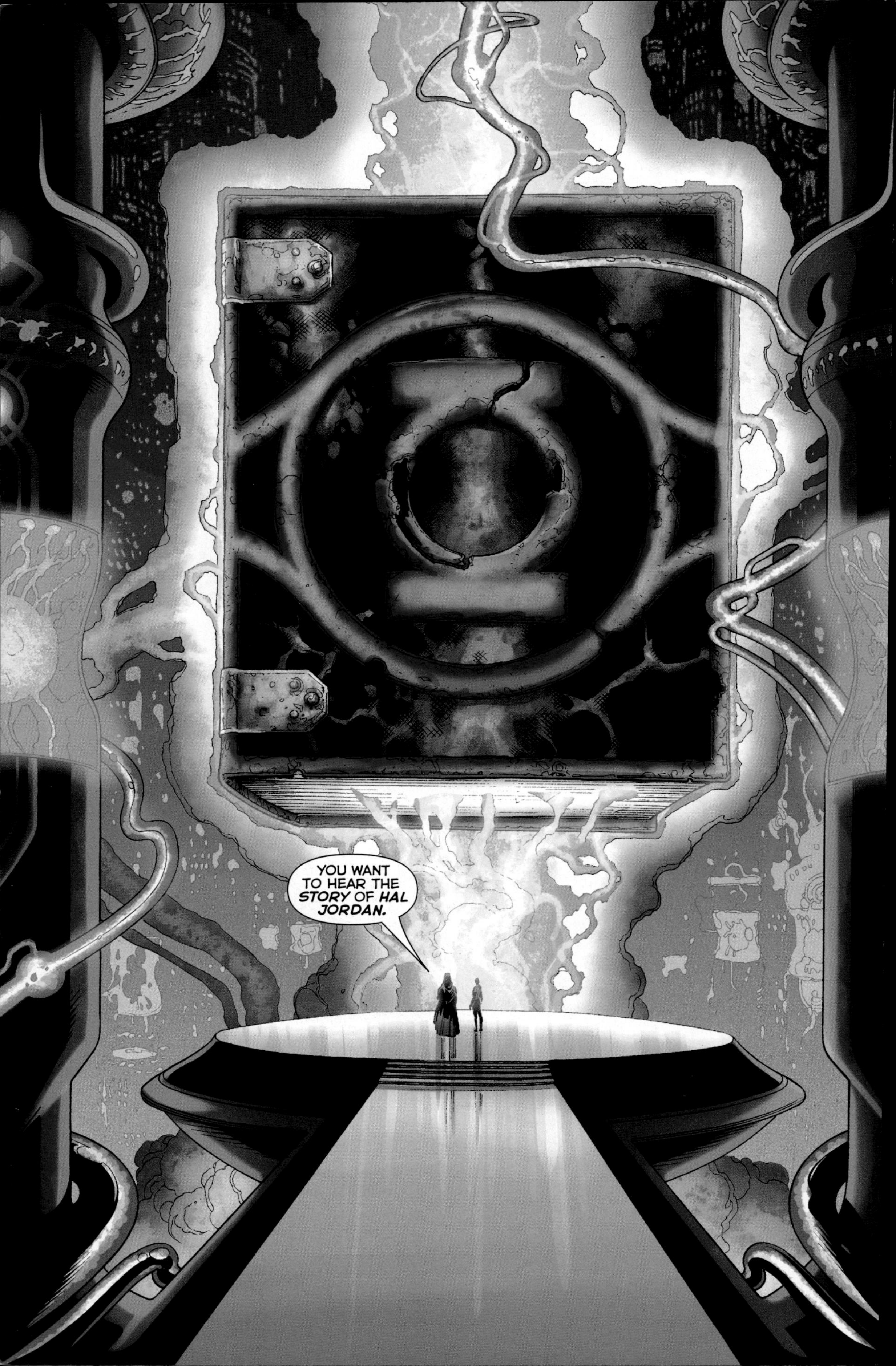
YOU WANT TO HEAR THE STORY OF HAL JORDAN.

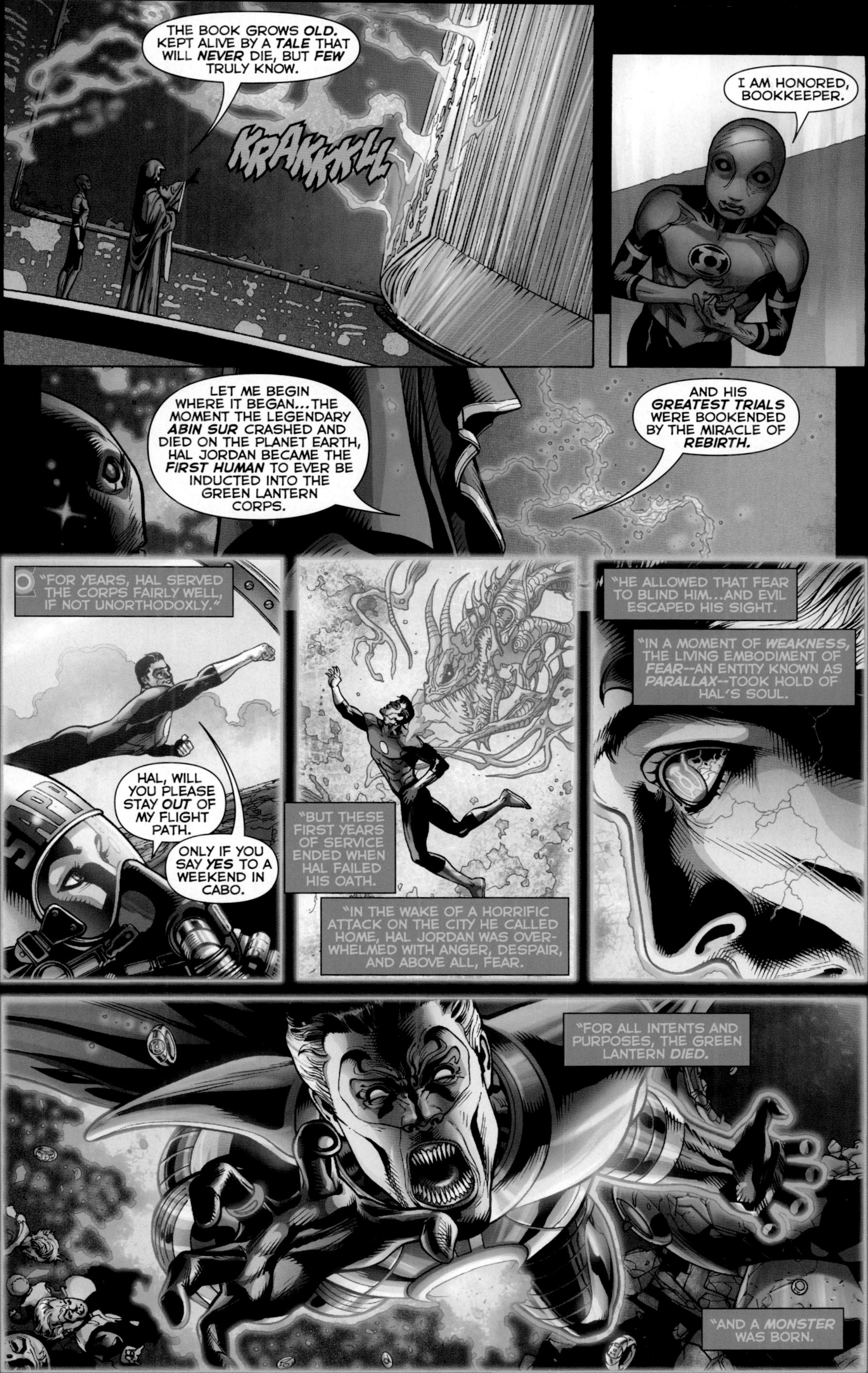
THE BOOK GROWS OLD. KEPT ALIVE BY A TALE THAT WILL NEVER DIE, BUT FEW TRULY KNOW.
KRAKKKLL
I AM HONORED, BOOKKEEPER.
LET ME BEGIN WHERE IT BEGAN... THE MOMENT THE LEGENDARY ABIN SUR CRASHED AND DIED ON THE PLANET EARTH, HAL JORDAN BECAME THE FIRST HUMAN TO EVER BE INDUCTED INTO THE GREEN LANTERN CORPS.
AND HIS GREATEST TRIALS WERE BOOKENDED BY THE MIRACLE OF REBIRTH.
"FOR YEARS, HAL SERVED THE CORPS FAIRLY WELL, IF NOT UNORTHODOXLY."
HAL, WILL YOU PLEASE STAY OUT OF MY FLIGHT PATH.
ONLY IF YOU SAY YES TO A WEEKEND IN CABO.
"BUT THESE FIRST YEARS OF SERVICE ENDED WHEN HAL FAILED HIS OATH.
"IN THE WAKE OF A HORRIFIC ATTACK ON THE CITY HE CALLED HOME, HAL JORDAN WAS OVERWHELMED WITH ANGER, DESPAIR, AND ABOVE ALL, FEAR.
"HE ALLOWED THAT FEAR TO BLIND HIM...AND EVIL ESCAPED HIS SIGHT.
"IN A MOMENT OF WEAKNESS, THE LIVING EMBODIMENT OF FEAR--AN ENTITY KNOWN AS PARALLAX--TOOK HOLD OF HAL'S SOUL.
"FOR ALL INTENTS AND PURPOSES, THE GREEN LANTERN DIED.
"AND A MONSTER WAS BORN.

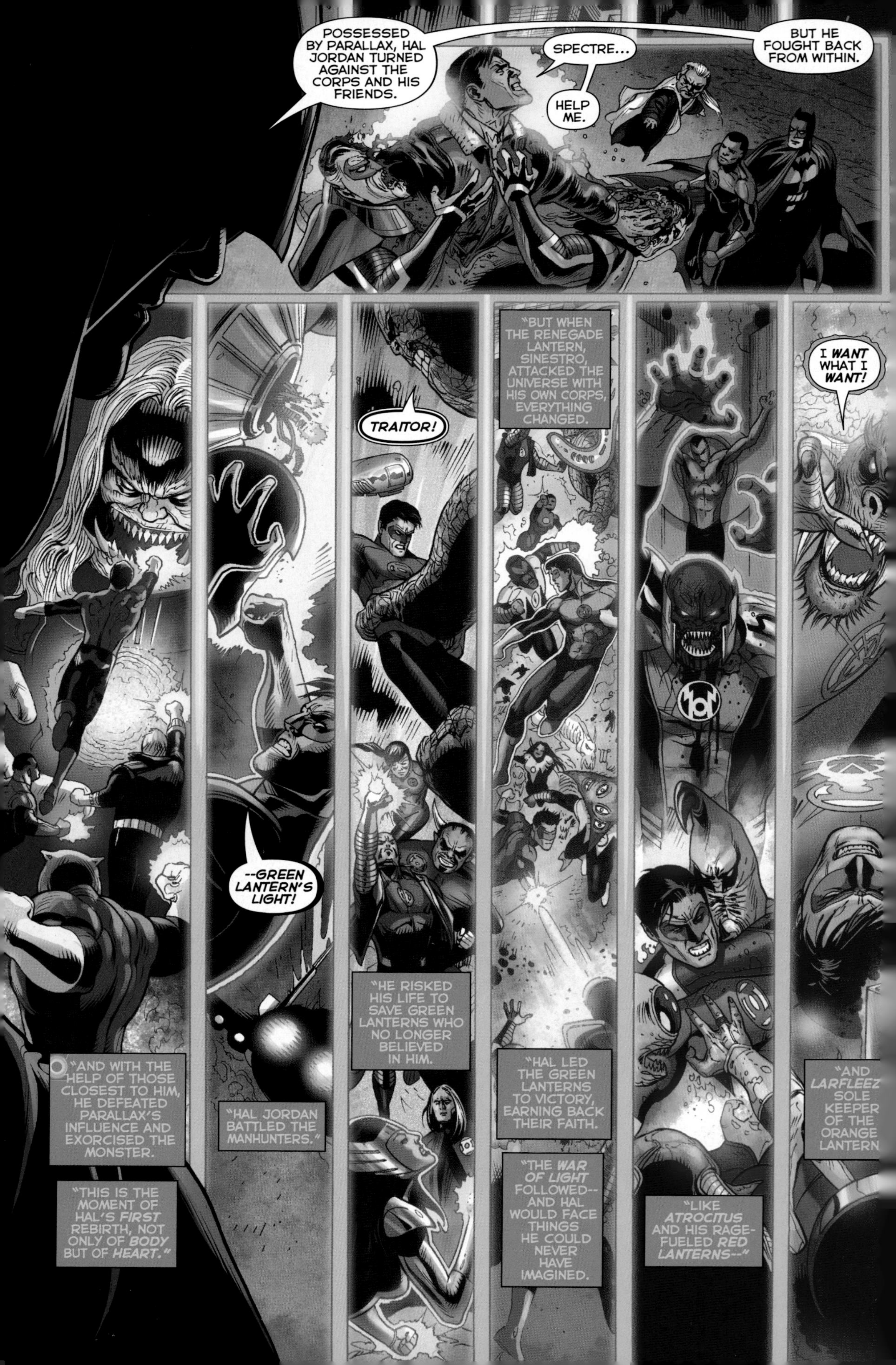

POSSESSED BY PARALLAX, HAL JORDAN TURNED AGAINST THE CORPS AND HIS FRIENDS.
SPECTRE...
HELP ME.
BUT HE FOUGHT BACK FROM WITHIN.
"AND WITH THE HELP OF THOSE CLOSEST TO HIM, HE DEFEATED PARALLAX'S INFLUENCE AND EXORCISED THE MONSTER.
"THIS IS THE MOMENT OF HAL'S FIRST REBIRTH, NOT ONLY OF BODY BUT OF HEART."
--GREEN LANTERN'S LIGHT!
"HAL JORDAN BATTLED THE MANHUNTERS."
TRAITOR!
"HE RISKED HIS LIFE TO SAVE GREEN LANTERNS WHO NO LONGER BELIEVED IN HIM.
"BUT WHEN THE RENEGADE LANTERN, SINESTRO, ATTACKED THE UNIVERSE WITH HIS OWN CORPS, EVERYTHING CHANGED.
"HAL LED THE GREEN LANTERNS TO VICTORY, EARNING BACK THEIR FAITH.
"THE WAR OF LIGHT FOLLOWED-- AND HAL WOULD FACE THINGS HE COULD NEVER HAVE IMAGINED.
"LIKE ATROCITUS AND HIS RAGE-FUELED RED LANTERNS--"
I WANT WHAT I WANT!
"AND LARFLEEZ SOLE KEEPER OF THE ORANGE LANTERN

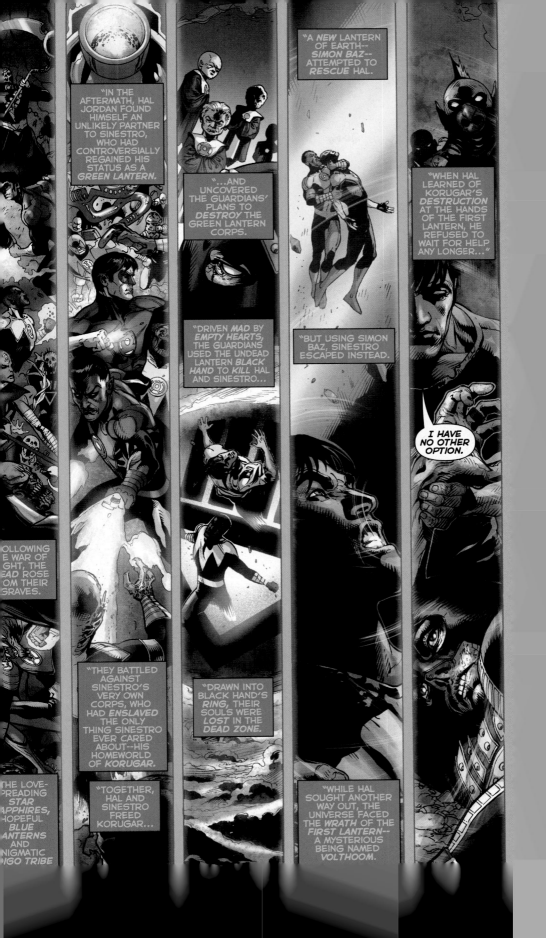

"IN THE AFTERMATH, HAL JORDAN FOUND HIMSELF AN UNLIKELY PARTNER TO SINESTRO, WHO HAD CONTROVERSIALLY REGAINED HIS STATUS AS A *GREEN LANTERN*.

"...AND UNCOVERED THE GUARDIANS' PLANS TO *DESTROY* THE GREEN LANTERN CORPS.

"A *NEW* LANTERN OF EARTH-- *SIMON BAZ*-- ATTEMPTED TO *RESCUE* HAL.

"WHEN HAL LEARNED OF KORUGAR'S *DESTRUCTION* AT THE HANDS OF THE FIRST LANTERN, HE REFUSED TO WAIT FOR HELP ANY LONGER..."

"DRIVEN *MAD* BY *EMPTY HEARTS*, THE GUARDIANS USED THE UNDEAD LANTERN *BLACK HAND* TO *KILL* HAL AND SINESTRO...

"BUT USING SIMON BAZ, SINESTRO ESCAPED INSTEAD.

OLLOWING E WAR OF GHT, THE EAD ROSE OM THEIR GRAVES.

I HAVE NO OTHER OPTION.

"THEY BATTLED AGAINST SINESTRO'S VERY OWN CORPS, WHO HAD *ENSLAVED* THE ONLY THING SINESTRO EVER CARED ABOUT--HIS HOMEWORLD OF *KORUGAR*.

"DRAWN INTO BLACK HAND'S *RING*, THEIR SOULS WERE *LOST* IN THE *DEAD ZONE*.

THE LOVE-PREADING *STAR* APPHIRES, HOPEFUL *BLUE* ANTERNS AND NIGMATIC DIGO TRIBE

"TOGETHER, HAL AND SINESTRO FREED KORUGAR...

"WHILE HAL SOUGHT ANOTHER WAY OUT, THE UNIVERSE FACED THE *WRATH* OF THE *FIRST LANTERN*-- A MYSTERIOUS BEING NAMED *VOLTHOOM*.

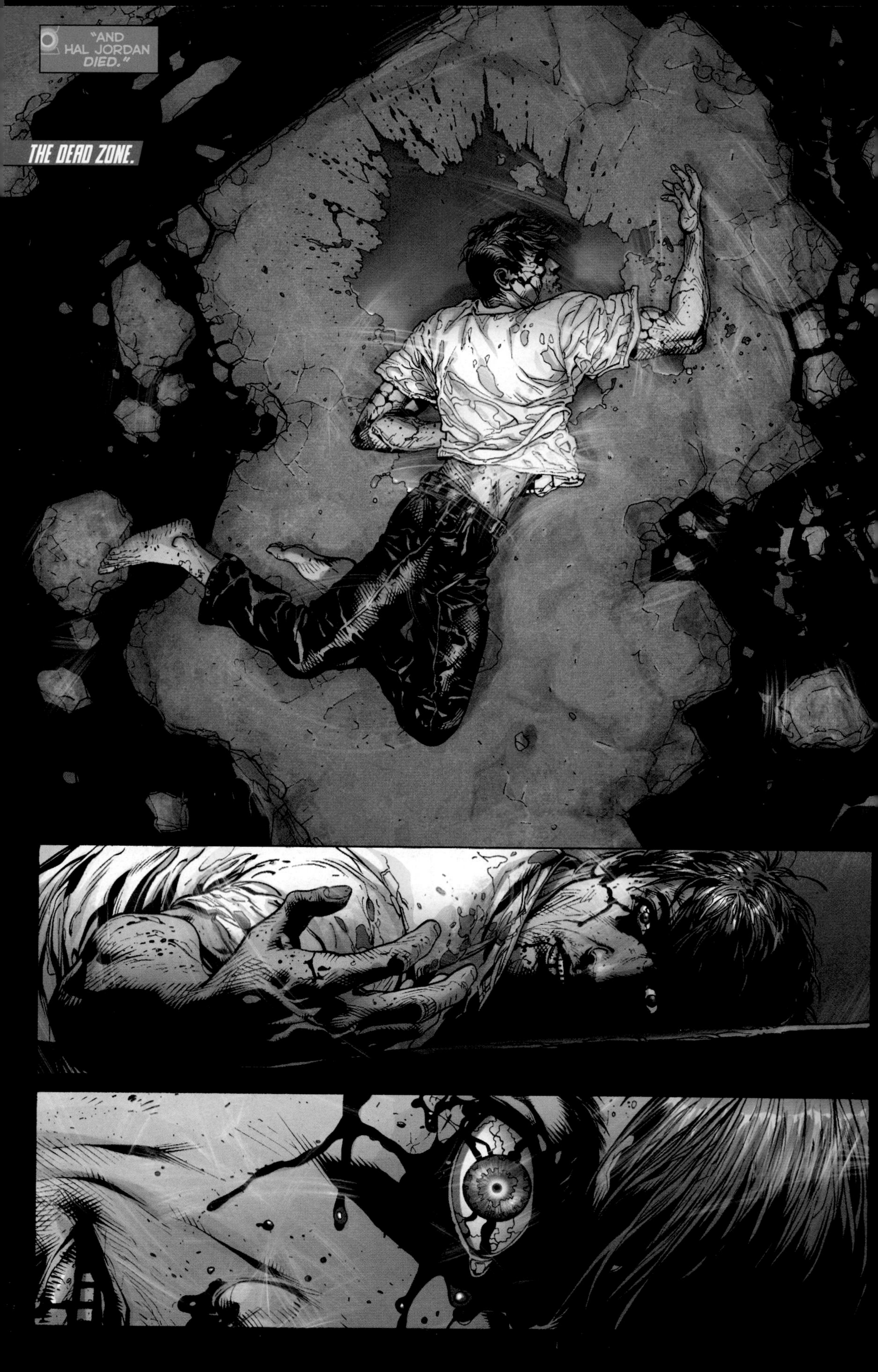
"AND HAL JORDAN DIED."
THE DEAD ZONE.

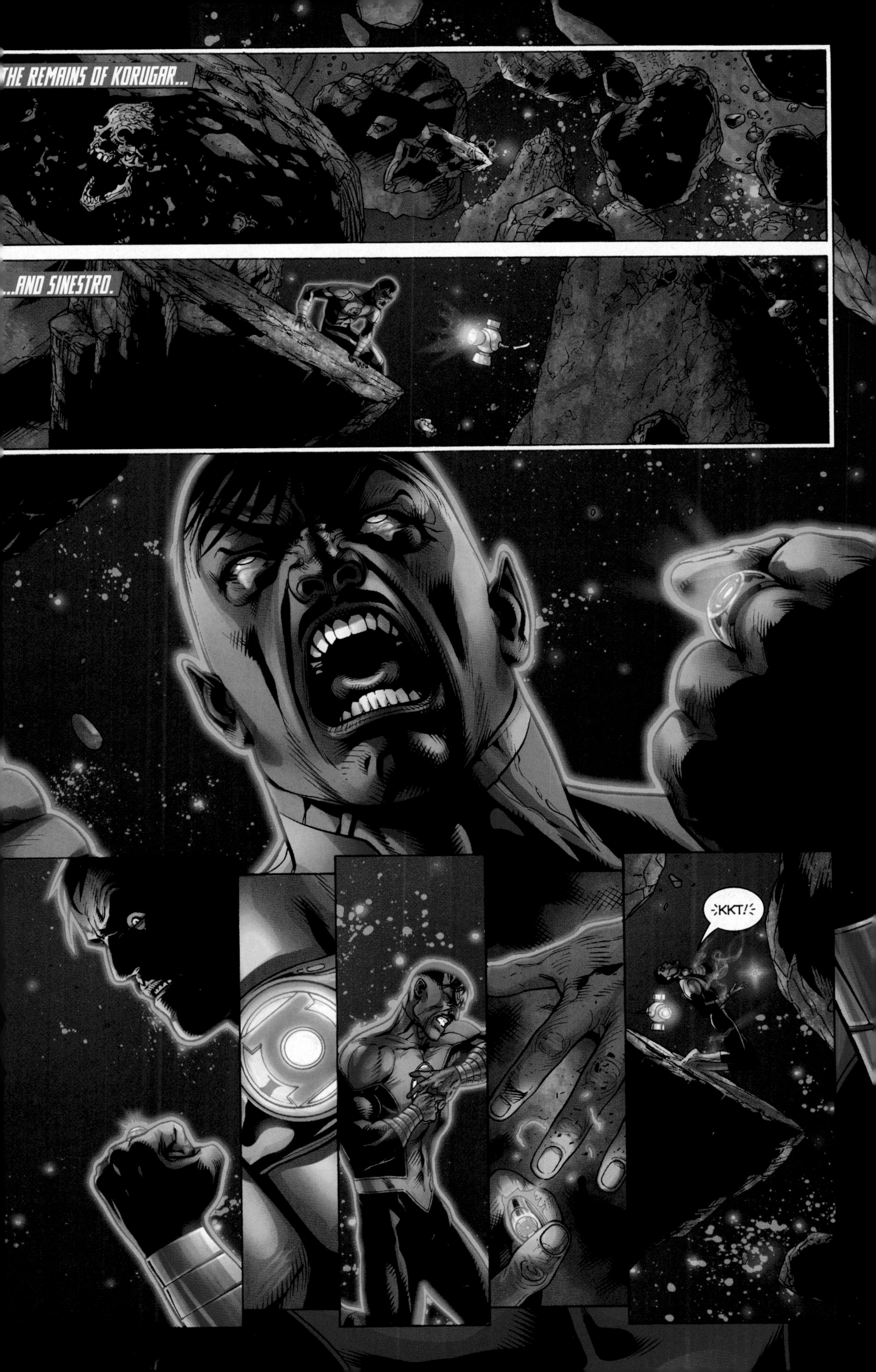
THE REMAINS OF KORUGAR...
...AND SINESTRO.
KKT!

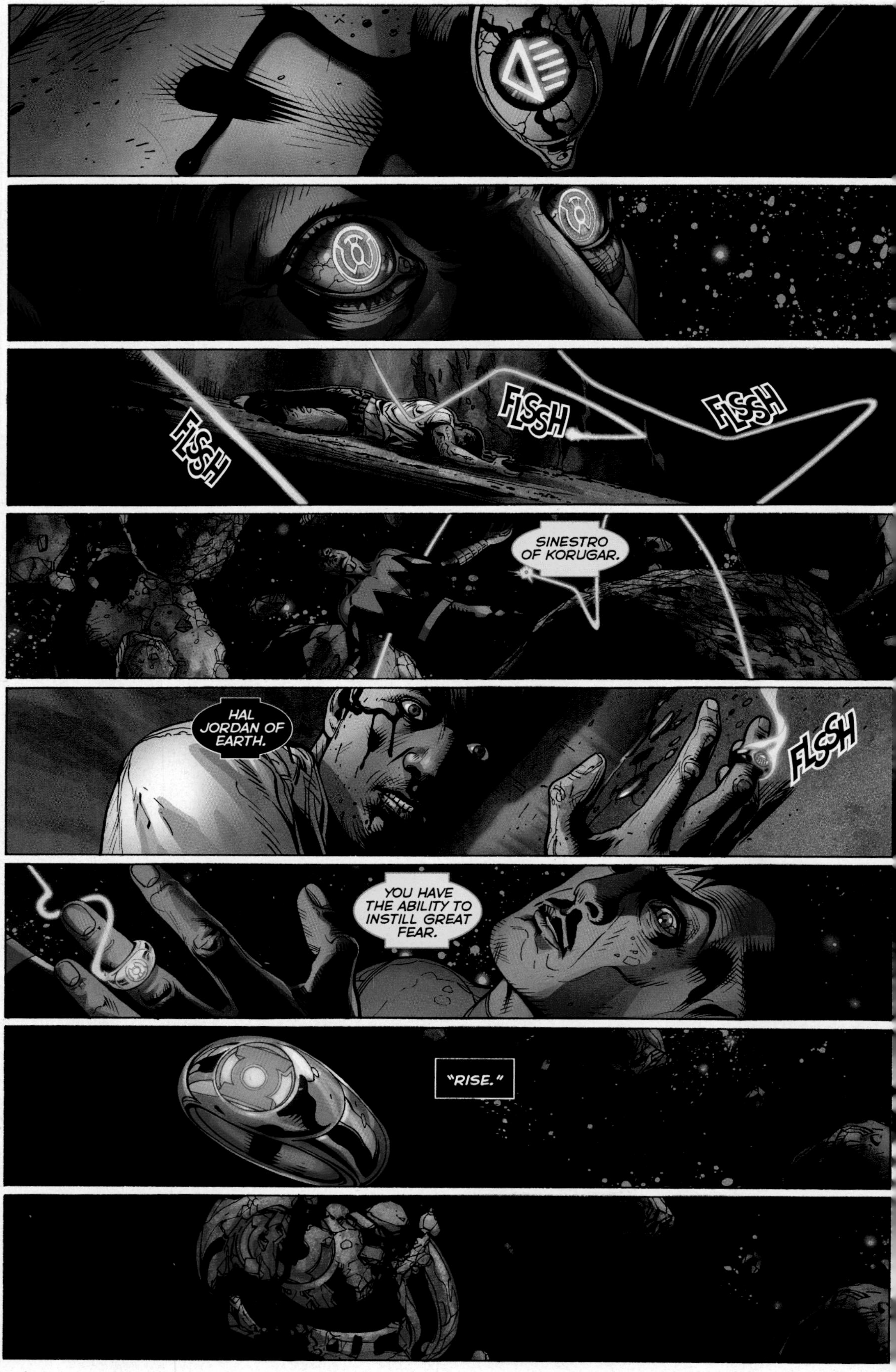

FLSSH
FLSSH
FLSSH
SINESTRO OF KORUGAR.
HAL JORDAN OF EARTH.
FLSSH
YOU HAVE THE ABILITY TO INSTILL GREAT FEAR.
"RISE."

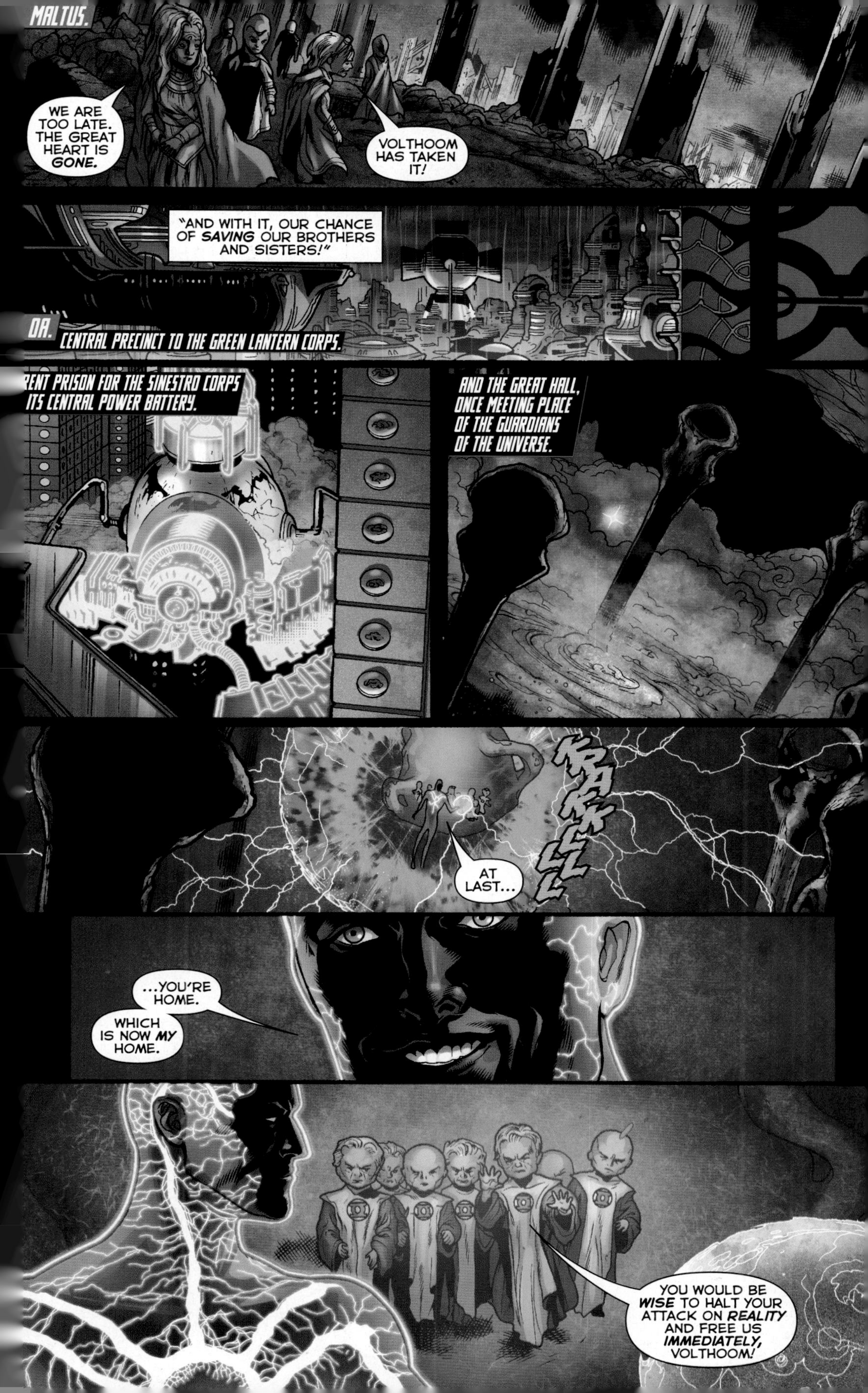
MALTUS.
WE ARE TOO LATE. THE GREAT HEART IS GONE.
VOLTHOOM HAS TAKEN IT!
"AND WITH IT, OUR CHANCE OF SAVING OUR BROTHERS AND SISTERS!"
OA. CENTRAL PRECINCT TO THE GREEN LANTERN CORPS.
RENT PRISON FOR THE SINESTRO CORPS ITS CENTRAL POWER BATTERY.
AND THE GREAT HALL, ONCE MEETING PLACE OF THE GUARDIANS OF THE UNIVERSE.
KRAKKLLL
AT LAST...
...YOU'RE HOME.
WHICH IS NOW MY HOME.
YOU WOULD BE WISE TO HALT YOUR ATTACK ON REALITY AND FREE US IMMEDIATELY, VOLTHOOM!

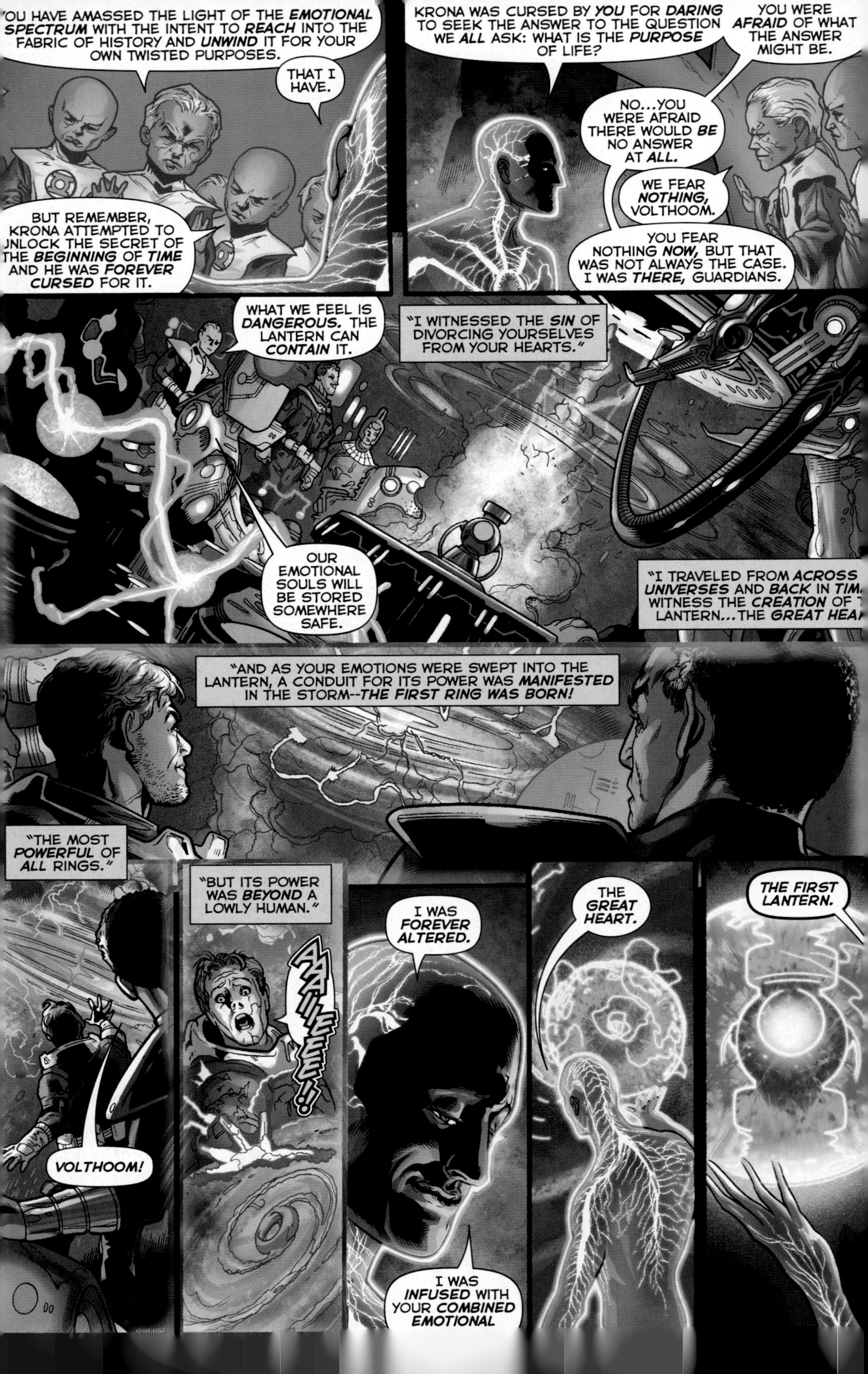

YOU HAVE AMASSED THE LIGHT OF THE EMOTIONAL SPECTRUM WITH THE INTENT TO REACH INTO THE FABRIC OF HISTORY AND UNWIND IT FOR YOUR OWN TWISTED PURPOSES.
THAT I HAVE.
BUT REMEMBER, KRONA ATTEMPTED TO UNLOCK THE SECRET OF THE BEGINNING OF TIME AND HE WAS FOREVER CURSED FOR IT.
KRONA WAS CURSED BY YOU FOR DARING TO SEEK THE ANSWER TO THE QUESTION WE ALL ASK: WHAT IS THE PURPOSE OF LIFE?
YOU WERE AFRAID OF WHAT THE ANSWER MIGHT BE.
NO...YOU WERE AFRAID THERE WOULD BE NO ANSWER AT ALL.
WE FEAR NOTHING, VOLTHOOM.
YOU FEAR NOTHING NOW, BUT THAT WAS NOT ALWAYS THE CASE. I WAS THERE, GUARDIANS.
WHAT WE FEEL IS DANGEROUS. THE LANTERN CAN CONTAIN IT.
"I WITNESSED THE SIN OF DIVORCING YOURSELVES FROM YOUR HEARTS."
OUR EMOTIONAL SOULS WILL BE STORED SOMEWHERE SAFE.
"I TRAVELED FROM ACROSS UNIVERSES AND BACK IN TIM WITNESS THE CREATION OF T LANTERN...THE GREAT HEA
"AND AS YOUR EMOTIONS WERE SWEPT INTO THE LANTERN, A CONDUIT FOR ITS POWER WAS MANIFESTED IN THE STORM--THE FIRST RING WAS BORN!
"THE MOST POWERFUL OF ALL RINGS."
VOLTHOOM!
"BUT ITS POWER WAS BEYOND A LOWLY HUMAN."
AAAIIEEEE!!
I WAS FOREVER ALTERED.
I WAS INFUSED WITH YOUR COMBINED EMOTIONAL
THE GREAT HEART.
THE FIRST LANTERN.

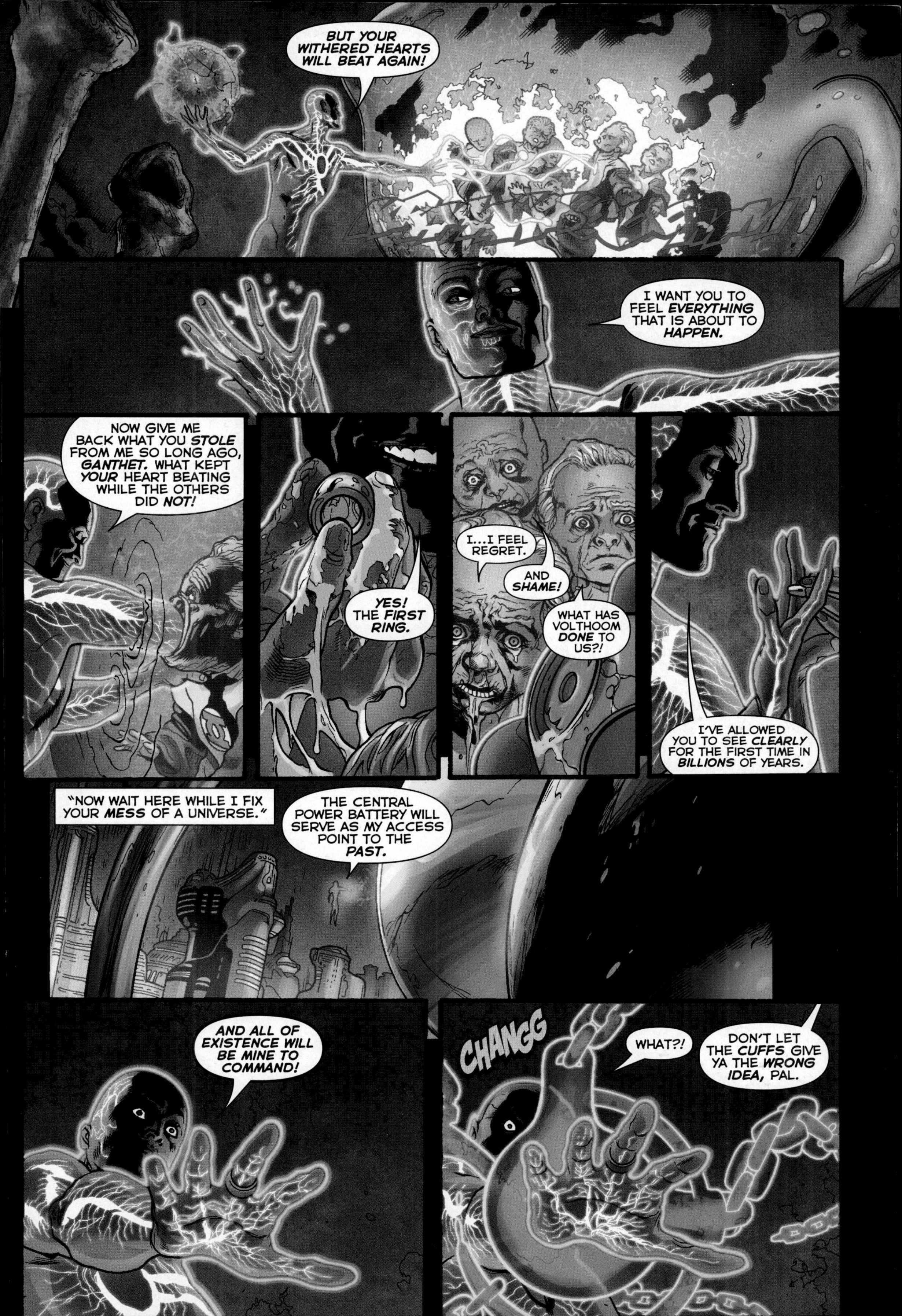

BUT YOUR WITHERED HEARTS WILL BEAT AGAIN!
I WANT YOU TO FEEL EVERYTHING THAT IS ABOUT TO HAPPEN.
NOW GIVE ME BACK WHAT YOU STOLE FROM ME SO LONG AGO, GANTHET. WHAT KEPT YOUR HEART BEATING WHILE THE OTHERS DID NOT!
YES! THE FIRST RING.
I...I FEEL REGRET.
AND SHAME!
WHAT HAS VOLTHOOM DONE TO US?!
I'VE ALLOWED YOU TO SEE CLEARLY FOR THE FIRST TIME IN BILLIONS OF YEARS.
"NOW WAIT HERE WHILE I FIX YOUR MESS OF A UNIVERSE."
THE CENTRAL POWER BATTERY WILL SERVE AS MY ACCESS POINT TO THE PAST.
AND ALL OF EXISTENCE WILL BE MINE TO COMMAND!
CHANGG
WHAT?!
DON'T LET THE CUFFS GIVE YA THE WRONG IDEA, PAL.

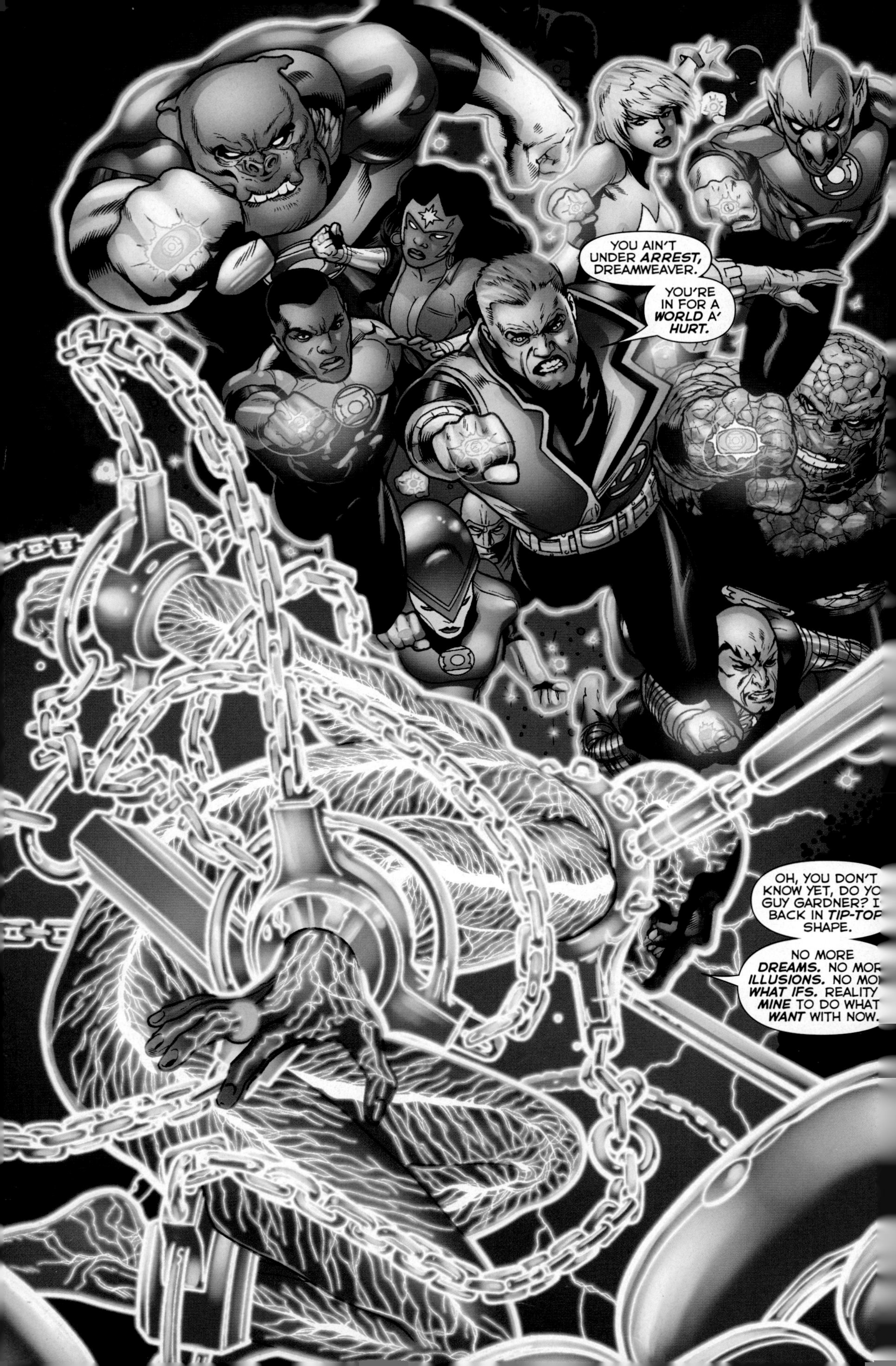
YOU AIN'T UNDER ARREST, DREAMWEAVER.
YOU'RE IN FOR A WORLD A' HURT.
OH, YOU DON'T KNOW YET, DO YO GUY GARDNER? I BACK IN TIP-TOP SHAPE.
NO MORE DREAMS. NO MOR ILLUSIONS. NO MO WHAT IFS. REALITY MINE TO DO WHAT WANT WITH NOW.

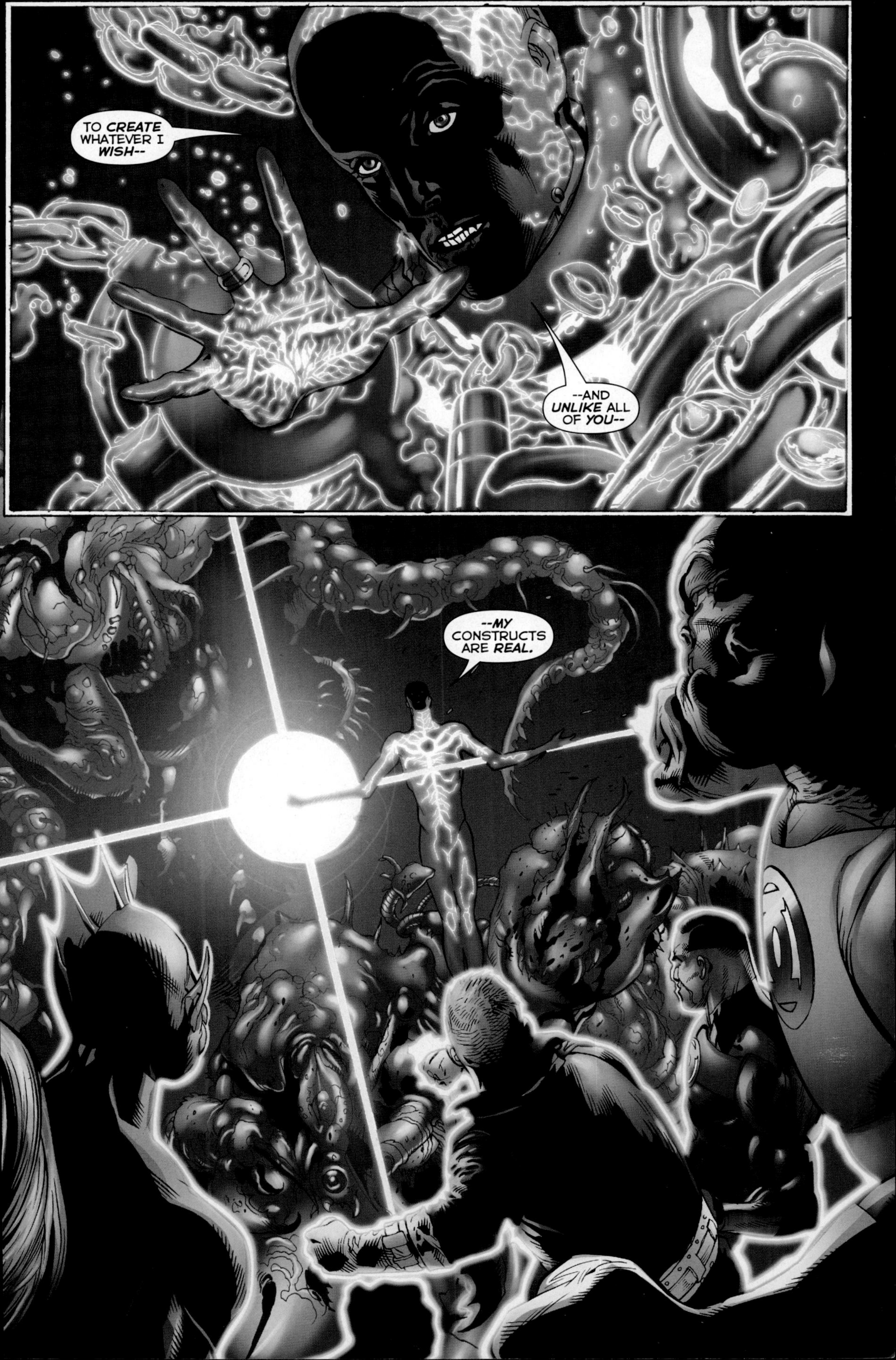
TO CREATE WHATEVER I WISH--
--AND UNLIKE ALL OF YOU--
--MY CONSTRUCTS ARE REAL.

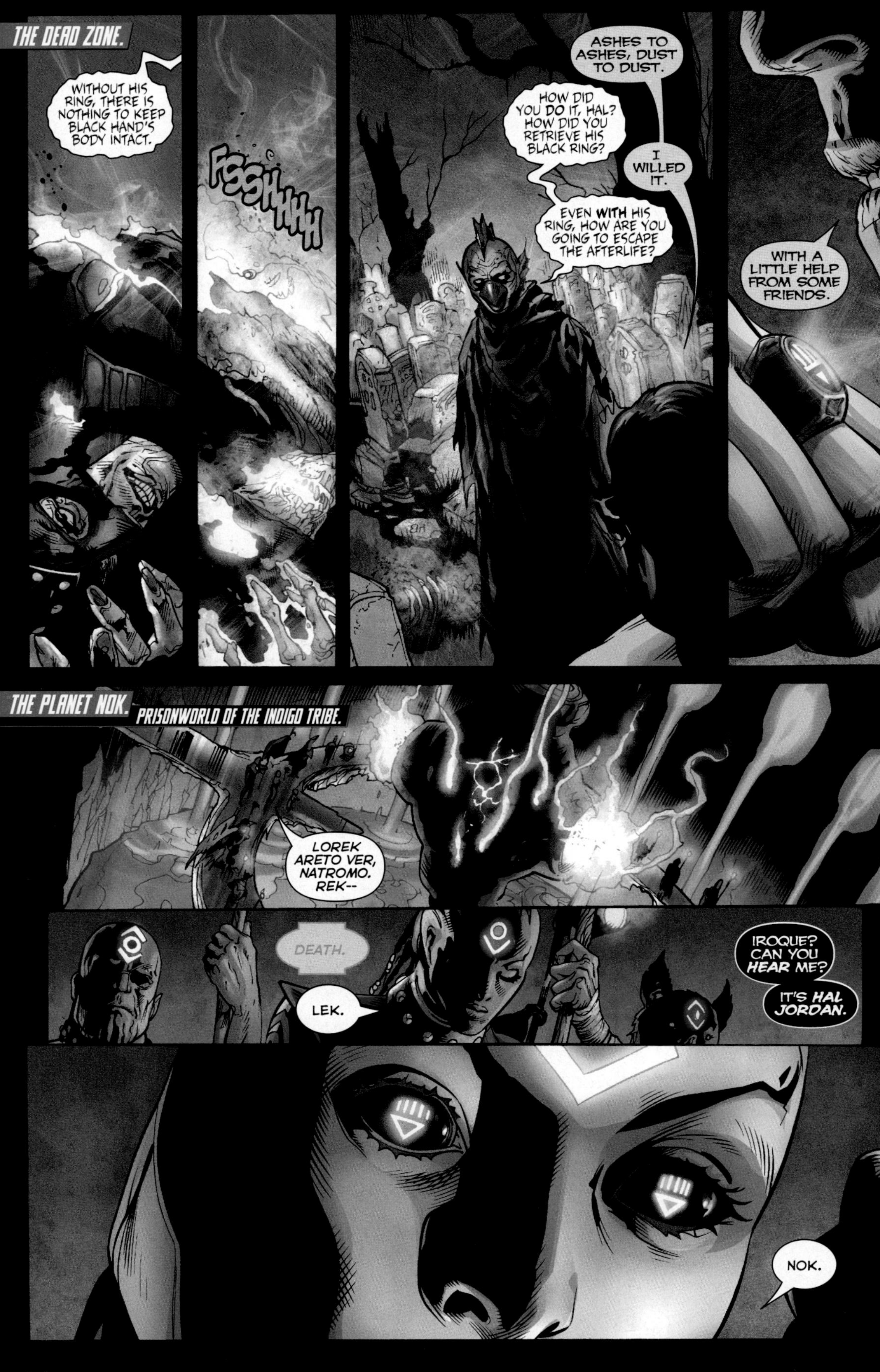
THE DEAD ZONE.
WITHOUT HIS RING, THERE IS NOTHING TO KEEP BLACK HAND'S BODY INTACT.
FSSHHHH
ASHES TO ASHES, DUST TO DUST.
HOW DID YOU DO IT, HAL? HOW DID YOU RETRIEVE HIS BLACK RING?
I WILLED IT.
EVEN WITH HIS RING, HOW ARE YOU GOING TO ESCAPE THE AFTERLIFE?
WITH A LITTLE HELP FROM SOME FRIENDS.
THE PLANET NOK.
PRISONWORLD OF THE INDIGO TRIBE.
LOREK ARETO VER, NATROMO. REK--
DEATH.
LEK.
IROQUE? CAN YOU HEAR ME?
IT'S HAL JORDAN.
NOK.

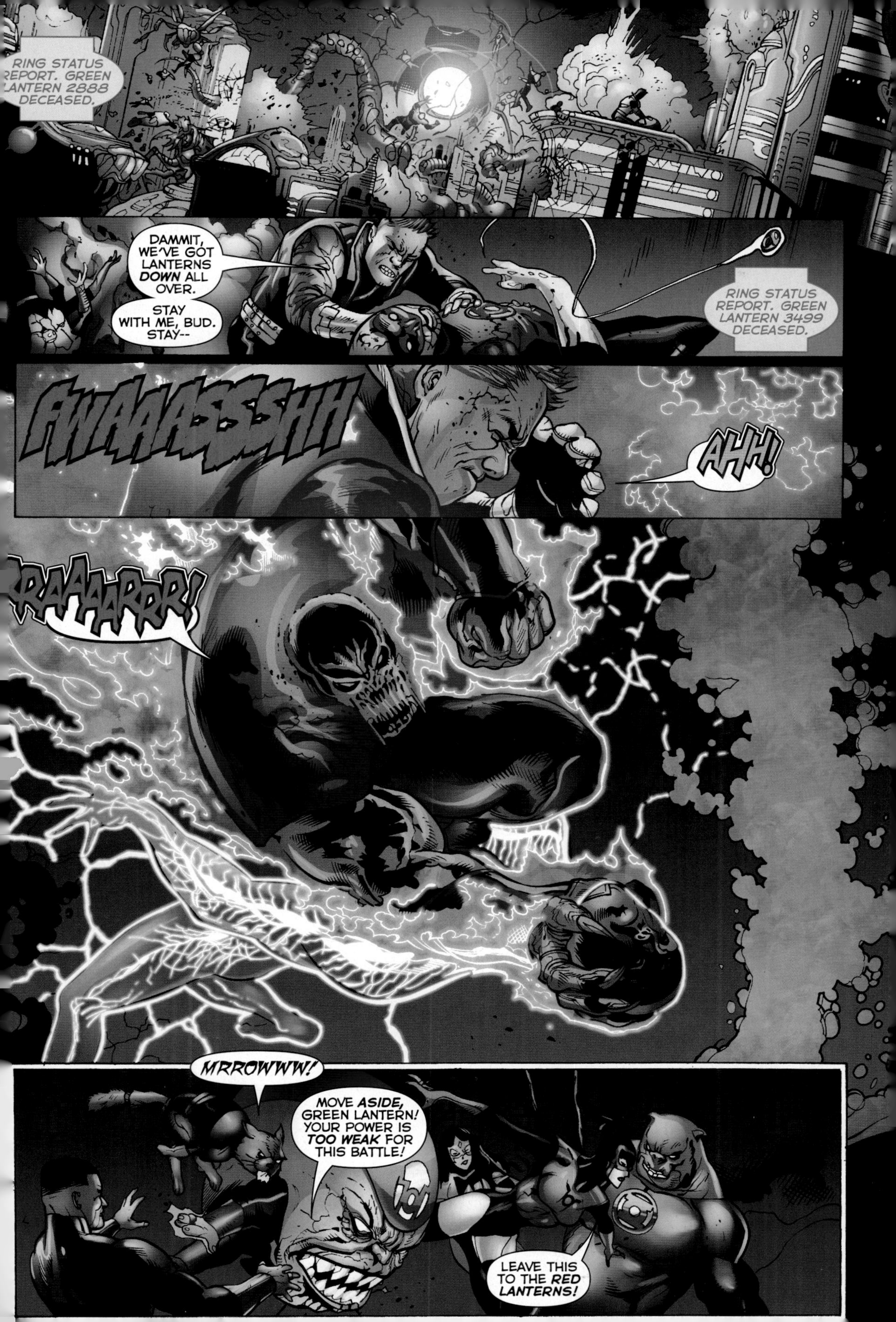
RING STATUS REPORT. GREEN LANTERN 2888 DECEASED.
DAMMIT, WE'VE GOT LANTERNS DOWN ALL OVER.
STAY WITH ME, BUD. STAY--
RING STATUS REPORT. GREEN LANTERN 3499 DECEASED.
FWAAAASSSHH
AHH!
RRAAAARRR!
MRROWWW!
MOVE ASIDE, GREEN LANTERN! YOUR POWER IS TOO WEAK FOR THIS BATTLE!
LEAVE THIS TO THE RED LANTERNS!

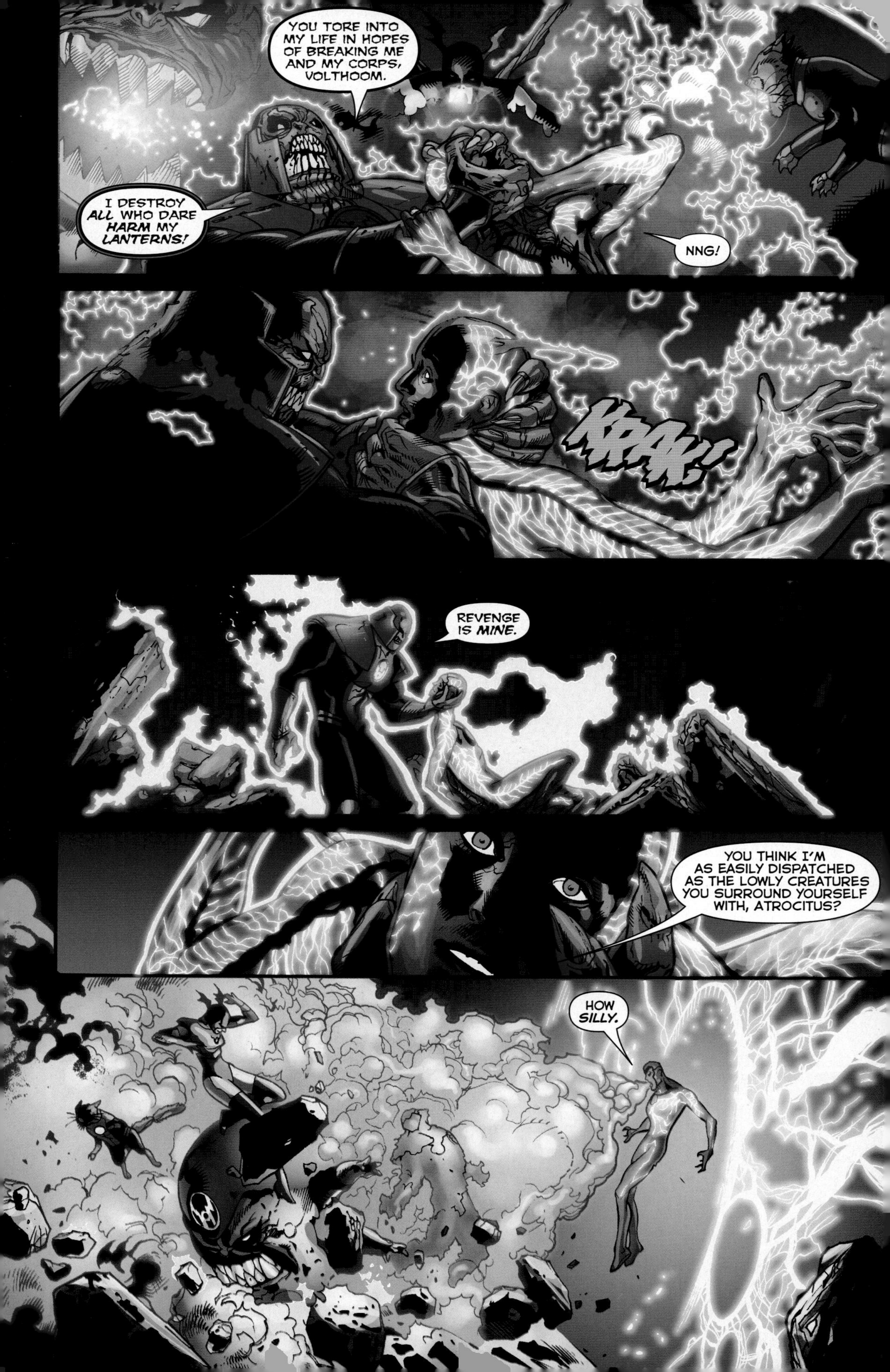
YOU TORE INTO MY LIFE IN HOPES OF BREAKING ME AND MY CORPS, VOLTHOOM.
I DESTROY ALL WHO DARE HARM MY LANTERNS!
NNG!
KRAK!!
REVENGE IS MINE.
YOU THINK I'M AS EASILY DISPATCHED AS THE LOWLY CREATURES YOU SURROUND YOURSELF WITH, ATROCITUS?
HOW SILLY.

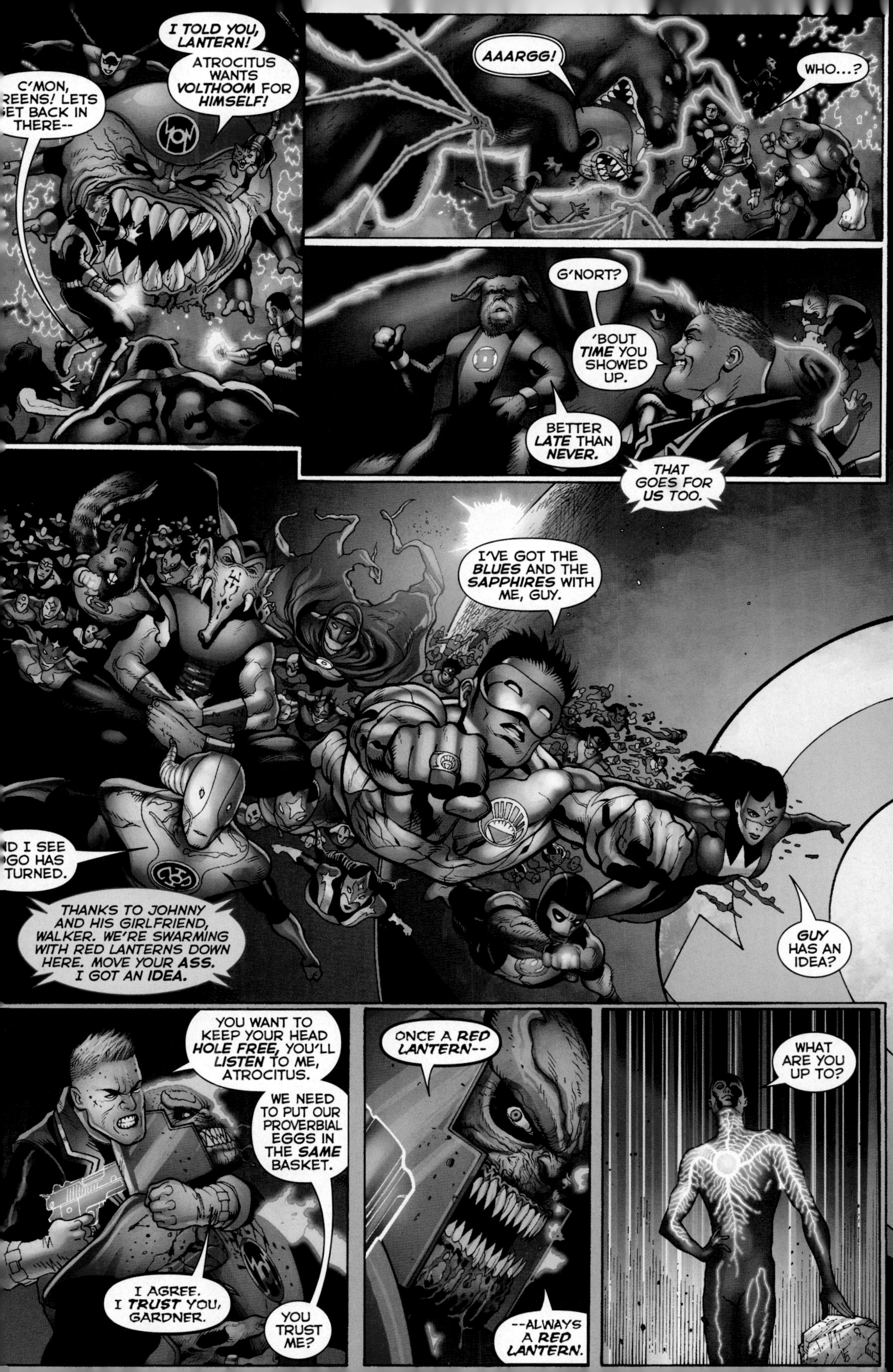
I TOLD YOU, LANTERN!
ATROCITUS WANTS VOLTHOOM FOR HIMSELF!
C'MON, REENS! LETS ET BACK IN THERE--
AAARGG!
WHO...?
G'NORT?
'BOUT TIME YOU SHOWED UP.
BETTER LATE THAN NEVER.
THAT GOES FOR US TOO.
I'VE GOT THE BLUES AND THE SAPPHIRES WITH ME, GUY.
ID I SEE OGO HAS TURNED.
THANKS TO JOHNNY AND HIS GIRLFRIEND, WALKER. WE'RE SWARMING WITH RED LANTERNS DOWN HERE. MOVE YOUR ASS. I GOT AN IDEA.
GUY HAS AN IDEA?
YOU WANT TO KEEP YOUR HEAD HOLE FREE, YOU'LL LISTEN TO ME, ATROCITUS.
WE NEED TO PUT OUR PROVERBIAL EGGS IN THE SAME BASKET.
I AGREE. I TRUST YOU, GARDNER.
YOU TRUST ME?
ONCE A RED LANTERN--
--ALWAYS A RED LANTERN.
WHAT ARE YOU UP TO?

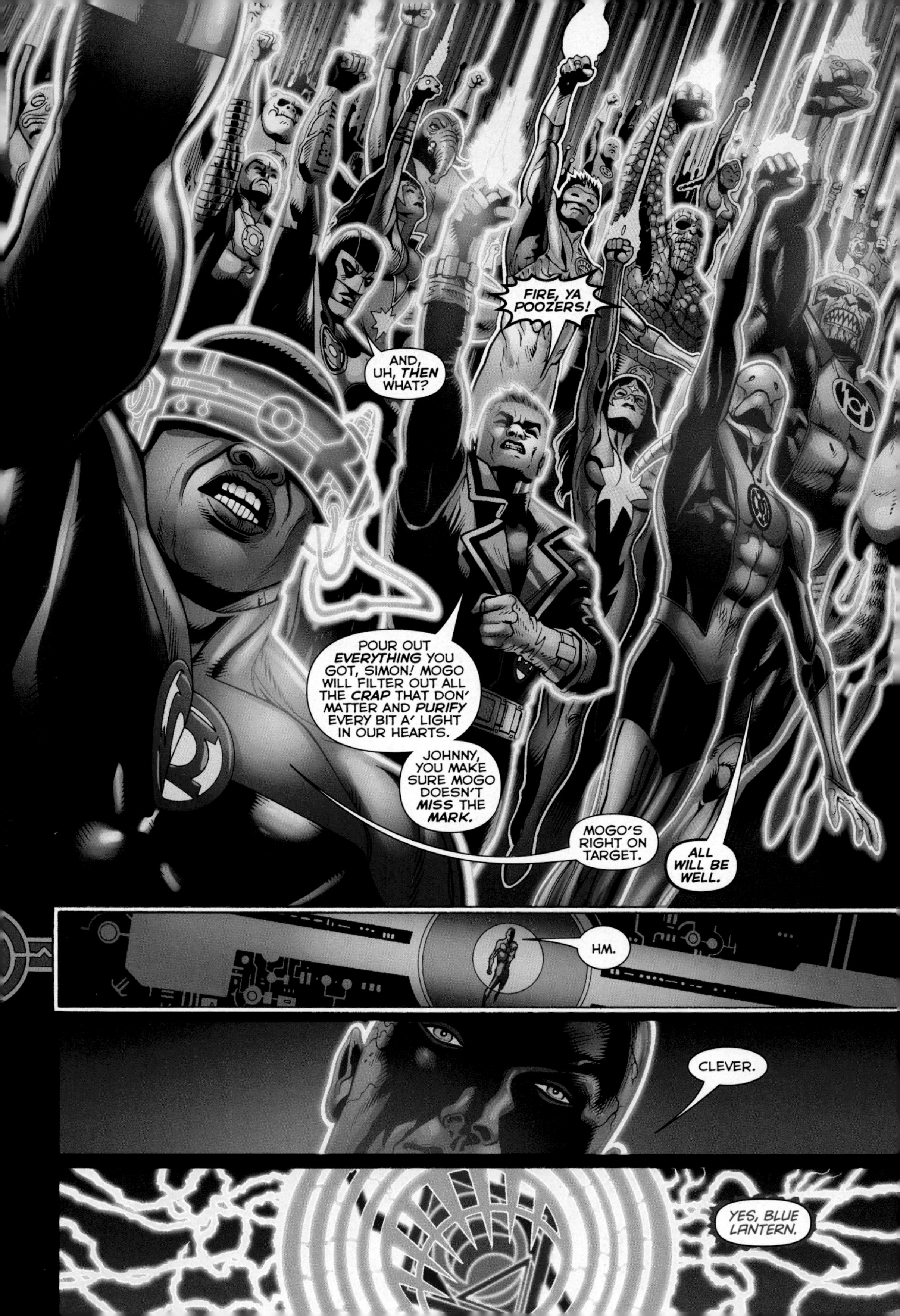
FIRE, YA POOZERS!
AND, UH, THEN WHAT?
POUR OUT EVERYTHING YOU GOT, SIMON! MOGO WILL FILTER OUT ALL THE CRAP THAT DON' MATTER AND PURIFY EVERY BIT A' LIGHT IN OUR HEARTS.
JOHNNY, YOU MAKE SURE MOGO DOESN'T MISS THE MARK.
MOGO'S RIGHT ON TARGET.
ALL WILL BE WELL.
HM.
CLEVER.
YES, BLUE LANTERN.

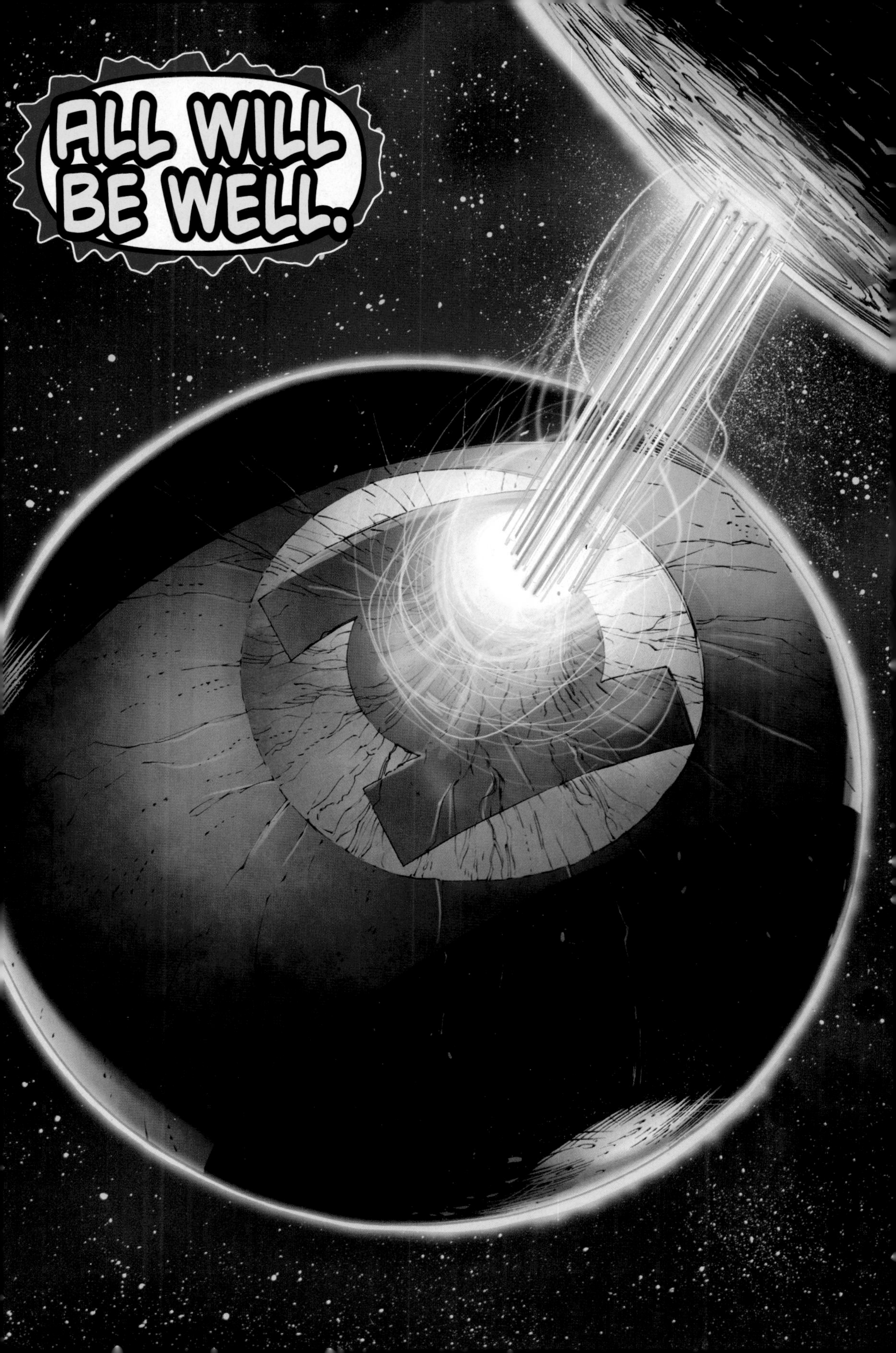
ALL WILL BE WELL.

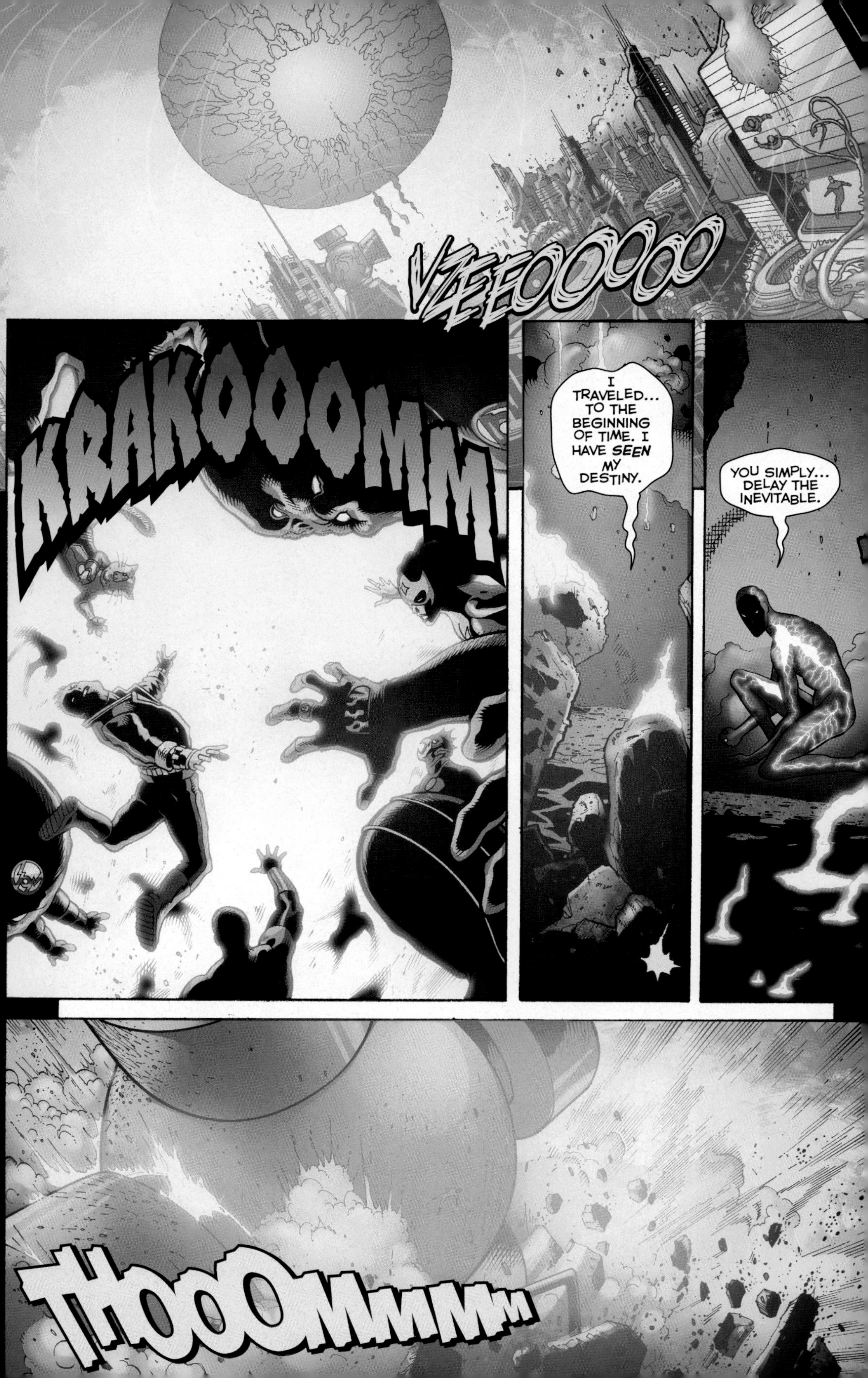
VZEEOOOOO
KRAKOOOMMM
I TRAVELED... TO THE BEGINNING OF TIME. I HAVE SEEN MY DESTINY.
YOU SIMPLY... DELAY THE INEVITABLE.
THOOOMMMMM

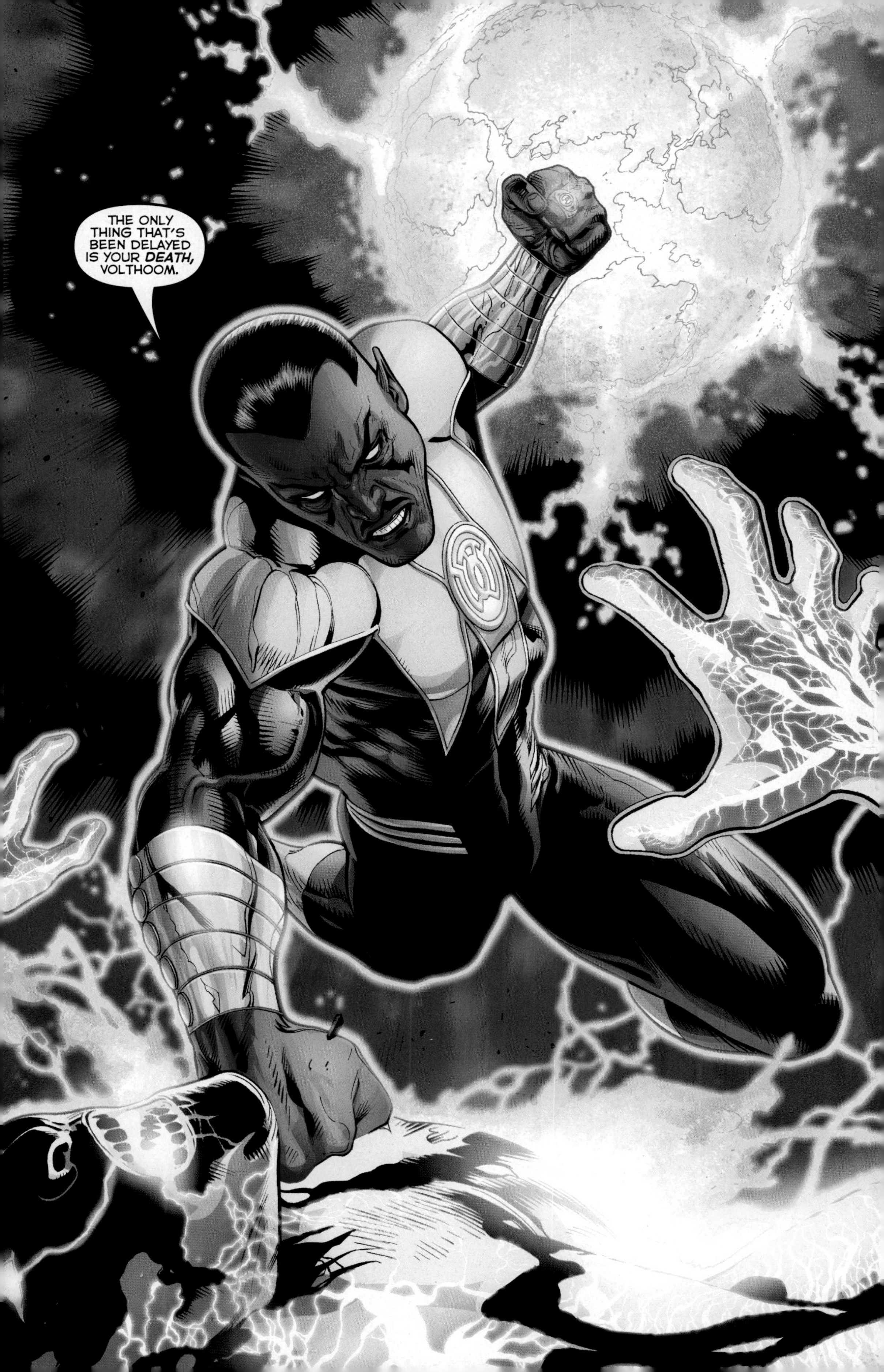
THE ONLY THING THAT'S BEEN DELAYED IS YOUR DEATH, VOLTHOOM.

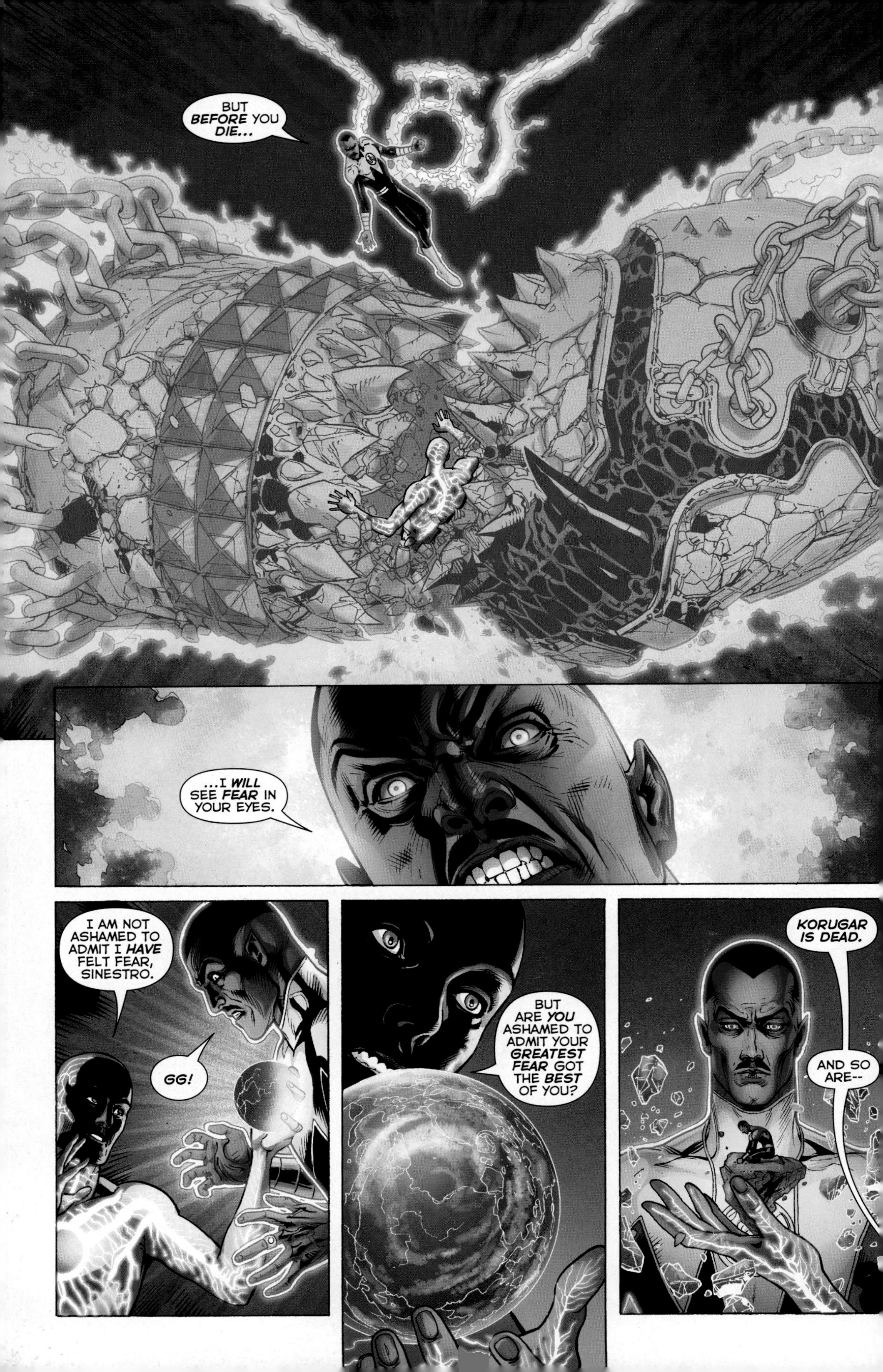
BUT BEFORE YOU DIE...
...I WILL SEE FEAR IN YOUR EYES.
I AM NOT ASHAMED TO ADMIT I HAVE FELT FEAR, SINESTRO.
GG!
BUT ARE YOU ASHAMED TO ADMIT YOUR GREATEST FEAR GOT THE BEST OF YOU?
KORUGAR IS DEAD.
AND SO ARE--

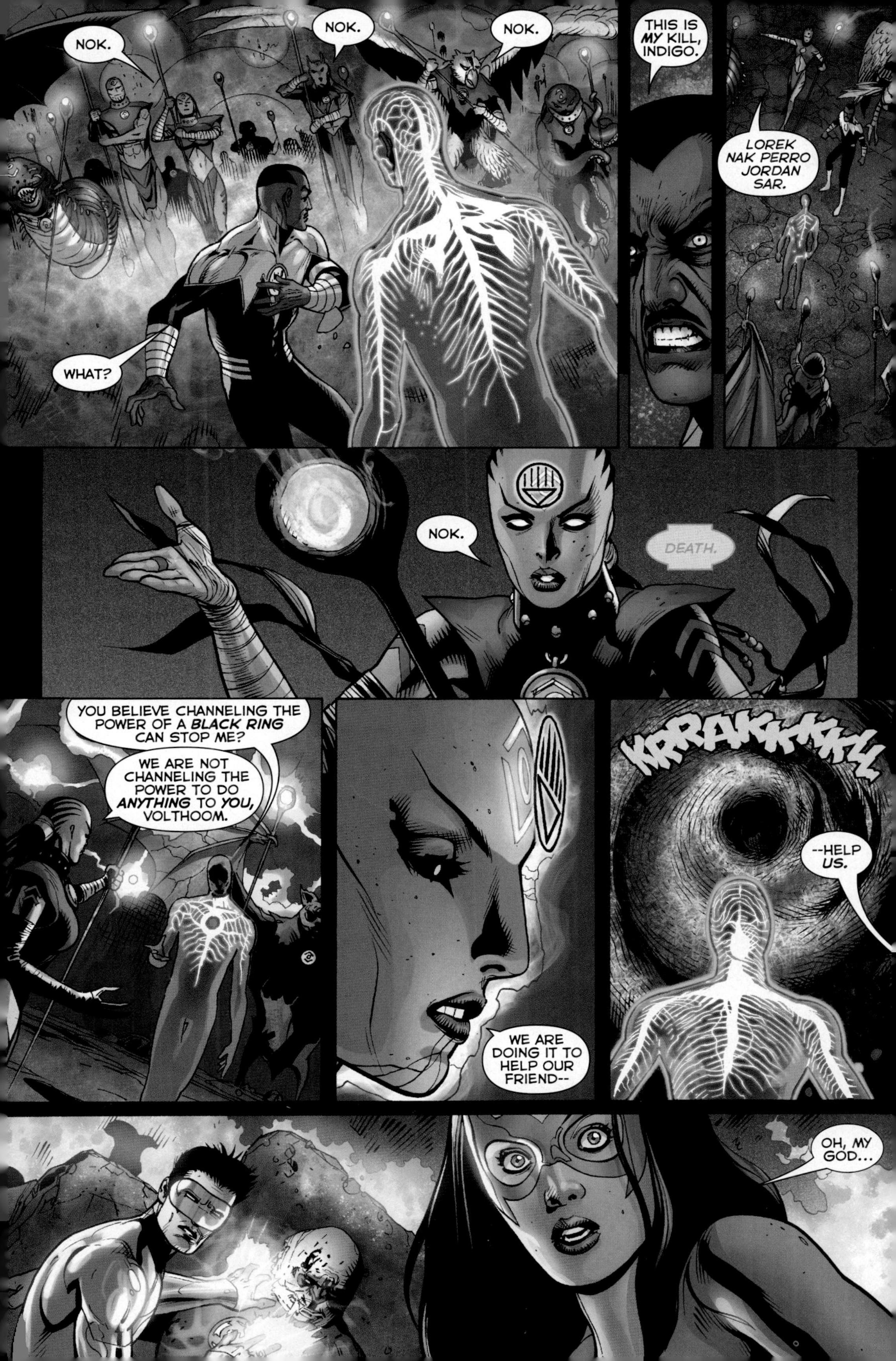
NOK.
NOK.
NOK.
WHAT?
THIS IS MY KILL, INDIGO.
LOREK NAK PERRO JORDAN SAR.
NOK.
DEATH.
YOU BELIEVE CHANNELING THE POWER OF A BLACK RING CAN STOP ME?
WE ARE NOT CHANNELING THE POWER TO DO ANYTHING TO YOU, VOLTHOOM.
WE ARE DOING IT TO HELP OUR FRIEND--
KRRAKKKKKL
--HELP US.
OH, MY GOD...

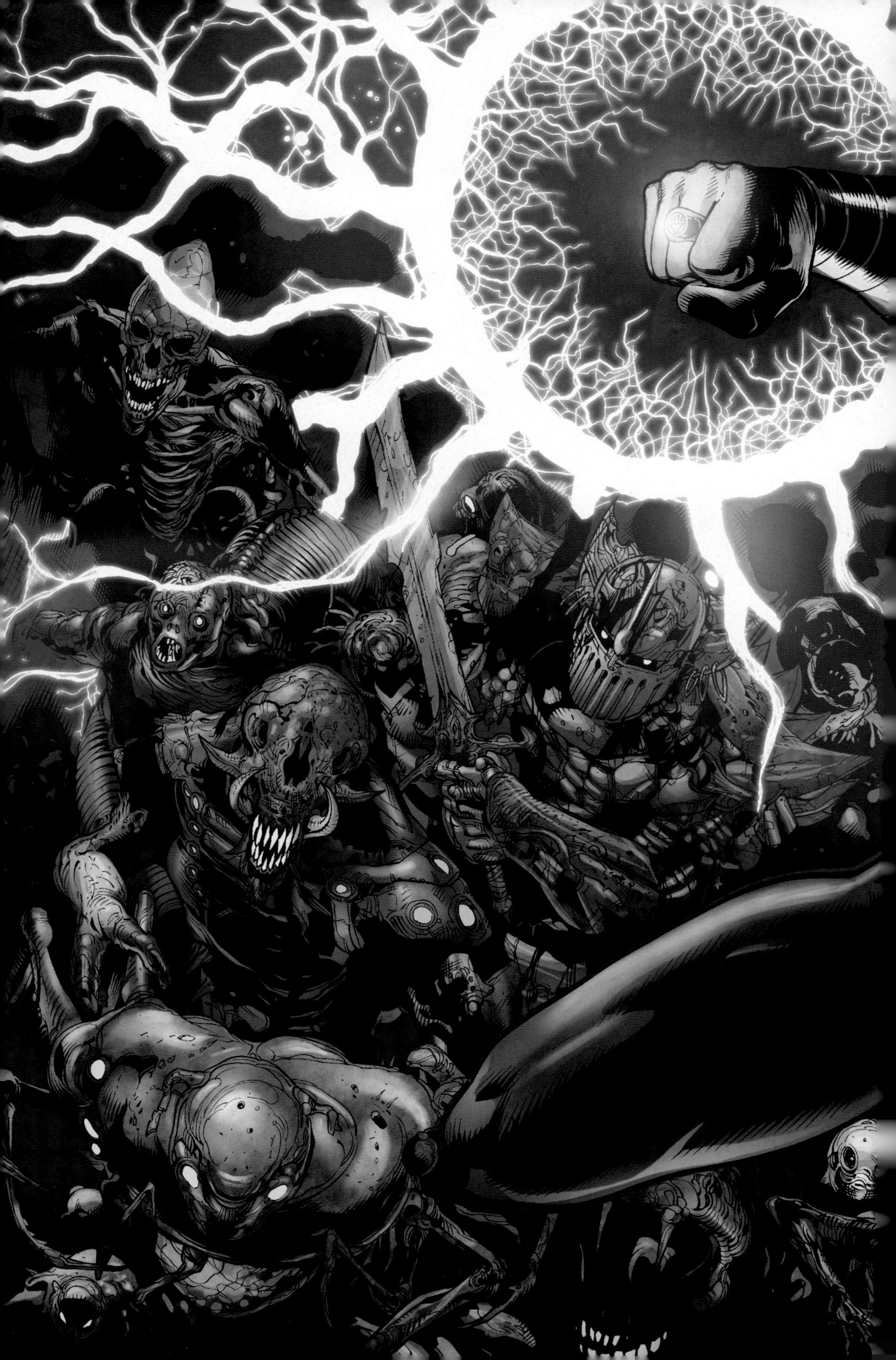

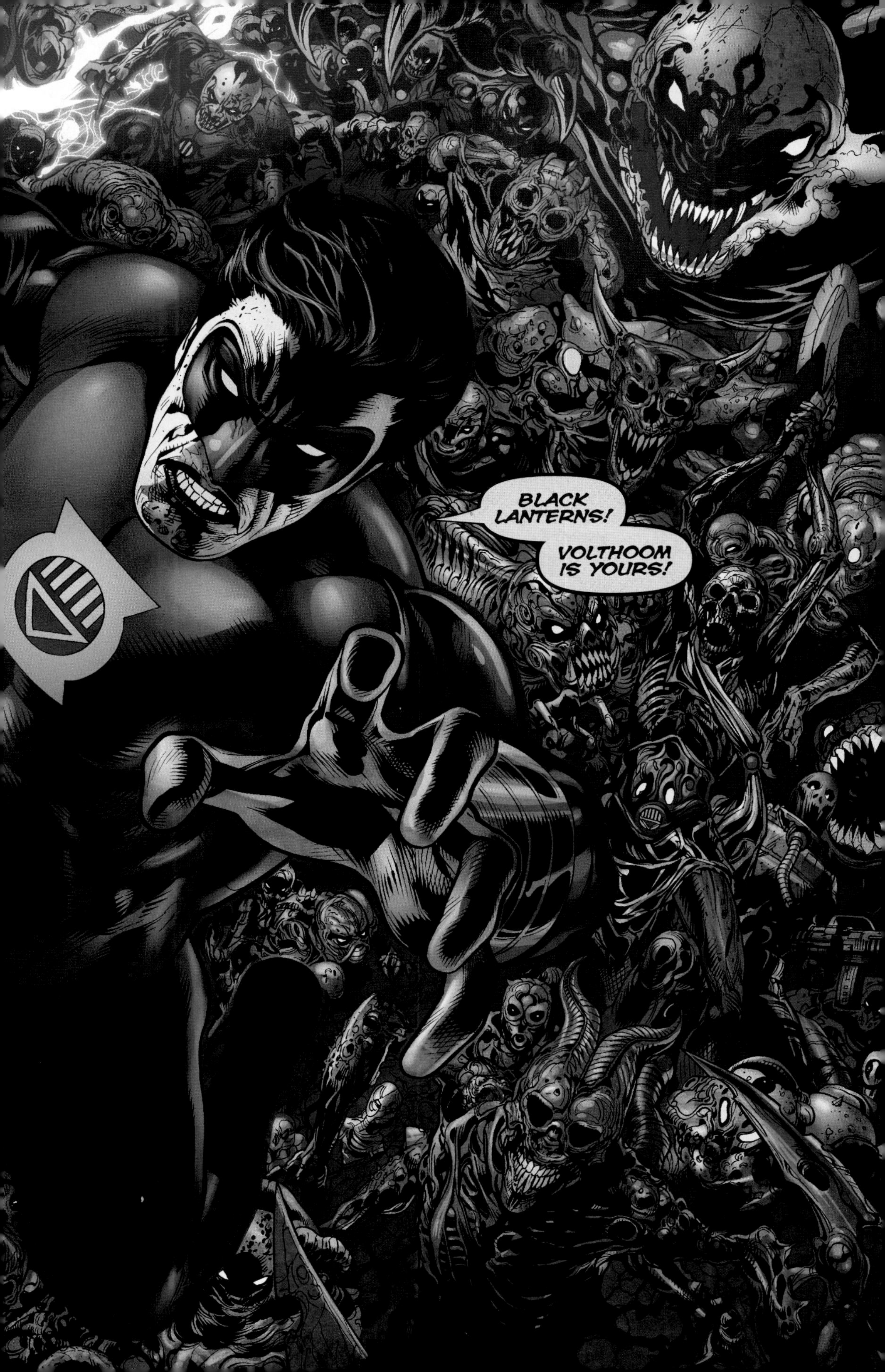
BLACK LANTERNS!
VOLTHOOM IS YOURS!

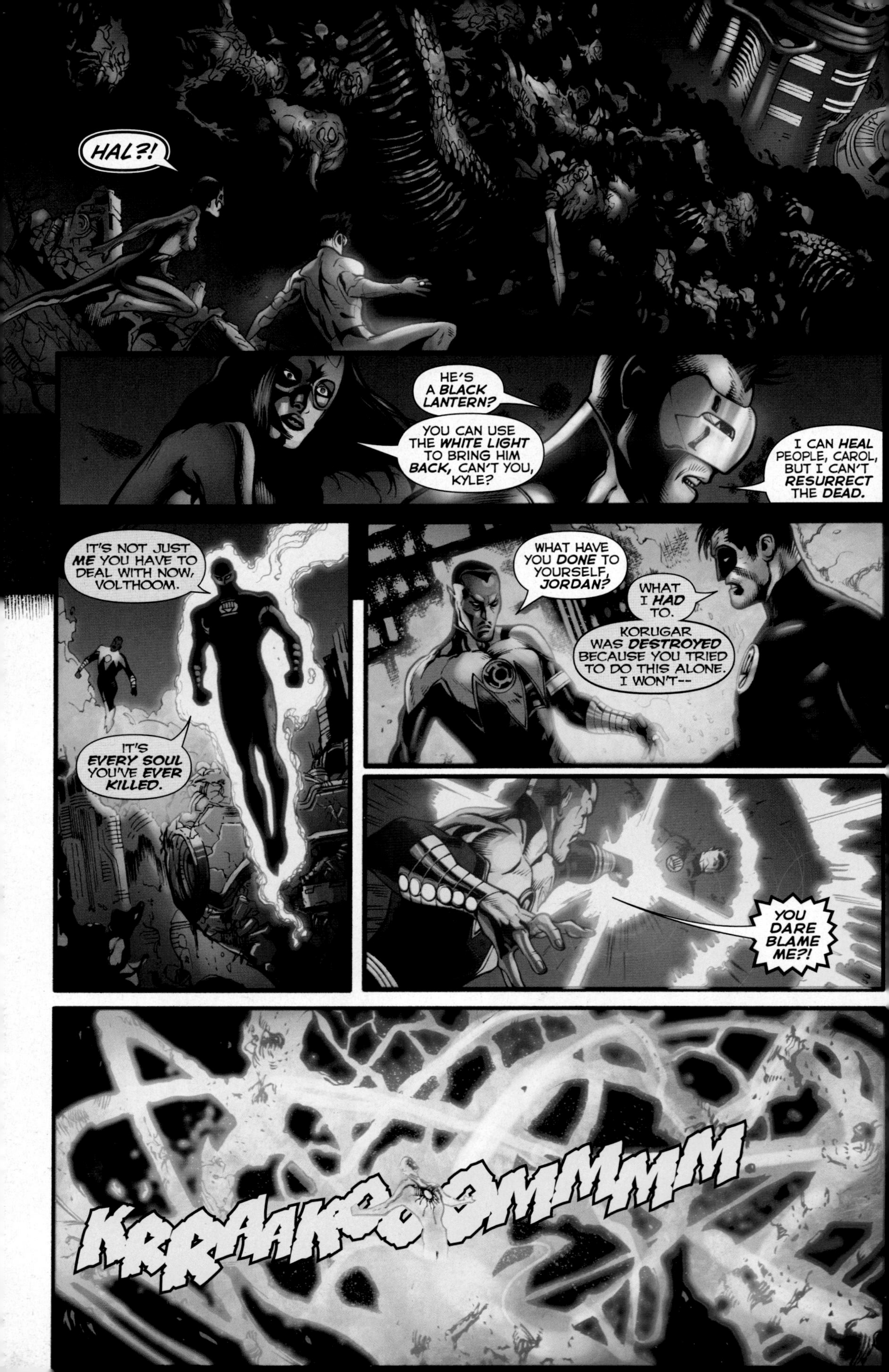
HAL?!
HE'S A BLACK LANTERN?
YOU CAN USE THE WHITE LIGHT TO BRING HIM BACK, CAN'T YOU, KYLE?
I CAN HEAL PEOPLE, CAROL, BUT I CAN'T RESURRECT THE DEAD.
IT'S NOT JUST ME YOU HAVE TO DEAL WITH NOW, VOLTHOOM.
IT'S EVERY SOUL YOU'VE EVER KILLED.
WHAT HAVE YOU DONE TO YOURSELF, JORDAN?
WHAT I HAD TO.
KORUGAR WAS DESTROYED BECAUSE YOU TRIED TO DO THIS ALONE. I WON'T--
YOU DARE BLAME ME?!
KRRAAKOOOMMMMM

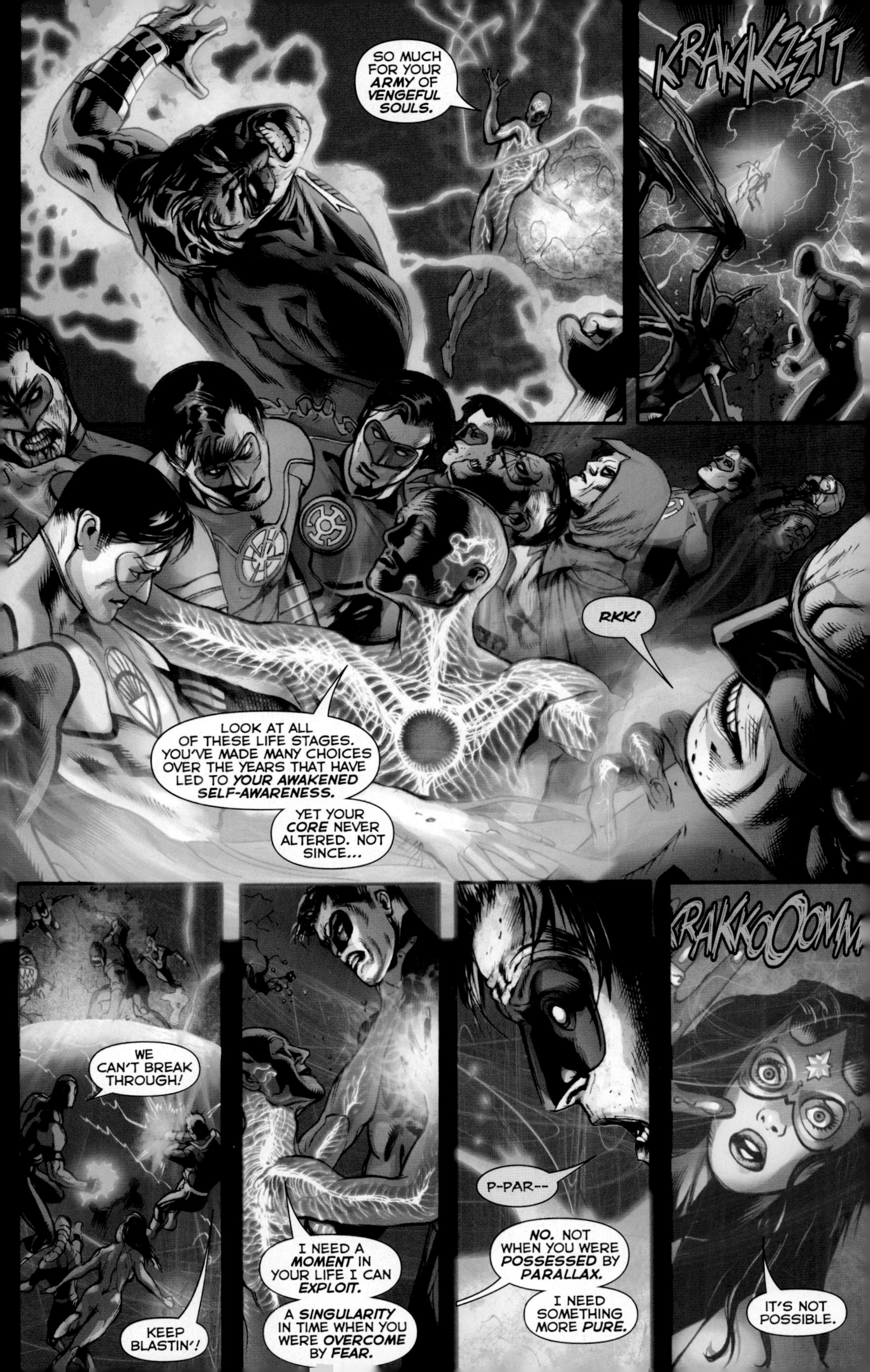
SO MUCH FOR YOUR ARMY OF VENGEFUL SOULS.
KRAKKZZTT
RKK!
LOOK AT ALL OF THESE LIFE STAGES. YOU'VE MADE MANY CHOICES OVER THE YEARS THAT HAVE LED TO YOUR AWAKENED SELF-AWARENESS.
YET YOUR CORE NEVER ALTERED. NOT SINCE...
WE CAN'T BREAK THROUGH!
KEEP BLASTIN'!
I NEED A MOMENT IN YOUR LIFE I CAN EXPLOIT.
A SINGULARITY IN TIME WHEN YOU WERE OVERCOME BY FEAR.
P-PAR--
NO. NOT WHEN YOU WERE POSSESSED BY PARALLAX.
I NEED SOMETHING MORE PURE.
KRAKKOOOMM
IT'S NOT POSSIBLE.

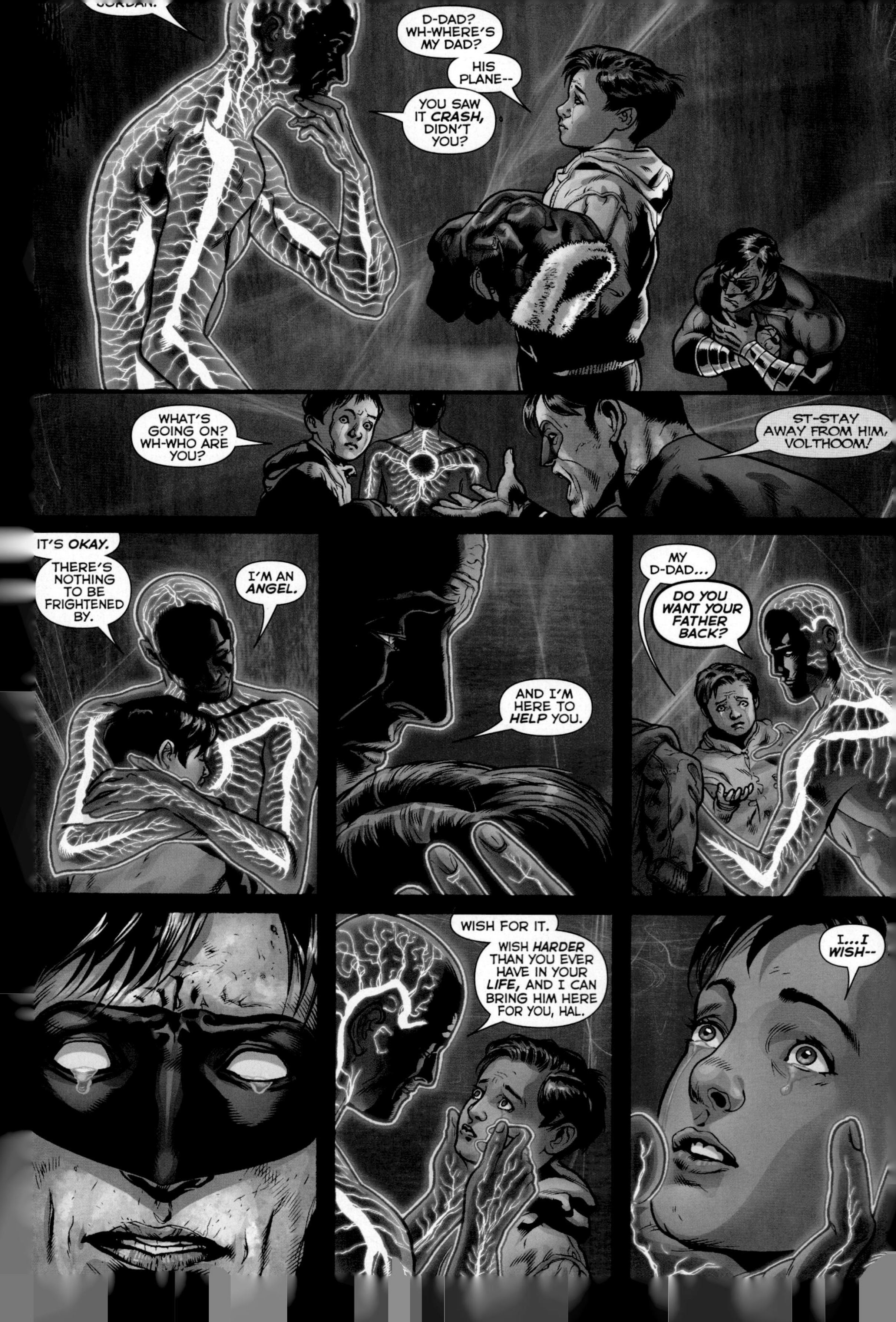
JORDAN.
D-DAD? WH-WHERE'S MY DAD?
HIS PLANE--
YOU SAW IT CRASH, DIDN'T YOU?
WHAT'S GOING ON? WH-WHO ARE YOU?
ST-STAY AWAY FROM HIM, VOLTHOOM!
IT'S OKAY.
THERE'S NOTHING TO BE FRIGHTENED BY.
I'M AN ANGEL.
AND I'M HERE TO HELP YOU.
MY D-DAD...
DO YOU WANT YOUR FATHER BACK?
WISH FOR IT.
WISH HARDER THAN YOU EVER HAVE IN YOUR LIFE, AND I CAN BRING HIM HERE FOR YOU, HAL.
I...I WISH--

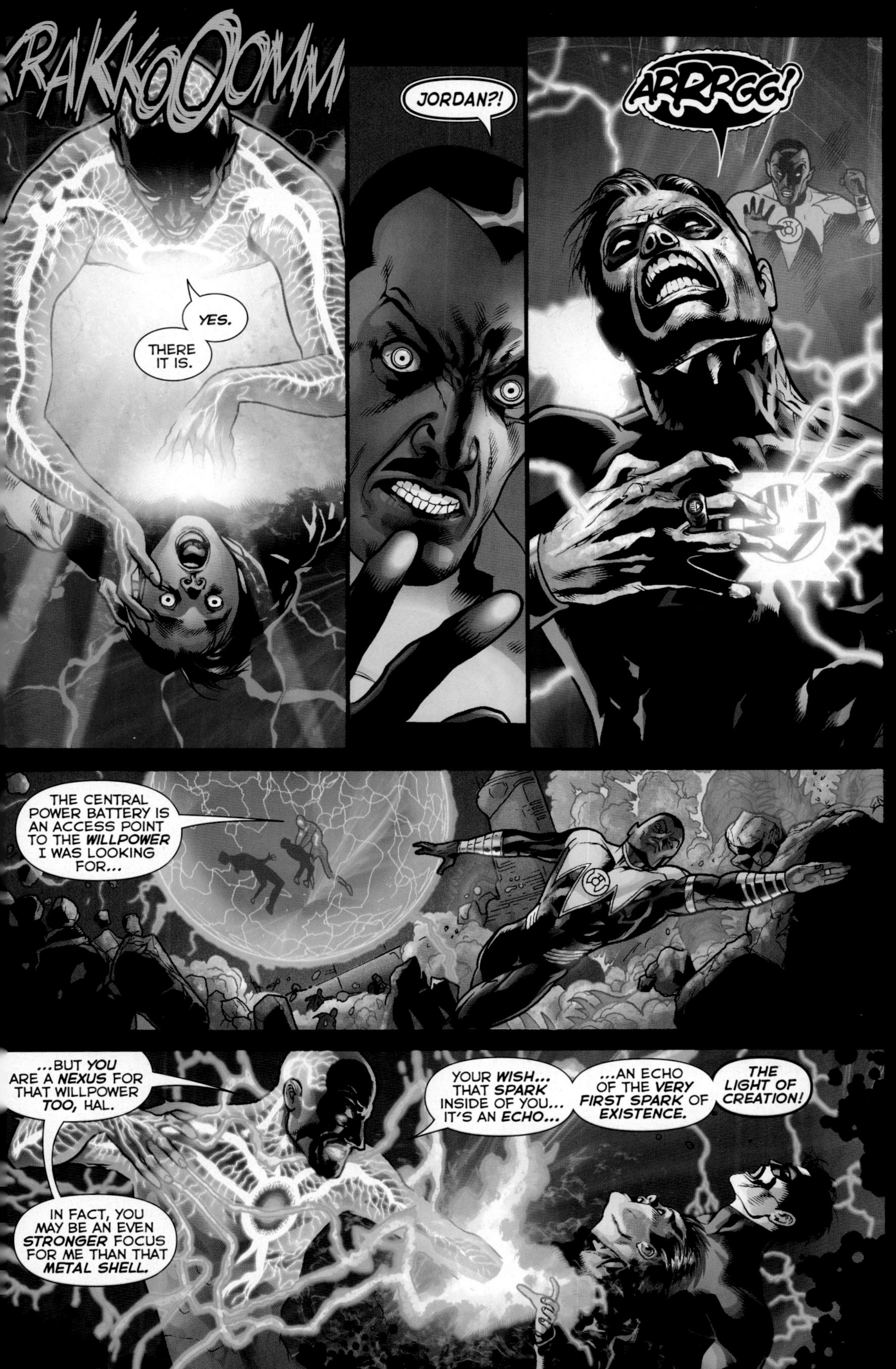
RAKKOOOMM
YES.
THERE IT IS.
JORDAN?!
ARRRGG!
THE CENTRAL POWER BATTERY IS AN ACCESS POINT TO THE WILLPOWER I WAS LOOKING FOR...
...BUT YOU ARE A NEXUS FOR THAT WILLPOWER TOO, HAL.
IN FACT, YOU MAY BE AN EVEN STRONGER FOCUS FOR ME THAN THAT METAL SHELL.
YOUR WISH... THAT SPARK INSIDE OF YOU... IT'S AN ECHO...
...AN ECHO OF THE VERY FIRST SPARK OF EXISTENCE.
THE LIGHT OF CREATION!

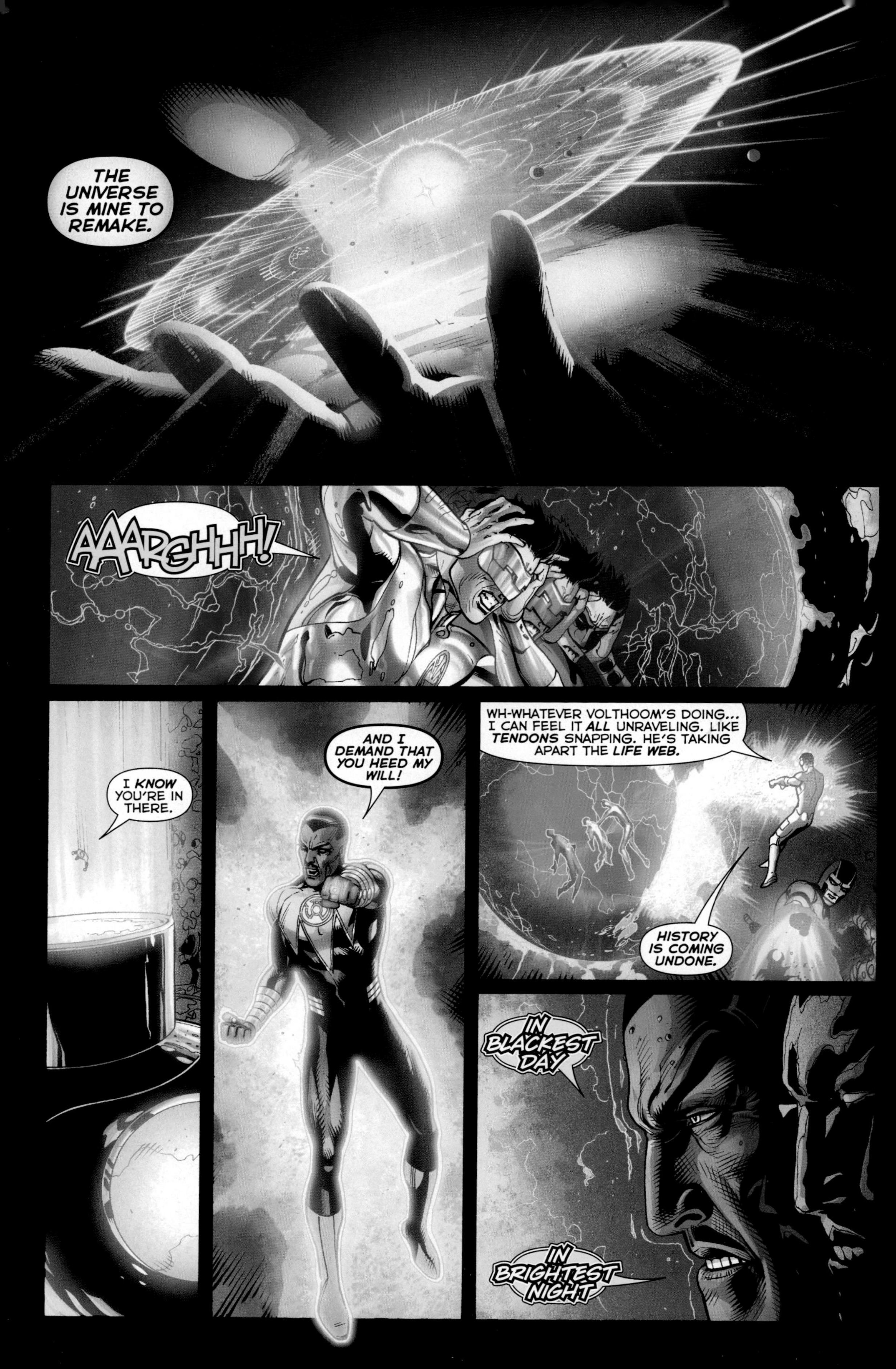
THE UNIVERSE IS MINE TO REMAKE.
AAARGHHH!
I KNOW YOU'RE IN THERE.
AND I DEMAND THAT YOU HEED MY WILL!
WH-WHATEVER VOLTHOOM'S DOING... I CAN FEEL IT ALL UNRAVELING. LIKE TENDONS SNAPPING. HE'S TAKING APART THE LIFE WEB.
HISTORY IS COMING UNDONE.
IN BLACKEST DAY
IN BRIGHTEST NIGHT

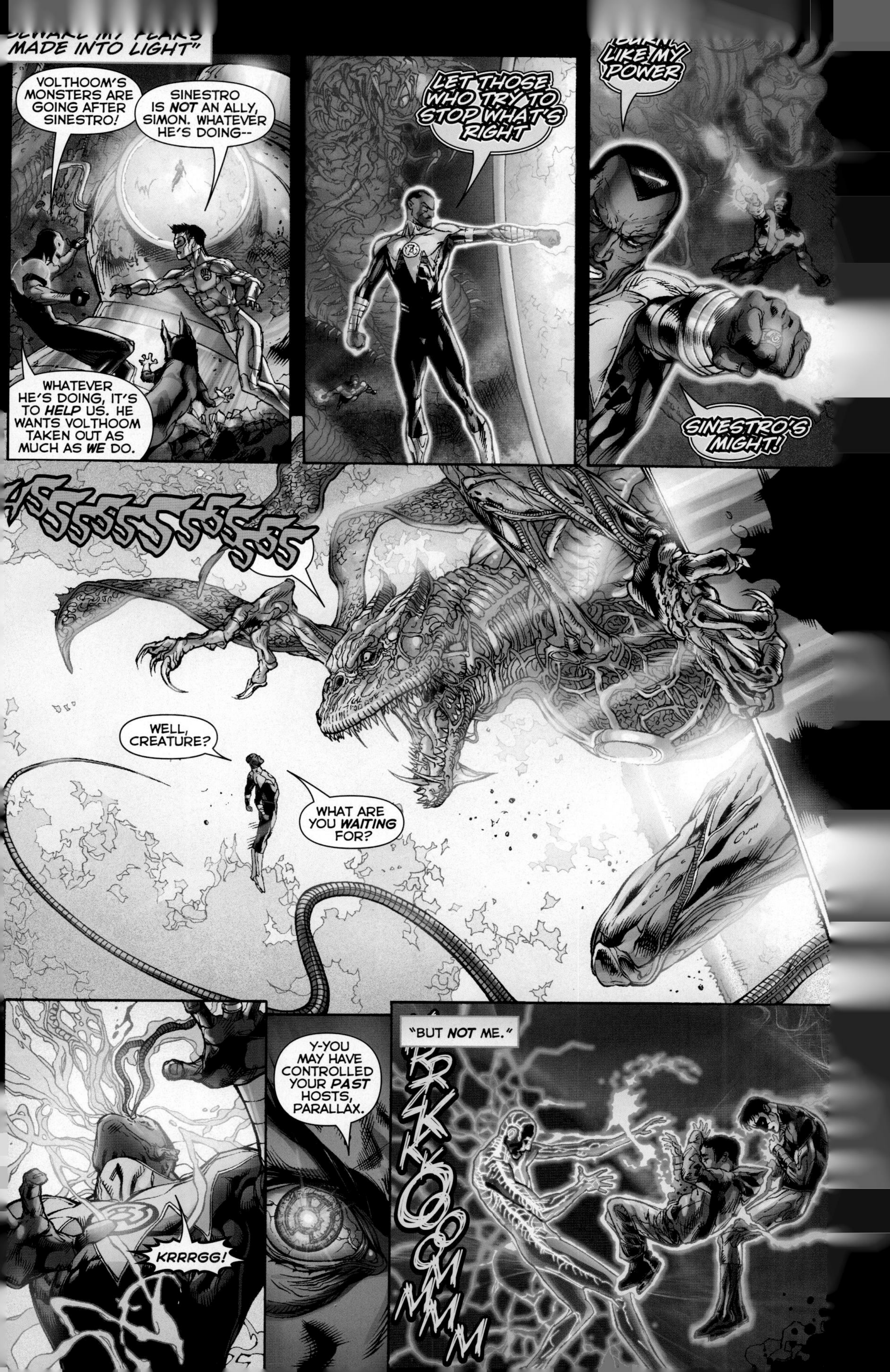
MADE INTO LIGHT"
VOLTHOOM'S MONSTERS ARE GOING AFTER SINESTRO!
SINESTRO IS NOT AN ALLY, SIMON. WHATEVER HE'S DOING--
WHATEVER HE'S DOING, IT'S TO HELP US. HE WANTS VOLTHOOM TAKEN OUT AS MUCH AS WE DO.
LET THOSE WHO TRY TO STOP WHAT'S RIGHT
LIKE MY POWER
SINESTRO'S MIGHT!
SSSSSSSSSSS
WELL, CREATURE?
WHAT ARE YOU WAITING FOR?
KRRRGG!
Y-YOU MAY HAVE CONTROLLED YOUR PAST HOSTS, PARALLAX.
"BUT NOT ME."
KRAKKOOOMMMM

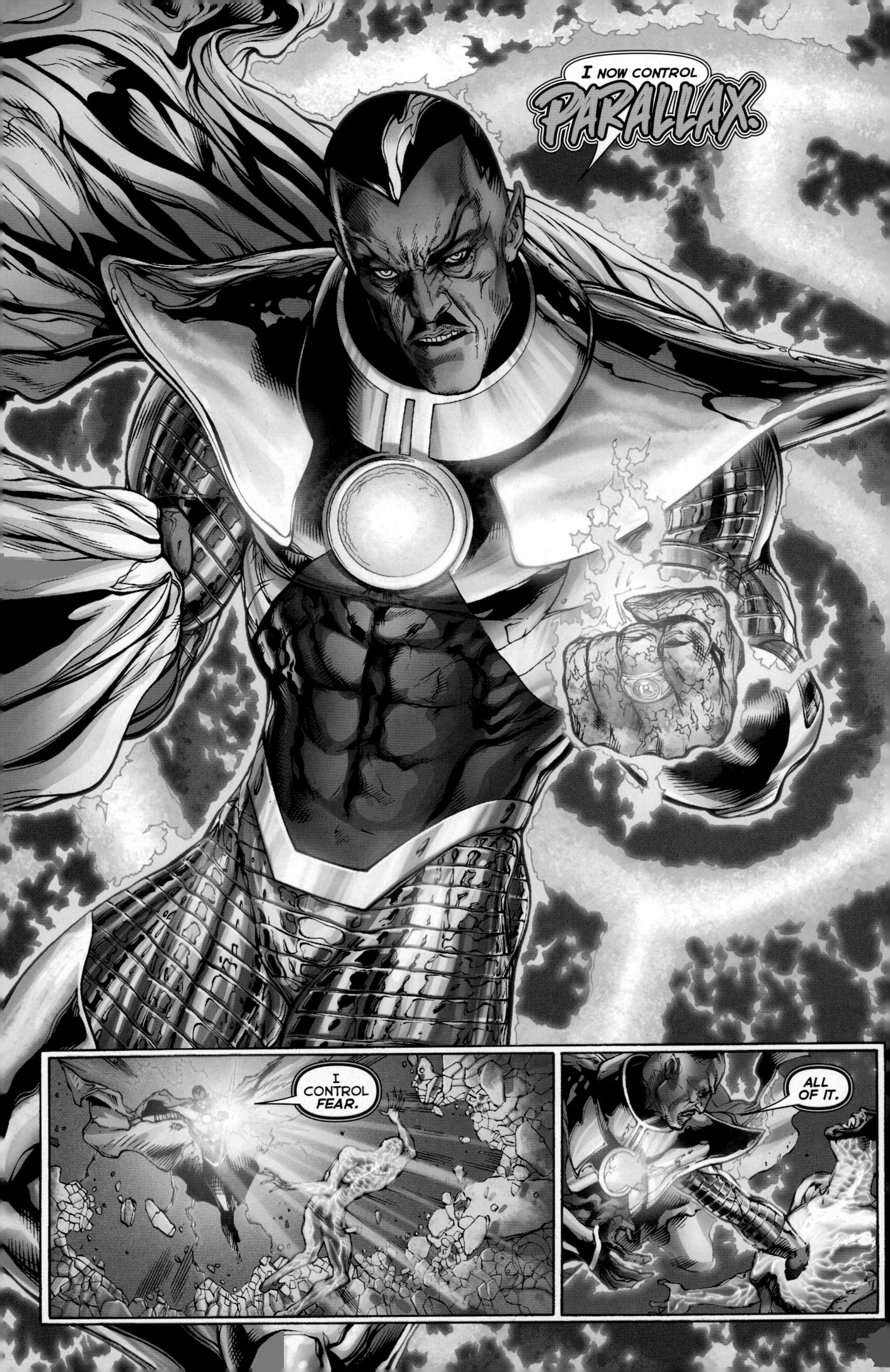
I NOW CONTROL PARALLAX.
I CONTROL FEAR.
ALL OF IT.

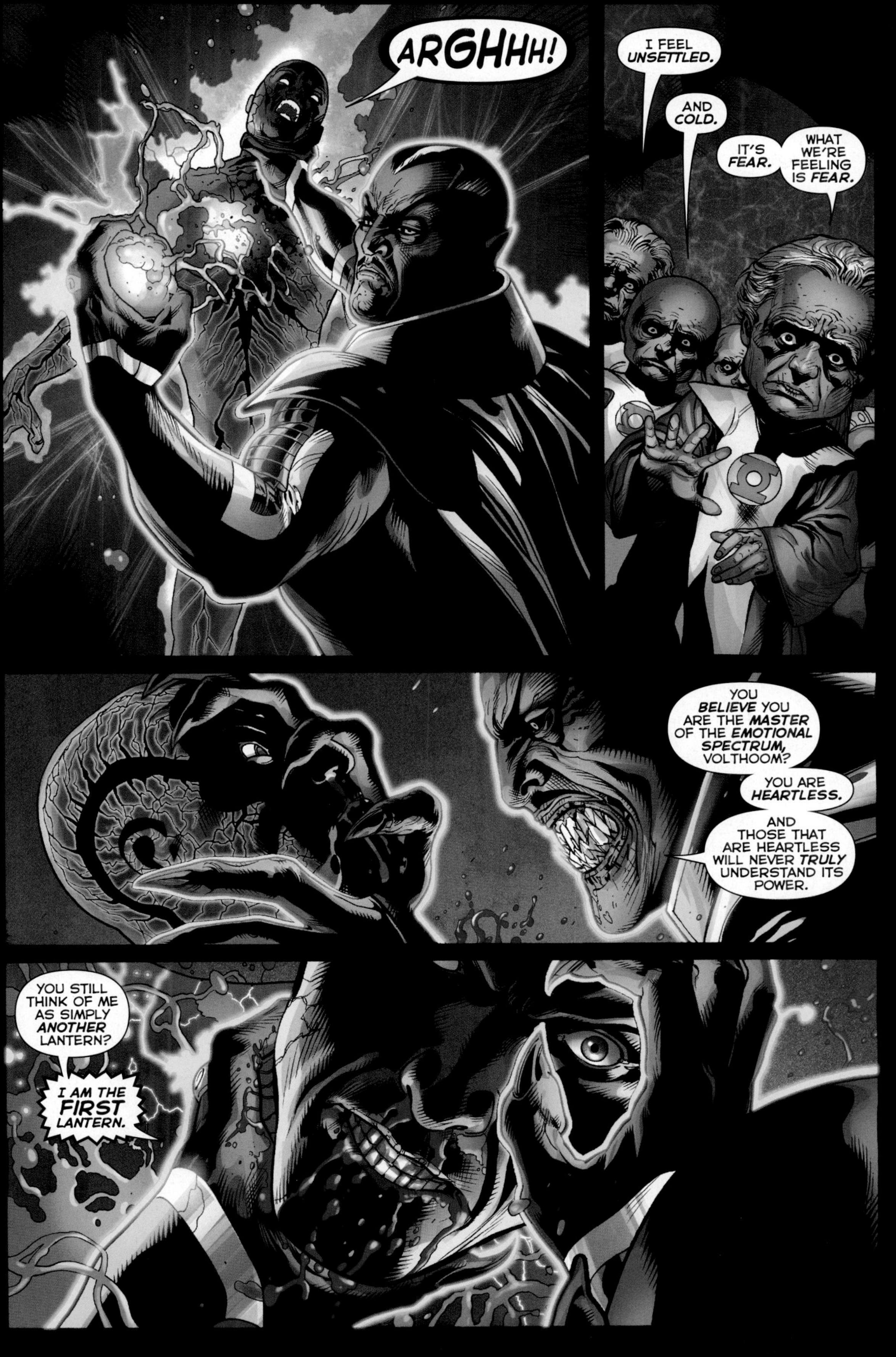
ARGHHH!
I FEEL UNSETTLED.
AND COLD.
IT'S FEAR.
WHAT WE'RE FEELING IS FEAR.
YOU BELIEVE YOU ARE THE MASTER OF THE EMOTIONAL SPECTRUM, VOLTHOOM?
YOU ARE HEARTLESS.
AND THOSE THAT ARE HEARTLESS WILL NEVER TRULY UNDERSTAND ITS POWER.
YOU STILL THINK OF ME AS SIMPLY ANOTHER LANTERN?
I AM THE FIRST LANTERN.

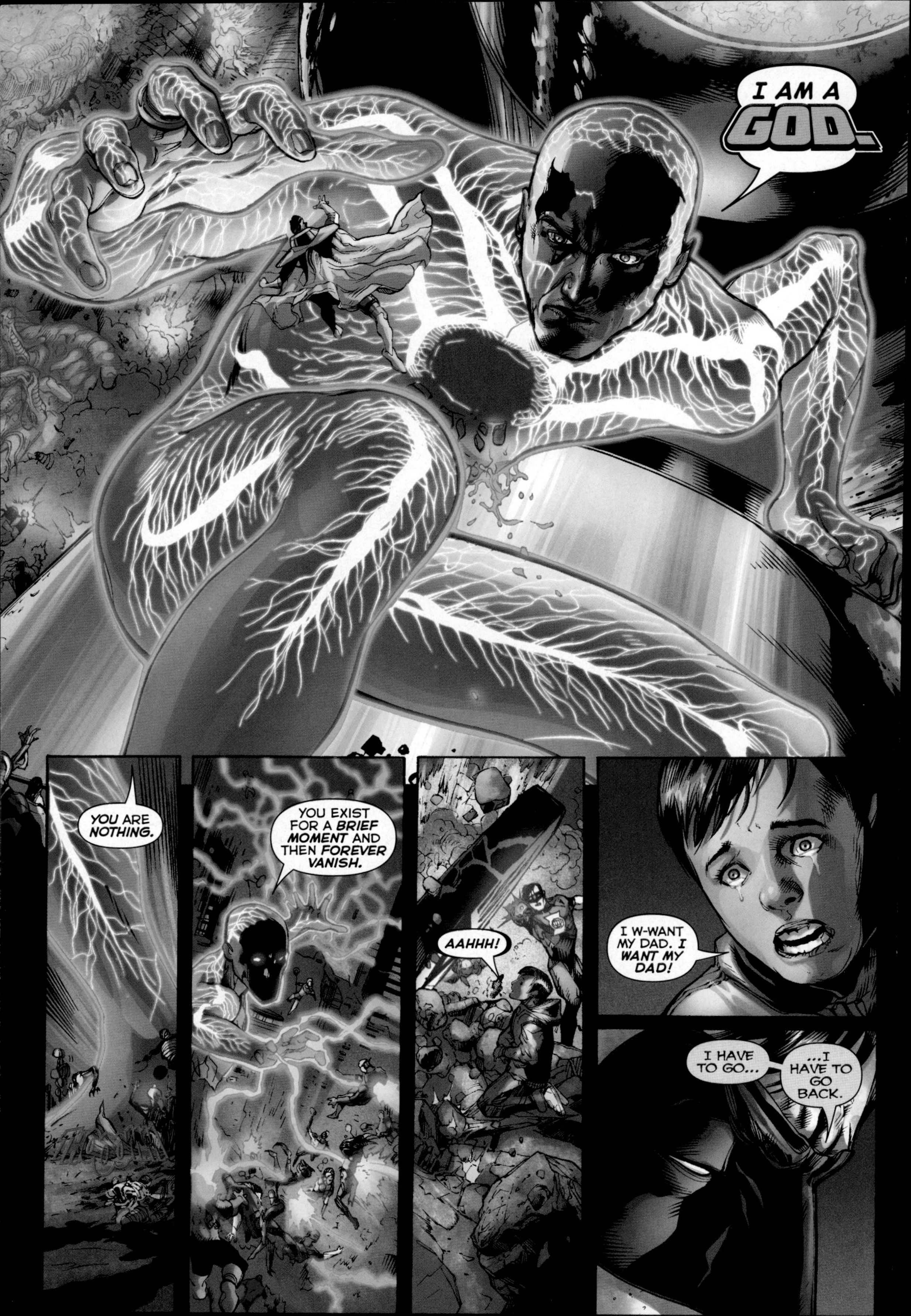
I AM A GOD.
YOU ARE NOTHING.
YOU EXIST FOR A BRIEF MOMENT AND THEN FOREVER VANISH.
AAHHH!
I W-WANT MY DAD. I WANT MY DAD!
I HAVE TO GO...
...I HAVE TO GO BACK.

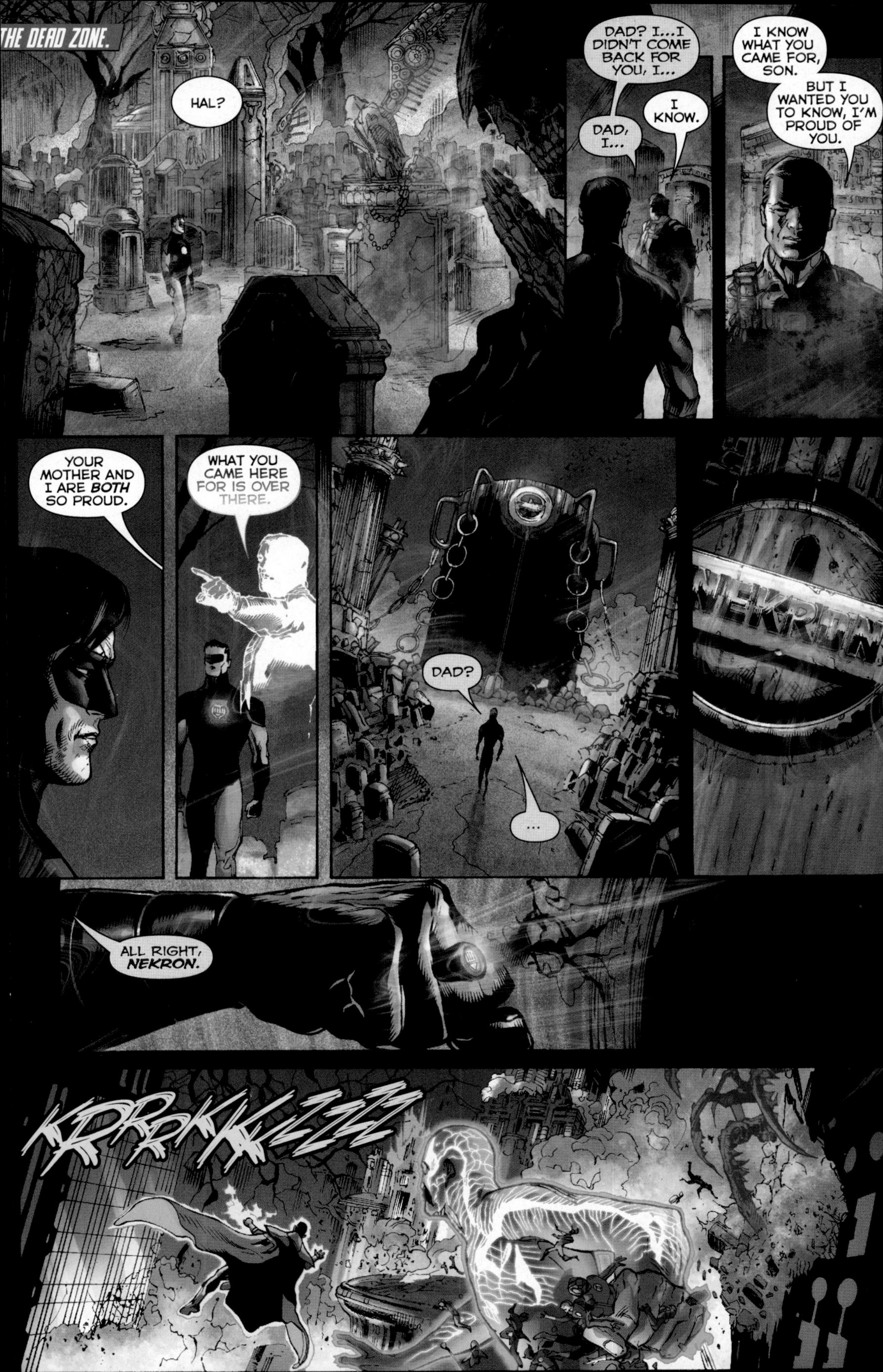
THE DEAD ZONE.
HAL?
DAD? I...I DIDN'T COME BACK FOR YOU, I...
DAD, I...
I KNOW.
I KNOW WHAT YOU CAME FOR, SON.
BUT I WANTED YOU TO KNOW, I'M PROUD OF YOU.
YOUR MOTHER AND I ARE BOTH SO PROUD.
WHAT YOU CAME HERE FOR IS OVER THERE.
DAD?
...
NEKRON
ALL RIGHT, NEKRON.
KRRKKZZZZ

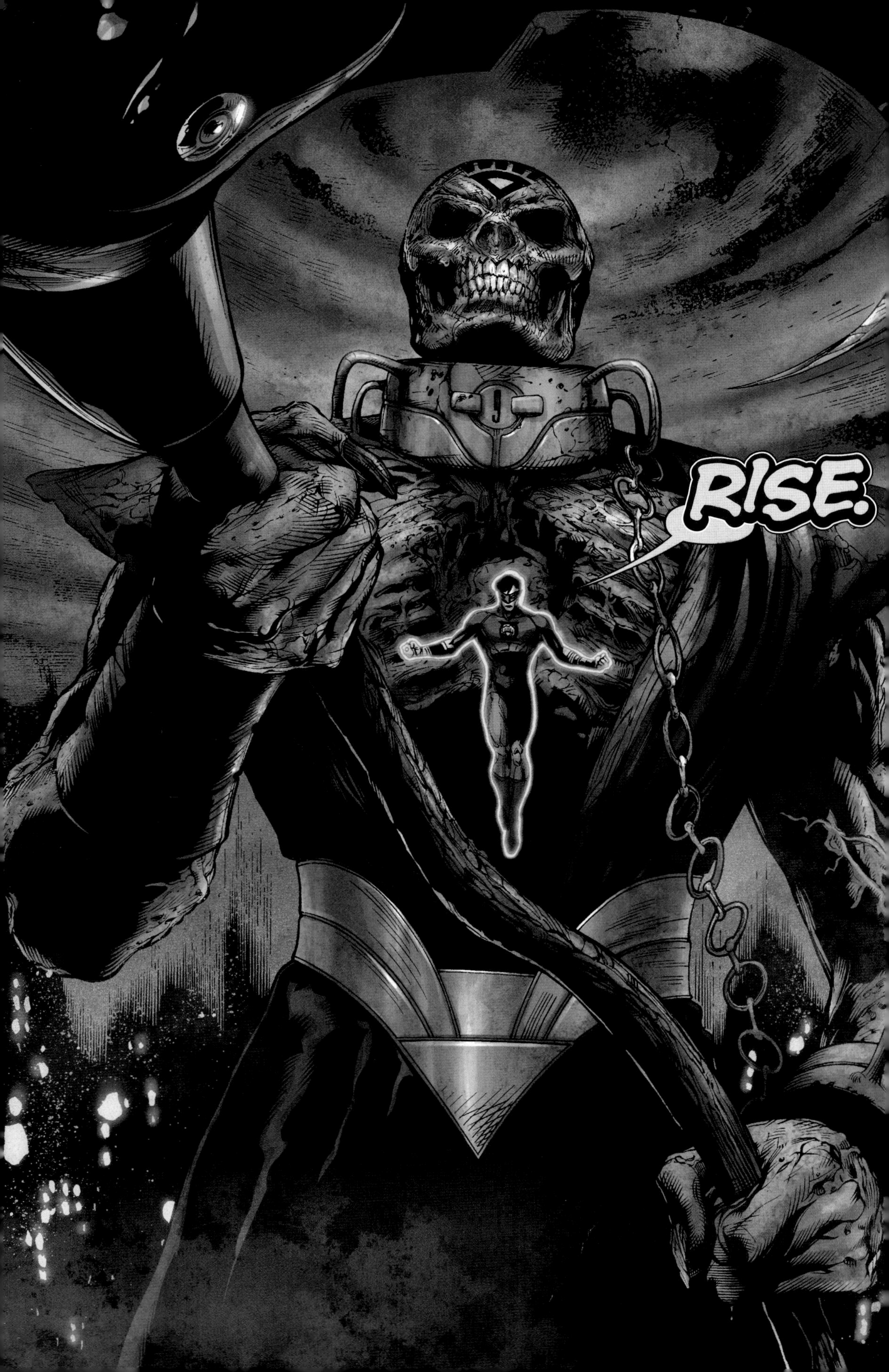
RISE.

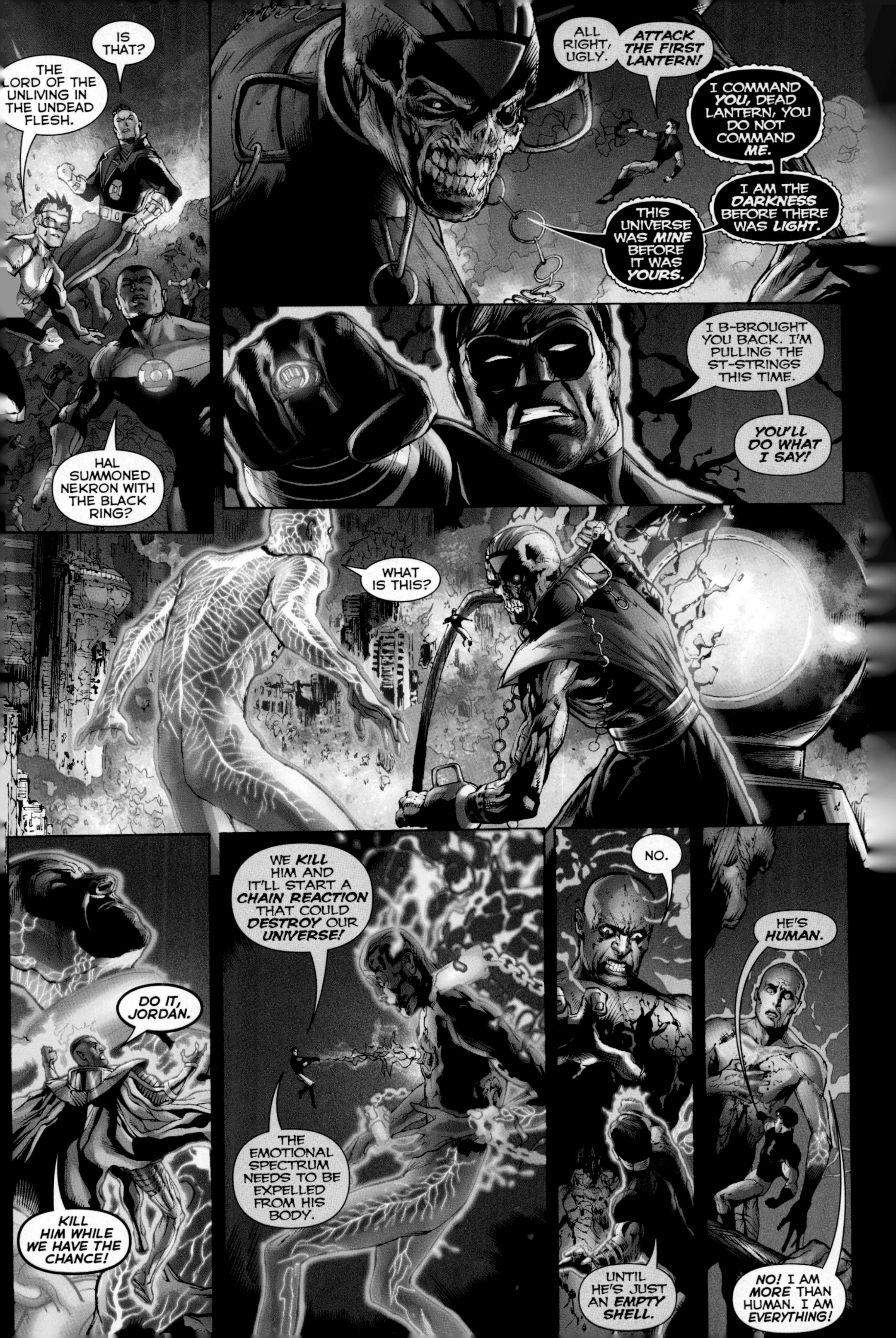
IS THAT?
THE LORD OF THE UNLIVING IN THE UNDEAD FLESH.
ALL RIGHT, UGLY. ATTACK THE FIRST LANTERN!
I COMMAND YOU, DEAD LANTERN, YOU DO NOT COMMAND ME.
I AM THE DARKNESS BEFORE THERE WAS LIGHT.
THIS UNIVERSE WAS MINE BEFORE IT WAS YOURS.
HAL SUMMONED NEKRON WITH THE BLACK RING?
I B-BROUGHT YOU BACK. I'M PULLING THE ST-STRINGS THIS TIME.
YOU'LL DO WHAT I SAY!
WHAT IS THIS?
DO IT, JORDAN.
KILL HIM WHILE WE HAVE THE CHANCE!
WE KILL HIM AND IT'LL START A CHAIN REACTION THAT COULD DESTROY OUR UNIVERSE!
THE EMOTIONAL SPECTRUM NEEDS TO BE EXPELLED FROM HIS BODY.
NO.
UNTIL HE'S JUST AN EMPTY SHELL.
HE'S HUMAN.
NO! I AM MORE THAN HUMAN. I AM EVERYTHING!

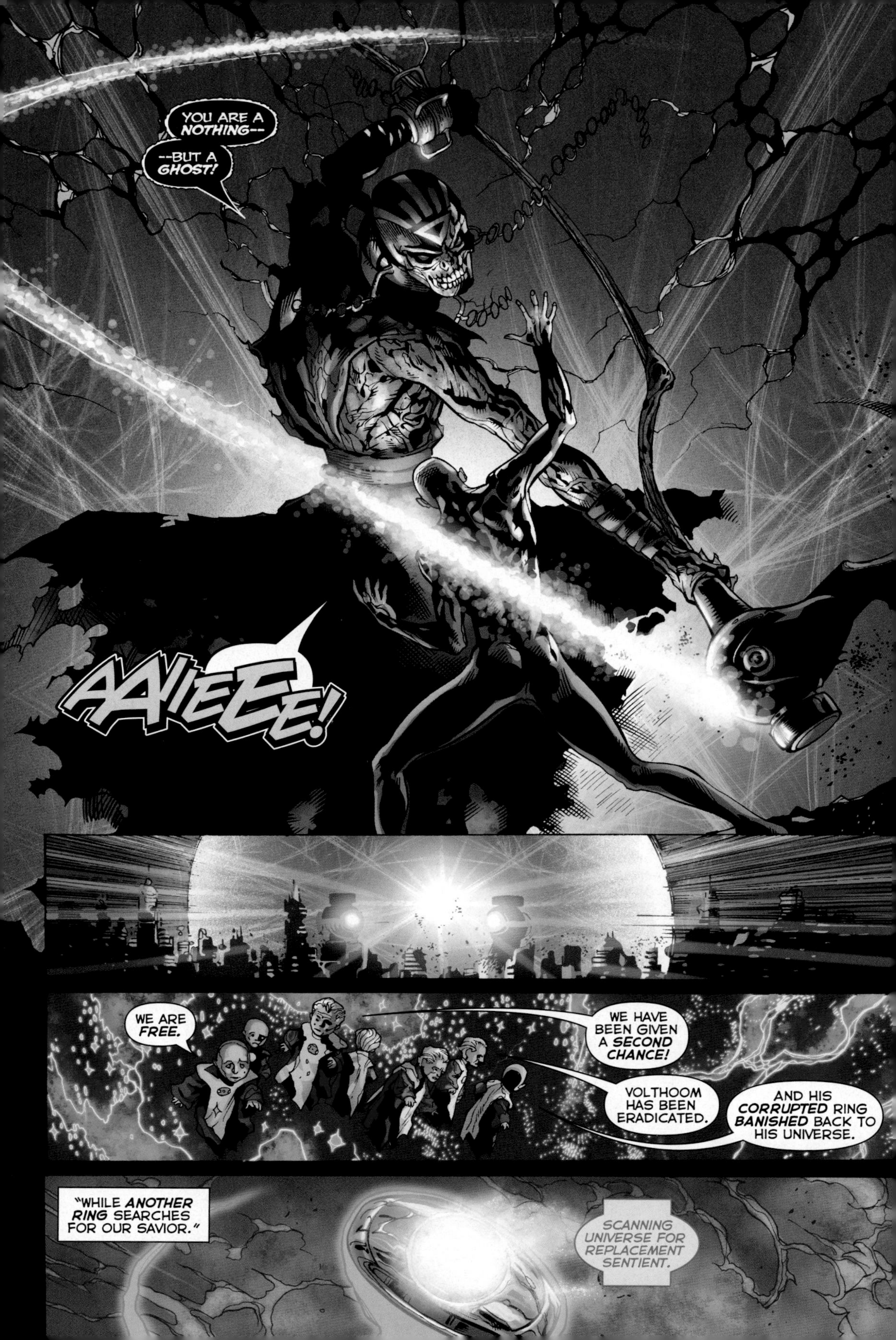
YOU ARE A NOTHING--
--BUT A GHOST!
AAIIEEEE!
WE ARE FREE.
WE HAVE BEEN GIVEN A SECOND CHANCE!
VOLTHOOM HAS BEEN ERADICATED.
AND HIS CORRUPTED RING BANISHED BACK TO HIS UNIVERSE.
"WHILE ANOTHER RING SEARCHES FOR OUR SAVIOR."
SCANNING UNIVERSE FOR REPLACEMENT SENTIENT.

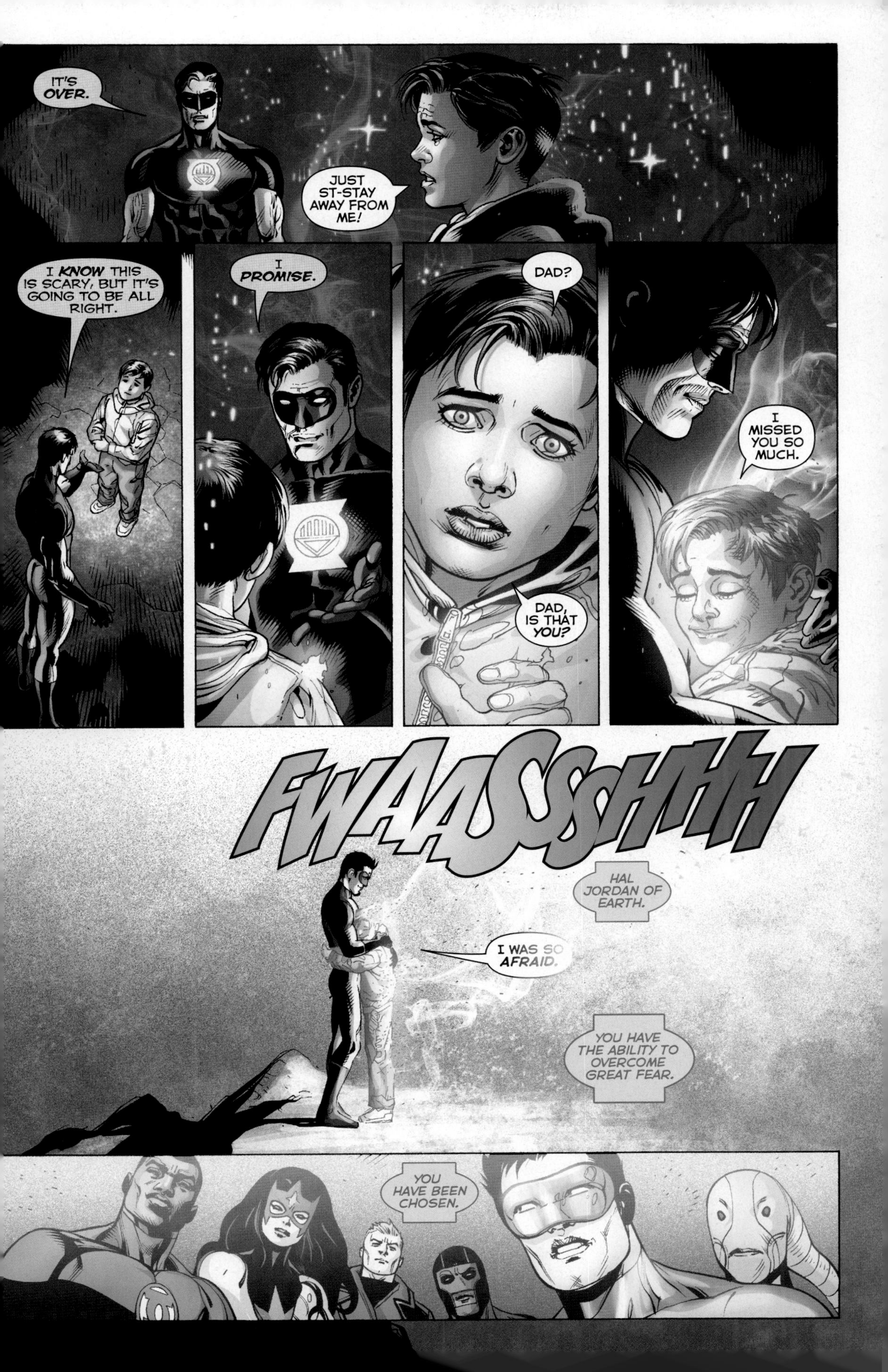
IT'S OVER.
JUST ST-STAY AWAY FROM ME!
I KNOW THIS IS SCARY, BUT IT'S GOING TO BE ALL RIGHT.
I PROMISE.
DAD?
DAD, IS THAT YOU?
I MISSED YOU SO MUCH.
FWAASSHHH
HAL JORDAN OF EARTH.
I WAS SO AFRAID.
YOU HAVE THE ABILITY TO OVERCOME GREAT FEAR.
YOU HAVE BEEN CHOSEN.

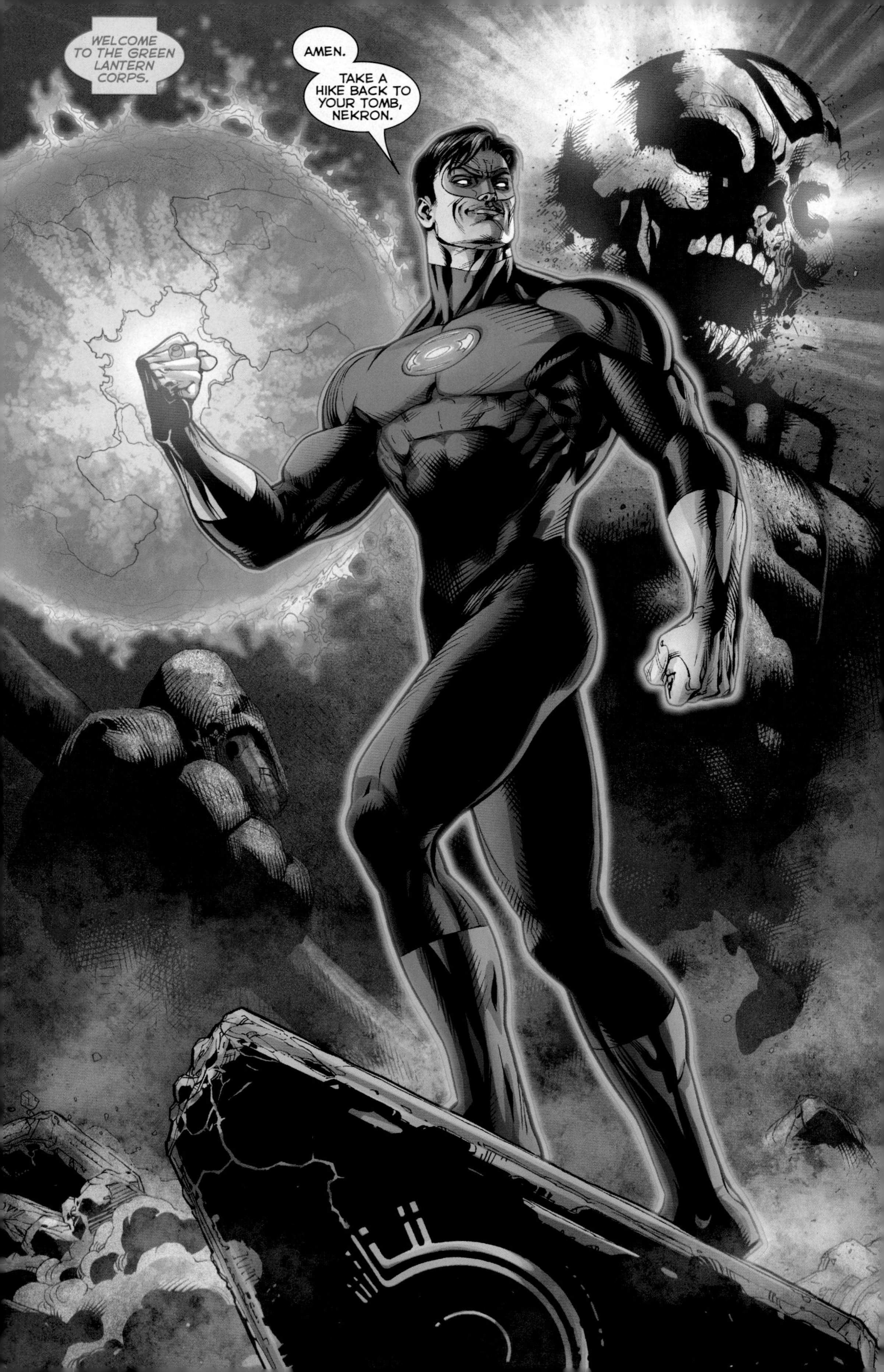
WELCOME TO THE GREEN LANTERN CORPS.
AMEN.
TAKE A HIKE BACK TO YOUR TOMB, NEKRON.

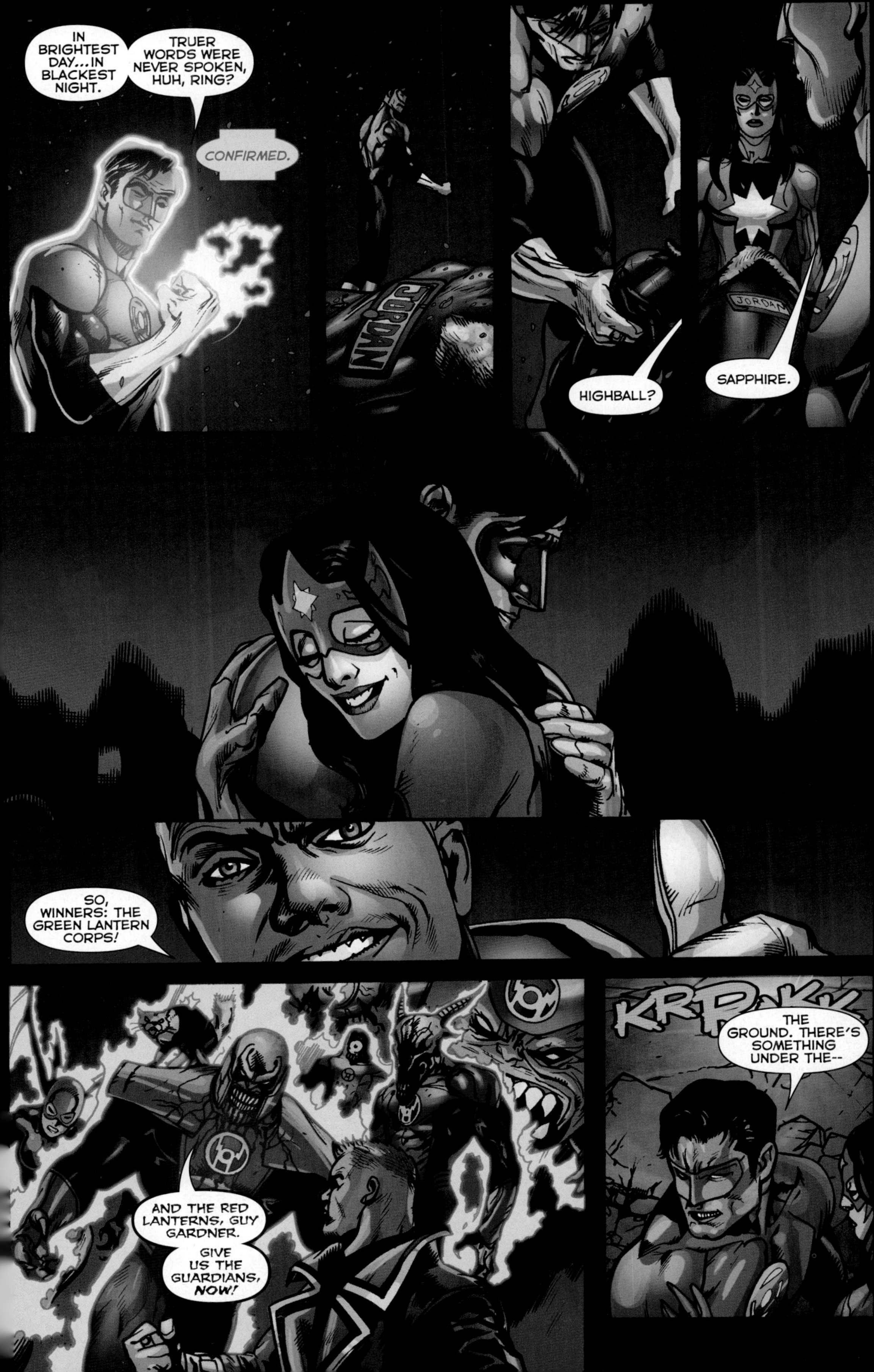
IN BRIGHTEST DAY...IN BLACKEST NIGHT.
TRUER WORDS WERE NEVER SPOKEN, HUH, RING?
CONFIRMED.
JORDAN
JORDAN
HIGHBALL?
SAPPHIRE.
SO, WINNERS: THE GREEN LANTERN CORPS!
AND THE RED LANTERNS, GUY GARDNER.
GIVE US THE GUARDIANS, *NOW!*
KRPKVL
THE GROUND. THERE'S SOMETHING UNDER THE--

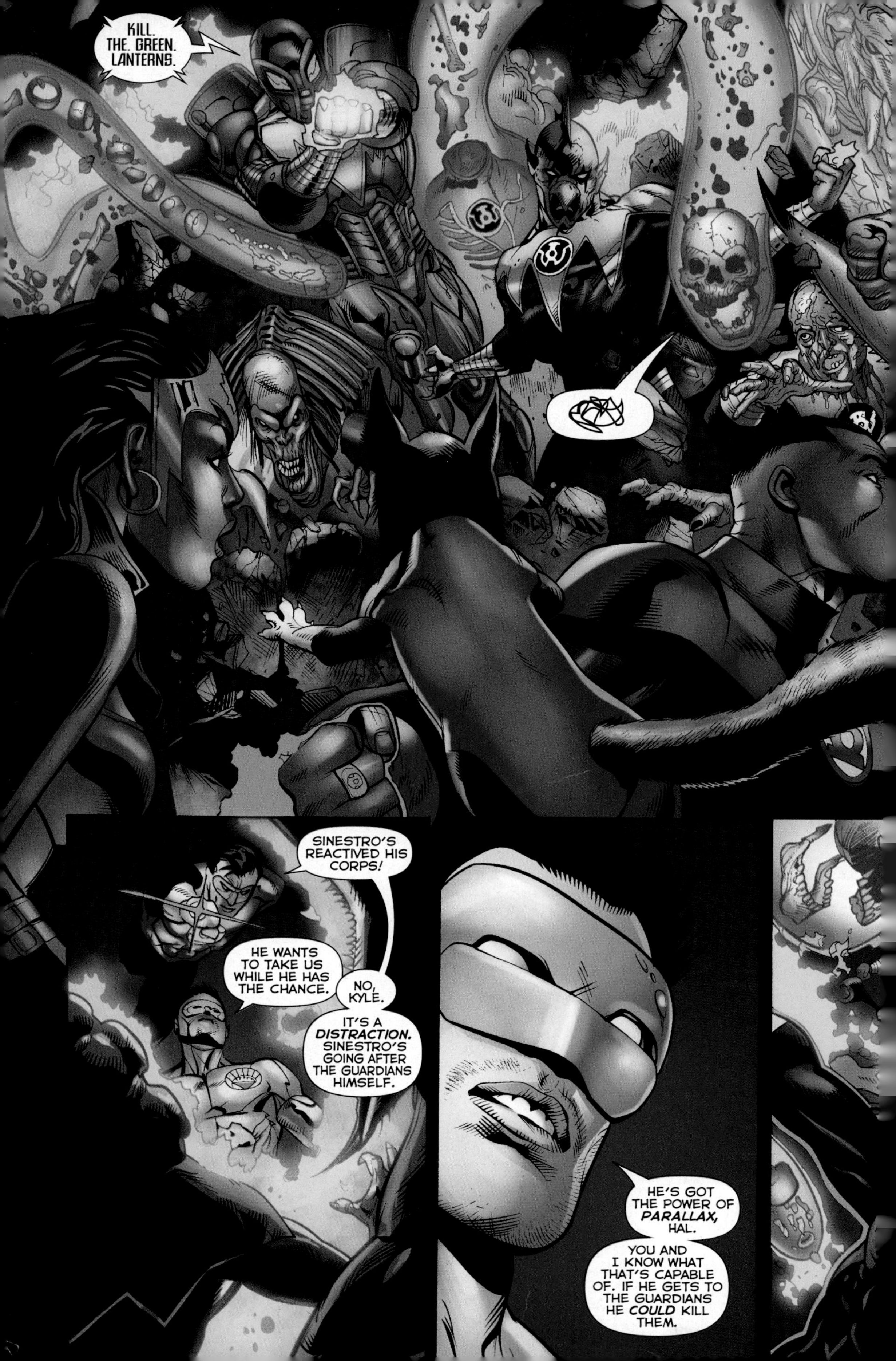
KILL. THE. GREEN. LANTERNS.
SINESTRO'S REACTIVED HIS CORPS!
HE WANTS TO TAKE US WHILE HE HAS THE CHANCE.
NO, KYLE.
IT'S A *DISTRACTION.* SINESTRO'S GOING AFTER THE GUARDIANS HIMSELF.
HE'S GOT THE POWER OF *PARALLAX,* HAL.
YOU AND I KNOW WHAT THAT'S CAPABLE OF. IF HE GETS TO THE GUARDIANS HE *COULD* KILL THEM.

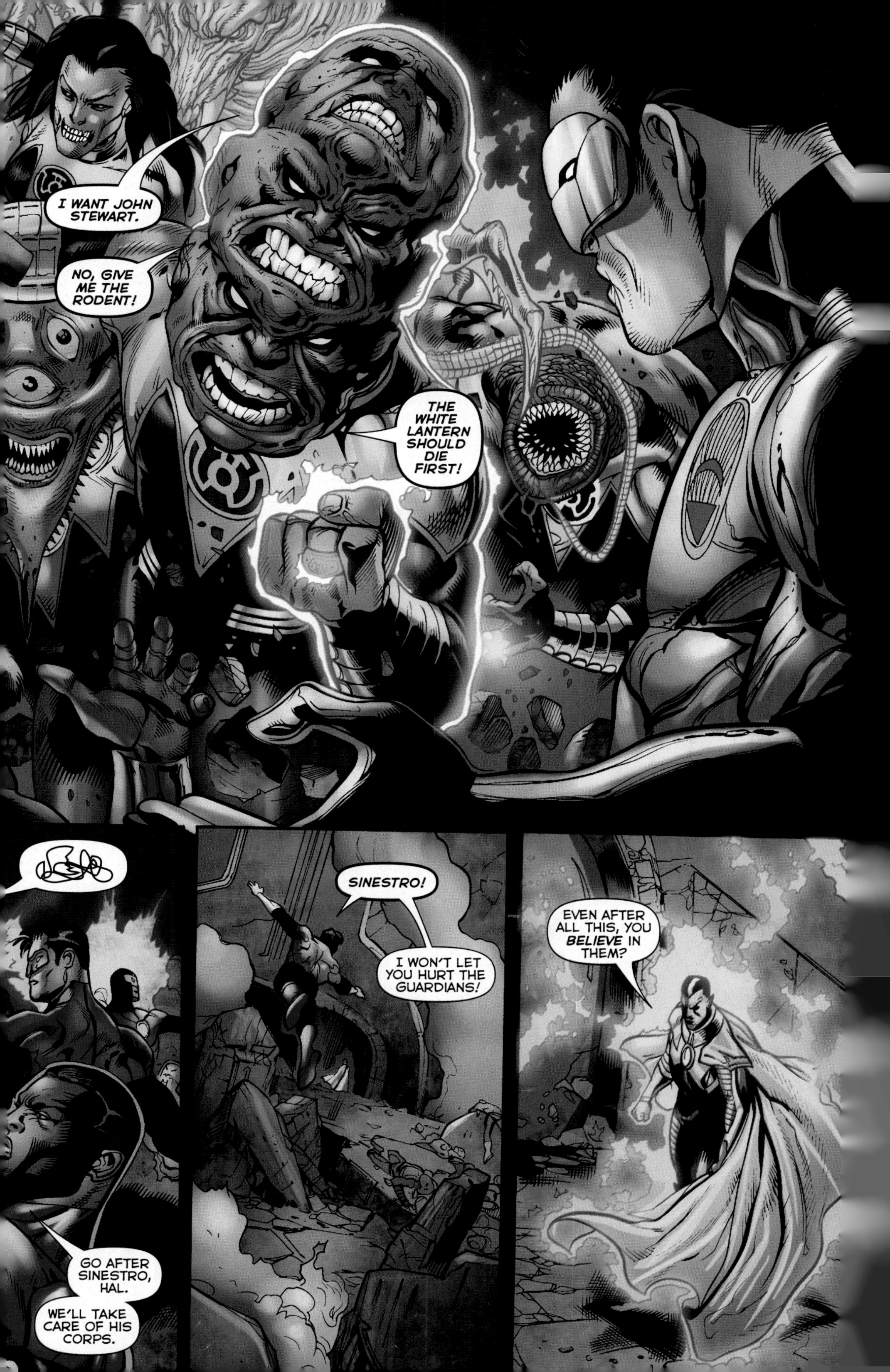

I WANT JOHN STEWART.
NO, GIVE ME THE RODENT!
THE WHITE LANTERN SHOULD DIE FIRST!
SINESTRO!
I WON'T LET YOU HURT THE GUARDIANS!
EVEN AFTER ALL THIS, YOU *BELIEVE* IN THEM?
GO AFTER SINESTRO, HAL.
WE'LL TAKE CARE OF HIS CORPS.

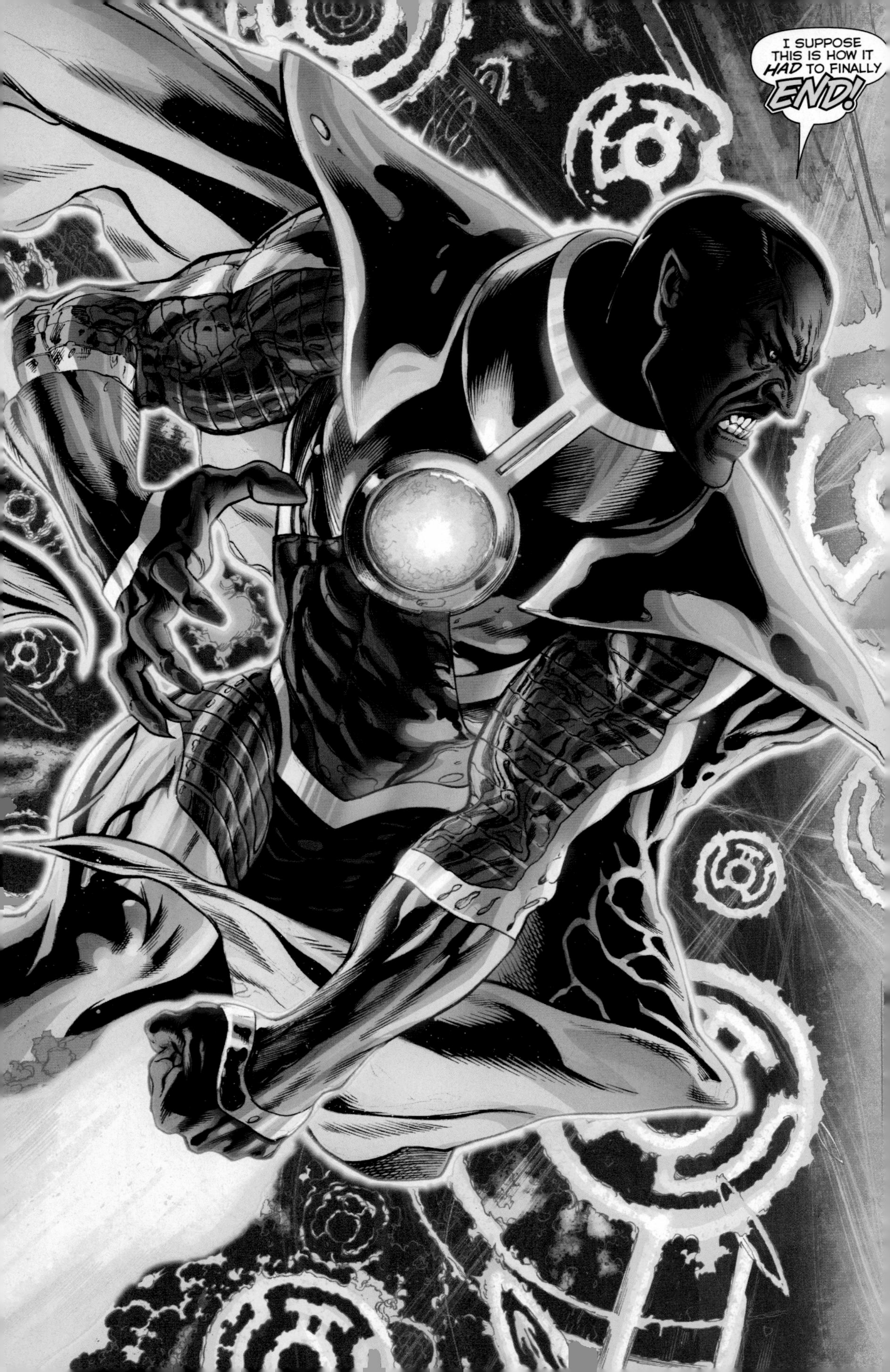
I SUPPOSE THIS IS HOW IT HAD TO FINALLY END!

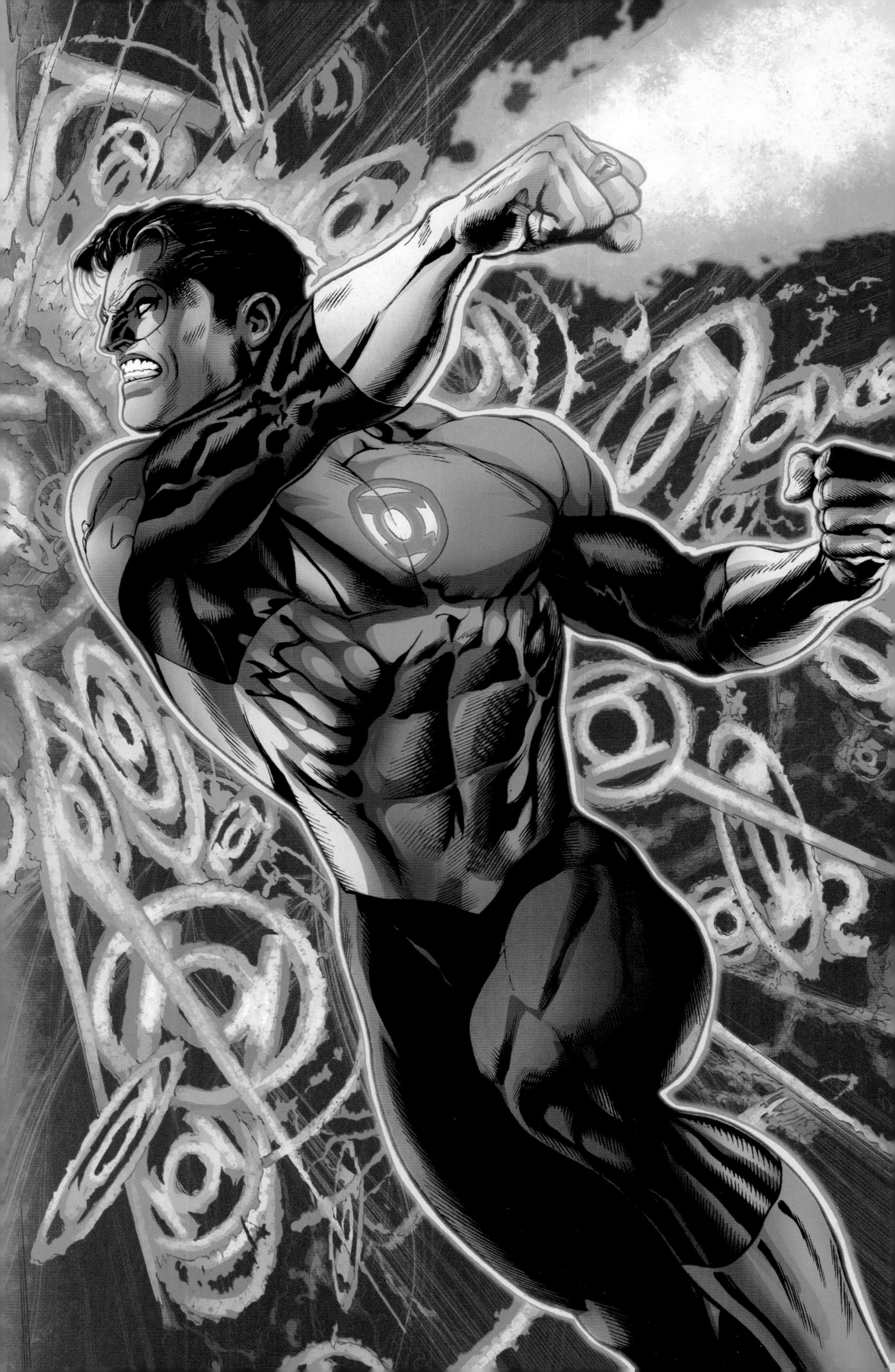

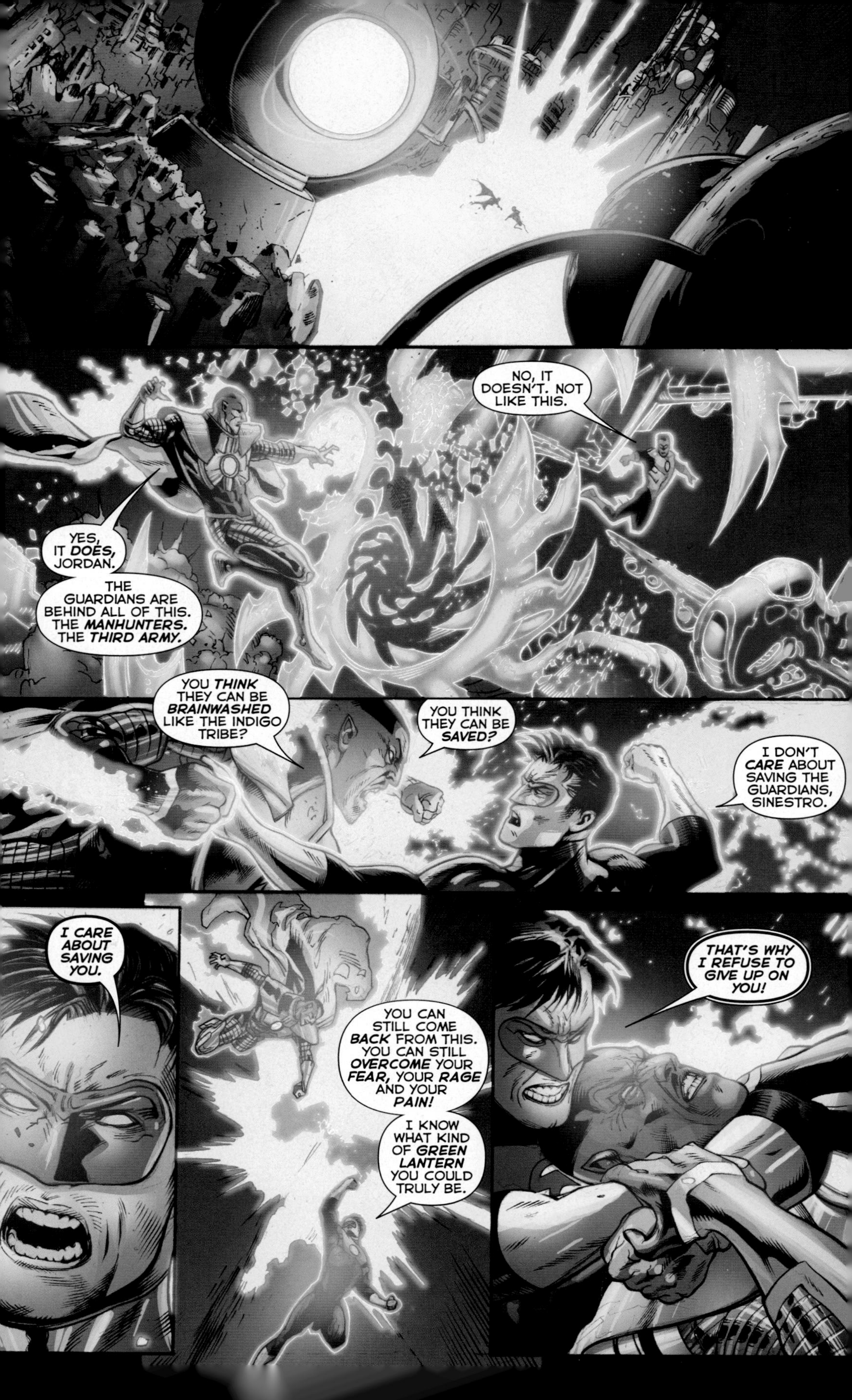
NO, IT DOESN'T. NOT LIKE THIS.
YES, IT DOES, JORDAN.
THE GUARDIANS ARE BEHIND ALL OF THIS. THE MANHUNTERS. THE THIRD ARMY.
YOU THINK THEY CAN BE BRAINWASHED LIKE THE INDIGO TRIBE?
YOU THINK THEY CAN BE SAVED?
I DON'T CARE ABOUT SAVING THE GUARDIANS, SINESTRO.
I CARE ABOUT SAVING YOU.
YOU CAN STILL COME BACK FROM THIS. YOU CAN STILL OVERCOME YOUR FEAR, YOUR RAGE AND YOUR PAIN!
I KNOW WHAT KIND OF GREEN LANTERN YOU COULD TRULY BE.
THAT'S WHY I REFUSE TO GIVE UP ON YOU!

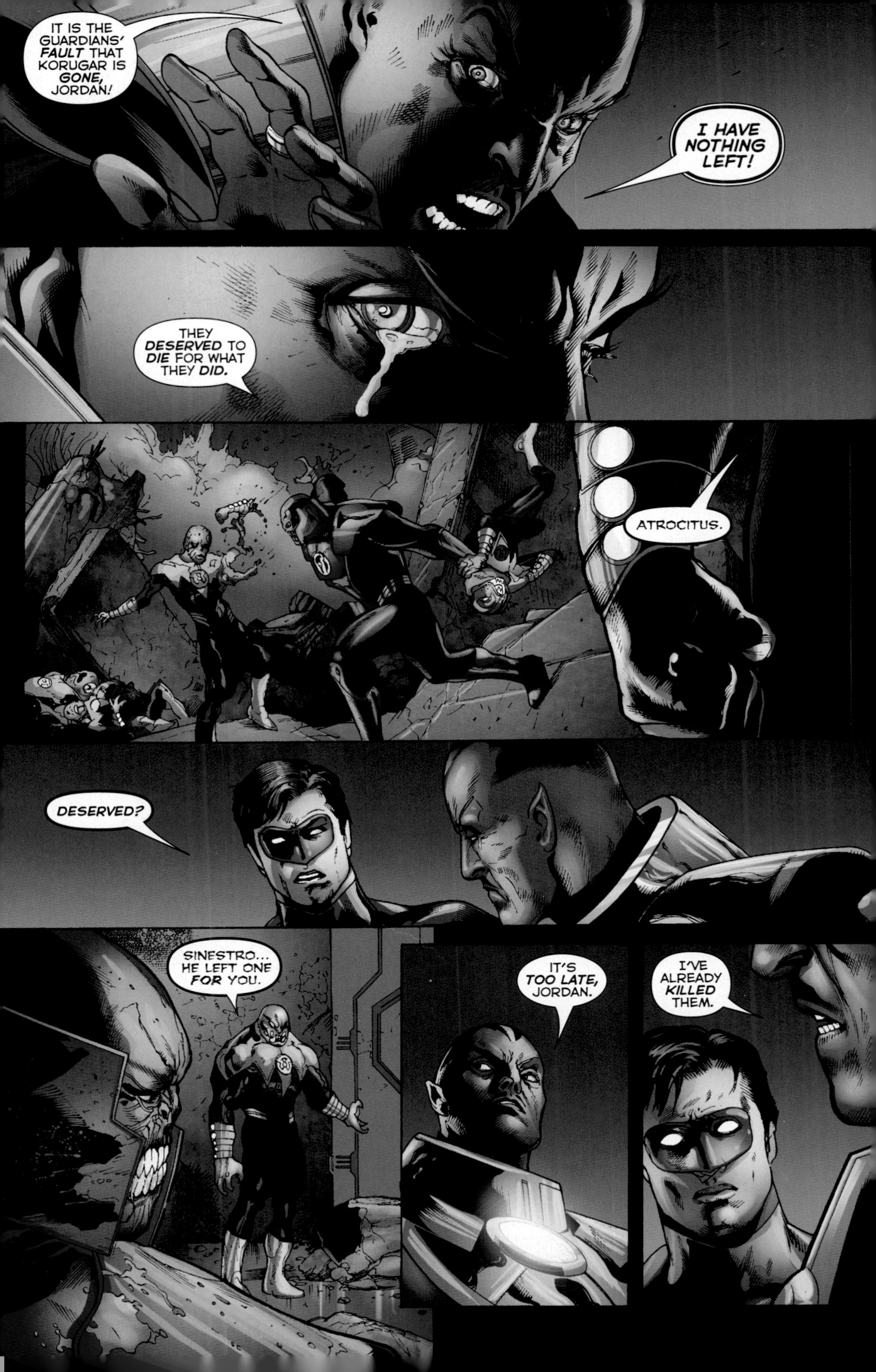
IT IS THE GUARDIANS' FAULT THAT KORUGAR IS GONE, JORDAN!
I HAVE NOTHING LEFT!
THEY DESERVED TO DIE FOR WHAT THEY DID.
ATROCITUS.
DESERVED?
SINESTRO... HE LEFT ONE FOR YOU.
IT'S TOO LATE, JORDAN.
I'VE ALREADY KILLED THEM.

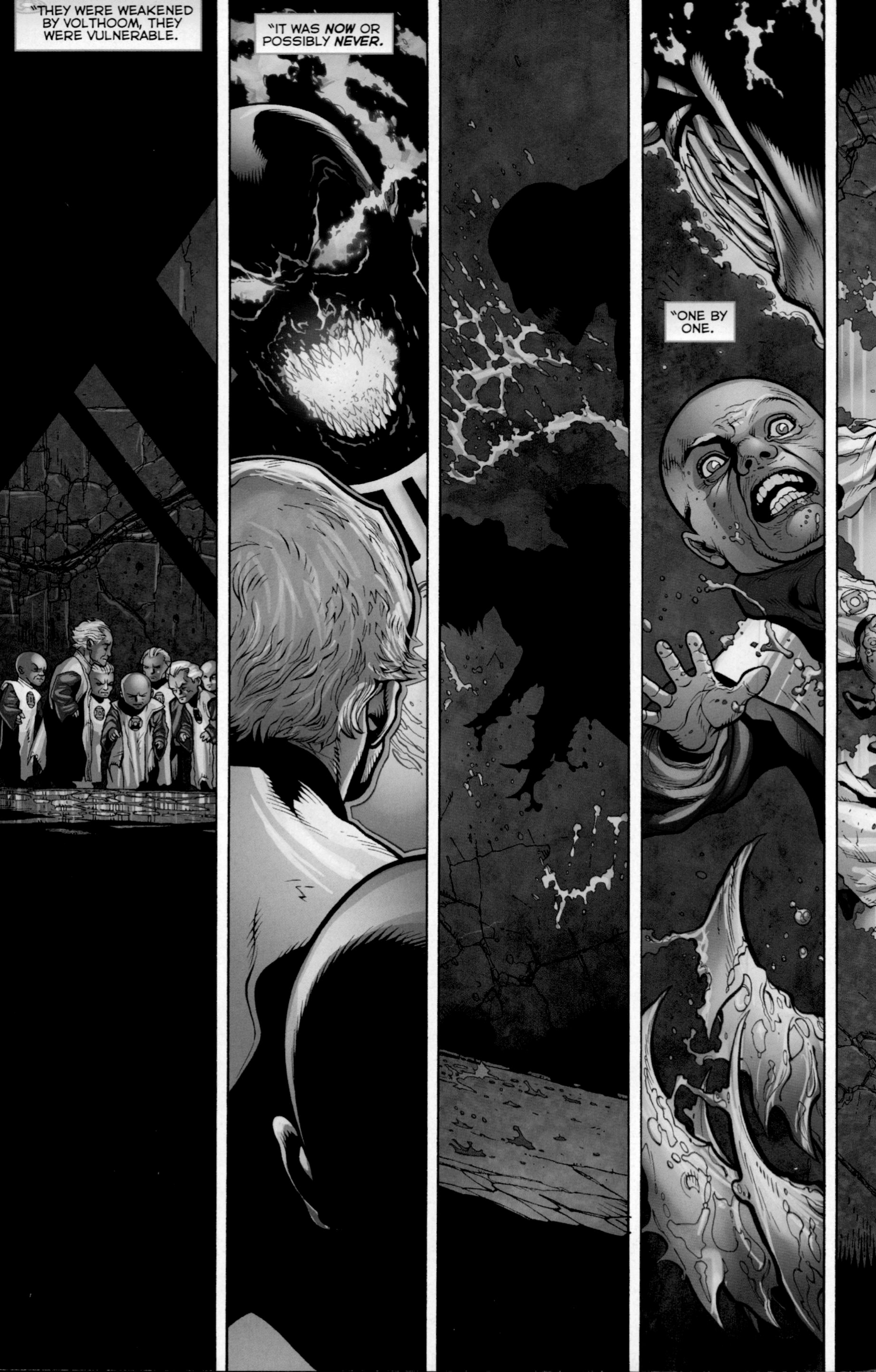
"THEY WERE WEAKENED BY VOLTHOOM, THEY WERE VULNERABLE.
"IT WAS NOW OR POSSIBLY NEVER.
"ONE BY ONE.

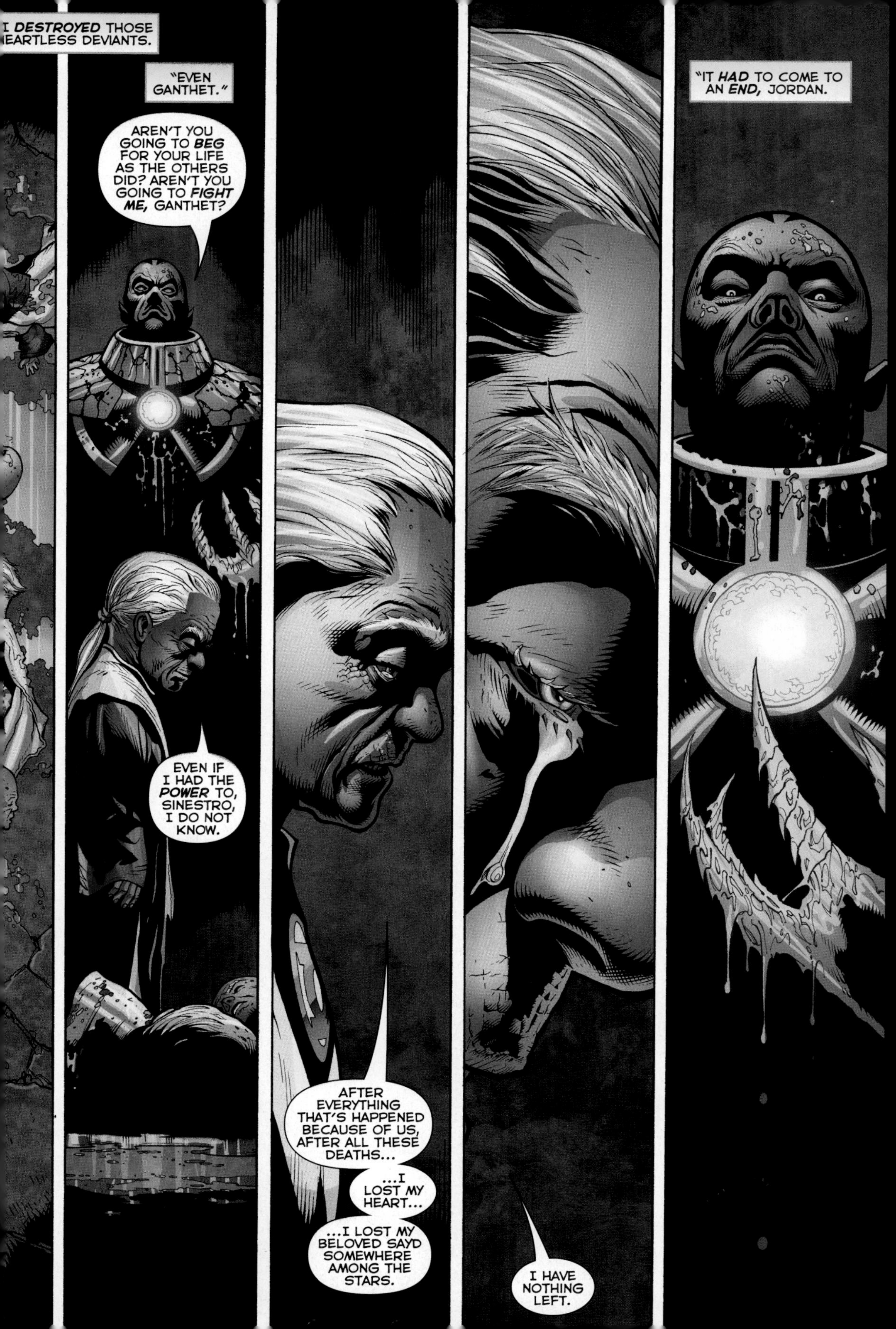

I DESTROYED THOSE HEARTLESS DEVIANTS.
"EVEN GANTHET."
AREN'T YOU GOING TO BEG FOR YOUR LIFE AS THE OTHERS DID? AREN'T YOU GOING TO FIGHT ME, GANTHET?
EVEN IF I HAD THE POWER TO, SINESTRO, I DO NOT KNOW.
AFTER EVERYTHING THAT'S HAPPENED BECAUSE OF US, AFTER ALL THESE DEATHS...
...I LOST MY HEART...
...I LOST MY BELOVED SAYD SOMEWHERE AMONG THE STARS.
I HAVE NOTHING LEFT.
"IT HAD TO COME TO AN END, JORDAN.

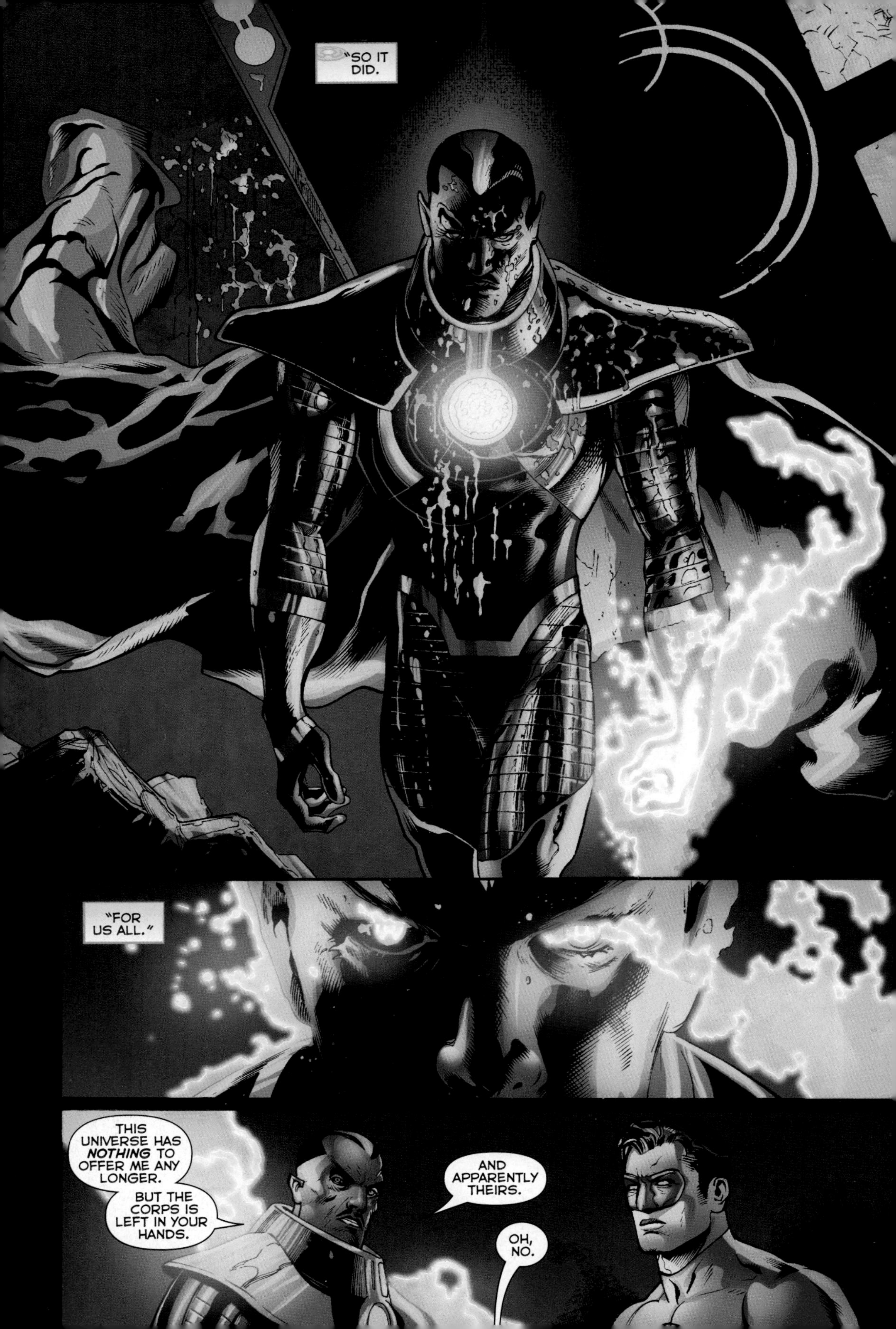
"SO IT DID.
"FOR US ALL."
THIS UNIVERSE HAS *NOTHING* TO OFFER ME ANY LONGER.
BUT THE CORPS IS LEFT IN YOUR HANDS.
AND APPARENTLY THEIRS.
OH, NO.

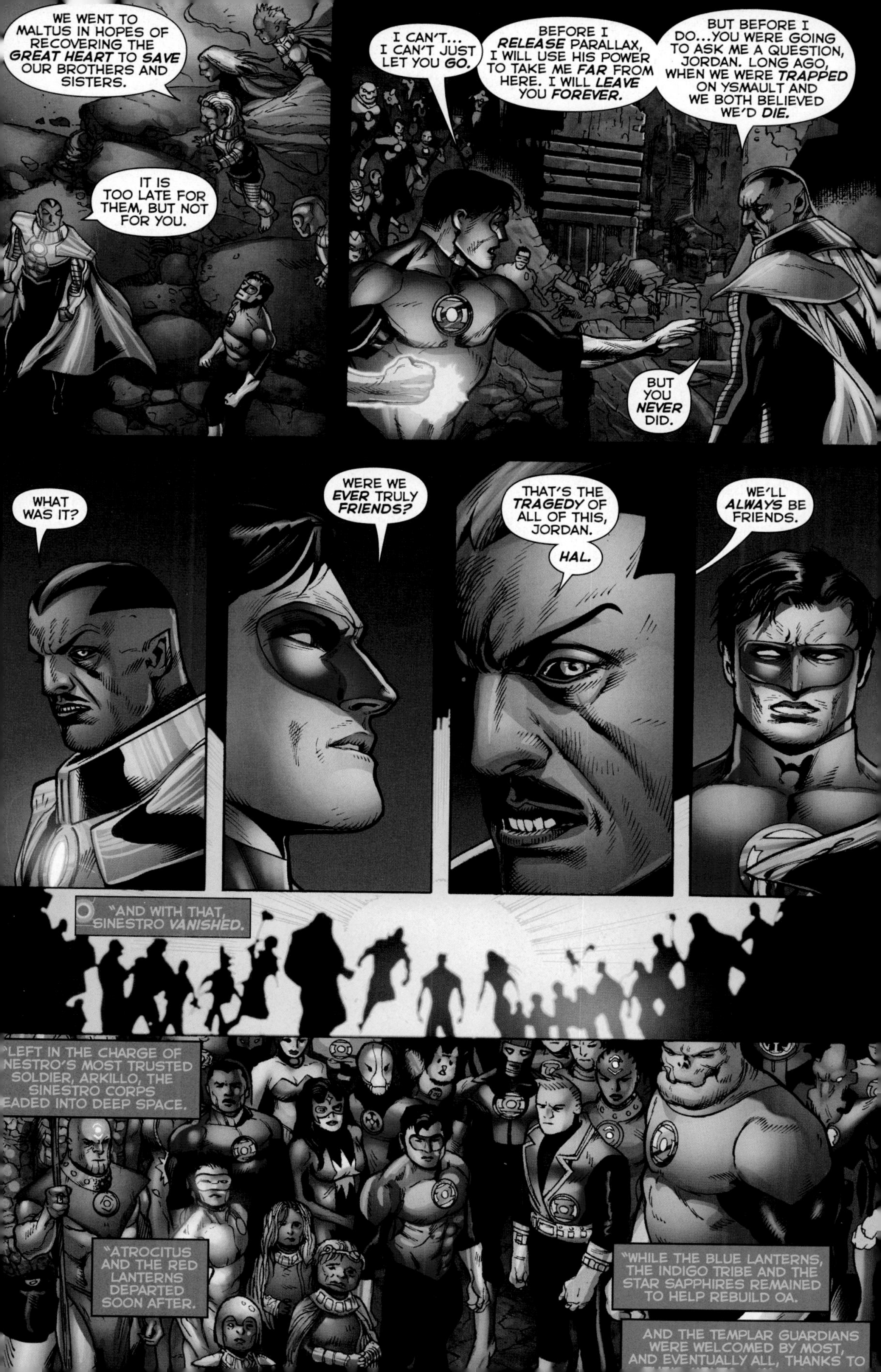
WE WENT TO MALTUS IN HOPES OF RECOVERING THE GREAT HEART TO SAVE OUR BROTHERS AND SISTERS.
IT IS TOO LATE FOR THEM, BUT NOT FOR YOU.
I CAN'T... I CAN'T JUST LET YOU GO.
BEFORE I RELEASE PARALLAX, I WILL USE HIS POWER TO TAKE ME FAR FROM HERE. I WILL LEAVE YOU FOREVER.
BUT BEFORE I DO...YOU WERE GOING TO ASK ME A QUESTION, JORDAN. LONG AGO, WHEN WE WERE TRAPPED ON YSMAULT AND WE BOTH BELIEVED WE'D DIE.
BUT YOU NEVER DID.
WHAT WAS IT?
WERE WE EVER TRULY FRIENDS?
THAT'S THE TRAGEDY OF ALL OF THIS, JORDAN.
HAL.
WE'LL ALWAYS BE FRIENDS.
"AND WITH THAT, SINESTRO VANISHED.
"LEFT IN THE CHARGE OF NESTRO'S MOST TRUSTED SOLDIER, ARKILLO, THE SINESTRO CORPS EADED INTO DEEP SPACE.
"ATROCITUS AND THE RED LANTERNS DEPARTED SOON AFTER.
"WHILE THE BLUE LANTERNS, THE INDIGO TRIBE AND THE STAR SAPPHIRES REMAINED TO HELP REBUILD OA.
AND THE TEMPLAR GUARDIANS WERE WELCOMED BY MOST, AND EVENTUALLY ALL, THANKS TO

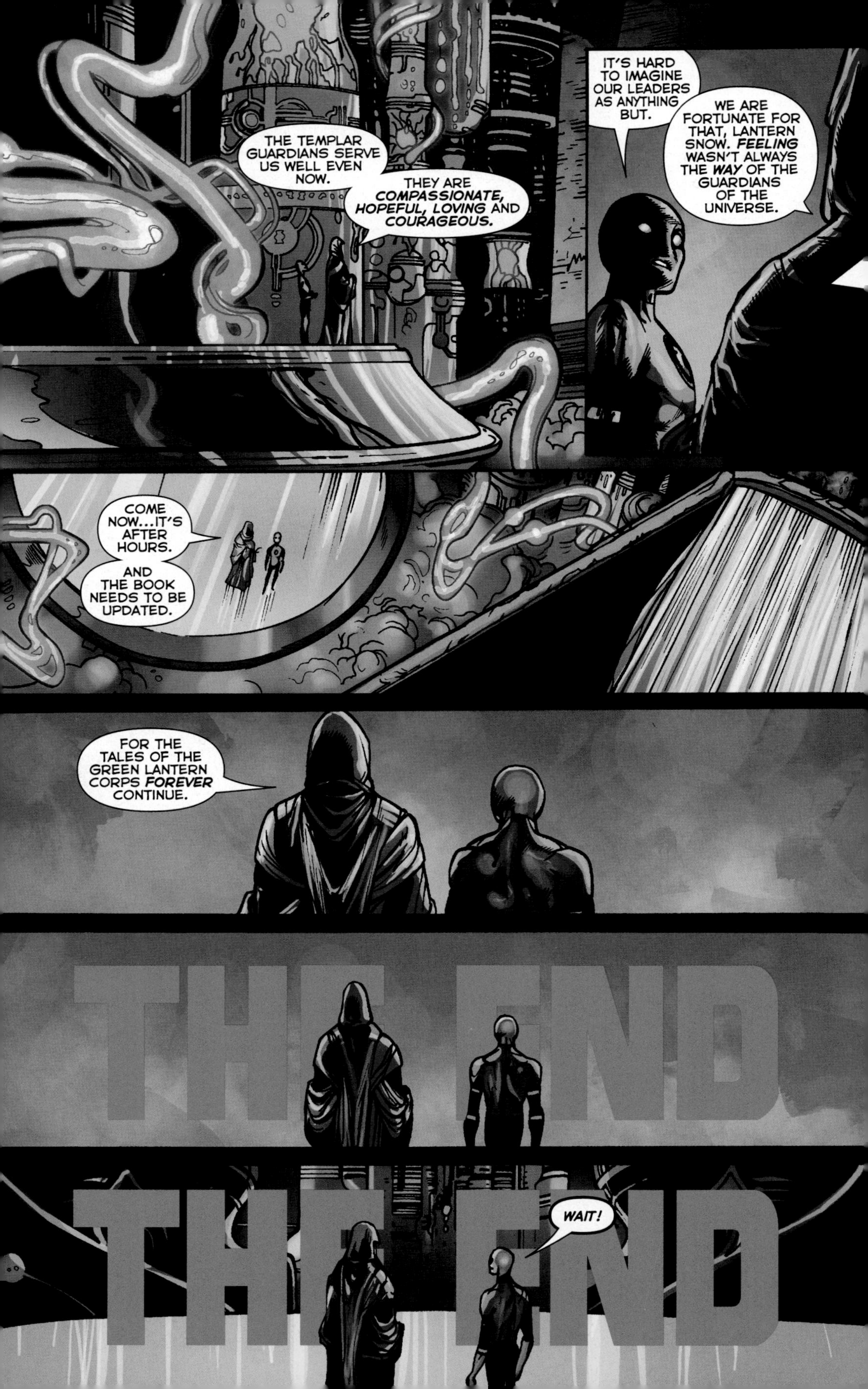
THE TEMPLAR GUARDIANS SERVE US WELL EVEN NOW.
THEY ARE *COMPASSIONATE, HOPEFUL, LOVING* AND *COURAGEOUS.*
IT'S HARD TO IMAGINE OUR LEADERS AS ANYTHING BUT.
WE ARE FORTUNATE FOR THAT, LANTERN SNOW. *FEELING* WASN'T ALWAYS THE *WAY* OF THE GUARDIANS OF THE UNIVERSE.
COME NOW...IT'S AFTER HOURS.
AND THE BOOK NEEDS TO BE UPDATED.
FOR THE TALES OF THE GREEN LANTERN CORPS *FOREVER* CONTINUE.
THE END
THE END
WAIT!

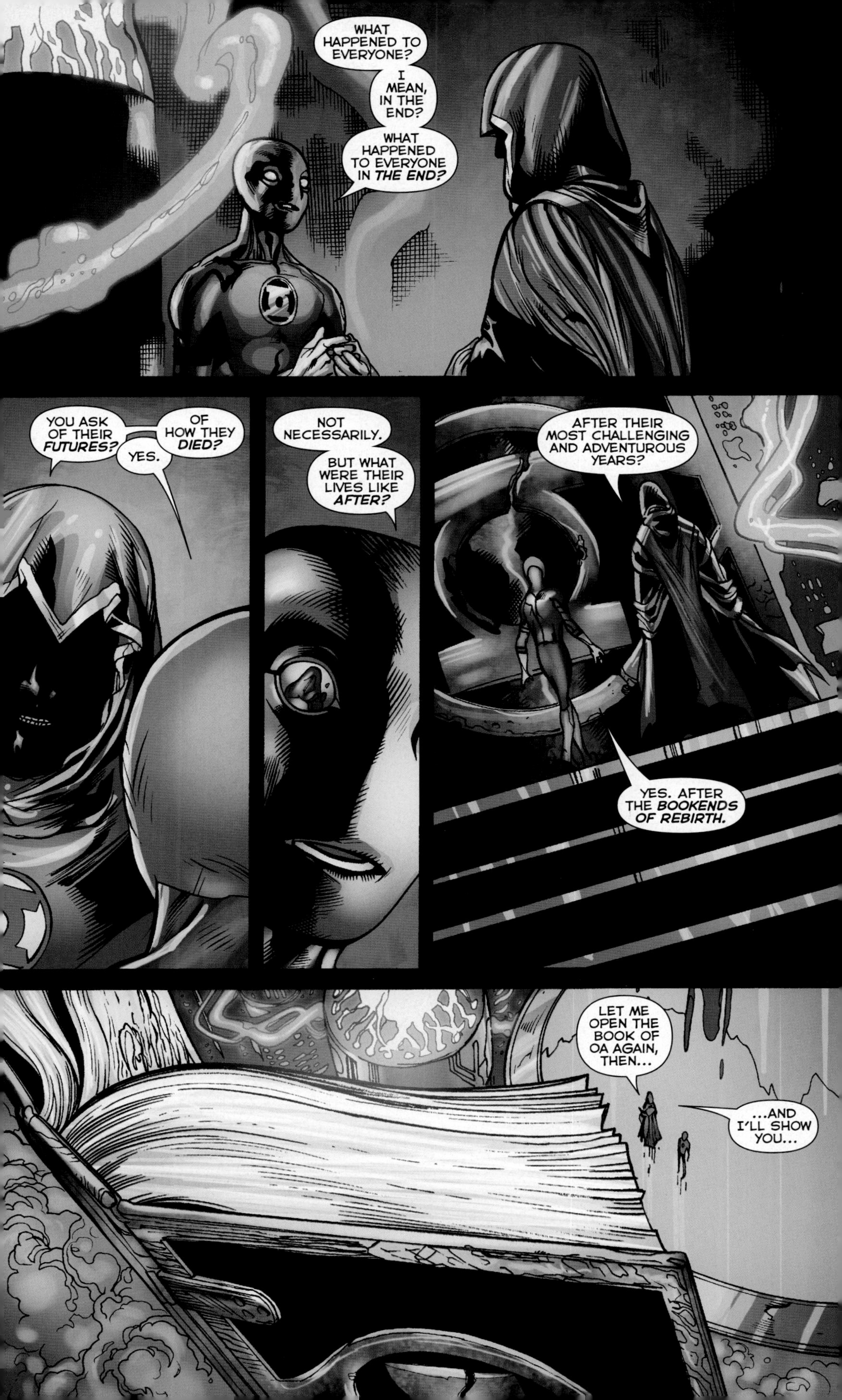
WHAT HAPPENED TO EVERYONE?
I MEAN, IN THE END?
WHAT HAPPENED TO EVERYONE IN *THE END?*
YOU ASK OF THEIR *FUTURES?*
OF HOW THEY *DIED?*
YES.
NOT NECESSARILY.
BUT WHAT WERE THEIR LIVES LIKE *AFTER?*
AFTER THEIR MOST CHALLENGING AND ADVENTUROUS YEARS?
YES. AFTER THE *BOOKENDS OF REBIRTH.*
LET ME OPEN THE BOOK OF OA AGAIN, THEN...
...AND I'LL SHOW YOU...

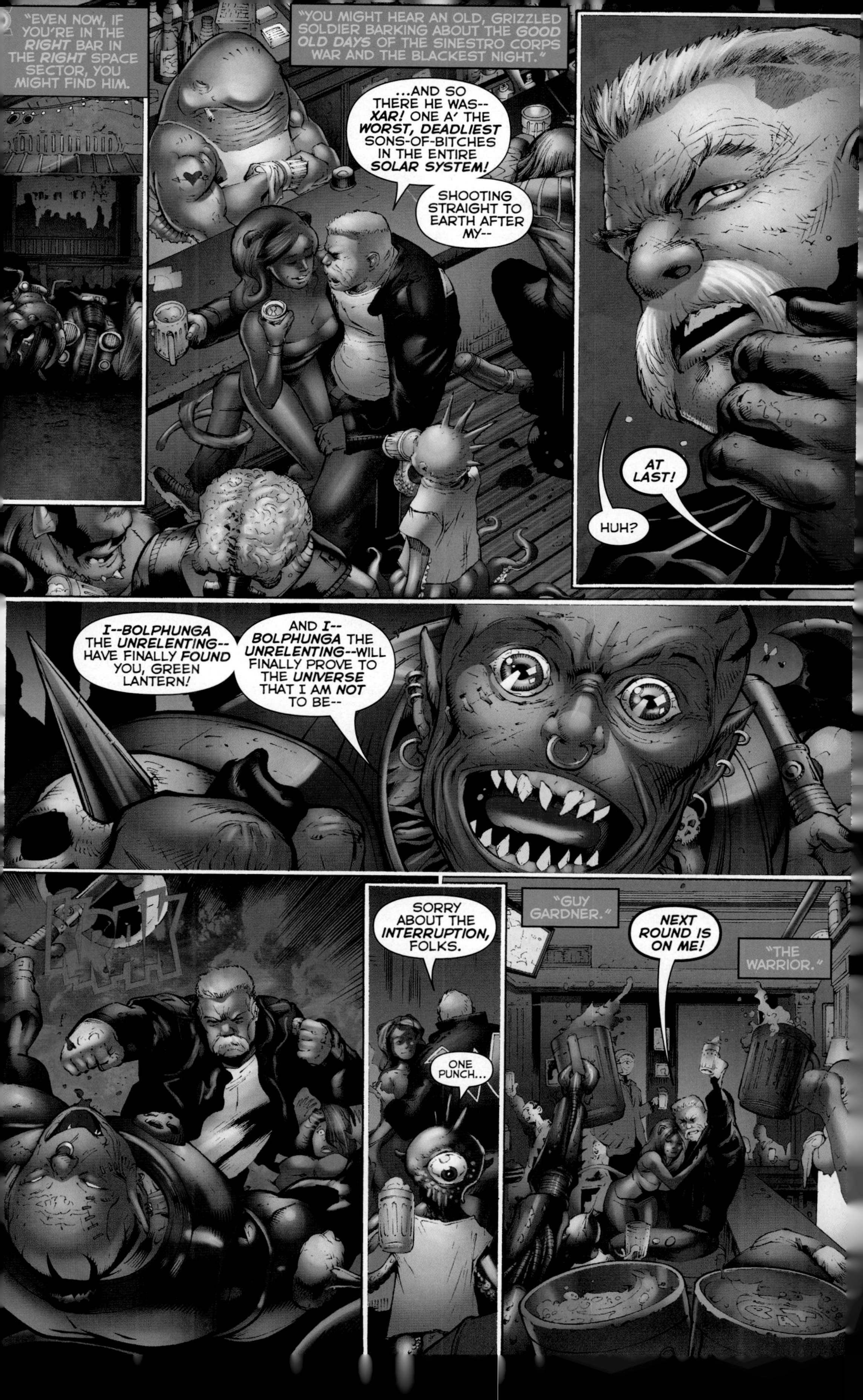
"EVEN NOW, IF YOU'RE IN THE RIGHT BAR IN THE RIGHT SPACE SECTOR, YOU MIGHT FIND HIM.
"YOU MIGHT HEAR AN OLD, GRIZZLED SOLDIER BARKING ABOUT THE GOOD OLD DAYS OF THE SINESTRO CORPS WAR AND THE BLACKEST NIGHT."
...AND SO THERE HE WAS-- XAR! ONE A' THE WORST, DEADLIEST SONS-OF-BITCHES IN THE ENTIRE SOLAR SYSTEM!
SHOOTING STRAIGHT TO EARTH AFTER MY--
AT LAST!
HUH?
I--BOLPHUNGA THE UNRELENTING--HAVE FINALLY FOUND YOU, GREEN LANTERN!
AND I--BOLPHUNGA THE UNRELENTING--WILL FINALLY PROVE TO THE UNIVERSE THAT I AM NOT TO BE--
SORRY ABOUT THE INTERRUPTION, FOLKS.
ONE PUNCH...
"GUY GARDNER."
NEXT ROUND IS ON ME!
"THE WARRIOR."

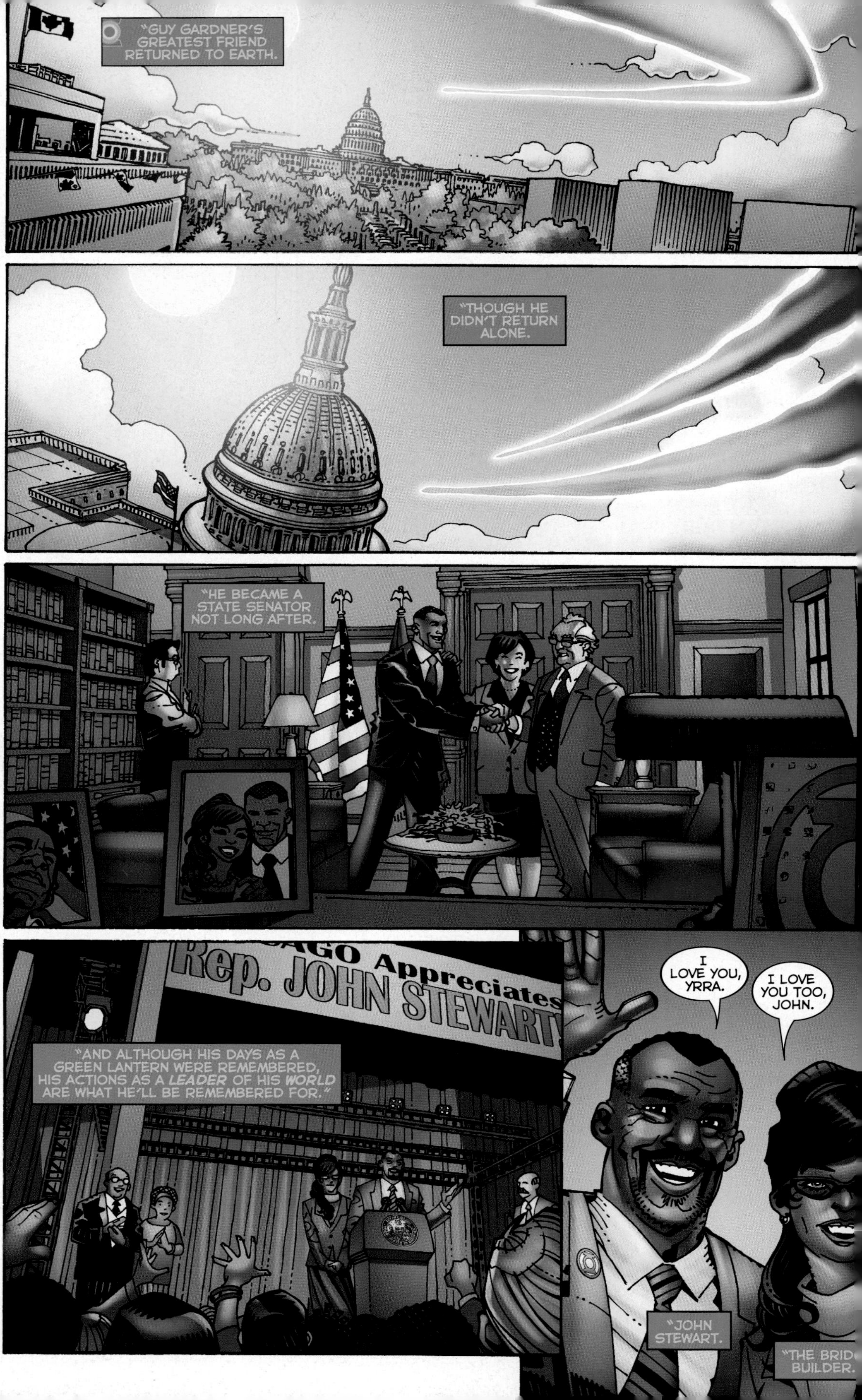
"GUY GARDNER'S GREATEST FRIEND RETURNED TO EARTH.
"THOUGH HE DIDN'T RETURN ALONE.
"HE BECAME A STATE SENATOR NOT LONG AFTER.
Rep. JOHN STEWART!
Appreciates
"AND ALTHOUGH HIS DAYS AS A GREEN LANTERN WERE REMEMBERED, HIS ACTIONS AS A *LEADER* OF HIS *WORLD* ARE WHAT HE'LL BE REMEMBERED FOR."
I LOVE YOU, YRRA.
I LOVE YOU TOO, JOHN.
"JOHN STEWART.
"THE BRID BUILDER.

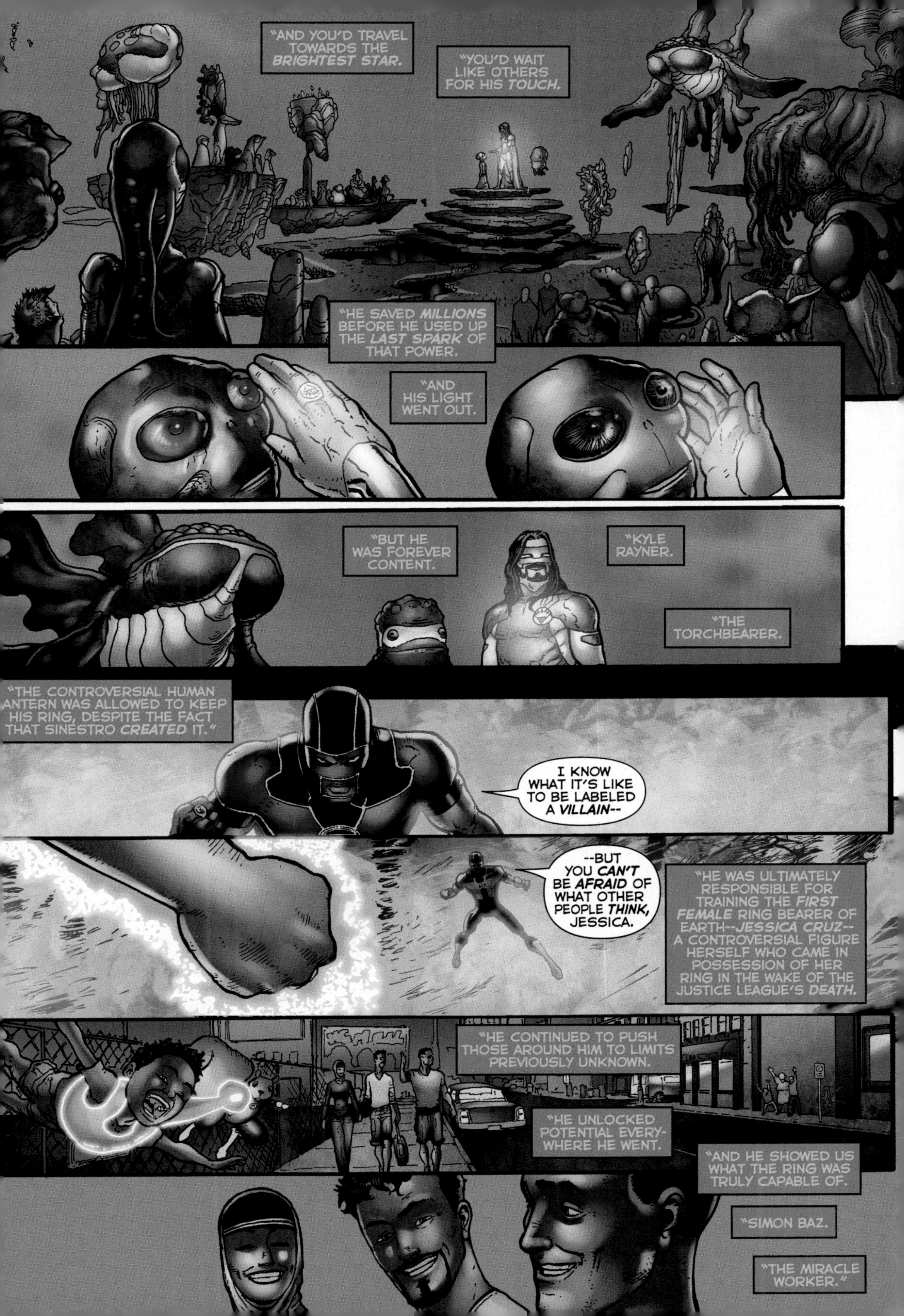
"AND YOU'D TRAVEL TOWARDS THE BRIGHTEST STAR.
"YOU'D WAIT LIKE OTHERS FOR HIS TOUCH.
"HE SAVED MILLIONS BEFORE HE USED UP THE LAST SPARK OF THAT POWER.
"AND HIS LIGHT WENT OUT.
"BUT HE WAS FOREVER CONTENT.
"KYLE RAYNER.
"THE TORCHBEARER.
"THE CONTROVERSIAL HUMAN LANTERN WAS ALLOWED TO KEEP HIS RING, DESPITE THE FACT THAT SINESTRO CREATED IT."
I KNOW WHAT IT'S LIKE TO BE LABELED A VILLAIN--
--BUT YOU CAN'T BE AFRAID OF WHAT OTHER PEOPLE THINK, JESSICA.
"HE WAS ULTIMATELY RESPONSIBLE FOR TRAINING THE FIRST FEMALE RING BEARER OF EARTH--JESSICA CRUZ--A CONTROVERSIAL FIGURE HERSELF WHO CAME IN POSSESSION OF HER RING IN THE WAKE OF THE JUSTICE LEAGUE'S DEATH.
"HE CONTINUED TO PUSH THOSE AROUND HIM TO LIMITS PREVIOUSLY UNKNOWN.
"HE UNLOCKED POTENTIAL EVERYWHERE HE WENT.
"AND HE SHOWED US WHAT THE RING WAS TRULY CAPABLE OF.
"SIMON BAZ.
"THE MIRACLE WORKER."

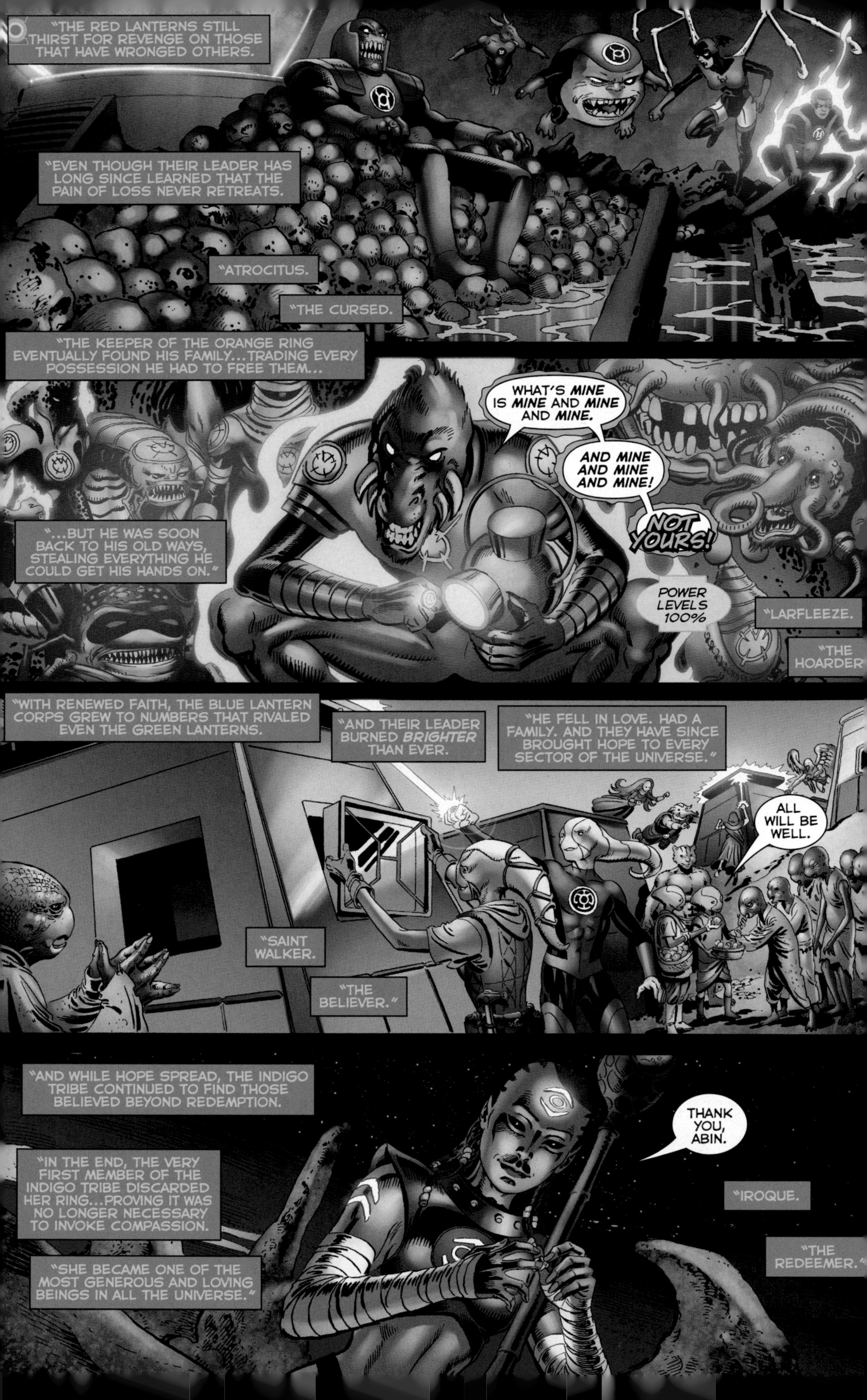
"THE RED LANTERNS STILL THIRST FOR REVENGE ON THOSE THAT HAVE WRONGED OTHERS.
"EVEN THOUGH THEIR LEADER HAS LONG SINCE LEARNED THAT THE PAIN OF LOSS NEVER RETREATS.
"ATROCITUS.
"THE CURSED.
"THE KEEPER OF THE ORANGE RING EVENTUALLY FOUND HIS FAMILY...TRADING EVERY POSSESSION HE HAD TO FREE THEM...
WHAT'S MINE IS MINE AND MINE AND MINE.
AND MINE AND MINE AND MINE!
NOT YOURS!
"...BUT HE WAS SOON BACK TO HIS OLD WAYS, STEALING EVERYTHING HE COULD GET HIS HANDS ON."
POWER LEVELS 100%
"LARFLEEZE.
"THE HOARDER
"WITH RENEWED FAITH, THE BLUE LANTERN CORPS GREW TO NUMBERS THAT RIVALED EVEN THE GREEN LANTERNS.
"AND THEIR LEADER BURNED BRIGHTER THAN EVER.
"HE FELL IN LOVE. HAD A FAMILY. AND THEY HAVE SINCE BROUGHT HOPE TO EVERY SECTOR OF THE UNIVERSE."
ALL WILL BE WELL.
"SAINT WALKER.
"THE BELIEVER."
"AND WHILE HOPE SPREAD, THE INDIGO TRIBE CONTINUED TO FIND THOSE BELIEVED BEYOND REDEMPTION.
THANK YOU, ABIN.
"IN THE END, THE VERY FIRST MEMBER OF THE INDIGO TRIBE DISCARDED HER RING...PROVING IT WAS NO LONGER NECESSARY TO INVOKE COMPASSION.
"IROQUE.
"SHE BECAME ONE OF THE MOST GENEROUS AND LOVING BEINGS IN ALL THE UNIVERSE."
"THE REDEEMER."

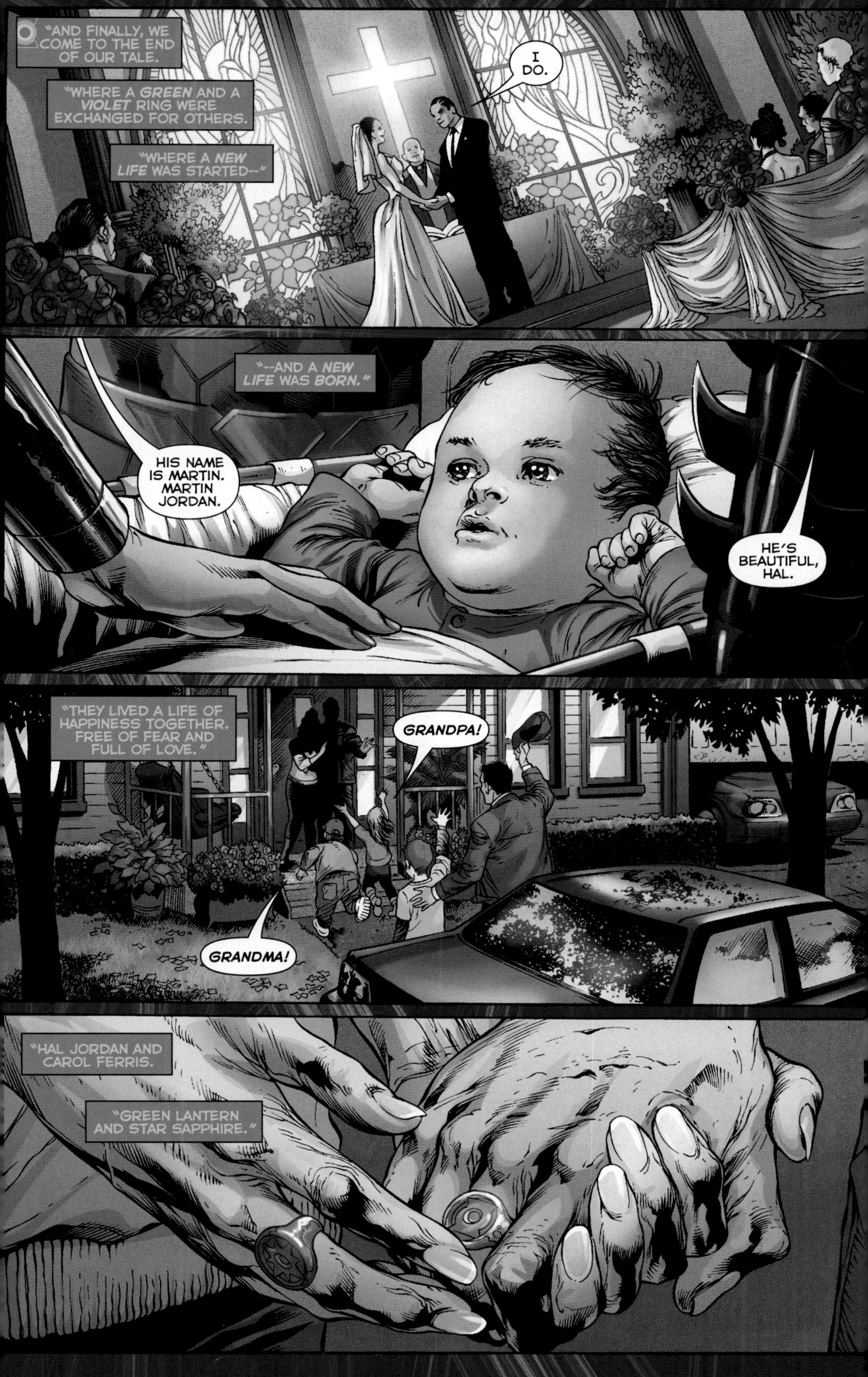
"AND FINALLY, WE COME TO THE END OF OUR TALE.
"WHERE A GREEN AND A VIOLET RING WERE EXCHANGED FOR OTHERS.
"WHERE A NEW LIFE WAS STARTED--"
I DO.
"--AND A NEW LIFE WAS BORN."
HIS NAME IS MARTIN. MARTIN JORDAN.
HE'S BEAUTIFUL, HAL.
"THEY LIVED A LIFE OF HAPPINESS TOGETHER. FREE OF FEAR AND FULL OF LOVE."
GRANDPA!
GRANDMA!
"HAL JORDAN AND CAROL FERRIS.
"GREEN LANTERN AND STAR SAPPHIRE."

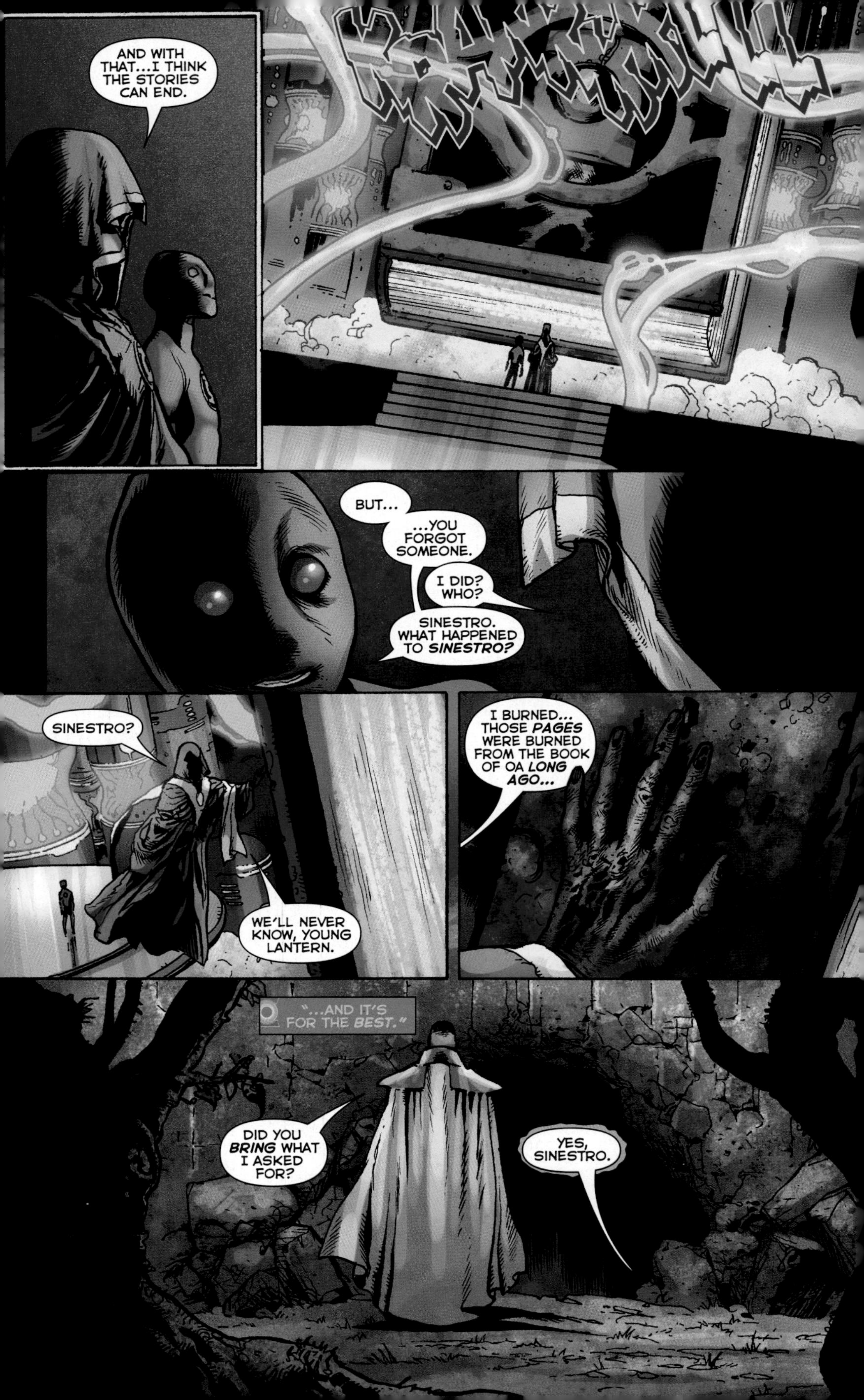
AND WITH THAT...I THINK THE STORIES CAN END.
BUT...
...YOU FORGOT SOMEONE.
I DID? WHO?
SINESTRO. WHAT HAPPENED TO SINESTRO?
SINESTRO?
WE'LL NEVER KNOW, YOUNG LANTERN.
I BURNED... THOSE PAGES WERE BURNED FROM THE BOOK OF OA LONG AGO...
"...AND IT'S FOR THE BEST."
DID YOU BRING WHAT I ASKED FOR?
YES, SINESTRO.

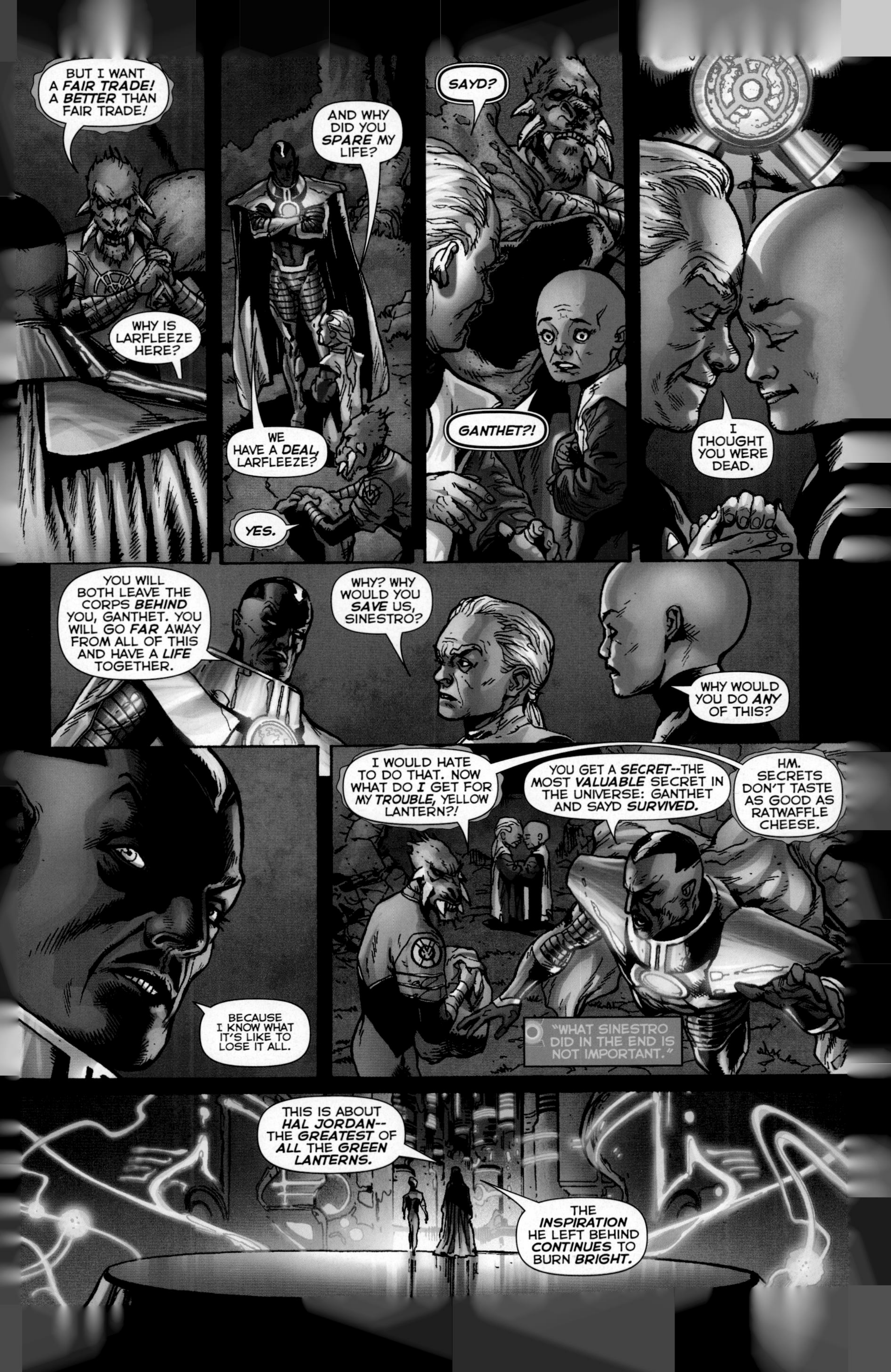
BUT I WANT A FAIR TRADE! A BETTER THAN FAIR TRADE!
WHY IS LARFLEEZE HERE?
AND WHY DID YOU SPARE MY LIFE?
WE HAVE A DEAL, LARFLEEZE?
YES.
SAYD?
GANTHET?!
I THOUGHT YOU WERE DEAD.
YOU WILL BOTH LEAVE THE CORPS BEHIND YOU, GANTHET. YOU WILL GO FAR AWAY FROM ALL OF THIS AND HAVE A LIFE TOGETHER.
WHY? WHY WOULD YOU SAVE US, SINESTRO?
WHY WOULD YOU DO ANY OF THIS?
BECAUSE I KNOW WHAT IT'S LIKE TO LOSE IT ALL.
I WOULD HATE TO DO THAT. NOW WHAT DO I GET FOR MY TROUBLE, YELLOW LANTERN?!
YOU GET A SECRET--THE MOST VALUABLE SECRET IN THE UNIVERSE: GANTHET AND SAYD SURVIVED.
HM. SECRETS DON'T TASTE AS GOOD AS RATWAFFLE CHEESE.
"WHAT SINESTRO DID IN THE END IS NOT IMPORTANT."
THIS IS ABOUT HAL JORDAN-- THE GREATEST OF ALL THE GREEN LANTERNS.
THE INSPIRATION HE LEFT BEHIND CONTINUES TO BURN BRIGHT.

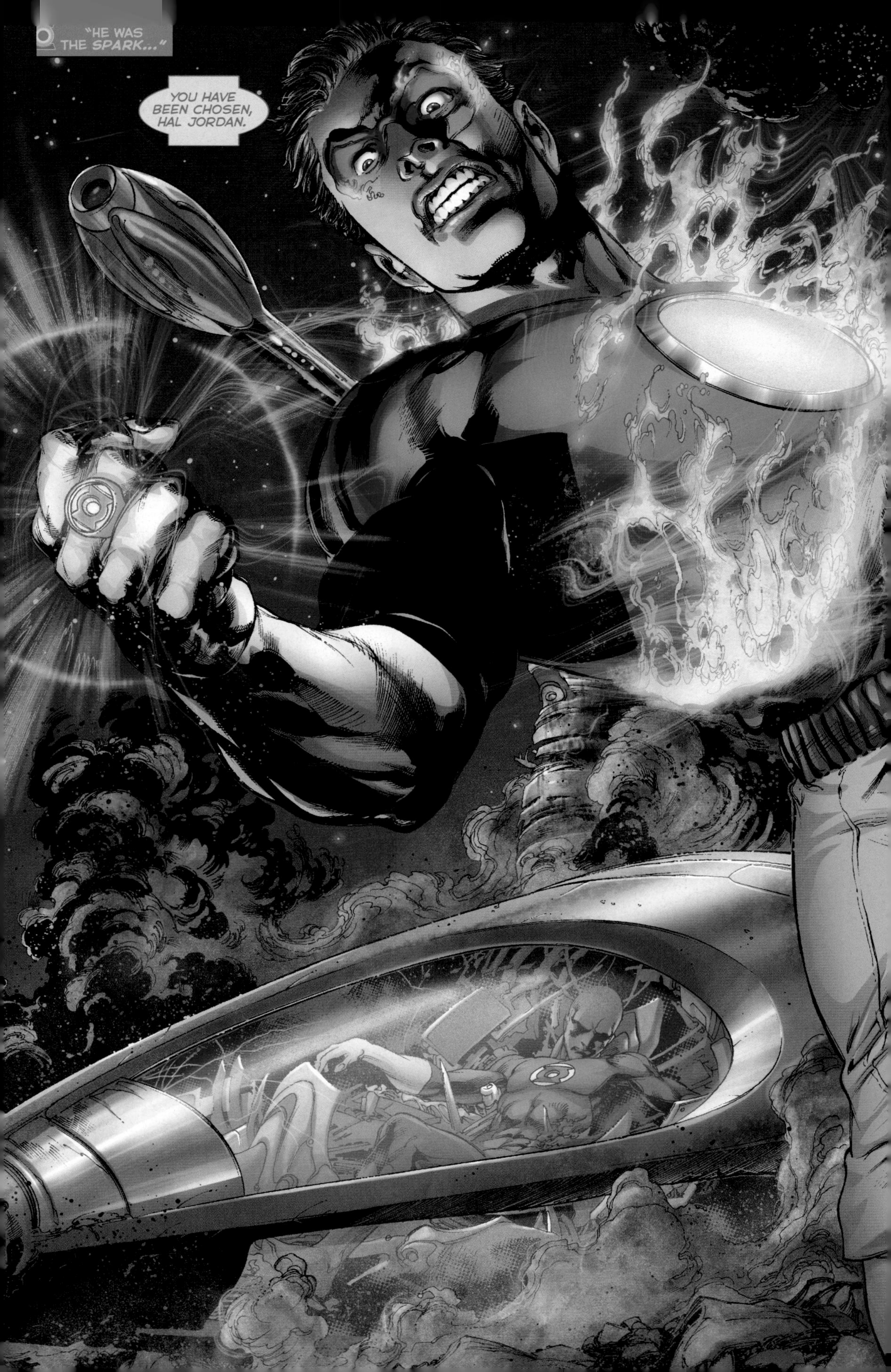
"HE WAS THE SPARK..."
YOU HAVE BEEN CHOSEN, HAL JORDAN.

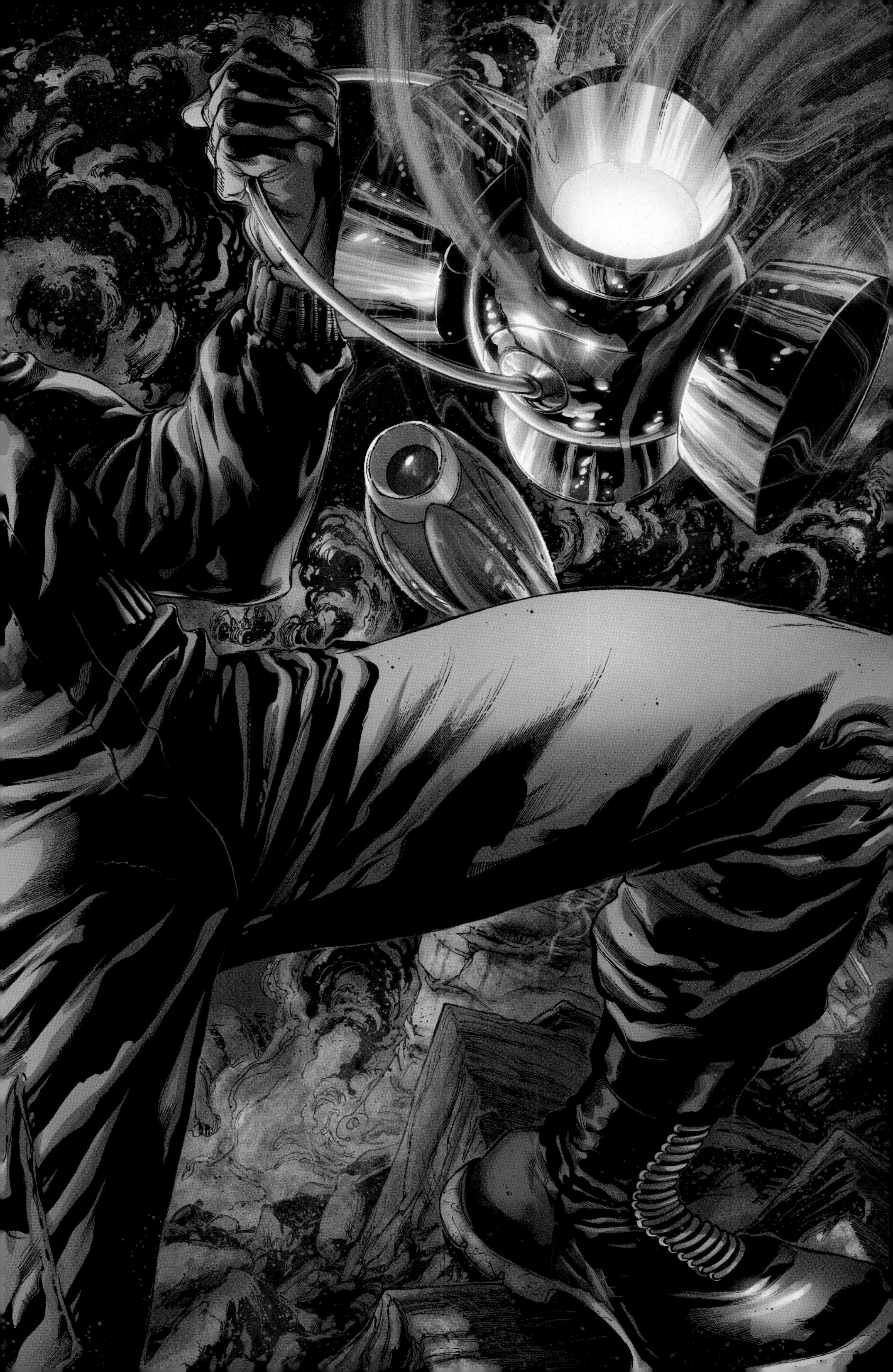

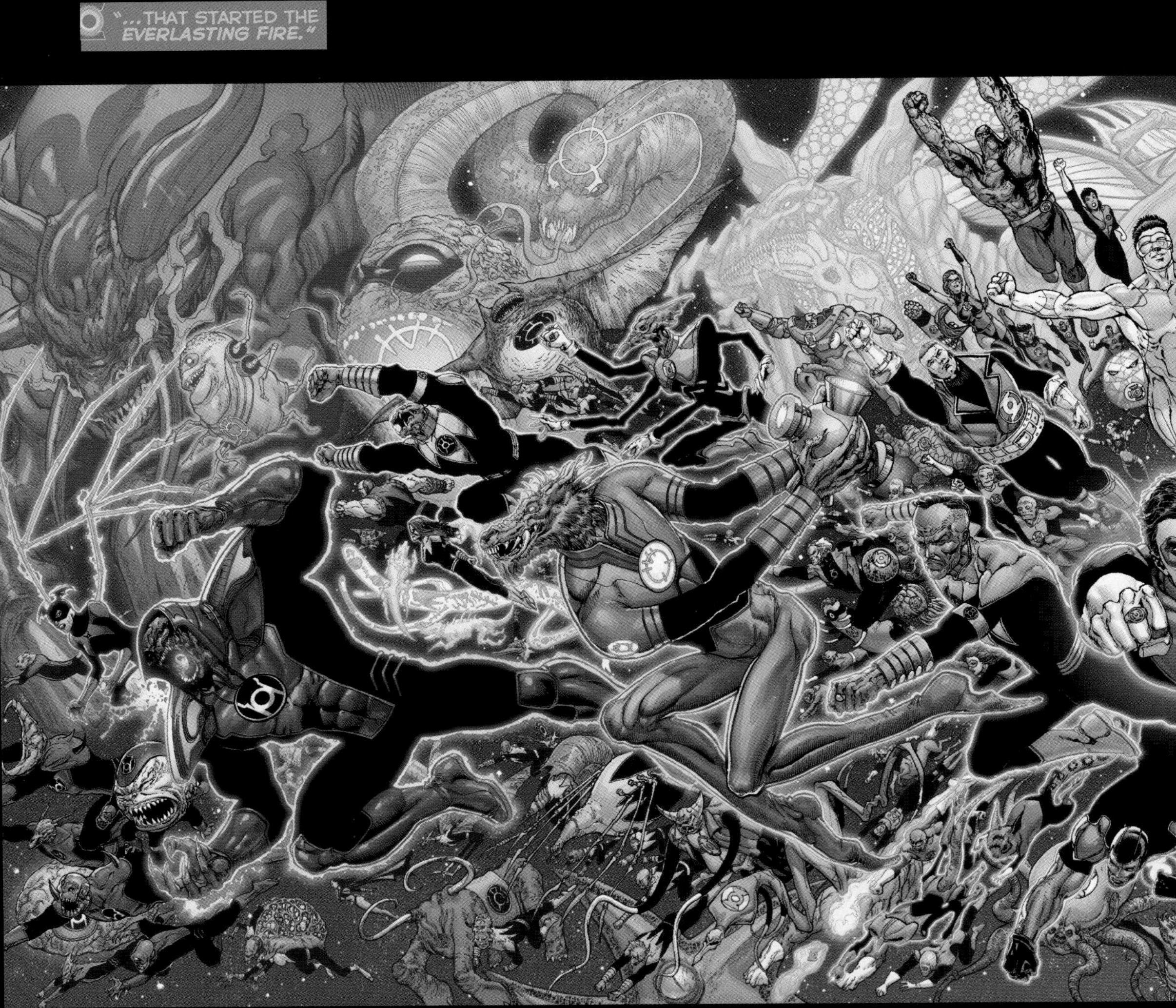
"...THAT STARTED THE EVERLASTING FIRE."

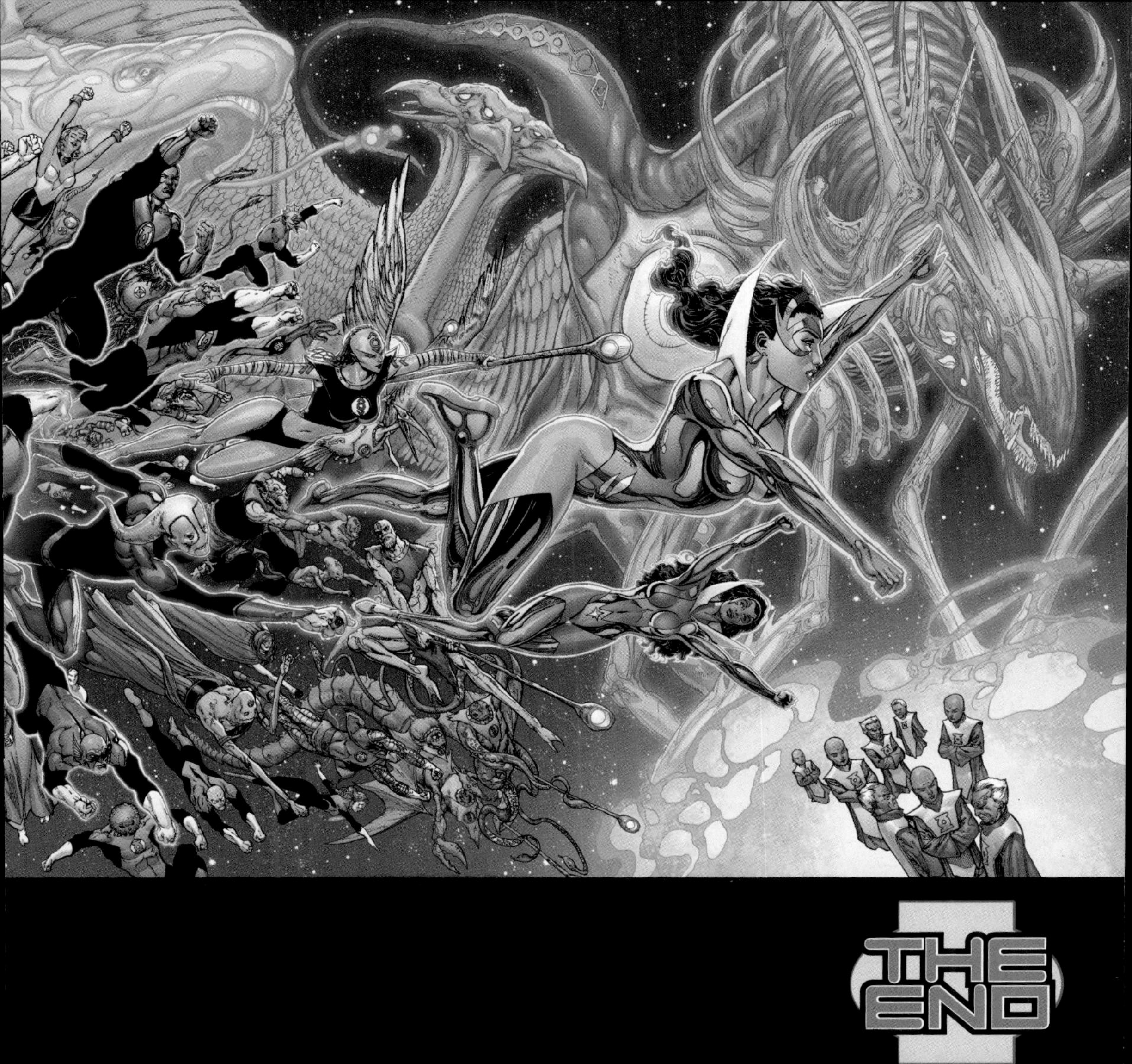
THE END

GREEN LANTERN #19
Fold-out cover by Gary Frank & Brad Anderson

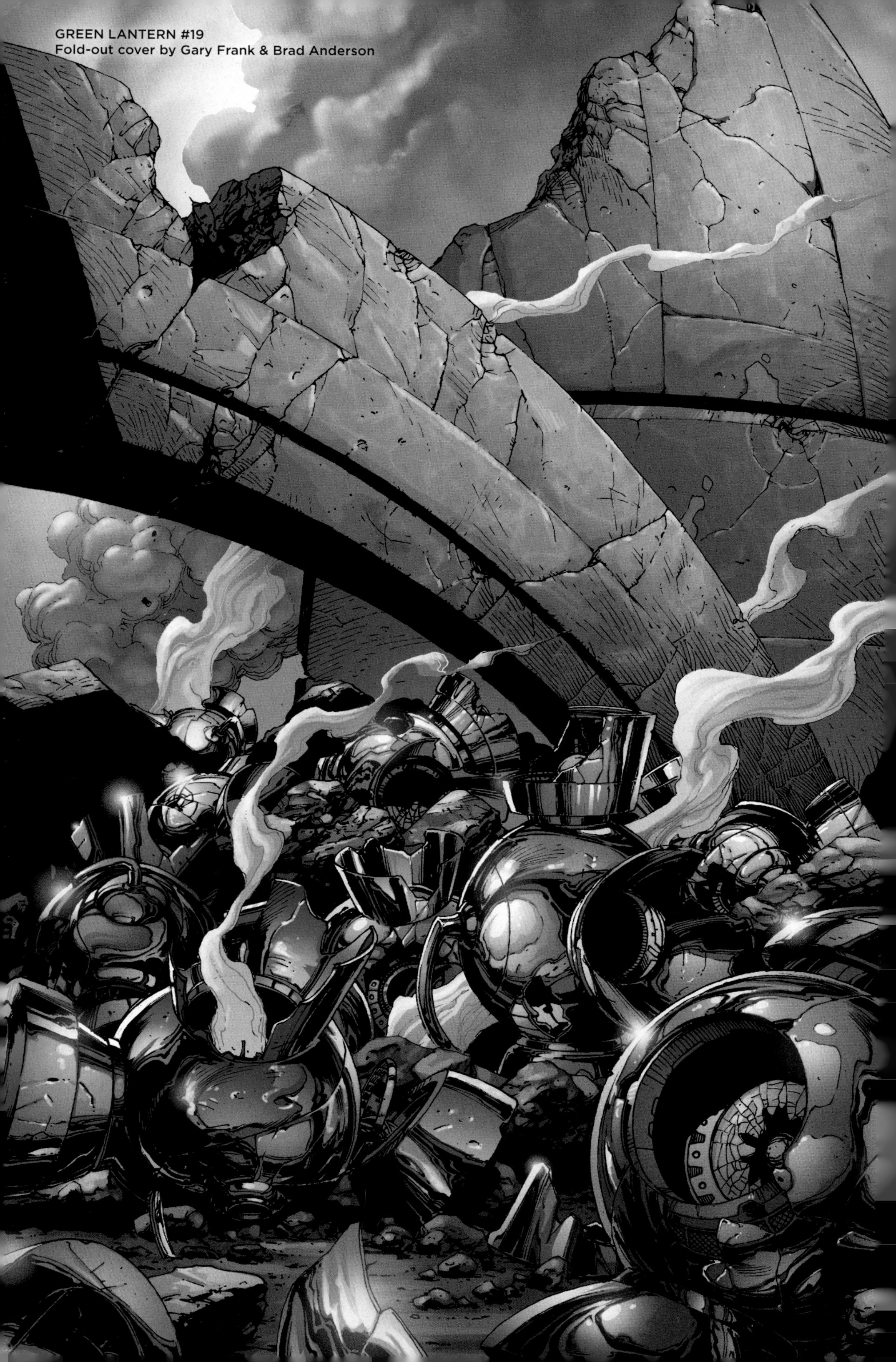

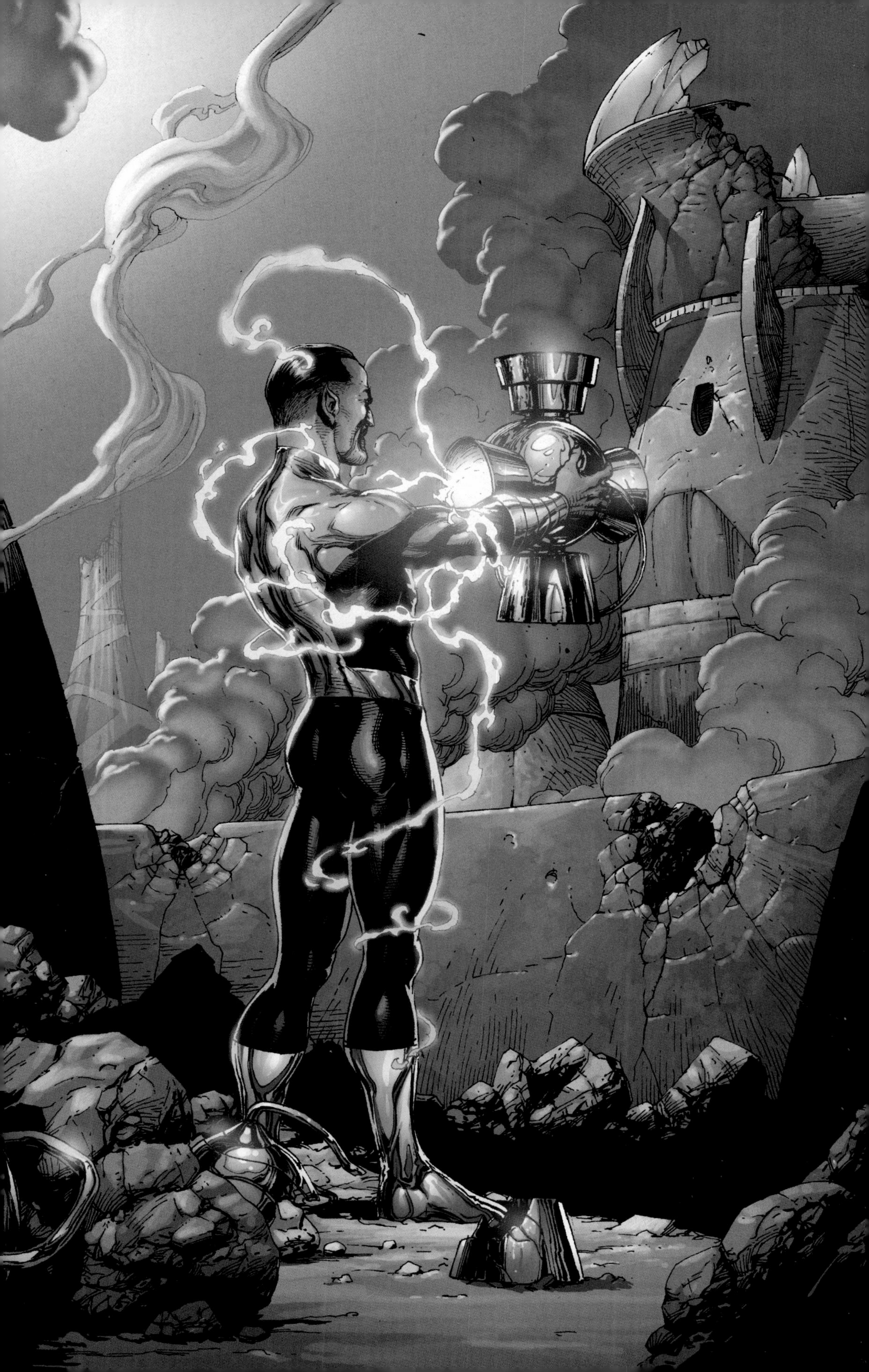

GREEN LANTERN #20
Wrap-around cover by Doug Mahnke & Alex Sinclair

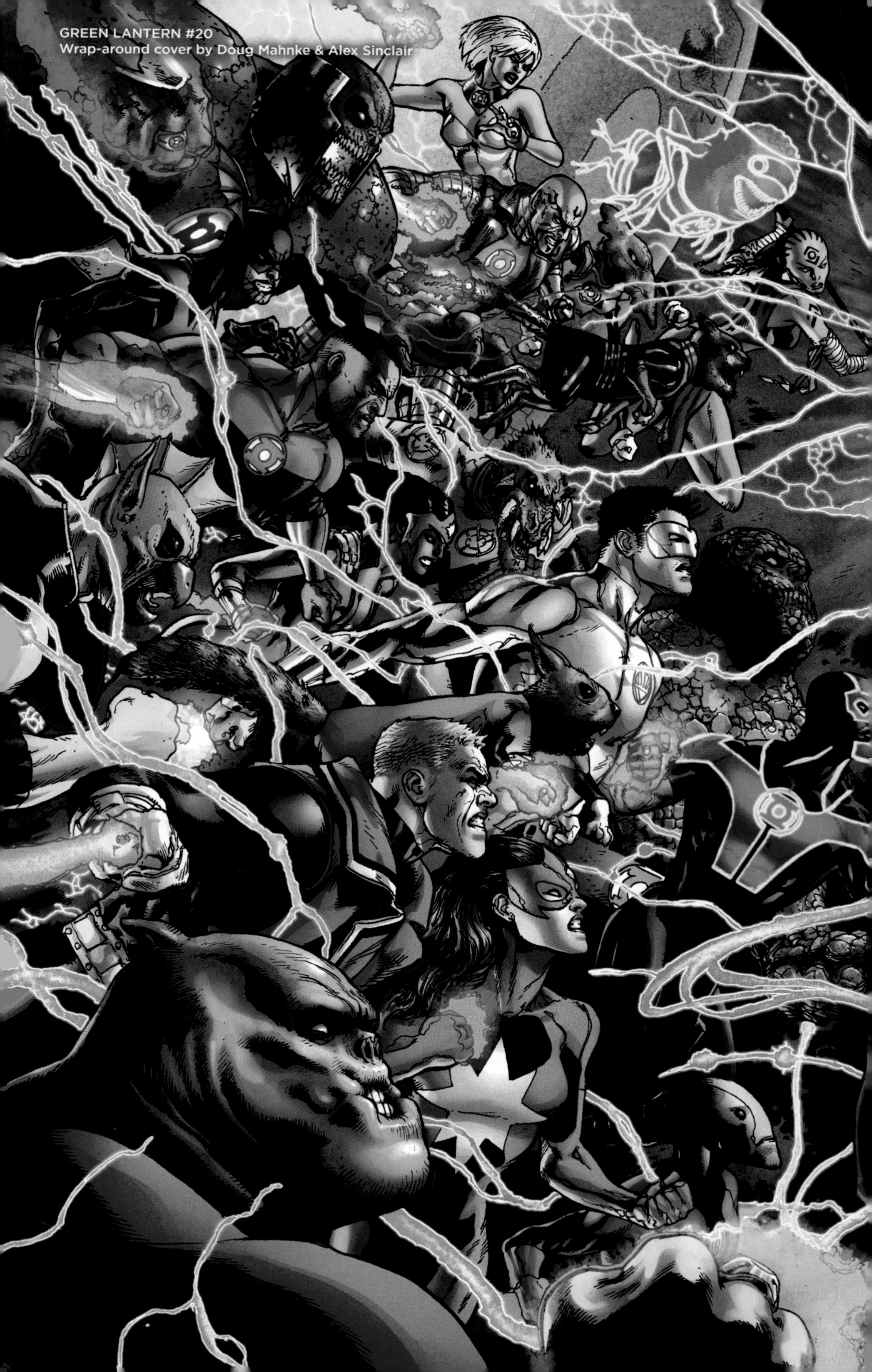

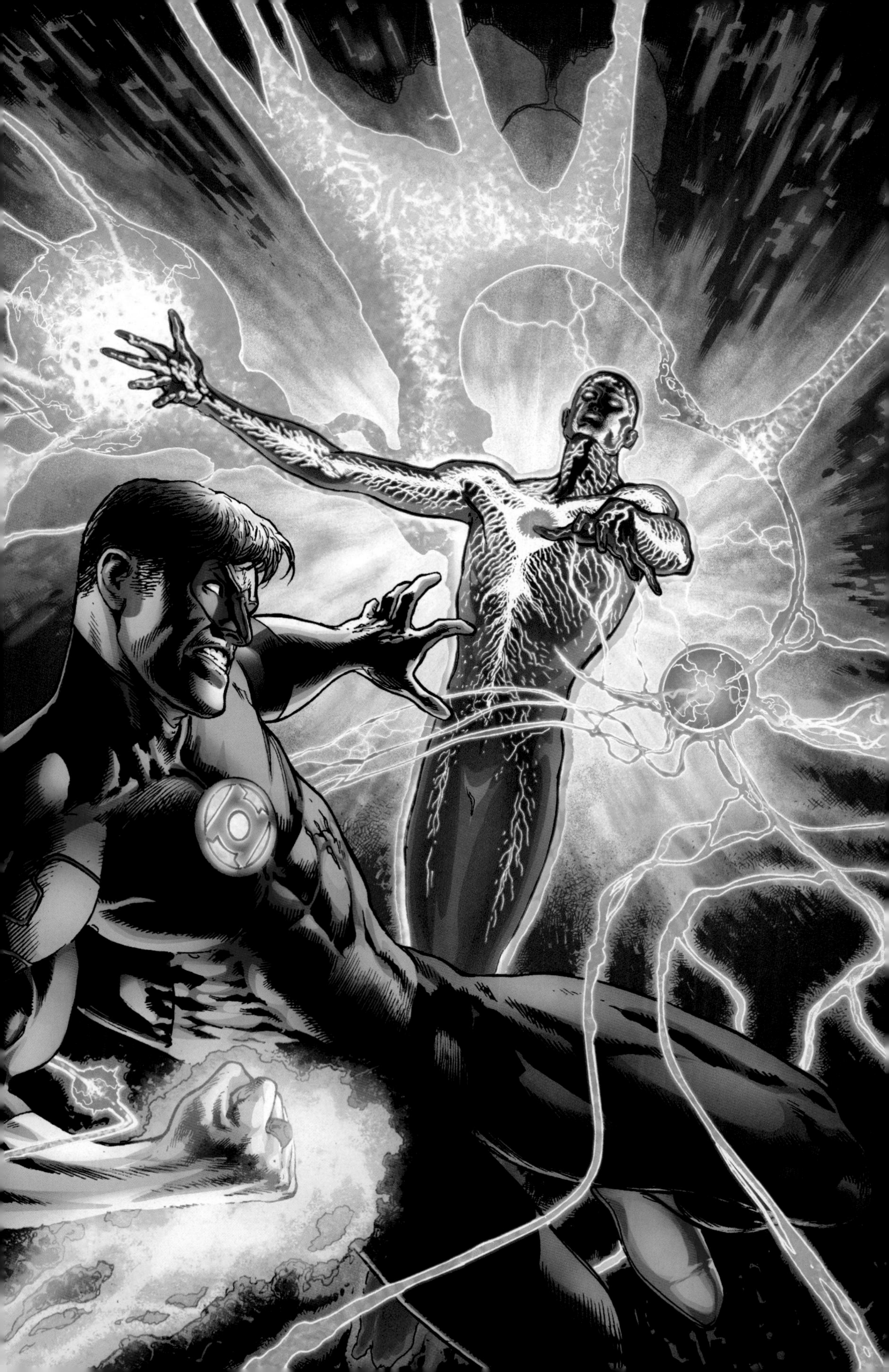

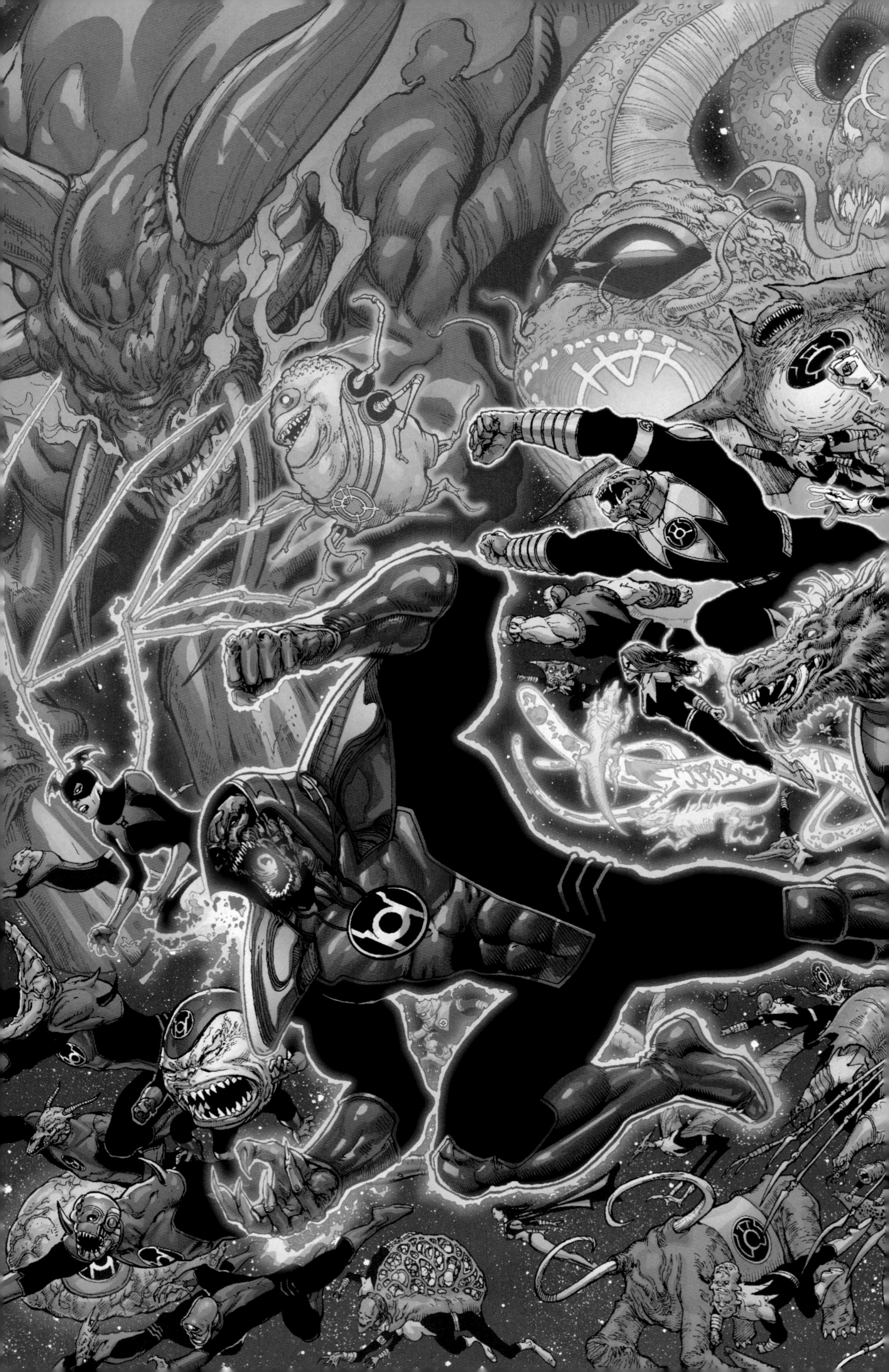

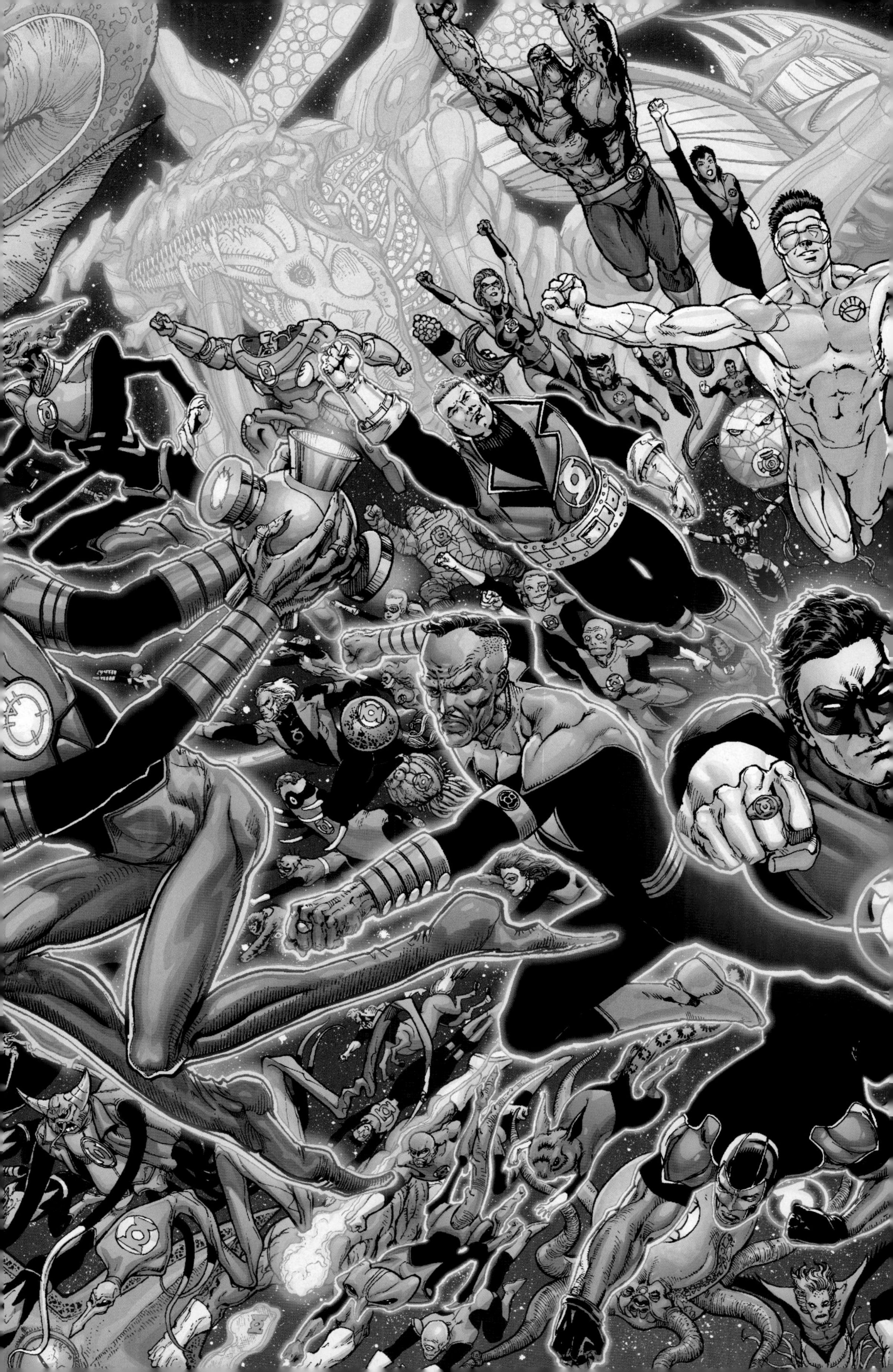

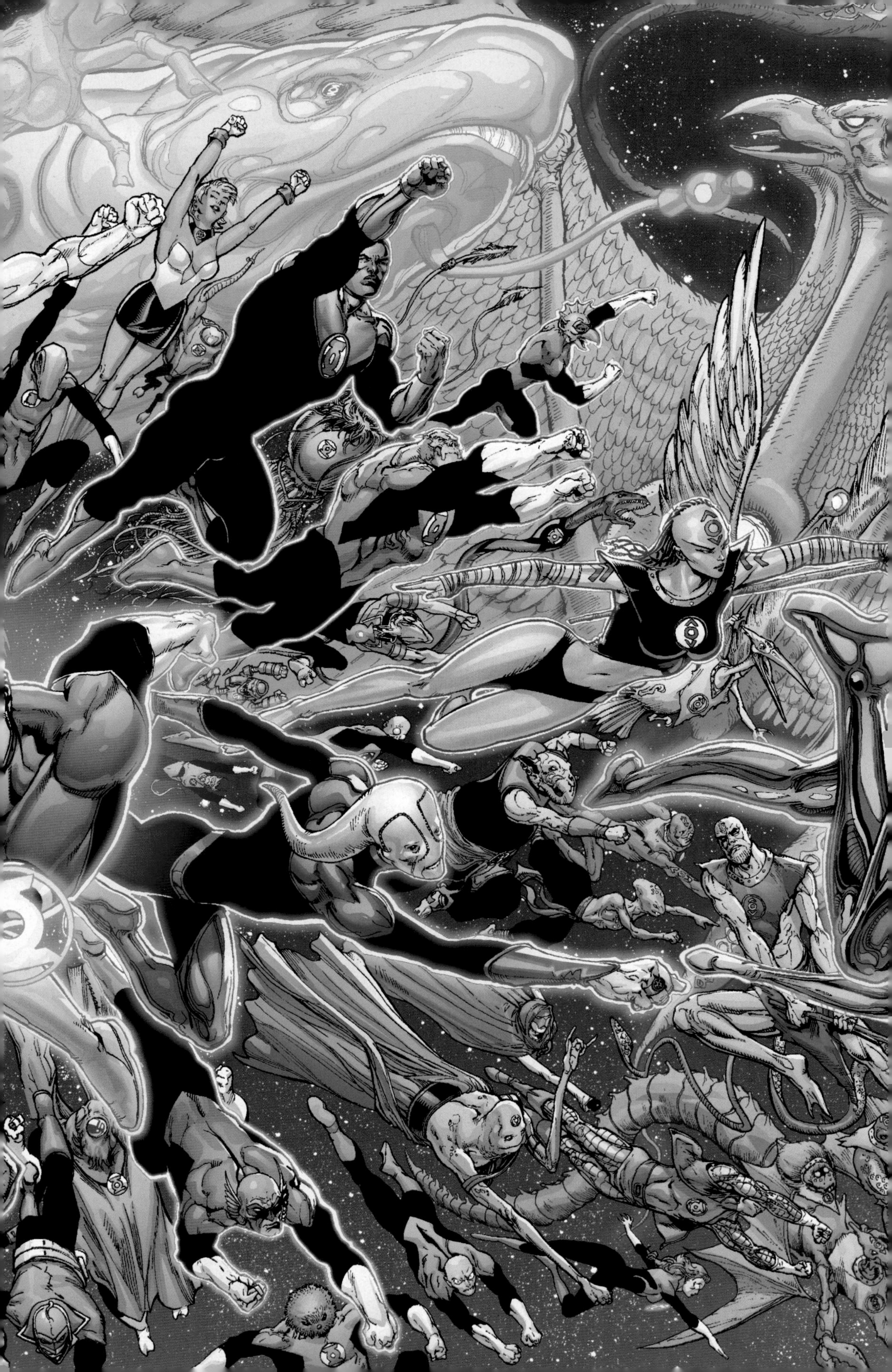

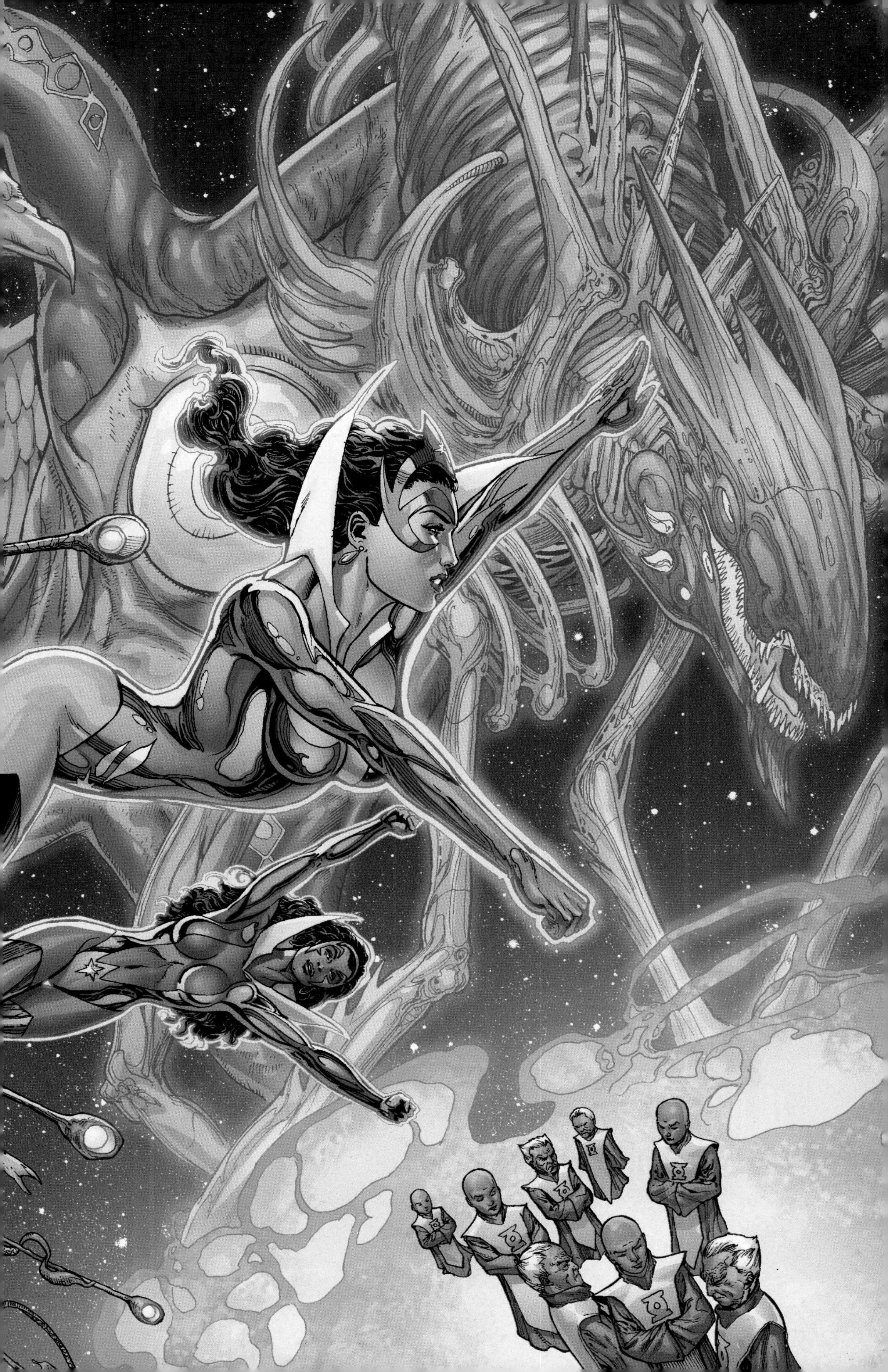

SO THE SAD NEWS:

With this collection Doug Mahnke and I are closing the GREEN LANTERN SAGA that began with GREEN LANTERN: REBIRTH #1. As every storyline was coming to a head, it felt like the right time. The book is still doing great. The characters are as vibrant as ever. Let's go out how we started – on a high note.

Counting up between the GREEN LANTERN monthly series, REBIRTH, BLACKEST NIGHT and the various one-shots and specials...that makes over 100 issues of GREEN LANTERN I've had the absolute privilege, pleasure and fortune to write.

I'm obviously ending my run with a little sadness because I love these characters, every single one of them. But I'm walking away feeling very proud of what we've done and very grateful for the opportunity to collaborate with so many fellow creators. It's that collaboration, and every reader out there, who have made this a truly special experience. It's hard to imagine a GREEN LANTERN universe without characters like Atrocitus, Larfleeze, Saint Walker, the Indigo Tribe or the rest of the gang anymore. And I can't count how many Lantern T-shirts of all colors I continue to see.

It was Dan DiDio and Peter Tomasi who I first spoke with about GREEN LANTERN. Dan was the Executive Editor of DC Comics at the time, and Pete my editor on JSA. They both wanted to relaunch GREEN LANTERN. My very first proposal that I could find dates back to September 2nd, 2003, meaning I've been working on GREEN LANTERN for nearly ten years in some way or another. I'll never forget Dan telling me his idea for the title, "Rebirth," he said.

Through BLACKEST NIGHT and BRIGHTEST DAY, literally, Peter Tomasi has always been there. From the incredibly long conversations and debate on REBIRTH to later writing GREEN LANTERN CORPS beginning with the conclusion of SINESTRO CORPS and up until today, Pete has been my creative partner in crime, and what GREEN LANTERN grew into would not have happened without him.

And, of course, look at the amazing artists I worked with: Ethan Van Sciver, your mad genius was key to everything we expanded the universe into – the endless energy you have for creation is unmatched. Ivan Reis and Joe Prado, you brought a scope only you two could deliver, culminating with BLACKEST NIGHT – and you're showing the world what JUSTICE LEAGUE should be. And Doug Mahnke...he's the current superstar I work with every month on GREEN LANTERN and have for years now. Doug, you're one of the most amazing and unique artists in the business. Your power, grit and sense of wonder can be seen at its very best in GREEN LANTERN #20. I'm fortunate enough to continue working with Doug as we head over to JUSTICE LEAGUE OF AMERICA.

We all owe a debt to Julius Schwartz, John Broome and Gil Kane for creating such an incredible foundation to build on with Hal Jordan and the Green Lantern Corps. Without them, there would be no Green Lantern.

Thank you again for reading – whether you started with REBIRTH or started with this – I sincerely appreciate your time and imagination.

IN BRIGHTEST DAY, IN BLACKEST NIGHT – ALL WILL BE WELL,

Geoff Johns

GEOFF JOHNS
GREEN LANTERN RETROSPECTIVE

GREEN LANTERN #0
UNUSED COVER PENCILS BY DOUG MAHNKE

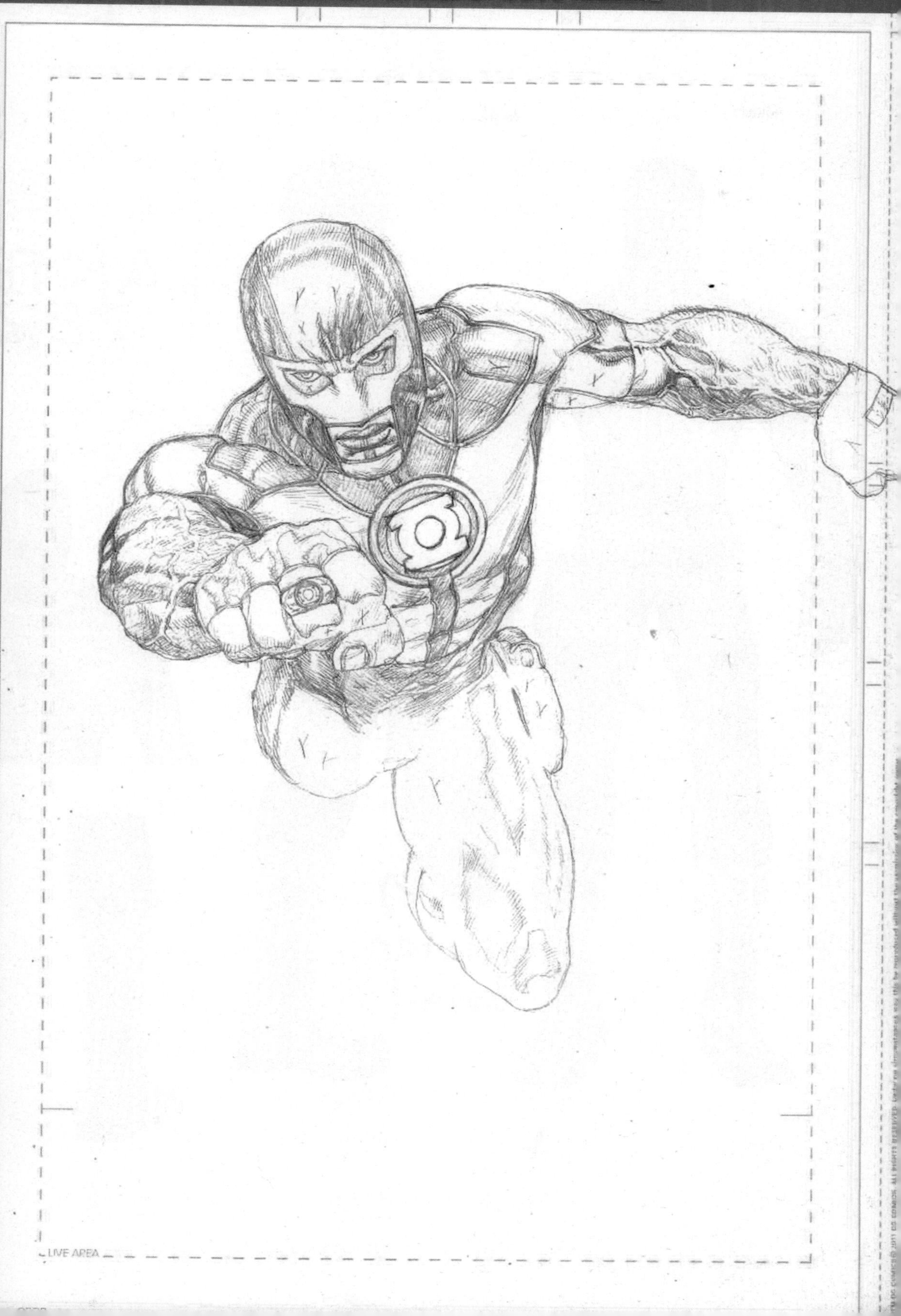
LIVE AREA

GREEN LANTERN: SIMON BAZ
CHARACTER DESIGN BY DOUG MAHNKE

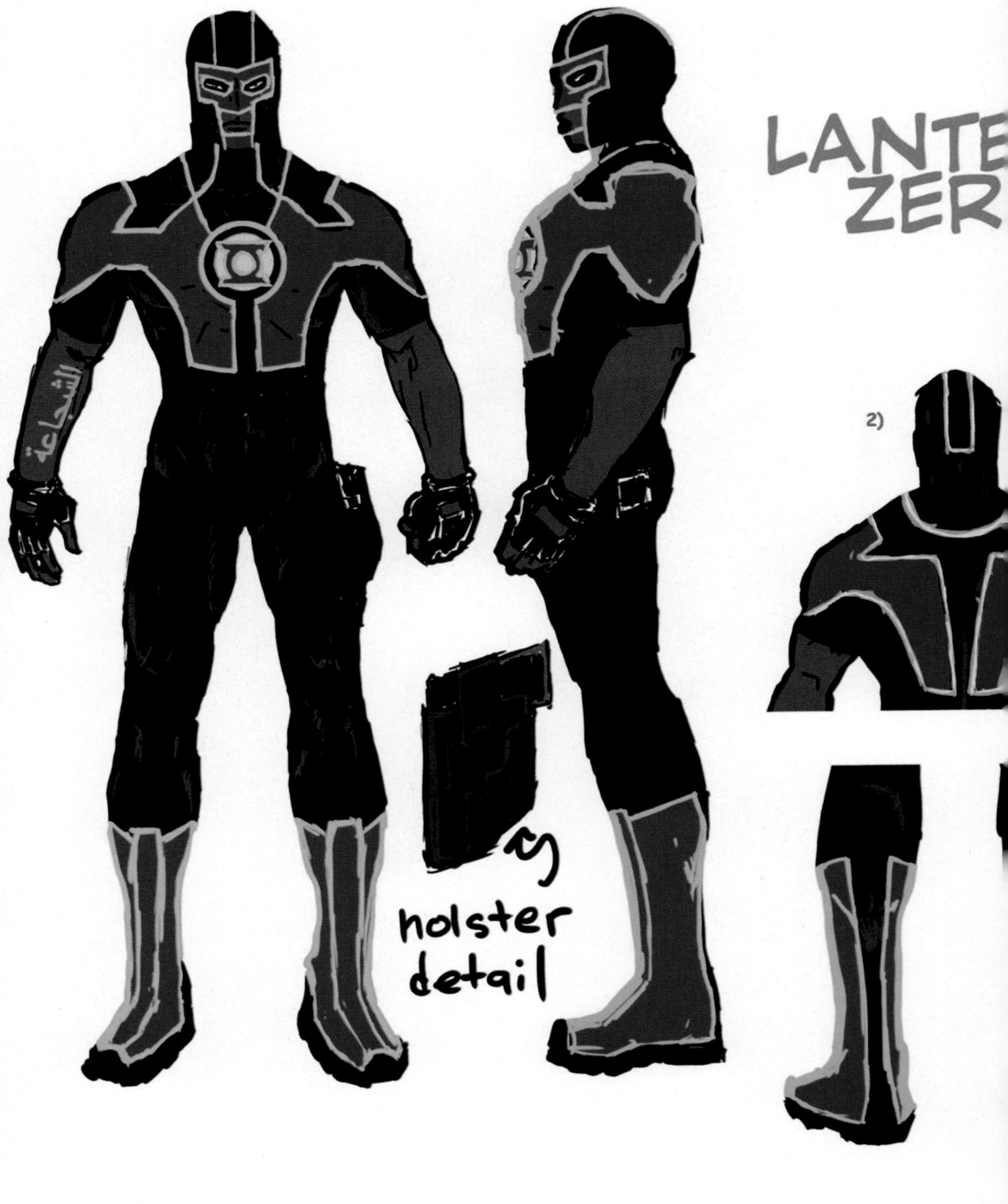
الشجاعة
holster detail
LANTE
ZER
2)

1)

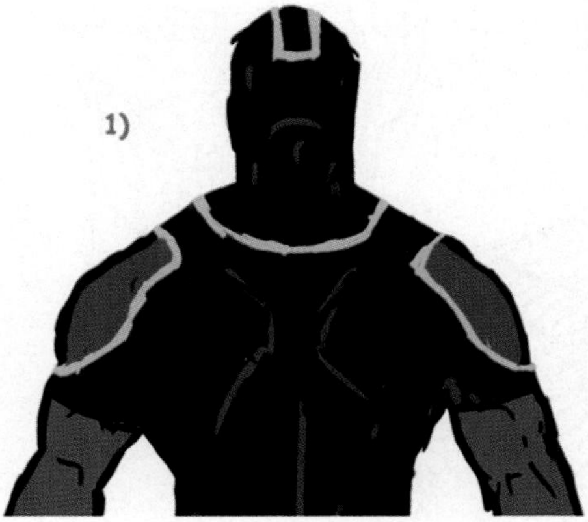

3)

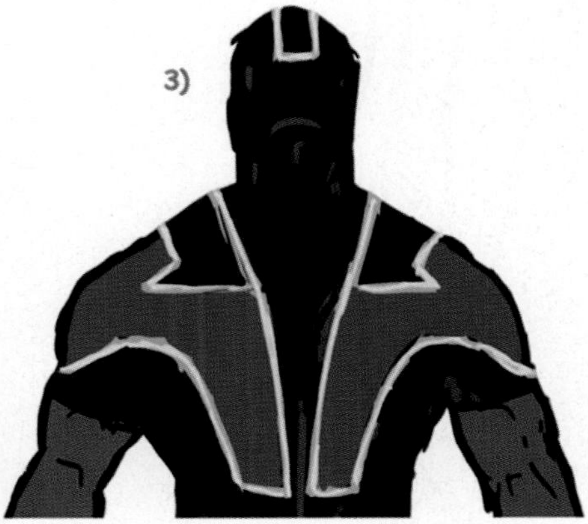

4)

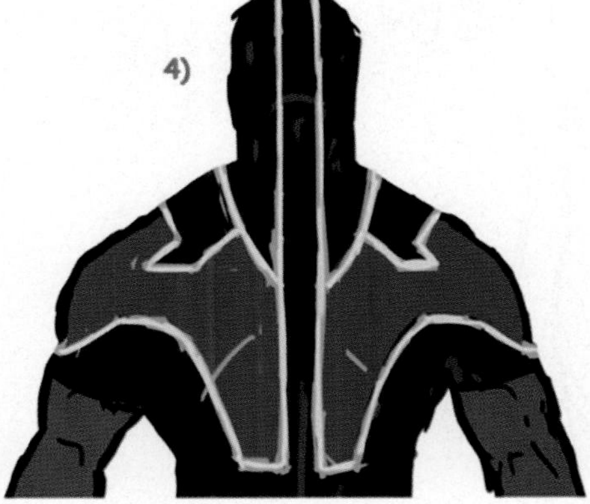

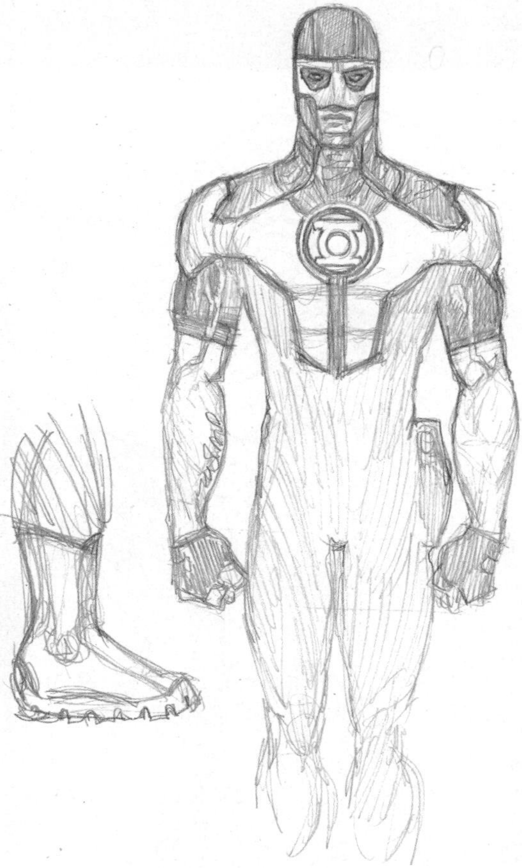

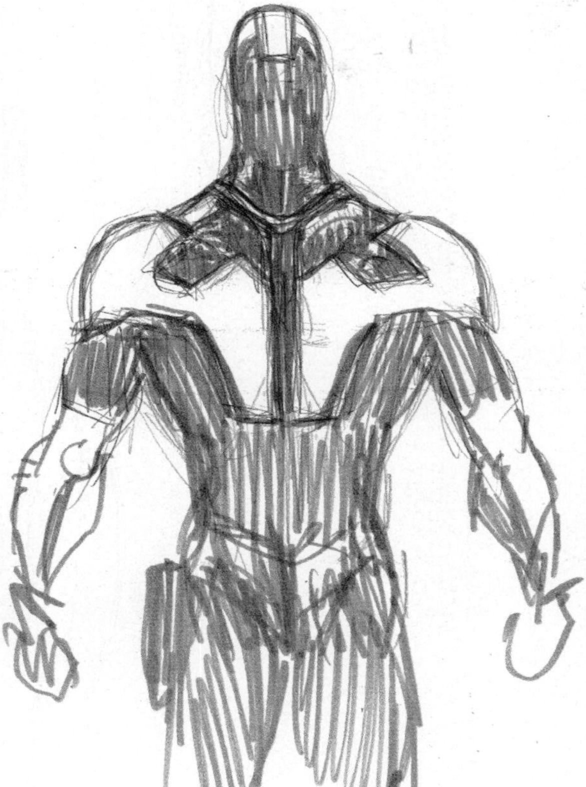

FIRST LANTERN
CHARACTER DESIGN BY DOUG MAHNKE

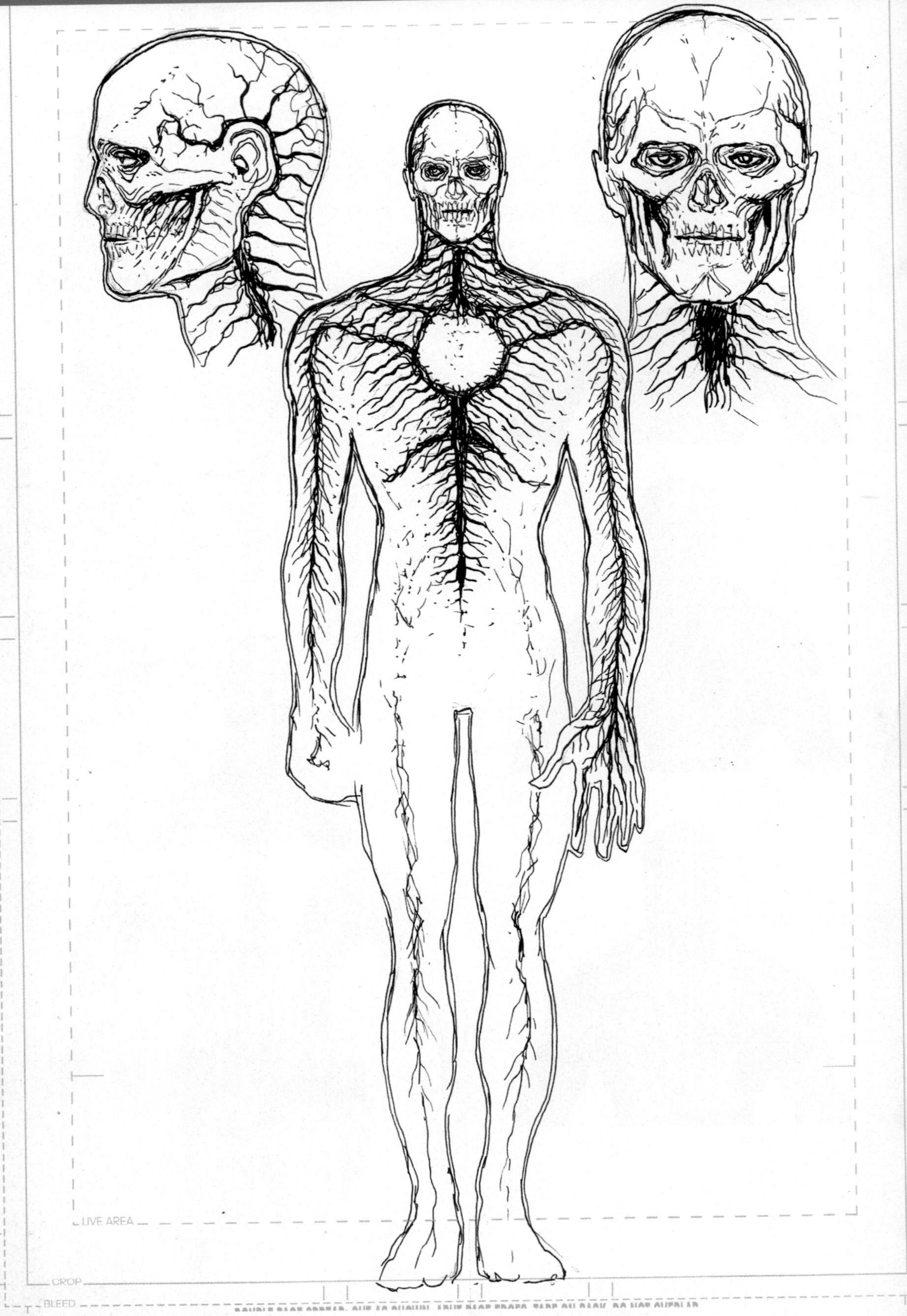
LIVE AREA
CROP
BLEED

FROM THE WRITER OF *THE FLASH* & *ACTION COMICS*

GEOFF JOHNS
BLACKEST NIGHT with IVAN REIS

BLACKEST NIGHT:
GREEN LANTERN

BLACKEST NIGHT:
GREEN LANTERN CORPS

Read the Entire Epic!

BLACKEST NIGHT

BLACKEST NIGHT:
GREEN LANTERN

BLACKEST NIGHT:
GREEN LANTERN
CORPS

BLACKEST NIGHT:
BLACK LANTERN
CORPS VOL. 1

BLACKEST NIGHT:
BLACK LANTERN
CORPS VOL. 2

BLACKEST NIGHT:
RISE OF THE BLACK
LANTERNS

BLACKEST NIGHT:
TALES OF THE CORPS

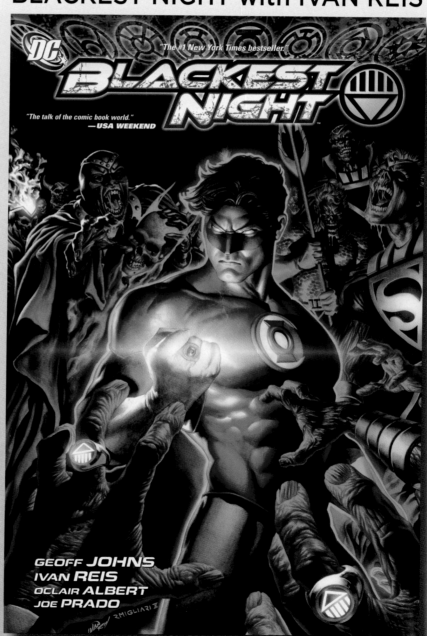

GEOFF **JOHNS**

IVAN **REIS**

OCLAIR **ALBERT**

JOE **PRADO**

DC COMICS™

FROM THE WRITER OF *JUSTICE LEAGUE* & *THE FLASH*

GEOFF JOHNS

GREEN LANTERN: REBIRTH

GREEN LANTERN:
BRIGHTEST DAY

GREEN LANTERN:
REBIRTH

GREEN LANTERN:
NO FEAR

GREEN LANTERN:
REVENGE OF THE
GREEN LANTERNS

GREEN LANTERN:
WANTED:
HAL JORDAN

GREEN LANTERN:
SINESTRO CORPS WAR

GREEN LANTERN:
SECRET ORIGIN

GREEN LANTERN:
RAGE OF THE RED
LANTERNS

GREEN LANTERN:
AGENT ORANGE

GREEN LANTERN:
BLACKEST NIGHT

GREEN LANTERN:
BRIGHTEST DAY

GREEN LANTERN:
WAR OF THE
GREEN LANTERNS

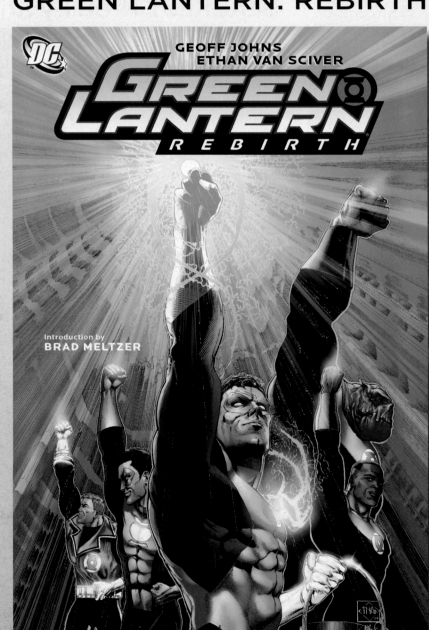

GEOFF JOHNS
ETHAN VAN SCIVER

GREEN LANTERN
REBIRTH

Introduction by
BRAD MELTZER

"The Green Lantern franchise is currently the best in the superhero genre."
—IGN

FROM THE PAGES OF *GREEN LANTERN*

GREEN LANTERN CORPS: RECHARGE

GEOFF JOHNS & DAVE GIBBONS
with PATRICK GLEASON

GREEN LANTERN
CORPS: SINS OF THE
STAR SAPPHIRE

EEN LANTERN
RPS: RECHARGE

EEN LANTERN
RPS: TO BE A
NTERN

EEN LANTERN
RPS: THE DARK
DE OF GREEN

EEN LANTERN
RPS: RING QUEST

EEN LANTERN
RPS: SINS OF THE
AR SAPPHIRE

EEN LANTERN
RPS: EMERALD
LIPSE

EEN LANTERN
RPS: BLACKEST
GHT

EEN LANTERN
RPS: REVOLT OF
E ALPHA LANTERNS

EEN LANTERN
RPS: THE
EAPONER

EEN LANTERN:
R OF THE GREEN
NTERNS

EEN LANTERN:
R OF THE GREEN
NTERNS AFTERMATH

Geoff Johns and Dave Gibbons
Patrick Gleason

DC COMICS™

*"This is the perfect place for people war[ ]
of the Green Lantern to start readin[g]
his adventures in order to see just how
dynamic his world really is."*
—COMPLEX MAGAZIN[E]

START AT THE BEGINNING

GREEN LANTERN
VOLUME 1: SINESTRO

**GREEN LANTERN
CORPS VOLUME 1:
FEARSOME**

**RED LANTERNS
VOLUME 1:
BLOOD AND RAGE**

**GREEN LANTERN:
NEW GUARDIANS
VOLUME 1:
THE RING BEARER**

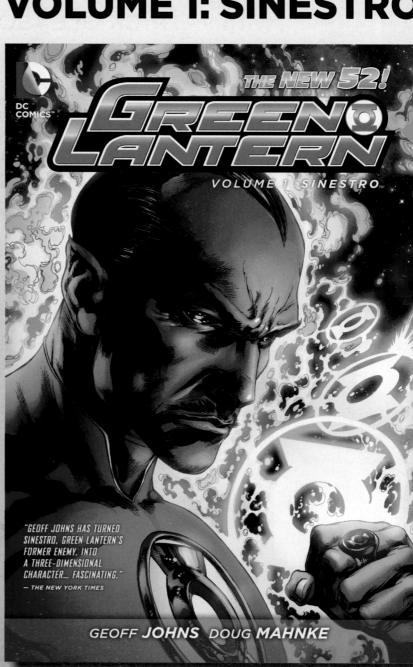

*"GEOFF JOHNS HAS TURNED
SINESTRO, GREEN LANTERN'S
FORMER ENEMY, INTO
A THREE-DIMENSIONAL
CHARACTER... FASCINATING."*
— THE NEW YORK TIMES

GEOFF JOHNS DOUG **MAHNKE**